CITIES AND GEOLOGY

"And for you that remain. . .you may pray for a safer future. . .not weighing the profit by an oration only. . .but contemplating the power of the city in the actions of the same day by day performance and thereby becoming enamoured of it. And when this power of the city shall seem great to you, consider then that this same was purchased by valiant men, and by men that knew their duty. . . ."

From the Funeral Oration of Pericles
in the "History of the War Fought
between Athens and Sparta," *by*
Thucydides the Athenian (460–399 B.C.),
using the translation of Thomas
Hobbes, published in 1628

Cities
and
Geology

ROBERT F. LEGGET

Formerly (1947–1969) Director,
Division of Building Research,
National Research Council of Canada, Ottawa

With a foreword by
Professor Quido Zaruba, D.Sc.
*Member of the Czechoslovak Academy
of Sciences, Prague, Czechoslovakia*

McGraw-Hill Book Company
New York
St. Louis
San Francisco
Düsseldorf
Johannesburg
Kuala Lumpur
London
Mexico
Montreal
New Delhi
Panama
Rio de Janeiro
Singapore
Sydney
Toronto

FRONTISPIECE
The city of Boulder at the foot of the Rocky Mountains,
a city that is appropriately the location of the headquarters of the Geological Society of America. (Courtesy
of the city of Boulder.)

ENDPAPERS
Reproduction of a portion of one of the maps of the subsurface of Paris, showing the old quarries described on
page 340. The underpinning along one of the Metro
routes can be clearly identified. (Reproduced by kind
permission of L'Inspecteur Général des Carrières, Paris,
France.)

CITIES AND GEOLOGY

34567890HDMM7987654

This book was set in Press Roman by Allen-Wayne
Technical Corp. The editors were Jack L. Farnsworth
and James W. Bradley; the designer was Merrill Haber;
and the production supervisor was Thomas J. Lo Pinto.
The drawings were done by Eric G. Hieber.
The printer was Halliday Lithograph Corporation; the
binder, The Maple Press Company.

LIBRARY OF CONGRESS CATALOGING IN
PUBLICATION DATA

Legget, Robert Ferguson.
    Cities and geology.

    Bibliography: p.
    1. Engineering geology.   2. Cities and towns
--Planning.   I. Title.
TA705.L39   624'.151'091732   72-12742
ISBM 0-07-037062-1

Contents

Foreword

The author of the well-known book *Geology and Engineering,* which contributed so much to the recognition of the importance of geology to civil engineering, set about an urgently needed task in showing the significance of geology for city planning. Two convincing reasons demonstrate that this new book of Robert Legget's is much needed and that it comes at a good time.

Firstly, there is the tremendous growth of towns and cities in the last few decades. This phenomenon affects every country in the world; the problems that it is creating know no national boundaries. They are so serious that they must be shared internationally, since the combined efforts of experts in many countries must be pooled if effective solutions are to be found.

Secondly, the development of cities and new settlements is in many cases too rushed to pay due regard to natural environment and particularly to geological conditions. It is very often forgotten that the geological history of land is so frequently an important guide to the planning of its future use. The author of this book shows that geological factors have been ignored even in recent manuals and comprehensive publications on urban planning. And yet urban geology should be the starting point, since without accurate knowledge of the subsurface conditions beneath land that is to be used for city growth, no sound planning can be carried out, the more so today since the areas now available for building are usually the least suitable ones. Neglect of geological structure can lead to serious economic loss.

This book reveals the applicability of the knowledge of geological conditions of the environment to sound urban planning and most-adequate land use. The general survey of the problem and the selection of topics show what can be accomplished when knowledge and experience cooperate. The text is presented in such a clear and accessible form that it will be readily understandable not only by civil engineers, who generally have some knowledge of geology, but also by architects, who are not usually instructed in this science but who are important agents in town planning, and by all those interested in the appearance of the landscape.

Since urban geology has been for many years past my own field of work and interest, I welcomed the news that Robert Legget was preparing this book. I have followed its development with close personal attention and have provided the author with some notes on problems of urban geology in my country.

In Czechoslovakia, with its complex geological structures and cities of very ancient foundation, I have seen not only what can happen when proper geological investigations have not been carried out in advance of planning but have seen also the great benefit that can result when they are. Czechoslovakia today presents many examples of the advantages of adequate study of urban geology, in keeping with the attention that has been devoted to all aspects of engineering geology for many years in this country.

The worldwide importance of the subject was shown by the fact that the first session on engineering geology ever held at one of the International Geological Congresses dealt with "Engineering Geology in Country Planning." This was in Prague in 1968 when the first meeting of the International Association of Engineering Geology was also held. The papers prepared for this session and now published (they are included in the references at the end of this book) came from authors in 10 different countries. This indicates clearly the wide international interest in this subject. The worldwide examples given in this book confirm that geological problems which affect the planning of cities are indeed shared by all countries.

It is with much pleasure that I have complied with the invitation of my friend, Dr. Robert Legget, to contribute a foreword to this masterly review of the importance of engineering geology in urban and environmental planning and of the great service it can render in this field.

QUIDO ZARUBA
President
International Association
of Engineering Geology

Prague,
Czechoslovakia
February 1972

Acknowledgments

My indebtedness to a large number of friends in many countries of the world will be clear from the pages that follow. In assembling information for examples that illustrate some of the varied ways in which geology influences the development of cities, and the supporting photographs and diagrams, I have been so greatly aided. Acknowledgments with the illustrations, mention of some names in the text, and of many more in the list of references at the end of the volume, give some indication of this assistance, even though there are many more whose names do not thus call for mention who have been similarly helpful. In every case I have tried to send direct acknowledgment, but I would like this general statement to be taken by all who have helped me as an additional personal record of appreciation.

For permission to quote copyright material, I am obliged to the Secretary (Local Government and Development) of the British Department of the Environment (page 516); the Director of the United Nations Center for Housing, Building and Planning (page 9); and the publishers of referenced volumes for a few shorter quotations. Quotations from publications generally of a more technical nature will be taken, I hope, as an indication of my sense of the value of the publications so cited. If, however, I have erred in using any such material without having obtained any necessary prior permission, I trust that I may be advised so that correction may be made, even as I hope that the constructive use of the quotations will be explanation of my error.

My long-standing interest in and concern for the use of geological information in urban and regional development were naturally and helpfully strengthened during my service with the Division of Building Research of the National Research Council of Canada. To my former colleagues I record the sense of my obligation for their tolerant understanding and constructive discussions. Correspondingly, I am grateful, for their interest in this volume and for their skilled assistance in guiding it through production, to Messrs. J. L. Farnsworth and J. W. Bradley of the McGraw-Hill Book Company.

Finally, it is a special pleasure to record my indebtedness to the engineering geologists of Czechoslovakia who have given me their friendship, and especially to Professor Quido Zaruba, who has honored me by writing the Foreword. This relatively small country has far more than its fair share of problems in engineering and urban geology, but the excellent manner in which these problems have been dealt with are reflected in the Czechoslovakian publications in this field, rightfully widely known. To Professor Zaruba and his wife I owe so great a debt that it is met only in part by all that this volume represents.

ROBERT F. LEGGET

Table of Metric Equivalents

1 mile = 1.609 km
1 yard = 0.914 m

1 in. = 2.54 cm

1 mile^2 = 258.999 hectares
$\quad\quad$ = 2.589 km^2
1 acre = 0.405 hectare
1 yard^2 = 0.836 m^2
1 ft^2 $\quad$ = 0.093 m^2
1 in.^{2} $\quad$ = 645.16 mm^2

1 yard^3 = 0.764 m^3
1 ft^3 $\quad$ = 0.0283 m^3
1 in.^{3} $\quad$ = 16.387 cm^3

1 gallon (Imp.) = 4.546 liters
1 gallon (U.S.) = 3.785 liters

1 ton = 1.016 tonnes

1 ton per ft^2 = 10,936 kg per m^2
1 lb per ft^2 $\quad$ = 4.882 kg per m^2
1 lb per in.^{2} $\quad$ = 0.070 kg per cm^2

1 km = 0.621 mile
1 m $\quad$ = 1.094 yards
$\quad\quad\quad$ = 3.280 ft
1 cm = 0.3937 in.

1 hectare = 0.0039 mile^2
$\quad\quad\quad\quad$ = 2.47 acres

1 m^2 $\quad$ = 1.196 yards^2
$\quad\quad\quad$ = 10.764 ft^2
1 cm^2 = 0.155 in.^{2}

1 m^3 $\quad$ = 1.308 yards^3
$\quad\quad\quad$ = 35.314 ft^3
1 cm^3 = 0.061 in.^{3}

1 liter = 0.201 gallon (Imp.)
$\quad\quad\quad$ = 0.264 gallon (U.S.)

1 tonne = 2,204.62 lb

1 kg per cm^2 = 14.20 lb per in.^{2}
$\quad\quad\quad\quad\quad$ = 2,048 lb per ft^2

CITIES AND GEOLOGY

chapter one

Growth of Cities

. . . a city such as vision
Builds from the purple crags and silver towers
Of battlemented cloud, as in derision
Of kingliest masonry; the ocean-floors
Pave it; the evening sky pavilions it;
    Its portals are inhabited
    By thunder-zoned winds.
                Percy Bysshe Shelley[1.1]
                (1792–1822)

The purpose of this book is to show how essential is geology in the planning and development of cities. Town and country planning is now accepted throughout the world as a vital public service, in place of the unorganized and uncontrolled use of land in earlier days. All such planning involves the optimum use of land so that the physical development of cities and regions may best meet the needs of people. The proper use of land—for buildings, for roads, for parks—can be achieved only if the nature of the ground and subsurface conditions is known with certainty. Since the science of *geology* is concerned with all aspects of the crust of the earth, the use of geological information, and of geological methods to obtain new information about local subsurface conditions, should therefore be an essential part of the physical planning of all cities.

This chapter sets the scene by presenting a brief summary of the phenomenal growth of the cities of the world today. To planners and to demographers this is a familiar picture. They will know also how extremely limited is the appreciation of this overall situation outside their own circles. It is essential that students, above all, should have an appreciation of the challenge presented to them by the rapid growth of world population. There follows in Chap. 2 a short historical review of the way in which geological features, almost always unrecognized, have influenced the development of cities down through the centuries. A general introduction to the art of planning as practiced today (Chap. 3) necessarily introduces also some of the ways in which geological conditions influence all such work. This leads directly to the main part of the book, with more detailed treatments of the geological implications of the main features of city development being presented in Chaps. 4 to 7.

In each of these chapters, examples are given of the influence of geology upon the aspects of urban development being considered. In some cities, knowledge of the local geology has been used to good effect; in others, where geology has been neglected, the distressing results of such neglect will be clearly evident. The hazards that geological conditions can present to cities is next considered in what is necessarily the longest chapter of the book, Chap. 8. Finally, and against the background provided by the preceding chapters, suggestions are advanced in Chap. 9 as to what cities can do to ensure that the geological conditions beneath and around them are used and controlled to public advantage. It is fortunately possible to show also what some cities have done in this direction.

The author has not hesitated in this final chapter to venture beyond the strictly factual character of the preceding eight chapters in presenting his own views as to what all cities should do—indeed, *must* do—if planning for the population challenge within the remainder of this century is to be well done. There must be good cities for the people of the world to live in; there must be pleasant environments for people to enjoy. Geology can help. This book essays to show how vital this help can be.

1.2 WORLD POPULATION GROWTH

In the year 1800 there were no more than 50 cities in the world with a population of more than 100,000. Today there are well over 1,000 urban centers of this size and over 100 cities with a population of more than 1 million.[1.2] * This phenomenal growth is a response to the increase in total population throughout the world and to the additional growth in urban populations due to the steady move from the country to the city. Neither of these trends can be stopped. When projected to the end of the twentieth century, the potential situation thus suggested is so remarkable that it must be supported by sound facts before being placed before the reader.

From the beginning of human history to the start of the Christian Era (the year A.D. 1) the total population of the world had grown to about one-quarter of a billion[†] people. This is the best estimate that can be made since, naturally, demographic statistics were then unknown. It is reasonably certain, however, that the total population of the world in the year 1750 was about 700 million, an increase of about three times in that many centuries. By 1900 the population had more than doubled, the total then being 1.6 billion. By 1965, in less than half the time required for a doubling of the population since 1750, the total had doubled again, to a new total of 3.3 billion.[1.3] These more recent figures are as accurate as such overall estimates can be; any error will not affect their overall significance, which can best be appreciated when seen in graphical form. Figure 1.1 presents these same figures conveniently plotted. The conclusion to which they point is obvious. Unless some major catastrophe takes place—and all will pray that this never comes to pass—the population of the world will be something like double what it was in 1965 before the twentieth century reaches its close.

There are some who suggest that the world cannot sustain this population since, if all available land were put to maximum use for agricultural purposes, there would still be, it is suggested, a world shortage of food after the total world popula-

---

*References thus indicated will be found in "References Cited in Text" (pages 553–575).
†By a billion is meant 1,000 million.

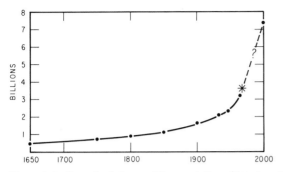

Figure 1.1 Growth of the world's population. *(Based on figures from the Encyclopaedia Britannica and, for recent years, publications of the United Nations.)*

tion passed about 5 billion.[1.4] Others make light of this suggestion and go further in stating that the world can support a much greater population than the 7 billion that seems probable for the year 2000. Here is ground for argument, but about the present net growth of world population there can be no argument whatsoever. The latest figures available in 1970 show that the total number of living persons on the face of the earth has increased by over 1 billion since the year 1950, and this is during a period that will be familiar to all readers.[1.5] If these figures are too vast to be comprehended, they can be expressed in another way. During the year 1970, the net increase of population (i.e., births less deaths) was about 138 for every single minute of time.

Despite the generally accepted accuracy of current demographic statistics, some observers may suggest that these figures are liable to error. They well may be, but the error—if any—will almost certainly be found to be in the low direction. Consider these estimates prepared by those who may be regarded as world experts in demography, the demographic staff of the United Nations. Their estimates for the total population of the world by the year 1980, prepared in the years indicated and based on the best available information at the time, were:[1.6]

Estimate in 1951 ...... 2,976 to 3,636 million

Estimate in 1954 ...... 3,295 to 3,990 million

Estimate in 1958 ...... 3,856 to 4,280 million

Making every possible allowance for errors and unforeseen factors, with the one great proviso that the world does not suffer a major catastrophe, it seems to be beyond any shadow of doubt that a doubling of the net population of the world as a whole before the end of the century is inevitable. There will be local variations, with the greater increases probably in warmer climates, but the projected increase in North America is not much less than the doubling that will be the overall pattern.

The consequence is that in the same period the world must at least double its physical plant to take care of this increase in the number of people. Since standards of living are steadily increasing throughout the world, and as more attention is paid to pollution control, the amount of new construction of all kinds necessary before the year 2000 will have to be more than equal to all the building that exists on the face of the earth today. And a very large proportion of this new building will be in cities. The land area used for cities that are to be built anew, or extended from existing cities, in the next 30 years will therefore be more than double that which is in use for such urban development today, and probably considerably more in view of yet another factor that must now be considered.

1.3 THE MOVE TO THE CITIES

From the start of the period of modern history, initiated by what was called the Industrial Revolution, one of the most remarkable aspects of population distribution has been the steady move from rural areas to towns and cities. There are some who regard this as a relatively recent phenomenon, due to the increasing mechanization of farming activities, necessitating a drop in farm employment. All available statistics show, however, that this is not the case. Indeed, any reading of ancient history will show that the "bright lights of the city" have always exercised a remarkable fascination for some people so that the trend from country to town is of long standing. It has, however, been most marked since the start of the nineteenth century, and it has now reached such proportions in all parts of the world that in the early years of the next century, with the major proviso made in the preceding section, more than one-half of the world's population will be urban dwellers. This is indicated in Fig. 1.2, which is based upon the best figures available in 1966.

The significance of this change in distribution may not be immediately apparent, but if thought be given to the millions of rural people in the developing countries of the world, countries where one does not expect to find large cities, then the profound importance of this trend will become clearer. This aspect of the overall picture is illustrated by the fact that within the decade of the sixties, the number of cities with a population of over 1 million located in the tropics, and not in the more temperate climates usually considered in such reviews, has increased from four to 14, and this in 10 years.[1.7]

The other side of the picture is seen when the situation in North America is considered. Figure 1.3 shows graphically that the move to the cities in both Canada and the United States is no new thing but has been almost steady for about 100 years. To those who know the continent, with its fertile farms, its pleasant farming communities, and little towns, the present situation is almost unbelievable. But these are census figures that are presented, and the end is not yet. More recent figures

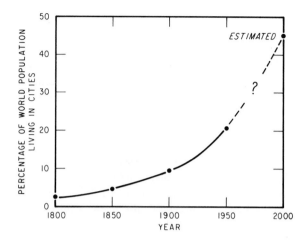

Figure 1.2 Growth of urban population in the world. *(Based on figures given in reference 1.7.)*

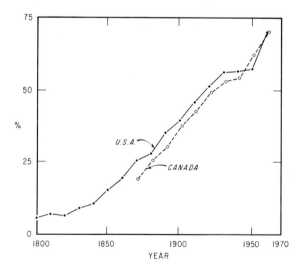

Figure 1.3 Growth of urban population in North America. *(Based on United States figures from the U.S. Bureau of the Census and Canadian figures from the Dominion Bureau of Statistics.)*

released by the U.S. Bureau of the Census show that, for the 100 largest metropolitan areas in the United States (in which live, incidentally, 57 percent of the total United States population), the growth of population between 1960 and 1968 was 13.2 percent as compared with a growth rate of only 9.3 percent for all other areas, including the smaller cities, with an overall national average of 11.4 percent.[1.8] Clearly, the present trend in North America is not only a move from the country to the cities but quite definitely to the larger cities.

Many sociological problems are involved, both in explaining the trend and in finding solutions for the difficulties within cities that the steady increase is creating. In the North American economy there is no real way of putting a stop to, or even slowing down, the trend. Attempts have been made to divert industry to the smaller cities but with only limited success. The formation of new towns has been tried, and is again being advocated, but even if these are successful, the main problems will persist. Problems are mentioned if only to show that they are not forgotten. In the present context, however, this trend is but a further major factor in confirming the certainty of a vast increase in the size and the number of cities throughout the world in the remainder of this century.

Table 1.1 translates these general figures to the local scene. It is sometimes easier to visualize general trends in terms of cities or countries with which one is familiar. The figures given are typical; they could be extended to cover all the main countries of the world, but the pattern would be unchanged—of a massive increase in the proportion of national populations that live in urban areas.

TABLE 1.1
Percentages of Populations in Urban Areas*

Country	Percentage (year)	Percentage (year)
United States	51.2 (1921)	69.9 (1960)
Canada	49.5 (1921)	69.6 (1961)
Australia	64.0 (1933)	81.9 (1961)
Belgium	57.3 (1920)	62.7 (1947)
Denmark	43.2 (1921)	69.9 (1955)
France	46.4 (1921)	55.9 (1954)
West Germany	70.5 (1939)	76.8 (1961)
Japan	18.1 (1920)	63.5 (1960)
Netherlands	45.6 (1920)	60.4 (1960)
Norway	29.6 (1920)	32.1 (1961)
Sweden	29.5 (1920)	51.9 (1962)
Switzerland	27.6 (1920)	41.9 (1960)
United Kingdom	79.3 (1921)	80.0 (1961)
U.S.S.R.	17.9 (1926)	47.9 (1959)

*Based by permission on table 3 in Peter Hall, ***World Cities***, World University Library, London, 1966.

One of the strangest aspects of this overall situation is that, on the international level, there is no major body that is directly concerned with this complex and critical problem of building for the population increase that is now taking place. There is nothing comparable (for example) with the World Health Organization or with the Food and Agriculture Organization, both of which have staffs of over 2,000 and annual budgets of over $30 million (U.S.). Within the United Nations organization there is only a small, but excellent, Center for Housing Building and Planning, with a staff of about 40 and an annual budget of $1 million. Their publications and reports fully substantiate what has been suggested about the growth of cities.

In a particularly valuable U.N. paper, the case of the Soviet Union is given to illustrate what has happened with planned cities.[1.9] The report states:

> No developed country has a higher number of specifically planned cities than the Soviet Union in which over the last four decades the urban population has grown from 26.3 million to 124.8 million. By 1980, it should reach 190 million with a 70 percent level of urbanization. Of the 900 new towns built between 1917 and 1965, 400 were established in new territory, many of them beyond the Urals, in an effort to open up the new mineral and farming resources. A subsidiary aim—to hold down growth in the old giants, Moscow and Leningrad—has proved less successful since both cities have tripled in size since the decision was taken in the 1930's to put a stop to their further development.

The paper concludes that, in the Soviet Union, and outside the largest cities, "the growth of the urban population has been a reflexion, not a forerunner, of expanding industrialization."

1.4 THE GROWTH OF CITIES

The history of ancient cities, their growth and decline, provides a fascinating reflection of the rise and fall of ancient civilizations. Babylon and Memphis (on the Nile) are each thought to have had a population at one time of about 80,000. Athens, at the height of its glory, is thought to have had a population of around 300,000, being probably the first city in all history to reach this size. Rome came to be a much larger center, being thought to have had a population of over 1 million people by A.D. 100. Nine hundred years later, Constantinople (Istanbul) was probably the leading city of Europe, with a population of around half a million; but in China, at about the same time, the city of Sian is thought to have had a million residents. The tide of history moved westward, with Paris in the ascendant, rising to a population of something like 300,000 by the mid-fourteenth century, while London was still a center of about 100,000. Other European cities rose steadily in size and influence, but by the year 1800 there was only one city in the world with more than 1 million inhabitants, the City of London.[1.10]

From that time on, the picture changes into one of almost unvaried growth, starting in England but soon spreading to Europe as the Industrial Revolution steadily transformed the economies of nations. The trend finally spread to countries elsewhere, with North America taking the lead early in the twentieth century, to be followed by the U.S.S.R. after 1918. By 1850, as showing how relatively recent has been the growth of what may be called modern cities, only Paris had joined London in having more than 1 million inhabitants. Even at the turn into the twentieth century, there were still only 12 cities of this magnitude—London, Paris, Berlin, and Vienna in Western Europe; Leningrad and Istanbul in Eastern Europe; New York, Chicago, and Philadelphia in North America; and Tokyo, Peiping, and Osaka in the Far East.

The position changed dramatically in the next 40 years. At the outbreak of the Second World War there were no less than 42 cities of over 1 million, located in every continent, with Sydney and Melbourne in Australia being well on the way to their places among the major cities of the world. And within 20 more years, by 1960, the number had increased by no less than 46, giving a total of 88 million-inhabitant cities in place of the two of just over a century before. As this book goes to press there are almost certainly over 100 of these major centers throughout the world, with some metropolitan areas now having populations in the vicinity of 10 million people.

A similar pattern holds for urban centers of less than 1 million inhabitants. Statistics are not readily available, since different countries use different yardsticks for their urban surveys. The figures given in Table 1.2, however, can be taken as a good indication of the overall picture since it is probable that the distribution of population has not changed markedly in the intervening years since 1955. As was indicated in the preceding section, the trend today is toward the larger centers, certainly in North America, so that the table represents in all probability a somewhat more favorable distribution than would be obtained from accurate statistics of today.

TABLE 1.2

Distribution of Population in Urban Areas*

Data for the world for 1955

Size of City or Town	Number	Population (millions)
More than 5,000	27,600	717
More than 20,000	5,500	507
More than 100,000	875	314
More than 500,000	153	158
More than 1,000,000	49	101

*Based by permission on a table in E. Jones, *Towns and Cities*, Oxford University Press, London, 1966.

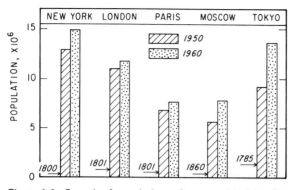

Figure 1.4 Growth of populations of some major cities. *(Based on figures given in Peter Hall,* World Cities, *World University Library, London,* 1966.)

Figures such as those in this table suffer from the disadvantage that they suggest a static condition, whereas the whole purport of this chapter is to demonstrate the dynamic situation throughout the world with regard to the growth of cities, up to the present and looking ahead in the foreseeable future. This is clearly evident from Figs. 1.1 and 1.2. To relate again the general situation to the particular, Fig. 1.4 has been prepared to illustrate for just a few typical cities the rate at which they have been expanding, a rate that will almost certainly increase in the years immediately ahead.

This spectacular rate of growth can well be appreciated merely by looking at the amount of construction work proceeding at any one time in any modern city. If this growth be associated with what has been shown earlier about the increase in the population of the world, and the very definite trend away from country living to city life, then the critical future of the cities of the world can be clearly seen. Since it is evident that the population of the world will double in something like the next 30 years, then the size of cities and towns will certainly be more than doubled in the same period.

The physical size of cities cannot be accurately gauged from their populations, in view of the wide variations in the patterns of living. In Edinburgh, Scotland, for example, parts of that most gracious city have a population density of only 35 per hectare, whereas in parts of Delhi and Calcutta, India, the density reaches the almost incredible figure of 1,550 per hectare. Here, too, there must be change, for wherever there is such crowding of human beings there is a challenge for some amelioration of the conditions of shelter that make such population densities possible. This means, inevitably, a still further increase in the area of land that is going to be used for urban development, the land that is the subject matter of this volume.

The vast extent of this land area is rarely appreciated since it is so difficult to obtain an overall view of town and country. Statistics alone can provide this overview.

For the year 1959 the situation in the continental United States (i.e., excluding the two new states of Alaska and Hawaii) is shown by the following figures: total land area 770,000,000 hectares; total land used for urban development 10,900,000 hectares; total land used for highways, railways, and airports outside urban areas 10,100,000 hectares.[1.11] A total area, therefore, of 21,000,000 hectares has been "developed" for human use, to a very large extent paved over or built upon so that the natural surface has disappeared. This represents about *2.75 percent* of the total land area of the United States. This is possibly the most remarkable figure to be cited in this brief chapter; when presented to many intelligent North Americans, it is greeted with plain disbelief. But the figures quoted are from the office of the Bureau of the Census of the United States and so must be taken as authentic.

Some warrant for them is given if the corresponding situation in Great Britain is considered. In a volume published as early as 1922, it was estimated that even at that time about 10 percent of the total land area of the United Kingdom had been "developed" for man's use.[1.12] Fifty years later, the percentage may be as high as 14 or 15 percent.[1.13] Similar figures could be provided for other countries, but since they will all be found to be so surprising, it will be preferable to leave readers of this volume in other countries to obtain the figures for themselves so that they can assure themselves as to the accuracy of the result they obtain.

Reverting to the figures that have been quoted for the United States, with merely a doubling of the area given over to cities and associated areas within the remaining years of this century, a simple calculation will confirm the accuracy of the official estimate of *36 million hectares—140,000 square miles—*that have to be taken out of natural use and paved or built upon by the year 2000 for the provision of services and buildings for man's use—36 million hectares in the United States alone![1.14] It is popularly said that in this great country "one million acres are being paved every year," and this is usually regarded as a wild exaggeration made by those interested in conservation. It is, most certainly, an understatement.

1.5 THE POPULATION CHALLENGE

The author realizes the risk that he runs in placing this short chapter at the start of this volume. Those who are familiar with the "population explosion" and its major consequences may be tempted to say, "Oh, no! Not again . . ."—being tired of this type of introduction. On the other hand, all those to whom the picture is new may be so appalled by the prospect that the growth of population presents that they will be tempted to say, "It just can't be true . . . the author is just building up a case for himself."

There is no question of "building a case" because the case is there for all to see. The statistics quoted can be checked from independent and unquestioned sources by the inquiring reader. While there may be some minor variations, some possibility of minor errors, some questioning of certain assumptions, there cannot be the slightest doubt about the accuracy of the overall picture that has been so briefly presented here. It has been placed first to provide the requisite background to all that follows. Above all, it will show why the author wishes to share his "concern"—to use that fine old word as the Quakers use it so eloquently—about the way in which this inevitable expansion of cities is going to be handled throughout the world. Above all, it is hoped that these summary figures will demonstrate to younger readers the challenge that they will face in the years immediately ahead. The students of today will be professional men approaching the peak of their powers as the twentieth century turns into the twenty-first. They will be living in a world with twice the population of today, in cities that are more than twice as extensive as those of today.

Behind all that follows, therefore, lies the undoubted fact that the land used to accommodate the growth of cities will, by the year 2000, be more than twice the area in use as this book goes to press. The amount of new land that will have to be used for the growth of cities in the United States alone—36 million hectares (140,000 square miles)—will equal the total area of England, Wales, Scotland, and Czechoslovakia combined. The geological character of all this land to be used for civic development in every country *must* be known with certainty if planning is to be well done and construction carried out safely and economically. This is the challenge to which this book can be merely an introduction.

chapter two

Geology and Ancient Cities

If a builder build a house for a man and do not
make its construction firm and the house which he
has built collapse and cause the death of the owner
of the house, that builder shall be put to death . . .
if it destroy property, he shall restore whatever it
destroyed, and because he did not make the house
which he built firm and it collapsed, he shall re-
build the house which collapsed at his own
expense.

Hammurabi, of Babylon[2.1]
(2067–2025 B.C.)

The crudeness of this method of dealing with weak building foundations can, perhaps, be overlooked when it is realized that the Code of Hammurabi was probably the first set of building regulations ever to be recorded and that it dates back almost 4,000 years. It is a significant document (as can be seen) and shows an appreciation of good building practice that is quite remarkable for so long ago. That it was used for the buildings in a great city that disappeared under desert sands, as will be briefly noted when this volume comes to its close, in no way invalidates the early indication it gives of an understanding of the necessity for good ground upon which to build the cities of old. It may be helpful to take a quick look backward before the challenge of the future is faced. Edmund Burke once said that "people will not look forward to posterity, who never look backward to their ancestors." This assuredly holds true for those engaged in any consideration of the use of the earth by man.

Ancient cities can usually be seen to have grown from small settlements founded for some clearly recognizable reason. The crossings of rivers at convenient fords provided one type of obviously desirable location for some permanent settlement. So also did ports at the mouths of rivers or on coasts where natural features provided good shelter. A supply of good drinking water was often a determinant for the precise location of some military encampments that might have to withstand siege. More frequently in such cases, a site would be chosen that gave natural defense security, as for example by building on the summit of a rocky crag or at the entrance to a pass through mountainous country. Even the supply of suitable building materials appears to have had some influence on early settlement, and the development of early mines naturally called for associated habitations. All these natural features—mines, good building stone, passes through mountains, rocky crags, good water supply, natural harbors, river mouths, and fords across streams—are the result of local geological conditions. Practically all ancient settlements, and so most ancient cities, were therefore located with the aid of what was very elementary geological reasoning, even though it was not recognized as such. Even the name geology was not generally used until the end of the eighteenth century, but it did not require the recognition by name of a branch of elementary scientific inquiry to enable early man to use his good judgment of the natural terrain in which he lived in deciding upon the location of his early settlements.

The "Old World" naturally presents a truly remarkable number of examples that illustrate this simple thesis. Now that travel between the New World and the Old is happily becoming so commonplace, especially for younger people, students being pre-eminent in these peaceable invasions, a brief glance will be taken at three locations in Europe that are readily accessible before turning to some examples to be found in Great Britain. Coastal cities present their own special contribution to any such review, however brief. And the New World has examples of its own with which this very "quick tour" may finish most appropriately as a short prelude to the main part of this volume.

2.2 THREE EUROPEAN EXAMPLES

Malta provides a good starting point. It is the main island of a small group known generally as the Maltese Islands, lying in the center of the Mediterranean Sea, about 97 km south of Sicily. Known around the world for the heroic defense mounted by its inhabitants during the Second World War, it was awarded—as an island—the George Cross by the King of England, and given a special citation by President Franklin Roosevelt, to mark this outstanding achievement. Although repeatedly bombed for more than 3 years, it never surrendered, continuing its strategic services, including the operation of its naval base. Few people ever ask how the inhabitants managed to survive such an ordeal. They were able to shelter in the natural caves to be found all over the island in the local limestone, but this is only one part of a long geological story.

Malta now supports a population of about 330,000, but not too many centuries ago its inhabitants could be numbered merely in the thousands. It achieved fame in the Middle Ages when it was selected as a permanent home by the Knights of the Order of St. John, an order known today around the world for its saving work in first aid. In A.D. 1113 the Order was formed as a military brotherhood, one of several arising from the Christian Crusades. In 1291 the Knights were forced to evacuate their fortress of Acre, still to be seen today in the northern part of Israel. They took up temporary residence, from 1291 to 1310, on the island of Cyprus, but in the latter year they occupied the lovely island of Rhodes after defeating the Saracens. In turn, they were displaced by the Turks in 1523, and they had then to find a new location in which to settle. Under the direction of an able Grand Master, a number of possible locations were studied by a group of eight Commissioners. Eventually Malta was chosen after the submission to the Grand Master of one of the earliest of reports on "engineering geology."

Reporting in 1524 to Viterbo, the Grand Master, the Commissioners stated that

the island of Malta was merely a rock of soft sandstone called tufa, about six or seven leagues long and three or four broad; that the surface of the rock was barely covered with more than three of four feet of earth which was likewise stony, and very unfit to grow corn or other grain; that it produced abundance of figs, melons, and different fruits; . . . that, except for a few springs in the middle of the island, there was no running water, not even wells: the want of which the inhabitants supplied by cisterns; that wood was so scarce as to be sold by the pound . . .[2.2]

Despite this somewhat discouraging report, but after a review of all the circumstances of the several locations investigated, it was decided to accept the offer of King Charles V of Spain—the gift of Malta and the small adjacent island of Gozo on condition that the Knights defended Tripoli. They landed on Malta in October 1530, the start of 250 years of steady development for the island.

In 1565 the Knights were attacked again by the Turks, but they resisted in one of the most famous sieges of the Middle Ages, a siege that was eventually lifted with the Knights victorious. It was this event that led them to erect defenses around the Grand Harbor and to plan and build the new city of Valetta, now the capital in place of Mdina, the old capital, and the only real settlement when the Knights arrived. With the aid of three military engineer-architects from Italy and Spain, a sound town plan was developed and the new town was born on 28 March 1566. By this time the Knights knew how to build with the excellent local stone; they were aided by Maltese

Figure 2.1 Malta. The Grand Harbor and Fort St. Angelo. *(Copyright photograph by Prof. J. Quentin Hughes.)*

builder-mason-architects. "It is remarkable," says Professor J. Quentin Hughes, who has written very interesting books on Malta, "that so small an island, under constant subservience to a foreign government, should have produced an architecture which is essentially Maltese in spite of passing fashions . . . and should have been able to use its native architects almost without exception."[2.3] It is this local building in Malta that was described by Disraeli as "its noble architecture [which equals] if it does not excel, any capital in Europe."

The main stone used for building is a globigerinal limestone of Miocene age that outcrops over much of the island. It was used for building in Roman times. An early description, in 1791, was by Deodat de Dolomieu, one of the Knights, who was a scientist of repute in those early days; dolomite was named after him. The limestone is found in two main beds, the lower one being the prime building stone, "rose coloured, warm and soft." An upper coralline limestone is not suitable for building, except for the most primitive walls.[2.4] Greensand and blue clay also outcrop on the island. The lower coralline limestone is variable, but much is of the character of marble, harder than the globigerina and thus in demand for foundations since the latter stone is susceptible to damage by water when freshly cut. There are quarries on the island, but most of the buildings of Malta were built of stone excavated from their basements, the globigerina forming about one-third of the surface of Malta. Stone excavated for drainage ditches was also used for building purposes. The Knights at one time had a regulation requiring that all house buildings in Valetta should be carried out with stone from Manderaggio, where they were excavating in this stone a small harbor for light craft.

The globigerina stone has to be protected from the infrequent rain and so is always coated with whitewash to form a protective skin. It is easily worked; slabs treated with warm oil provided good floors with a hardened finish. For the carving that distinguishes so much of the building in Malta, exposure to the air after the carving of new stone will lead to the formation of a hard "crust" (as it is described) that, if not damaged, will protect the sharpness of the carving indefinitely. Stone that is not carved within a year or two after its being set in position must be removed and replaced with new stone. There must be few if any other cities in which building basements have served first as quarries and then as cisterns for water supply, few if any locations in which planning and building have been so definitely influenced by local geology.

Crossing over to Italy and going north, Venice is an obvious stopping point. This world-famous city, located at the head of the Adriatic Sea, dates back to the seventh century. Some of the population of the adjacent mainland then moved out onto a cluster of small islands, known locally as "barene," in the center of a large lagoon, as a safety measure. Extending along the shore for 56 km, 10 km in width, the lagoon has an area of 545,000 hectares. Three local rivers were diverted, a sea-protection wall built with three inlets for the tide, and the city gradually developed by building upon piles driven into the "mud" of the lagoon, the accumulation of river silt that creates the barene. Only within the past century has Venice been connected with the adjacent mainland, first by a railway bridge and in 1935 by a highway bridge. Its isolated position was well used in establishing its preeminence as a medieval mercantile power; its position as a renowned center of art is known to all. Problems of high water, however, have plagued the city for centuries, although only in recent decades to an alarming degree. Combinations of changes in atmospheric pressure, heavy rain, high tides, winds, and mass movements of the water of the Adriatic Sea (known as "seiches") have caused periods of unusually high water (*acque alte*) from time to time. One of the most serious was in 1966. It is from this year that most serious study has been given to the future of this noble city, study that has been well publicized around the world.

Records of 58 *acque alte* during the 100 years prior to 1966 showed that 48 had occurred in the last 35 years, but 30 in the last 10 years. Two additional factors were recognized as being of increasing importance—the gradual rise in the level of the sea and the progressive subsidence of the bed of the lagoon. These two more-permanent features, when combined with occasional combinations of the natural forces just listed, help to explain the growing frequency of flooding at Venice. Nothing can be done, naturally, about the general rise in sea level (an amount of 15 cm in a century having been observed at Venice), but the subsidence of the ground beneath the lagoon appears to be due to human activity so that it should be possible to control it. Subsidence has also been increasing, from 1 mm per year in the period 1909–1925 to 5 mm per year in the period 1953–1961. A number of reasons have been discussed. Some think that movements of the underlying bedrock are responsible; others, that the

Figure 2.2 Venice. General view showing the surrounding lagoon. *(Courtesy Il Directore Generale, Ente Nationale Italiano per il Turismo, Rome.)*

extraction of natural gas from under the delta of the River Po may have had some effect. More probable, however, since it is a phenomenon found elsewhere in the world, is the consolidation of the soil upon which the city rests as a result of excessive pumping of groundwater from aquifers beneath. Yet a further factor is the recent development of a large industrial development about 3.2 km from the city on the shore of the adjacent mainland, imposing new loads on the sediments of the lagoon. There appears to be some correlation between the observed subsidence and the pumping from the 7,000 wells that have been in use. Drilling for gas and oil in the vicinity of Venice has now been prohibited. Efforts are being made to reduce the pumping of groundwater.[2.5] These are but the start of the major rehabilitation project embarked upon by the Government of Italy in October of 1971 with an initial planned expenditure of $400 million.[2.6] Well-wishings for the success of this venture will be worldwide.

Very different are the subsidence problems that have to be faced in the ancient town of Kutná Hora, located in eastern Bohemia, some 65 km to the east of Prague, Czechoslovakia. Its development defies all the rules that usually governed the growth of medieval towns. The discovery of silver-rich veins in the local rocks toward the end of the thirteenth century led to the start of settlement. For several decades people were attracted to the locality, living in small villages close to the deposits, villages that were later amalgamated into one town. At the start of the fourteenth century, silver mining was well established. In 1528 there were minted in Kutná Hora, by hand, coins known as "Prague groschen," being in widespread use as currency. Kutná Hora had then a population of 60,000 and had become the second largest town of Bohemia. At the turn into the fifteenth century the King of Bohemia promulgated the first European codification of mining laws (*Jus regale montanorum*) for use at Kutná Hora; it was soon in use in many other countries. Silver mining started to decline at the end of the sixteenth century and today is nonexistent. But the town remains, with its problems, and one can still visit one of the old mine workings and even see the ancient coins minted by hand just as they were made over four centuries ago.

The natural conditions of the area around Kutná Hora were not at all favorable for the founding of a large town. There is no local waterway of importance, no convenient transportation routes come near, and the physiography of the terrain around was not suited to easy defense in time of war. The town is located in a broad depression, the topography of which is naturally controlled by the geological structure of the area. To the north the depression is closed by three hills made up of crystalline schists, chiefly gneiss. On the hill slopes and over the bottom of the depression are relics of Cretaceous marine sediments, mainly sandy limestones and marlstones. A small stream (the Vrchlice) runs through the area, its bed cut down into a canyon-shaped valley in the local crystalline rocks. Mining activity in these same rocks greatly disturbed the continuity of the bedrock underlying the old town. The presence of old waste dumps of excavated gneiss and of heaps of slag from the old foundries complicates many surface features. The old mine workings, the full extent of which, as also their exact location, cannot now be determined with any accuracy, have led to surface subsidence in

Figure 2.3 Kutná Hora, Czechoslovakia. Supporting old buildings damaged by ground settlements due to mining. *(Photograph by R. F. Legget.)*

many parts of the town. The subsidences are quite irregular, in location and in timing, but many beautiful old buildings and many of great historic interest have been damaged. Temporary supports are used to the extent that is possible, and no new building is now permitted above the mined-out area.

The hydrogeological conditions beneath the town and its surroundings were also strongly affected by the old mines. Originally, the local bedrock was generally impermeable, but mining seriously disturbed this condition. Water in the mines was drained into numerous sumps, galleries, and along open joints in the rock and then pumped to disposal at the surface. At the present time, the mines are flooded, and so the level of the groundwater is the same as the level in the Vrchlice stream. Surface water infiltrates into the old mine workings. As the groundwater flows through the fractured bedrock and over old spoil heaps, it is enriched with soluble sulfates, and this makes it quite unsuitable for use, for example, in making concrete. Many of the wells originally used lost their water as the mines were developed and interfered seriously with groundwater conditions. Eventually, the town lost its established supply of water from wells, and, as early as the fifteenth century, a town water supply had to be installed. Water was brought to the town in wooden pipes from supplies in the Cenomanian sandstones near the town and led into several fountains, one beautiful example of which still

Figure 2.4 Kutná Hora, Czechoslovakia. The ancient public water fountain for water distribution. Note the roadway of granite setts. The figure
on the left is that of Dr. Zaruba, author of the Foreword to this book.
(Photograph by R. F. Legget.)

stands. A new water supply was installed at the beginning of the twentieth century,
drawing water that is suitable for human use from an old mine pit. Naturally, these
very complex geological conditions have been most carefully studied. A major survey
was reported on in 1949, summarizing an extensive geological survey aided by over
500 borings. Engineering-geological maps (to be discussed in Chap. 3) were prepared
and are used in the development of new sections of Kutná Hora, where building now
proceeds without fear of trouble from these interesting old mine workings.[2.7]

2.3 SOME ANCIENT CITIES OF ENGLAND

Many more examples, of equal interest, could be cited from Europe, but since Great
Britain will be generally more familiar to North American visitors, attention will now
be directed to a few British examples. It has been said that Great Britain contains more
varied geological conditions for its size than any other part of the world. This is
reflected by what one finds as soon as one asks what are the geological formations
underneath some of the more famous of British buildings. This is the sort of question

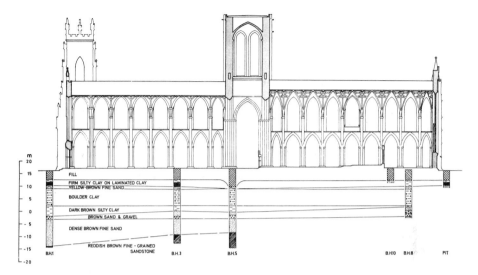

Figure 2.5 York Minster, England. A cross section through the great church showing test boring results obtained prior to the reconstruction of 1970. *(Courtesy of Ove Arup and Partners, consulting engineers; D. J. Dowrick, the Institution of Civil Engineers; and the Concrete Society.)*

that can add so much to the enjoyment of travel. Such inquiries can be an introduction to the delights of serendipity, the art of finding that for which you are not looking. But one does not even have to ask questions if one lands in the southeast of England and travels in the lovely county of Kent. There can be seen churches and other older buildings built of flints, easily recognizable stones that are indicators of the presence nearby of the great Chalk strata that distinguish so much of southern England.

Even names provide clues to local geology. Stamford in Lincolnshire is a modernized version of "Stone-ford," an important town in medieval times. It was settled by Anglo-Saxons who used the local River Welland as one of the corridors up which they penetrated to the center of England. Oolitic limestone slopes down to the river on both banks, and so gave a solid, or "stone," ford that was well used in earlier times.[2.8] The cathedrals of England naturally attract visitors by their beauty and variety. A few questions will reveal that many of the better known of these lovely churches have suffered from foundation trouble, especially under the large central towers that were a special feature of Norman building. The towers of Winchester, Gloucester, and Worcester fell in the twelfth century; Lincoln, among others, in the thirteenth; and Ely and Norwich in the fourteenth.[2.9] York Minster is one of the largest (and most beautiful) of medieval buildings in northern Europe. It has had more recent troubles, a survey in 1965 revealing serious cracks in the superstructure and differential settlements of as much as 230 mm. The underpinning and reparation of this cathedral church was a civil engineering task of great complexity, now successfully completed. It started with an exploration of what was underneath the great building. Test borings, some put down within the church itself using special electrically driven drills in order to minimize noise, revealed the situation shown in Fig. 2.5. A depth of filled ground up to 8 m was found near the central space, and this was probably responsible for the serious settlement of the northwest pier. The differential settlements throughout the building were probably due to the stratum of brown clay, especially since this was found to contain laminations of sand. Visitors in the future will never suspect all this as they admire the graceful lines and beauty of the Minster, but, like every other building, it is supported, now safely, by the ground beneath it with all its inevitable variety.[2.10]

Salisbury is a small English city widely known around the world if only because of the lovely spire of its early English cathedral, the tallest spire in England. Like so many of the older cities of that famous island, it was founded by the Romans, who fortified a nearby hill known as Old Sarum, calling the fortress Sorbiodunum. It was later captured by the Saxons, and then by the Normans, the name changing each time and eventually becoming Salisbury. One can examine the top of the fortress hill today and still find Roman artifacts, such as pieces of Samian pottery. But Salisbury is now located on the plain below, this being one case in which a complete town was moved from one location to another for the best of geological reasons—to get a safe and certain water supply. The wells supplying the hill-top fortress had become so depleted that it was no longer a satisfactory place for its increasing population. There is a pleasant local story about Bishop Poore, who was responsible for the move in A.D. 1219 from the hilltop to the plain below, ordering an arrow to be shot from the heights of Old Sarum into the valley below, with the new Cathedral to be built at the spot where the arrow fell. Be that as it may, the junction of the Rivers Avon and Wily provided an admirable town site, as may be seen today. Bishop Poore must have been an unusual man, for the new town was laid out with some degree of order, quite unlike the usual nonplanning of medieval towns.[2.11] He must have known or been advised about the geology of building stones, for it is on record that "Alia de Bruyère, the lady of Downshay, covenanted to supply for twelve years from Downshay quarries all the marble for the building of Salisbury Cathedral."[2.12]

Downshay is now a pleasant, small manor house close by the famous quarries of Purbeck in Dorsetshire that are still in use. For over 700 years these famous quarries on the "Isle of Purbeck" on the south coast of England have been supplying excellent building stone, two recent services being for the restoration of the Temple Church, London, and Exeter Cathedral, after the damage they sustained in the Second World War. Quarrymen have always lived close by, many in the village of Worth Matravers, in which every house is of local stone, as is the local fourteenth century inn and most of the farms around. The most famous local stone is widely known as "Purbeck marble," an Upper Jurassic limestone containing many fossil shells of the freshwater gastropod

Paludina that contribute to its decorative quality. The quarries are almost 48 km from Salisbury so that haulage of the stone for the cathedral must have been an enterprise of some difficulty. Immediately beneath the Purbeck beds are the even more famous Portland beds from which Portland Stone, one of the most popular of all British building stones, is quarried. It is an oolitic limestone of even texture. It was a favorite with Sir Christopher Wren, who is said to have used more than a million tonnes. It is to be seen in St. Paul's Cathedral and many other Wren churches in London, the Cenotaph in Whitehall, and even in the plinth of the King Charles statue at Charing Cross, in which may clearly be seen some of the characteristic Portland-bed fossils.[2.13]

Ninety-seven km due north of Portland is another famous source of excellent building stone that has been in use since the time of the Roman occupation of Britain. Bath Stone takes its name from the city that grew up at the crossing of the River Avon by the Fosseway, the great Roman road from the southwest to Lincoln. Known as Acquae Sulis, it soon became famous for its warm baths and medicinal waters. There are records of visitors coming to "take the waters" during the first four centuries of the Christian Era, showing that it was as fashionable a place then as in more recent years. The Romans discovered the great spring that still flows (at a rate of 1.8 million liters per day with a constant temperature of 49°C), developed the area around, and built magnificent bathing facilities, of the local Bath Stone, but all was lost and forgotten after the Saxons sacked the town in the year 577. Excavations in 1727 first revealed traces of the buried Roman center. It was not until late in the nineteenth century that real study was given, concurrent with careful excavation, to what lay beneath the streets of the central part of Bath.

The hot springs have been known and have been in continuous use since the time of Queen Elizabeth I. Today one may visit the famous Pump Room and taste the waters. The author fully agrees with the verdict of Sam Weller that they have "a wery strong flavour o' warm flat-irons." But one forgets this when walking down into the ancient Roman Bath, the lower section of which is still in excellent condition, the Bath Stone as good as new, even though now in place for almost 2,000 years. The King's Bath is still lined with the original lead sheets installed by the Romans. One can see the masonry conduit they built to convey the spring water, the lead box-shaped pipe in which water was led into the Bath, the jewels and other trinkets that visitors of those far-off days threw "into the fountain" just as is done today. And one can see, among the artifacts, a set of Roman dice, one of which is even loaded.[2.14]

The local geology is responsible for all this work of the Romans—the ford across the river, the hot springs, the excellent building stone. The Bath-Bristol area is underlain by folded and faulted Paleozoic rocks over which have been deposited a succession of Jurassic sediments that now form limestones, tough clays, and fuller's earth. These beds are almost horizontal, in general, but subsequent earth movements and surface erosion have resulted in a complex pattern of local geology that makes the area possibly the most interesting of all parts of Great Britain in demonstrating the effect of geological conditions on local building. The Bath Stone, about which more will be said

Figure 2.6 Bath, England. The Roman Bath, with the remains of Roman columns built of Bath Stone on the left; the famous Pump Room can be seen above. *(Photograph by R. F. Legget.)*

in Chap. 7, comes from a stratum of limestone known as the Great Oolite that caps many of the hills around. The stone has assisted in giving to Bath its delightful appearance, the architecture of its buildings being renowned, its fine Crescents having such great appeal to all lovers of good building. But even they have been affected by another aspect of the local geology. Camden Crescent, for example, is incomplete since part of it collapsed as a result of the great Hedgemead landslide of 1790. All round the city can be seen evidences of landslides, large and small. They are now well recognized, and all planning for the further development of Bath is taking fully into account these difficult geological features.[2.15]

In the neighboring city of Bristol there are similarly interesting geological features, notably old coal mine workings and spoil dumps that add to the complications of building in one part of the city.[2.16] There is also an old church that provides striking evidence of the problems met with in connection with its foundations. The Temple Church stands on Victoria Street, on the site of an oval church built by the Knights Templar but destroyed in 1312. The new church was nearing completion in the year 1390, its tower only partially complete, when work was stopped for a time, being resumed only in 1460. In this interval, because the tower had been founded on "marshy ground" (the site is close to the River Avon), it settled considerably but unevenly. A new start was therefore made, probably with better foundation design, and the remainder of the tower was built vertically. Figure 2.7 shows the tower as it is today, the departure from the vertical of the lower section being about 1.2 m, the unusual change at the midpoint being one of the most vivid examples known to the author of the influence of geology upon building in cities.[2.17]

There is so much to admire in the fine building practice of the Romans that one further example of their work may be briefly noted in concluding this glance at geology and building in Great Britain.

Figure 2.7 Temple Church, Bristol, England. The lamppost is vertical, demonstrating the movement of the tower; note the change in inclination of the tower below the upper section. *(Photograph by R. F. Legget.)*

Figure 2.8 Bristol, England. Entrance to some of the ancient cellars that lie beneath the older part of the city. *(Courtesy of the City Archivist, Miss E. Ralph, and the City Public Relations Office.)*

It was in A.D. 43 that the Emperor Claudius sent an army of 50,000 men, under A. Plautius Silvanus, to invade Britain; in a very short time they had subdued the land previously but briefly invaded by Julius Caesar. Settlement followed quickly. Under the successor to Plautius, P. Ostorium Scapula, the great road running northwest from the crossing of the Thames, now known as Watling Street, was soon being pushed forward by the Roman military engineers. They probably had an innate sense of geological appreciation, if only because Vitruvius had written his famous *Ten Books on Architecture* (and engineering) a century before.[2.18] His eighth book makes clear the importance of geology in connection with finding water, as do other parts of his remarkable work with regard to building and town planning. Just when Watling Street reached the estuary of the River Dee is not known with certainty, but pigs of Roman lead have been found that can be dated about A.D. 74, showing that by that year the Romans were working the lead mines of Flintshire and shipping lead to Chester. From then on, Chester became a strategic point in Roman development, as a road center, a port, and a full-scale legionary fortress.

The Roman city had an area of 24 hectares, enclosed by a wall, remains of which

can be seen in the modern city of today. Somehow, the Romans discovered the New
Red Sandstone as an excellent building stone. They opened up a quarry at Runcorn on
the River Mersey 24 km away; it is still in use, having supplied stone in recent years for
the restoration of Chester Cathedral.[2.19] Chester is still an important center after
almost 2,000 years and despite a geological catastrophe. This was the silting up of the
River Dee, and so the end of Chester as an ocean port. Since this happened in the
Middle Ages, there is no record of how quickly it took place, but it is on record that
the whole or a major part of the annual tribute owed by the citizens to the King was
remitted on account of "the influx of Sand and the silting up of gravel" in 1445,
1485, and 1486. Merchants had to move their mooring grounds further down the estuary; eventually a real alternative had to be found for the seagoing traffic in the Irish
Sea and this was found in Liverpool, a relatively small port in the adjacent estuary of
the River Mersey.[2.20] What Chester lost, Liverpool gained, becoming in modern times
one of the great ports of the world and the second port of the United Kingdom. Sand
and silt, however, remain a problem, over 10 million tonnes having to be dredged every
year from the famous Liverpool entrance channel, formed by about 32 km of rock-
faced submerged revetments.[2.21]

2.4 SOME COASTAL CITIES

It was but natural that almost all early cities were located either on the seacoast or on
the banks of rivers, in view of general reliance upon water transport. This same imperative has led also to the founding of new cities at the sites of natural or even of artificial
harbors that have been developed to take care of increases in ocean shipping. Location
near the sea or on river banks carried with it its own hazards, however, as all too many
examples from history show only too well. The erosion of some seashores by the
natural action of winds and waves, the corresponding silting up of openings from the
sea through the drift of eroded material along coast lines (known as *littoral drift*), the
meandering of rivers and the erosion of river banks—all these are examples of natural
processes that are studied as a vital part of physical geology, processes that are still
being studied, so complex are the interactions of the various forces at work. It is not
surprising, therefore, that early builders were unacquainted with these phenomena and
sometimes carried out works in connection with their maritime cities that only served
to increase these location problems.

Alexander the Great, for example, great general that he was, could not have been
expected to appreciate fully the consequences of one of the devices he had to use in
order to capture the ancient city of Tyre, now known as Sur, in Lebanon. Originally,
the city was strategically located upon an island. In order to capture it, as he did in
332 B.C., Alexander constructed a solid causeway from the mainland to the island.
The city fell but the causeway remained. There is appreciable littoral drift along this
part of the eastern Mediterranean coast, with the result that it was blocked in its movement along the coast, gradually building up around the causeway, the modern city

appearing to be on a regular part of the mainland.[2.22] In other cases, natural causes without any aid from man have notably changed coastal features. The natural silting of the estuary of the River Dee in England has been noted. The Gulf of Ephesus in Asia Minor, when visited by Saint Paul, extended inward from the coast a distance of 24 km; today the ancient port works are on dry land far from the sea, and the whole area has changed.[2.23]

Visitors to the modern city of Rome would be incredulous if told that the city they enjoy was once a port, boats being able to sail even into the great Roman sewer, still in use, famous through 2,000 years as the Cloaca Maxima. Through the centuries, silting of the River Tiber has raised the level of its bed and so of its water level, which is today almost at the springing line of the 3.6-m arched roof of the Cloaca. Embankment walls have been built along the river banks, but their effect is debatable. Although small vessels did at one time sail up to Rome, its main shipping was through the great port of Ostia. Now an inland city, Ostia was a port of eminence 2,000 years ago. Its entrance was protected by two breakwaters, following the Greek tradition in harbor design, a tradition that appears to have been followed without consideration of the effect of this interference with natural coastal action. The Emperor Claudius developed the great port when silting had already interfered with the smaller natural harbor. The area enclosed by the breakwaters was no less than 565 hectares; the great masonry wharves were 2.4 km long. A lighthouse 60 m high stood at the entrance, all these works being of a magnitude and character that even today can evince nothing but admiration coupled with wonder. But all are now gone or buried in the sands, victims of the inexorable effects of geological processes.[2.24]

Roman engineers also carried out maritime works in England, one of the most notable being the protection works they constructed in the low-lying land around the Wash, that unusual feature of the east coast of England. The remains can still be seen. Since the time of the Roman occupation, careful land-reclamation work has reclaimed almost 20,000 hectares of land from the sea, following the example of the Dutch with their great works in the Zuider Zee. But to the north of the Wash is one of the most telling of all examples of coastal erosion, along the Holderness coast of Yorkshire, immediately to the north of the mouth of the River Humber. Here 55 km of the coast consists of cliffs of boulder clay, a material readily eroded by the action of the sea. Records of the changes in this line of coast are available for almost 2,000 years, and these show that 21,500 hectares of land have been lost since Roman times. Loss of land is bad enough, but through the years at least 28 towns have slowly disappeared into the sea. *The Lost Towns of the Yorkshire Coast* is the melancholy title of a notable volume in which this remarkable example of geological destruction is described in detail.[2.25] And the erosion still goes on, pill boxes erected as recently as the Second World War now being partially buried in the sand as their sites have been eroded by the sea.[2.26]

Previous references have been made to the remarkable variation of geology in the British Isles. This is shown by the phenomenal variety of the coast line of England,

Wales, and Scotland and correspondingly by the effects of coastal action upon the towns and cities located on it. Down in the "West Country" of Cornwall, there still persists the legend of Lyonesse, a tradition that in this rocky area there was once a solid land link between Land's End and the Scilly Isles, with a major town located on what are today known as the Seven Stones, lonely crags arising from the sea. There is no proof to substantiate the legend, but the fact that it has persisted in local lore down through the centuries is an interesting reflection on geological influences upon early settlements.

On the Welsh coast there are other examples, notably the castle and town of Harlech. The castle was built by King Edward I in 1286 and included a watergate, proof indeed that it was on the coast, early written records showing that there was an active port close to the castle at what is now the town of Harlech. But today, only 700 years later, both are far from the sea, the adjoining Morfa Harlech having begun its growth as a shingle spit to the south of the town. The Scottish coast has its own examples, too, one of the most interesting being on the east side of the country in Aberdeenshire. Here, between the modern Fraserburgh and Peterhead, a sand spit grew centuries ago and formed a large tidal inlet on which was established the Royal Burgh of Rattray. It is known with some degree of certainty that in the year 1720 the entrance to the harbor was choked with blown sand from adjacent dunes—yet another process in physical geology—and it could not be cleared. The harbor was rendered useless; the Royal Burgh was so seriously affected that its population drifted away, and today nothing at all is left except the ruins of an ancient church.[2.27]

Further to the south, in Fifeshire, the Royal Burgh of St. Andrews stands on its Old Red Sandstone cliffs, but erosion is at work here too. Quoting from the "Report of the Royal Commission on Coast Erosion and Afforestation," which, although dated 1911, is still one of the most important works on this subject:

> This erosion [on the East Sands] has been going on for a long time, and within the last ten years the coastline appears to have receded about 20 to 30 feet. The erosion principally affects the property belonging to the University of St. Andrews, and it appears to have been accelerated by the removal of materials under the authority of the Corporation [of St. Andrews]—who claim the foreshore—from the beach. The representative of the Corporation who gave evidence admitted that the removal greatly assisted the erosion.[2.28]

Here the hand of man has aided geological processes; but there is an even more striking example of this from the south coast of England.

On the south coast of Devonshire, in Start Bay, there used to be a small fishing village called Hallsands, located above a shingle beach and backed by a steep rock cliff. The shingle is very mixed, some of the pebbles having traveled long distances along the coast as part of the littoral drift. For many years, the beach was in a stable condition, records showing this for well over a century. It was a very small village but important to the 126 people who lived there in the 37 houses, crowded close to the sea. In 1897 the great dockyard at Devonport was enlarged and large quantities of material were required for the construction work. Permission was given by the British Board of Trade for the contractor to dredge shingle from below the beach at Hallsands; by 1902, and despite strong local protests, 660,000 tonnes had been removed. Dredging was then stopped, but the damage had been done. Despite the construction of a seawall, the level of the beach had dropped by 5.7 m, and without the natural protection provided by the shingle beach, waves washed right over the wall. Some villagers moved away, but most stayed on until, on 25 to 27 January 1917, there occurred a combination of high spring tides and strong northeast winds that led to such storm conditions that 24 of the remaining 26 houses were destroyed.[2.29]

The village of Hallsands will long remain in the records of engineering and geology as a telling example of what the misguided work of man for one town can do to another, even as a further but final example from along the south coast of England will be a continuing reminder of what Nature can do on her own. One of the most distinguished of all the honorary positions that, with their great and long-standing

Figure 2.9 Brookland, Kent, England. The square bell tower of St. Augustine's Church, parts of which were built in the thirteenth century, located on the ground instead of on top of the church tower. *(Photograph by R. F. Legget; courtesy of Rev. N. G. O'Connor, Rector of the Romney Marsh Group of Parishes.)*

Figure 2.10 Brookland, Kent, England. Interior of St. Augustine's Church showing deformation of columns and arches; parts of the church date back to the thirteenth century; it contains the finest of the remaining 38 lead fonts in England. *(Photograph by R. F. Legget; courtesy of Rev. N. G. O'Connor, Rector of the Romney Marsh Group of Parishes.)*

traditions, the British still preserve is that of "Warden of the Cinque Ports," the very name betraying the ancient origin of the post. The five ports were Hastings, Romney, Hythe, Dover, and Sandwich, to which were later added Winchelsea and Rye. Sir Winston Churchill held this ancient office at the time of his death. Winchelsea, Rye, Romney, and Sandwich are now far removed from the sea and so have long since ceased to be the ports on which their early fame was based. The first three have been cut off from the sea by the formation of Romney Marsh, almost 25,900 hectares in extent and formed in large measure by the largest and most remarkable of the shingle beaches of England, 98 percent of which is made up of flint pebbles eroded from the adjacent White Cliffs of the famous Chalk of southern England. But the office of the "Warden of the Cinque Ports" remains, as a delightful link with the past, even as it is also so fitting a symbol of an important part of the message of this book.

As one travels over the Marsh, now a prosperous farming area famous for its sheep and the site of one of England's modern nuclear power stations, there are signs here of conditions beneath the surface for those who know that "sight is a faculty; seeing, an art."[2.30] The ancient church in the tiny village of Brookland, almost in the center of the marsh, has a most unusual appearance, puzzling at first until one realizes that the steeple-shaped belfry is situated on the ground by the side of the church instead of on top of the tower. A first glance inside the church confirms the reason for this precaution on the part of the early builders, for there is serious differential settlement even under the relatively light loads of the church structure without its belfry, a certain reminder of the "marshy ground" on which this church had also to be built. This would now be called organic terrain, peat, or (in Canada) muskeg, material with low bearing strength and high water content resulting in considerable subsidence when it is placed under load.

2.5 SOME CITIES OF THE NEW WORLD

The "New World" is a strange expression to have to use when the civilization of the Incas of Peru is thought of, but the term is conveniently applied to the countries of American continents in distinction to the older lands of Europe and the East. The origin of the Incas, however, and other early races of Central and South America is lost in the mists of history, becoming known and so recorded only from the time of the Spanish invasion. "Every schoolboy knows" that the Spaniards found a remark- ably well-developed but simple civilization in Peru located in some of the most rugged terrain that it is possible to imagine. A narrow strip of land separates the cordillera from the sea, but the works of the Incas were not stopped by the mountains, moun- tains that include some of the highest peaks in the Americas. Their justly famous road ran through the mountains, paved with bitumen, which they had learned to use, for much of its total length of about 6,500 km. They constructed masterpieces of water- carrying canals and tunnels for bringing water from the high mountains to the waste places on the coast.[2.31] Their use of cut stone for building staggers the imagination, even today, for they used blocks weighing up to 305 tonnes, transporting them without any mechanical aids for distances up to 80 km, over rivers and up ravines, setting them in place (after polishing them) with joints so true that a knife blade cannot be inserted. Recent studies have confirmed an old legend about their softening rock for finishing with the juice of certain leaves, then polishing the surfaces with sand and water.[2.32] Granites and porphyries were among the rocks they used; they seem to have made bricks also. Assuredly of all ancient peoples, the Incas occupy a unique place in the uses made of geology.

It is tempting to dwell further on the remarkable work of the Incas, on the geology of the remarkable cliff dwellings of New Mexico, or on the recent discoveries at the great city of Teotihuacan near Mexico City, but the term "New World" was used to invite attention to the influence of geology in the siting and development of some of the more modern cities of North America.[2.33] With a vast continent to be settled, it is but natural that physical features of the landscape should have determined so clearly and so often the location of the early settlements that grew into the cities of today. The oldest port in North America, St. John's, Newfoundland, is located on an

Figure 2.11   Machu Picchu, Peru. Remains of the great Inca city with Huyana Picchu in the background; the inset shows an example of the remarkable joints in stonework achieved by the Incas. *(Courtesy of the Director, Empressa Nacionale de Turismo, Lima, Peru, and the Peruvian Embassy, Ottawa.)*

enclosed harbor that is almost completely landlocked, the result of the gouging out of the relatively soft St. John shale by glacial action. San Francisco, on the Pacific coast, is located on a rocky peninsula that forms a magnificently enclosed harbor, approached through the famous Golden Gate, a peninsula the geology of which will call for mention later in this volume. New Orleans was founded in 1717 as a settlement on the natural levee forming the east bank of the Mississippi River as close to the head of the great delta as then seemed desirable, spreading across the adjacent flatlands to Lake Pontchartrain.[2.34] Although the location is geologically understandable for a small settlement, it has served to provide New Orleans with some unusual foundation problems as it has developed into the great city of today.

New York, on the other hand, developed from the small Indian settlement of Manhattan that was quite naturally founded on the rocky island between the Hudson River and Long Island Sound, with the result that the excellent rock foundations available almost all over the island have been put to good effect. The early skyscrapers were a reflection of the sound and strong foundation beds provided by the Manhattan schist. What was good for building foundations added complications to the construction of underground utilities and especially of the subways so essential to the modern city. All these underground railways had to be built relatively close to the surface, as pedestrians on many New York streets appreciate vividly when a subway train passes beneath them and they are walking near a ventilation grating.

The city of Boston has developed from one of the earliest settlements in northeastern America, John Winthrop and 300 fellow colonists arriving in 1630 to found a settlement in what was, for them, truly the New World. During their first year they tried two sites but found them unsatisfactory geologically; finally, they moved to the peninsula of Shawmut, and this is now the center of the modern city. They had tried a rocky tract north of Boston and then the slopes of a drumlin in what is now Charlestown, but the dense glacial till there yielded little water. On the Shawmut peninsula, however, they found several large springs and so were able to ensure a supply of good water, so essential for all human habitation. Excavations in the modern city have disclosed the alternating strata of tills and gravel that, under natural conditions, led to an artesian condition of the local groundwater that the early settlers probably tapped.[2.35]

In Canada the same pattern of settlement is found. One of the first of the tiny permanent settlements established by France to become a fine modern city is that now known as Quebec City. Here a magnificent rocky headland is so striking a feature of the north bank of the River St. Lawrence that it has been called the "Gibraltar of North America." It was an obvious location for a fortification, and so here the settlement was started, thanks to the great exposure of shale and limestone that make up Cape Diamond, rocks of Middle Ordovician age that have been the subject of many learned discussions among geologists. The early explorers went on up the great river until eventually they were stopped by what are now called the Lachine Rapids, the first interference with normal navigation to be met with all the way from the open

Atlantic, about 1,600 km away. Here, in 1546, Jacques Cartier landed on what he found to be a large island featured by a regal-looking hill, near the foot of which the first permanent settlement was established many years later (in 1609) by Samuel de Champlain. The rapids are caused by dikes in the local black shale. "Mount Royal," from which Montreal took its name, represents the remains of an old plutonic intrusion of Lower Devonian age. Around these two striking geological features the metropolis of modern Canada has developed into a gracious city.

Champlain pushed his explorations further to the west, going up the Ottawa River for the first time in 1613 and being halted in his canoe journey first by rapids at what is now the town of Hawkesbury and 96 km further on by a magnificent fall in the river that he named Chaudière and that necessitated two portages. Almost 200 years later, settlers from New England followed his route up the Ottawa River and established a small settlement at the first of these portages around the Chaudière Falls. They called it Hull. It was followed a few years later by another settlement on the

Figure 2.12 Montreal, Quebec, Canada. The great modern city that has grown up at the foot of the Lachine Rapids on the St. Lawrence, seen in the foreground with an ocean vessel approaching the first lock on the St. Lawrence Seaway; the view shows the 1967 "Expo" on the island in the center and Mount Royal—one of the Monteregian Hills—surrounded by the city. *(Courtesy of the Public Relations Department, City of Montreal; Mr. Paul Ledec.)*

south bank below the Falls, and this eventually became Ottawa, capital city of the Dominion of Canada. The early water routes of North America provide many other examples of settlements started by reason of geological impediments to canoe navigation that have developed into great modern cities, Chicago being an unusual example, its location at the entrance of what is now the Chicago Drainage Canal, leading from Lake Michigan to the upper reaches of the Mississippi River, clearly indicating its early links with water travel.

The same dependence upon local geological conditions will be found for the smaller cities of North America as for the larger urban areas. The group of cities in northern New York State, along the Mohawk Valley, constitute a good example. Albany was located at the head of normal navigation on the Hudson River and Troy at the junction of the Hudson and Mohawk Rivers. Deposits of industrial minerals have aided the development of Albany; molding sand from the Albany lake plain with limestone from the nearby Helderberg escarpment combined with iron ore from the Adirondacks to make it an important iron center at the time of the American Civil War. Local clay deposits and suitable limestone have made it a center for the manufacture of portland cement. Glacial action influenced the formation of the Mohawk Valley and left a legacy of buried gravel deposits, now used for local water supplies, in old glacial valleys. Available water power from the Genessee River cutting its way across the strike of the country rocks enabled Rochester to become at one time the world's largest flour-milling center. The neighboring city of Syracuse owes its origin to the natural brine that was discharged from local rocks, leading to an important salt industry.[2.36] Mention of salt is a reminder of the importance of mining to urban development.

Great mines, so obviously dependent upon local geology, have also had their part in the location of towns and cities. Some of these have had limited lives as mines have become exhausted, but others have their future assured by reason of the ore reserves adjacent to them. Butte, Montana, with its great copper mines, is an important example. So also is Sudbury in Canada, with the great ore bodies of the Sudbury basin providing so much of the world's nickel supply. New discoveries of nickel ore in northern Manitoba have led to the establishment within recent years of an entirely new town, planned from the start in relation to the local terrain. Possibly the most remarkable example of all is from another "new" country, the great modern city of Johannesburg in South Africa having grown out of the small mining camp first established when the great gold ores of the "Reef" were first discovered. Later in this volume the effects of this geological setting will be described.

2.6   CONCLUSION

These few examples from the pages of history, taken almost at random, could be duplicated many times over, but always to the same effect—how the fate of some early cities was dependent upon local geological conditions and the action of natural forces

upon them; how by some of his own actions man has interfered with nature, sometimes with disastrous results to the cities that were his own creation; how the location
of most cities has been determined, although usually unwittingly, by geological factors,
of which water supply has always been one of importance.

Some readers may have been surprised at the stress that has been laid upon the
dynamic character of natural processes, but the dynamic impermanence of nature was
familiar long ago to William Shakespeare. In *Troilus and Cressida*, one of his characters
says:

> When I have seen the hungry ocean gain
> Advantage of the kingdom of the shore,
> And the firm soil win of the water'y main,
> Increasing store, with loss, and loss with store . . .

And this was 400 years ago. The message has been repeated many times, but it seems
that it must regularly be learned afresh—the surface of the earth is *not* fixed and
immovable but is constantly subject to the play upon it of natural forces, the combined effect of which is but one of the many facets of the study of geology.

These examples from the past are cited by way of introduction to the main part
of this volume, which deals with the conscious and deliberate consideration of geology
not only in the siting of cities but with their planning in every respect, and then in the
actual prosecution of these plans as cities are built, as they expand, and as they change
in the course of time. It will be shown that, with the geological information available
today—about the details of local geology and the working of natural physical processes—there is no excuse for a repetition of any of the mishaps or mistakes of the
past. These have been cited only with constructive intent. The builders of old did the
best they could with the knowledge then available; it is easy to look back from the
vantage point of today and see where they could have done differently. It should *not*
be possible for an observer at the end of this century similarly to look back over the
preceding few decades, back to the seventies, and see similar mistakes.

chapter three

Planning
and
Geology

Earth has not anything to show more fair:
Dull would he be of soul who could pass by
A sight so touching in its majesty:
This City now doth, like a garment, wear
The beauty of the morning; silent, bare,
Ships, towers, domes, theatres, and temples lie
Open unto the fields, and to the sky;
All bright and glittering in the smokeless air.

William Wordsworth[3.1]
(1770–1850)

This is a pen picture of the cities that should be. William Wordsworth may not be very highly regarded by some of the poets of today, but he did record in these well-known words the vision that he one day saw of a noble city at its best, leaving a challenge to all who are concerned with the planning of cities that yet may be. He was also one of the first to point to the necessity of *Planning with Nature*, if some of his lyrical lines be read in a modern context. It is through proper planning that the cities which the world must have to house its expanding population can be, and must be, much more than mere agglomerations of streets and buildings. The city beautiful is still a worthy goal for all who are concerned with urban development. Geology has its part to play in achieving this end.

It cannot be gainsaid that cities over the years, many of which are beautiful indeed, including the city described so feelingly by William Wordsworth, were developed without very much conscious or organized planning. As with many other human activities, however, it was possible for gifted individuals by their intuition or genius (call it what you will) to achieve on their own in urban planning of earlier years results that today would be realized only by conscious corporate effort. The world is the better for their work. Some cities just grew, with no deliberate effort at planning of any sort. In many cases their deficiencies are now concealed by the glamour that age alone has given them. In others, in which building was carried out in defiance of Nature, time has taken its toll of the mistakes so that what is seen today is the residue that by chance did conform with sound precepts of planning.

Even today, there are still all too many examples of urban developments carried out without adequate planning and in disregard of almost elementary consideration of geological features. Fortunately, the consequences of this precipitate neglect do not usually lead to actual troubles or difficulties, even though they can so often result in urban communities that are aesthetically unsatisfying and operationally inefficient. The necessity for advance planning for all urban developments is, however, finally coming to be generally accepted. There are few modern cities that do not include planning in their normal operations, with civic engineering and architectural offices well alerted to the need for the integrated planning of all their work. Planning boards abound. The literature on urban planning is expanding rapidly. Public discussions of proposed plans are no longer the unusual phenomena that they were not too many years ago. Meetings to discuss urban planning have now taken their rightful place among professional gatherings. What then is involved in the planning process?

3.2 ELEMENTS OF PLANNING

No succinct and yet meaningful definition of the word "planning" in the urban context has yet been developed. In view of the complex municipal functions and services that must be included in any true planning project, it is doubtful if there ever will be. And yet the concept that the word conveys is generally familiar to all interested in urban development—the coordination for public benefit of the design, construction, and operation of the many publicly provided services that together make up the physical communities of today. Attempts to give a general definition are no new thing since planning, contrary to the understanding of many newcomers to the field, is not something that started in the sixties. President Franklin D. Roosevelt, for example, said in 1932 that

> the major part of all city and regional plans must consist of proposals that will help to secure a better balance than hitherto in the distribution of industries and population, both within cities, and between cities and country districts. With the aid of well-conceived plans, based on sound economic principles and with a high social purpose, we shall be able to prevent much waste of money and unwholesome conditions in the environment of dwellings, such as has occurred too often as a result of want of planning in the past.[3.2]

These words still hold true today, 41 years later. Lewis Mumford has written many notable books and papers about the modern city that have already stimulated two generations. As early as 1938 he wrote that

> the task of regional planning . . . is to make the region ready to sustain the richest types of human culture and the fullest span of human life, offering a home to every type of character and disposition and human mood: creating and preserving objective fields of response to man's deeper subjective needs.[3.3]

Eloquent words, such as these, are helpful in a general sense, even though they illustrate the difficulty of defining specifically what urban planning comprehends. The only really satisfactory way of dealing with planning in general is that followed in a masterly paper "The State of the Art of Planning," by W. S. Pollard and D. W. Moore, that was honored by a high award of the American Society of Civil Engineers to whom it was presented and by whom it was published.[3.4] By permission of Mr. Pollard and the society, Fig. 3.1 is a reproduction (with a slight addition) of the first illuminating diagram in this paper, upon which the following suggestions are based.

PLANNING RELATIONSHIPS

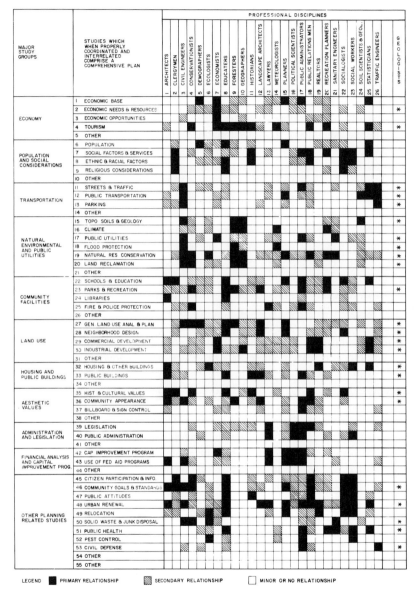

Figure 3.1 Professional disciplines in planning relationships; figure 1 in *The State of the Art of Planning*, reference 3.4, with the addition noted. *(Courtesy of W. S. Pollard, Jr., and D. W. Moore; and the American Society of Civil Engineers.)*

Figure 3-1 shows at a glance the quite remarkable relationships that are possible and that must be considered in the urban planning process. Even the order in which the main areas of study are listed can be questioned, illustrating at the outset the complexity of the planning process. There are some who would place first "Population and Social Considerations"; others, perhaps, "Land Use." Here are two vital aspects of urban development, but even they cannot be considered without constant attention to their "Economy." Since no city can live by itself, "Transportation" facilities must enter into planning considerations at an early stage, as must also the provision of "Community Facilities." These cannot exist without "Public Utilities" together with "Housing and Public Buildings." In a well-planned city "Aesthetic Values" must be given full consideration in the decision-making process. "Administration and Legislation" are necessary procedures for the approval and implementation of final plans. These procedures must always be subject to "Financial Analysis," with the necessary provision of "Capital" for carrying out the works that are planned.

One item from the left-hand list has yet to be mentioned, the "Natural Environment," since all that has so far been described, if it is to be implemented, has to be located in a natural environment, the character of which must clearly be known before overall coordination of plans can proceed. Consideration of the natural environment is no more important than the other major subdivisions since, unless land is to be used, for example, there is no urgent necessity for its nature to be known with certainty. At the same time, without a satisfactory natural environment in which to locate a new city, or to extend an existing city, all the other factors quickly become theoretical and eventually irrelevant. It could, therefore, be suggested that the existence of, and information about, a satisfactory natural environment is *primus inter pares*. It will be seen that in listing the professional disciplines that may be involved in the planning process, Pollard and Moore have carefully avoided any invidious comparisons by placing them in alphabetical order! It is this author who has had the temerity, for the sake of emphasis in this context, to separate "Geologists" and to extend slightly the listing of functions that their work can and usually will influence. It will clearly be seen how vital their role is, no more important than that of other professions, but basic to the successful start of planning, since without knowledge of the ground on which building is to take place no planning can be carried out with any certainty.

There are more than 1,400 squares in this interesting diagram, each one a potential function in the planning process, and well over 500 that are operative functions. It is small wonder, then, that so complex a network of relationships defies accurate definition. Certain basic principles for the "optimization of the environment" become evident from a detailed study of the "system" (for that is what it is) thus so conveniently delineated. These are stated by the originators of this chart as follows: that plans must be realized and not merely used as the basis for more planning; that citizens at large must share in the commitment to an urban plan; that day-to-day decisions must be made within the context of the overall plan; that the plan should be constantly in use and work upon it should never stop; and that the plan must be susceptible to changes in technology and so remain flexible but definite for present needs. Some of these suggestions are of demonstrated relevance to similar charts that accompany the original paper, charts showing the 30 types and groups of organizations that have some contact with urban planning and the interest of the community as a whole, and of individual citizens, in different aspects of the planning process. Remaining charts illustrate graphically the many steps that are involved in the implementation of an agreed-upon overall urban plan.

It will be seen that there is nothing unusual or mysterious about the items listed in detail on the left-hand side of Fig. 3.1. They are all functions that are already well recognized in city life, functions that are already the responsibility of individual professional groups such as engineers and architects. In the past, however, these separate functions have all too often been carried out without reference to other parallel functions, not only those in the private segment but also in the public sector in large municipalities or regions where adequate lines of internal communication did not exist. The art of planning, therefore, is no new discipline of itself but rather the skillful and effective coordination and correlation of a considerable number of individual functions, all related to the development of the urban community. The modern city is so complex that it is only when all aspects of its development can be viewed, in this way, against a broad background of the city or region as a whole, or as a "system" (to use the word of the hour), that the achievement of excellence can be approached. And it is excellence of every physical aspect of the cities of the future that must be the goal of all concerned with urban planning so that they may be, indeed, good places in which to live.

Consideration of the environment—geology—is, therefore, one of the most vital parts of this whole complex process, a part without which the planning operation cannot proceed with any degree of certainty or true efficiency. Sound information about the ground in the area being planned, and for the region immediately adjoining, is a prime essential of the basic data that must be assembled for even the overall general planning that will always precede the more detailed planning of individual facilities. This means knowledge not only of what the surface of the ground looks like but of what lies beneath the surface, the character of the materials that make up the land on which the city is to grow and the position and nature of the water in the ground beneath the site being planned, since this can have a profound influence upon building at the surface. It follows, therefore, that all concerned with the planning process must have at least a general appreciation of the methods followed in geology to obtain the information about the ground that is so necessary. This information must be represented in convenient form so that it can be coordinated with other relevant information in formulating the overall plan. The obvious way of doing this is through the medium of maps. Maps are the usual framework for the recording of proposals for the use of land so that the provision of geological information on maps is but an extension of a well-recognized and generally accepted practice. Geological maps, however, have to show three dimensions and not two; they are, therefore, somewhat unusual and will need some explanation in the pages that follow.

This summary of urban and regional planning has been presented so briefly since its general character is well recognized by those interested in the future of cities. The place of geology in the overall planning process is so fundamental that even the reference that has been made to this might seem to be almost belaboring the obvious. Would that this were so. If it were, indeed, so obvious, there would be only limited need for a volume such as this. Unfortunately, the reverse has been the case up to very recently. Not only has the relevance of geology to planning not been appreciated, but the whole subject of the terrain and natural environment has been all too often neglected. Planning has been generally carried out on beautifully pre-pared topographical maps that showed where natural features were located but that gave no indication as to what they were—no information about even the surface materials let alone what lay beneath the surface, no information about the water that exists beneath the ground and that can influence surface conditions so markedly.

To those who do appreciate the importance of terrain conditions in planning, this suggestion of widespread neglect might appear to be a personal idiosyncracy of the writer. If only to show how widespread has been this neglect, a slight diversion into the recent past will be made that will demonstrate beyond doubt that proper attention to geology in urban and regional planning is indeed long overdue. What follows is presented in no foolishly critical sense. Geologists have themselves to blame, to a degree, for the fact that the results of their scientific work have not been utilized in the past as they should have been. The few cases of neglect that are cited will give all the more emphasis to what can now be seen to be such a vital need in planning, and will confirm the pioneer value of the examples that will later be given of what is now being done to link the science of geology with the art of planning.

3.3   EARLIER NEGLECT OF GEOLOGY

Chapter 2 presented a small selection of examples from the past, all showing how geology had unconsciously influenced the development of cities in earlier days. Many readers will be able to add to the cases therein cited examples that they themselves have studied—examples that may serve to remind them of a city some features of which they had puzzled over, not realizing that geology might have been the determin-ing factor. One would expect, therefore, that in the many volumes recording recent detailed studies of different aspects of urban development that may now be found on the shelves of planning or geographical libraries, there would be found innumerable references to geology. Strangely, exactly the reverse is usually the case. It is only very occasionally that geology comes in for mention at all in even the best of such books. To take an example almost at random, there was published in 1969 an excellent and most interesting study, *The Impact of Railways on Victorian Cities,* the examples chosen being from Great Britain.[3.5] This 467-page volume can be

warmly recommended to those interested in this particular aspect of urban development. It will be found, however, that it contains not a single reference to geology
or even indirectly to geological conditions as having had any influence whatever upon
the topic with which the volume deals. Those who know the railways leading to
major British cities will find this surprising, especially if they recall the tunnels through
the Bunter sandstone through which two of the main railway approaches to the city
of Liverpool are made and the steep grades and occasional tunnels that feature the
lines going to the north from the London terminals. Regrettably, this is typical.

The books of Lewis Mumford have already been mentioned, appreciatively.
The author admires the works of this master writer so much that it is with diffidence
and regret (but with Dr. Mumford's knowledge) that he has to point out that even in
such masterpieces as *The City in History*[3.6] and the earlier *The Culture of Cities*[3.7]
one will look in vain for the word "geology" or any of its derivatives. The influence
of geology is clear for all readers to see; it was probably so obvious to this distinguished
author that it may have seemed to him to call for no special recognition. So influential
are his books, especially with planners, that this neglect may possibly have had some
influence on the long-delayed acceptance of geology as one of the vital determining
factors in the art of planning. A mere glance at these great books suggests examples
that could well have been included in this volume. There is a quotation from
Herodotus, for example, in the first of the works noted above, with regard to the
building of Babylon, describing how "the soil they got from the cutting was made
into bricks and when a sufficient number were completed, they baked the brick in
kilns" and then used the finished bricks for the building of the city (see page 17).
The move of Old Sarum to the new Salisbury is described but not the very basic
geological reason (see page 25). The story of the founding of Venice by a group of
refugees from Padua is yet another delightful example—but the temptation to dip
further into this fascinating volume must be resisted since it has been mentioned
here only as a very special example of the way in which geology has lacked recognition
as an important factor in the planning process.

A publication of the American Society of Civil Engineers has already been
mentioned, again appreciatively. This society publishes as no. 49 in its well-known
series of "Manuals and Reports on Engineering Practice" a fine *Urban Planning
Guide.*[3.8] This is a volume of 299 pages that contains 10 chapters, contributed by
nine distinguished members of the Society. It is a veritable compendium of information
on almost all major aspects of urban planning, with a wealth of useful references to
other publications. It can, therefore, be warmly recommended, apart from one remarkable omission—the treatment of the natural environment in which urban planning has
to be carried out. A careful reading of the text reveals only three uses of the word
"geology" or any one of its derivatives. In the fine chapter on "Residential Land
Planning" it is stated, "In many cases, it is necessary at this preliminary stage to
make soils or geological studies . . . ," and one of these cases is later given this
suggestion: "The soils engineer and geologist are vital members of the team in the

planning of hillside developments." That is all, apart from a short paragraph that is favored with a subsubheading–"Topography, Geology and Soil Condition"–in the chapter "Industrial Land Planning." Here it is explained that "The geology and soil conditions are a contributing factor in the selections of sites for plant location." There follow six lines of very general advice, concluding with this remarkable suggestion: "Soft soils requiring expensive foundations should be avoided whenever possible."

When such an authoritative guide as this manual pays such scant attention to geological conditions in urban planning, it is small wonder that engineers and others concerned with planning have failed to appreciate how their work can be assisted by adequate preliminary consideration of the geological conditions underlying land that is to be planned for urban development. Even more remarkable, however, is the complete neglect of geology in another ASCE paper, also published in April 1969, with the topical title "Civil Engineering and Urban Systems."[3.9] The paper is a lucid explanation of a fine concept that is given the label "urban systems engineering," in keeping with the current use of the word "system" to indicate that correlation of functions that has always been a feature of good civil engineering, although not often recognized by any title. The authors rightly remind their readers, "Engineering has often been described as the art of making science useful." They proceed to list the disciplines that contribute knowledge to civil engineering in the context of urban planning, and these are "Physics, chemistry, thermodynamics, fluid mechanics, properties of materials, mechanics, economics . . . mathematics . . . city planning, law, politics, public administration, sociology, political science, anthropology, the physical, natural and health sciences etc." And geology? It is not mentioned.

Enough has been said, even with these few selected examples, to show that the neglect of geology is a very real omission from much current thinking about urban and regional planning. Many pages could be filled with similar extracts from or commentaries upon complete volumes devoted to planning but containing no reference whatever to geological conditions. Engineering papers have been cited, but exactly the same would be found in corresponding papers by architects. Beautifully printed maps and reports showing carefully prepared master plans for important regions can be seen that take no account at all of the local geology. There are some exceptions, naturally, and examples will be mentioned later in this chapter, but these are the exceptions, the rule being that geology is a factor in planning generally neglected. In all too many cases, it has been given due recognition only when trouble has developed and has been found to be due to some previously neglected aspect of subsurface conditions.

It may appropriately be asked how master plans have been implemented without trouble in view of this widespread neglect of terrain conditions. In many cases, sites that were satisfactory from the topographic point of view were, automatically but really by chance and in no way due to the insight of the planners involved, reasonably satisfactory from the geological point of view. There is at least one of the "new towns" that have been developed in North America in the last two decades that was

Figure 3.2 Dawson City, Yukon Territory, Canada. Differential settlement of buildings due to underlying ice-laden perennially frozen soil (permafrost); the building on the right is approximately vertical. *(Photograph by R. J. E. Brown; courtesy of the Division of Building Research, National Research Council of Canada, N. B. Hutcheon, Director, DBR/NRC.)*

planned and built without any consideration of the local geology at all. The owners were lucky. They might not have been. There is another new town in the northern part of the continent that was built in accordance with a fine master plan but without appreciation of the fact that the site chosen was near the southern limit of discontinuous permafrost, a ground feature of the far north that will shortly be explained.

As luck would have it—and that is the only expression that applies—the site was exactly on the border of the permafrost, the probable existence of which could have been foretold in this particular area merely by looking at aerial photographs in an office without even going onto the site. But aerial photographs were not looked at, certainly by those capable of interpreting them adequately, and so buildings were erected on ground that was perennially frozen. Disturbance of the natural cover and of the surface soil combined with heat loss from the buildings soon thawed this frozen material, with results that must be left to the imagination. The resulting troubles have all been corrected so that visitors to this fine community today would find it hard to believe that troubles ever existed. But they did, through neglect of ground conditions that could so easily have been foretold. This must have been the experience, on a modified scale and without the complications introduced by permafrost, in many new towns, but the mistakes have been found and duly corrected with no record left to testify to the neglect of geology in the planning process.

3.4   GEOLOGY AND PLANNING

No more will be said about prior neglect of geology, for it is the purpose of this book to show how much its consideration can *add* to sound planning. Henceforward the approach will be the positive one, demonstrating what geology can do, illustrated to the maximum extent possible by examples of what the application of geological studies has been able to achieve. It will be taken for granted that geology *must* be considered in all urban and regional planning. Accordingly, those who are to be connected in any way at all with planning must have at least a general appreciation of what geology is— the terms that are widely used to describe its findings and the methods employed in exploring the nature of the earth's crust.

Graduate engineers, certainly of recent years, will usually have taken an introductory course in geology, and so engineering (and geological) readers can skip this section and proceed in their reading to Sec. 3.5. Architects do not usually have this advantage, nor do those who are drawn into the planning process from other disciplines, either professionally or as representative citizens on advisory boards. For all such readers, the shortest possible outline of geology will therefore be presented so that its relevance to planning may be appreciated. It is not necessary to be expert in earth science, but it is necessary to be able to appreciate the information that is provided about an area to be planned by those who are the experts. The science is one of quite general interest. It has rightly been called "the people's science" since it affects so much of everyday living—the true appreciation of scenery, for example. It can, therefore, be studied by anyone interested in the outdoors and through the reading of helpful books, some of which are listed at the end of this volume.

It is through geological studies that it is possible to "see" what is beneath the grass in the fields of a virgin area that is to be developed, to understand why springs occur where they do, usually on sloping ground, what happens to the rainwater that falls on the area, what materials will be found when excavation starts and so whether there will be any sand and gravel that can usefully be taken out before building commences, whether there is any possibility of even more valuable minerals being found beneath the planning area, whether there is any danger of encountering buried caverns that will interfere with foundation construction. It will be seen from this short list that it is fundamental to an appreciation of geology to think of the crust of the earth in three-dimensional terms. This is probably the only unusual change in mental attitude that will be required, since in all ordinary living it is so natural to look only on the surface of the land as its beauty is enjoyed, its unusual features studied, or even its possible use for utilitarian purposes considered.

It does require a little mental effort to remember that immediately beneath the apparently well-established surface lies a complex of solid materials, usually starting with soil but eventually becoming solid rock, even at great depths such as the 900- to 1200-m depths to bedrock beneath the Canadian prairies. Some of the illustrations in this book, such as the geological sections and block diagrams, may assist in developing this three-dimensional sense. There is a British book on physical geology (*The Earth's Crust*, by Dudley Stamp) that is illustrated with many photographs of three-dimensional, colored, block models that portray vividly the interrelation of surface features and underlying geology; it is listed at the end of this volume. The great cuts that now have to be excavated for modern highways also show this clearly with respect to the solid materials of the crust. There will almost always be ground-water present beneath the surface also, even though this may be another feature of the earth that is first a little difficult to appreciate. If, however, thought be given to looking down a simple well to the quiet water at the bottom, then it will be realized that the water that is seen there must be a small part of the vast body of water in the ground that would be similarly tapped if wells were sunk in other adjacent locations. It is to the study of this complex subsurface structure, as well as the way in which it is evidenced at the ground level, that the earth sciences are devoted.

Geology, the oldest and basic member of what are now called the *earth sciences*, may be more rigorously defined as that branch of natural science that is devoted to the study of the physical features of the earth, the character and structure of the rocks composing it, the forces at work in altering it, and the record of the animals and plants that have lived on its lands and inhabited its former seas. The study of fossil animals and plants is known as *paleontology*. This is a subject that will probably not enter into the discussions in this volume, even though the study of microfossils has been used to assist in major civil engineering works such as the proposed tunnel beneath the English Channel, correlation of the Chalk rock between its exposure in France and in England having been effected in this way. *Stratigraphy* uses the fossil record and other aids to determine the order of rocks as they are found in the earth's crust; the names of the different rock strata thus determined will come in for frequent reference as geological conditions beneath different urban areas are reviewed.

This study will be intimately concerned with the materials that make up the crust of the earth. They are three—rock, soil, and water. The detailed study of rocks is known as *petrology*, and the more detailed study of individual minerals as *mineralogy*. Both are aided by the relatively newly recognized study of *geochemistry*. The prefix *geo-* is always an indicator of some branch of the now broadly based subdivisions of geology or of one of the earth sciences closely associated with it. *Geophysics*, for

Figure 3.3 Lake St. John district, Quebec, Canada. Newly formed creek caused by a major landslide—an aerial view looking down and showing evidence of groundwater (dark) in newly formed banks. *(Photograph by W. J. Eden; courtesy of DBR/NRC.)*

example, indicates the application of some of the methods of physics to the exploration of the character of the earth and especially of the earth's crust. *Geotechnique* is a fine new term that is coming into general use to describe the engineering study of soils and rocks, thus encompassing what engineers call *soil mechanics* and the corresponding study of *rock mechanics* as well as other scientific aids to determining what are sometimes called the "engineering properties" of earth materials.

Soils will come in for repeated mention. This term *soil* is used to describe all the unconsolidated, or fragmented, material in the earth's crust, as distinct from the term *rock*, which connotes the solid material from which soils are derived. The name soil was always used in this way from the earliest days of geology, but when scientific agricultural studies grew to be of importance and the topsoil was intensively studied for agricultural purposes, it was perhaps natural that agricultural soil scientists (pedologists) should have started to use the single word when soil near the surface was being investigated. In the literature the word "soil" is therefore used in both senses, but the meaning will always be clear from the context. In this book, it is always used in its original broad sense, and "topsoil" is used when only the soil near the surface is meant. Some soils have been formed in place by the progressive disintegration of the rock still to be found beneath them. They are known as *residual soils* and are generally found in areas with warm climates. Other soils have been moved to their present positions from their place of origin by the action of wind, or of water, or of ice (in glaciers). They are correspondingly known as *transported soils*. They are more commonly found in areas with temperate or colder climates, many having been deposited in the last million years, in what is known to geologists as the *Pleistocene epoch*, an important part of the *Quaternary system*, the most recent subdivision of the long period of geological time.

Figure 3.4 Grand Manan, New Brunswick, Canada. Typical exposure of water-transported soils showing alternating layers of sand and gravel, all gravel and boulders being rounded through water action. *(Photograph by R. F. Legget.)*

Pleistocene geology is therefore a branch of unusual importance in urban and regional studies since about three-quarters of the surface of the earth, other than under the sea and that part covered by ice or fresh water, consists of soil and not bedrock. The geological problems most commonly met with in urban and regional planning, therefore, may be expected to be problems associated with soils. Soil and rock are naturally exposed in the beds of all the oceans; *submarine geology* is now assuming an importance all its own, both scientifically and because of the aid it can give to the prosecution of engineering works that are supported by the sea bottom, especially on the continental shelf. Since soil is a material easily moved, it will be appreciated that the changes which are constantly taking place all over the surface of the globe are evidenced chiefly by the movement of soil—as by soil erosion, for example. The study of the present form of the surface of the earth and of the forces that are at work all the time in changing was formerly known as *physical geology*, although commonly called *geomorphology* in keeping with practice in the German language. These modifying processes are usually associated with water and only to a minor extent with wind—water above the earth's surface in seas, rivers, and lakes, and water beneath the surface described generally as *groundwater*. The movement of water itself is a part of the science of *hydrology*, but this always has strong geological overtones, the blending of the two disciplines being somewhat naturally known as *hydrogeology*.

These names are mentioned so that the reader may be familiar with them as he comes across them in the remainder of this volume or in reading some of the references to which attention will be directed. Fortunately, the elements of geology are straightforward and so can be readily understood. Nothing more than an understanding of the principal geological terms, coupled with an appreciation of the dynamic character of geological processes always at work on the surface of the earth and the ability to "see" into the crust of the earth in visualizing the three-dimensional structure of the crust, will be necessary for the nongeological reader in reading the following pages and in following the influence that geology has exercised on so much of urban development. The study of geology starts in the field so that all observant citizens as they travel can see for themselves evidences of geological action, if they will look for them. In this way they can come to understand some of the more common landforms of today and gain a meaningful appreciation of scenery. The science itself has naturally gone far beyond the initial field observations (upon which, however, it is still basically founded) so that the most sophisticated equipment and intricate laboratory techniques, mathematical inquiries, statistical studies, and computer applications are all parts of its methodology today, just as with the other main branches of natural science. Although so simple in its essentials and so relevant to the things of everyday, geology is indeed one of the great scientific disciplines. A glance at any current geological journal, such as the *Bulletin of the Geological Society of America*, will quickly dispel any impression that the science is standing still or is not keeping pace with other and parallel advances in the onward march of science.

It is with the application of the essentials of geology that this volume is concerned. One of the most important of the general concepts is what is called the *geological cycle*, the name given to the continuing process by which the face of the earth is altered. Solid rock is eroded in some way; the products of erosion are transported by wind, water, or ice; they are deposited where they form new beds that, in the course of time, will be compressed and altered so as to form solid rock; these new strata will eventually be moved from their original position by the equivalent of earthquake action; erosion will start again, and so the cycle continues. This simple outline is perhaps a little difficult to comprehend in general terms, but it can be better visualized if some well-known rocky cliff by lake, river, or sea is pictured in the mind's eye. Rock fragments are always breaking away from all rocky cliffs; in many cases they will accumulate at the foot of the cliffs in huge piles of "scree." If this is in contact with water, some will be washed away at times of high water or by storms and become shingle on the beach, at first large in size but gradually becoming smaller as the fragments are worn down by the action of the waves. Shingle will become pebbles, and pebbles eventually become sand. Some sand and even pebbles may long remain in the same place, but much will be further ground down into silt and eventually to clay, very fine particles that will settle in still water and finally come to rest in beds that are initially flat.

Figure 3.5 Hong Kong. A deep cutting in residual soil formed by weathering of local bedrock and including boulders of unchanged rock. *(Photograph by Peter Lumb, University of Hong Kong.)*

In the course of time—geological time, of a duration to be measured in millions of years—these beds of clay will become shale; beds of sand will become sandstone; beds of pebbles can become conglomerate; beds of the remains of small marine animals will become limestone—all known as *sedimentary rocks*. Volcanic eruptions and other violent earth movements provide evidence of the existence of molten rock in the earth's interior, some extruded in the form of the lava to be seen today. Rocks of this character are known as *igneous rocks;* they include the oldest rocks that are known, dating back to about 5,000 million years ago. Some sedimentary rocks will be affected by heat and pressure in times of geological upheaval and will change in character into what are known as *metamorphic rocks*, slate and marble being such derivatives from shale and limestone. A conglomerate is, perhaps, one of the most interesting types of rock to examine—hard and solid as any rock can be, it can be seen to have been formed by an assemblage of rounded pebbles that have been bound together in a matrix by a process that it is almost impossible to visualize. The constituent pebbles were formed by the erosion of solid rock faces millions of years ago, transported just as pebbles are today, and deposited in a large bed that, in the course of time, was transformed into the solid rock which can be seen today. Wind and wave, ice and frost are still wearing rocks away today. Natural heat and moisture are still disintegrating solid rock into residual soil that may eventually be transported. So the geological cycle continues and will continue as far ahead as man can contemplate.

There is, therefore, a great natural system by which rock strata have been formed, and this is now recognized as ensuring that, apart from the occasional effects of violent upheavals, the younger rocks will lie above older rocks. Sedimentary or metamorphic rocks that contain fossils have built-in "time indicators" since fossils will be distinctive for any one period. It is in this way that the relative ages of rocks can be determined, great groups of rocks, divided into major time intervals, being given special names. Through quite remarkable laboratory methods it is now possible to determine the actual age of many rock types with a reasonable degree of certainty. All rocks, therefore, have a built-in history, and it is this that provides geology with one of its most fascinating aspects. The resulting geological time scale will not be of any direct consequence in the application of geology in planning, but since it may be of some general interest, Fig. 3.7 is included to show it in simple graphical form. Names of the different eras and periods will be frequently used to describe rock formations. It is to be recalled that it is the Pleistocene epoch—the last million years—that is of such unusual importance in planning work since it was in this span of time that most of the soils now encountered on the earth's surface were formed.

Within this last subdivision of geological time, the earth was subjected to varying climatic conditions, both colder and warmer than the climate of today. One significant result was that large parts of the Northern and Southern Hemispheres were repeatedly covered by ice, vast extensions of the relatively small remaining ice caps of today. These tremendous *continental glaciers* advanced and retreated, leaving behind them in many places traces of their presence in beds of glacial soils formed by the grinding of solid rock by ice action, moraines, and other features of the glaciers. At

Figure 3.6 McAdoo, Pennsylvania. Typical large rock cutting on Interstate Highway 81, south of McAdoo, showing a syncline in the Pottsville formation with gray conglomeratic sandstone overlain by red sandstones and shales. *(Courtesy of Department of Transportation, Pennsylvania, D.C. Sims, Deputy Secretary for Highway Administration and D.M. Hoskins, Assistant State Geologist.)*

times, the depth of ice was over 1.6 km. This great load on the thin crust of the earth had the natural result of depressing the level of the solid land beneath the ice so that the relative elevations of land and sea were changed appreciably. As the ice receded, the level of the land rose again; it is still rising, very slowly, following the last glaciation of North America, which took place about 11,000 years ago. Accordingly, it is not uncommon to find deposits of sand and gravel that were once very clearly an ocean beach at elevations now high above present sea level. The existence of such "raised beaches" on the earth's surface is significant in the modern use of the earth's surface, but exactly the same sort of oscillation of sea level has been going on throughout the whole range of geological time. This will explain why sedimentary rocks are now found far from and far above the present oceans—coal deposits near the South Pole at an elevation of over 3,350 m, even the top of Mount Everest being of limestone. The unraveling of these many stages in the development of the earth's surface as it is known today is but one of the many fascinating aspects of geology.

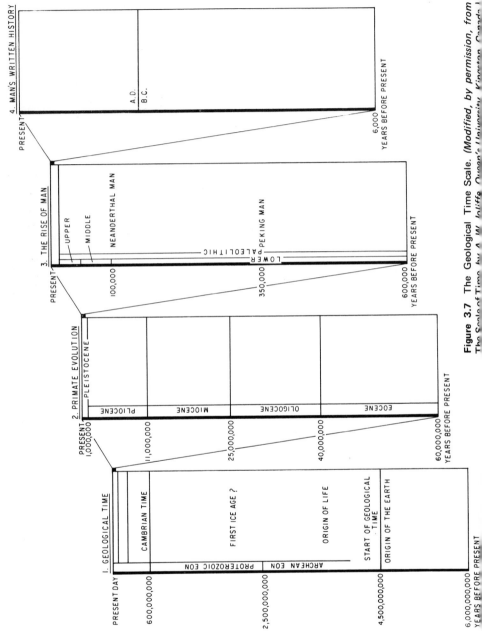

Figure 3.7 The Geological Time Scale. *(Modified, by permission, from The Scale of Time by A. W. Jolliffe, Queen's University, Kingston, Canada.)*

Especially complex is the determination of the relation of many strata of glacial soils to the successive glaciations in the Pleistocene epoch. These studies have direct relevance to the use of the land under which they occur. The maximum extent of the ice sheets in North America will show that this is a facet of geology not confined to far-northern Canada. It is true that almost all of mainland Canada, but not quite all, was covered in the successive North American glaciations, although much of the Queen Elizabeth Archipelago in the Arctic strangely did not have this experience. The most recent glaciation extended as far south as New York City, south of Columbus, Ohio, and as far as Des Moines, Iowa, then trending northward but always to the south of the Canadian border. Earlier glaciations had extended even as far south as St. Louis and Lawrence, Kansas. In Europe, much of the British Isles, all of Scandinavia, many parts of the U.S.S.R., much of Germany and Poland, and most of Switzerland, as well as the higher parts of other mountainous areas, were once ice-covered. Glacial soils, therefore, are to be expected throughout the tremendous area of the Northern Hemisphere thus roughly sketched. In other parts of the world,

Figure 3.8 Near Messina, New York. "Friends of the Pleistocene" inspecting a new exposure of Wisconsin glacial till during the construction of the St. Lawrence Seaway; angular rock fragments, embedded in the soil matrix, can clearly be seen. *(Photograph by R. F. Legget.)*

the soils encountered will be residual soils, even though they may have been transported either by wind or by water.

Permafrost has been mentioned. This word is used to describe the condition
of the ground when its temperature is always below the freezing point of water. Most
of Alaska, the northern half of Canada, and much of the Soviet Union today are
underlain by permafrost. In earlier geological time much larger areas were similarly
frozen, with results, in some places, that can still affect modern building. If the
frozen ground should consist of solid rock, the frozen condition will have no serious
consequences, but if the ground is soil, then all water held between the solid grains
of soil material will be in the form of ice. Should the surface of such material be
disturbed in summertime, the ice will probably melt and so completely change the
character of the soil. This may have very serious effects, if not anticipated, and it is this
fact that makes the planning of all developments in northern regions so vitally dependent upon accurate knowledge of ground and ground-temperature conditions.

This broad indication of the types of soil to be expected in different parts of the
world is a good indication of the relevance of geology to the assessment of terrain
for human use. It will be clear that if such use involves excavation of any magnitude,
soils (and rocks) will be exposed to view that have never been seen before in human
history. This applies whether the excavation be in virgin land or in the middle of an
old city. In each case, geological information will be revealed that may possibly be

Figure 3.9 Inuvik, Northwest Territories, Canada. Effect of the melting of
massive ground ice at the surface of a gravel pit when excavation had
facilitated the melting; the scale is given by the hat and windbreaker.
(Photograph by G. H. Johnston; courtesy of DBR/NRC.)

of great scientific value. Accordingly, geologists will be found who will have an interest not only in seeing the scientific information they have gathered put to good use but also in availing themselves of the opportunity of seeing for the first time exposures presented by excavations. Geology and planning can, therefore, demonstrate a true partnership of the science and the art in all such cooperative endeavors.

3.5 PLANNING AND GEOLOGY

A new city can never be planned and designed in total disregard of its environment, upon which it cannot be just imposed. It must fit at least with the topographic limitations of the chosen site. It will be influenced inevitably by the geological conditions beneath the surface of the site. Before considering the applications of geology to urban and regional planning in any detail, therefore, it may be useful to glance briefly at some of the more obvious influences that terrain can have upon overall planning. Fundamentally, a new urban center must incorporate the landscape of its site as an integral part of its plan. Requirements of the regional plan must be reconciled with the main environmental features. The plan must take account of geological and foundation conditions, respecting the agricultural importance of some soils and protecting the original character of the landscape to the extent that is possible. Drainage of the site and the supply of water and of building materials are all geological factors that must be given consideration. Assurance must be had that the plan will not interfere with the winning of building materials (especially sand and gravel) that may lie under part of the site but rather allow for their extraction prior to use of this part of the area for building. The necessity for "looking below the surface" as a part of the planning process must therefore be appreciated from the very earliest stages of site consideration.

As an example of the geological features that must be most carefully studied, consider the use of flood plains, widened valley floors immediately adjacent to river channels, that always appear to be such ideal areas for building. They will be underlain, sometimes to quite appreciable depths, by recently deposited alluvial material. They will occasionally be inundated during flood periods of the river. Since river flows are always variable, inundation may not take place every year. In some cases it may be an infrequent occurrence, but it requires only one period of flooding of developed land to wreak sometimes incredible damage. From meteorological, hydrological, and geological investigations it should always be possible to determine with reasonable accuracy whether flooding of a flood plain is a possibility, and even to determine the probability of flooding within stated terms of years. The shape and width of the flood plain will be controlled by the topography of the region, by the gradient of the river, by the annual discharge of the river and especially by the variation of this throughout the year, and by the amount of sediment being transported by the stream. A flood plain, therefore, is an organic part of the landscape, an essential part of the stream channel required for the safe conduct of flood waters.

Attractive for urban development though flood plains may appear to be, they provide unusual problems with building, quite apart from the ever-present hazard of possible flooding. Foundations on flood-plain sites are always difficult and so are expensive to construct. Foundation excavations will require pumping; foundation walls must be designed and constructed so as to be watertight because of the high water table that will exist at the site; in some cases, buildings must be designed to resist hydrostatic uplift; all services such as sewers and waterlines will have to be installed with difficulty and with the probability of repeated immersion as the water table rises in flood periods. All these features will add greatly to the cost of construction, despite the "obvious" advantages of the site. Flood-plain soil deposits are frequently loose sandy loams with no regularity in deposition, thus providing most variable foundation bed conditions. With their inevitably high moisture content, their bearing capacity will be very limited and variable, requiring unusual precautions in foundation design.

Quite apart from difficulties in actual building on flood plains, such areas suffer from undesirable microclimatic features induced by the inevitably high water tables coupled with the type of soil usually forming the surface strata. Ground mists will be common and atmospheric humidity usually high. On the other hand, the existence of alluvial soils will make such areas most suitable for agricultural land, the high water table being an advantage rather than the reverse. Although the growing of farm crops may not be suitable for an urban development, such areas also provide ideal parklands and recreation areas. With such uses, so desirable from the geological point of view, occasional flooding of the site will be of no consequence. Indeed, if the sediment carried by the adjoining river is suitable material, the flooding may be an advantage to sustained growth of grass and other vegetation in just the same way as the flooding of the River Nile has for centuries been of benefit to Egypt.

It is of interest to note that in Central Europe the builders of medieval towns generally avoided building on flood plains. They were rightly afraid of floods, and they knew well the difficulty of construction on the wet ground found adjacent to rivers. The old parts of the older cities of Europe will usually be found to be located on the higher ground provided by river terraces, well above flood-water levels. This wise practice, not based consciously on geology but utilizing the same kind of "horse sense" that the application of geology properly involves, has been widely forgotten in more recent years. Study of the growth of European cities will show that from the early years of the second half of the last century, intensive building on flood plains has proceeded under the pressures of imprudent development of urban living.

This is illustrated even in such a notable city as Prague. The banks of the Vltava (Moldau) River were used for building toward the end of the nineteenth century. High embankments were constructed along the river banks to protect such lands, in effect making the river in some sections into a canal. Under the protection of these banks, intensive building followed, even though the foundation bed materials were poor. Today it is found that the rows of houses thus built so close to the river are an impediment to reasonable traffic improvements. The original lovely character of the river banks was destroyed and many historical sites were covered up by this thoughtless regulation of the river.

Many other similar examples could be given, all showing how the older practice of leaving areas adjacent to river banks in their natural condition has been forgotten in the scramble for urban land, an older practice that geology is now reconfirming. It may be said that protection of flood plains from indiscriminate building is "obvious." So also are all other basic principles of sound design, in urban development as elsewhere. Obvious or not, the proper use of flood plains in urban areas has to be generally rediscovered. It is here that, through the presentation of geological facts, the necessary arguments for the protection of such lands can be supported and implemented without having to rely on references to earlier practices, good as they may have been.

The same experience can be encountered with the use of sloping ground. Topographical maps can show the angle of slope of such areas, but they cannot indicate the significance of the degree of inclination. In the area round London, for example, slopes have failed that were formed naturally in the London clay as flat as 9° to the horizontal, a slope that nobody would ordinarily question.[3.10] If the geology, as well as the topography, of such areas is carefully studied, the necessity of exercising the greatest care in interfering with the stability of such sensitive slopes will be obvious and much trouble can be avoided. In southern Scandinavia and in eastern Canada, sloping ground that appears to be perfectly stable may be underlain by sensitive marine clays that have the unfortunate property of liquefying when disturbed (because of the internal structure). What may appear to be stable slopes today may actually be the scars of old landslides in these difficult clays, a fact that can be determined by geological investigation aided by the use of aerial photographs.

So also with steep rock slopes. Exposed bedrock will often be shown on topographical maps. Its presence will suggest to all who have any appreciation of geology that the soil cover where rock is not exposed may be shallow. Yet there have been all too many cases where this "obvious" warning went unheeded. Plans have been prepared showing street layouts and water and sewer lines without regard to the fact that all excavation might have to be in rock. Some plans of this sort have actually been carried into effect, with what extra trouble and expense can well be imagined. Steep rocky hillsides are often the last relic of the original countryside, and as such should be preserved whenever possible as points of scenic interest quite apart from the utilitarian advantage of avoiding heavy expense in excavating through solid rock. In many cases, naturally, bedrock cannot be avoided in the development of an urban plan. Even here, however, the exact geological character of the bedrock must be known with certainty if trouble is to be avoided.

The city of Prague may again be mentioned as an example since geologically it is an unusually interesting area that illustrates in so many excellent ways the influence that geology can exercise on urban development. Some of the steep slopes in the city are formed of Ordovician slates. The stability of these rocks is controlled by the strike and dip of the strata relative to the inclination of the slope. When streets were laid out parallel to the strike of the beds dipping down the slope, the equilibrium of the entire hillside could easily be disturbed by construction works that could cause the slate to slide along its bedding planes Failures of this sort have occurred due to the undercutting of a slope for the widening of a road and even by trench excavation for the installation of sewers. In the northeastern part of Prague, deep excavation for the construction of roads cut into the hillsides in the same direction as the strata resulted in serious rockslides and even in the fracturing of retaining walls.[3.11] Such problems can be avoided if streets are located so as to cross the strike of the rock strata. This can be done only if the details of the local geology are known with certainty. If planning can be so aided, then excavation will be easier to carry out and slope failures can be avoided. The steeper the slopes in solid rock, the more detailed must be the relevant geological investigation before any plans can be completed.

If a planning area includes abandoned quarries or sand and gravel pits, these may show on a topographic map merely as local depressions. Vegetation may have grown up to such an extent that only a close examination of the ground, coupled with study of the history of the area, will reveal the old workings. All such locations must be the subject of detailed geological investigation since their abandonment may have been for geological rather than for economic reasons, and these could have some effect upon the future use of such areas. On the other hand, when the detailed geology of such areas has been determined, this may suggest ways in which the old workings can be incorporated into an overall plan with advantage instead of being regarded merely as an impediment to the orderly development of well-graded streets. In a few areas, notably those with limestone as the local bedrock, underground quarries may be found that have ceased to be operative. Later in this volume examples will be

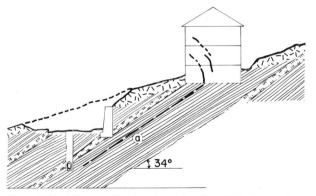

Figure 3.10 Diagram showing how the dip of sloping rock strata can affect engineering structures. *(Based on fig. 14-6 in* Inzenyrska Geologie, *Prague, 1957, courtesy of the authors, Q. Zaruba and V. Mencl.)*

given of very efficient use of such man-made caves, naturally only after the most inten-sive geological examination to ensure the safety of the underground supports and roofs.

There are also limestone regions in which natural caves may exist beneath the surface, sometimes with little or no evidence at the surface to indicate that caverns do exist. These cavities are due to the slow solution of the limestone by percolating groundwater. If exposed at the surface, they give rise to what is known as *karst topography*, the name derived from a mountain range in Yugoslavia near one of the most famous of all these "pockmarked" terrains. The same phenomenon can occur if gypsum is present in the bedrock formation, and for the same reason. It may be very difficult to judge merely from observations of the ground surface how extensive such caverns are, but a general geological reconnaissance of the area will indicate to the experienced observer the probable extent of the hazard, a hazard that will naturally affect all planning of the area in question. Figure 3.12 illustrates how complex can be the siting of even individual buildings in such areas. It shows the site of a central heating plant for a health spa in East Moravia in Central Europe. The site originally proposed (*a*) was found by test to be situated immediately above some karst caves. Boreholes sunk at the second choice for a site (*b*) also encountered large cavities beneath what might have been the foundation if these studies had not been carried out. The site finally used (*c*) was still of such a character that reinforced concrete slabs had to be used to bridge across open fissures in the local Devonian limestone, but the plant was successfully completed.

Figure 3.11 Kueilin, Kwangsi Province, S. China. Karst topography in limestone, illustrating how limestone surfaces now covered by soil can be extremely irregular. *(Photograph by J. Silar, Prague.)*

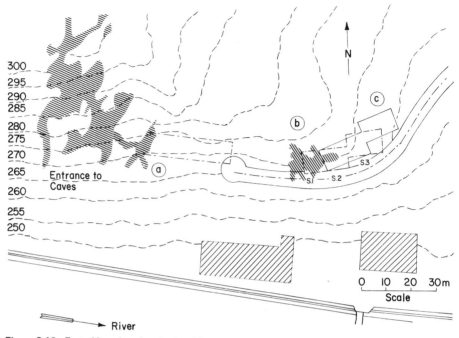

Figure 3.12 East Moravia, Czechoslovakia. Location of heating plant showing the alternative sites investigated; the significance of (*a*), (*b*), and (*c*) is indicated in the text. *(Based on fig. 14-8 in* Inzenyrska Geologie, *Prague, 1957, courtesy of the authors, Q. Zaruba and V. Mencl.)*

Leaching by groundwater of the salt beds that are sometimes found forming part of bedrock, when local geology is appropriate, can cause serious settlement of the ground surface. Over long periods of time the growth of vegetation may conceal the true nature of depressions in the ground caused in this way, and so they might also be unsuspected in a planning exercise in which geology was not given full attention. This is not a theoretical danger. A number of communities in central Germany have had to be permanently relocated because of ground subsidence due to solution of underlying salt beds. *Faults*, major breaks in the continuity of solid rock strata, may be similarly concealed at the surface and yet in some cases may be potential causes of disturbance at ground level. In all cases, faults should be avoided on sites upon which permanent buildings are to be erected. They, too, can be determined by careful geological study of the region within which the planning area is located. Even so simple a matter as the drainage of a site, apparently so straightforward a matter topographically, can be influenced by geological factors that may not be superficially evident.

When planning starts, for urban community or region, the area to be developed is not the equivalent, therefore, of a piece of blank paper ready for the free materialization of the ideas of the designer, but it is rather an environment that has been exposed for a very long period to the effects of many natural modifying factors. The present-day surface of the earth is the product of most complicated geological, hydrogeological, climatic, and other processes, knowledge of which assists in recognition of probable trends of future terrain changes. Development of new communities and the charting of regional development must, therefore, take account of this fundamental organic and dynamic character of Nature so that the works of man may fit as harmoniously as possible into the environment and not disturb its biological equilibrium any more than is essential. To conserve the soundness and productive power of a region for the use of future generations is a basic requirement of overall planning, and one that should be observed as a guide in the prosecution of all engineering works. As Francis Bacon said so perciptiently almost 400 years ago: "Nature to be commanded must be obeyed."

Obedience to Nature could well be the motto of every planning agency. Much has naturally been achieved along exactly these lines. Nothing on these pages is intended to convey any suggestion that geology has always been completely neglected in the development of modern cities and in the planning of the regions that are today being recognized so widely. Many engineers and architects in their collaborative work consciously or unconsciously take into account all features of the terrain with which they are dealing, often without using the name "geology," even though they are instinctively using geological approaches in their planning work. As will shortly be seen, much has already been achieved in the way of regional geological mapping with the needs of urban and regional planning specifically in view. This, however, is but a beginning of the widespread use of geology that must, in the future, feature all urban and regional planning work from which, until relatively recent times, it has been in general so conspicuously absent.

There are a few manuals and books dealing with planning that, in contrast with the examples cited earlier, have given some attention to geology as one of the contributing disciplines to the overall work of architects and engineers. In 1969 there was published a particularly noteworthy example of what is, so happily, a new trend. This volume is even graced with the title *Design with Nature*, and this indicates accurately the approach that it takes.[3.12] The author—Professor Ian McHarg—is, significantly, a landscape architect and planner, head of the Department of Landscape Architecture and Regional Planning at the University of Pennsylvania. His most attractive volume, with an introduction by Lewis Mumford, shows by means of a series of vivid examples, taken from the author's professional practice, how geology can be used in the planning process. Designing with Nature is indeed the whole approach of Professor McHarg. He has developed a technique of plotting on base maps each of the significant factors contributing to an overall regional plan and then superimposing these to see where they conflict. The positive graphical guidance thus given is clearly evident, especially when color is used, the proper allocation of space for urbanization, recreation, and conservation being well delineated.

In an early example, Professor McHarg groups his factors under the headings "Physiographical Obstructions" and "Social-Cost Values." The former include slope, drainage, bedrock geology, and soils; the latter, such items as historical values, forest and wildlife values, and residential values. In a later example (of Staten Island), a new subdivision is followed, major groupings being climate, geology, physiography, hydrology, pedology, vegetation, wildlife, and land use. In explaining the special place that Staten Island could have occupied, Ian McHarg says: "It is a special place—its geological history made it so. Silurian schists form the spine of the island, but the great Wisconsin glacier of Pleistocene time left its mark, for there lies the evidence of the terminal moraine. There are glacial lakes, ocean beaches, rivers, marshes, forests, old sand dunes, and even satellite islands." And in further comment, this: "The serpentine ridge and the diabase dike of Staten Island can only be comprehended in terms of historical geology. The superficial expression of the island is a consequence of Pleistocene glaciation. The climatic processes over time have modified the geological formations, which account for the current physiography, drainage, and distribution of soils." Here is the message of this book well expressed indeed by a distinguished regional planner in relation to the significance attaching to geology in his own work.

It must be recalled that the general approach of this notable volume, so well described by the resounding title—*Design with Nature*—is with relation to the planning of whole regions. That the approach it makes is not universally acclaimed may be indicated by one remarkable critique of Professor McHarg's techniques: ". . . the basic criterion for any land use is economic, and if a certain use is demanded by the economic life of the community, it will be built regardless of physical characteristics of the property, and if a use is not required, all the physically suitable land in the world will not create a demand for that use."[3.13] Others point out regularly that decisions on land use must be based on economic and political pressures. One cannot deny that this has been the case, all too often, in the past. Economic factors must certainly be given due weight, and the realities of political considerations cannot be forgotten or overlooked. But in view of what has happened to the newly developed parts of far too many cities, and of the still greater expansion of all cities that can even now be foretold, a continuation of hard-bitten approaches like this to planning in disregard of all natural features, good and bad, can lead to environments that can only be contemplated with regret that verges on shame. Geology, and all other relevant disciplines, simply must be given due consideration in the future planning of cities if disasters are to be avoided and man-made environments ensured that are at least conducive to decent living and reasonable civic pride. The fact that due consideration for geology in planning work can, in many cases, be shown to save money will usually win over the most recalcitrant of critics.

3.6 GEOLOGICAL METHODS AND MAPS

Geology, then, must be accepted as one of the major scientific disciplines supporting the work of engineers and architects and all others concerned with the planning of regions and urban centers. Naturally, it is not necessary or even desirable that those who are to use the results of geological investigations in their planning work should know in any detail how geologists go about their work of preparing the geological maps and reports that can prove to be of such vital importance to them. But it will be useful and helpful if they have at least a general idea of how these results are achieved. They will then be able better to appreciate the significance of geological information and be able to discuss with understanding with those responsible their general approach to the study of the region or area involved. A brief outline of geological methods will therefore next be presented, together with an introduction to the nature of geological maps, following which the application of this work to specific areas will be discussed with a broad spectrum of examples.

Topographical maps are naturally the first requirement of the geologist for his own field studies. It is not without significance that topographical mapping has always been closely associated with the geological work of the U.S. Geological Survey. Armed with the appropriate maps, to the largest scale that is available, the geologist then embarks upon his own field studies. Despite all the advances in sophisticated advanced methods of terrain study, such as will shortly be noted, there is no substitute for examination of the area being studied on foot and with that instinct for seeing beneath the surface that is second nature to all field geologists. Every detail of significance is recorded carefully on the base map, exactly where it is observed. Exposures of bedrock, the type of rock that is exposed, the nature of the jointing to be seen in exposed rock and especially any indication of faulting (or fracture) of rock strata, the presence and compass direction of any glacial striae such as may be found on polished glaciated rock surfaces, and naturally the presence of any fossils in bedrock—all these are typical of the information that must be patiently gathered and recorded. Soil, too, must be similarly recorded, with notes as to type, any variations and sudden changes, and especially any indications of groundwater (such as springs) within it. "Wet grounds" are always of special importance as are also the plants to be found in such places, some knowledge of *botany* being always of value to a geologist since some plants are reliable indicators of groundwater.

There is one detailed type of observation that must be explained with the aid of the accompanying Fig. 3.13 since it is so important and since it will assist in the understanding of how geologists can determine conditions beneath the surface from observations on the ground. When rock strata are exposed, it will often be seen that they are arranged in clearly defined beds. This will be a sign that they are either sedimentary or metamorphic rocks. Originally, these beds were horizontal or very close to this, if only because of the way they were deposited. Now they may be inclined, sometimes quite steeply, through earth movements of the past. Many strata can be seen to have been distorted into great curved shapes. It is, therefore, necessary to record the exact direction now taken by each bed at every exposure so that, by the piecing together of all these items of evidence, it may be possible to reconstruct a picture of the form taken by the beds beneath the surface, especially if a number of different exposures of the same bed can be observed and measured. These measure-

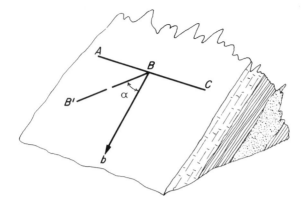

Strike is the compass direction of *ABC*
Angle of dip is the angle α
Lines *ABC* and *BB'* are in same horizontal plane
Lines *ABC* and *Bb* are on exposed rock surface

Figure 3.13 Diagram illustrating the terms "dip" and "strike" as used to define the position of the surfaces of rock strata.

ments are known as the *dip* and *strike* of the beds. The dip is the angle made with the horizontal by a line running down the surface of a dipping bed exactly at a right angle to the strike—which is the compass direction of a line across an exposure of the rock that is horizontal. With these two numbers for each exposure of a stratum of sloping rock, it is possible to define exactly the direction of the surface of the bed at that point.

Naturally, geologists have to use a form of "shorthand" to record all this diverse information upon small sections of topographical maps. There is reasonable agreement as to the signs that are used for this purpose. When all possible observations have been made it is then the task of the geologist to attempt their correlation. This is often tedious work, frequently necessitating further field studies in areas of unusual complexity. But ultimately it will be possible to prepare a preliminary geological map for the area. It must be remembered that geological maps have to attempt to show three dimensions more vividly than in the case of topographical maps. The key to this extension of the mapping concept is a clear indication of the angle of dip for all rock strata. If this is done, and the traces of the contacts between adjacent rock beds at the surface clearly indicated, then it is possible by means of ingenious geometrical methods to determine from the map the thickness of the different beds shown at different locations and to build up a picture of the underground structure. This is usually shown at the side of most geological maps in the form of a cross section taken along some suitable line (marked on the map), and it is with these geological sections that users of geological maps for planning purposes will be chiefly concerned. They are always clear, vividly portraying the underground structure of

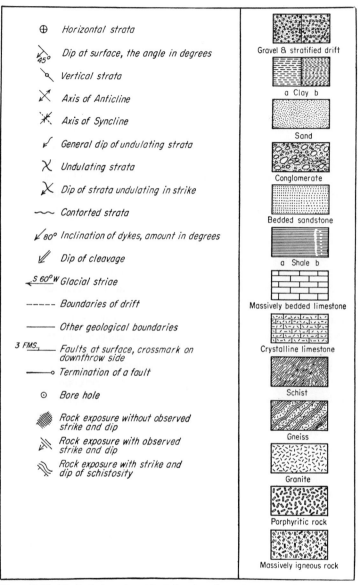

Horizontal strata

Dip at surface, the angle in degrees

Vertical strata

Axis of Anticline

Axis of Syncline

General dip of undulating strata

Undulating strata

Dip of strata undulating in strike

Contorted strata

Inclination of dykes, amount in degrees

Dip of cleavage

Glacial striae

Boundaries of drift

Other geological boundaries

Faults at surface, crossmark on downthrow side

Termination of a fault

Bore hole

Rock exposure without observed strike and dip

Rock exposure with observed strike and dip

Rock exposure with strike and dip of schistosity

Gravel & stratified drift

a Clay b

Sand

Conglomerate

Bedded sandstone

a Shale b

Massively bedded limestone

Crystalline limestone

Schist

Gneiss

Granite

Porphyritic rock

Massively igneous rock

Figure 3.14 Typical signs (graphical shorthand) used on geological maps. (The signs shown are generally in accord with the practice of the U.S. Geological Survey, but all geological maps include a guide to the signs used and these should always be consulted; the American Geological Institute of Washington, D.C., publishes useful "Data Sheets" giving a more complete set of examples.)

the rocks exposed at the surface along the chosen line; they are a most helpful aid in gaining that three-dimensional picture of the area being planned that is so essential.

The plotting of bedrock only has been discussed so far. When bedrock is either at or close to the surface of the ground, it will be shown on the local geological maps. In some areas, however, such as the plains of the Midwest and the Canadian prairies, bedrock may sometimes be at very great depths beneath the surface. Bedrock maps can still be prepared, but they will now have to be based on the results of deep borings. Far more important, and essential for all activities on the ground surface, will be the geological maps of the overlying soils. In areas that are thickly covered with deposits of glacial soils, these "drift maps" (as they used to be called in European countries) are of the greatest importance. They are prepared in exactly the same way as bedrock maps, with the possible addition of information obtained through shallow borings, an operation that can be very easily conducted in soil. Transported soils will also be found to be arranged in beds. Usually these will still be horizontal, in view of their geological youth, but any variations from this must duly be noted.

There will be found for most developed areas yet a third set of maps, these being maps that show the variation of the soils near and at the surface of the ground (topsoil) as prepared by agricultural soil scientists (pedologists). There is now a very well-developing science of such topsoil mapping, the results of which are of vital importance to agriculture. If a profile through the soil near the surface is examined, it will usually be found that different "horizons" of soil transformation—from the basic soil material beneath—can be observed. Three horizons are generally recognized, known as "A," "B," and "C." Figure 3.15 shows that the C horizon grades into the unaltered fragmented material that, to engineers and to geologists, is also known as soil. Readers need not be concerned about this slight semantic difficulty since all three disciplines work closely together with reasonable understanding; the context in which the word *soil* is used will always show whether the more general use is intended or the use that would be aided if *topsoil* were to be used instead. The value of agricultural soil maps is appreciable, quite apart from their use in agriculture, whenever development work involves the soil close to ground surface. For road location, airport location, and similar operations that, on relatively level ground, do not involve much excavation, the use of pedological soil maps can be of real assistance.

So well developed is this "engineering" use of pedological information that many highway departments, for example, will be found to have worked out (and published) complete systems of correlation between the many different agricultural soils types in their area (usually known by local names) and the basic engineering properties of these soils. With county soil maps now such a widespread feature throughout North America, the value of this most satisfactory interdisciplinary correlation can well be imagined. The engineering properties of soils constitute one of the significant contributions to this general area by civil engineering, through work in soil mechanics laboratories where techniques for the determination of all major physical properties of soils are now in wide use, following standardized test methods.

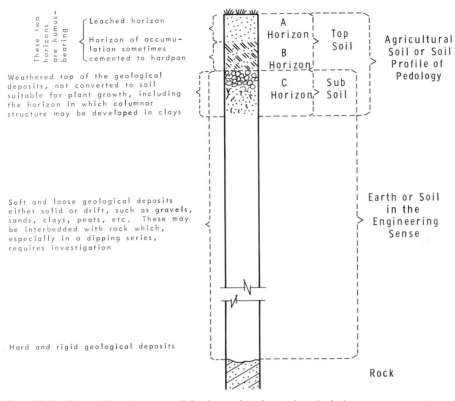

Figure 3.15 The relation between soil in the engineering and geological sense and the pedological use of the word. *(Courtesy of the British Standards Institution from the British Standard* Code of Practice for Site Investigation, 1957.)

These properties will call for frequent mention in the chapters that follow and so need not be detailed here. In any final geological-engineering report upon a planning area, however, the indication that the results of these tests give as to the usefulness of local soils will always be an important feature. For more specialized investigations, the mechanical properties of rocks will be similarly useful, properties determined in rock mechanics laboratories that are so similar to soil mechanics laboratories that *geotechnical properties* of soil and rocks is probably a much better way of describing this vital information.

It will now be seen that, although geological field work remains the foundation upon which regional geological information is based, it is today supplemented by many excellent scientific aids in the laboratory. In geological laboratories, rock samples collected during field studies will be tested, and they, too, can be subjected today to a surprising array of special tests. Among the most interesting are those that permit the determination of the age of rocks, and soils, to be carried out with reasonable accuracy. The "carbon-14" method is perhaps the most commonly mentioned of these test procedures, but there are now other methods available in a field that is a most active area of research.

Research activity will have been implicit as a background for much that has already been said, so very briefly, about the procurement of information about the geology of any region. It is, therefore, appropriate to note here that workers in the earth sciences as a whole are just as dedicated to pushing back the frontiers of knowledge in their special area through research as are those engaged in chemistry. physics, and biology. And geological and geotechnical research has the added complexity that much of it must be carried out in the field, the meshing of theoretical, laboratory, and field research in the earth sciences making it one of the most exciting of all scientific fields in which to work.

It is as a result of these research efforts that new field methods are now supplementing basic geological field work. Through very specialized laboratory techniques, it is now possible to detect minute quantities of elements in samples of water, soil, and even in vegetation, that may have come from rocks buried beneath surface soils. *Geochemical* and *geobotanical prospecting* are now well-recognized and highly developed field techniques that, although used chiefly in prospecting for ore deposits, have their uses also in detailed geological mapping for other purposes. *Geophysical* methods have been in use now for many years and are still powerful tools that can supplement surface observations. There are four main types of physical tests applied at the surface in order to determine the main lines of subsurface structure: *electrical methods*, involving the passage of electric currents through the ground between buried electrodes; *seismic methods*, involving the measurement of the rate of transmission of seismic vibrations artificially produced; *magnetic methods*, depending upon accurate measurement of the earth's magnetic field; and *gravimetric methods*, utilizing extremely sensitive instruments for measuring slight changes in gravimetric attraction. Although much oversimplified, these capsule descriptions will show that a variety of methods is available from which choice can be made, depending upon local conditions. It has to be remembered, however, that the results obtained are always indirect and must be checked by direct observation or measurement such as can be made with the aid of test drilling. Correlation is frequently very close, but it cannot be relied upon unquestioningly.

Aerial photography has yet to be mentioned. Although first used over 100 years ago, it has been only in relatively recent years that this quite remarkable technique has demonstrated its real potential in aiding geological reconnaissance. The use of color films has been a major factor in this latest significant development since great accuracy in color rendition can now be obtained, permitting a degree of "photointerpretation" that was previously unattainable with black and white photography. Even with black and white prints, however, much was possible, especially in view of the very wide coverage now available through national air photo libraries. (The whole of Canada, second largest country of the world, has, for example, now been photographed from the air.) It has proved to be especially valuable in the more remote parts of the world. Special mention may be made of regions in the north underlain by permafrost.

Figure 3.16 Charlesbourg, Quebec, Canada. Typical aerial photograph showing how ground forms may be distinguished; the radial planning of the town is uncommon. *(Courtesy of the National Air Photo Library, Dept. of Energy, Mines and Resources, Ottawa, Canada.)*

Photointerpretation of this type of terrain has been so well developed that it is possible, with reasonable certainty, to delineate from aerial photographs of the boundary region those areas that are underlain by frozen ground and those that are not, mainly through detection of differing vegetation. An example already cited indicates how important this advance in geological reconnaissance from the air can prove to be.

There are even further advances to record briefly, such as the use of stereoscopic aerial photography. When stereoscopic exposures are made on color film, the results can be almost startling in the reality they present when viewed through appropriate instruments. Machine plotting of contours can now be undertaken almost automatically from good stereo aerial photographs, and this, too, can aid geological interpretation. High-altitude flying is an advance of more recent years that is resulting in even greater potential for this aid to work on the ground. Finally, the use of special infrared film, giving thermal infrared images, is opening up entirely new fields of photointerpretation that suggest quite exciting possibilities for the future. The use of side-scanning radar has already been used successfully to photograph from great heights such an area as that in California in which the great San Andreas fault is so important a feature. The high-energy radar beam penetrated all surface vegetation, producing a clear photograph of the underlying bedrock—reproduced later in this volume.

Interesting and exciting as are these new developments, inviting further discussion, they must be left with this brief mention since it is with the results that they can achieve that this volume is concerned. Enough has probably been said to show that there are now available to geologists a variety of techniques for their study of the earth's crust. All these can be brought to play, if and when necessary, in the detailed study of the geology of a region that is made with the specific purpose of assisting in the preparation of a sound plan for the development of the area. Sometimes such regional studies will be specially commissioned and carried out in close association with the planning authority. In other cases, a special report (and possibly map) will be prepared for a planning organization based on appreciation of their needs for planning purposes but utilizing geological information already available. Such studies will naturally be of a general character only, sufficient for the proper appreciation of all terrain features in the process of planning but not adequate for the design of the foundations of individual structures.

This part of the implementation of the overall plan will call for individual site investigations for each structure or group of structures, carried out in much greater detail than will be necessary for planning purposes, with special attention given to the engineering properties of the soil and rock encountered and to local groundwater conditions.

The third and final stage in subsurface investigation in urban planning and development is that which is carried out when construction begins—continuing examination of all soil and rock that are exposed in excavation and the correlation of this information with the predictions from test boring, and with existing knowledge of the local geology. These are the three progressive stages in this essential part of all urban development. The second and the third are dependent upon the first. Examples will therefore next be presented of some typical appreciations of geology in relation to urban and regional planning, some specially prepared, some the summation of years of attention to the geology of specific areas, but all providing city planners with a vital part of the background information they must have if their work is to be well done.

3.7 SOME EXAMPLES

Washington, D.C.

No better introduction to the use that can be made of geology as a basic factor in regional planning could be imagined than the brochure entitled *Natural Features of the Washington Metropolitan Area*, published in January 1968 by the Metropolitan Washington Council of Governments (COG), subtitled appropriately *An Ecological Reconnaissance*.[3.14] This beautifully produced 50-page brochure was financed, in part, through an urban planning grant from the federal Department of Housing and Urban Development under the provisions of the (U.S.) Housing Act of 1954, a welcome indication of the interest of senior government in this type of approach to planning. The purpose of the report is stated to be "to present and analyze, under one cover, certain basic data essential to an understanding of the natural environment of the Washington Metropolitan Area. Within this urban region, approximately 25 square miles per year—or about one per cent of the metropolitan area annually—will be converted from farm, swamp, and hillside to subdivision, street and park between now and the year 2000." This prediction is an interesting confirmation, for one important city, of the overall figures presented in Chap. 1, figures that—at first sight—might have appeared to be so absurdly large. The metropolitan region that includes Washington is 610,000 hectares in area, measuring about 112 km wide and 89 km long. It is situated between the Atlantic Ocean and the Appalachian Mountains. Its geology is therefore varied, including several geological provinces, covering a period of geological time of as much as 600 million years. Map No. 1 in this impressive publication shows the generalized geology of the area.

A concise text accompanies this first map, contributed by Dr. Charles F. Withington, and explains in outline the four main provinces—the coastal plain, the Piedmont province, the Triassic lowland, and the Blue Ridge complex—each of which is clearly indicated on the accompanying map. It is further explained how geology influences some of the key factors in urban development, 11 factors being listed with their significance. Typical are slope stability, foundation conditions, excavation characteristics, groundwater features, and suitability for septic tanks. Maps that follow show generalized industrial mineral distribution (this being a $25 million a year industry in the area), ground elevations, the slope of the ground, soil distribution, streams and

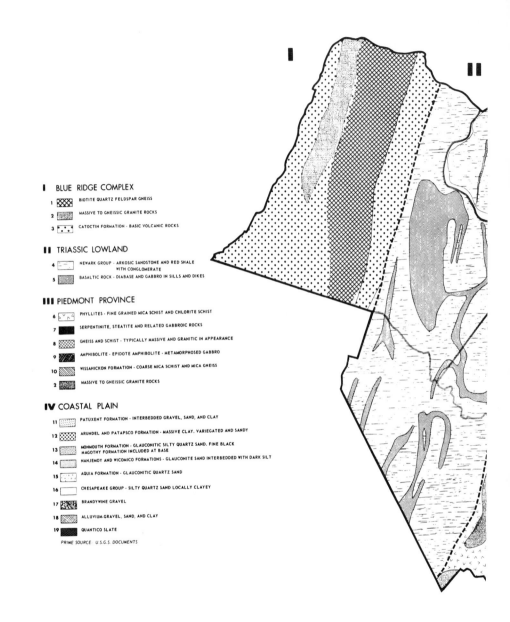

I BLUE RIDGE COMPLEX

1   BIOTITE QUARTZ FELDSPAR GNEISS

2   MASSIVE TO GNEISSIC GRANITE ROCKS

3   CATOCTIN FORMATION - BASIC VOLCANIC ROCKS

II TRIASSIC LOWLAND

4   NEWARK GROUP - ARKOSIC SANDSTONE AND RED SHALE
                WITH CONGLOMERATE

5   BASALTIC ROCK - DIABASE AND GABBRO IN SILLS AND DIKES

III PIEDMONT PROVINCE

6   PHYLLITES - FINE GRAINED MICA SCHIST AND CHLORITE SCHIST

7   SERPENTINITE, STEATITE AND RELATED GABBROIC ROCKS

8   GNEISS AND SCHIST - TYPICALLY MASSIVE AND GRANITIC IN APPEARANCE

9   AMPHIBOLITE - EPIDOTE AMPHIBOLITE - METAMORPHOSED GABBRO

10   WISSAHICKON FORMATION - COARSE MICA SCHIST AND MICA GNEISS

2   MASSIVE TO GNEISSIC GRANITE ROCKS

IV COASTAL PLAIN

11   PATUXENT FORMATION - INTERBEDDED GRAVEL, SAND, AND CLAY

12   ARUNDEL AND PATAPSCO FORMATION - MASSIVE CLAY, VARIEGATED AND SANDY

13   MONMOUTH FORMATION - GLAUCONITIC SILTY QUARTZ SAND. FINE BLACK
               MAGOTHY FORMATION INCLUDED AT BASE

14   NANJEMOY AND WICOMICO FORMATIONS - GLAUCONITE SAND INTERBEDDED WITH DARK SILT

15   AQUIA FORMATION - GLAUCONITIC QUARTZ SAND

16   CHESAPEAKE GROUP - SILTY QUARTZ SAND LOCALLY CLAYEY

17   BRANDYWINE GRAVEL

18   ALLUVIUM-GRAVEL, SAND, AND CLAY

19   QUANTICO SLATE

PRIME SOURCE: U.S.G.S. DOCUMENTS

Figure 3.17 Washington, D.C. Generalized geology of the Washington metropolitan area, based on U.S. Geological Survey publications. *(Map No. 1 in reference 3.14; courtesy of the Metropolitan Washington Council of Governments.)*

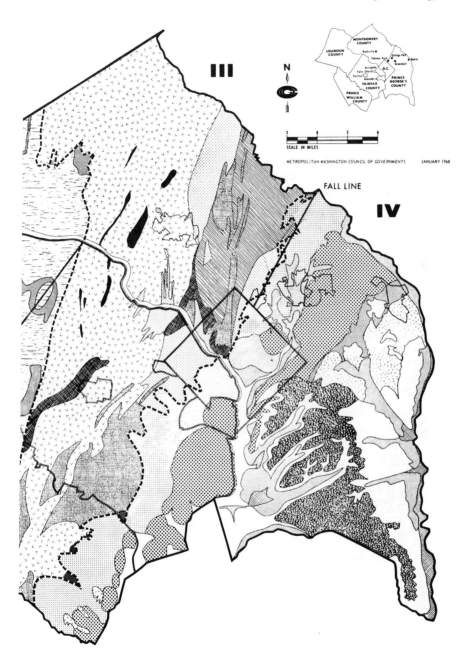

III

IV

FALL LINE

N

SCALE IN MILES

METROPOLITAN WASHINGTON COUNCIL OF GOVERNMENTS   JANUARY 1968

drainage basins, the presence of flood plains, groundwater distribution, woodlands—all with supporting statistics and explanatory notes—and, finally, a general map that is a composite of all the natural features previously delineated. This was obtained by superposition (not unlike the procedure advocated by Professor McHarg) and is accompanied by notes on the policies that must be considered in the further development of the area, and their relation to the natural environment so excellently illustrated in the report. It is impossible even to glance through these pages without being made aware of the profound influence of geology upon the natural features of the area. A reading of the text confirms this in a manner that is not possible in such a very generalized treatment of the subject as has so far been presented in these pages.

The information thus assembled was drawn from many sources. The geology of the Washington area has been studied by the U.S. Geological Survey (the headquarters of which has always been in the area) since 1882. Dr. N. H. Darton, of the Survey, started his observations in 1891 and was able to publish a masterly report in 1950, summarizing his studies over a period of 50 years.[3.15] There must be few, if any, cities that have had the benefit of such devoted attention to their geology from one individual for half a century. His work has been carried on by other members of the Survey staff, including Dr. Withington. In 1961 a detailed engineering-geologic study was started of the 112,500 hectares of the inner urban area that is yielding a series of modern geological maps, on a scale of 1:24,000, that depict not only the major lithologic units but also the general engineering properties of these units and the mineral resources of the area. In this, and the following brief notes on specific examples, few details of the local geology will be given since these are essentially of local interest. In every case, however, the references cited will prove to be a guide to the literature in which such detailed information can be found.

In the case of the Washington area, the USGS has naturally published quite a number of reports and papers during the 70 years in which it has been studying its own local geology. All this information was put to good use in providing a background and guide to the test-drilling program necessary for the second phase of subsurface investigation for the Washington subway, the construction of which started in 1969. Here the route had to be determined by considerations other than geological, but this made the geology to be encountered along the route all the more important. Almost 2,000 test borings were put down in detailed investigations, but previous geological studies indicated that about 40 percent of the subway would be in the Piedmont province and the remainder in coastal deposits, with possibly 40 percent of the length in rock tunnel.[3.16] One can be sure, in view of the long history of geological observation in the capital, that all the geology exposed during the subway construction will be carefully observed and accurately recorded.

San Francisco Bay Area

One of the pioneer studies of the engineering geology of a region in North America was that carried out by the USGS in the San Francisco Bay area, leading to publication of two fine maps at the end of the fifties. In 1957 there was published a map showing the "Areal and Engineering Geology of the Oakland West Quadrangle, California," by Dr. Dorothy H. Radbruch, and in the following year a corresponding map of the "Geology of the San Francisco North Quadrangle, California," by Drs. J. Schlocker, M. G. Bonilla, and D. H. Radbruch.[3.17] Both sheets present not only excellently reproduced geological maps of the land area shown but long descriptions of the geology and tables giving generalized descriptions of the engineering properties of the earth materials encountered. More will be said later about the valuable summary information that can be thus presented, but these early tables gave such information as permeability, slope stability, and foundation characteristics. Geological sections complete the quite remarkable coverage that is presented on these single sheets.

The origin of the project may well be quoted from the legend on the San Francisco sheet:

> [The San Francisco Bay] area was selected because its strategic location both as the focal point of development for a large part of the west coast and as the gateway to trans-pacific commerce, has made it one of the outstanding centers of continuous expansion and construction in the nation. The study in no way pretends to supplant detailed site studies. Rather it tries to supply an accurate background picture of the lithology and of the geologic processes that change or modify the earth materials involved. As much of the quadrangle that does lie beneath the bay is hidden by streets, buildings and other man-made structures, geologic observations were confined largely to undeveloped lots and to current excavations for utility lines and building foundations and had to be supplemented by data obtained from boreholes and earlier foundation construction. Several thousand logs of boreholes drilled by private firms as well as federal, state, county and municipal agencies provided data that were invaluable in filling out the geologic story of the area.

This work of the late fifties is now being supplemented by a major new project, the first of seven pilot studies planned by the (U.S.) Departments of the Interior and Housing and Urban Development. Commencing on 1 January 1970, the project is

> a regional scale demonstration on project to test the usefulness of environmental resource data in improving comprehensive urban planning and decision-making. The study will attempt to determine those data most useful for these purposes and the most effective ways of interpreting and presenting such data. The study will provide information on areas of earthquake fault hazards and landslide potential, and response of San Francisco margin lands to earthquake shock. Flood-prone areas, and those useful for solid waste disposal, and subsurface fluid waste storage will be identified. Water and mineral resources—particularly those of major urban significance such as sand and gravel—will be inventoried. Findings of the unique study—to be carried out by a multidisciplinary team of U.S. Geological Survey earth scientists and engineers working in close cooperation with Bay area planners—will provide valuable guidelines to similar efforts throughout the nation.[3.18]

Figure 3.18 San Francisco, California. Aerial view of the city showing in general the area covered by the engineering-geological map mentioned in the text; the Golden Gate may be seen at the top of the photograph. *(Courtesy of San Francisco Convention and Visitors Bureau.)*

The other areas in which similar projects were contemplated were Denver, Puget Sound, Connecticut Valley, Pittsburgh, Washington, D.C., Baltimore, and either Atlanta or Miami. The eventual results of these studies will indeed be of great and widespread value and should encourage the prosecution of many similar cooperative ventures of geologists, engineers, and planning authorities.

Portland, Oregon

Regional geological information is presented in a rather different, but equally useful, manner in the case of a study of the geology of the Portland region in Oregon, field work for which was contemporaneous with that for San Francisco. An area of 270,000 hectares was mapped in detail. If only to indicate the amount of work represented by the resulting map, field work was conducted every summer from 1948 to 1955 (with the exception of one year) by Dr. D. E. Trimble and assistants. An unusually interesting geological map of this whole area was prepared, printed in the usual vivid colors and accompanied by a geological section, in the margin, the scale being 1:62,500 (or about one mile to the inch).[3.19] The explanation accompanying the map is in the form of what may be called a "standard" geological report, a clearly written account of the area and its geology in a 119-page report, in the cover of which the map is included.

The study is explained thus: "The investigations were intended to provide basic geological information broadly applicable to the construction industry for use in the investigation of foundation conditions and in the search for earth materials for construction. The data, however, are equally useful in the search for industrial minerals, in the development of groundwater resources, and in a great many other

Figure 3.19 Portland, Oregon. Aerial view of a typical valley in the basaltic rocks in the western part of the city, which form most attractive scenery; a landslide has taken place in the area on the left, but this has been stabilized by the rock toe adjacent to the roadway. *(Courtesy of the Oregon State Highway Division and W. H. Stuart.)*

ways." One of these other ways will be, naturally, to assist with any regional and urban planning in the region, even though this is not specifically stated in the text since the map and accompanying explanation give exactly that general geological background that has been stressed as essential for the efficient carrying out of urban and regional planning. The latter part of the report deals with landslide potential in the area, with useful information on local industrial mineral deposits and on local soils in relation to construction.

The local soils are unusual since they include large deposits of loess (a wind-deposited, fine-grained soil that often creates difficulties in construction) and deeply weathered soils. It is remarkable that in a region relatively so far to the north, the process of laterization (a special type of weathering) should have proceeded to such depths as are found in the Portland area, some cases exceeding 30.5 m. Knowledge of the properties of these special soil types is quite essential in advance of all planning. This excellent report is typical of the best type of local geological study. It is introduced here since, although its title gives no indication of its engineering character and even though planning is not specifically mentioned as one of its potential uses, it is exactly the sort of valuable general geological review of an important area that can be of such great use in the planning process. Search should always be made, prior to the start of planning, for any possible reports of this type for every area for which special geological investigations have not been initiated as a part of the background to planning operations.

Some Far Eastern Studies

If only to make quite clear that studies such as are under discussion are not confined to North America, note may be made of some areal studies carried out in the Far East. Almost by chance, the author came across an early example of what one individual can do, in a paper published in 1940 on foundation conditions in the fabled city of *Mandalay* in northern Burma.[3.20] F. D. L. Wooltorton, a civil engineer, prepared a report on the foundation soil conditions in this city, a précis of which was published in a London engineering journal. This was in the very early days of soil mechanics, but the paper gives remarkably useful information about the local *kyatti* soil that is usually found immediately underlying the better-known black cotton soil so widespread in the East. Geological conditions in *Hong Kong* will call for mention in later chapters since the weathering of the local granite into residual soil gives rise to serious problems when engineering work has to be carried out in it. It is therefore of interest to note that in May 1962 there was held a Conference on Hong Kong Soils at which nine papers were presented covering all the main aspects of the local soils of this small but important area.[3.21] The total area of the colony is less than 107,000 hectares, but the proceedings of a discussion of its soil conditions fill a useful volume of 149 pages.

A somewhat similar conference was held in September 1964 in *Calcutta*, India, and again a most useful volume resulted that will be of great use to all concerned with developmental activity in this crowded metropolis.[3.22] Appreciative reference was therein made to a 1940 publication of the Geological Survey of India that described "The Geology and Underground Water Supply of Calcutta, Bengal." Since Calcutta lies in the alluvial plain of the great Ganges River, bedrock is at a great depth below the surface, so deep that no test boring has yet penetrated to rock. Records of tube wells sunk to more than 305 m below the surface have revealed deeply buried peat beds with sand beds and also clay in which calcareous nodules known as *kankar* are found. For planning purposes, therefore, the detailed properties of the soils that form the entire surface of the city and surroundings have to be known with certainty. The 1964 conference made a great contribution to providing this information in convenient and usable form.

Use of Pedological Information

The great value of surveys of surface soils has been mentioned; a typical case from *Australia* may be mentioned as an example. In 1959 there was published by the New South Wales Department of Agriculture's Soil Survey Unit a report of their survey of the municipality of *Ku-Ring-Gai*, an extensive area located about 9.6 km

Figure 3.20 Hong Kong. Typical exposure of residual soil, grading from the solid *in situ* granite up to surface soils and showing blocks of granite still unweathered. *(Courtesy of Peter Lumb, University of Hong Kong.)*

to the north of the city of Sydney and its lovely harbor.[3.23] Troubles had been experienced in the suburbs of the city with the cracking of walls of domestic buildings due to differential soil movements beneath their foundations. The Commonwealth Experimental Building Station in conjunction with the Soil Physics Section of the Commonwealth Scientific Industrial and Research Organization decided to investigate the matter in the municipality of Ku-Ring-Gai, and the N.S.W. Soil Survey Unit was asked to make the survey, CEBS being responsible for the correlation of the results with engineering properties and foundation behavior. The report deals with local climate, vegetation, and geology, The area is underlain by two formations of *Triassic* age, the Wianamatta shale and the Hawkesbury sandstone. Weathering and laterization has created the local soils from these rocks, the depth to weathering being in places between 7.6 and 9.1 m. Soils were sampled to depths of 2.1 m, 17 soil series being recognized and grouped into four soil "associations," and these are shown on the map that accompanies the report, the value of which has been attested to by local building officials.

One of the many treatments of the correlation of pedological soil classifications with engineering properties of soils is to be found in the excellent handbook of the *Michigan* State Highway Department, *Field Manual of Soil Engineering*, now in its fourth edition.[3.24] Although prepared for use in highway design and construction and allied engineering work (such as for airfields), this manual can serve equally well for planning purposes in Michigan and is a most useful guide for those working in other areas to whom comparable local comparative information is not immediately available. For those who wish to consult a general review of this important inter-disciplinary collaboration, a bulletin issued by the *Illinois* State Geological Survey Division can be commended. Entitled "Coordinated Mapping of Geology and Soils for Land-Use Planning," it is issued as No. 29 in the Survey's series of Environmental Geology Notes.[3.25] The number in this series is indicative of the attention that the Illinois Survey has been paying to the importance of geology in the environment, in company with most of the other state geological surveys. The progress made by these state organizations in the application of geology to engineering and to environmental and planning problems, as a natural consequence of their long-standing interests in local industrial mineral supplies, is most encouraging. This work has resulted in so many excellent examples that might be cited in this context that regret must be recorded at the impossibility of citing even one report from each of the surveys now active in this field. At the risk of inviting invidious comparisons, attention will be directed to six examples; it must be emphasized that these are typical of a steadily growing number of such reports coming from many surveys.

Some Examples from State Surveys

The *Kansas* State Geological Survey, with headquarters at the University of Kansas in Lawrence, issued in June 1968 a 63-page report describing "A Pilot Study of Land-Use Planning and Environmental Geology" that can prove to be of special use to those who are thinking of embarking upon studies of this kind.[3.26] It is, as its title suggests, an exploration of the many factors that have to be considered in making regional geological studies designed to assist with the planning of land use. Copies were issued with a definite invitation to readers to submit comments and criticisms. In the planning of the work described, an Urban Geology Advisory Council (inter-disciplinary) was assembled to review and criticize preliminary plans. A pilot area of one mile square was selected, a little more than 1.6 km to the west of the city limits of Lawrence. Previous experiences in the general area, summarized in the report, had included starting a housing development on land below which (unknown to the developer) limestone existed close to the surface, with consequent trouble and expense, and the building of a complex of apartments without due consideration of spring floods, resulting in serious flooding of first-floor apartments. There were, therefore, good guidelines for developing the framework of the study. Community interests and activities were inventoried—transportation by road, rail, and air, pipelines, solid-waste disposal, liquid-waste disposal, foundation construction, utility installation, landscaping and land-clearing, mineral-waste extraction, and the provision of recreational and open spaces. These items, which are listed to show how useful a guide the report itself can be, were offset against a corresponding list of physical factors. When field studies were complete, the results were plotted on individual maps (to a scale of 1:25,000) for each physical factor, then assembled, and the results correlated as is explained in the text. Especially useful are some concluding suggestions for future studies of the same type based on the experience gained, and clearly explained by the author, Dr. Paul Hilpman.

Typical of the work of the *Missouri* Division of Geological Survey and Water Resources, of the State Department of Business and Administration, is their treatment of the Maxville quadrangle in the northeast corner of Jefferson County, which itself is in the northeast corner of the state. In May 1968 the Survey published a regular geological map of the quadrangle with an accompanying set of explanatory notes and a geological profile, all printed on the back of the map. In itself, this excellent map, with its accompanying geological section, would be helpful in planning, but it is supplemented by a second map of the whole area to the same scale (1:24,000) showing the engineering geology of the quadrangle.[3.27] This shows, equally clearly, the alluvial soil deposits in the river and stream valleys and, for the remainder of the area, the soils grouped into six units, depending on the underlying bedrock with simple indica-tions as to their suitability in engineering use. The explanatory text is issued as a separate, folding, eight-page pamphlet that describes very clearly all the materials to be encountered in carrying out engineering work in this area. On the back of the engineering geology map are printed two large tables, the first giving details of the engineering characteristics of all the soils shown on the map and the second, corre-sponding interpretations as to such matters as use as fill, susceptibility to erosion, drainage properties, and general limitations affecting its use. Below the tables are seven block diagrams that must prove to be most useful to those unfamiliar with geology since they show so clearly the three-dimensional aspect of some of the local land-use problems, previously stressed as being of such importance.

In *Michigan*, yet another pattern is found. Report of Investigation No. 13 was published by the Geological Survey Division of the state's Department of Natural Resources; it deals with the "Geology for Environmental Planning in Monroe County," located in the extreme southeast corner of the state.[3.28] The study was prepared by Professor Andrew T. Mozola of the Department of Geology of Wayne State University in Detroit. It is published as a well-produced, photo-offset, letter-sized report, with many illustrations embodied in the text, and accompanied by five folding maps of the county, one sheet of cross sections through the area, and a bedrock map and chart of stratigraphic succession for the whole state. The five maps show, respectively: the bedrock geology, the bedrock surface topography, the thickness of soil all over the county, the glacial deposits, and the piezometric water level in the ground for the whole area. As can be imagined from this listing, the report presents a great deal of information in surprisingly compact form for an area having quite unusual geological problems that can have profound effect upon planning. The county is underlain by Paleozoic rock strata dipping gently northwest. Bedrock consists generally of limestone, with some sandstones and shales. Glacial soils cover practically all the bedrock surface, in places to depths of 49 m. Over most of the county, however, depth to bedrock is not more than 9 m. The result is that over most of the area, except in large urban areas, water supplies are obtained from wells drilled in the bedrock. Domestic wastes are disposed of through septic tanks that discharge into the soil and so complicate the overall groundwater situation, which is, therefore, susceptible

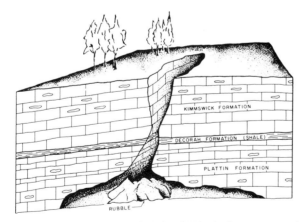

Figure 3.21 Missouri. Typical simple block diagram as used to illustrate geological structure three dimensionally; this example shows soil overlying cavernous limestone. *(Figure 5 on the back of the map in reference 3.27, courtesy of the Missouri Division of Geological Survey and Water Resources, W. B. Howe, State Geologist.)*

to contamination. Knowledge of geology is, therefore, crucial to land-use planning for this one reason alone. An earlier report in the same series, also by Professor Mozola (No. 3 on Wayne County), gives rather more general explanation about groundwater conditions and can be strongly commended as a useful introduction to this important part of geological study for planning purposes.[3.29]

Another of the Environmental Geology Notes, No. 33, from the *Illinois* State Geological Survey Division, can be used to illustrate a somewhat similar approach taken by this organization. Entitled "Geology for Planning in De Kalb County, Illinois," it was prepared by Dr. David L. Gross of the Survey staff.[3.30] It is a summary of a report specifically prepared to assist the De Kalb County Planning Department with their work, the department requesting the Survey to provide them with information on waste disposal, groundwater availability, sand and gravel resources, and suitability of the land for highway and subdivision development and for septic systems. The county is a predominantly rural area in northern Illinois, approximately 96 km west of Chicago. The city of DeKalb is the site of Northern Illinois University and is located in the center of the county. With growing population, and its location midway between Chicago and Rockford, it is expected that the county will develop rapidly. The attention being paid to planning, and to geology as a prerequisite to planning, is indicative of the forward-looking administration of the county.

The official report to the Planning Department was accompanied by maps to a scale of 1:125,000 (or about 1:120,000). These have been reduced to a scale of 1:250,000 for presentation, by photo-offset, as illustrations bound with the text of the bulletin. The three steps taken in pursuing this study are outlined: differentiation of all geological units within the county by field mapping, subsurface exploration, and laboratory investigations; evaluation of these geologic units in terms of mineral resources and engineering properties; and preparation of maps based on the assembled information in which areas are graded for specific land uses. Ingenious graphical symbols are used on the maps in place of the usual color printing, demonstrating what economies can be introduced in the presentation of such a summary report when necessary. Five maps are included, showing surficial deposits, groundwater conditions, sand and gravel resources, suitability of areas for solid waste disposal, and suitability of areas for general construction. As a guide to preliminary planning, and to further and more detailed investigations, these small-scale maps should prove to be of great value.

Continuing eastward, yet another approach to this overall problem of making geological information readily available and useful for planning is to be found in a typical publication of the *Ohio* Division of Geological Survey of the Department of Natural Resources of the state of Ohio. Professor George W. White, of the University of Illinois, is the author of a report that deals with the "Glacial Geology of Wayne County, Ohio."[3.31] (The duplication of county names is purely coincidental.) This is a county in the northeast of Ohio, its center about 80 km south of Lake Erie, that is completely covered with glacial soils, having no bedrock exposures. Planners,

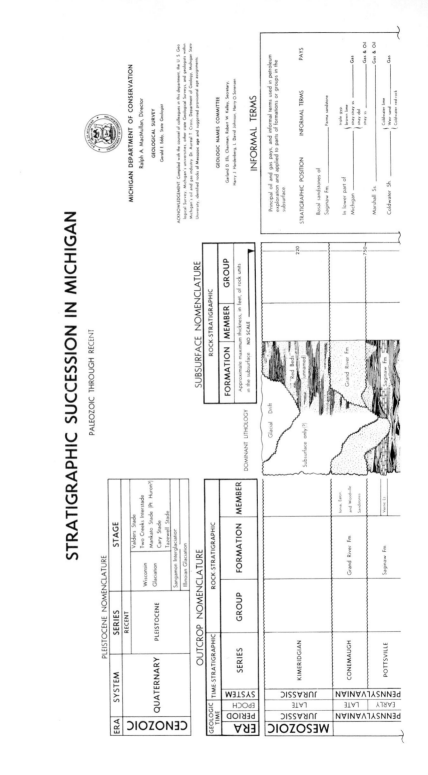

STRATIGRAPHIC SUCCESSION IN MICHIGAN

PALEOZOIC THROUGH RECENT

MICHIGAN DEPARTMENT OF CONSERVATION

Ralph A. MacMullan, Director

GEOLOGICAL SURVEY

Gerald E. Eddy, State Geologist

ACKNOWLEDGMENT: Compiled with the counsel of colleagues in this department, the U. S. Geological Survey, Michigan's universities, other state Geological Surveys, and geologists within Michigan's oil and gas industry. Dr. Aureal T. Cross, Department of Geology, Michigan State University, identified rocks of Mesozoic age and suggested provisional age assignments.

GEOLOGIC NAMES COMMITTEE

Garland D. Ells, Chairman; Robert W. Kelley, Secretary;
Harry J. Hardenberg, L. David Johnson, Harry O. Sorensen

INFORMAL TERMS

Principal oil and gas pays, and informal terms used in petroleum exploration and applied to parts of formations or groups in the subsurface

STRATIGRAPHIC POSITION	INFORMAL TERMS	PAYS
Basal sandstones of Saginaw Fm.	Parma sandstone	
In lower part of Michigan	triple gyp	
	brown lime	Gas
	stray stray ss.	
	stray dol	Gas & Oil
	stray ss	
Marshall Ss.	Cold-water lime	Gas & Oil
Cold-water Sh.	Weir sand	Gas
	Cold-water red rock	

PLEISTOCENE NOMENCLATURE

ERA	SYSTEM	SERIES	STAGE
CENOZOIC	QUATERNARY	RECENT	
		PLEISTOCENE	Valders Stade / Two Creeks Interstade / Mankato Stade (Pt. Huron?) / Cary Stade / Tazewell Stade (Wisconsin Glaciation)
			Sangamon Interglaciation
			Illinoian Glaciation

SUBSURFACE NOMENCLATURE

ROCK-STRATIGRAPHIC		
FORMATION	MEMBER	GROUP

Approximate maximum thickness, in feet, of rock units in the subsurface. NO SCALE

DOMINANT LITHOLOGY

Glacial Drift

"Red Beds" (unnamed)

Subsurface only(?)

Grand River Fm

Saginaw Fm.

220

750

OUTCROP NOMENCLATURE

GEOLOGIC TIME				TIME-STRATIGRAPHIC	ROCK-STRATIGRAPHIC		
ERA	PERIOD	EPOCH	SYSTEM	SERIES	GROUP	FORMATION	MEMBER
MESOZOIC	JURASSIC	LATE	JURASSIC	KIMERIDGIAN			
	PENNSYLVANIAN	LATE	PENNSYLVANIAN	CONEMAUGH		Grand River Fm	Ionia, Eaton, and Woodville Sandstones
		EARLY		POTTSVILLE		Saginaw Fm	Verne Ls.

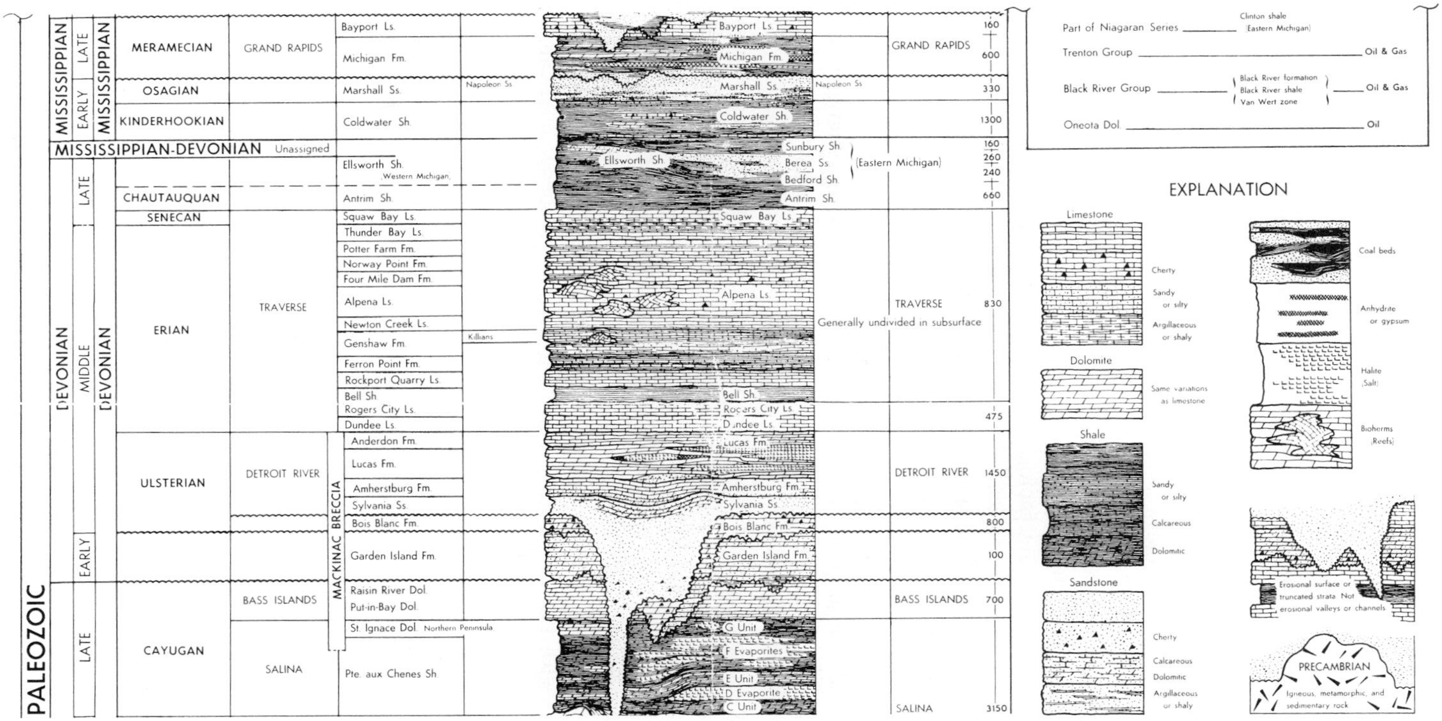

Figure 3.22 Michigan. Parts of a typical geological stratigraphic section showing rocks underlying Michigan. *(Chart accompanying references 3.28 and 3.29, courtesy of the Michigan Geological Survey Division, A. E. Slaughter, State Geologist.)*

95

therefore, will be concerned with the types of soils to be encountered, and these can be properly described only against a full understanding of the glacial history of the region. This Professor White gives in his lucid text, which is illustrated with records of shallow boreholes and with cross sections taken through sand and gravel pits and also along a cut in one of the state's new superhighways.

One of the especially interesting features of this report is its demonstration of the reciprocal benefit from geological-planning-engineering collaboration, since the description of the soils of Wayne County could not have been made as complete as it is without the information gleaned from engineering excavations. A color-printed map of the county to a scale of 1:62,500 accompanies the report, showing not only all the main soil types but also significant geological features, such as alluvial fans and flood plains. It requires only a very broad general knowledge of glacial geology to appreciate the significance of the soil types and landforms shown on the map and described in the text, and so the report and map can prove to be most useful sources of vital planning information. Most geological surveys will be found to publish geological reports of this type, not specifically directed to planning purposes but of real use in planning work. Another notable example is the report on the "Pleistocene Stratigraphy of *Illinois*," by H. B. Willman and J. C. Frye, a masterly 204-page review of the glacial geology of the entire state of Illinois.[3.32]

After *Cities and Geology* had been prepared, the Geological Survey of *Alabama*, in cooperation with the USGS, published the first number in their new Atlas series that is so good, and so relevant to the purpose of this volume, that it must be given this all-too-brief reference. "Environmental Geology and Hydrology, Madison County, Alabama, Meridianville Quadrangle" is the title of a fine color-printed 72-page atlas that exemplifies admirably, for one county, the main sections of this volume. The introduction deals with the "population explosion"; resources, topography, climate, and water and land use are all well discussed against a basic appreciation of the geology of Madison County, located in the Tennessee Valley on the northern border of Alabama. The use of excellent colored maps for each section of the atlas is particularly effective, justifying the page size, which is even larger than that of the Washington folio. Financed by the City of Huntsville, Madison County, and the State and Federal Geological Surveys, the atlas can be warmly commended to all who wish to see "cities and geology" in action.[3.33]

Some Canadian Examples

Since *Montreal* has a history as a settled community of over 300 years, and is the seat of McGill University and l'Université de Montréal, having been for a short time the headquarters of the Geological Survey of Canada, it is natural that there should have been built up an appreciable collection of geological literature about the city and its environs. This vast quantity of information was assessed and correlated by the City Planning Department (Service d'Urbanisme), the results being published in their *Bulletin Technique* No. 4 in February 1966.[3.34] This is another outstanding document in the field under review, comparable, although different in style and in size (through the use of folding colored maps), to that for the Washington area so warmly commended at the outset of this section.

The Bulletin considers not only the Island of Montreal, on which the city is located, itself an area 58 km long by 11 km wide, but also a broad region around, the total area depicted in the maps being about 780,000 hectares. The Bulletin is entitled "Physical Characteristics of the Region" and is printed, as is usual, in both English and French. The Director of the Department when it was issued explains that the Bulletin is addressed to "all those who are interested in the planning of large urban agglomerations" and that it was undertaken "as part of the programme of the Planning Department towards the preparation of a master plan for the region . . . ." And the bedrock geology is the first topic to be discussed, illustrated by a color-printed geological map that is so well printed, in such vivid colors, and that shows such a complex pattern for the local geology that it could well be mistaken for a fine example of modern nonobjective art.

The scale is about 1:300,000, each sheet therefore measuring about 38 by 51 cm, easy to handle and yet clear to read. These details of presentation are mentioned only because of the great importance of winning the attention of those involved in planning policy (such as members of advisory planning boards) who are not familiar with geology and who may have to be persuaded as to the need for such consideration of the natural environment as a preliminary to the process of detailed planning. The Washington area report is outstanding in this regard, the only possible minor flaw in its presentation being its overall page size (28 by 35 cm) so that copies will not fit into any normal files—but possibly this is a designed advantage since the brochure has to be given special office treatment! The finished size of the Montreal brochure is standard letter size (22 by 28 cm), which is convenient, but it does involve the use of folded maps, as do three of the state Survey reports that have just been described. Convenience in presentation should not be forgotten, subsidiary though it is to the content of reports and maps.

Reverting now to the content of the city of Montreal Planning Department's fine production, the bedrock geology of the Montreal region is concisely described in the textual matter that prefaces the first map. The second section deals with the local surficial deposits, all glacial soils apart from some recent alluvium; a second map vividly illustrates these. Relief and drainage characteristics are shown on three maps— a contour map showing land form, a special map indicating land slopes, and a map showing the outlines of the main drainage basins of the district from which the drainage pattern can be deduced. A map of the local forest cover completes this excellent graphical presentation. The brochure closes with some brief notes on the implications of its contents for planning, with an indication of the further information that is necessary for completing the overall picture of the natural environment of the region around and including Canada's metropolis.

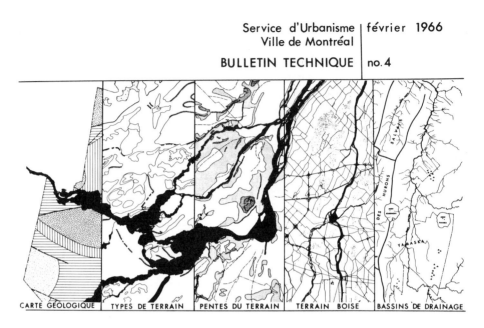

Service d'Urbanisme | février **1966**
Ville de Montréal

BULLETIN TECHNIQUE | no. 4

CARACTÉRISTIQUES PHYSIQUES

Figure 3.23 Montreal, Quebec, Canada. Cover of the bulletin described in the text (reference 3.34) showing the five main types of maps included. *(Courtesy of the City Planning Department, Montreal, Guy R. Legault, Director.)*

More detailed investigations have naturally been made in the city proper, this work having been initiated as a joint project of the city of Montreal, through its Public Works Department, and the Geological Survey of Canada. A notable joint paper summarizes the first results of this work, giving a fine overview of the geology of the city as a whole.[3.35] Geological sections are used to good advantage in this paper, showing that the major escarpment that distinguishes the western end of the city is not "solid rock" as most citizens imagine but consists of thick deposits of local glacial tills, rock level being more than 30 m below the surface. Those who would like to read in French a companion general account of the geology underlying this first city of Canada can do so by referring to the *Proceedings of the Sixth International Conference on Soil Mechanics and Foundation Engineering* that was held in Montreal in 1965 and that naturally featured a lecture on this subject.[3.36] Work continues on the accumulation of subsurface geological records, as will be related in Chap. 9 when this more detailed aspect of the urban subsurface is considered.

Another notable Canadian document in this field is one that has already come to be known as the *Saskatoon Folio*, even though its full title is *Physical Environment*

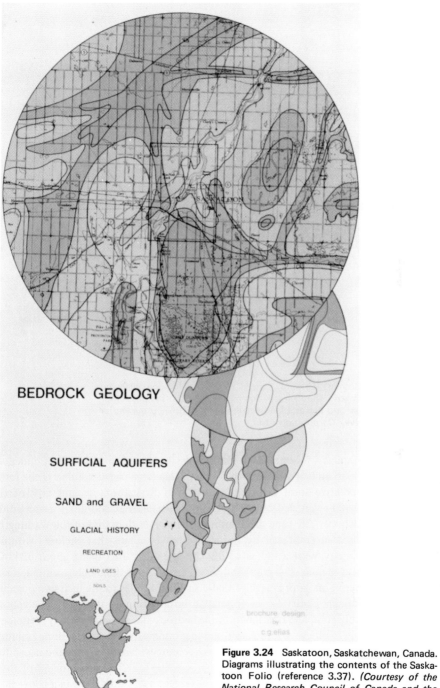

BEDROCK GEOLOGY

SURFICIAL AQUIFERS

SAND and GRAVEL

GLACIAL HISTORY

RECREATION

LAND USES

SOILS

brochure design
by
c.g.elias

Figure 3.24 Saskatoon, Saskatchewan, Canada. Diagrams illustrating the contents of the Saskatoon Folio (reference 3.37). *(Courtesy of the National Research Council of Canada and the Saskatchewan Research Council.)*

Figure 3.25 Scarborough, Ontario, Canada. Aerial view looking northwest from over Lake Ontario showing the Scarborough Bluffs (see page 366), and the golf course and pastoral land above them, in 1947. *(Courtesy of the Lockwood Survey Corporation Ltd.)*

of Saskatoon, Canada.[3.37] Published jointly by the National Research Council of Canada and the Saskatchewan Research Council, this large-paged volume is the result of a truly cooperative local effort in the city of Saskatoon, second city of the province of Saskatchewan, led by Dr. Earl A. Christiansen as coordinator and editor of the resulting volume. The page size is even slightly larger than that of the Washington area volume. The area embraced by the study, however, was that enclosed within a circle around the city with a radius of 32 km, the total area being about 324,000 hectares. The folio includes 54 maps and diagrams, most of them color-printed, many of the maps covering most of a page so that a scale of 4 miles to the inch was possible, resulting in reasonable clarity for even detailed information on the maps. The volume contains reasonably complete treatments of the bedrock and surficial geology, pedology, climate, and geotechnology—with subsections on groundwater resources, slope stability, engineering properties of tills, sand and gravel resources, land use, and land capability for outdoor recreation, for agriculture, and for irrigation. The need for 68 of these large pages is readily explained by the broad coverage that is thus given in a convenient form of all important phases of the physical environment of this prairie city, easily appreciated by the nontechnical reader and adequate for all general phases of local

Figure 3.26 Scarborough, Ontario, Canada. The same view as Fig. 3.25 fifteen years later, in 1962; the gulley on the right can be identified in both views and the main road. *(Courtesy of the Lockwood Survey Corporation Ltd.)*

planning. A foreword to the volume explains that it is the hope of those concerned with the volume that it will serve as an example which other Canadian cities may be encouraged to follow.

In dealing with geological studies around cities, it is inevitable that attention should be directed to the larger cities of the world. Smaller cities, however, need exactly the same sort of assistance in the assessment of their physical environment. It may, therefore, be useful to mention that the smaller Ontario city of *Kingston* (population 75,000) has had the advantage of useful studies of its terrain prepared by members of the staffs of its university and military college, a 13-page report from the Royal Military College in 1958 and a 21-page preliminary report in 1969 from members of the staffs in geology and civil engineering at Queen's University, whose studies of the local geology and geotechnical features continues, in association with their teaching work.[3.38] This is a useful pattern for colleges in smaller centers.

An alternative approach is to have such studies carried out by state or provincial organizations, such as was the case for the area around the small southwestern Ontario city of *Galt*. The surficial geology of this area was studied by Dr. Paul Karrow and reported on through a geological circular issued by the Department of Mines of *Ontario*.[3.39] This Department, similar to many of the state Surveys, has a long list of useful publications, many of which can assist with local planning efforts. Some of the key papers on the unusual Pleistocene geology of the *Toronto* region have been issued by this department, one of the most recent (also authored by Dr. Karrow) being on the Pleistocene geology of the *Scarborough* area, to the east of Toronto, an area that includes the famous Scarborough Bluffs, shown in Figs. 3.25 and 3.26.[3.40]

Three Special Cases

From the many other reports now publicly available that show how geology is at last becoming an accepted preliminary to planning procedures, three will be briefly described. All deal with the application of geology to particular local problems. The first is another case from *Illinois*, where, on the morning of 21 June 1970, the village of Crescent City, about 120 km south of Chicago, was heavily damaged by explosions and fires resulting from the derailing within the village limits of 11 railroad tank cars containing propane. Fortunately, no lives were lost, but about 70 people (mainly firemen) were injured. Much of the village, which has a population of just under 600, was destroyed. The Illinois Department of Local Government Affairs quickly engaged a firm of architect-planners to prepare a plan for rebuilding the village. The firm requested the State Geological Survey Division to provide information on the geology and mineral resources of the vicinity. A survey was conducted for the 9.6-km-square area centered on the village. A report was prepared, using information in the Survey files supplemented by some field studies, and was published in September 1970 as one of the Environmental Geology Note Series already mentioned, just three months after the accident.[3.41] No unusual geological features were found, but the report drew attention to the economic asset provided by the possibility of natural gas storage in an arch-shaped underground structure in the underlying St. Peter sandstone. Information on other natural features, such as have been described for many of the foregoing examples, is conveniently summarized in the report, which must have been of real value in the replanning of this devastated village.

Quite different was the request addressed to the U.S. Geological Survey by the Air Force Academy Construction Agency for assistance in an assessment of the site chosen for the new Air Force Academy 17.6 km north of *Colorado Springs*. Once the site had been selected, speed became the order of the day. The result was that the field work for the geological mapping of the 7,250 hectares site was completed in just over one calendar month. The resulting geological map of the site and descriptive text were delivered five days after the field work was completed and incorporated in the first general plan for the Academy submitted to the U.S. Air Force by the appointed architect-engineer. The expedition with which this work was done, as well as the preceding example, are mentioned not as something to be emulated but in tribute to, and as showing how geologists can produce fast results when necessity demands this. The USGS naturally continued its work at the Academy site, especially in connection with the performance and interpretation of pumping tests on water wells. More detailed site investigation, and testing of earth materials, was carried out in advance of construction. During construction careful observations were made on all excavations and other features of geological interest. All this

Figure 3.27 Colorado Springs, Colorado. Aerial view of the Air Force Academy site during construction in November 1956. (1) Grading in progress; (2) backfill being placed against major retaining walls; (3) rows of caissons for the classroom building. *(Courtesy of the Commanding Officer, U.S. Air Force Academy.)*

information was combined into a masterly report, published as a 93-page, printed, illustrated, letter-sized paper by the Survey in 1967.[3.42] This is one of the most comprehensive records that this author has ever seen of all three phases of the use of geology in the development of what was, really, the building of a new small city.

Finally, yet another "rush job" was the request addressed to the U.S. Department of the Interior by the National Aeronautics and Space Administration (NASA) for an assessment of environmental conditions and resources of southwestern *Mississippi*, with special reference to the possible reuse of the Mississippi Test Facility of NASA. The request was received on 4 February 1970; the deadline was 27 February 1970. The area of the site itself was about 5,200 hectares, but the surrounding "buffer zone" included 52,000 hectares and the areal study would have to extend beyond this. The assignment would appear to have been an impossible one, but it was done, as requested, through the remarkable aid now available of remote sensing from high-flying aircraft, coupled with an interdisciplinary team effort, the results of which have fortunately been made publicly available in a most significant color-printed report of the U.S. Geological Survey (Geographic Application Program).[3.43] The cover of the report is a fine, color infrared photograph of the test site taken from the plane assigned to this project from a height of more than 16 km on 17 February; this remarkable view is a fitting introduction to a notable report that may well prove to be a pioneer document, in that it demonstrates so well what can be done in civilian activity using techniques and methods previously thought of mainly in the context of national defense.

The 58-page report is accompanied by a map prepared from one of the enlarged photographs, two of which are included as large folding sheets. The text is a singularly concise account of the team effort that was directed toward assessing 19 potential uses of the test facility site in relation to 16 environmental factors. Clearly it would be impracticable to summarize what is already a summary account. It was, however, the use of color infrared photography that permitted such a quick assessment of the changes that had taken place in the region in the last 18 years, by comparing the specially taken high-altitude views with earlier terrain pictures. The high-altitude photographs were taken from an Air Weather Service/NASA RB-57F plane equipped with seven cameras. Helicopters were used at the time of the overflight to get "ground-truth" photographs. Prints were back in Washington five days after the special mission was planned, two of the days having been spent waiting for clear weather. Thermal infrared and side-scanning-radar imagery were not used in this exercise so that there are even further possibilities ahead in this expanding field of investigation so well demonstrated in this report. The photographs that were obtained were used by geologists, hydrologists, those studying forestry and agricultural land use, and for indications of areas suitable for outdoor recreation. The report justly observes that "the use of [infrared] film in conjunction with the RB-57F aircraft camera system and with future space satellite systems should prove to be one of the most important scientific advances in increasing capability to conduct world-wide regional studies."

3.8   TERRAIN EVALUATION

It must be remembered that this remarkable use of high-flying aircraft as an aid to geological reconnaissance is but an extension of a technique that has been in use for over a century. The specific application of aerial photography to the evaluation of terrain can be traced back to the days of the First World War, with publications dating back to the thirties that are still of value. It was, perhaps, the demands of the Second World War that led to the most significant advances not only in aerial photointerpretation but in recognition of the need for evaluation of different terrains for specific purposes, such as the trafficability of different types of vehicles over difficult ground. Such uses of aerial photographs might appear to be somewhat removed from the application of geology in the planning of regions and urban areas. This, however, would be a first impression only and one quite incorrect since further consideration will serve to show that determination of soil type and other geological surface manifestations have been greatly aided by the use of aerial photography. Although some of the initial expectations have yet to be fully realized, enough has been achieved to warrant at least brief mention of the subject before directing attention to the probabilities for the future in linking geology with planning work, especially in view of recent work in Australia.

It is now well established that study of aerial photographs can give a good general idea of local geology, especially if some limited ground study has indicated the controlling features of the local topography presented by the underlying geological structure. This facility has been put to good use in general terrain studies where large areas are involved, such as for studies of road location, railway planning, and the location of airports. A typical example was its use for the locating of a new airport at Martinsburg, West Virginia, in the ridge and valley country of that part of the Appalachians, the topography of which renders detailed geological field studies rather more difficult than usual.[3.44] Aerial photographs proved their worth in an office reconnaissance of the whole of the great delta of the Mackenzie River in the Canadian Arctic when search had to be made for the site of an entirely new town to replace the settlement of Aklavik due to difficulties with local permafrost conditions at this older settlement.[3.45] In advance of the very short open season for studies in the field, it was possible to gain a good general idea of geological conditions around the rim of the delta (in an office 4,800 km away) and so to select 12 potential new town sites. Visits to these eliminated eight. More detailed field studies led eventually to the selection of the gravel-based site now occupied by the new town of Inuvik on the eastern edge of the delta, foundation conditions having been proved to be just as had been predicted from the aerial photointerpretation.

Extension of the same sort of photointerpretation has made it possible for *permafrost* conditions to be determined from the air with reasonable certainty, especially at the southern limit of the permafrost area in Canada.[3.46] Ten summers of field work for the purpose of "spot checks" on deductions from aerial photographs

Figure 3.28 Inuvik, Northwest Territories, Canada. Aerial view of this new town, the locating of which is described in reference 3.45, showing the east channel of the Mackenzie River on the left and the change from the gravelly hill on which the town is located to the edge of the tundra. *(Courtesy of the National Air Photo Library, Dept. of Energy, Mines and Resources, Ottawa, and K. R. Greenaway.)*

went into the preparation of the Canadian Permafrost Map on which this southern limit is shown, the map having proved to be most useful in planning exercises for northern development and for specific site selection.[3.47] Field work is naturally always necessary to confirm preliminary predictions thus obtained, but this practice is really no different from the detailed site investigation that is needed for normal urban development, even with the existence of the most detailed regional geological map used for preparation of general plans. A further extension of the same techniques has been made in Canada in connection with the necessary detection of *muskeg* areas—muskeg being an Indian word used to describe organic terrain ("peatlands"), of which there are over 130 million hectares in the Dominion. These shallow deposits do not provide good sites for the building of roads or buildings, and so evaluation of terrain has the objective, in many cases, of determining where such areas are so that they can be avoided in planning work. Color photography has been put to good use in this special application of aerial photointerpretation, to such an extent that determination of the main organic types of muskeg can be distinguished from heights of 1,500 m and less.[3.48]

Urban development in permafrost and muskeg areas will always be extremely limited, but it is appropriate to note that even in such inhospitable areas, these modern techniques of terrain evaluation have been so successfully applied. Some of the most advanced work in this field has been carried out on the other side of the world by Aitchison and Grant of the Australian CSIRO Division of Applied Geomechanics, some of their work having been carried out also in inhospitable areas in northern and western Australia, yet the exact antithesis of the Canadian north, showing the versatility of these aerial reconnaissance methods.[3.49] As a part of their work, these Australian workers have prepared a most useful review of their significant work in developing terrain evaluation for engineering. This has appeared in a volume devoted to the more general subject of *Land Evaluation*, its publication being indicative of the attention already devoted to this broad subject in this southern continent.[3.50] In their worldwide review they direct attention to the significant work done in South Africa, in terrains not unlike some in Australia. It is to the latter, however, that reference must be restricted.

Terrain evaluation as viewed by Aitchison and Grant is for engineering purposes, with engineers as the potential users. They have concentrated attention upon four parameters: (1) slope characteristics, (2) underlying geology, (3) soil characteristics, and (4) vegetation characteristics. In their work they have been assisted by the somewhat unusual general geological conditions found in so much of Australia where "there are no young or old mountains and the terrain can be considered as being composed as a series of surfaces, separated by slopes between them and containing within them isolated remnants of other surfaces or isolated volcanic hills, necks etc." It has been possible, therefore, to develop nine main classes of slope conditions and similarly to develop corresponding classifications for the other parameters and to subdivide them also. Through a system of number combinations, therefore, it is possible to record terrain characteristics in such a form that they can be computerized, stored, and retrieved when needed. It is significant that drainage does not appear as one of the main parameters, an indication of the low rainfall that characterizes so much of Australia, but the system that Aitchison and Grant have developed—to which they

LITHOLOGY   Claystone, siltstone, sandstone, some limestone, mostly ferruginized (ferruginous sandstone, ironstone), and silicified (silcrete, porcellanite, opal)

OCCURRENCE   Continuous throughout most of terrain pattern

TOPOGRAPHY   Rough, rocky, steep to gently sloping dissection slopes

INCLUSIONS   Terrain units 2.1.01, 2.2.01, 3.2.03, 4.2.00, and 4.3.00 of terrain pattern 23, province 43.001

TERRAIN COMPONENTS

Terrain component No.	Dominance	Occurrence	Slope		Soil description	USC	PPF
			Parallel to major axis	Transverse to major axis			
322 002 22 or 322 002 02	Low	Slope adjacent to drainage	Planar to 2°	Convex to 2°	Rock outcrop, pockets of gravel or gravelly soil	—	—
334 002 22	Dominant	Long slope from higher terrain units	Planar to 5°	Convex to 10°	Rock outcrop, pockets of gravel or gravelly soil	—	—
421 00 02	Very low	Shallow drainage floor	Concave to 2°	Planar to 1°	Rock outcrop, pockets of gravel of gravelly soil	—	—
653 002 20	Subdominant	Slope from steeper terrain units	Concave to 20°	Convex to 5°	Rock outcrop, pockets of gravel of gravelly soil	—	—

Figure 3.29 Australia. Two typical pages, showing the system of land evaluation described in the test for Terrain Unit 3.5.03. *(From* Terrain Classification for Engineering Properties of the Rolling Down Province, Queensland, *K. Grant, CSIRO, 1968, courtesy of the author and of G. D. Aitchison, Chief of Applied Geomechanics Division, Australia.)*

DIAGRAMMATIC REPRESENTATION OF TOPOGRAPHY AND ARRANGEMENT OF
TERRAIN COMPONENTS WITHIN TERRAIN UNIT

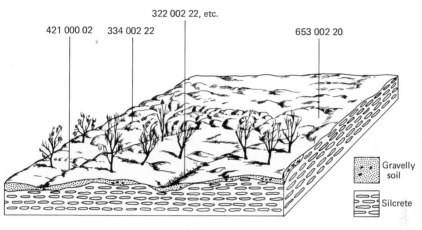

322 002 22, etc.

421 000 02   334 002 22   653 002 20

Gravelly
soil

Silcrete

Parameters of terrain unit

Local relief	Length to	Width to
amplitude to (ft)	2 miles	2 miles

Surface cover			Vegetation				Terrain parameters		
Description	Shape	Diameter to (in.)	Description	Spacing to (ft)	Tree height to (ft)	Girth diam. to (in.)	Local relief amplitude to (ft)	Length to (yds)	Width to (yds)
Silcrete, some ironstone	Angular Rounded	4 1	Grassland, spinifex to 50% cover or open woodland, gidyea, occasional whitewood, beef-wood, spinifex to 50% cover	100	20	8	10	200	100
Silcrete, some ironstone	Angular Rounded	4 1	Grassland, spinifex to 50% cover	—	—	—	50	1,000	500
Nil			Open woodland, gidyea, occasional whitewood, beef-wood, spinifex to 50% cover	100	20	8	3	1,000	20
Silcrete, some ironstone	Angular Rounded	4 1	Lancewood thickets, much fallen timber, spinifex to 50% cover	10	20	8	20	500	200

Figure 3.29   (continued)

have applied the label PUCE (Pattern-Unit-Component-Evaluation)—is so adaptable that
it can readily be applied to quite different sorts of terrain. The evaluation procedure
naturally starts with critical examination of aerial photographs. Sampling sites are
chosen while this first phase is in progress. The initial results are taken into the field,
studied, amended and corrected as may be found necessary by detailed investigation,

and finally prepared in proper form for publication and use.

In order to illustrate how results obtained by the PUCE system are recorded, Fig. 3.29 is reproduced through the kindness of Dr. Aitchison from one of the published reports. This publication recorded the results of studies in an area of northern Queensland known as the Rolling Downs. The accompanying photograph (at least one photograph accompanying each individual description) shows the country described. This "scrub country," as it might be called in North America, is typical of much of that considered in this report. The descriptions are self-explanatory, apart only from the coding numbers, but these are the keys to the computerization of the results of the survey, the machine storage being naturally supplementary to the visual presentation of the report.

It will be clear, even from this summary account, that, as Grant says, "terrain evaluation does not replace site investigation or engineering geology . . . it is a logical extension of engineering geology." The system could not possibly be used except against a background knowledge of and working familiarity with geology. The "provinces," for example, of the classification scheme are the main geological time subdivisions encountered in Australia (from *Archeozoic* to *Cainozoic*). Appreciation of the local geology is the key to the successful recording of the significant terrain features. When these are recorded, they will always evidence the importance that geology occupies in the assessment of the terrain. This is well shown by published examples of this system at work and by the terrain maps that are, perhaps, the ultimate product of the whole procedure. In effect, these are engineering-geological maps, even though prepared in this somewhat unusual manner. They are effective examples of the final product of most of the procedures so far described to which more detailed attention must now be directed.

3.9 ENGINEERING–GEOLOGICAL MAPS

The developments described in the two preceding sections pointed to the evolution of special maps that would combine the scientific information shown on the normal type of geological map with the interpretation of this information in terms of the use to which the ground so delineated might be put. In several of the cases mentioned, tables accompany either geological reports or maps giving the correlation of geological formations, or of individual soil and rock types, with engineering properties and terrain characteristics. In the case of the example from the Missouri Division of Geological Survey and Water Resources, companion maps are published together in the same enclosure, one showing the geology of Jefferson County and the other what is called the engineering geology of the same area. The final result of the Australian system of terrain evaluation is, as has just been noted, an engineering-geological map of the area that has been assessed.

The use of the word "engineering" should be no impediment to appreciation of the very broad use of maps of this character, especially for planning purposes.

The term "engineering properties" has come into wide use to describe those physical properties of soil and rock that must be known with reasonable certainty, in addition to their geological descriptions, before land composed of these earth materials can safely be considered for use in urban or any other type of development. In like manner, the term "engineering-geological maps" has gradually come into use and is now widely accepted as common usage, even though all concerned with urban and regional planning, whether architects or engineers, will need to make equal use of these significant aids to sound planning. That they are a relatively new concept in North America must be admitted. That they provide a singularly useful and efficient method of presenting geological information for all urban and regional planning purposes will, it is hoped, be clear when this section has been read.

As with many such concepts, it is quite impossible to say that engineering-geological maps were ever "invented" at any time or by any person. They have gradually evolved, and are indeed still evolving, as steadily increasing attention is being paid to the importance of geology in planning. European practice, in this instance, has been ahead of that in North America, but there is mutual liaison between the Old World and the New in this as in most scientific endeavors so that future progress will benefit from this increasing international collaboration. In North America much has already been accomplished, not always under the name of "engineering-geological maps" but certainly with this concept in view. Work of the U.S. Geological Survey in the San Francisco area has already been mentioned appreciatively.

Reference must also be made to the very extensive work that has been carried out by engineering geologists in the greater Los Angeles area. There is a notable and large volume of most valuable papers dealing with engineering-geological problems in this area alone to which attention may be directed.[3.51] The area has been plagued (if that is not too mild a word) by a variety of landslide problems, especially as land developers have increased their use of hillside areas, in earlier days with results that were all too often unfortunate. Today, there are legal restrictions upon such hillside developments. Most constructive efforts have been and are being made to see that geology is given every consideration in all planning and development work in this great and growing urban area, which could itself be used as a single illustration to demonstrate most of the matters discussed in this volume. Since, however, so much has already been published about "geology and Los Angeles," and since so many of the problems there are determined by local climatic and geological conditions, attention will rather be directed to another area where geological maps are now being developed, while recording this tribute to all the fine work done in and around "L.A."

Denver, Colorado, is another rapidly growing urban conurbation located in a magnificent natural setting close to the foothills of the Rocky Mountains, the significant geology of the region of which it is the urban center being obvious to even the most casual observer. With the city of Boulder about 32 km to the northwest, and satellite communities such as Littleton around Denver itself, there are many common problems to be faced in the steady development of this important area. Early in

1967 a controversy developed over the proposed subdivision of a small hillside tract near Boulder. City officials, in the face of strong objections on the grounds of the hazards attached to soil and geological conditions along this eastern margin of the adjacent Front Range, sought for specific terrain information. They turned to the U.S. Geological Survey, as a result of which a manuscript copy of a geological map of the Boulder quadrangle was promptly placed in open, or public, files so that it could be officially consulted. This was a geological map, however, and so questions inevitably arose about the interpretation of the geology that it showed in relation to problems of local land development. Almost coincidentally with this specific request, the Denver Regional Council of Governments (DRCOG)—formerly the Inter-County Regional Planning Commission—requested the U.S. Geological Survey to conduct a regional planning study of geological conditions as they affect the use of land along the eastern margin of the mountains near Denver. A cooperative engineering-geological research project was therefore started in August 1967, this being the first such project between the USGS and a regional planning organization. Initially, the project was financed cooperatively among the regional planning commission, several city and county governments in the region, and USGS. Since July 1968 it has been financed by the Denver Regional Council of Governments and the USGS.

This cooperative study, covering an area of 116,000 hectares, much of it already urbanized, is therefore in progress as this book is published. Three of the resulting engineering-geological maps had been released in preliminary form by 1971, together with accompanying reports.[3.52] They cover the city of Boulder and adjacent areas and the area around the city of Golden. Each map covers an area of 14,200 hectares. Eight maps will eventually cover the whole of the area served by DRCOG. (Progress has been slowed up by a number of factors, including the tragic deaths of two of the geologists who started the work.) The two objectives of the program are "to supply DRCOG with engineering geology information for planning use in a part of the Denver metropolitan area that is rapidly becoming urbanized, mainly by augmenting existing geological information with engineering geology information . . . [and] . . . to explore how geologic and engineering geologic information can be made more understandable and useful to more non-geologists, in part by developing methods of representation of map information, text arrangements, and verbal expression." The second objective can be seen to be a research project into the preparation of engineering-geological maps so that the whole program has a significance that extends far beyond the immediate needs of the Denver area, important as they are. It has the added advantage that the meetings that are being held in association with the work—with planners, builders, and civic groups—is developing in the district an awareness of the importance of geology in general and of the local geology in particular, as a vital and essential aid to good planning.

Probably not unconnected with the project was the passage by the General Assembly of the State of Colorado in 1967 of an amendment to the State Land Subdivision regulations specifically permitting inclusion in the land subdivision

Figure 3.30 Denver, Colorado. Aerial view of the city, with its imposing backdrop of the Rocky Mountains, looking west. *(Courtesy of Denver Convention and Visitors Bureau.)*

of criteria dealing with such geological items as "earth testing for the determination of possible earth and rock creep, sliding on Bentonitic shales . . . ."[3.53] More recently, the city of Lakewood, one of the suburban municipalities due west of Denver, has included in its planning ordinance a requirement that "investigation by competent engineering geologists shall be considered as a requirement prior to future subdivision or land development . . . ." More specifically: "Accompanying the preliminary plat the developer shall furnish a preliminary geological report by an Engineering Geologist indicating the degree of compatibility of the existing geologic, topographic, and drainage features of the area with the proposed development . . . ."[3.54] And as a result of the first phase of the Denver area program, the Jefferson County Planning Department revised part of their county plan, thus indicating for the first time in this region the influence of geological considerations in regional planning.

The work now being carried out in the development of these engineering-geological maps is more than merely an office adjustment of existing geological maps. Further field work is necessary to check on all significant surface features; laboratory tests upon typical materials of each map area have to be conducted and assessed; engineering practice and difficulties previously experienced with excavation or other earthwork have to be studied; and finally the specific needs of planners in the particular type of terrain that is being mapped must be determined. In the preparation of the engineering-geological maps, geological names of formations will not normally be necessary, and so they will be either eliminated or abbreviated. What is much more important is the type of material in each geological subdivision. Special characteristics of any of the prevalent local materials must be indicated, such as the swelling characteristics of the Pierre shale in the Denver area. Relative ease of excavation is another important feature of the materials shown on the map that should be described, difficult as this is. Past landslides and potential landslide areas can be indicated, as can springs and other evidences of high water table beneath the surface being mapped. The resulting map will still show surface indications of the underlying geology but interpreted so that an appreciation of the map can guide those responsible in determining suitable areas for building, those best fitted for recreational purposes, and those where geological hazards may be encountered.

The amount of information to be presented in this way is so extensive that it is not practicable to include it all on the map itself. Tables, such as those already mentioned in earlier examples, are planned for the Denver area maps. The Boulder map, for example, is accompanied by three tables—for igneous and metamorphic rocks, for sedimentary rocks, and for surficial deposits (or soils) of the map area, each with the following main subdivisions, against each of which is a concise account for each geological unit in the map:

Equivalent geological unit (the geological name)

Description and thickness

Other features (such as jointing)

Topographic form and surface relief

Weathering and ancient soils

Workability (e.g., in excavation)

Surface drainage and erosion

Groundwater

Suitability for waste disposal

Foundation stability

Slope stability

Probable earthquake stability

Use

It is of more than usual interest to find that practice in the preparation and use of engineering-geological maps has a long-standing history in Europe, and especially in the countries of Eastern Europe. An extensive literature on this one subject has developed. Even though the original papers are naturally written in languages that are not commonly used by English-speaking peoples, many papers have the courteous benefit of an abstract in English, and, as will shortly be noted, there are now some publications in English describing this important work. As indicating the progress that has been made, attention may be directed to a *Bibliography and Index of Engineering Geological Mapping, Part 1*, by Dr. J. Hruska, published by Geofond in Prague, Czechoslovakia.[3.55] This small book has been produced by computer offprint, clear indication of the detailed attention being given to this matter by Czechoslovakian geologists. The Index lists a total of 131 reports and/or maps, mainly from Czechoslovakia, East Germany, and Poland (with 45, 36, and 40 entries, respectively), but with a few items from Hungary, Romania, the U.S.S.R., and Yugoslavia. The more extensive publications from these latter countries are to be listed in future parts of this significant publication—produced in English, by computer, in Prague.

Famous in geological circles throughout Eastern Europe is the pioneer engineering-geological map of Warsaw published as long ago as 1936 by Professors Sujkowski and Rozycki. The map was produced as four sheets, being based upon study of the records of several thousand test borings and test pits. The first three sheets show the geological conditions at the ground surface and at depths below the surface of 5 m and 10 m, respectively. In view of the magnitude and extent of underground excavations beneath all cities, a feature of urban areas that will be described later in this volume, the value of this knowledge of geological conditions at such depths below the surface will be obvious. The fourth sheet shows the contours of the underlying Tertiary clays and, in addition, the locations and age of disused sand and loam pits, old quarries and ponds, and the abandoned earlier channels of the Vistula River, exactly the sort of information that is so difficult to assemble in haste (as it often has to be in the absence of such maps as this) but which can be of vital importance in the construction of civic works. All four sheets were prepared to a scale of 1:20,000; the maps were supplemented by geological sections.[3.56]

As with developments in parallel fields, it was in the years immediately following the Second World War that activity in these countries resumed. One of the first of the postwar productions was an engineering-geological map of the central area of Prague to a scale of 1:12,000 by Dr. Q. Zaruba. This showed the geological conditions existing at a depth of 2 m beneath the surface. This information is of unusual importance in Prague since the central part of the ancient city is underlain by an appreciable depth of "made ground," consisting of the rubble of old buildings either demolished or destroyed by fire centuries ago.[3.57] Important work has been done in the U.S.S.R., notably by Drs. Popov and Kolomenskii of the Moscow Geological Prospecting Institute. An account of their approach to the preparation of engineering-geological maps is available in English.[3.58] Attention will be directed to the latest thinking in this field in Czechoslovakia, although tribute must be paid also to a remarkably comprehensive folio of maps for planning purposes issued in Hungary.[3.59] In all these countries, the device of using several sheets of the same area to delineate different features, which can then be correlated, is generally followed rather than the use of one map accompanied by explanatory tables.

The remarkable progress that has been made in Czechoslovakia in engineering-geological studies generally, and particularly in their use of engineering-geological maps, derives in part from work done on important transportation construction works before the Second World War. For the construction of a new railway line from Bystrica to Divisky, for example, a geological map to a scale of 1:25,000 was prepared. Some parts of the route, especially those subject to landslides, were mapped on a scale of 1:1,000 (or about 1 inch to 83 feet). For the construction of a new express highway from Brno, in Moravia, to Gottwaldov, a part of the valley of the Morava River was mapped geologically to a scale of 1:2,000. Zoned maps for a number of river valleys in Slovakia had been prepared as early as the fifties, technical properties of rocks being graphically expressed. The zones developed on the maps are areas in which the geology provides roughly identical conditions for the construction of hydroelectric and other river works. As this work has progressed, experience has been shared and methods of mapping steadily developed. Ingenious graphical devices, involving the use both of color and of different sorts of black and white markings, have been developed to the point where one color-printed map can demonstrate the main features of the three-dimensional structure of the ground in the area covered by the map sheet.

To illustrate the sort of mapping that is now being done in Czechoslovakia for engineering and planning purposes, a set of four sheets constituting the "map" for one area will be described in general terms.

Sheet A will be a detailed geological map showing the pre-Quaternary bedrock, the surficial material (soil), and filled ground, with appropriate thicknesses. Brown hatching shows the bedrock; the lines are broken if the bedrock is more than 10 m below ground-surface level. The surficial deposits are shown in color, the lower layer represented by colored horizontal stripes. (In Prague a third soil layer rarely occurs; if it does, it can be indicated by vertical stripes.) The thickness of the soil from the surface is given by roman numerals. Isoclines of the thickness of the surficial deposits are denoted by continuous thin lines or by broken lines if the thickness exceeds 10 m. Fill material is shown by red hatching; if thicker than 2 m the thickness is noted in meters.

Sheet B will show the engineering-geological characteristics of the area and some geomorphological and hydrogeological information. The map will show these features in broad detail, there being plotted such features as hazardous slopes, landslides, eroded gulleys, undermined areas, open-cast and underground mines, areas containing mineral resources not yet mined, and areas in which building is restricted in order that the natural environment shall be preserved. In addition, the engineering properties of rocks, such as ease of excavation, depth of weathering, and compressibility, are represented by symbols. Colored circles are used to denote the chemical characteristics of groundwater.

Sheet C is usually a map of the sources of the information that is incorporated into the other maps, or (as it is called) the documentation map. Test pits, test borings, excavations, etc., from which information has been used are marked with appropriate symbols. Locations from which samples have been taken for laboratory testing, or where field analyses have been made or other special tests, are marked with colored symbols. This map also shows quarries, both those in operation and those that have been abandoned, wells, and springs.

Sheet D is the map that shows the correlation of all the engineering-geological information shown on the other maps, with the terrain and the uses to which the set of maps is to be put. It will suggest evaluations of the information given in maps *A* and *B* with special reference to urban development and construction of industrial or transportation structures. By means of the well-known "semaphore" colors—red, yellow, and green, used with the conventional meanings attached to them for ease in use—the map area is divided into regions that are unsuitable, usable, and suitable for development. A synoptic table arranged in a series of columns but printed on the map gives a short listing of these leading features in a form that is easy to read.

From these descriptive notes, at least a general idea of these remarkable Czechoslovakian maps can be obtained. It is unfortunate that it is impossible to reproduce even one of the sheets in full with this volume. As Dr. Quido Zaruba, who has contributed in so many ways to this volume, observes: "The compilation of engineering-geological maps on a scale of 1:5,000 is relatively expensive but it is worth while . . . for this reason, we have so far restricted their preparation to the areas of economic importance, where a large industrial or urban development is planned, or in the case of the reclamation of devastated areas."[3.60]

Czechoslovakian geologists have described their progressive development of engineering-geological mapping in many publications and in languages other than their own. Their work has been graciously acknowledged, to give just one example, by officers of the Bureau de Recherches Geologique et Minières of France, who have also made use of similar graphical techniques for the production of their own engineering-geological maps, a most useful discussion of their work having been published in 1969.[3.61]

The work in Czechoslovakia has been conducted in close collaboration with corresponding efforts in other Eastern European countries. It is not surprising, therefore, to find that under the aegis of the Permanent Commission on Geology of COMECON (the economic union of the U.S.S.R., Czechoslovakia, Poland, Romania, Hungary, and East Germany) there has been developed, and published, a code of practice, or standard, for the preparation of engineering-geological maps. This is a significant document. Like all such codes, it is a very generalized document, especially since it covers a lot of ground. As is always the case with any technical standard, it has been continually under review, and its further development is being assisted by

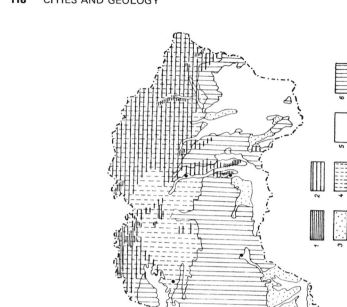

Figure 3.31 Slovakia, Czechoslovakia. Map illustrating location and intensity of landslides in the Carpathian Mountains of Czechoslovakia. (1) Areas heavily affected by slides; (2) areas with considerable tendency for slides; (3) areas of cohesive soils in which topography is not conducive to slides; (4) areas of weak rocks favorable to slides; (5) areas of sand and gravel not favorable to slides; (6) areas of competent rocks not favorable to slides. *(Figure App. 1, page 72, in reference 3.26, courtesy of the author, M. Matula, Bratislava.)*

an international working group, which meets under the auspices of UNESCO. There is in prospect, therefore, a truly international standard for the preparation of engineering-geology maps that, as it comes into national use, will greatly assist international cooperation in this important field.

The rules set forth in the COMECON document were followed as closely as possible in the engineering-geological assessment of the Czechoslovakian Carpathians, a complete volume on which, accompanied by a regional map to a scale of 1:200,000 covering almost the whole of Slovakia, has been published in English.[3.62] Professor Milan Matula and his collaborators at the Comenius University in Bratislava were not daunted by the extreme complexity of the geology, and especially of the engineering-geological features, of the Carpathians—complexity that is responsible in large degree for the natural beauty of this lovely region—but have brought together their many studies into this synthesis. The master map, with the explanation that the 225-page volume provides, will be of great benefit to all future and more detailed studies within this important region, even as it shows to those who do not know the Carpathians, and who may never have the pleasure of visiting them, the real significance of geological studies from the point of view of their use in planning and engineering and how the dominating features of even complex geology can be conveniently recorded on paper for use in this way.

From this brief review it can be seen that there is much activity in several parts of the world in the development of sound techniques for the preparation of engineering-geological maps. They can be regarded as the best of all methods for recording and transmitting the basic information about terrain and ground conditions that is so essential for planning purposes. The fact that both in Australia and in Czechoslovakia the aid of computers has already been invoked for the speedy processing of information will be an indication of the forward-looking thinking that is already being devoted to this important matter. But computers are only tools; they can utilize only the information that is obtained through the skilled hard work of geologists and engineers. Although most useful, they are but supplementary to the type of field studies and laboratory investigations that have been so briefly summarized in the foregoing description of how information on the ground is obtained for use in the planning process.

Significant also are the indications that have been given of the international cooperation that has already featured some parts of the developments described. Now that there has been formed an International Association of Engineering Geology, there will exist a formal channel of communication to supplement that happy exchange between scientists of different countries that has always been so distinctive a feature of geology in general, as of other natural sciences, and which is certainly featuring already the steady growth of engineering geology. The building job that the whole world faces in the remaining years of this century is so vast that such international cooperation will be essential, as well as desirable, if the planning of good cities is to be properly assisted by geological endeavor. With confidence, therefore, the steady development of engineering-geological maps for this purpose can be anticipated not only nationally but also internationally, with the possibility of useful international standards as guidelines already within sight.

3.10 CONCLUSIONS

"Buildings banned until sewage can be handled." How often are news headings of this type seen, unfortunately in ever-increasing number, as the pressure for residential accommodation around great cities forces the rapid development of raw land. In many cases, health requirements make it essential that the use of septic tanks be banned because the soil conditions are such that effluent from tanks will discharge into impermeable clay soil that simply cannot serve as the natural filter that is always assumed at the point of discharge. Residential construction in such areas must be prohibited until proper sewers can be installed, leading to adequate sewage-treatment plants, so that clay soils are not expected to do the impossible.

In other cases, on very porous sand and gravel, the permeability of the ground may be such that effluent from septic tanks will pass through the ground so quickly that it will foul the groundwater beneath and so pollute potential, or actual, sources of drinking and domestic water. These are but two of the main reasons why the disposal of domestic sewage can, of itself, interfere so seriously with building developments. As will clearly be seen, this is due to ground conditions that could easily have been determined in advance of any plans for building if only geology had been appreciated as one of the physical factors that must be fully investigated before plans for any sort of development are prepared, even in a general way.

Many pages could be used to give other examples demonstrating the interrelation of the various major factors involved when land is "developed" for urban use. Water supply and the installation of the necessary pipes or tunnels in proper relation with street layouts; the interrelation of roadway arrangements to give convenience and efficiency to traffic, and the installation of necessary traffic controls at critical locations before roadways are finished; the location of bridges so that they do not interfere with later installation of services; decisions as to when and whether electrical power-supply cables shall be buried or left suspended from poles—the list is almost endless, if all aspects of planning are to be considered in advance, as they must be if planning is to be well done and efficiency and economy ensured. In combination, all these features constitute the complex *system* (to use again this popular word of the present age) that is the modern town and city. And all depend, ultimately and basically, upon the ground. They cannot be planned as they should be without knowledge of the geological conditions underlying the site.

This simple statement can be made without any qualification for all urban and regional planning even on the most favorable terrain. It cannot be known with certainty if the terrain is favorable until investigation has shown what lies beneath the surface. In such cases, the application of geology will be in the nature of an insurance policy. It can be neglected—sometimes, in very favorable locations, without causing trouble—but the risk is great. The minimal expenditure on the geological investigations required for a master plan will be so small a part of the total planning cost that it cannot be financial restrictions that have caused, up to now, so widespread neglect of the science that should be in the forefront of all planning work. It may be that geologists have not taken active enough steps to see that the practical value of their scientific studies is appreciated in the cities in which they live and work. Whatever the reason, the picture is changing and changing rapidly, as it is hoped that this chapter alone has demonstrated.

There has been sketched in outline only the availability for most urban regions of basic geological information that will show the types of rock and soil that will be encountered in areas being planned for development. The way in which this scientific information can be assessed with special reference to the practical needs of planners, and produced in convenient form for use as engineering-geological maps, with or without supplementary reports, has been outlined. The existence in many areas of published papers on the local geology, which can always give a start to more detailed study, must always be remembered. When unusual geological features exist on land to be built upon, special studies will be necessary even for the preparation of a master plan in order that the possibility of safe development may be assured before any specific plans are drawn. Publications such as those of Professor McHarg show from the viewpoint of the planner how vital geology can be in the overall assessment of an area that is to be taken out of its natural use and built upon for the use of man.

All this is the first phase of the interrelation of geology with the planning and development of cities. It will not come amiss to point out again that, once the master plan has been developed and approved, and the probability of actual building emerges, the second phase in the use of geology comes into view. This is the detailed investigation of building sites and the intensive study of small areas that are to be used for special purposes in civic development. This phase cannot very usefully be generalized; it must be treated with direct reference to the type of structure or ground use that is involved in the detailed planning. Accordingly, the following chapters deal with the main groupings of these specific parts of urban (and regional) development. Considerations of water naturally come first, and so the next chapter presents a general survey of the role of hydrogeology in the building and maintenance of cities. The foundations of all structures is, perhaps, that part of the building of cities that is most obviously dependent, completely, upon satisfactory underlying geological conditions. Foundations, therefore, constitute the subject matter of Chap. 5, and they inevitably lead to consideration of some of the problems of open excavation within urban areas. Open excavations are always seen and are often the object of keen observation by interested citizens. Underground excavations, however, are frequently not only not known, even by interested citizens, but are rarely appreciated. It may be to some a surprise to find a complete chapter devoted to excavations far below the streets of cities, but such a figure as the 112 km of tunnels beneath the streets of the Canadian city of Edmonton will help to show how important this part of urban building is, again obviously dependent for its successful prosecution upon full knowledge, in advance of excavation, of the geological conditions that are going to be encountered.

Most of the materials used in the building of cities have natural origins. In the case of building stone, sand, gravel, and crushed stone, direct use of industrial minerals is involved. With lime, cement, gypsum, and other similar products, some processing will be involved, but the natural origin of the materials is still obvious. And materials can have a profound influence upon the character of a city. The geology of these natural materials must be known if they are to be used well. Not only are materials brought into a city, but waste materials have to be disposed of; here, too, geology has its part to play in somewhat unexpected directions, as Chap. 7 will make clear. Finally, the unusual geological features and characteristics of some areas, such as have been so far mentioned only in general terms, must be considered in some detail since the geological hazards to which some cities are exposed necessitate unusual attention to local geological conditions. Landslide areas will perhaps be the most familiar, but all cities must be aware of their relation to seismic areas to ensure that local building regulations are correct. They are, however, merely two of a long list of geological hazards (presented in Chap. 8) that must be known, at least in general terms, by all engaged upon urban and regional planning just in case they should ever have to face the problems that such hazards can present.

These five main divisions into which the second phase of the overall subject has been subdivided are all implicit in the early consideration of geology in preliminary planning. There they need be considered, usually, only as a part of the general influence of ground conditions upon the master plan. It is only in the specific planning work preliminary to building that these matters have to be considered in detail, as will shortly be explained. And it is only when construction work actually starts that the reality of subsurface conditions, previously deduced from surface studies and test borings, becomes evident and the underlying geology of the site can be seen. Then the third phase in this use of geology commences. Actual geological conditions must be accurately observed throughout all excavation and foundation work so that predictions used in design can be checked and their accuracy determined. Even with the most assiduous preliminary geological investigations and the most carefully located and executed test borings, one can never be absolutely certain about any underground conditions until excavation shows them as they really are. Geologists will here have a scientific interest as well, since only by observing excavations can they see for themselves the actual formations of rock and soil that their studies will have predicted. In most cases, they will have the chance of observing underground conditions that have never been seen before and may never be seen again, certainly in the foreseeable future. Records of the geology thus observed can, therefore, be useful not only as an essential part of construction documentation but also from the purely scientific point of view.

This information is invaluable not only of itself but as contributing to the general fund of knowledge about the subsurface conditions in the area immediately around the construction site, to the direct benefit of all building that may be carried out in the vicinity in the future. One would imagine that every city would have arrangements for collecting, storing, and making publicly available this type of really vital information, information of no direct monetary value but information that cannot be obtained in any other way. Every city should have such arrangements. Very few do, to the extent that can be seen desirable. Some cities have none. "What every city should do," therefore, is to ensure that it does obtain this information before it is lost forever. This is the main suggestion of the final chapter. Inevitably it leads to consideration of more general topics, such as the conservation of geological and other natural features around cities without some reference to which a book such as this would not be complete.

Geology, therefore, has an important role to play in ensuring that the growth of existing cities and the development of "new towns" and, inevitably, of new cities is carried out with efficiency, with economy, and with due regard for all that can make cities beautiful. When citizens of any community come to see how geology has influenced the growth of their town or city, their interest in its future planning will be enhanced, and, possibly of more importance, they may be led to an appreciation of the beauties of nature and the need to conserve all that is possible. For all engaged in the practice of planning, a general understanding of geology, its methods and its achievements, should become as second nature so that the physical characteristics of the environment will be instinctively considered at the outset of looking into the development of every new area to be used for community purposes. So vital is this necessary appreciation of the requirement of designing with Nature that an earlier paragraph will be repeated to bring this chapter to a fitting close.

When planning starts, for urban community or region, the area to be developed is not the equivalent of a piece of blank paper ready for the free materialization of the ideas of the designer, but it is rather an environment that has been exposed for a very long period to the effects of many natural modifying factors. The present-day surface of the earth is the product of most complicated geological, hydro-geological, climatic, and other processes, knowledge of which assists in recognition of probable trends of future terrain changes. Development of new communities and the charting of regional development must, therefore, take account of this fundamental organic and dynamic character of Nature so that the works of man may fit as harmoniously as possible into the environment and not disturb the biological equilibrium any more than is essential. To conserve the soundness and productive power of a region for the use of future generations is a basic requirement of overall planning and one that should be observed as a guide in the prosecuting of all engineering works. To repeat what Francis Bacon said so percipiently almost 400 years ago:

"NATURE TO BE COMMANDED MUST BE OBEYED"

chapter four

Hydrogeology of Cities

There should be a natural abundance of springs and
fountains in the town, or, if there is a deficiency
of them, great reservoirs may be established for
the collection of rainwater, such as will not fail
when the inhabitants are cut off from the country
by war . . . . For the elements which we use most
and oftenest for the support of the body contribute most to health, and among these are water and
air. Wherefore, in all wise states, if there is a want
of pure water, and the supply is not all equally
good, the drinking water ought to be separated
from that which is used for other purposes.

Aristotle
(384–322 B.C.)
Jowett translation[4.1]

The vital importance of water supply to cities has been well recognized from the beginning of history, the words of Aristotle being but a reminder of this continuing feature of all urban development. Many early settlements were located specifically because of an available supply of water; all settlements had to be certain of enough water for the needs of their inhabitants; some early towns were relocated, as shown in Chap. 2, when their supply of water failed. Geology is always a determining factor in the occurrence of water and in conveying it for use in cities.

The existence of water on the surface of the earth distinguishes this planet from others in the solar system. It is estimated that there are 1.25 billion cubic km of water on the earth, but of this vast total 97 percent is in the oceans and is salt. Of the remaining 37.5 million cubic km of fresh water, about 87 percent is locked up, occurring as ice in the polar regions and in glaciers, all but 10 percent of it in Antartica. This leaves just about 4.7 million cubic km of fresh water that is really water; of this quantity, about 90 percent is stored beneath the surface of the earth as groundwater. There is still left a very small fraction of the total—about one-hundredth of 1 percent—but it is this relatively small quantity that makes life possible since it is the water to be found in streams, rivers, lakes, and the atmosphere.[4.2]

Although the total quantity of water on the earth's surface has not changed during the 4 or 5 billion years of its existence, the small quantity upon which life depends is always moving. This may give the impression that water is sometimes "lost," especially when there is talk of severe water shortages, but this is never the case. The constant change in the location of this water is governed by well-recognized natural laws that, together, constitute what is known as the *hydrological cycle*. An appreciation of the main features of this cycle is essential for an understanding of the influence of geology on the movement of water, and so upon all aspects of city planning in which water is involved, and they are many.

The cycle is in continuous operation, in every way a dynamic natural phenomenon. Breaking into it, consider first rain falling from the clouds onto the surface of the earth. That part which falls on the sea or upon the surface of rivers or lakes is added directly to the great volume of what is commonly called *surface water*. Of the

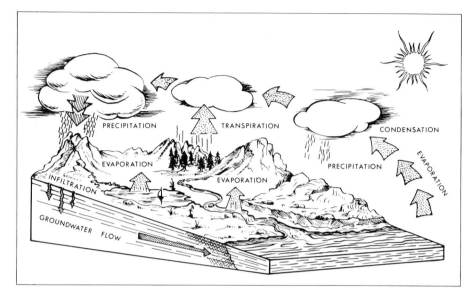

Figure 4.1 The hydrological cycle. *(Reproduced from reference 4.2, courtesy of the Department of the Environment, Ottawa, Canada, and E. R. Peterson.)*

rain water that falls on the land, some will run along the surface (especially if this is solid rock or soil well protected by vegetation such as grass) down any slope that leads to the nearest ditch or stream. Thence it will flow on to rivers, lakes, and eventually the sea. Some rain, however, will sink into the surface of the earth if the ground is pervious. As it seeps downward, it will dampen the soil through which it is moving, and in most cases it will eventually reach the upper surface of the body of water that is almost always found within the earth's crust, the great reservoir of *groundwater*. This surface, known generally as the *water table*, will vary in level, rising as more water is added to the groundwater by seepage from the surface or in other ways. Through springs, and seepage into the beds of streams, rivers, and lakes, the excess groundwater will be gradually lost from the upper part of the natural reservoir, and so the level of the water table will remain reasonably constant, unless and until it is interfered with by man.

The groundwater lost in this way helps to supply the flow of streams and rivers. This fact explains why they still go on flowing when no rain is falling. Eventually all the water that has fallen as rain will find its way back to the sea, apart only from that part which is drawn up directly into the atmosphere by evaporation from the surfaces of open water and running streams, or from the ground through transpiration from the leaves of vegetation. Evaporation is constantly taking place from the surface of the sea, at differing rates depending upon temperature and other conditions of the atmosphere. The water vapor is moved by the winds. Clouds are formed. Eventually they will precipitate rain, and so the cycle continues, perpetually.

   This is a simple outline of a wonderful natural process that in its detailed operation is remarkably complex. *Hydrology* is the study of the entire cycle and its implications for man. *Hydrogeology* is the associated study of the influence of geology on the movement of water, mainly groundwater, but it will shortly be seen that geological influences also have a bearing on other parts of the cycle. Figure 4.1 illustrates the outlines of the hydrological cycle. It may possibly make more real than can the use of words the dynamic aspect of this continually operating cycle, the vital water on which life depends being always in motion. Nothing can interfere with the overall working of the cycle, day in and day out. By his engineering works, however, man can have a local and temporary effect upon this natural movement of water, as for example by the building of a dam. The natural cycle itself can be subject to serious local variations. Floods, for example, are no new thing. They have taken place at intervals from time immemorial, due to local combinations of climatic and other natural conditions. Rainfall varies, with occasional long droughts in some places and catastrophic storms in others. These are natural variations that have to be considered in overall planning. In a similar way, the needs of urban settlements for a good water supply and for efficient means of disposal of water that has been used have to be planned with full appreciation of all the natural determining factors, of which geology is one. It is the purpose of this chapter to show how this has been done by citing a series of examples from varied cities throughout the world, examples providing experience that should assist in the planning of cities for the future in all major aspects in which water is involved.

4.2 RAINFALL

Records of local rainfall are one of the basic tools of the planner. Either directly, if records have been obtained locally for a long enough period, or by correlation of such local records as are available with the nearest longer-term records, an overall picture of the variation of rainfall throughout the year, and from year to year, must be obtained. For the world as a whole, the average annual precipitation is about 0.68 m, but local rainfall varies from desert regions, where there may be only a shower at very rare intervals, to mountainous areas, with over 10.2 m per year. The reference to mountains will be an indication of the profound influence that topography has upon rainfall, and topography is a reflection of the local geology.

   Although this interrelation of topography and rainfall is generally recognized as a regional phenomenon, heavy rainfall being experienced for example on coastal areas backed by high mountains as on the west coast of Canada, it is a factor that cannot always be neglected in considerations of smaller areas. The city of Vancouver on the west coast of Canada may be cited as an example. Beautifully located at the mouth of the Fraser River, the city extends to the south over the flat, low-lying land of the Fraser delta and to the north to the foot of, and indeed up the lower slopes of, mountains of the Pacific Range of the Coast Mountains that here come right to the edge of the sea. Good records are available from a number of long-term-rainfall gauges within the city area, and these show that the average annual rainfall within the city limits varies from 0.76 m in the south to over 3.0 m in the north, a ratio of over 4:1, a variation caused directly by the geologic setting of the city.

Rainfall records must, therefore, always be considered in relation to local topography in order to ensure that no such variations are involved. Since it is desirable to have an overall picture of the local rainfall situation for many aspects of planning, it may be useful to introduce readers to a simple means of plotting rainfall in association with local average monthly temperatures. Figure 4.2 shows typical records for Ottawa, Washington, D.C., and Prague plotted in the form of *hythergraphs*. One has simply to look at a few typical hythergraphs, especially if they are for cities that one knows, to become familiar with the overall impression of local climate that these graphs so quickly present. Hythergraphs are essential tools in all planning.

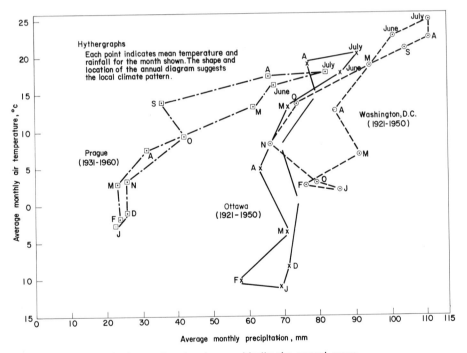

Figure 4.2 Typical hythergraphs, showing graphically the annual mean climates of Washington, D.C., Ottawa, and Prague; plotted points combine the mean monthly temperatures and precipitation for the months indicated by letters.

4.3 SURFACE WATER

The flow of streams and rivers is another important element in the information needed for planning. It is conveniently described as the *runoff* from the *catchment areas* of streams and rivers. "Catchment area" is a term that really describes itself. It is the natural basin, the runoff from which constitutes the flow of a river at any measuring point. The runoff will vary throughout the year, normally from a low flow at the end of summer to peak flows in late spring. The magnitude of this variation in flow throughout the year can be a critical factor in planning. It depends on a number of physical features. The River St. Lawrence, for example, has a variation (at Montreal) of only 2:1 because of the "balancing effect" of the Great Lakes acting as storage reservoirs. On the other hand, and in the case of most rivers, the variation is a great deal more than this (up to 100:1) where there are no lakes to provide storage and where the geology of the catchment area is such that much of the rainfall flows off directly without seeping into the ground to add to groundwater storage. A general knowledge of the geology of catchment areas is important, therefore, in considerations of river flow. A British study gave some typical figures for runoff at two different points on the River Exe in Devonshire, the lower one just above the range of tidal influence, and the other near the head of the river.[4.3] The dry-weather flow for the whole catchment area is (proportionately) almost four times that for the upper part of the area alone. The reason is that most of the bedrock underlying the upper part of the catchment area consists of igneous Devonian measures with low permeability, thus providing no groundwater storage, whereas the New Red Sandstone underlies much of the remainder of the catchment. This rock, being reasonably porous, does provide groundwater storage and this serves to maintain river flow in dry weather. Flooding in springtime will therefore be more serious from the upper part of this river than for the main river at its mouth. And the danger of floods in urban areas is one of the hazards that all planners must consider.

Geology is one of the main determinants of variation in river flow but there are others, sometimes more important. In the case of rivers in northern climates, river flow in springtime will be affected, sometimes seriously, by the incidence of frost. If the ground surface of a catchment area freezes before snow falls, it may remain frozen until the spring under the later snow cover and thus induce quick runoff in the spring. Some disastrous floods in North America, such as on the Red River, to be mentioned later in this chapter, have been due to this cause. The denudation of catchment areas of their protective cover of trees, and, in extreme cases, of the vegetation growing in soil, can certainly have a serious effect on runoff. Normal vegetation cover is one natural means of holding water as rain falls, giving it a chance to seep into the ground rather than to run off directly to the nearest stream. The degree to which this protection is effective may be a matter of debate, but the world-wide efforts now being made for the conservation of forests and of soil testify to the importance of this additional factor in the variation in the runoff of rivers.

The significance of urban development in connection with runoff will be apparent. When streets are paved, all rainfall will be forced to run off down the drains that must be provided as a part of roadway design. The paving of large areas for the parking of automobiles, as for example around North American "shopping centers," provides a vivid demonstration of this geological activity of man, especially if such an area is watched during a heavy rainstorm. It can readily be seen that this covering up of the natural ground surface will have a profound effect upon groundwater conditions beneath the paved area, in addition to giving what may be called "instant runoff." That this is no new phenomenon is shown by this interesting extract from the last will and testament of Benjamin Franklin (1706–1790):

> And, having considered that the covering of a groundplot of the city with build-ings and pavements, which carry off most of the rain and prevent its soaking into the Earth and renewing and purifying the Springs, whence the water of wells must gradually grow worse, and in time be unfit for use, as I find has happened in all old cities, I recommend that at the end of the first hundred years, if not done before, the corporation of the city [Philadelphia] . . . [bring] by pipes, the water of Wissahickon Creek into the town, so as to supply the inhabitants . . . .[4.4]

And this was written almost 200 years ago. Franklin left the sum of £1,000 to his native city of Boston, and the same amount to Philadelphia, calculating that, at the end of the 100 years mentioned in his will, this sum by compounding would have increased to over £130,000. This fine old man considered that this fund could then assist with the building of the city's waterworks.

Although so far-seeing with respect to the need, Franklin could not see that so soon after his death the demands of public health would necessitate the action that he anticipated for a century later. It was on 27 January 1801 that the mayor and members of the city council attended the formal opening of Philadelphia's first water-works, water from the Schuykill being pumped through two steam-operated pumping stations and delivered into a simple system of wooden water mains.[4.5] The whole project was the ingenious concept of Benjamin Latrobe and included a tunnel 1.8 m in diameter and over 915 m long excavated under the city, one of the first urban tunnels of North America. The provision of pure water to cities has been a prime municipal responsibility throughout North America ever since that auspicious day, as it had already become in older European cities even in the eighteenth century, a direct result of man's interference with natural geological conditions.

4.4 GROUNDWATER

Rainfall and surface flow are familiar to all. Groundwater, however, will not normally be as familiar a natural feature to city dwellers, even though those who live in rural areas usually well know how important is the supply of water that they obtain from the reservoir of groundwater through wells or springs. It will be evident, from the foregoing brief discussion of surface runoff, that groundwater is of vital importance to all urban development. An understanding of the essentials of groundwater occurrence is therefore most necessary for all who are to be concerned with town and country planning. Fortunately, the main features are extremely simple, once the three-dimensional aspect of the ground to be used for development has been grasped. The surface that can be seen is naturally important, but equally so is the constitution of the ground beneath the surface. The necessity for thinking of the ground as just the upper surface of the block of soil and rock that underlies it, and of remembering that subsurface conditions can have an important influence on the use of the ground surface, will be a recurring theme throughout this whole volume. It is not a difficult concept to visualize. Looking into an excavation, peering down a well, or watching a test-boring operation in progress will help to make real the fact that the natural surface of the ground is a reflection of the materials beneath it.

The water to be seen at the bottom of a well or the seepage that can be observed in most deep excavations is an indication of the body of water that is stored in the interstices of the soil or rock below the water table (defined previously). Coarse sand and gravel will naturally contain relatively large amounts of water. This simple fact illustrates the dependence of groundwater occurrence on geology. The type of soil or rock determines not only the quantity of water held within it but also the ability of this water to flow when conditions are appropriate. The latter characteristic is called the *permeability* of the material. Clays, for example, have a high *porosity*, but the pores between the minute particles that make up the solid clay matter are so small that the water is tightly held and so will not flow. Sandstone rock, on the other hand, although quite hard and solid, can be so constituted that some of the pores within it, between the grains of sand of which it is made up, will be open, thus allowing water to flow through it, slowly but quite definitely.

Permeable soils and rocks can therefore hold water and release it, permitting the flow of groundwater through them if subsurface conditions are appropriate. When they hold water they are called *aquifers*, a Latin word that conveniently describes these important geological strata. There are, correspondingly, many types of rock and some soils (such as clays) that are impermeable either completely or to such a degree that no water can usefully be obtained from them. They will naturally act as barriers to the flow of groundwater, sometimes usefully but sometimes with disadvantage to the convenient use of the water in adjacent aquifers. Many rocks, and even stiff clays, will be found in their natural position in the ground to be fractured by jointing. These joints will naturally provide channels through which groundwater can flow. Even impermeable rocks, therefore, may yield water if they are jointed and if other subsurface conditions are appropriate. The availability and possible utilization of groundwater at any site that is to be developed can, therefore, be determined only after a thorough study of the subsurface conditions.

Against this general review of groundwater, some of its more detailed aspects may now be considered. In Fig. 4.3, some simple diagrams illustrate the interrelation

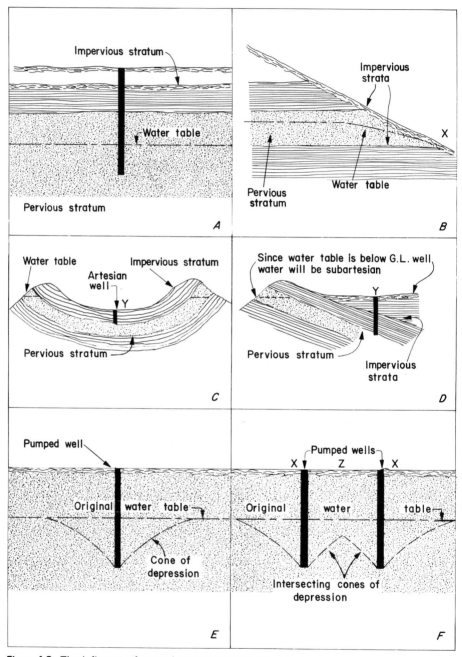

Figure 4.3   The influence of ground structures upon groundwater occurrence, the several sketches being explained in the text.

of permeable and impermeable strata. Diagram *A* illustrates the ordinary occurrence of groundwater as found in a well that has been dug through clay, for example, to water-bearing sand below. If the surface of the ground is inclined, as shown in diagram *B*, and with the arrangement of strata shown, groundwater will seep out at the surface at the point *X*. This is the sort of condition that leads to the springs that are so common a feature of rural hillsides. It is easy to imagine variations of these basic combinations of strata. The next two diagrams illustrate the effect that an impermeable stratum can have in confining groundwater. The groundwater thus "trapped" will be under pressure, but it cannot escape from its confinement until holes are drilled to it, as indicated at *Y* in the diagrams. As soon as these drill holes go through the impermeable strata, the trapped water will force its way up the holes under pressure. If the drill-casing pipe is extended above the surface, water will rise in this pipe until it is at the same level as the free water table. This condition, when groundwater is under such pressure that it will rise above ground level in a well or borehole, is known as *artesian water* (after Artois in France).

Finally, if groundwater is removed from the ground by pumping, the water level will naturally be drawn down. When this happens water will flow from all the aquifer around toward the point of abstraction of the groundwater. When pumping has been carried on long enough to give a condition of equilibrium, the flow of water from around the well must equal exactly the amount being removed. To induce this flow toward the well, there must be the necessary gradient, and so the surface of the water table will be as shown in diagram *E*. The shape of the curved surface of the water table can be calculated mathematically; it is known as the *cone of depression*. This is a very important concept in connection with the use of groundwater. If, for example, pumped wells are spaced too closely together, the cones of depression will interfere with one another (as shown in sketch *F*), and a full yield will not be obtained. And if anyone is depending on a stable level for the water table at a point such as *Z*, then he will be seriously affected by the pumping at *X*. Pumping in the city of Liverpool, England, in a rock called the Bunter sandstone, has affected groundwater levels as much as 3.2 km away.

Subsurface conditions are not usually as simple as those shown in these diagrams, but the principles thus illustrated are always applicable. When, therefore, water is pumped from a well, this will affect an appreciable area around the well. If impure water, such as sewage, is dumped into the ground or down a well or any other opening, it will immediately foul the groundwater that it joins. If groundwater has to be lowered (as is often the case) in order to carry out deep excavation work, this lowering will, again, affect an appreciable area around the excavation. The possible effect of this must be investigated in advance of the start of the excavation work. If the level of a lake is to be raised, or lowered, the groundwater conditions all around the lake will be affected, often for considerable distances. When the first Aswan Dam was built on the River Nile in Egypt, the reservoir that it created caused so extensive a change to groundwater conditions in the surrounding country that the water supplies at oases 160 km away were increased.

The complete interrelation of the geology of any area, such as a potential town site, the rain that falls upon it, the flow of any streams or rivers that pass through it, and the reservoir of groundwater beneath it, will now be clear. The study of these physical features is conveniently described as the hydrogeology of the area. It is related not only to water supply but also to the disposal of waste water after human use and of storm water running off streets and buildings. Flooding of rivers can have a profound influence upon the use to which low-lying land can be put in urban development. The position of the water table can seriously affect the performance of foundations, just as it can be of critical importance in all excavation work. In Rotterdam, the high water table that features that Dutch city was put to good effect when complete sections of prefabricated concrete tunnel sections for a new subway were actually floated into place, through the center of the city, using excavations in which the groundwater had been allowed to come up again to its normal level (see page 309). In other cities excessive pumping of groundwater has caused serious settlement of the ground surface. Later in this chapter examples will be given to illustrate these and other effects. Throughout other chapters it will be impossible to describe some examples without almost incidental reference to some aspects of the local hydrogeology. A comprehensive example will first be described, but even before this it will be desirable to discuss briefly the quality of natural waters, and their temperatures, since these properties naturally affect the use of water for urban purposes.

4.5 QUALITY OF NATURAL WATER

As rain clouds form and as rain falls to the ground, impurities in the atmosphere will be absorbed in minute quantities, with the result that rainwater is never "pure water" in a strict sense. When it comes into contact with the ground, either as surface water or as groundwater, it will be in intimate contact with soil or rock. In the course of time, and if in contact with materials that have any soluble constituents, it will acquire minor constituents from these materials, thus departing still further from a scientifically pure condition. All natural waters, therefore, contain some dissolved solid or gaseous materials, and these small amounts determine the quality of the water. Before water can be used in any way for human purposes, its quality must be tested. Standard tests for water quality are an invariable part of all water-supply arrangements.

"Hard water" and "soft water" are terms in common usage. Hardness of water is the result of contact with rocks containing calcium or magnesium carbonate or calcium or magnesium sulfate. Soft water is an expression really indicating the absence of hardness. Such relatively purer waters will have been in contact with igneous or metamorphic rocks containing no soluble constituents. The degree of hardness is measured by determining the number of parts of different chemical salts per million parts of water. Truly pure water, for example, will dissolve only 20 ppm of calcium carbonate or 28 ppm of magnesium carbonate, but if the water contains any carbon dioxide, as rainwater usually will, then it can dissolve much larger quantities. If the content of calcium carbonate exceeds 200 ppm, then it will have to be treated chemically to reduce the hardness before it can be used generally as "potable water."

An important part of water-supply engineering is, therefore, the testing and treatment of water quality. Of concern here is the fact that practically every constituent of water, when so determined by test, will be geological in origin. If, for example, a stream to be used for water supply is known to flow over limestone rock, the water will be suspect before even the first test is performed upon it. It is sometimes said, almost in jest but quite accurately, that an engineer or geologist can tell you something about the local geology of an area merely by washing his hands under a tap connected with the local water supply. When unusual impurities are found in water, then a first place for inquiry as to their source is the geology of the materials with which the water has been in contact. Iron salts, for example, can be very troublesome, affecting not only the taste of water but causing staining of materials with which it is used. They are particularly troublesome if water is to be used for the dying industry. Geological study in advance of development will assist in tracing the source of such impurities and so with the necessary treatment of the water, or the finding of an alternative supply.

The presence of high concentrations of calcium and magnesium sulfates in groundwater can be very serious if they are not detected and concrete structures are founded in ground containing such water. Rapid deterioration of concrete in western Canada in the early years of the present century led to a major research program that resulted first in a recognition of the sulfate content of prairie soils as the cause of the trouble, and then to the invention of a special sulfate-resistant cement that is now almost universally used in areas in North America featured by sulfate-bearing groundwater.[4.6] The problem is not peculiar to North America. In England, a detailed survey has shown that sulfates of calcium and magnesium occur widely in the Mesozoic and Tertiary clays that are quite widely distributed. Some areas in most countries will possess this undesirable feature, but it is one that can readily be detected by well-planned preliminary-site investigations.

There are other areas where impurities (so called) in natural water prove to be advantageous. The most famous beers of the world will be found to possess their special qualities due to the geological quality of the water used in brewing. Pilsner beers of Czechoslovakia are world famous, brewed in long-established breweries in the pleasant town of Pilzen to the west of Prague from local water that is quite soft, containing only small but vital quantities of solids. The ales brewed in Burton-on-Trent in England, also widely known, are made from hard water obtained from valley gravels and Keuper sandstones. It was once humorously calculated that drinkers of Burton ales consume at least 158,760 kilograms of solid gypsum every year. So also with other noted drinks. Scotch whisky derives at least some of its unusual properties from the fact that it is distilled only in certain areas of the north of Scotland where the available water has been found through the years to have exactly the right properties. It gains these by flowing in contact with igneous rocks and through the peat that is the usual surface cover in that lovely area. One famous company that operates several distilleries once arranged for each of the distilleries to use water from one of the others, a research project of special appeal. It was found that, although the whisky produced in each distillery during the test was excellent, it was "entirely different from that produced before [they] temporarily exchanged the waters." It would take more than even geology to explain such a result.[4.7] One delightful and erudite writer on this vital topic even goes so far as to say that there is a difference between whisky made from water that comes "off granite through peat" and that made from water "off peat into granite."[4.8] This probably represents an unsolved geochemical problem.

4.6 GROUNDWATER TEMPERATURES

Another important property of groundwater is its temperature. There is general familiarity with the fact that spring water is generally cool and that there are parts of the world where very hot water comes out of the ground. More than this general

Figure 4.4 The distillery at Bunnahabhain, Isle of Islay, Scotland, illustrating typical "granite and peat" topography conducive to the distilling of Scotch whisky. *(Courtesy of the Scottish Tourist Board, Edinburgh.)*

impression is necessary in urban planning work, however, in view of the demands now being made upon groundwater resources. If the temperature of groundwater is carefully measured over an appreciable period of time, it will be found to be sensibly constant. This temperature will be found usually to be almost but not quite the same as the average annual air temperature throughout the year for the same location. This can be readily understood if the "insulating effect" of the upper few meters of the ground is considered.

Until relatively recently, this fact was of no very great practical significance, although it did give a pleasantly cool supply of water whenever groundwater was used directly for this purpose. Today, however, in many cities this condition of groundwater is providing a valuable, but variable, "sink" for absorbing the heat from buildings that are equipped with air-conditioning systems. Using cool groundwater in this way, by pumping it into the air-conditioning system and then back again to the ground, is an obvious and apparently economical means of achieving desired degrees of cooling. With the sudden increase in the demand for air-conditioning in so many modern cities, the demands upon groundwater for this purpose have also increased. So serious has the matter become that outright prohibition of the use of groundwater for this purpose has had to be imposed in some cities. In others, strict controls have had to be exercised. Some theaters in New York, for example, are permitted to use groundwater for cooling, but only on condition that a closed circuit is used for all water pumped in this way (in order to obviate any possibility of contamination) and that all water so used is returned to the ground by means of wells.

The reverse problem—of having hot groundwater—is rarely met with, except in some special areas, but there is on record at least one case (the town of Riverside in California) where the temperature of the local groundwater was so high that a cooling system had to be installed.[4.9] Usually, however, such hot waters are found to have such a high content of minerals that they cannot be used for normal water-supply purposes. On the other hand, the mineral contents are often found to have therapeutic effects, with the result that "mineral springs" have been an aid to medicine since the earliest period of human history. The Roman baths at what is now the city of Bath in England (see page 27) are typical of early examples. The many cities and towns that incorporate the word "springs" in their names will usually be found to be the site of such mineral-water occurrences. Karlovy Vary (formerly Karlsbad Springs) in northwestern Czechoslovakia is a world–famous example of more recent years; its waters come through a group of about 30 springs, the main discharge being the Vridlo Spring. Water temperatures range up to $65°C$ and about three times as much CO_2 gas as water is emitted. The waters contain up to 6,500 mg per liter of dissolved solids.[4.10]

The heat associated with such waters comes from the internal heat of the earth, just as some of the water itself probably derives from within the earth sphere rather than from rain. Most of the hot water so encountered, however, is groundwater that has been heated by the passage through it of heated magmatic gases that do come

Figure 4.5 Karlova Vary, Czechoslovakia. One of the hot springs. *(Photograph by R. F. Legget.)*

from below the earth's crust. This combination is most vividly demonstrated by the *geysers* that are so spectacular a feature of some small areas in New Zealand, Italy, Iceland, and the United States. "Old Faithful" in Yellowstone Park, Wyoming, is a world-famous example. Since almost all of the conveniently available hot springs have already been developed, in a number of cases having been directly responsible for the founding of a town or city around them, they will not normally come within the purview of planners of new towns.

They call for this brief mention, however, since in several parts of the world intensive search is now being carried out for new sources of natural heat beneath the surface of the earth as an economic and convenient means of generating power. Already more than 1 million kilowatts are being generated from this source in Italy—the pioneer, with its Larderello field generating power since 1905—New Zealand, Japan, Mexico, the U.S.S.R., and the United States. The Geysers area, 144 km north of San Francisco, has been known as an area where natural steam came out of the ground since the days of the early prospectors (1847), but it was only in 1922 that the first very small power plant was installed to utilize this source of heat. Pacific

Gas and Electric Company now operates a power station with an installed capacity of almost 200,000 kilowatts utilizing this unique source of heat, to be increased to 600,000 kilowatts by 1975. In 1971 the President of the United States signed an act passed by the Congress opening up federal lands in the western states for the development of geothermal power. Further developments in the use of this pollution-free and most economical power source may therefore be anticipated.[4.11]

It is in the small northern country of Iceland, however, that "hot groundwater" has been put to the most extensive and remarkable use. Nearly one-half of the total population of the country (just under 200,000) live in houses that are heated by natural heat. Practically the entire population of the pleasant capital city of Reykjavik are now served in this way, with the result that the city is probably the most smokefree of all capital cities of the world. Hot springs have been known in Iceland since time immemorial, as have active volcanoes, but it was not until about 1925 that modern utilization of the hot water evidenced in the country's many hot springs and geysers was really started. Today, 72,000 of the 80,000 inhabitants of the capital city live in naturally heated houses. The heat comes from groundwater obtained from three areas—Reykip, with 70 free-flowing wells, 300 to 600 m deep, giving 300 liters per second at 86°C; Laugarnes, in the center of the city, with 11 boreholes, 650 to 2,200 m deep, giving about 300 liters per second at 130°C; and Ellidaar, in the eastern part of the city, discovered only in 1967, where 5 boreholes, 860 to 1,600 m deep, give 165 liters per second at 100°C. Over 100,000 m² of land are

Figure 4.6 Reykjavik, Iceland. Storage tanks for the natural hot water used to heat buildings in this capital city. *(Courtesy of J. Gislason, Director, Orkustofnun, Reykjavik.)*

now covered by glass and heated by natural heat, most of the enclosed area being used for cultivation. All the many swimming pools throughout the country are similarly warmed to convenient temperatures. The unusually comfortable living conditions enjoyed by Icelanders are provided, therefore, by nature—aided by excellent modern engineering practice in thus controlling for public convenience the heat given by groundwater.[4.12]

4.7 HYDROGEOLOGY OF WINNIPEG, CANADA

The city of Winnipeg in western Canada illustrates most of the main features of the hydrogeology of cities. Capital of the province of Manitoba, it started as a small trading post to which the first settlers came in 1812. Now a great metropolitan area, it has a population of well over half a million. It is located at the junction of the smaller Assiniboine River (coming from the west) with the Red River, which flows generally due north from its source in the Dakotas, entering Lake Winnipeg near the town of Selkirk at latitude 50°10′N. It stands on relatively flat prairie soils about 80 km to the west of the edge of the outcropping igneous rocks of the Precambrian Shield. An interested visitor might assume that it had few problems in connection with water, especially after finding that its average annual rainfall is only 0.48 m. Further inquiry would show how wrong first impressions can be, one of the important lessons given by Winnipeg being to show how vitally important are the geological conditions beneath the city. Three-dimensional thinking is essential for an appreciation of the hydrogeology of this important urban area.

Figure 4.7 is a geological cross section running east to west through the city, as shown in the key map, the distance included in the section being about 96 km. The general dip of the bedrock to the west is clearly shown, the Precambrian rocks being overlain by sandstone of the Winnipeg formation, then by a great thickness of limestones and dolomites. (The exaggerated vertical scale makes the dip of the rocks appear to be much steeper than is in fact the case; the dip to the west is only about 91.4 m every 32.2 km). The rocks are covered to varying depths by soil. Within the city area, compact glacial till overlies the dolomitic limestone, and so acts as a seal to the groundwater that is contained in the upper 15 to 30 m. This water has its main source in rainfall upon areas well to the east of Winnipeg, where pervious soils are exposed at the surface. Some also comes from the west, the general pattern of groundwater flow being shown on the section. The sandstone is naturally a good aquifer, but, unfortunately, the water it contains is saline and so not fit for normal use. The water in the upper portion of the carbonate formation, however, is of good quality, although somewhat hard, as is usual with water in contact with limestones.

The first wells were put down about 1840 and started a steady increase in demand upon this confined aquifer. Today there are over 200 industrial and commercial wells in the city area and thousands of domestic wells. Although river water was used for the public supply by the original Winnipeg Water Works Company, ground-

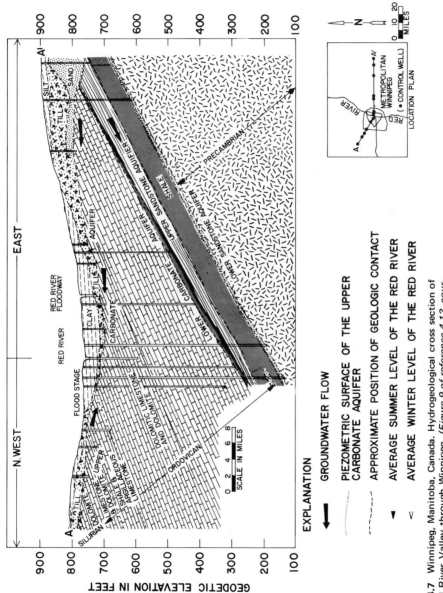

Figure 4.7 Winnipeg, Manitoba, Canada. Hydrogeological cross section of the Red River Valley through Winnipeg. (*Figure 9 of reference 4.13, courtesy of the National Research Council of Canada and F. W. Render.*)

water was pumped as the main supply starting in 1900, some 10 years after the municipality had purchased the private company. The rate of pumping increased from about 4 million liters per day in 1900 to over 40 million liters per day in May 1919. In that month the city brought into use the Greater Winnipeg Aqueduct, through which excellent water was brought to the city from the Lake of the Woods area to the east. The dramatic effect upon the rate of pumping is shown in Fig. 4.8. This record shows that pumping is again increasing, the rate now being about 12 million liters per day.

From early records it is known that before the start of major pumping of the groundwater the water table would come very close to the surface of the ground when a well or borehole penetrated through the protecting stratum of glacial drift and allowed the groundwater to "find its own level." (This condition is known as *subartesian*.) There were even some flowing wells in one part of what is now the built-up city area. Pumping had the natural effect of lowering the water table. Where previously there had been flowing wells, the water table fell to 12 m below the surface. As soon as the major pumping stopped in 1919, the water table started to rise again, and in due course it came back almost to its natural position. Today, with increased pumping, it is again dropping. The dynamic nature of the system is illustrated by the fact that, if one calculates the distance that the water table should have dropped if

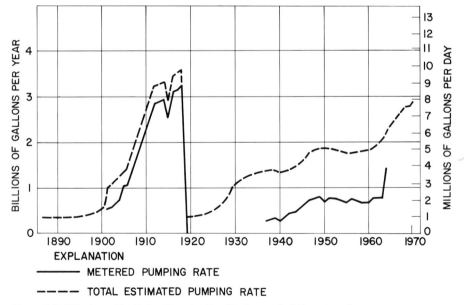

EXPLANATION

———————— METERED PUMPING RATE

— — — — TOTAL ESTIMATED PUMPING RATE

Figure 4.8 Winnipeg, Manitoba, Canada. Graphical record of the rates of pumping groundwater for the city's water supply. *(Figure 3 of reference 4.13, courtesy of the National Research Council of Canada and F. W. Render.)*

there were no replenishment of the supply beneath the city, this is found to be about 183 m. The maximum measured drawdown has been no more than 18.3 m, showing that the reservoir of groundwater is being constantly replenished. The system has now stabilized, the amount pumped out of the bedrock being just about balanced by the inflow from the surface soils to the east and west of the city.

The salinity of the water contained in the sandstone is possibly due to flow over *evaporites*. Salt concentration is about the same as that in sea water (35,000 mg per liter). Reference to Fig. 4.7 will show that some wells have penetrated the sandstone. This has naturally released the groundwater held in it under pressure, and so some limited contamination of the relatively pure water in the limestone has occurred. Possibly related to this salinity is the fact that the groundwater encountered right at the surface in the Winnipeg area (in damp ground near the surface) has a high sulfate content. This reacts with concrete if this is made with ordinary portland cement. All concrete structures in contact with the ground must, therefore, be most carefully mixed and placed, using the special sulfate-resistant cement that is now readily available.

This, however, is but one aspect of the influence of local water conditions upon construction practice. Far more serious is the fact that if any excavation for foundations or other purposes penetrates into the glacial till, the pressure of the groundwater beneath may break through the till and rise to its free level, thus flooding the excavation. Before any deep excavations are made, therefore, detailed knowledge of the local groundwater situation is essential. The same danger is present when piles or caissons are used for the founding of heavy structures. If possible, they penetrate as far as the upper structure of the till on which they are then founded. Many cases are on record in which this was not done, and the till was penetrated in the absence of the information on local groundwater conditions that is now available, with consequent difficulty with the water thus encountered. One excavation in which groundwater was encountered somewhat unexpectedly was a preliminary trial pit put down in connection with the Red River Floodway that now bypasses the city. One excellent result of this incident was the completion of a most thorough investigation of the entire hydrogeological situation in the Winnipeg area, upon the published record of which this account is largely based.[4.13]

The floodway was constructed in 1961–1965 after this great city had been devastated by a most serious flood on the Red River in 1950. Historical records had shown that floods of this magnitude had occurred in the earliest days of settlement so that flooding had to be accepted as a natural phenomenon that might occur again. To a large extent, the flooding is due to snow conditions in the Red River Valley and the incidence of frost in the preceding fall season. The floodway was therefore designed to have a peak capacity of 1,700 m^3 of water per second, or rather more than one-half the maximum flood flow in 1950. It is about 48 km long and the excavation involved was over 76 million m^3, or about 40 percent of all the excavation necessary for the Panama Canal. Large concrete intake and outlet structures as well as

Figure 4.9 Winnipeg, Manitoba, Canada. The Winnipeg Floodway in use,
looking south (toward the city), the Red River being on the right. (*Figure
19 of reference 4.13, courtesy of the National Research Council of Canada
and F. W. Render.*)

the substructures for 10 bridges had to be constructed. That all were completed
satisfactorily is tribute to the information that was available about the geological
and groundwater conditions that would be encountered. The floodway has already
proved its worth since it went into action in the spring of 1965 for the first time.
Normally it is an "empty ditch," and since the channel is up to 19.5 m deep, with an
average depth of about 9 m, it has naturally interfered with the groundwater situation
all along its route. Within a year after completion of the work, however, a new
equilibrium position had been reached, and those dependent upon groundwater in
the affected area were able to adjust their operations to the new conditions.

Not many cities have a hydrogeological situation that includes quite so many
features as does the metropolitan area of Winnipeg, but almost all cities include some
of them. It will now be clear why an appreciation of the three-dimensional structure
of the earth beneath every urban area is so essential to an understanding of each one
of the separate aspects of water that have here been so briefly discussed. All planning
must be based on similar "block thinking" since subsurface conditions can have so
direct an influence upon what is done at the surface of the ground.

4.8 WATER SUPPLY

Against the general background that has been presented of the integrated water
"system" of a city, specific aspects of water in cities will now be considered. Water

supply naturally comes first, since the existence of all cities depends upon an adequate and safe supply of good water. All modern cities now have piped water supplies to residences and industrial users. This convenience has naturally led to an increase in the use of water, as have modern domestic devices such as washing machines and air conditioners. The demands of industry have correspondingly increased. The average consumption of water in electrified rural and urban dwellings is now between 150 and 230 liters per day (lpd). Municipal water systems, supplying both domestic and industrial demands, have now to supply from 450 to 760 lpd. Many large industries need so much water that they have their own systems. It takes, for example, 45 liters of water to refine 4.5 liters of gasoline; 260 tonnes of water to manufacture 1 tonne of sulfite wood pulp; 272,000 liters of water to make 1 tonne of steel. The demand for water seems to be insatiable since not only is there the increase in demand due to increase in population, but there is this additional increase due to increasing individual demand both domestic and industrial. Water supply, therefore, is a key factor in all planning of urban growth. Geology is one of the main determinants in all water supply systems.[4.14]

The city of Denver, Colorado, now the center of a metropolitan area of over 1 million, cannot get enough water for its needs on the eastern slopes of the Rockies, on which it is located, and so has had to construct expensive tunnels in order to tap water that would normally flow down the western slopes. The state of California, with its population having increased in 30 years from about 7 million in 1940 to almost 20 million in 1970, has had to consider water supply from the point of view of the state as a whole. It is now building a great system that will convey water through a major aqueduct 714.5 km from reservoirs in the northern parts of the state to the great urban agglomerations of the south. Israel, a small country facing a critical water situation, has correspondingly constructed a small aqueduct to convey water pumped out of Lake Gennesaret (the "Sea of Galilee") in the north 240 km to settlements on the edge of the desertlike Negev in the south. The same widespread search for water is to be found all round the world as many larger cities have to go further and further afield in order to supplement their existing water-supply systems.

The main sources of water for city use may be reviewed briefly prior to the presentation of summary accounts of the geology of some outstanding systems. Cities that are located on lakes can obtain their supplies readily, if the lake water is of good quality, by pumping directly from the lake supply. Examples are most of the cities on the Great Lakes, such as Chicago and Toronto, each with extensive underwater structures at the intake ends of pumping mains, the construction of which always involves detailed geological knowledge of the lake beds. Cities on river banks can also have direct pumped supplies if the river water is suitable. Montreal on the River St. Lawrence and Prague on the River Vltava are well-known cities that obtain their supplies in this way. Pumping through wells and boreholes from the groundwater underlying urban areas is another very old but still widespread source of public water, although the effects of overpumping have caused much trouble in some areas. When these local sources are not sufficient to supply city needs, then the main recourse is to find an undeveloped area, the water on which can be collected in impounding reservoirs and then piped to the city in need. The city of Liverpool in England carried out one of the first major modern developments of this kind in the Old World with its Vrynwy works in central Wales in the 1880s, but the practice is now common around the world. San Francisco, for example, has a notable water supply from the Yosemite National Park through its Hetch-Hetchy aqueduct, the water generating power as it flows down to serve the city's needs.

Many major cities, as will shortly be seen, combine two or even three of these sources of supply as the demand upon them for more water continues to increase. Some cities use combinations of two of the schemes for reasons of economy and safety. Des Moines, Iowa, for example, has for many years obtained its water supply from the Raccoon River, not directly but by pumping from collecting galleries (of concrete pipe) buried in water-bearing sands, the water thus collected seeping through the sand from the river that is 60 m away. The natural sand beds act as splendid filters.[4.15] Some of the great industrial cities of the Ruhr have similar systems, as also does Göteborg in Sweden. The city of Kano in northern Nigeria has a somewhat similar scheme, except for the fact that the concrete wells from which its supply is pumped were sunk in position in the sand of the dry bed of the local river that flows on the surface only in times of flood. The wells capture the flow of groundwater in the sand, and this continues throughout the year.[4.16] Finally, there are naturally a number of unusual sources of water supply that do not fall within the main categories listed; each is a special case by itself. A number will be briefly described.

Although the engineering features of all these water-supply projects are peculiar to the city involved, and affect only that city, the geological aspects are not so confined. The geology that is utilized and the water that is taken are each part of a continuum, all of which must be considered in the planning stages, for the water that one city takes for its use may thus be removed for potential use by a neighboring city, especially if groundwater is involved. Accordingly, in a number of countries, the first steps have fortunately been taken to deal with water-supply problems on a natural basis rather than on the basis of artificial political divisions. In Great Britain, for example, the Water Resources Act of 1963 established river authorities that have complete jurisdiction over all water within the catchment area of their river. These authorities, now in operation, have the duty of licensing *all* abstraction of water, including groundwater, from their areas and of controlling the pollution caused by discharges of used water. Considering the water resources of a catchment area necessarily means thinking of it in overall geological terms. Geology, therefore, is one of the bases upon which the developing work of the authorities is founded.[4.17] In Canada, a pioneer effort was the establishment in 1957 of the Ontario Water Resources Commission that has complete jurisdiction over all the catchment areas within the Province of Ontario, and also over the use made throughout the province of water taken from the Great Lakes on which Ontario borders. From the start of its important work, the commission has recognized the importance of geology in all its operations. Planning in Ontario, therefore, necessarily involves close consultation with the Water Resources Commission and its staff in all matters affecting water. Geology is therefore in the planning picture from the start.[4.18]

4.9 WATER SUPPLY OF LONDON

London, England, is served by a water-supply system that is not only one of the largest in the world but one that demonstrates quite remarkable geological features. The Metropolitan Water Board (MWB), established in 1903, is now responsible for the supply of water to a population of over 6 million people, living in an area of 140,000 hectares. This area includes most of what is popularly thought of as "London," extending in the west to the weir across the River Thames at Teddington and to Dartford in the east, well down toward the river's mouth. During the year 1969–1970, the Thames supplied 70 percent of the total supply, the smaller River Lea 16 percent, and water from wells 14 percent.[4.19]

Records of water supply in London go back almost 800 years. Water was originally drawn directly from the Thames and its small tributaries, but, at the urging of King Henry III, the Lord of the Manor of Tyburn (Gilbert Sanforde) made a grant to the city in the year 1237 allowing them to convey water from springs on his property to the City in "pipes of lead." This was the beginning of one of the most extensive uses of groundwater for public water supply of which there is any record. By the sixteenth century, springs were being so well used that further supply had to be pumped from the Thames, at first by horse-driven pumps, later by the frequently illustrated waterwheel arrangement in the first archway of London Bridge. Possibly more significant was the work of the New River Company in 1613 in bringing by gravity spring water from springs to the north (in Hertforshire) to a round pond at Clerkenwell (in the city). The MWB appropriately has its head office building today on this site. Guiding genius of this company of "adventurers" was Sir Hugh Myddleton. He used local clay for forming the banks of the New River; the records also mention "loads of Chalk," the local bedrock. Geology, as a name, had not then been invented, but it seems fairly certain that, even at this early date, a good appreciation of the fundamentals of geology was being put to good use in this early water-supply system.[4.20]

The first pumped well appears to have been put down in 1837. Thereafter an increasing amount of water was obtained in this way. When the MWB was established, the New River Company was supplying between one-third and one-half of its supply of over 180 million lpd from pumped wells. Today, over 225 million lpd are obtained from groundwater alone, through 52 well stations, about half on each side of the river. The source of this remarkable supply is the great London Basin, shown diagrammatically in Fig. 4.10. The term "basin" is really inaccurate since the subsurface formation is actually a trough with its axis WSW to ENE. The Chalk is relatively impermeable, but it is jointed and fissured, with the result that it holds great quantities of water. This reaches it, as can so clearly be seen in the diagram, from

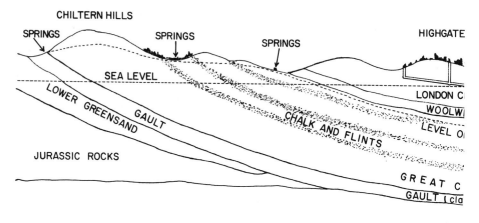

Figure 4.10 London, England. Geological section across the London Basin. Vertical scale exaggerated 40 times. *(Courtesy of the Metropolitan Water Board, London, E. C. Reed, Chief Engineer.)*

the rainfall that descends on the Chiltern Hills and South Downs. Adding to the geological good fortune of London is the deep stratum of impervious London clay that underlies the entire urban area and serves as a tight seal on the water in the clay. In earlier days, therefore, when the clay was pierced by a borehole, the groundwater would rise even beyond the surface of the ground, giving artesian flow, but the many years of pumping have now lowered the water table so that in places it is 60 m below the surface. Near the eastern boundary, this pumping has already had the effect of making some wells brackish, due to infiltration of sea water. It is unlikely, therefore, that any increase in the amount pumped out of the Chalk can be allowed.

Although the London Basin is obviously the most interesting feature of London's water supply from the geological point of view, there are current developments with equal—although not so obvious—interest. The MWB abstract water from the River Thames through special intakes above Teddington Weir (the western limit of their area), but they may not take water when the flow over the weir is less than 643.5 million lpd or reduce the flow below this quantity. It is led into storage reservoirs, treated, pumped, and then supplied throughout the board's area. A similar arrangement is followed with water from the River Lea. The runoff at Teddington Weir is the responsibility of an authority with the delightful name of the Thames Conservancy.

In an effort to increase the flow of the Thames, especially in times of low flow, the Conservancy embarked in 1965 on a pilot project of pumping groundwater from the upper and middle Chalk and feeding this supply into a tributary of the Thames. The small valleys of the River Lambourne and the Winterbourne Stream were chosen, and a 3-year experimental program was carried out. Nine boreholes were used for

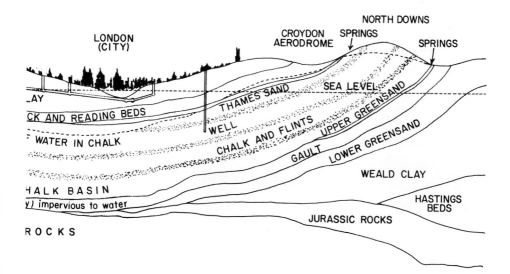

pumping during the period May to October. Infiltration from the streambeds and seepage of rainfall in the ordinary way during the remaining winter months essentially restored the water table by spring of each year. Careful ecological studies were carried out to ensure that this variation from the natural pattern of flow was not causing any untoward biological effects. The influence of the pumping on neighboring properties was also studied. The results were most satisfactory. It is now estimated that over a 10-year period a net gain in the flow of the River Thames of up to 378.5 million lpd at the end of a severe dry period can be obtained, at an estimated cost of one-third to one-quarter of the cost of conventional balancing reservoirs, and yet with no loss of farm land. This significant experiment, which shows such potential for the future of London's water supply, was possible only because of appropriate geological conditions beneath the catchment areas studied, conditions that were most thoroughly investigated before the experimental pumping was started.[4.21]

4.10 WATER SUPPLY OF NEW YORK

The development of the early water supply to what is today the great metropolitan area of New York is a most complex story. It involves the old Manhattan Company and the involved political maneuverings that preceded the establishment of the administration of the great city of today with its five boroughs. Water was initially secured from local shallow wells, the rocky character of so much of the island of Manhattan severely limiting the possibilities of this source. Pumping from the rivers around the island followed. Epidemics of serious diseases and the great fire of

Figure 4.11 Thames Valley, England. Pumping station for experimental recharging of tributary streams to the River Thames. *(Courtesy of the Thames Conservancy, E. J. Brettell, Chief Engineer, Reading.)*

16 December 1835 combined to lead to action for a safer supply. With a vision that can be admired even today, the civic authorities finally agreed to go 48 km north of the city to the small Croton Watershed, to build there one of the first great dams of North America, conveying the water in an aqueduct to the city crossing the Harlem River on the famous High Bridge. The new water supply, the pressure in which permitted a fountain 15 m high to be a central feature of the celebrations, was officially dedicated on 14 October 1842, truly a pioneer undertaking.

This was the beginning of the great system of aqueducts that today supply most of the water for the New York area. Following the Croton works came the Catskill system, bringing water over 160 km to the city. The Catskill works involved two large dams and some of the major tunnels of the United States. They were significant in this present context since the successive chief engineers to the Board of Water Supply were assisted in all their works by a group of distinguished geologists, one of whom was Dr. Charles P. Berkey, who later became an acknowledged leader in this new field of applied geology. Later came the even more extensive Delaware River project, water again being brought almost 160 km through another great tunnel system to serve the ever-increasing population of the city. Again, geology was used in assisting with the construction of all the engineering works involved in this immense project, the written records of which are of great assistance to all engineering geologists. Today, work is under way on still further tunnels beneath the city for water distribution.[4.22]

These applications of geology to the construction of dams, bridges, and tunnels, although pioneering efforts in the early days of the New York water supply, are today happily standard practice on almost all civil engineering work. There is, however, one part of the water supply to the New York area that presents some unique features. To the east of the island of Manhattan lies Long Island, about 192 km long with a maximum width of 35 km. It constitutes an important coastal plain bordering on New York State and Connecticut. It is divided, politically, into four counties, the two smallest (at the western end) being also boroughs of New York. Figure 4.13 shows the geological sequence underlying a typical section through Long Island. As can be seen, the bedrock that is so prominent a feature of Manhattan is close to the surface at the northern side of the island but is 600 m below the surface on the southern coast. The overlying beds are almost all water-bearing, only the Raritan and Gardiner clay beds failing to be good sources of water. The surface glacial deposits were deposited during the ice movements that featured the Pleistocene epoch; they are pervious enough to allow rainfall, under natural conditions, to seep through to the beds of sands and gravels below.

When settlement of Long Island started, groundwater conditions were in equilibrium. Seepage of rainfall into the ground surface kept the water table high, flow

Figure 4.12 Dr. C. P. Berkey in the field—a portrait that is included in view of his great contributions to engineering geology in general and to the geology of the water supply to New York City in particular.

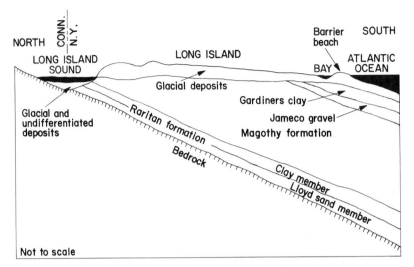

Figure 4.13 Long Island, New York. Diagrammatic section showing general relationships of the major rock units of the groundwater reservoir of Nassau County, Long Island. *(Figure 2 of "Changing Pattern of Groundwater Distribution on Long Island," courtesy of the Director, U.S. Geological Survey.)*

through springs and into the small water courses on the island, with possibly some seepage into the sea, maintaining the balance. Beneath the sea, the groundwater was naturally sea water but, because of the different specific gravities of fresh and salt water, there was a state of equilibrium between the two beneath the island, the fresh water resting on top of the salt water at a depth of possibly 300 m. The first settlers got good water supply from springs and shallow wells. They disposed of their waste water in cesspools that drained back into the water-bearing beds. Eventually, and inevitably, this seepage began contaminating private wells. Larger and deeper public wells were the next stage; they could be so placed as to minimize danger from pollution. Generally these wells drew water from the Jameco gravel and the Magothy formation, which, with the underlying Raritan formation, is of Cretaceous age, the Jameco and Gardiner beds being Pleistocene deposits. Even with increased pumping from these public wells, equilibrium was not seriously disturbed since most of the water found its way back into the water-bearing beds after use.

The next stage of development involved the "servicing" of developed areas in Kings County (Brooklyn), and this involved the paving of streets and the installation of sewers. These excellent improvements carried the waste water direct to the sea, or Long Island Sound, so that it was not returned to the water-bearing beds from which supplies were being drawn in ever-increasing amounts. The result was that there was a serious drop in the water table. In the Brooklyn area, where 283.9 million lpd was being pumped by 1936 on an average day, the construction of sewers and the paving of streets had combined to lower the water table to as much as 10.7 m below sea level. This naturally allowed sea water to encroach, and serious contamination of some well supplies resulted. The situation was naturally continually under expert review. The final outcome was that, by 1947, virtually all pumping of groundwater for public supply had ceased, and Brooklyn and the area around was being supplied from the surface water available through the New York Board of Water Supply. Groundwater could still be pumped in Brooklyn for air-conditioning purposes, but only on condition that it was returned directly to the ground from which it came.

The water table therefore rose again, but even this most satisfactory result brought problems in its train. During the period of heavy pumping and water-table retreat, subways and other structures located below the surface of the ground had been built without experiencing any problems due to groundwater. As the groundwater slowly came back nearly to its original position, flooding of basements and subway tunnels occurred until the necessary remedial measures were taken to secure local control of the water table. There could be no better example of the completely integrated "system" that must be considered when the hydrogeology of city areas is involved. Today, groundwater conditions beneath Long Island exhibit all phases of the development just recited for the western end. At the eastern end, natural conditions still remain; then come settlements of individual houses with individual wells; then the use of public wells; further to the west, urban areas that are sewered but that still derive their water by pumping from below, the water table therefore having been lowered to a serious degree; and finally the well-developed area finishing in Brooklyn that now gets all its water supply from the New York system, the water table still slowly coming up toward its natural position but with groundwater con- taminated by sea water to a degree that is not known with certainty since it is not now used for public supply.

The extent of the use of groundwater for public supply is shown by the fact that, in 1963, an average amount of about 1,438 million lpd was being pumped out of Long Island wells. It has been suggested that "this pumpage probably represents one of the largest such uses of a single well-defined groundwater reservoir anywhere in the world." Future planning of conservation measures includes the use of recharge wells, reclamation of water from sewage, and desalination of sea water, matters that are touched upon later in this chapter. The implications for all future city planning on Long Island are obvious. Planning can be undertaken only with full cognizance of the exact groundwater situation in the area involved. Fortunately, a great deal of relevant information is publicly available through the joint efforts of the U.S. Geologi- cal Survey and the New York State Water Resources Commission. A most informative "Atlas of Long Island's Water Resources" has been prepared jointly by the two agencies; it can be recommended to all interested in the use of groundwater anywhere as showing in vivid pictorial form the complications of the Long Island situation. And when readers of this volume have occasion to land at the J. F. Kennedy International Airport, they may perhaps recall that they are landing on top of this quite remarkable reservoir of groundwater, from which so much of the water used throughout Long Island is drawn.[4.23]

4.11 SOME OTHER NOTABLE WATER-SUPPLY SYSTEMS

Every water-supply system, from the simplest well to the great reservoir and aqueduct projects for major cities, is dependent upon satisfactory geological conditions for its successful operation. There are therefore countless examples that could be cited to illustrate how the supply of water to urban communities has been integrated with overall planning. Only a small selection can be presented, supplementing the accounts just presented of the major systems for London and New York. Selection is not easy, but the examples that follow, each very briefly described, will at least indicate the information that is available for those who wish to have a more complete review of the water-supply side of city development. The examples have been chosen to illustrate somewhat unusual geological conditions, but there are few water-supply projects that do not present at least some geological features that require special attention. Water-supply systems of remarkable geological interest serving the great European cities of Prague and Vienna could well be described, but attention will, rather, be directed to projects in some of the more distant parts of the world.

Sydney, Australia

Water supply to the great metropolitan area of Sydney, New South Wales, now with a population of well over 2 million, has an unbroken history since the days of the first settlement. It is recorded that on 26 January 1788 "sufficient ground was cleared for the encamping of the officer's guard and the convicts who had been landed . . . at the head of the cove, near the run of fresh water, which stole silently along through the very thick wood . . . ." The Tank Stream, thus so pleasantly described, supplied water to the little settlement from 1788 to 1826. "It still flows, a dark and hidden stream, beneath the shops and offices of modern Sydney," but it had become polluted before it was abandoned as the main water supply in 1826. Groundwater was next used, a supply being obtained by tunneling for "Busby's Bore" in a corner of Hyde Park, but this supply also became insufficient. In 1886 the first water was brought to the city from the Nepean watershed to the north, collected by means of a wire across the Nepean River at Pheasant's Nest. This was the beginning of a series of notable collecting projects, using larger catchments, all further removed from the city, and involving the construction of many notable civil engineering works. Geology added its complications since valuable coal seams underlay some of the dam sites needed for the water supply projects. The NSW Mines Department laid down stringent limitations upon coal mining in the vicinity of the dams that were built on such unusual sites, and beneath the reservoirs they form; no troubles have been reported either of leakage or settlement. The last of these major projects was the

Warragamba scheme that included the building of the largest dam in the Southern Hemisphere across the Warragamba River. This great structure, 120 m high but only 330 m long at its crest, because of the precipitous gorge in which it is built, would call for mention not only because of its size but also because the sandstone rock on which it is founded caused complications during construction, requiring most expert geological advice. Observations on this dam since its construction are adding an important chapter to the records of engineering geology.[4.24]

Hong Kong

The small crown colony of Hong Kong, with a total area of less than 103,000 hectares, has a rapidly increasing population that is already over 3 million. It has good rainfall, but this naturally varies year by year. Its water problem is therefore primarily one of storage since the supply obtained from runoff from the rocky hills that make up so much of the colony has now been supplemented by water from China. The Chinese have reversed the flow of the Shih Ma River and pump its water through eight

Figure 4.14 New South Wales, Australia. Warragamba Dam for the water supply of metropolitan Sydney. *(Courtesy of the Metropolitan Water, Sewage and Drainage Board, Secretary S. R. Smith, Sydney.)*

pumping stations, aided by six large reservoirs, to a point just north of the Hong Kong border. The colony is taking 67,500 million liters of this water per year, giving the Chinese almost £1,000,000 in foreign exchange. Storage, however, is difficult since there are no natural large reservoir sites amid the Hong Kong hills. Every advantage has been taken for the building of small storage reservoirs, but for major storage it was finally decided to convert an inlet from the sea to hold fresh water instead of sea water. The Plover Cove project has converted an area of 1,110 hectares into a main fresh-water reservoir. Intensive study of the geology of the sea bed revealed about 10.5 m of soft clay overlying 1.5 m of stronger clays beneath which is bedrock of granite in various stages of weathering. Dredging removed all the soft clay, the stiffer clay being left as the bottom of the reservoir to act as a seal against penetration of sea water once the reservoir was filled. The main dam is 2,070 m long and 45 m high, but with only 16.7 m above water level. Geologically it is interesting because of the extensive use made of decomposed granite, and granodiorite, from the hillsides overlooking the famous harbor. So rapidly has the demand for water increased that work is to start in 1971 on an even larger project at High Island, involving still further use of the sea bed as a reservoir site.[4.25]

Gibraltar

It is naturally the cities with limited area around them that have the greatest problems in providing good water supply. One of the most remarkable examples of this is the colony and city of Gibraltar. Because of its strategic location and remarkable bastionlike Rock, it is well known around the world. Despite this, its problems with

Figure 4.15 Hong Kong. The upper part of the Plover Cove Reservoir Dam, the larger part of which is below water level. *(Courtesy of Binnie and Partners, Geoffrey Binnie, and Scott Wilson, Kirkpatrick and Partners, Hong Kong, joint consulting engineers.)*

Figure 4.16 Gibraltar. The artificial catchment area for obtaining rain-water for the city's use; one of the collecting troughs may be seen about half way up the covered slope; the dark patch near the entrance to the Rock is an area in which corrugated iron sheets had been temporarily displaced by wind. *(Photograph by R. F. Legget.)*

water supply are not widely appreciated. Even though its situation is unique—fortunately for other cities—the solution to its problem is of such interest that it warrants brief reference. The great Rock consists of hard and compact Jurassic limestone, with some shale, providing no supply of spring water. Some water is obtained from wells in the sandy flat area between the Rock and the Spanish border; some of this can be used for potable supplies, but brackish water has to be kept separate and is not used for human consumption. The main part of the local supply is obtained, however, by aiding nature in collecting the rainfall that descends on the east side of the Rock by means of an "artificial catchment area." This has been achieved by covering 9.7 hectares of the steeply sloping rock face with corrugated iron sheets, tightly lapped together, and draining into concrete collecting trenches. The upper trench leads directly into the interior of the Rock in which large reservoirs have been excavated by mining. The lower supply, water from the wells, etc., is pumped into these underground storage reservoirs that are so extensive that they are served by a small railway for maintenance personnel. The competent nature of the limestone has been put to good effect in these extensive excavations since no supporting structures are necessary. Water has also to be imported by ship, so great is now the local demand, and desalination of sea water will probably have to be used in the future.[4.26]

Juneau, Alaska

Far removed from Gibraltar, but with a similarly confined location, is the capital city of Juneau in Alaska. It has been built on a small coastal plain on Douglas Sound, a section of the 1,600-km long Inland Passage that distinguishes the northwest coast of North America. The restriction of the site by mountains is well shown by the fact that, even in this isolated location, a large steel bridge has had to be constructed across the channel to give access to building sites on Douglas Island. Water supply for the city was obtained from Gold Creek well above the town and from wells in Last Chance Basin through which the creek flows. Cold-weather problems caused many difficulties, and so a new supply system had to be developed. A tunnel had been driven in 1898 by a mining company that intended in this way to drain the gravels of the Last Chance Basin in the expectation of discovering gold. Their efforts were defeated when the heading broke through into the gravels, the tunnel being flooded. Another company tried in 1902 to wash the gravels into the tunnel. Some success was achieved, but a flash flood in 1905 plugged the tunnel and brought operations to a halt. The tunnel was then abandoned and became clogged with debris, but it was still connected with the water-bearing gravels. Having been driven through sound basalt-gabbro rock, the tunnel itself was found to be quite sound when it was investigated as a possible conduit for water. The tunnel was cleaned out, a concrete connection with the water-bearing gravels was constructed with proper controls, and connections to the city reservoir made at the lower end of the tunnel that now serves as the major aqueduct. Gravity flow from wells in the gravels is normally sufficient, but water can also be pumped when necessary. The large diameter of the tunnel results in low velocities, and so the rock around the tunnel acts as a heat-exchanger, warming the water slightly from its initial temperature of about 5°C throughout the year, thus eliminating the previous problems with winter freezing.[4.27]

Vancouver, British Columbia

Almost 1,600 km south of Juneau, but on the same coast, lies the city of Vancouver, western metropolis of Canada. Serving a population of almost 1 million is the Greater Vancouver Water District, established in 1926. It has been given complete control over catchment areas of three small rivers with an area of 58,500 hectares. They are located immediately to the north of Burrard Inlet on which the city is located, in the Pacific Range of the Coast Mountains that includes peaks of almost 1,500 m within sight of the city. The high rainfall ensures good runoff, and this is stored for city use in reservoirs created by dams on the small rivers. Large pipes convey the water by gravity from the reservoirs to the water district, the crossing of Burrard Inlet being effected by a notable pressure tunnel, the construction of which was a difficult operation due to the geological conditions encountered. Since the water comes from catchment areas underlain by igneous rocks, its quality is remarkable—hardness rarely exceeding 10 ppm, total dissolved solids only 23 ppm—so that chlorination is all the treatment that is required. This wonderful water supply is really fortuitous, since the city was founded not as a result of any careful city planning but in connection with the terminus of the Canadian Pacific Railway on Canada's west coast. There are few major urban areas throughout the world that are so fortunate as to have a gravity supply of pure water available within 16 km of the civic center. The growth of Vancouver has certainly been aided by this good fortune.[4.28]

Sheikhdom of Kuwait

Kuwait, although only 1.6 million hectares in extent, has become well known because of the great quantity of oil obtained from beneath its surface, now over 2 million barrels of petroleum per day. Located at the head of the Arabian Gulf, it has an average annual rainfall of only 8 cm. This all comes during the winter months of November to May, sometimes as intense local storms but more generally as light winter showers. Temperatures range from 51 to -7°C. Post-Miocene rocks underlie the generally inhospitable surface of the country, the northern part being generally

Figure 4.17   Vancouver, British Columbia, Canada. A general view of the city from the south, showing the adjacent Coast Range in which are located the reservoirs for the city's water supply. *(Courtesy of the Greater Vancouver Visitors and Convention Bureau.)*

a gravelly plain. The Dibdibba formation, thought to be of Pleistocene age, consists predominantly of sand and gravel and serves as an aquifer, as do also underlying formations of limestone. The oil reserves are in more deeply underlying Cretaceous sandstones and limestones. Regional dip of the strata is to the east and northeast. Settlers in the area, prior to the recent oil developments, were able to get water from shallow wells; dug wells were also used, but all the water so obtained was brackish due to contact with some of the local rock formations. Drilling for oil started in 1936, and further brackish-water supplies were discovered in this way. Two major sources were thus developed, the water being distilled for potable use but used directly for other purposes. In 1960, fresh groundwater was surprisingly discovered by "a rig drilling brackish water wells for the Basra Road construction [being] accidentally sited on the wrong location when moved during a sand storm." Careful studies revealed that this fresh water is surrounded and underlain by brackish water. The details of the local geological structure are such that, from inflow at the surface following winter rains, some water is retained in the Dibdibba cemented sandstone before being rendered brackish. Now, 32 million lpd are obtained from this source, which is here described to emphasize the existence of groundwater beneath even the most unexpected areas.[4.29]

Honolulu

Honolulu, capital city of the state of Hawaii, is located on the island of Oahu, one of the eight inhabited Hawaiian Islands that are now so well and favorably known for their natural beauty and hospitable climate. The islands are the peaks of a vast underwater series of volcanic mountains. Mount Kaala in Oahu is 1,220 m high, but since the sea around has depths going to 4,500 m, it can be seen that these peaks are amongst the highest mountains in the world. Some of the volcanoes are still active, but not on Oahu. The islands are therefore formed of volcanic lava, a rock that is generally highly permeable. Since the islands are blessed with good rainfall and as the generally rugged terrain exposes the rocks, water seeps into the ground continually and so gives excellent local supplies. But because the rocks are so permeable, their open pore structure is also filled with sea water beneath the surface of the sea and so deep below the islands. The conjunction of the fresh and salt water held in the rocky foundations to the Hawaiian Islands is one of the most remarkable examples of a hydrogeological phenomenon that is becoming of increasing importance.

The phenomenon is generally known as the *Ghyben-Herzberg effect*, since its nature was first recognized by W. Badon Ghyben of the Netherlands in 1889 and apparently quite independently by B. Herzberg in Germany in 1901. As with many such discoveries in science, other scientists had noticed the phenomenon but had not described it so clearly as the two men mentioned, whose names are given here since readers may come across them in reading about groundwater. The situation with which their names are now associated is, in principle, very simple; it is readily

Figure 4.18 Honolulu, Hawaii. View inside one of the Maui wells, or tunnels, giving an impression of the flow of water through the porous rock, the photograph being taken before the lower part of the tunnel was allowed to fill up. *(Courtesy of the Board of Water Supply, Honolulu, G. Yuen, Manager and Chief Engineer.)*

visualized. Because sea water is about one-fortieth heavier than fresh water, due to its salt content, it follows that the fresh water will, if undisturbed, "float" (so to speak) on the top of the sea water. The depth to which the fresh water will extend below sea level will be 40 times the height of the lens of fresh water. There will be no dividing line between salt water and fresh, but experience has shown that the actual occurrence of both types of water in a permeable formation, such as the lava rocks of Hawaii, does approximate to this theoretical pattern when undisturbed.

Inhabitants of Oahu, relatively few in number until recent times, relied upon the flow of surface streams for their water supply until 1879, when the great reservoir of groundwater underlying the island was discovered. Due to impermeable surface deposits, the groundwater was then under artesian pressure in many parts of the island. This was tapped by the first well drilled (in 1879), a well that was the forerunner of more than 400 wells that had been drilled by 1910. By 1923, the groundwater level in the area of Honolulu had dropped 6.9 m below its original level (which was only 12.6 m above the sea) and in so doing had disturbed the delicate balance between salt and fresh water, with the result that some wells had "salted up." As the geology of the island was studied, and the sensitive balance of water conditions was determined, measures were taken to control the use of this valuable asset. The Honolulu Board of Water Supply was established in 1929 to control and manage the water supply to the city. In 1959, through a merger with the former Suburban Water System, the board was given control over all the water in the island of Oahu. It has scientifically developed the former rather crude methods used for "skimming off" the fresh water from the upper surface of the great underground reservoir. This is now done by means of deep shafts, some distance from the coast, some vertical and some inclined, at the foot of which horizontal adits are constructed as collecting galleries for the water seeping through the porous rock. The location of these galleries is determined on the basis of detailed geological studies, since they must follow the general line of the lava flows. Some are more than 300 m long. Water is abstracted from the galleries by strong pumps and so fed into the Board's distribution system. The U.S. Geological Survey has officially designated these unusual installations as "Maui-type basal water tunnels," but they are more popularly known as "Maui wells," even though so far removed in size and arrangements from what one normally thinks of as a well. The principle employed, however, is just the same, the additional complication at Honolulu being the absolute necessity of maintaining the delicate balance between seawater and fresh water.[4.30]

4.12 SALT-WATER INTRUSION

The remarkable water-supply system of Honolulu has been described at some length because it illustrates in such a constructive way the balance that can be maintained along coasts formed of permeable materials, either soil or rock. It will be obvious that the situation in Oahu is far from being unique. Along all coast lines below which groundwater is found, this same delicate balance will exist. Such a condition has already been noted in connection with the groundwater below Long Island, New York. Reference had to be made there to the fact that some wells had become brackish by infiltration of sea water. Unfortunately this situation has been allowed to develop at all too many coastal locations around the world. The problems thus created have therefore been studied in Israel, the United Kingdom, the Netherlands, and Japan, as well as in North America. Overpumping from wells located close to the coast has been the usual cause of this intrusion of seawater. It is understandable that, when demand for water increases, an obvious solution is to increase pumping rates—unless those responsible have a very clear idea indeed of the delicate hydrogeological situation with which they will be interfering. What makes the matter the more serious is that, once this balance is disturbed, it is difficult and time consuming to restore the natural condition, and sometimes impossible.

The problem of restoration is, however, being vigorously tackled in different parts of the world. Enough is now known of groundwater movement so that, in the development of new urban areas near the sea, salt-water intrusion should never be allowed to develop. The planning of local water-supply arrangements should always be carried out with full knowledge of the dangers of overpumping near the sea coast. Existing situations, however, have to be dealt with, and there is always the possibility of accidental salt-water intrusion. Accordingly, brief reference may usefully be made to a notable example of remedial measures involving the development and operation of what is called a *sea-water barrier*.

The south coastal basin of southern California is well known, if only because of the great agglomeration of urban development that now distinguishes it. It is formed of unconsolidated sedimentary deposits of great complexity that are generally pervious. The great plain therefore constitutes a vast underground reservoir of groundwater from which increasing water supply has been drawn. Oil is also found beneath the plain, and its extraction has led to further pumping of groundwater. Sea-water intrusion first became a problem in the 1940s. A quarter of a century later, 17.6 km of the southern Californian coastline had been affected. Critical contamination with seawater extends inland for about 3.2 km in places, averaging about 2.4 km. Beginning in 1950, however, the Los Angeles County Flood Control District embarked on a major control program. Some early work was done by actually constructing barrier walls of puddled clay, but the main county program has been the installation of a steadily increasing number of recharge wells, close to the coast. The wells range in depth from about 45 to 180 m. They are located most carefully in relation to the local geological conditions, the length of perforated surface, through which fresh water is recharged into the ground, being determined in exact alignment with appropriate aquifers. Twelve wells had been installed along a 2.4-km length of coast by 1965; the ultimate program for the 17.6 km of coastline affected being 75 recharge wells through which will be fed a volume of 2.1 m^3 per second of fresh water, obtained from the Metropolitan Water District of Los Angeles, and brought by its great aqueduct from the Colorado River. Design of the wells has been progressively improved since the program started. Helpful accounts of all phases of this unusual project have been published so that much useful information is available for others who have to deal with similar problems.[4.31]

4.13 RECHARGING GROUNDWATER

So much has already been presented about abstracting groundwater for human use that the foregoing reference to recharging water into the ground may strike an unusual note for some readers. The way in which nature replenishes groundwater was briefly mentioned in the account of the hydrogeology of Winnipeg, a state of balance having there been achieved between withdrawal of groundwater for use in the city and its natural replenishment. This state of equilibrium has not always been possible to achieve. There are all too many locations, in many parts of the world, where over-pumping has seriously depleted groundwater supply, even without the consequent intrusion of sea water or contamination of the supply from other underground sources. Since water is never "lost," the water so taken from the ground must be disposed of somewhere, usually down sewers and drains to neighboring watercourses. The idea of disposing of surface water by putting it back again into the ground probably often occurred to users in earlier times, but it was not until the latter part of the nineteenth century that specific planning of this reuse of water was started.

"Artificial groundwater recharge" is the formal name that has been given to this procedure. It is now widely practiced and is gradually becoming a basic part of water planning, when local conditions (especially geological) are appropriate. The first attempts to replace water on any major scale appear to have been made in Northampton, England, in 1881, using the underlying Lias limestone. Experiments were conducted with the Chalk of the London Basin, also in England, as early as 1890. Later, old shafts and adits in the Chalk were used as media for the recharging of water, and it proved possible to measure the percentage of the replaced water that was later repumped for further use. There are in Sweden over 20 municipalities that obtain their water supply from groundwater that is, to some extent, replenished by artificial recharge. The Hague, de facto capital of the Netherlands, has a large modern part of its water supply utilizing this procedure. And many cities in the United States are similarly assisted in maintaining their public water supplies. Wells are sometimes used by a more general method, as by the employment of spreading grounds, specially prepared flat areas of permeable ground that are flooded at regular intervals.

Los Angeles again provides an outstanding example of this phase of water supply, the agencies responsible being the Metropolitan Water District of Los Angeles, which serves six counties in this populous area, and the Los Angeles County Flood Control District. The general nature of the geology of the Los Angeles area was mentioned on page 165. It will be appreciated that, provided the detailed stratigraphy of the soils underlying any proposed site is known with certainty, then water-spreading beds can be planned and constructed with confidence. Well over 40 hectares of land are now in use in the Los Angeles area for this purpose. Experience has gradually been accumulated in the operation of the spreading grounds, with consequent increased efficiency in their use. Accurate records of all water are maintained. These have shown, for example, that water infiltrating into some of the upper beds reaches the North Hollywood Pumping Station 1 year later, a vivid reminder of the flow of groundwater beneath the surface, but flow at a necessarily very low velocity. It is this slow process of percolation that aids in the purification of water so recharged into the ground. Naturally, there is a limit to the degree of purification that can be achieved, but the efficacy of these natural filter beds is shown by the fact that not only water but also effluents from sewage plants are in regular use today for recharging ground-water supplies. Naturally, the effluents are first refined to a high degree of purity, but the final reclamation of such waste water is the result of its passage through the

Figure 4.19 Tel Aviv, Israel. Spreading ground for the infiltration of treated effluent for recharging groundwater. *(Courtesy of the Mekorot Water Co. Ltd., and Y. Rabinowitch, City Engineer, Tel Aviv.)*

pervious beds into which it is recharged. This procedure is now being followed, naturally under close control, in California, but an unusual example can be cited from the small country of Israel.[4.32]

One of the main planning problems of Israel is that of an adequate water supply. Already, almost 90 percent of its available water is being put to use, and this includes not only pumping from wells penetrating the groundwater beneath the sandy coastal plain but also the use of the water that is now being pumped from Lake Gennesaret and transmitted by a large pipe conduit to the southern part of the country. Pumping from wells along the coast has already been interfered with by salt-water intrusion, but the demand for water still increases with increasing population and industrialization. The sewage from the area of Tel Aviv (there being a population of over 800,000 in and around this new city) has been discharged directly into the Mediterranean. Collected in a main truck sewer, its flow was to be reversed in 1970 to a new treatment center 17.6 km away. It will first be led to treatment lagoons, the location of which has been most carefully selected. They are underlain by an impervious clay stratum so that none of the waste water can infiltrate into the ground from the lagoons. Anaerobic and aerobic action will be induced for treatment of the wastes and reasonably full treatment ensured before the waste water is allowed to enter the spreading lagoons. These are to be located on sand so that infiltration will take place with consequent slow flow (about 2 m daily) toward the area selected for the location of the recovery wells, through which the refined groundwater will be pumped for use in the city area. Salinity (which is not affected by percolation through the ground) is expected to be a problem so that it is anticipated that the water thus reclaimed will have to be mixed with purer water to give the necessary standard for public supply. It can, however, be used directly for the irrigation that is of such great importance to Israel. There must be few water projects that are so completely dependent upon local geological conditions for their existence.[4.33]

4.14 DISPOSAL OF WASTE WATER

The disposal of waste water, either from industry or after domestic use, might seem at first glance to be a matter of engineering significance only. The design of sewerage and drainage systems, as also the design of sewage-treatment plants, does indeed constitute an important part of that branch of civil engineering most commonly known as sanitary engineering, although now sometimes described as *environmental engineering*. The example from Israel that has just been cited will show, however, that geology may have an important role to play even in this part of the general system of water use in cities. And this goes beyond the normal applications of geology in site selection and in the carrying out of civil engineering construction work, applications that will be considered in Chap. 5. Every gardener knows that to dispose of minute quantities of liquid waste, he can dig a hole in his garden, put the liquid in "and forget about it." Enough has already been said about the interrelation of groundwater and surface flow to show that this simply cannot and never must be done with regard to waste water in any appreciable quantity.

Some of the problems are illustrated by the experience of the Rocky Mountain Arsenal of the U.S. Army, located near Denver, Colorado. Liquid wastes from the manufacturing processes in this plant seeped downward from receiving ponds into a shallow aquifer. This seepage appeared to have contaminated groundwater to such a degree that apparently damage was done to some crops irrigated by this water. As an alternative solution, a lined reservoir 43.3 hectares in extent was constructed, together with necessary observation wells all around it to ensure its safe operation. Its capacity was limited, however, and so to gain extra capacity for the liquid wastes, a very deep waste-water well was sunk. Extending to a depth of 3,420 m below the surface, the well is believed to be the deepest ever sunk for such a purpose. It was designed to dispose of the waste liquid by seepage into the 300-m thick Fountain formation of porous sandstone that is overlain by an impermeable stratum of shale, 900 m thick, which would act as a safe seal. The well extends to the underlying Precambrian granite and starts with a diameter of 60 cm at the surface. Together with a treatment plant to remove colloidal solids from the liquid before it was put down the well, the well was estimated to have cost over $1 million. It went into operation in March 1962. In April of the same year, observations disclosed the start of a series of minor earthquake shocks in the Denver area, over 700 being registered by November 1965. These were attributed to the effect on the complex rock structure into which the well had been drilled of the vast quantities of liquid being pumped into the well under pressure, at times almost 11.4 million liters per month. Many difficult questions arose when this unusual situation was studied in depth, but there was no doubt about the correlation of the pumping and the incidence of the earthquake shocks. Pumping into the well was stopped in February 1966.[4.34]

This extreme case is cited to illustrate the problems that can arise when waste water is disposed of underground, but to this must be added the fact that many deep wells are being used quite satisfactorily for this purpose. The petroleum industry, for example, has for many years used deep-well disposal for the brine pumped out of many oil fields in the procurement of crude oil, without experiencing unusual difficulties. The use of recharging wells for countering sea-water intrusion has shown how such "reverse wells" may be used to good effect. But accurate geological knowledge of the complete subsurface at the recharging site is absolutely essential before disposal of waste water in this way can even be considered, to ensure that permeable strata are available and that their use will in no way interfere with existing groundwater in other aquifers. And there is naturally a limit to the extent to which such underground storage can be used so that deep-well disposal is not, by any means, the complete long-term answer to waste-water disposal.

The same requirement—for detailed and accurate geological information—is equally necessary for surface disposal of waste liquids. In the fringe areas around many cities, septic tanks are used for the partial treatment of domestic wastes, discharging into adjacent areas through the usual network of tile drains. This is a satisfactory solution until such time as proper sewerage is available, but only if the ground conditions are suitable for the percolation of sewage-tank effluents. There are all too many cases of septic-tank installations installed without accurate geological information, sometimes with hazardous results. Suburban land division and development has actually been halted in some cases because of unsuitable ground conditions for septic tanks. The location of septic tanks serving lake- and riverside cottages is an important matter often overlooked. There must be sufficient travel for the tank effluent through the soil for its reasonable purification before it seeps into river or lake. Geological studies are again an essential prerequisite for such installations.

The growing use of sewage lagoons, as a cheap substitute for sewage-treatment plants, is increasing the seriousness of this problem, since sewage lagoons must be impermeable to prevent the escape of untreated sewage into permeable ground beneath, where it may contaminate groundwater. Fortunately, the use of sewage lagoons in urban areas is usually a temporary expedient, sometimes preferable to the widespread use of individual septic tanks, and a solution that can be used when local ground conditions do not permit the use of septic tanks. Despite their temporary character, however, their design and installation require the utmost care, as does also their maintenance and protection from interference should any other developments take place in adjacent areas.

Typical of the apparently quite innocent developments that can cause real trouble was the experience at a relatively new housing development in a dry area, located on gently sloping ground. All waste water from this pleasant area (from septic-tank effluents, watering of gardens, etc.) percolated slowly downhill, following the underlying bedrock. A new irrigation canal was constructed near the bottom of the sloping ground. It was not given an impermeable lining, and so a small amount of leakage was to be expected once it was put into use, enough to seep down to the bedrock, completely saturating a triangular prism of ground beneath the canal. This saturated ground, being regularly supplied from the irrigation water, formed a perfect "water dam" in the way of the natural flow from the housing area, previously uninterrupted. Trapped by this unusual and unseen dam, the seepage from the housing area gradually accumulated, with a consequent slow rise in the water table. Fortunately, the problem was recognized in good time, but if this had not been done, the entire housing development would have been in jeopardy.

Another extreme example, now completely corrected, may finally be mentioned not in any critical sense but to illustrate in a most graphical way some of the fundamentals of groundwater that must always be kept in mind in urban development. The town of Bellevue, Ohio, is now well served by an excellent sewage-treatment plant built in conformity with all the requirements of the State Board of Health. The town is located over cavernous limestone. With such convenient receptables available, it was small wonder that in earlier days 1,500 sinkholes had been put down into the limestone caverns into which all types of waste, including domestic sewage, was dumped. On 26 June 1937 an unusually heavy rainstorm, almost a "cloudburst," occurred, with between 17.3 and 20.3 cm of rain falling in 9 hours. All the ordinary facilities for handling the runoff of this "storm water" were overloaded; all underground caverns were filled. Flooding onto the surface occurred, geysers 4.5 to 6 m high breaking through the streets in the lower parts of the town. Much of the town was therefore flooded, and not merely with rainwater, for the underground caverns discharged their content of wastes, a grim reminder indeed that water "poured into the ground" does not just disappear but is still a part of the vast and intricate water "system" that must be fully considered in all urban planning.[4.35]

4.15 DRAINAGE

The example just cited shows clearly that the effective drainage of storm water and other excess flows is also not merely a matter of good engineering but one that may have significant geological controls. These will become the more important as the worldwide movement toward adequate treatment of all waste waters before discharge gathers momentum, in response to the growing demands for pollution control on all fronts. In most older cities, storm water has been conveyed for discharge in the same sewerage system as that used for domestic and industrial wastes. After heavy rains, this places a severe burden upon the capacity of sewage-treatment plants. Some cities have a dual system of sewers, one for the direct discharge of storm water and the other for conveying sewage to its treatment plant, an ideal arrangement that will be given increasing attention in future urban planning. Older cities, however, must seek for solutions utilizing their existing sewerage systems. One significant development may be mentioned, this being the planned use of excavated caverns deep beneath the ground for storage of storm water. It is a solution obviously completely dependent for its success on appropriate local geological conditions.

The city of Chicago is underlain by competent bedrock mainly of Silurian age, including shales, sandstone, and dolomitic and calcareous limestones, in all of which tunneling can be carried out satisfactorily. It has been proposed that storm water falling onto city streets should be dropped from the surface through 1.2-m-diameter vertical shafts to large excavated caverns capable of holding the flow from a 100-year flood. The caverns would be connected by a 32-km-long tunnel, 9 m wide by 18 m high, to an underground pumping station that would gradually pump the storm water back to the surface, some for discharge into the nearby Illinois River. It is further proposed that some of the water would be pumped into a large surface reservoir that would serve as the upper pool of a 1.3-million-kilowatt pumped-storage hydroelectric installation, operating on the same principles as those plants, all parts of which are located above ground. The engineering implications of this imaginative proposal will be obvious. It is here mentioned since it may well prove to be the forerunner of a number of such installations in major cities, faced with disposing the runoff from heavy storms. No such projects can be contemplated unless local geological conditions are entirely suitable.[4.36]

Discussion of geological aspects of drainage provisions would involve repetition of much that has already been said. There is, however, one special feature of drainage that must be mentioned briefly, this being the quality of drainage water from abandoned excavations, especially from mines. As cities extend their boundaries, it is inevitable that some will find included in their limits old mines that have long since been disused. The water that accumulates in such old mine workings is frequently found to be highly acidic; if not detected before discharge into ordinary water courses, damage to the ecological balance of the stream or river may result. There are, unfortunately, all too many cases on record of serious damage to fish and other forms of life by drainage from abandoned coal mines in particular. Problems are sometimes accentuated because of difficulties of assessing responsibility, but the matter is a geological hazard that must be watched for whenever old mining workings are included in a planning area.

Drainage from abandoned coal mines can be particularly troublesome, as has been found in the region of the Appalachian coal basin, for example. The root cause of the problem is usually the oxidation of pyrite and similar materials, leading to the formation of an acidic condition of the water that comes in contact with them, with consequent further chemical reactions when such water leaves the mines or spoil dumps. States and provinces that have to deal with this problem have been gradually introducing the necessary regulations, which inevitably involve a study of the mine geology so that the source of troublesome drainage can be determined, preliminary to the development of adequate remedial measures. Public pressure for attention to all forms of pollution has fortunately had the effect in some places of accelerating attention to this particular groundwater problem.[4.37]

4.16 FLOODS AND FLOOD PLAINS

Floods have called for repeated reference in this chapter. They constitute one of the most serious hazards that cities have to face. Unlike fires, however, which can be fought and usually extinguished, floods have to be accepted once they occur. Preventive works have to be planned and executed a long time ahead. Flood prevention and flood precautions must, therefore, be an integral part of long-term urban planning. Floods may be of three main kinds. They may be local floods due to unusually heavy rainfall on the paved streets and impermeable roofs of cities, "flash floods" that were touched upon in the preceding section. They may be due to flood flow in rivers and streams that pass through an urban area. Or, in the case of coastal cities, they may be due to unusual combinations of tidal and wind conditions. This third type is so unusual that it may well be left for consideration in Chap. 8. The second type of flood, however, is of frequent occurrence in some cities and towns, and it has very definite geological overtones.

Excessive flow in time of spring runoff is a perfectly natural phenomenon so that some river flooding has to be accepted as a part of the natural order. In Sec. 4.3 the dangerous combination in northern areas of early frosts coming before snowfall was explained. The great floodway that has had to be constructed around the city of Winnipeg (Sec. 4.7) shows what expenditure may be involved in the construction of preventive measures against such natural occurrences. It is now incontrovertible that the works of man—in cutting down forests and in using improper agricultural methods on cleared land—have intensified the danger of flooding in many catchment areas. Modern hydrological investigations make it possible to predict with reasonable accuracy the probable magnitude of the flood flow in any river or stream over a stated number of years. (Reference has already been made to a "100-year flood.") With this information available, it is possible to design the necessary preventive works in urban areas. These will always be costly and of questionable economy since they will be called into use so seldom. It is, therefore, of vital concern to city authorities to support any measures that will reduce the magnitude of peak flood flows.

This can only be done by work in the catchment area above the city in question. To this extent at least, therefore, urban planning cannot stop at the city boundaries but must comprehend to a degree the catchment areas that feed all watercourses that come into the planning area. Flood control is usually thought of as being achieved through the construction of strategically located large dams that can impound water in time of flood, releasing it to increase river flow at low-water periods. This is vital and important engineering work, geology playing its usual part in relation to the foundation of all structures and the impermeability of reservoirs. There are, however, less spectacular and complementary flood-control measures in which geology is more directly involved, these being the establishment of good agricultural practices (such as contour plowing on sloping land) and the construction of "little dams" and other soil conservation measures designed to delay immediate runoff of heavy rains and induce percolation into the ground. The relevance of geology to all phases of soil conservation (as such work is now generically described) is so obvious that it need only be mentioned to be appreciated, exact information on subsurface conditions throughout a catchment area being a prerequisite for all conservation planning.

There is one important aspect of flooding within urban areas to which attention must be directed, this being the use (or misuse) of flood plains. It is a common feature of rivers, when flowing through broad valleys, to overflow their banks regularly in time of flood. The annual flooding of the banks of the River Nile has already been mentioned, but exactly the same thing occurs, although on much smaller scales, on most normal rivers. These flat areas that are so regularly inundated are known as

Figure 4.20 Vanport, Oregon. Looking northwest over the flood plain of the Columbia River during the serious flood of May–June 1948; the railroad embankment to left of center had been acting as a levee until it was breached, affecting 20,000 people and resulting in 13 deaths. *(Courtesy of the U.S. Corps of Engineers, Portland Divisional Office, and W. H. Stuart.)*

flood plains. They are usually reasonably flat and naturally immediately adjacent to rivers; they are, therefore, apparently ideal for building areas. The danger of using such flood plains, and especially for residential building, will be obvious, and yet in all too many older cities this is exactly what has been done, with consequent serious damage and inconvenience coupled frequently with loud demands for the provision of costly flood-protection works. Control over the use of all flood plains in urban areas is absolutely essential.

The geological hazards of building on flood plains were touched upon in Chap. 3 (page 65). Flooding, in itself a geological hazard, is naturally the main danger, but the subsurface of flood plains usually consists of low-strength soils, with high ground-water levels making the design and construction of foundations equally difficult. It was flooding of a flood plain used for residential construction that caused such havoc in Etobicoke, Ontario, when Hurricane Hazel resulted in catastrophic rainfall in the vicinity of Toronto in 1954, thus leading to high flood flow on Etobicoke Creek; 80 lives were lost and 25 millions of dollars damage caused by this one flood. Replanning has eliminated further danger of this sort, but the occurrence is a most telling example of what can happen.[4.38]

With adequate preliminary geological and hydrological studies, it is possible now to avoid the misuse of flood plains in urban planning, generally restricting their use to purposes other than building, such as parks and playing fields. The real problems arise in the case of municipalities that have not had the benefit of such advice in their development so that they find themselves today with extensive building development in flood-plain areas. It has been reported that in 1971 there are still 5,200 cities and towns of significant size in the United States, part or all of which are located in flood plains. Since the early fifties, 360 communities in 15 states have adopted regulations regarding the use of flood plains, and 500 more in 41 states had such regulations under consideration in 1971. The magnitude of the problem that still remains will be obvious.

Illustrative of the problems that flood plains present is the town of Prairie du Chien, a town of 6,000 people in Wisconsin on the Mississippi River. The great valley is here 2,400 m wide confined between high cliffs, the river being in two channels, each about 300 m wide. Due to the location of the town, much of it is flooded whenever spring flood level is high. Careful study has suggested that 48 buildings in the lower part of the town should be torn down, 157 relocated, and 33 raised in their present locations above the 100-year-flood level.[4.39] Reference to raising buildings indicates one relatively easy solution, if it is used in advance of building—the placing of fill over flood-plain areas to give a working surface well above all possible normal flood levels. This can be done, however, if subsurface conditions are known with accuracy—a qualification that will have to be mentioned repeatedly throughout this volume, indicative of the essential requirement for all urban planning of adequate knowledge of the urban geology of all planning areas.

4.17 CONCLUSION

The hydrogeology of cities can now be seen to be a vital key to all successful urban planning. Without water a city cannot exist. Its procurement in sufficient quantity and of good quality both for domestic and industrial use is a primary civic service. Correspondingly, the safe and sanitary disposal of all waste water—or, rather, water that has been used, since it is never "wasted"—is an equally important service. Both use and disposal are closely interrelated with many other aspects of water in relation to the life and well-being of cities, the utilization of water within urban areas being indeed a "system" and it must be so considered. And geology exercises critical control over most phases of water use and procurement so that, without adequate geological information, planning in respect of water cannot be carried out effectively and may even, in extreme cases, be bad planning.

The means whereby local geological information is obtained and should be recorded for local use through the use of engineering-geological maps has already been explained (see page 110). Since the idea that water, and especially groundwater, is an integral part of the local geology will be a new concept to some readers, it may usefully be noted here that study of local geology must include study of all aspects of the local water regime. And this does not mean engaging "water diviners" (or "dowsers," as they are sometimes known)—individuals who aver that they can "find water" by the activation of a forked twig that they carry. There may possibly be something to this supposed peculiar personal attribute, for many well-known people are said to have had the ability to "divine water," but the whole subject has become so surrounded with charlatanry that it is worthy of no more than this brief passing reference, especially since no "diviner" can ever find water if the underlying geological conditions are not appropriate for the local occurrence of water.[4.40] Sound study of all phases of the local geology is, therefore, the basic requirement for water planning.

This will be the more important as the insatiable demand for water from existing cities and industries continues to increase and as new supplies have to be found for cities and industries yet to be created. Alarming figures could be quoted for the future prospects for water supply in some of the well-developed countries of the world, notably the United States; the already critical water situation in Israel has been mentioned. Let it suffice to say that every effort must be made to see that water is used as efficiently as is possible, coupled with long-term planning for future sources to be drawn upon when there are any available. Typical is the work of the Saskatchewan Research Council in studying the deep prairie-soil deposits beneath the urban areas of this western Canadian province. By deep drilling through the thousand or so meters of soil, buried channels have been discovered in the underlying bedrock surface, often gravel-filled and serving as major channels for groundwater flow. Already this work gives promise of answering long-standing questions about the relative flows of the North and South Saskatchewan Rivers, but more importantly the studies have shown the potential that exists for appreciable new sources of water supply, even though heavy pumping may be involved.

Adequate water supplies hold the key to the development of many parts of the world that have not yet achieved their full potential. The imaginative Indus Valley project, building upon the earlier experience of some of the extensive water projects of India, is typical of the worldwide attention now being given to the proper use of water for human welfare. In all this work, geology will have a critical role, and nowhere more so than in the planning of all aspects of water in the cities of the future.

chapter five
Foundations of Cities

The foundations of these works should be dug out of the solid ground, if it can be found, and carried down into solid ground as far as the magnitude of the work shall seem to require . . . . If, however, solid ground cannot be found, but the place proves to be nothing but a heap of loose earth to the very bottom, or a marsh, then it must be dug up and cleared out and set with piles made of charred alder or olive wood or oak, and these must be driven down by machinery . . . .

Vitruvius
The Ten Books of Architecture
book III, chap. IV, paras. 1 and 2
Morgan translation[5.1]

The growth of cities means the creation of many structures. Not only are buildings of many sizes and types required for industry, residence, recreation, and civic services, but roads must be built, bridges constructed, airports developed, and a wide variety of ancillary construction carried out. All these constructions—from the greatest of skyscrapers to the most mundane of roadway pavements—are structures, planned and designed by engineers and architects, in order to transfer the loads they carry to the ground beneath. Geological conditions beneath urban areas provide, therefore, the ultimate support for all that makes possible the physical plant of all cities.

The fact that every structure, whether in town or country, whether large or small, transfers the loads it carries to the ground beneath, so that accurate knowledge of local geological conditions is essential for assurance of the safety of all structures, is such an obvious truism that to mention it might seem to be belaboring the obvious. As is the case, however, with so many things that are obvious, the old tag that "familiarity breeds contempt" is here again only too true, as the long history of building makes all too clear. The "obvious" must therefore be delineated and explained, since the planning of all urban areas must start from an appreciation of the vital significance of the underlying geology for all that is to be built over it.

Until quite recent years, underlying geological conditions were even a determining factor of some local architecture. The skyline of the southern part of Manhattan Island, the central core of the great city of New York, has for long been familiar around the world. Not so familiar has been the fact that the construction of New York's skyscrapers, starting near the turn into the twentieth century, was possible on such a scale mainly because the underlying foundation conditions (the solid Manhattan schist) permitted unusually heavy foundation loads to be carried safely. In contrast, it is only within recent years that the skyline of London has included any buildings higher than the "towers, domes, theatres, and temples" written about with such feeling by William Wordsworth more than a century ago. Geology provides the explanation, foundations in London having to be supported by the London clay, which, although so favorable a feature from the point of view of water supply, prevented the erection of tall buildings until the advent of modern foundation engineering. Today, the

London skyline is changing, slowly, as tall buildings make their appearance. Fortunately, it will be many years before the contrast between the view from Westminster Bridge and that from the Staten Island ferry fails to remind the informed observer of the significance of the local geology beneath London and New York.

Now that engineers are studying and testing soils just as they do the other structural materials that they use, in what is known as the science of soil mechanics, it is possible to compensate in design for the great difference in strength and character between the Manhattan schist and the London clay. Limitations upon building height are, therefore, today more a matter of economics and aesthetics than of foundation design. This is shown even in Mexico City, where, as will later be related, foundation bed conditions have been as difficult and troublesome as beneath any major city of the world. Figure 5.13 shows that even Mexico City now has its skyscrapers, but, again, it will be many years before the buildings of Mexico City fail to remind the astute observer of conditions beneath them. In Prague, one has to go down steps, rather than the more usual mounting of steps, to enter many of the older buildings in that lovely 1,000-year-old city. This is not as the designers of these ancient buildings intended but is, again, a reflection of subsurface conditions. Through the centuries, the general ground level of the old city of Prague has been gradually raised by the accumulation of debris from old buildings as they were dismantled or destroyed, until today the general street level in the "Old City" is more than 2 m higher than the original ground surface, to match which all the older buildings were designed.

Examples could be multiplied from around the world, but this would lead to a tedious recital. Rather will examples come up for mention in appropriate places when more detailed aspects of the building of cities are being discussed. It must be observed, however, that one of the main reasons for the general neglect of foundation bed conditions in planning work is the fact that so few serious foundation failures ever occur. It follows that, once foundations are installed and covered up, they are quite naturally forgotten as the beauty or utility of the superstructures erected upon them is admired. Although complete foundation failures are so rare as to be almost unknown to all but specialists, the performance of foundations is not always exactly as good as is intended, with the result that superstructures of buildings may be unduly strained by uneven settlement. In severe cases this will show up as cracking, especially in plaster. In the most extreme cases, when danger may be imminent, buildings may have to be "underpinned." This intricate engineering operation involves going under a building that is in distress for any reason and providing it with new foundations, carried down to the appropriate foundation bed that will safely provide the support desired. Foundation engineers train themselves to watch out for any diagonal cracking that may display itself in buildings that they visit, this being often a telltale signal that untoward settlement has occurred. Cracking that is not diagonal will rarely be related to the foundations; even diagonal cracking, in the rare cases when it can be seen, may be due to other reasons. It is now mentioned, however, to emphasize from yet another direction the vital importance in the building of cities of accurate knowledge of the subsurface conditions and the proper use of this information in foundation design.

The Leaning Tower of Pisa in Italy provides one of the best-known examples of a foundation deficiency, its unusual tilt having probably made it so renowned. The cause of the tilt will be discussed later. It is, however, not alone among the famous buildings of the world to have been influenced by foundation behavior. The Taj Mahal in Agra, India, is another world-renowned building, renowned for its unique design and intrinsic beauty that those who have seen it find so difficult to convey in words. Even the Taj Mahal, however, does not float in the air (although by moonlight one can imagine that it does) but rests upon solid and mundane foundations. The critical visitor can find cracks even here, in the cellar on the north side and in the eastern part of the superstructure, signs of foundation trouble many years ago caused by erosion by the adjacent River Jamuna, trouble that was satisfactorily dealt with so that there has been no recent settlement.

Brief reference has already been made, in Chap. 2, to the foundation troubles experienced by some of the cathedrals in England. One of these noble churches displays today an unusual result of foundation failure that is generally taken to be an

Figure 5.1 Wells, Somerset, England. The great inverted arches beneath the central tower of Wells Cathedral, the purpose of which is explained in the text. *(Photograph by Peter Barker of Peter Barker Photographers Ltd., Clevedon, Somerset, England.)*

architectural feature of unusual attraction. The cathedral Church of St. Andrew in the lovely little city of Wells, Somerset, is the seat of the Bishop of Bath and Wells. It is built on a site that probably had its first church by A.D. 705. The present cathedral was started in the year 1184, building continuing for almost 200 years until the interior as now known was substantially completed by about 1360. The church is founded on late Pleistocene gravel in which the water table is close to the surface. Records show that an earthquake in 1248 damaged the structure. The great central tower was raised by Dean Godelee in 1321 but, naturally, without the aid of any sound advice about geology or engineering. Serious settlement took place. The whole cathedral chapter was summoned in 1338 to consider what steps should be taken in view of the "shattered condition of the Fabric." Under Bishop Ralph of Shrewsbury (whose magnificent tomb is in the cathedral) the damage was halted and rectified by the ingenious device of building dual inverted arches on three sides of the central space, the quire screen providing the necessary support on the remaining side. The inverted arches are today one of the attractive features of this cathedral but few visitors realize that they are looking at an ingenious correction of poor foundation conditions. The stone of which the church is built is Doulting stone, obtained from a quarry in the inferior Oolite beds, first used by the Romans, then used to build the cathedral, and still used to make necessary repairs today, 600 years later.[5.2]

Beneath every building, therefore, and beneath every roadway, every bridge, and every airport runway, there must be geological strata that have been found adequate to support the loads that these structures have to carry. Determination of the

Figure 5.2 Edinburgh, Scotland. The north end of the Shrine, with its casket, in the Scottish National War Memorial atop Edinburgh Rock; the bedrock can be seen projecting from the floor to the right of the pedestal. *(Courtesy of Captain K. R. Haywood, Secretary to the Scottish National War Memorial Records Committee, Edinburgh.)*

location and characteristics of these strata is the starting point for sound foundation design. The strata may be rock but more generally will be soil. Rarely will bedrock be right at the surface, but there are some cases where this does occur, one of the most delightful examples being in the War Memorial Chamber in Edinburgh Castle, a Scottish building that is widely known probably because of the wide distribution (undoubtedly by expatriate Scots) of the famous view from Princes Street. In this lovely chamber, the architect had the inspiration to bring the solid rock of the castle through the floor so that the central pedestal is visibly founded upon the rock. This world-famous craggy rock consists of a plug of fresh, hard basalt emplaced in Carbon-iferous sediments. These consist of alternating sandstones, shales, and marls, and they may be seen to the east of the rock, underlying the famous esplanade. Ice movement has been from the west and this has exposed the basalt on the northern, western, and

Figure 5.3 Oslo, Norway. Cut-away model of modern office building in Fridtjof Nansen's Plass, showing variation in foundation rock surface. *(Courtesy of the Norwegian Geotechnical Institute, L. Bjerrum, Director.)*

southern flanks of the plug, leaving grooves at places in the exposed bedrock. Viewed in plan, the rock and esplanade can be seen to constitute a "classical example of crag-and-tail structure" often found in relation to ice movement. Unfortunately, the great rock is not quite as stable as folklore would suggest. There have been landslides in the boulder clay in the northern face of the tail, and periodic falls of blocks of the basalt have occurred in recent years. Remedial works have been necessary. To assist with any further corrective measures, a detailed engineering-geological study of the rock was carried out in 1966–1967.[5.3]

In fitting contrast there may be mentioned a modern commercial building in the Norwegian capital city of Oslo. Adjacent to the famous city hall, on Fridtjof Nansen's Plass, this eight-story building is entered from the street through a pleasant entrance hall, nothing in which suggests that the building differs in any way from all those similar buildings that are founded on soil or rock through a one- or two-level basement. Figure 5.3 shows what a deceptive impression is thus gained by practically all visitors to this pleasant building. One corner of the structure is founded on concrete piers resting directly on rock, but so serious has been the erosion of the rock surface at this particular site, by glacial action, that the opposite corner of the building is supported on steel piles 50 m long, as shown in the photograph of the model prepared by the Norwegian Geotechnical Institute, which assisted with the foundation design. Piles had to be used since the soil over the rock consists of soft and sensitive glacial clays, as determined by subsurface exploration carried out in advance of design.[5.4]

5.2   THE DESIGN OF FOUNDATIONS

The terms "foundation" and "foundation bed" have been used in the foregoing introduction. They indicate the two essentials of foundation design. The foundation is that part of the structure that is in contact with the ground and through which loads are transferred from the structure to the ground. The foundation bed (or beds) is the geological stratum (or strata) upon which the foundation itself is supported. The distinction is important since it helps to clarify the position of the geologist in relation to foundation work. The design of the foundation itself is strictly the preserve of the civil engineer, a vital part of his structural design that he can prepare only when he has available the most accurate and complete information about the foundation beds on which he is to build. This information is obtained for all but the smallest building sites by means of test boring and soil and rock sampling, field engineering operations that are now a part of the general field of geotechnical engineering (which includes soil and rock mechanics). Applied geology is an essential part of geotechnical work, necessarily so since without an appreciation of the general geology underlying a site, test borings can be economically wasteful and, in extreme cases, even misleading.

For all but small building sites, accordingly, the first phase of subsurface investigation is a study of the geology of the site. In many cases, and for all ordinary sites in those cities that maintain adequate subsurface records (as described in Chap. 9), enough geological information will be available on record to enable the test-boring program to be properly designed without delay. Where such information is not conveniently available, it will have to be sought out by study of all available geological publications about the whole area around the site. In the case of all major projects, unless the local geology is already well known and recorded, a detailed geological survey of the site will be necessary. This is almost always the case with major engineering structures. From the point of view of overall planning, a broad appreciation of the geology of the area being planned is quite essential, as already explained in Chap. 3 and as will be further illustrated in Chap. 9. In this chapter, the more detailed geological considerations that affect foundation design and construction are described and illustrated from actual practice so that the problems faced by engineers in their work when implementing the results of planning may be appreciated by all involved.

Geological conditions at any building site may be one of three general types:

1. Solid rock may be exposed at the surface or lie so close to it that structures can be founded upon rock with a minimum of excavation.

2. Bedrock may lie below the surface at such a distance that loads can be transferred to it, when necessary, by foundation units such as piles or caissons.

3. Bedrock may lie so far below the surface that it would be uneconomical, and sometimes quite impossible, to transfer loads to it, and so all foundations must rest upon the overlying soil strata.

It will be obvious that when condition 2 exists, it may not be necessary to transfer loads to the underlying bedrock in the case of relatively light structures, especially so in the case of surface structures such as road and airport pavements, so that such cases will be a variant of condition 3.

That part of the city of New York at the south end of Manhattan Island is an example of condition 1, as has already been explained. Many of the cities around the Great Lakes, such as Chicago and Detroit, are examples of condition 2, as will be seen when examples of actual foundation designs in Chicago are described, the underlying Niagara dolomite being approximately 30 m beneath ground surface. The city of London, England, typifies condition 3, but so also do the cities of the Canadian prairies and of the Great Plains of the United States, bedrock in some cases (such as the city of Saskatoon, Saskatchewan) being as much as 1,000 m beneath the surface. Examples to be cited in the following pages will illustrate all three conditions that provide a useful general guide to overall concepts of foundation conditions such as are required in planning considerations.

The geological determinants in these three groupings of subsurface conditions are particularly helpful to those who are not engineers since it is common practice to talk about "deep" and "shallow" foundations in engineering discussions. The two groupings relate directly to foundations on the one hand, as discussed by the engineer, and foundation beds, as will be considered by the geotechnical workers including geologists. They are not, therefore, contradictory. There is no agreed-upon definition of what is a deep or a shallow foundation, but as a rough guide, any foundations that have to be taken more than 10 m beneath surface level would generally be classed as deep, those above this depth being correspondingly called shallow. What is far more important than any agreed use of these terms is a general understanding of the way in which the foundation beds carry the loads transmitted to them by the foundation. The loads do not "disappear" into the ground. This may appear to be a foolish statement, and yet, all too often, one can hear this suggestion made by those who have not stopped to think about the fundamentals of foundation action.

Figure 5.4 illustrates in simple graphical form these fundamentals that must be appreciated by everyone concerned with planning and building. The reaction of the foundation beds must be equal to the load placed upon them from the structure. Soil or rock in contact with the underside of the foundation, no matter what form this may be, must be stressed to exactly the same degree as the lower side of the structure itself. The unit bearing pressure in the ground must therefore equal the imposed unit pressure from the building, usually expressed as so many kilograms per square meter or in similar units. Since the foundation strata form a continuous mass, the stress at the immediate surface of contact will gradually be dissipated through the strata that underlie the foundation. On the basis of certain simplifying assumptions as to the nature of the ground, it is possible to calculate mathematically the way in which the unit stress in the ground gradually decreases as it "spreads out" with increasing dis-

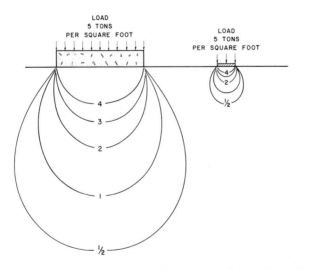

Figure 5.4 The so-called bulb of pressure, a diagram illustrating the decrease in unit pressure in the ground beneath a loaded foundation.

tance from the foundation. Typical results of such calculations are illustrated in the diagram. It will be obvious why this aspect of foundation design is known as the "bulb of pressure," but this label may be misleading. The lines are there on the diagram merely to illustrate the particular state of stress at these locations, but throughout the whole mass that is supporting the structure there is a continuous stress condition, gradually decreasing in intensity.

Once this general picture of the way in which loads are sustained by the ground is appreciated, then it will be clear that the most important lesson to be learned from this diagram is that the subsurface conditions beneath any foundation *must* be known with certainty to a considerable depth. A good working rule, the reason for which can be appreciated from the diagram, is that subsurface conditions must be accurately known—always—to a depth of at least twice the width of a foundation. That this is no mere theory is shown by many examples of structures that have suffered from serious settlement because of the lack of adequate strength in some soil stratum deep below the surface, sometimes unsuspected until trouble has developed. Dr. Terzaghi, the revered founder of the modern science of soil mechanics, related many cases of this sort that he had encountered in his worldwide practice. Typical was a group of buildings being erected on a tidal flat. The subsoil was explored to a depth of 27.4 m. Because of the high compressibility of the soil strata near the ground surface, it was decided to found these buildings (none of which was more than 12 m wide) on piles 21 to 27 m long, at which depth borings had shown firm ground to exist. Settlement of the buildings started even during construction and within 2 years had amounted to more than 0.6 m. When further subsurface investigations were made, it was found that the settlement was due to the consolidation of a stratum of soft clay 9 m thick located at about 34.5 m below the ground surface.[5.5] This is not an unusual case; it has the advantage of showing that the subsurface must be known with certainty to an appreciable depth below the bottom of the foundation—in this case the tips of the piles—and not merely to the bottom of the building.

The design of foundations is complicated by the fact that the engineer-designer must have a good idea of how his foundation is going to be constructed before he can embody its design in final contract documents. In some cases, construction procedures may place restrictions upon the actual choice of foundation type, especially in ground that contains much groundwater. The final choice of a construction method will naturally be the responsibility of the contractor, subject always to the agreement of the designing engineer, but preliminary consideration of probable construction methods by the designer is yet another reason for the absolute necessity of accurate subsurface information. When deep excavations have to be made for the basement sections of large buildings, and so for their foundations, the construction of the foundation may well prove to be the most difficult part of the whole building project. Examples will be given later, but the matter is mentioned here in order to emphasize the vital importance of ground conditions not only in the design stage but also through construction, until all work below the surface level is complete and the erection of superstructures can proceed. And it is in the carrying out of construction, especially of major excavation, that geologists may sometimes earn a "bonus" for their work by being enabled to see subsurface conditions of unusual geological interest that would otherwise never be revealed. Geology, therefore, has a most important role to play in this unusually interesting part of civil engineering, a role that is the more significant in that no two foundation problems are ever the same. This is why foundation design and construction can so truly be described as an art, experience playing so vital a role, but an art that can be and must be aided by all the help that the science of geology can provide.

5.3   SUBSURFACE EXPLORATION

Geology has its most important role to play in foundation work in assisting with necessary determination of subsurface conditions at building sites. This extends not only through the preliminary study of geological records and, when necessary, the carrying out of detailed geological studies of the geology at the site, but also in the planning of the test-boring program. Unless test borings are planned in close association with what is known of the local geology, they will, at the least, be less than fully effective. Reasonable familiarity with the local geology is therefore an essential requirement for at least one of those charged with arrangements for test boring. As the results of boring become available, they must be plotted and studied in intimate association with local geology so that the program can be adjusted, if necessary, to ensure the most effective use possible of every hole that is put down. Even though the total expenditure on test borings will be a very small fraction of the total cost of a building project, every dollar that is spent should be spent as effectively as possible. Geology can be a firm determinant of this requirement.

In the first place, the approximate depth to rock must be known so that suitable boring plant can be assured. If it is known in advance that no rock will be encountered, but only soil, then the necessary equipment for soil sampling will be all that is necessary. Should there be, however, any possibility of boulders being encountered during drilling, then equipment capable of drilling through them can be ordered in advance, with consequent monetary saving and convenience. A prime requirement, therefore, is to know whether the soils to be encountered are *residual soils* or *transported soils.* True residual soils will gradually phase into unweathered bedrock, the upper surface of which may be very irregular. Boulders of unweathered rock are sometimes encountered in the middle of a mass of residual soil, but this possibility will be known to those who are familiar with the local terrain.

Transported soils, on the other hand, will vary widely. They may be fine-grained loessal-type soils, probably wind-deposited, that are encountered in all parts of the world. They may be alluvial soils if located along lakes and rivers. Glacial soils, on the other hand, will be found only to the north (or south) of the southern (or northern) limit of glaciation, boundaries now known throughout the world with reasonable certainty. If transported by water, they may not be too dissimilar, superficially, from residual soils that have been so moved, but if deposited by outwash from glaciers, then great heterogenity is to be expected. Boulders will feature many glacial tills, and they may even be found in glacial lake clays. They may be of great size, as may be seen from many a monument formed by a large glacial erratic that could not easily be moved from a building site. They may be missed by test borings, but if encountered they must be penetrated and cored so that their size may be determined and their exact petrological character may be found in order to ensure that they are glacial erratics. This necessitates having rock-drilling equipment available for the test-boring operation.

On all these matters, geology can be a useful guide. It will be no more than this since the whole purpose of the test boring is to determine with as much accuracy as possible what are the subsurface conditions that geology can only suggest as probable. It is for this reason that the correlation of the plotted records of all test borings with the general picture of the local geology already available is so essential a part of the field control work that is a vital part of every test-boring program. All that has been said about the solid materials to be encountered applies with equal force to the determination of groundwater conditions, and also to the detection of buried gas. Admittedly this will be unusual, but in certain glacial clays the decaying of vegetation of earlier ages sometimes results in pockets of methane that may be encountered even in test borings. If there is any possibility at all of such occurrences, all necessary safety precautions must be taken in the drilling operation, and the possibility mentioned in contract documents, even if gas is not encountered in the test drilling.

Whenever groundwater is encountered in test holes, its level must be recorded. If possible, some holes should be equipped with perforated casings, left in place, and capped so that groundwater levels may be observed for as long a period as possible before construction commences. In most places, the water table will be found to vary in elevation throughout the year; if this information can be obtained, it is a further aid to efficiency in construction. Not only must the position of groundwater be determined with accuracy (and its movement, when this is possible) but also an indication of its quality. Samples can easily be taken from test holes so that they may be analyzed for any traces of undesirable features, such as the presence of sulfates. If this simple precaution had always been taken, much damage to underground concrete in western Canada could have been avoided, since special sulfate-resisting cement could have been specified for the concrete, once the sulfates had been detected.

When rock is encountered in test boring, it should always be a requirement that it must be cored to a certain minimum specified depth, say, 3 m. The cores so obtained can then be examined so that the character of the rock can be determined in order to ensure that the drill hole has penetrated bedrock and not a boulder. Great care must be taken in basing any assumptions as to the rock surface beneath the ground merely on the basis of the results of a few test borings, especially in glaciated country. One of the common features of massive glacial action is to carve out from solid bedrock deep grooves that will later be filled in with glacial soils. "Buried valleys" undetected by test boring have probably caused more trouble in excavation than all other problems in excavation work, apart only from one other matter that will shortly be mentioned. Figure 5.5 shows a building well known to the author that is founded throughout on limestone bedrock. A 23-m-long extension was needed to the rear of the building (facing the camera). Fortunately, the presence of a buried valley in the vicinity was suspected, since the Ottawa area has been glaciated. A test boring put down 22.5 m from the corner on the right went down 27 m without encountering rock, at which point boring was stopped and a decision made to use another site where bedrock was near the surface.

Since the existence of, or the lack of, adequate subsurface information will inevitably have to be mentioned in many of the brief case histories that follow, possibly enough has now been said to make clear the vital interconnection between local geology and all test-boring programs. There is, however, one more aspect that must be mentioned since, in critical cases, it can lead to incredible difficulties if not handled properly in preliminary site study. This is the requirement that a test-boring program shall give exact information as to the character of the materials to be encountered during excavation or pile driving. Rock cores have been mentioned. Not only must the character of the rock be observed from these but also the soundness of the rock and the amount of jointing. The latter will be indicated by the percentage recovery of the

Figure 5.5 Ottawa, Canada. Rear of the Building Research Centre, Montreal Road Laboratories of the National Research Council of Canada; all the buildings shown are founded on rock, but the text relates the findings from a test boring put down only 23 m from the rear corner of the main building. *(Photograph by L. G. Smith, courtesy of DBR/NRC.)*

core that is drilled, but only if the drillers have strict instructions to record accurately the core recovery. Information such as this is essential for the clear-cut separation of the excavation that has to be made in contract documents into "rock" and "soil." The details of this distinction come within the province of civil engineering, but it will be obvious that payments for the two classes of excavation will be very different in view of the different equipment necessary for the two operations. If the material actually encountered in excavation differs appreciably from that shown on the contract drawings, based on the subsurface exploration program, then financial arguments will result at the end of the contract, sometimes involving very substantial sums of money. Every possible care must, therefore, be taken to get the most accurate classification possible of all materials that will be encountered, in advance of the preparation of the contract documents.

From the many hundreds of cases that are now on record, a small but unfortunately typical example may be mentioned. The boilerhouse basement for a large building in Massachusetts involved excavation to a depth of 7 m. Only one test hole was put down in the boilerhouse area, and only to 4.3 m. Instead of the glacial overburden encountered over the rest of the site, the contractor encountered bedrock at a depth of 4.5 m in the deeper excavation. The bedrock was hard schistose sandstone of Pennsylvanian age (the Rhode Island formation). Blasting could not be used, but, fortunately, the contractor was able to remove the rock with a large tractor ripper, although at greatly increased cost. His claim for extra payment led to the "usual" argument; although payment was granted, all the trouble could have been avoided if test boring had been adequately carried out.[5,6]

Soil sampling is today a well-developed technique, so-called undisturbed samples being obtainable now from great depths, using special sampling tools. If sealed with special wax immediately upon being taken out of the tool, soil samples will retain their natural moisture content, and so their natural characteristics, until opened up in a laboratory for examination. In glaciated areas, very tough glacial till is often encountered just above the level of bedrock, which is sometimes of considerable thickness. The normal sampling tools will not easily penetrate this material. In earlier days, it was often called *hardpan*; its excavation can be almost as difficult as the removal of solid rock. Frequently the sinking of test holes in soil has been and still is carried out by "washing out" the hole with water under pressure, the flow of water bringing with it up the hole the fragments of soil material that can then be caught and retained in a proper receptacle at the drill head. Compact glacial till has usually derived its toughness from ice pressure, with the result that, in the presence of water, it will disintegrate into its constituent particles of silt, sand, and gravel. A "wash boring" into compact glacial till will, therefore, give no indication whatever of the tough and compact nature of the till but result merely in a wet mass of loose soil particles. How often such misleading results from wash borings have led to difficulties with excavation is impossible to estimate, but it is an undoubted fact that some of the most extensive legal suits regarding claims for extra payment for excavation have been due to this simple

Figure 5.6   Czechoslovakia. Weathered sandy marl, the rock disintegration being the result of periglacial action; i.e., at one time it was perennially frozen. *(Photograph by Q. Zaruba, Prague.)*

error. Geologists, therefore, will (if they are wise) assist their engineering confrères by *never* using the term "hardpan" but rather sounding due notes of warning if there is any likelihood of compact glacial till being encountered in foundation excavations.

Brief reference must be made to permafrost, even in relation to foundations in other than Arctic regions. The nature of permafrost—a frozen condition of ground—was explained in Chap. 3. In northern regions, enough is now known of the occurrence of permafrost for it to be detected during early site investigation and the necessary precautions taken in design. There are, however, many glaciated areas, especially in Europe, where the condition of permafrost that existed in glacial eras had a serious effect upon some types of bedrock. The Chalk of England, for example, is found in some areas to be disintegrated to depths up to 6 m due to the action of frost in glacial periods; if undetected, such a poor condition of what might be assumed to be "solid rock" can lead to serious complications.[5.7] The problem is particularly serious in central Europe. In glacial periods the continental ice sheet spread over the greater part of northern Europe, the glaciation of the Alps then being more extensive than it is today. A belt roughly 500 km wide that intervened between the glaciated areas was characterized by permafrost conditions, with a very cold and dry climate. Under these circumstances, the exposed soil and underlying bedrock were affected in glacial periods by strong physical weathering and deep perennial freezing.

Weathering is evidenced in this area by thick accumulations of slope detritus and extensive boulder fields, preserved on many solid rock slopes. The relics of perennially frozen ground are deep wedgelike fissures that were filled with ice in glacial periods. When the ice thawed in interglacial periods, loam or sand would fill the fissures. Frost wedges up to 6 m thick have also been preserved in the upper layers of bedrock. The freezing also sometimes produced loosening or distortion of near-surface layers, especially in thin-bedded or schistose rocks. In the zone of permafrost, the schists today may be heavily jointed and contorted, cavities again being filled with detritus or loam. The freezing of water produced considerable stresses in surface layers, causing irregular uplift in places and undulation or even folding of the surface. The compressibility of bedrock that has been disturbed by deep Pleistocene freezing is very high. In Bohemia, near Prague, tests have shown it to be three times that of sandy gravel. Because of this weakening of previously solid strata, and even more so because of the extreme irregularity of weathering due to permafrost, the foundation of structures in areas that have been affected by weathering due to Pleistocene permafrost is always a matter requiring the very greatest care.

It will now be clear that subsurface exploration in urban areas does not mean rushing out immediately to the proposed building site with a test-drilling rig. On the contrary, before any test drilling is contemplated, careful search must be made for all available local geological information either in published reports and maps or from the results of foundation studies for nearby sites. Local historical records should also be studied; they can sometimes reveal information of unusual value. When a new parking garage was planned for the center of Ottawa, to be located immediately

Figure 5.7 Prague, Czechoslovakia. Test drilling into the bed of the Vltava River adjacent to the fourteenth-century Charles Bridge, with Hradcany Castle and the Cathedral Church of St. Vitus in the background. *(Photograph by Q. Zaruba, Prague.)*

behind the Chateau Laurier Hotel, the Canadian National Railway engineers responsible knew that the site chosen had been used 140 years before by the (British) Royal Engineers when building the Rideau Canal. They consulted those with knowledge of this old work and were thus guided to the Public Archives of Canada. Here they were provided not only with an old map showing a quarry from which came the stone for the locks of the canal, exactly on the site planned for the garage but also an old photograph showing the disused quarry just before it was filled in. Test drilling was thus greatly aided, construction starting against the background of this accurate subsurface information.

Another historical example is provided by the construction of the foundation for a new million-dollar library for St. Mary's University in Halifax, Nova Scotia. Old-timers in the city could remember seeing some filling being done on the proposed site. The Clerks of Works knew the Provincial Archives and so went there, being guided to an old ordnance map of this part of the city dated 1784. This showed the location of an old creek—where the Royal Navy used to fill their water casks! This map was coordinated with a map of 1836 and confirmed that the site proposed for the library was where an old swamp had been, through which the creek had flowed, whereas bedrock was clearly near the surface not very far away. By moving the site of the building merely 15 m, on the basis of this ancient information (aided by detailed site studies), bedrock was found within easy digging distance, and upon this the library was founded.

Finally, brief mention must be made of the way in which the results of subsurface information are presented for consideration by owners, municipal authorities, planners, and others concerned with urban development. Records of geological formations on maps, profiles of test borings, and photographs of any available exposures can all help to build up the three-dimensional picture of the subsurface without which no sound decision about building, or even planning, can be made. But these aids can be greatly assisted by the use of three-dimensional models. The simplest way in which these can be developed is by the placing on a solid base, indicating the building site to scale, of vertical sticks, colored to show different strata, exactly on the locations of the test holes they represent. As more test results are added, a picture of the subsurface will quickly be built up, easily visualized by the juxtaposition of the different colors. When the expense is warranted, complete models in suitable transparent plastic material can be built up, but the careful use of simple stick models will usually suffice to give all concerned a vivid picture of what is beneath the ground, the development of which they are considering.

5.4 AN EXAMPLE OF SITE INVESTIGATION

Since no two foundation projects are ever the same, in view of the variability of soil and rock, it follows that there can be no such thing as a really "typical" example of a study of the subsurface of a building site. Every study will have special features depending upon the nature of the project, the size and the geology of the site. In order, however, to indicate how such work is organized and carried out, a recent study of a somewhat difficult site will be outlined.

The University of Alberta is located at Edmonton, capital city of the province of Alberta, Canada. Its campus has a fine site on the south bank of the North Saskatchewan River, which here flows in a valley about 54 m deep. Since the valley sides slope in places at about 30° and have a local history of landslides and since the campus extends to the river, it was decided that a detailed study of the northern section of the campus should be made prior to any decisions being made about the location of new buildings in this general area. A committee was therefore established, under the chairmanship of the university's dean of engineering, having members from the departments of geology and civil engineering, together with representatives of the university's planning office and the provincial public works department. This group guided a thorough study of the local geology, following which detailed investigations of the river problems and of the engineering properties of the soils and rock encountered were undertaken, the latter being naturally the major part of the project. Results of the work have been published in convenient form for general information.[5.8]

Figure 5.8 is an aerial view of the northern part of the university's property and illustrates some features of the local geology. The flat plain on which the university stands consists of lacustrine sediments of glacial Lake Edmonton, generally highly plastic clays, overlying glacial till of high density and good strength. Sedimentary rocks of Upper Cretaceous age outcrop along the river bank; they consist of inter-bedded shales, sandstone, and coal, dipping 9.6 m per km (about 1 in 250) to the southwest. The river has eroded into the shale an average of 9 m in the last 6,500 years, its bed now consisting of thin layers of mobile sand and gravel overlying the shale that is exposed in the banks. Erosion of the banks has been taking place, the south bank (of interest to the university) having receded 12.6 m in 83 years. The site is underlain by two buried valleys, the major preglacial valley on the west being filled with Saskatchewan sands and gravels to a depth of 24 m. Fortunately, both buried valleys slope toward the present river valley, and their lowest elevations are above the present river level. They therefore assist local drainage to some extent and are an advantage rather than the problem that such valleys often present. Some seepage of groundwater does occur, and this contributes to small rock slides at river level.

The geotechnical engineering part of the study involved the drilling of 30 test holes to depths from 30 to 45 m, 152 to 203 mm in diameter, penetration tests being carried out in the test holes when appropriate. Slope indicators and piezometers were installed for long-term observations of any change in slopes and in groundwater levels. Samples of all soils and rock encountered were thoroughly tested in the laboratory and the test results used in detailed analyses of the existing slopes. This was done separately for the eastern and western sections under study since the natural slopes differed appreciably in these two parts of the area. All this work was done with full consideration of the geological features of the site. The two buried valleys affected

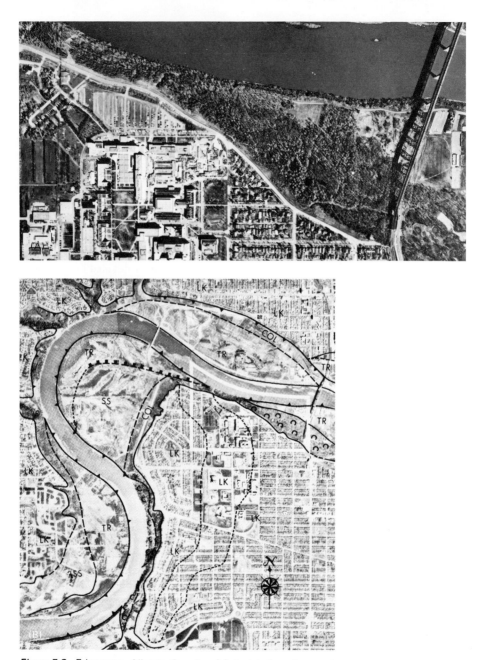

Figure 5.8 Edmonton, Alberta, Canada. (a) Aerial view of part of the campus of the University of Alberta for which an extensive geotechnical investigation was made. *(Photograph courtesy of the University of Alberta and S. Thomson.)* (b) Aerial view of the region, including the test area of part *(a)*, with interpretations of the surficial geology marked on as a part of the geotechnical study described in the text. *(Figure 1 of reference 5.8 by courtesy of the National Research Council of Canada and S. Thomson.)*

the groundwater levels and this geological feature had considerable influence upon considerations of the stability of the slopes, even though there is no surface indication of either valley on the upland or on the slopes.

Conclusions from the study, in addition to the recommended continuation of the recording of slope angles and groundwater levels, were that the university should allow for a setback of 45 m from the top of the valley slope until certain remedial works were undertaken and that no encroachment at all on to the present valley slopes, for any purpose, should be permitted without the advice of a qualified geotechnical engineer. The remedial works suggested were: (1) subsurface drainage to be installed in both the eastern and western areas in order to increase the stability of the valley slopes (a somewhat detailed matter, explained in the report on the study); and (2) protection of the river banks on the western section of the site to prevent further erosion and so stabilize the exposed rock, the form of protection to be the subject of detailed economic and engineering investigation. These very practical suggestions give clear guide lines for the immediate planning of new university buildings in an area of almost 40 hectares.

5.5 THE FOUNDATIONS OF THREE MONUMENTS

Before a discussion is attempted of some general features of the problems that may be encountered in foundation work, it may be helpful to describe a few examples of actual cases from cities around the world. Some of those selected were designed and constructed long before the days of modern foundation engineering. Others show what can now be done on even the most difficult sites. All are described quite briefly, but references are given to complete descriptions that are contained in the literature of engineering. The practice of describing for general benefit even serious difficulties in design and construction is a distinguishing feature of the profession of civil engineering that could be more widely followed with advantage. Since some of the heaviest individual foundation loads from urban structures come from tall monuments, three examples of these somewhat unusual "buildings" will be given first, starting naturally with the Leaning Tower of Pisa.

Leaning Tower of Pisa, Italy

Pisa is a pleasant city of about 100,000 people located at the head of the Arno Delta, 19 km northeast of Leghorn on the northwest coast of Italy. The famous tower was started in the year 1174 but not completed until 1350. It has continued to tilt very slowly since its construction, the technical description of its failing being that it suffers from differential settlement. If it had settled evenly all around, it would be today just another beautiful tower. And it certainly would have settled since, with its circular slab foundation (19.2 m in diameter with a 4.5 m hole in the center), it exerts a unit pressure on the ground beneath of 88 tonnes per m^2. It rests on a bed of clayey sand 3.1 m thick underlain by 6.4 m of sand, materials that might suggest admirable foundation conditions. Beneath the sand, however, is a stratum of brackish clay of unknown thickness and limited strength, and it is this material, stressed by the load coming from the foundation 8.5 m above, that is believed to be the cause of the differential settlement. Most detailed studies have been conducted of the foundation beds in recent years, as a result of which remedial measures have been devised that should retain indefinitely for the world this unique and quite delightful monumental building[5.9]

Washington Monument

Equally well known in the Western Hemisphere is the Washington Monument in Washington, D.C., not that it is tilted today, even though at one time it was found to be slightly out of plumb to the extent of about 44 mm. Its commanding position, however, facing the Capitol Building down the gardens with their reflecting pools, makes it well known to all visitors to the capital city of the United States, while its

Figure 5.9 Washington, D.C. The Washington Monument. *(Courtesy of the U.S. National Park Service.)*

Figure 5.10 Houston, Texas. The San Jacinto Monument. *(Courtesy of the Houston Chamber of Commerce.)*

purpose in commemorating the first President of the Republic makes it of symbolic importance to all United States citizens. Started in 1848 by public subscription, it was not completed until 1880 and then only with funds appropriated by Congress. By 1854 it was only 46 m high. When work was resumed in 1876, a committee of engineers under General T. L. Casey found the top to be out of plumb. By a very ingenious system of loading, they corrected this tilt, and the great shaft was completed to its full height of 169 m above the foundation. The monument then weighed 82,500 tonnes. For the work in 1876, test borings were put down but only to a depth of 5.4 m, such was the state of the art of foundation engineering at that time. Further investigations in 1931 showed most complex subsurface conditions below the sand and gravel stratum on which the foundation rests, including a bed of soft blue clay overlying the bedrock about 27.4 m below present ground level, and it is probable that the variable bearing capacity of this stratum was responsible for the initial differential settlement and for the total settlement today of about 152 mm. The 1931 studies suggested no further need for action, apart from ensuring that the ground around the monument is not disturbed, so that this well-known extensive green lawn must long continue to be the pleasant oasis that it is today near the heart of the great city.[5.10]

San Jacinto Monument, Houston, Texas

Thirty-two km to the southeast of the city of Houston, Texas, and not far from the Houston Ship Channel, is another noble column. Faced with buff-colored Texas marble, the San Jacinto Monument is 167.4 m high, with the Star of Texas on the top; it was built in the 1930s. Test borings showed that the site proposed for the monument was underlain by a deep stratum of clay, with some silt and sand, extending to a depth of more than 67.9 m. The total dead load imposed on the ground by the monument is over 35,000 tonnes, the foundation structure being a monolithic reinforced concrete raft 37.6 m square. This is carried directly by the clay on the basis of a careful design prepared using the fundamental principles of soil mechanics, even though they were just coming to be recognized when the monument was designed. Samples of the clay were tested in what would be regarded today as rather simple laboratory equipment. The consolidation characteristics of the clay were determined, and an estimate of total settlement of the foundations was prepared. Settlement readings have been taken on the monument now for over 30 years, total settlement being about 25 cm. Since, however, the whole Houston area is subsiding (as will be noted in Chap. 8), the accuracy of this differential settlement is open to a little doubt, but the monument has "performed" well and as anticipated.[5.11]

5.6 SOME BUILDING FOUNDATION PROBLEMS

Winchester, England

Winchester, the ancient capital of Saxon England, is one of the smaller cathedral cities of England; it is in Hampshire, some 96 km from London. It is a particularly lovely old place dominated by its splendid cathedral church, commenced in the year 1079 on the site of an older Saxon church. The site was admirable from the point of view of water supply, and fishing, as also for natural drainage, but the monk-builders of that early period would have been prevented from studying the foundation beds on which they were to build—if it may be assumed that they did go so far—by the high water table. In all probability this has not varied greatly through the years. The Norman church was extended, and changed in part, starting in 1202; the great nave was changed from Norman to Perpendicular Gothic by the famous Bishop William of Wykeham in the closing years of the fourteenth century. Since it contains examples of every order of architecture from Saxon up to those of recent times, the cathedral has long been a treasure of English building. Much alarm was therefore experienced when a study of the fabric at the start of the present century revealed serious settlements in parts of the cathedral (as much as 76 mm in the presbytery) and so serious a condition of many parts of the building that its future safety was in doubt.

The Dean of Winchester asked one of the leading British civil engineers of the time, Sir Francis Fox, to study the situation with the architects to the cathedral. A trial excavation revealed that the great piers and buttresses of the church were founded

Figure 5.11 Winchester, England. The statue of William Walker in Winchester Cathedral—the diver who, single-handedly, carried out the underpinning of the exterior piers of this great church. *(Courtesy of A. W. Kerr, Photographer, Kingswood, Surrey.)*

upon a raft of beech logs, in some cases complete trees being found, all laid in two directions at just about the level of the water table. Some were still sound; others had rotted, an indication of probable variation in the position of the groundwater. Under the Norman walls, short (1.5 to 1.8 m) oak piles had been driven into the underlying marly clay. Further exploration was difficult since the groundwater was very dark in color as well as being septic from the graves around. The dark color of the water was explained when a stratum of about 2.4 m of peat was found underlying 1.8 m of marly clay. Below the peat, the existence of which readily explained the settlements, was a thin stratum of silt and then a thick bed of gravel and flints overlying the chalk bedrock.

Figure 5.12 Winchester, England. Excavation for the construction of a new hotel, showing the header for the wellpoint dewatering system as a horizontal pipe just below the bank of soil below the hoarding, with the cathedral in the background. *(Courtesy of James Drewitt and Son Ltd., contractors, Bournemouth, and E. E. Green, consulting engineer.)*

An extensive scheme of reconstruction was prepared involving the shoring of the outside of the building, supporting the great arch vaulting inside to prevent collapse, using steel tie rods when necessary in association with an extensive scheme of high-pressure grouting in all the damaged masonry, and then underpinning all of the exterior walls down to the bed of gravel. This last operation had to be carried out in the complete darkness created by the black groundwater, since with the equipment available at that time, pumping would probably have removed some of the silt and possibly disturbed the foundation beds in other ways. The entire job was done by one man, an expert diver named William Walker, in a period of 5½ years, his work being regularly inspected by Sir Francis Fox, also in a diver's suit. The work involved excavating from beneath the walls, piers, etc., in successive pits, down to the gravel, and then placing concrete by hand up to the underside of the masonry of the walls. All was successfully completed and the walls of the cathedral have shown no signs of any structural trouble since then. It was reopened, with the reconstruction complete, at a great service held on 14 July 1912.[5.12] A statue of William Walker was later placed in the cathedral in grateful recognition of his notable work, possibly a unique tribute to a real builder.

Fifty years after this work, a new hotel had to be built within little more than 51 m of the cathedral. The record of the earlier work was available but the same groundwater condition had to be dealt with, naturally without damage to the cathedral. There are now available, however, devices called *wellpoints* for controlled pumping of water in excavation work, and these were used with complete success and with no ill effects on the structure of the great church. Wellpoints consist of special heads for attaching to small-diameter steel pipes, their bodies (of the same diameter as the pipe) being formed of strong metallic wire mesh of such dimensions that it will allow water to pass through easily but will not permit the passage of any but the very finest soil particles. Wellpoints are used in closely spaced rows to surround an area that has to be pumped dry, all connected into a larger pipe "header." The cone of depression (see page 134) from each wellpoint quickly intersects those of the two adjoining points, with the result that relatively limited disturbance of the local groundwater situation is caused, except immediately adjacent to the row of wellpoints and—naturally—within the area they surround that will be quickly dried out.

This advance in construction methods permitted the drying out of the excavation for the hotel with no difficulty. Naturally, the most careful records were maintained, including groundwater levels in test holes around the site, the most important of which was actually inside the cathedral. With excavation complete, and the building of the superstructure proceeding, the groundwater was allowed to regain its normal position, the foundation of the hotel having been designed accordingly. Of special interest is the fact that about one-third of the excavation for the building had been completed before the general contractor had even been appointed, much less started work—and all by archeologists! They found and recorded archeological "treasure trove," including remains of a Roman villa and of a Roman road.[5.13] In a similar way, the laborious hand excavation by Mr. Walker had revealed unexpected items from the past, including a rats' nest in which were pieces of parchment that, when deciphered, showed that they were from a service form of 700 years ago, and a carpenter's rule between 300 and 400 years old.

Mexico City

Very different are foundation conditions beneath Mexico City. Located in a majestic natural basin at an elevation of about 2,300 m above the sea, this great old city of the New World has been built on soils that constitute one of the most difficult of all foundation bed conditions. Layers of bentonitic clays of volcanic origin alternate with strata of sand, and all are highly charged with water, the original water table having been close to the surface. Pumping in earlier years from beneath the surface (now rigidly controlled) and local drainage measures combined to cause a general lowering of the ground level, even without loads from buildings. When buildings were

Figure 5.13 Mexico City, Mexico. The Palace of Fine Arts and the adjacent Tower Latino Americana, the differing foundations under which are described in the text. *(Courtesy of the Departamento de Turismo, Mexico, D.F.)*

placed on these soils, without adequate foundation designs, further serious settlements occurred, totally and differentially. Foundation conditions in Mexico City are therefore well known around the world to all who are interested in foundations. Examples of the settlement of buildings, and even of the ground itself, are spectacular. To mention but one example, the justly famous Palace of Fine Arts, a massive classical style masonry building with a total weight of over 58,500 tonnes, has settled more than 3 m and in addition has suffered very serious differential settlement, with consequent damage.

The Palace of Fine Arts is located on Juarez Avenue. It is indeed a strange coincidence that also on Juarez Avenue and just on the opposite corner from the Palace at San Juan de Letran Avenue (i.e., exactly facing) is Mexico City's first major "skyscraper," an elegant 43-story building of modern style, founded and carried successfully on exactly the same difficult foundation beds. Probably nowhere in the world is there such a juxtaposition of two great buildings that illustrate foundation engineering at its worst and at its best, both founded on most unusual geological strata. The

Tower Latino Americana was completed in 1951 and is performing with complete success, exactly as was anticipated in design. A most extensive and careful investigation of the subsurface was carried out in advance of design. A series of test borings was put down to a depth of 70 m below ground level, undisturbed samples of soil being taken at every change in soil type. In a typical boring, over 30 distinctly different strata of soil types were sampled and tested. They included volcanic ash, pumice sand, and even some gravel. The results of laboratory tests on the soil samples and study of the local groundwater situation enabled one of the most ingenious foundation designs yet applied to a large building to be successfully prepared and eventually constructed.

This foundation achievement was essentially a matter of excellent engineering, but it was so closely allied with detailed knowledge of every aspect of the underlying geology that a summary description of the construction may not be inappropriate. Once the properties of the various foundation beds were known, it was possible to design a foundation structure consisting of a concrete slab supported on end-bearing piles driven to good bearing on a stratum of sand 33.5 m below ground surface. These piles would go right through the first and thickest stratum of volcanic clay, the cause of most of the famous settlements. The piles were driven from the bottom of a relatively shallow excavation, 2.5 m deep, the material excavated being debris with sand and clay humus in which a quantity of Aztec pottery remains were found. The major problem was in excavating for the two basements required and for the foundation slab structure, the necessary depth being 13 m, and this with the groundwater close to the surface. The site was therefore surrounded with a solid wall of wooden sheet piling that, swelling when in contact with water, gave a good tight enclosure. Excavation then proceeded, but only partially down to the full depth. The gridiron of concrete beams needed for the foundation was placed in specially prepared trenches excavated to the full depth of 13 m. The panels between intersecting beams were then excavated one by one, the foundation slab concreted between them and as soon as possible loaded with sand and gravel, to give a load on the underlying ground equivalent to a good part of the total load to be expected from the building. This "false loading" was completed when the foundation was finished and then gradually removed, with a slow restoration of the groundwater to its original position permitted as the steel superstructure and its cladding were steadily erected.

Anticipated settlements, due to the transfer of the total weight of the building (only 24,000 tonnes as compared with the 58,500 tonnes of the Palace of Fine Arts) to the piles, from the piles to the sand-bearing stratum and through it to the strata below, were carefully calculated. The building has naturally been under close observation since completion and settlements have been exactly as calculated almost 20 years ago. Since the ground in Mexico City may settle quite apart from any settlement of well-founded buildings, the first floor of this great building was designed to be movable so that it could be adjusted, if necessary, to give access always at street level. It has not been necessary to make any adjustment to the floor, tribute not only to the design of the foundation but to the way in which interference with groundwater conditions in

Mexico City is now under control. Earlier reference was made to the fact that, with modern foundation design methods, it is now possible to erect large buildings on very poor foundation strata. The Tower Latino Americana is a splendid demonstration of what can now be done in the design and construction of foundations on one of the least desirable of building sites (from the foundation bed point of view), provided—and this was an essential part of the whole project—that subsurface geological conditions are known with certainty and with accuracy.[5.14]

Ottawa, Canada

Some of the public buildings erected in the late nineteenth and early twentieth centuries caused unusually heavy loads to be carried by foundation beds of soil. There appears to be, however, only one monumental building of that time that came close to having a complete foundation failure, even though there did occur some failures of commercial structures. (The most notable of these was the collapse of the grain elevator at Transcona, Winnipeg, Manitoba, which keeled over when it was first filled in 1913.) The monumental building in question is also located in Canada, near the center of the capital city of Ottawa. Ordovician limestone bedrock is available at or near the surface in many parts of Ottawa, but in other places it has been eroded by ice, and the depressions are usually filled with a sensitive marine clay. By ill chance, it was in one of the clay-filled areas that a building for a National Museum was located. Completed in the year 1910 after many difficulties with construction, the museum building has a somewhat unusual appearance today, as can be seen from Fig. 5.14, due to the necessary removal of a large tower over the front entrance. The total weight of the building is about 66,000 tonnes. As indicating one little-recognized aspect of foundation work, if the museum were completely filled to the maximum designed load on all floors, the "live load" would still be less than 2 percent of the dead load of the building itself.

In the construction of the massive sandstone structure, which is founded throughout on spread footings, a large excavation was necessary, and this (fortunately) removed an amount of soil equal in weight to 35 percent of the weight of the building itself. This reduced the stresses set up in the underlying soil, which consists of about 15 m of the sensitive clay with a very limited bearing capacity, overlying glacial till. Even so, the increase in stress in the soil was over 44 tonnes per m^2 under some footings but only 11 tonnes per m^2 under others. These figures were developed in the course of a study of the foundations of this building in 1953; they were clearly not appreciated at the time the building was erected. The result, inevitably, was serious differential settlement between different parts of the massive building, as much as 25 mm being visible in one corridor in the basement, which the original architect had very thoughtfully lined with glazed white tile so that the slightest effect of settlement showed up very clearly. The greatest loads on the underlying clay were set up under the massive entrance porch, with the result that this started to pull away from the rest of the building, more lightly loaded, a separation of over 25 mm having occurred near the roof line before the great tower over the porch was taken down in 1916, as a safety measure. Thereafter settlements continued but at a decreasing rate, as the moisture content in the clay gradually approached the equilibrium condition similar to that which had existed before the building was erected. Subsequent reconstruction of the interior of the building has removed almost all trace of the serious strains to which it was subjected and, apart from the missing tower, the outside of the building appears to be quite normal.

Since it is so prominent a building in Ottawa, and since its strange history is a matter of public record, there has been much uninformed public discussion about its safety. Years ago, a distinguished geologist who knew little about soils ventured the opinion that the troubles had been due to a fault that (so he said) ran under the building. This myth has persisted, despite full explanations of the real cause of the settlements—the overloading of the underlying soil. Settlement records have been taken regularly for about 20 years, and these show that present settlement is so insignificant that the building has virtually reached its final position. Calls for the removal of the building persist, however, despite its historical value and current utility, and despite the fact that it is now perfectly safe for any loads that can possibly be transmitted from it to the clay beneath. These local details are recited to illustrate the social problems that can result from what was inadequate foundation design, an experience that should never happen in this age, with foundation engineering and subsurface exploration so well developed. But satisfactory foundation designs require ceaseless vigilence in all preliminary work and absolute certainty as to ground conditions, this being the part with which the geologist can make so valuable a contribution.[5.15]

Figure 5.14 Ottawa, Canada. The National Museum Building, the inset view showing the main entrance to the building as constructed and before the tower had to be removed as a safety measure. *(Courtesy of C. J. Mackenzie, Secretary General, National Museums of Canada, Ottawa.)*

Victoria, Canada

Yet another of Canada's famous buildings may finally be described, not that the Dominion has any extra share of "problem buildings" but because, through excellent maintenance engineering, this particular building is the subject of the longest set of accurate settlement measurements known to exist anywhere for any building. These records were started because of initial difficulties that were entirely due to site conditions. The Empress Hotel occupies a central and prominent position in the pleasant city of Victoria, located on Vancouver Island on Canada's west coast, capital city of the province of British Columbia. Opened in 1908 "when the West was young," the Empress (as it is known to most Canadians) has become an institution, as gracious hotels can do, afternoon tea at the Empress being a ceremony that is an invariable feature of many visits to Victoria. It was built and is still owned by the Canadian Pacific Railway Company, the president of which company in the early years of the century was Sir Thomas Shaughnessy, a legendary figure in railroad history. He decided on the location of the hotel, at the head of an inlet of the sea that was being developed as the inner harbor of Victoria and immediately adjacent to the new legislative buildings of the province. When chosen, the site was a muddy bay (James Bay) completely flooded at high tide. The engineering staff that would be responsible protested as to the unsuitability of the site for a large building, but Sir Thomas, being the man he was, had his way, and there the hotel was built.

The city of Victoria ceded the land and built a sea wall across the bay to enclose the desired site, pumping from the harbor an average of 3.9 m of fill over the entire area to bring it up to the level required for building. Borings were naturally taken, in 1904, and again in 1913 when the hotel was extended; shafts were also excavated, presumably for visual inspection of the soils encountered. These can be fully appreciated only against the recent geological history of the Victoria area. When the last glacier retreated from this area about 13,000 years ago, the land had been so depressed by the great load of ice that the sea level was 83.8 m above its present level, relative to the land. Rebound of the land had occurred by about 11,000 years ago, but in this period a blanket of silty clay (the Victoria clay) had been deposited over the entire area to depths up to 30 m. During the next 2,000 years, the level of the sea dropped to 9 or 12 m below its present level, thus exposing the newly deposited clay. The clay therefore dried out near its surface, giving the Victoria clay its characteristic weathered crust that, at the hotel site, is about 4.6 m thick. After that, the sea level rose to its present elevation, and a new layer of sediment was deposited over the weathered surface of the Victoria clay. These geological details are given to illustrate how geology can explain a soil profile that would otherwise be puzzling.

A log of a typical boring at this interesting site shows 9.7 m of dredged material overlying the original surface, then 3.3 m of "soft mud," 2.7 m of "hard yellow clay," and 13.5 m of "blue clay on gravel and sand." The "blue clay" is the Victoria clay and the "hard yellow clay" the weathered crust of this deposit. With such soil conditions,

Figure 5.15 Victoria, British Columbia, Canada. The Empress Hotel. *(Photograph by C. B. Crawford, courtesy of DBR/NRC.)*

the original foundation engineers naturally decided to use piles. Timber piles were therefore driven to support all footings. If these had been driven to the underlying sand and gravel, they would have provided good bearing, but for reasons that cannot now be determined, and although the piles on the western side of the hotel were thus driven to this good bearing material, the piles over most of the site were driven only into the blue clay. The loads from the heavy masonry building were appreciable, and so settlements were soon observed, most acutely when additions were made to the hotel in 1913. Newly appointed foundation engineers clearly appreciated, even at that early date, what had happened and attempted to undo some of the damage by arranging for large quantities of soil from under the south end of the building to be excavated; these voids were made permanent by concrete construction and are there today. Metallic studs were also installed in an ornamental stone course that ran all round the hotel building, and settlement observations were then started. In 1970, therefore, almost 60 years of settlement records were available and, kindly provided by the CPR, were the subject of a detailed research study aided by modern soil mechanics techniques. This enabled the history of the foundation to be traced back to its start and assurance to be given confirming that the future settlement would be very small indeed so that the building was in good condition for long-continued use.[5.16]

The surface of the hotel site must have started to settle as soon as the pumping of the fill upon it was completed, partly because of the natural compaction of the pumped material but also because of the consolidation of the underlying Victoria clay owing to the weight of this fill material. (Six m of fill would be a load of about 11 tonnes per m^2 on the original surface.) This initial settlement of about 60 cm affected the entire site. When the piles were driven after the necessary excavation for the basement of the hotel, and the footings had been loaded with the weight of the superstructure, settlement continued due to this additional loading, except where the piles rested on the firm sand and gravel. Accordingly, the northeast corner of the building remained at the elevation it was at when constructed, but the southeast corner (where the Victoria clay was thickest and where the piles did not rest on the sand and gravel) had settled 0.48 m by the time of the construction work in 1913, and it has settled about 0.24 m since then. There is today, therefore, a difference in level between these two extreme corners of the original hotel building (since substantially enlarged with no foundation problems like this) of 0.72 m. The building is so large and was so very well constructed that it shows no evidence of this unusual condition. No visitors to this famous hostelry would ever suspect that the polished floors were not exactly level. Only those who have read the notable paper describing the recent studies would be tempted to see if they could find evidence of the differential settlement. Rolling billiard balls on the corridor floors would be about the only way to confirm inside the building what the levelling surveys have shown outside the building, but this would be a pastime inappropriate for the Empress Hotel of Victoria. It remains a splendid building and a classic example of the influence of geological site conditions upon long-term building performance.

Johannesburg, South Africa

Seldom if ever before have four complete blocks in the center of a large modern city been closed off for a great building complex, and excavated to beyond 22.86 m below street level, as was the case in the middle of Johannesburg in the late sixties. A 202.7-m-high office tower and an associated office building are the main features of the 2.4-hectare Carlton Center, located in the heart of this South African metropolis. Necessary excavation resulted in a 120.9- by 152.4-m hole in the city's center, excavation in one corner being planned to go to 29 m. Subsurface conditions consist of a complex system of igneous and metamorphic rocks—diabase, dolerite, quartzite, and shale—weathered to depths varying up to about 30.5 m and overlain by a thin veneer of transported soil. The boundary between transported and residual soils can always be distinguished by a "pebble layer" that is an unvarying indicator in the vicinity. Since groundwater was present in the weathered rock, pumping was therefore essential.

Water-level gauges were consequently installed in all the streets around the site. Regular movement monitoring was carried out to ensure that no damage accrued to neighboring buildings. All these had been carefully surveyed and recorded before excavation started. Support of the excavation involving a ringbeam of prestressed concrete wide enough to be used as a roadway makes the engineering features of this project of great interest. In this context, however, accurate knowledge of all subsurface conditions made possible the safe and efficient carrying out of this immense excavation in so critical a location.[5.17]

5.7 PROBLEMS WITH ROAD FOUNDATIONS

The foundations for roads and airport runways, since they carry loads so much smaller than those from large buildings, might be expected to present no special problems arising from the geology of the ground over which they are built. It is true that, with

Figure 5.16 Johannesburg, South Africa. Excavation for the multiblock Carlton Center; the large strut and the beam around the perimeter are of reinforced concrete; scale is given by the size of men. *(Photograph by R. F. Legget.)*

the application of modern soil mechanics, with good construction practices, and rigid inspection of every square meter of road foundation bed, good all-weather roads can now be constructed without difficulty. Geological problems may be encountered in excavating the cuts through which roads or runways may pass and in the selection of material to be used for the large fills that often feature modern highways as an alternative to costly bridges, when grades have to be eliminated. Even with "firm-looking ground" as a subbase for road construction, however, troubles can arise if the nature of the natural material to be covered up is not fully investigated.

It is, for example, all too easy to have such field inspections carried out in dry weather and to forget that the road must be satisfactory under all weather conditions. Even in sunny Florida it rains, sometimes, and sometimes very heavily. Trouble has been experienced there through nonrecognition of the change in property of the local Okachobee rock (a type of limestone) when wet as compared with its satisfactory performance when dry. In northern Canada, glacial tills can be encountered that, although appearing to be tough and compact, are actually in a relatively porous state due to their location near the center of ice movement. When dry, they appear to be quite satisfactory, but when wet they can soon acquire the consistency of the local *soupe aux pois*.

These are, however, problems that should be readily identified if preliminary investigations are properly carried out with full appreciation of the local geology. A somewhat extreme example will be described in more detail since it illustrates so clearly what can happen even with excavation in "solid rock." The California Department of Highways decided to route the Southern Freeway, as a part of the network of modern highways serving the central area of San Francisco, through the Potrero Hill area of the city above an existing tunnel of the Southern Pacific Railroad, one-half a kilometer long, built in 1906. The tunnel had been lined with unreinforced concrete walls and invert, with a roof arch of six courses of brick over the two tracks. Late in 1966 the general contractor for the road started his excavation and had completed it by the following September. In order to protect property adjacent to the big cut, an arched and rock-bolted retaining wall up to 16.5 m high was constructed along the east side of the excavation. All this was in the local Franciscan formation (through which the tunnel had been excavated) that consists of folded strata of shales with sandstone boulders in them and some serpentine present, the rock being badly fractured although quite solid. The maximum depth of the excavation for the road was about 18 m and the minimum clearance over the tunnel was 8 m.

One might imagine that with this clearance, and in solid rock, all would have been well, but even before excavation was complete, owners of buildings adjacent to the cut had noticed cracks in walls and roofs; cracks appeared next in sidewalks; and then water and gas mains began to fracture. By the time the excavation was finished, the tracks in the railroad tunnel were found to be "rough," or slightly out of alignment, and then movement was detected in the concrete walls and invert of the tunnel and in the brick roof arch. Inclinometers were installed to measure the

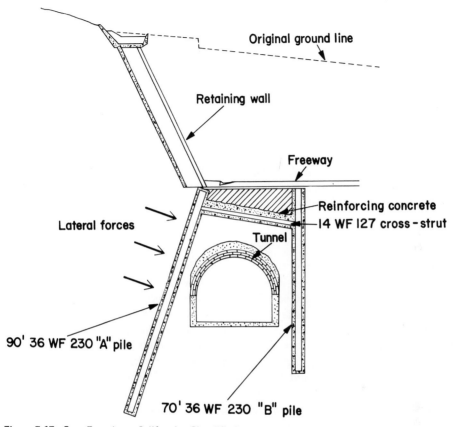

Figure 5.17 San Francisco, California. Simplified cross section through new freeway cutting and the Southern Pacific railroad tunnel, showing the basis of the remedial measures described in the text. *(Courtesy of the American Society of Civil Engineers and J. P. Nicoletti and J. M. Keith, from reference 5.18.)*

movement that was obviously taking place in the tunnel, the serious nature of which can be appreciated from the fact that the tunnel is the only access to the San Francisco terminus of the Southern Pacific system. A maximum rate of movement of 0.6 mm per day was observed, the entire western side of the tunnel moving inward. Studies were being made concurrently of possible solutions to the problem; the method adopted is shown in Fig. 5.17. Repairs had to be carried out so that they would not interfere with rail traffic and would cause minimum interference with the highway.

Using three large truck-mounted drill rigs, a total of sixty 1.07-m-diameter holes were drilled to a total length of 1,450 m, half being inclined holes drilled to depths of 27.4 m. Into the holes were inserted 0.9-m-wide flange steel beams weighing 342 kg per m. These were immediately concreted in place, with pumped concrete made with high-early-strength cement. The steel struts between the pairs of piles were then inserted in specially excavated trenches and tightly wedged in place before being embedded in weak concrete, which then constituted a good foundation for the road surfacing. A decrease in the movement was first observed after only nine frames had been installed. One month after the completion of this unusual rehabilitation job, movement had virtually stopped. No serious maintenance problems with the tunnel have since been experienced. The concept of the strut design proposed by engineers of the railroad company was the transfer of the load that was clearly actuating the movement of the west wall of the tunnel by means of a strong-enough framework to the continuous body of rock on the east side of the tunnel. The movement of the rock appeared to have been the result of the release of internal stresses in the rock by the deep excavation for the road, a salutary reminder of the state of stress in which "solid rock" deep below ground surface always exists.[5.18]

5.8   GENERAL FOUNDATION PROBLEMS

These examples are but a few from the almost innumerable cases from all parts of the world that could be cited in a review such as this of the geological aspects of foundation in cities. All would be different in some respect, as have been the foregoing examples, even though the basic feature of all—that of safely transferring loads from structures to the ground below—is always the same. The foregoing cases were selected to illustrate some of the more important special features of foundation work as influenced by local geology so that actual experience with foundations might be appreciated before the presentation of the more general comments that now follow. Fundamental to all projects is the absolute necessity for the most accurate knowledge practicable of the subsurface conditions of all building sites to depths of at least twice the width of the structure to be erected, no matter what the character of the site may be. This precept cannot be repeated too often since, in the past, it has so often been neglected. It will now be clear, however, that more than a superficial study of the local geology and the putting down of a few boreholes is necessary, one important supplement being a careful study of the actual history of building sites if there is any chance that they may have been built on previously, or used for any other purpose.

The danger that unsuspected boulders can create must be emphasized. They may be encountered in both residual and transported soils. Caution must always be exercised if the geological background to test-boring programs suggests even a faint possibility of boulders being encountered. It is far better to spend a small amount of extra money in advance of construction for this extra check on the possible presence of boulders than to run the risk of having construction seriously interfered with if they are encountered. The problems that groundwater can create in the construction of foundations has been touched upon. In the case of Winchester Cathedral, the influence of varying groundwtaer level showed itself in the decay of some of the timber piles; further examples will be given later. The chief significance of the Winchester buildings, however, is the influence upon construction of improved means of pumping groundwater (when this has to be done), wellpoints being now very widely used for "drying up" wet excavations. The carrying out of excavation for almost all foundations is a reminder of the importance of construction methods in this part of building work. In some cases, the construction of a foundation is quite the most difficult part of a building project. Great ingenuity has therefore been applied to minimizing construction difficulties, as will be seen from examples shortly to be cited.

Finally, the discovery of the Roman remains in the excavation for the hotel at Winchester is a typical indication of the reciprocal service to science that foundation work can give. In many cases, the geological conditions revealed by excavation are not unusual but rather are just what was expected from preliminary deductions. Even in these cases, however, excavation does enable geologists to procure samples of the materials exposed that would never otherwise be obtainable. Sometimes, geological strata will be exposed that were not expected, or variations in well-known geological conditions will be revealed. Geological observation of excavation work should, therefore, be a two-way street; examples will be given to illustrate this most desirable and often rewarding cooperation.

5.9 PROBLEMS WITH SOIL

Preliminary geological study will show whether a building site, or town site, lies in an area that has been glaciated or not. The boundary of glaciation is usually fairly well defined. The soils to be encountered will usually differ appreciably in the two types of country. Glacial soils will be more heterogeneous so that test borings will give less dependable results. It follows that a larger number of test borings can usually be justified in areas underlain by glacial soil than when residual soils are encountered. Despite all the care that is taken, great variations can still be encountered between adjacent holes, such as a sudden drop in level of a stratum of glacial till of as much as 4.6 m in a horizontal distance of less than 3 m. The effect that this actual condition had on excavation can well be imagined. Such possible variations must, therefore, be expected. No assumption of uniform conditions between adjacent boreholes should ever be made. The presence of boulders in many glacial deposits has already been stressed. It must always be anticipated and arrangements made for drilling through, and coring, any "rock" that may be encountered in test borings. The drill cores will permit determination of the rock type to be made. Correlation of this with knowledge of the local bedrock will give almost certain assurance that a boulder has, or has not, been encountered. This precaution is necessary because glacial erratics (as they are usually called by geologists) can be of remarkable size, a well-known example at Glen Miller, in Ontario, Canada, measuring 7.6 m in a vertical direction and about 10.7 m horizontally.

Boulders may still be encountered in glacial soils that have been "water sorted," a term used to describe the separation of fine from coarser soil particles when glacial material has been transported by running water and deposited either in streams, rivers, deltas, or lake bottoms. Many deposits of pure sand will be found in glaciated country, but even here care must be exercised. Depending on the way in which the sand has been deposited, it may be in either a very dense state or a loose state, with relatively low density. In the latter case, it may have to be consolidated to a greater density before being used as a foundation bed, since otherwise vibrations from any structure above might have a serious effect upon it. There are a number of engineering techniques available for this process of densification. *Loess* is an unusual type of soil encountered in many parts of the world. It consists of uniformly graded silt-sized particles that have been deposited by wind action, in effect, "wind-blown dust." It usually exhibits no stratification, but it can be encountered in beds over 100 m thick. Consisting of unweathered soil particles, it has an intricate internal structure that can be modified by water. As a foundation material, it is therefore suspect. In Chap. 8, examples will be given showing what a hazard it can be.

The geological history of glacial clay deposits is of unusual importance since the properties of clay can differ markedly, depending on whether they were deposited in fresh-water lakes or in the sea. In Scandinavia, and in the St. Lawrence Valley

Figure 5.18 San Joaquin Valley, California. Test plot for determining subsidence features following wetting of loess, after 14 months of operation. *(Courtesy of the California Department of Water Resources, L. B. James, Chief Geologist.)*

in northeastern North America, are large deposits of marine glacial clays that have quite unusual properties derived from their mode of deposition. All around the Great Lakes, on the other hand, are glacial clays (of similar superficial appearance) that were deposited in great fresh-water lakes, with correspondingly differing properties. The techniques of modern geotechnical studies—for obtaining undisturbed samples even of sand, and for testing all types of soils in the laboratory—now permit the accurate advance determination of the properties of soils in place, with consequent benefit to foundation design. Local geology remains, however, the starting point for all such investigations.

It is sometimes found that during the deposition of glacial clays, organic matter has been embedded in the clay matrix. In the course of time, such material can disintegrate, and methane gas may be formed. This will usually be in pockets and so create no major problems, but, if not detected, even pockets of methane can cause nasty explosions. If study of the local geology suggests any possibility of the presence of methane, the engineers in charge of excavation work should be warned judiciously so that the necessary cautionary measures can be taken. Methane can exhibit itself in unusual ways. On a large open excavation project in Toronto, Canada, the site had to be surrounded by steel-sheet piling and wellpoints in order that groundwater might be controlled, the site being adjacent to Lake Ontario. The pumping discharge from the main wellpoint header was located at a convenient point above the natural ground surface outside the excavation area. Quite by chance a workman one day struck a match in the vicinity of the discharge pipe, then discharging water at full capacity. He was somewhat surprised when a flame lit up at the upper lip of the water-filled pipe. This was due to methane, being pumped from the subsurface with the ground-water. This unusual flame burned steadily as long as the wellpoint system was in operation. The possible presence of methane in glacial clays must not be overlooked, therefore, particularly in urban foundation studies, for it can be a real hazard.[5.19]

Modern study of soils now includes mineralogical examination of the constituent particles in all but familiar soils. The results are often helpful in explaining unusual soil properties. *Clay mineralogy* is now an important branch of the main science of mineralogy. It is of special importance in the study of residual clays. In the process of disintegration (or "weathering") of the parent bed rock from which residual soils are formed, complex chemical reactions can occur, leading to the formation of minerals that may affect profoundly the properties of the resulting clays. *Laterites* and "black cotton soils" are two widely distributed and well-recognized residual soils, the properties of which are readily determined. In some tropical locations residual soils may be encountered that are relatively "young" and that will therefore be still strongly influenced by the nature of the parent rock from which they have been derived. Two such soils may look alike, and have the same feel, but differ markedly in their engineering properties. Any residual soils derived from volcanic rocks or volcanic ash should be suspect and subjected to the most rigorous testing before use. The presence of a mineral called *goethite* (an iron oxide) in such a soil caused unusual difficulties

Figure 5.19 London, England. Foundation stone for the main building of the University of London in its final position after being laid by H. M. King George V, but supported in this position while excavation proceeds around it. *(Photograph by R. F. Legget.)*

in construction on a large dam in east Africa, until its presence was determined. It has since been encountered on other engineering works.[5.20] The fact that residual soils are universally found in the tropical regions of the world, where a great increase in urban construction is to be expected in the years immediately ahead, makes the whole subject of residual soils one of unusual importance. So also is the fact that disintegration of parent rock may often be far from uniform with the result that masses of unweathered rock (the equivalent of boulders) may be encountered, as building experiences at Hong Kong and Singapore have made clear.[5.21,5.22]

5.10 PROBLEMS WITH ROCK

There are few popular impressions with regard to foundations that are more misleading than the idea that to "build on solid rock" is to avoid all possibility of difficulties. Certainly if the rock of a foundation bed is truly "solid," the chances of trouble developing are few. From what has just been said, however, about the weathering or rocks in tropical areas, a useful reminder is given of the fact that rocks are not mystical materials but rather are natural formations, of great variety, formed of complex assemblages of mineral particles and, in most cases, having been subject to great stresses and strains in the geological past. Nothing can therefore be assumed about rock strata that are found to be available as foundation beds. They must be investigated just as carefully as soil strata. Again, this involves in the first place a geological appreciation of the local rock in general, to be followed by more detailed investigation by means of diamond drilling and core examination. The correlation of all test-drilling results with an overall picture of the local geology is, if anything, even more important with rocks than with soils.

In general, igneous rocks will be found to be the most uniform and free from objectionable features; sedimentary rocks will be most suspect, with metamorphic rocks usually in an intermediate classification. The dip and strike of rock strata will have an important bearing upon their performance in foundations. Even so "solid" a rock as the Manhattan schist has caused troubles due to its steep dip and slippage upon its joint planes. Dr. Jacob Feld has reported a number of such cases in a series of notable papers on foundations in the New York area. In one case, a block of schist with a volume of 460 m^3 slid down a seam that had apparently been enlarged by tree roots, the movement triggered by frost action. This rock fall crushed a building below.[5.23] In other cases in the New York area, where incipient slipping on such inclined joint planes has been suspected, surface strata have been stabilized by being anchored with deep-drilled rock anchors to strata (of the same rock) well below the surface and so in no danger of moving. A case has been reported from West Germany of an eight-story reinforced concrete office building, founded on sloping ground with its foundations taken into what was presumed to be solid rock. After five stories had been erected, the load was such that the foundation started to move down the slope. It was stopped only by the drilling of 150 holes into a stratum of quartzite at a depth of about 6 m below the surface; steel dowels were grouted into the holes so that, in effect, the building was "riveted" onto its true foundation bed.[5.24]

The dip of rock strata must, therefore, always be most carefully studied, as must also the possibility of there being any faults on the building site. *Faults* in bedrock, even the smallest, are not usually isolated phenomena but are generally

Figure 5.20 Bronx, New York. Rock slip in broken Manhattan mica schist having a dip of 65°, due to the action of tree roots. *(Courtesy of Jacob Feld, consulting engineer, New York.)*

associated with other faulting in the same formation. Here is a matter on which local geological studies must always be fully consulted before test drilling on a building site commences. Even though reports on local geology, and maps that accompany them, will rarely go into such detail that the location of faults can be predicted with accuracy, they will at least give an indication of the possibility of faults being encountered. In the test drilling for a building in Ottawa, Canada (an area generally underlain by Ordovician limestones), holes were carefully spaced at 15-m intervals and good cores obtained from all. Those in charge of the drilling, however, failed to consult the main report on the local geology, the accompnaying map of which actually showed a probable fault crossing this building site. Excavation revealed the fault, nicely located between two rows of drill holes; much difficult extra excavation had to be carried out, with consequent delay in the completion of the building project.[5.25]

The limestone in the Ottawa area is not generally cavernous, but in many other locations the action of groundwater may be found to have enlarged joint planes in limestone and, in extreme cases, to have formed actual cavities beneath what appears to be a solid-rock surface. Fissures, many wide enough to be grouted up, are regularly encountered in foundation excavations in the area of St. Louis, Missouri. Such imperfect rock was encountered in the foundations for the great Gateway Arch and for the adjoining Mansion House Center, both adjacent to the Mississippi River. The local St. Louis formation is one of the Mississippian limestones, horizontally bedded and water-bearing. The groundwater level, incidentally, stays relatively constant throughout the year, at about 3 m above the level of the highest flood level known for the river, being determined by the level of the existing sewer system. The water table slopes toward the river but is affected by changes in river level only to a minor degree. Rock surface was found to vary irregularly from about 11 to 13.7 m below street level; overlying material consisted of variable sand, silt, and clay mixtures. All column loads were on individual piers drilled deep into the limestone until sound bearing could be assured. Grouting at 14 kg per cm^2 was carried out whenever found to be necessary. Every pier location was individually studied in order to determine the highest elevation at which the pier could be founded. Predrilling indicated whether grouting would be needed or not; cores were obtained in all cases for depths of about 3 m below the enlarged base of each of the cylindrical holes for the piers.[5.26]

Unusually difficult problems are encountered if the local bedrock is an over-

Figure 5.21 La Tuque, Quebec, Canada. A typical geological fault in Precambrian rocks of the Grenville Province. *(Photograph by R. F. Legget.)*

consolidated clay shale, a material that "looks like rock but behaves like soil." This description is really an oversimplification, and yet it conveys something of the difficulties that some shale rocks create. Typical is the Bearpaw formation, an Upper Cretaceous rock found in a large part of western Canada; the Pierre shale of the midwestern United States is similar. The material is a clay shale, the shaly characteristic having been induced by the very high pressures exerted on clay by the overlying ice of deep glaciers. The shale has reacted to the removal of this great load in the same way as any other material would—by an elastic rebound occurring immediately after the load was removed and a time-dependent rebound that is still occurring very slowly and that involves a slow softening of the material. Landslides all along the banks of the South Saskatchewan River, where they are formed of the Bearpaw shale, are clear indication of the long-term instability of this material.[5.27] When excavation is carried out in such materials, they have to be treated like soft rock with appropriate equipment. If the excavation is at all deep, the bottom will then consist of this over-consolidated material that, until this time, has been constrained by the weight of overlying shale. With the removal of even this small surcharge, rebound will occur unless the excavation is immediately covered up and loaded (from the structure) with a load at least equal to the weight of the shale that has been removed. And even in that case, if water can make contact with the newly excavated shale, swelling can still take place even under the load of the structure, sometimes with serious effects to the structure.

Most of the recorded experiences with this difficult material have been in connection with massive structures such as dams and canals. With the extension of cities in areas underlain by these shales, it is desirable that all concerned with foundations should be alerted to their undesirable properties. Dr. R. M. Hardy, of Edmonton, has fortunately recorded some of his experiences in investigating problems with the very similar preconsolidated clay shales of the mountainous area of western Canada; these behave in a corresponding manner. The shales contain a high percentage of the mineral montmorillonite, which has the property of taking up water into its structure with undesirable swelling effects. In one example, two circular tanks 30 m in diameter with 3.3-m-thick side walls and conical bottoms extending to a depth of 5.4 m below the surface were located close together in excavations in these shales, the distance between center lines being only 36 m. Within a few months after construction, the bottom of one tank had cracked but not the other. Investigations showed that seepage water had been able to reach the interface between the underlying shale and the cracked tank but had not done so in the case of the other. Swelling had resulted from this relatively minor feature. Another example involved the foundations for a steam power plant. Excavation in preconsolidated strata of preconsolidated shales and sandstones (with some coal) was carried out in the fall of the year and left open during the winter. Concreting of foundations started in the spring. Movements were noticed shortly thereafter. These were found to be due to seepage water in a coal seam causing swelling in the overlying clay shale, but only in a limited area, the coal seam not being continuous. The movement started only when water movement was possible with the change in weather. The corrective measures taken included the installation of wells through the concrete mat foundation to relieve the pressure buildup in the coal seam.[5.28] Clay shales are therefore rocks to be watched carefully in all preliminary site studies in view of their possibly unusual properties.

There is yet another problem that can be encountered with some types of shale; it must be mentioned, even though it is a problem of infrequent occurrence so that this is a note of caution rather than one of alarm. Some shales are found to contain free gypsum, and others have pyrite in them, two minerals that can be oxidized into other minerals when environmental conditions are exactly right. Bacterial action assists in this process, a possibility long suspected but now proved beyond doubt. Two cases of heaving of building basement floors founded on shale have occurred in Ottawa; bacteria were found in each case to be a contributing factor. Very warm basements, some fissuring of the rock, and a change in groundwater level were all factors that contributed to the unusual causes of this floor heaving. Detailed mineralogical studies have been fully reported.[5.29] An allied, but even rarer, problem is the occurrence of anhydrite in shale. If water gains access to this material, it will hydrate to form gypsum, also with increase in volume. There is on record the case of a very loud boom being heard one night in the town of Paint Rock, Texas. It was found the next day to have been due to a massive rock uplift on a nearby ranch. The uplift occurred along a stream channel in which water had been standing; it amounted to as much as 3 m. Some readers may tend to write this off as just another "Texas story," but the case is well authenticated. It serves to show the necessity for a most careful study of all bedrock that is to be used as a foundation bed in urban areas, and particularly if the rock is a shale.[5.30]

5.11 PROBLEMS WITH FILL AND FILLED GROUND

Some of the most difficult of foundation design problems occur when a building site is found to consist of an upper layer of "made ground" (to use an old but singularly descriptive term). In the older cities of Europe the accumulation of debris and rubble from buildings now long since destroyed will often give an artificial ground level to the entire central areas. The city of Prague, for example, as was mentioned earlier, has a normal level of its central area as much as 6 m higher than the original ground surface. Quite the most remarkable example of this type of filled ground is the city of Warsaw, about which more will be said in Chap. 7. Even in the New World, however, the same feature is to be found in those cities that are called "older" by North American standards. The city of Boston, for example, in its central section is found to be underlain by as much as 2 m of rubble fill, the remains of older buildings now demolished, repeating the pattern of European cities. Fortunately, the existence of filled ground of this sort is usually well known, locally, and so can be anticipated when test boring is planned. Detection of the original ground level will not usually be difficult from the

Figure 5.22 Ottawa, Canada. Looking into a test pit excavated in the floor of a modern building founded on black shale in which significant mineralogical change had taken place. *(Photograph by P. Goudreau, courtesy of DBR/NRC.)*

borings, but it is unusually important that it should be located with all reasonable accuracy.

When the fill consists of rubble from masonry or brick masonry buildings, it may provide an even better foundation bed material than the natural ground. It requires, however, merely a glance at Fig. 5.4 to be reminded that all it can do is to provide a hard crust to the ground to be stressed, presenting to the foundation engineer a particularly interesting problem in foundation design. More serious, however, is the case when the fill to be penetrated consists of refuse, in the form of what is now termed a "sanitary land fill" that has been completed and come to reasonable equilibrium, frequently with a lush growth of vegetation on its surface that may completely conceal the existence of heterogenous material underneath. As will be clear from what is said in Chap. 7 about the disposal of garbage from cities, the tendency to use building sites of this sort is bound to increase as the quantity of garbage to be

(a)

(b)

Figure 5.23 Warsaw, Poland. *(a)* A general view in the vicinity of Nowolipki Street in 1945, after the destruction of the city; *(b)* a view taken in 1962 from almost the same spot showing a part of the reconstructed city built over the rubble of the buildings that were demolished. *(Photograph by L. Jabrzemski. Courtesy of Polska Agencja Interpress, Michal Sadowski, Editor-in-Chief.)*

disposed of from cities continues to increase and the availability of good building sites correspondingly decreases. Such sites require extra special care in preliminary investigation, studies in which geological advice can be of the greatest importance. The original ground level must be known with accuracy and, if possible, the original state of that surface. The local groundwater situation is of vital significance. If the site is underlain by any basin-shaped impermeable strata, then the leachate from the garbage will have collected in this, and, in the course of time, it may have become toxic. Not only must such groundwater problems be anticipated (in older disposal sites) but also the possible presence of methane derived from the decay of vegetable matter.

The author knows of one tragic case in which a fine new housing development was built on an old sanitary land fill without any subsurface investigation of the site. When the houses were occupied, methane was found in some of the basements; it was traced easily to the decay of organic matter in the underlying garbage. And there was available no immediate solution to the resulting problem that can so readily be imagined. It is the task of the foundation engineer to devise suitable foundation designs for structures that must be located on such areas. In the future, with sanitary land fills now being rigorously controlled, the problems will be more simple, although on all such filled areas there will always be some problems if they are used for anything other than open spaces, or for the support of very light structures indeed. The greatest problems of all naturally arise when buildings have been erected on such fills without adequate sub-surface exploration. In southwestern Ontario there have been, most unfortunately, some explosions in houses built on sites under which was sanitary fill, in which methane had been generated, so that the problem here touched upon is a very real one and in no way theoretical. The geologist can help in avoiding such critical situations by including in his studies a meticulous investigation of the history of all city building sites on which he is consulted in order to see if there is the slightest chance that the site in question has been used, in the past, for refuse disposal of any kind. If it has, then extra precautions must be taken with all subsurface exploration and many more test holes put down than would normally be the case. The expenditure on these can be easily justified by reference to all too many examples of filled sites that were not so investigated.

A closely allied problem with geological overtones is the filling of old quarries in urban areas, as they become uneconomical in operation and the space they occupy becomes correspondingly more valuable for development as real estate. Many such quarries are deep; some cover large areas of ground. In no case that the author has ever seen was the fill in them being placed in accordance with good modern construction practice. In every known case the fill has been dumped in, usually by end-dumping, with the result that the heterogeneous mixture of soils and other material used for fill will be unconsolidated and thus liable to continuing settlement for a long time, quite apart from the settlement that will be induced in it when it is loaded. Unlike sanitary land fills, filled-in quarries can, and do, occur in central city areas that are eminently desirable for development. Again, preliminary investigation must include a diligent search for records of earlier quarrying operations in all cities in which this has been possible. The carrying out of test borings must be to depths such that the final rock level reached in the quarry can be determined with absolute certainty. One of the many land requirements for future civic development will be absolute control over the filling of quarries so that, when brought up to normal ground level, they can be used with confidence once the state of the fill material has been determined. All fill must be placed in thin layers and thoroughly compacted. These comments have been directed toward the filling of quarries. They apply also, to some degree, to the use of filled-up sand and gravel pits in urban areas. Such pits are fortunately not usually very deep, in contrast with quarries, but the same principles hold. If used as building sites, the bottom surface of the buried pit must be determined with accuracy, and the natural strata below this, as must also the state of the fill material so that the foundation engineer can properly design the foundations that are to be constructed.

The pressure for the development of such areas within city boundaries has been touched upon. It leads directly to yet another problem of fill, the use of what may be called marginal lands, such as swamps and tidal flats, that must have fill placed over them if they are to be made usable. Many think that this is a relatively modern development but history proves otherwise, the long experience in Holland in land reclamation being perhaps the main example. Even in North America, there are records of using "mud flats" by the placing of fill material upon them going back for 150 years, one early case being in Cambridge, Massachusetts. Today, however, there is such demand for land in urban areas that the use of such marginal lands is being rapidly increased. The author is well aware of the social problems involved in the use of such land, problems related to the preservation of some of those areas as natural wildlife reservations. He shares with others the hope that all appropriate "wet lands" (to use another descriptive term) can be preserved as a part of the natural heritage of man. The comments that follow on the use of such areas are based on the assumption that ecological questions have been faced and answered so that the marginal land to be used for building purposes has been designated for this purpose to general agreement.

The problems to be faced in such developments are mainly engineering, but, as usual, they depend upon the geology underlying the area to be filled. This must be determined in advance of any plans for filling, if only in the interests of economy but also to ensure that no difficulties will be experienced in the placing of the fill. It is surprising to find, in many cases, that organic material on the surface extends to shallow depths only. An example was provided by an area of swamp developed for a large shopping plaza that proved to have depths of only 0.6 to 1.5 m of organic silt overlying good sand that provided satisfactory foundations.[5.31] Other areas have soft and therefore weak soils going to considerable depths. If this situation is accurately determined in advance of construction, suitable methods can be employed to increase the strength of such soils so that normal foundation designs can be used. Methods that have been used successfully include the loading of the area to be developed with fill to considerably greater depths than will ultimately be required. The extra load causes extra consolidation of the weak soils, and so an increase in their strengths, and this will be generally retained after the excess fill has been removed and used elsewhere. Alternatively, drainage of very wet soils can be effected by the use of sand drains, columns of sand (like piles) formed in the soft soils with suitable equipment that will act as channels for water forced out of the surrounding wet material with consequent improvement in its properties.

There are to be found examples of land reclamation in almost every developed country. In India, the Bombay Back Bay reclamation project is an outstanding example. In Hong Kong, a major runway for its important international airport was built on land reclaimed from the sea, as was the main runway for the airport serving Gibraltar. In Japan, great progress has been made in reclaiming much-needed land from the sea by the controlled deposition of industrial waste, and the products of garbage incinerators. Further reference to this aspect of filled land will be found in Chap. 7, since it links two geological problems. The Netherlands provides without question the most famous example of all of winning land from the sea. When work in progress at present is completed, well before the end of the present century, 7 percent of the total land area of this compact and lovely land will have been created by reclamation, or 10 percent of all of its arable land. This epic feat of engineering is an example of what can be done by a relatively small country, working against great difficulties, but always on the basis of the most complete preliminary information possible about all areas to be gained from the sea.[5.32]

There may be mentioned as an example one of the best-known areas of such marginal land in North America that has not yet been extensively used. The Hackensack Meadows consist of a large area of low-lying land between the cities of Newark and New York, bounded on the east by the high land of the New Jersey Palisades. All travelers going south from New York by road, rail, or air (if visibility permits) see this vast area of swampland that has been described as "once a glacial lake, the Meadows is an inhospitable mix of sand, silt and clay topped with a layer of black organic mud, green reeds and swamp grass: for generations the area has been used as a refuse dump for the New York–New Jersey metropolitan area, so a thick layer of garbage blankets much of the marsh." Plans have been announced for its rehabilitation and use; when implemented, these will involve some such procedures as have been herein discussed. Much test boring has been done over the swamp. Borings have revealed the existence of two pre-Pleistocene buried valleys cut more than 30 m below present sea level into the underlying Triassic sandstone, one extending under the city of Newark, the other underlying the eastern margin of the Meadows. Light buildings have been erected on the Meadows in its northern section. Test borings for these revealed between 1.8 to 2.1 m of highly compressible surface tidal deposit, "meadowmat," or fibrous peat, overlying a thin stratum of still varved clay below which is a deep (7.5- to 22.5-m) deposit of soft to firm varved clay. Compact glacial till then overlies the sandstone bedrock. On these foundation beds one-story buildings

Figure 5.24 The Netherlands. The new town of Emmeloord in the Noordoostpolder. *(Courtesy of the Ministerie Verkeer en Waterstaat, The Hague.)*

have been founded, and have performed well, by being placed on specially selected and carefully placed fill resting directly on the stiff varved clay, after removal of the fibrous material. This shows what can be done with a minimum disturbance of natural conditions, based on careful study of the properties of the materials of the foundation beds.[5.33]

5.12 PROBLEMS WITH WATER

Much has already been said in this chapter about water. This is because there is rarely a foundation project that involves any appreciable amount of excavation that does not involve dealing with some groundwater. Other examples will inevitably be touched upon briefly in the remaining chapters just because groundwater is so all-pervasive in below-ground operations. Mention has been made of the methods now used for controlling such water in excavation, frequently by controlled pumping with well-points. It will have been noted that references to groundwater have not been confined to those examples in which excavation was carried out in soil. Fissured and jointed rock can be more troublesome with water problems than many soils. Correspondingly, in very porous rocks, pumping with wellpoints can be effective, surprising though this may appear. The Miami oolite is a soft white rock composed of calcium carbonate formed from minute marine organisms. It is porous and usually water-bearing. Deep excavations, although avoided in earlier years, are now regularly carried out in Florida in this rock with the aid of strategically placed wellpoints. In a similar manner, these versatile units can be successfully used in clays that present water problems, the suction from pumping creating a slight vacuum at the base of each wellpoint, which has the effect of creating unbalanced pressure at the nearest exposed face where atmospheric pressure will retard the issue of water from fine fissures and joints in the clay.[5.34]

There are potential problems with water that have to be considered after a building project has been completed. The maximum possible level of the water table must be predicted with all the certainty that is possible since, if it is to rise above the base level of the foundation structure, hydrostatic uplift pressures must be included

Figure 5.25 Key West, Florida. A wellpoint installation keeping dry an excavation in Miami oolite. *(Courtesy of the Moretrench Corporation and Powell Brothers Construction Company.)*

in design. For buried tanks, and similar structures that may possibly be at times empty of their normal loads, this matter is of unusual importance. Surprising though it may seem, there are records of concrete sewage tanks, buried in water-bearing ground, moving upward when empty. In contrast, the superintendent of the Ley Creek Sewage plant at Syracuse, New York, must set in operation a wellpoint pumping system that surrounds his treatment tanks before they are emptied for cleaning, so as to lower the water table and so obviate any danger of upward movement of the tanks.[5.35] This is but one of the many such installations that could be mentioned, all of which have been given this safety measure by reason of accurate advance knowledge of subsurface conditions, including the level of groundwater throughout the whole year. It must never be forgotten that water tables in general will vary in level throughout a 12-month period so that long-term observations of groundwater are quite essential.

Yet another maintenance problem, dependent upon the variation of the local water table, arises when a structure is founded on timber piles. Wood is one of the most remarkable and useful of all building materials. It is, however, organic in nature, and as a result it can deteriorate. Normally, when kept always dry, or always below water, it will last indefinitely, but it is susceptible to rotting if it is subject to alternating wetting and drying. It can readily be seen that if the water table beneath a building that is founded on wooden piles varies appreciably throughout the year, serious damage may result. Unfortunately, there are all too many examples of this maintenance problem. The great Cathedral of Strasbourg, with its wonderful clock, was built at a time when such technical problems were not appreciated. It was started in the year 1439, its stone footings supported on timber piles. Installation of a new drainage system in the eighteenth century interfered with the local groundwater conditions, with subsequent damage to the piles, necessitating a major foundation underpinning operation in the early years of the present century.[5.36] In the New World, the famous building housing the Boston Public Library, also supported by timber piles, was found to be cracking about 1929. Careful investigations showed that some of the piles had completely rotted, with the result that about 40 percent of the building had to be underpinned. A fine piece of "engineering detective work" (as it may well be called) traced the trouble to the probability of leakage into an adjacent sewer, although construction of the Boylston Street Tunnel of the Boston subway may have contributed. Remedial measures were adopted to prevent further trouble; these included the use of recharging wells.[5.37]

The central part of the city of Milwaukee, Wisconsin, is underlain by variable soils due to the local geological history of its lakefront section. The local watertable is generally high. Near the waterfront, the Northwestern Mutual Life Insurance Company erected a fine head office building in classical style in 1912. In 1930 a major addition had to be built, completing the use of an entire city block by this company. The extension was founded on timber piles, grouped under mass concrete footings. In order to ensure satisfactory performance of these footings, especially since the two buildings were united to form one structure, the architects included in

Figure 5.26 Milwaukee, Wisconsin. Head office building of the North-western Mutual Life Insurance Company, the later part being in the rear. *(Courtesy of the company, L. Clarey, Building Superintendent.)*

their design the provision in every concrete footing of a 10-cm pipe, suitably capped at the level of the subbasement floor. The maintenance staff of this fine building has faithfully recorded the groundwater levels in each of these observation wells ever since, readings being taken every month. Occasionally there will be a drop in the water level at a few locations, in which case water is fed in to the pipes until the normal level is restored. It goes without saying that the foundations have performed perfectly. Having had the privilege of examining this installation, through the courtesy of the company's officers responsible for its maintenance, the author can testify to its essential simplicity and the minimum demand it makes upon the maintenance staff while yet providing a continuing safeguard against unexpected change in sub-surface conditions beneath this important and beautiful building.[5.38] Whenever possible, should the precaution be necessary, such a system of observation wells should always be installed during construction when the cost is a mere bagatelle as compared to what investigations within a completed building can cost.

There is one further aspect of water and foundations that the author mentions with regret, since he is a tree-lover and wants to see the cities of the future given all the charm and serenity that beautiful trees can bestow. Trees can, however, ruin buildings. They are living things and require water, much water, for their growth. Young leaves can contain up to 90 percent of their weight in water; even tree trunks can contain 50 percent. Although the formation of 100 g of cellulose (the main content of wood) requires 55 g of water, a tree will lose correspondingly by transpiration almost 100,000 g of water, or 1,000 times as much as its own gain in weight. This water is obtained from the soil in which the tree grows through its root system, which may account for 10 percent of the total weight of a tree. Formed mainly of fine roots feeding into the few main thick roots to be seen when a tree is uprooted, the root system of an oak tree, for example, can total several hundred kilometers. When the Suez Canal was excavated, roots of a tamarisk tree were found at a depth of 30 m below ground level. Correspondingly, tree roots have been traced for a horizontal distance of 30 m from the tree itself. This is the intricate system of feeder channels through which a tree obtains its essential water supply. If growing in sandy or gravely soils and water supply fails, as by a sudden lowering of the water table, trees will quickly die. If in clay soils, especially those with high natural-moisture contents, trees will draw water from the minute pores within the clay. As the clay dries out, the root system will spread into the clay that still contains water. Some trees are greater users of water than others, and so more of a hazard when growing in clays that have the unfortunate property of shrinkage with decreasing water content. The broad-leafed desiduous trees are the worst "offenders"—poplar, alder, aspen, willow, and elm in that order, followed by maple, birch, ash, beech, and oak.[5.39]

Normally trees will draw their water supply from the upper part of the soil (topsoil) in which they grow, which is itself supplied by percolation of rain. In times of normal rainfall, this will be a system in equilibrium even for the heavy water users. When, however, a period of low rainfall is experienced, the deep-seated root system will go into action and draw water from previously unaffected clay. And if this is a shrinkable clay, shrinkage will inevitably follow, with unfortunate results for any buildings, streets, or other structures that may be supported by it. Experiments in Ottawa, Canada, have shown surprising movements in the local Leda clay in a dry summer. A vertical settlement of 13 mm at a distance of 6 m from a row of elm trees, and at a depth of 3.9 m, was typical and shows clearly what damage can be wrought in this way in periods of very dry weather on buildings founded on shrinkable clay.[5.40]

Older residential buildings in the center of the city of Ottawa provide all-too-good examples of the differential settlements (and, in a few cases, actual failures) caused by the elm trees that so grace the roads in which they stand, following a number of dry summers. Figure 5.27 shows the effect even on sidewalks. Ottawa is very far from unique in this respect, however. Examples are on record from Africa, Australia, Burma, China, India, Palestine, the Sudan, Belgium, and Texas. There are probably very few areas of the world where some evidence of cracking in buildings founded on clay soils, due to trees, could not be found. Some remarkable examples have been recorded from Great Britain. Typical was the case of brick two-story houses so badly cracked that their corners had to be shored up, and all due to Lombardy poplars within 6 m of the houses. A large theater, built of brick, in Stamford Hill, London, was seriously cracked because of the root action from a row of Lombardy poplars that had been planted presumably to act as a screen for the large expanse of brick wall at the rear of the theater building, the wall that cracked—to the extent of 44 mm at the top. For special local reasons, the remedy in this case involved deep underpinning of the wall in question.[5.41]

The solution of this unusual problem involves, as always, accurate foreknowledge of the subsurface conditions. If it is found, through tests on soil samples in the laboratory, that buildings have to be founded upon shrinkable clay, then the necessary precautions must be taken in design. Footings should be taken down as deep as practicable, but, of much greater importance, landscaping near the structures must be strictly controlled, particularly with regard to the siting of trees. A good working rule is to ensure that no tree is placed nearer to buildings on such foundation beds than a distance equal to the total height to which the tree may be expected to grow. Landscape architects may object to such a requirement, but they should be convinced if shown some of the examples, in detail, that have been summarized in the foregoing paragraphs. If trouble develops after a building has been erected, then the easiest solution is to remove the offending trees, regrettable though this procedure may be. If for any reason such a course is not possible, then the only solution is to underpin that part of the foundation that has been or may be affected. This is always a costly

Figure 5.27   Ottawa, Canada. The sidewalk of Metcalfe Street in Ottawa, showing the effect of differential drainage of the underlying clay soil by tree roots, the settlement being due to differential shrinkage of soil. *(Photograph by M. Bozozuk, courtesy of DBR/NRC.)*

Figure 5.28 London, England. Cracks in a major building due to the poplar trees that can be seen on the right, necessitating temporary supports as may be seen. *(Photograph by A. W. Skempton, London.)*

procedure, and so the economics of the situation call for special study. Cracks that have developed can be covered up, but a more desirable procedure is to get nature to reverse itself, by restoring the natural moisture content of the clay after the trouble-causing trees have been removed. To suggest that cracks in a building can be cured by the simple procedure of cutting down a tree and leaving a garden hose running continuously for some days will cause surprise to the uninformed, but it is a simple solution that works, even as it is also a vivid reminder of the importance of the exact state of the unseen materials upon which buildings are founded.

Reference must again be made, in concluding this section, to the quality of groundwater, since this is an aspect of subsurface investigation that can so easily be overlooked. The presence of sulfates in groundwater in excessive quantity was mentioned in Chap. 4 as one dangerous aspect if it is not detected. There are certain areas of the world, such as western Canada, where this problem is now widely recognized and so always anticipated in studying foundation sites. It is a problem that exists in many other locations, however, sometimes quite locally, and so should never be discounted as a possibility. Large areas of England have groundwater with appreciable sulfate content. There is on record an example of what can happen to a large complex of buildings when it is not detected. The St. Helier Hospital at Carshalton in Surrey (not too far from London) was built in 1938; it has a capacity of 750 beds, the main accommodation being provided by four multistory ward blocks with central services contained in one main service block, subways connecting the different parts of the complex. The foundations were of concrete all placed on a brown clay stratum that overlies the well-known London clay. In March 1959 some of the foundation concrete was exposed during maintenance work and was found to be seriously deteriorated. This led to a more general study that showed that the foundations were deteriorating steadily. "Samples of the substrata taken by boreholes showed that while the ground was of adequate load-bearing strength, the sulfate content was very high. It was evident that much of the existing concrete had suffered from chemical attack and the cement, which was of a high aluminous type, had weakened through these conditions and the warm damp atmosphere." In a major underpinning operation, the entire building complex had to be provided with new foundations, at what trouble and expense can best be imagined.[5.42]

5.13   PROBLEMS OF OPEN EXCAVATION

Once subsurface conditions have been determined and the design of a foundation completed, its translation into actuality becomes the job of the appointed contractor. As will already be evident, the construction of foundations is a specialized part of construction practice requiring great skill and wide experience for its successful prosecution. The contractor will have just as much interest as the designing engineer

Figure 5.29   Western Canada. Damage done to the concrete roof of a heating tunnel by sulfate-bearing groundwater, ordinary portland cement having been used. *(Photograph by J. J. Hamilton, courtesy of DBR/NRC.)*

in subsurface conditions since these indicate the materials with which he will have to deal in his work. In most sets of contract documents covering the construction of foundations, special care is taken to describe as accurately as possible the materials that will be encountered, and the groundwater conditions that will be met when the contract is carried out. It is only with this knowledge that the contractor can decide, in association with the designing engineer, how he is going to carry out his responsibilities.

Since practically every foundation involves some excavation, the carrying out of excavation in the confined areas available for such work is usually the first major part of the building contract. It will reveal whether the predictions as to subsurface conditions based on test borings are correct. Ground conditions must, therefore, be very carefully watched as they are uncovered to ensure that the methods being used are suitable and to permit of changes in construction planning when necessary. This will not usually call for any geological assistance, but geologists will have their own interest in the sections uncovered by the excavation, as will be briefly indicated at the end of the chapter. Because all successful excavation work depends upon adequate foreknowledge of what is to be excavated, this part of construction work, however, does have considerable geological significance. Two major excavation jobs will therefore be briefly described. They are so large as to be far from typical, but each illustrates usefully how accurate subsurface information was put to good use.

One of the largest automobile parking garages in the world is that which lies under Pershing Square in the heart of Los Angeles, generally unsuspected by visitors to this part of this vast city as they look at the pleasant gardens and growing trees that make the square such a pleasant urban oasis. Beneath the gardens, however, is a three-level garage capable of holding 2,000 automobiles, the lowest level about 9.7 m below street level. The garage occupies an area of about 2 hectares. It was opened in 1952 after a fast construction schedule. Careful preliminary investigation of the subsurface and the necessary soil testing had shown that all excavation would be in clean, fine brown sand, sand and gravel mixed with a little clay, fine gray sand and silt, and a local siltstone commonly known as Puenete shale. The area would generally be dry, but some groundwater at a depth of about 6 m was expected in the northern part of the square. Excavation was carried out over the entire site by 2-m^3 shovels that were even able to excavate the shale, although with difficulty. (Incidentally, hauling away the 200,000 m^3 of excavation was permitted only between the hours of 6 P.M. and 2 A.M.) The relatively limited quantity of groundwater was handled easily by intermittent pumping from a deep sump well at the north end of the site.

Because of the generally dry site and its great area, an ingenious system was developed for foundation construction. Excavation was carried out in two 4.8-m lifts. Concurrently, a large drill rig surrounded the entire site with 1.5-m-diameter holes spaced at 2.7-m centers, going to below final grade level, and belled out at their bottoms for the placing by hand of concrete footings. In these holes, precast concrete

Figure 5.30   Los Angeles, California. Excavation of Pershing Square in 1951 for the construction of the parking garage now hidden beneath the central garden. *(Courtesy of the American Society of Civil Engineers, from reference 5.43.)*

columns were then placed, each weighing 9 tonnes. Soil was left in place at its angle of repose up to the tops of these columns while the rest of the excavation was completed, the foundations placed for the whole garage except for the one bay around its entire perimeter. As the massive concrete structure rose to its finished level, 75 cm below finished garden level, it was used to support struts that were then fixed to the individual columns all around the site. With these supports in place, the remaining excavation of the sloping bank could be completed, and the final perimeter bay of the garage constructed, incorporating the precast columns placed when the job began.[5.43]

Entirely different were the problems faced in the design and construction of the foundations for the "two tallest buildings in the world" (when they were built), constituting, with many ancillary structures, the $600 million New York World Trade Center near the lower end of Manhattan Island. These great buildings are supported on concrete piers founded directly on the Manhattan schist that has already been mentioned as permitting the erection of skyscrapers of this magnitude. Rock level, however, was about 21.3 m below street level and the six-story basement had to reach also to this depth. Maps dating back as far as to the year 1783 were studied to obtain information about the development of the site. This historical investigation showed that in that year the shoreline of the Hudson River ran two blocks inland from the present shoreline. Along it had been built rock-filled cribs, timber wharves, and other structures. Long since covered up by miscellaneous fill, these old structures were founded upon mixed strata of organic silt (near the river) overlying inorganic silt and sand—all water-bearing. Groundwater, therefore, was not far from the present ground surface. Because of all the streets, buildings, and buried services surrounding the building site, it was quite impossible to contemplate lowering the water table around

Figure 5.31 New York City. Excavation for the World Trade Center, the scale being indicated by the figures of the visiting group and the subway tunnel crossing the site; the tiebacks supporting the temporary walls are to be seen on the right. *(Courtesy of the Port Authority of New York and New Jersey, M. S. Kapp, Chief Engineer.)*

the site, even under controlled pumping. After a study of all possible alternatives, it was decided to surround the entire site with a wall of concrete placed by means of a "slurry trench."

This ingenious construction process involves the careful excavation of a narrow trench, using special excavating equipment, on the line of the required wall, the trench being filled with a thick slurry of bentonite and water, a practice similar to the use of "drilling mud" in mining. When excavation is complete, and the trench filled with the slurry, concrete is then placed starting at the bottom of the trench by deposition with a submerged (or "tremie") pipe, grillages of steel reinforcing having first been placed in the trench to be encased in the concrete. As the concrete rises, the bentonite is displaced, and so the safety of the trench sides is assured through the intricate operation. When the concrete has cured, excavation can then proceed up to the walls. Because of their great height, when excavation was carried to full depth, the walls at the World Trade Center were anchored back by inclined steel tiebacks drilled into and grouted into the underlying schist. All the excavation from this vast hole in the heart of Manhattan was trucked to an adjacent site in the Hudson River that has been surrounded by a sheet-pile retaining structure. Dumped into the enclosed water, the fill has given a new section of land in this highly valued area, estimated to be worth $90 million to the City of New York.

Since the space excavated contained two circular tunnels in which subway trains were operating, stretching from one side to the other and supported during excavation on a steel truss bridge, the entire project was one of unusual fascination to all who are interested in unusual foundation construction. But almost all who visit the two great towers will probably be so fascinated by what they see above ground that they will give no thought to the rock below, nor to all that went into the design and construction of the works below ground upon which the great buildings now rest so securely.[5.44]

5.14   UNUSUAL CONSTRUCTION METHODS

All who are concerned with the physical aspects of the growth and development of existing cities know well that they must accept the foundation bed materials that underlie the city, poor as they may be in some cases. They must rely upon the ingenuity of engineers and contractors to devise ways of founding the buildings that are needed for the proper extension of the city and its facilities when these poor building sites have to be used. It may therefore be helpful if, in conclusion, a few examples are given showing how unsatisfactory building sites can be used, once the full facts about the subsurface conditions are known.

When the geological conditions under a building site consist of a deep stratum of very soft or very weak clay, any load placed upon such material will naturally lead to considerable settlement. Such material is, however, sustaining itself in a quite stable condition at levels below the surface. If, therefore, enough of the weak soil can be removed as would have exactly the same weight as the building to be placed upon it, and replaced by the building, then the building should "float" as it displaces its equivalent weight of soil. The idea is simple, but, because it has to be considered for sites under which the soil is weak in bearing, it is unusually difficult to execute in practice. It seems certain that some of the early pioneer civil engineers appreciated the idea, the Albion Mill building in London built by Samuel Wyatt in 1783-1786 being founded in something like this manner.[5.45] Of modern examples that were quite definitely designed in this way and successfully constructed, the main building of the New York Telephone Company at Albany, New York, holds pride of place. The local subsurface conditions consist of a stratum of Albany clay overlying bedrock, the clay having very low bearing capacity and being known to be difficult to handle in excavation. The building, erected in 1930 as an extension to existing facilities, measures 28 by 35 m, with three basements and 11 stories above ground. Designed for a live load of 735 kg per m², it was estimated that the bearing load to be imposed on the foundation bed would be 2,200 kg per m². Details of the unusual construction job that its building involved need not be given, but the design was successfully completed, and the building is still performing excellently.[5.46] Similar "floating foundations" will be of special importance in tropical areas, as building sites near major rivers have to be used, often underlain by deep deposits of alluvial material. This lends special importance to the use of this type of foundation for a building in Georgetown, Guyana. Other significant buildings founded in this way, of which records are available in the literature of foundation engineering, have been erected in Scotland and in Boston, Massachusetts.[5.47]

Figure 5.32 Georgetown, Guyana. The concrete box structure in the center is a floating foundation for the millhouse of a new sugar mill; excavation was carried out to the required depth in the individual cells. *(Photograph by E. Crowch, courtesy of H. Q. Golder, consulting engineer, Toronto.)*

Figure 5.33 Tokyo, Japan. Commercial building with five stories below ground and nine above being constructed by the Takenaka Caisson process, the structure seen being the concrete basement of the complete building that will be sunk to final depth by controlled excavation. *(Courtesy of the Takanaka Komuten Co. Ltd. and the Building Research Institute of Japan, K. Kagague, Director, and K. Kamimura, Chief of Information.)*

An alternative type of foundation design for buildings that must be founded on deep strata of relatively weak soil (when deep basements can be used) is to build the lowest section of the basement of the building on the surface of the undisturbed ground and then to force it into the ground by the weight of the upper stories of the building steadily built up above the initial basement. A special "cutting edge" must first be laid out around the perimeter of the building, upon which the building structure (usually of concrete) is then erected. Soil conditions must be known with absolute certainty to ensure uniform penetration of what may be called the "building caisson" and to obviate any possible difficulties in the excavation. This has naturally to be carried out under strict supervision and relatively slowly if the building is to sink accurately to its final position. Although this idea has long been used in the practice of civil engineering for the construction of bridge piers of relatively small cross-sectional area, the bold concept of applying the idea to building construction appears to have been developed first in Japan, where the subsoil conditions underlying much of the great city of Tokyo are eminently suitable (and correspondingly most difficult for ordinary foundation methods).

It was first tried out, successfully, in 1934 and since then has been applied to increasingly larger structures, ultimately to the construction of the Nikkatsu Building, which occupies a complete city block, has four basements, nine stories above ground, and a three-story penthouse. Well over 20 buildings in Tokyo have now been built in this way.[5.48] The idea has now been applied also in Europe, a 530-car parking garage, with seven levels below grade, having been constructed in Geneva, Switzerland, in the same manner. Here subsurface conditions consisted of 7.5 m of water-bearing sand and gravel overlying 21.3 m of soft clay that grades into a good firm clay on which the caisson was founded. The versatile mineral bentonite was put to good use again, as a lubricant this time, injected in an annular ring around the caisson formed by the slightly wider diameter of the cutting shoe as compared with the structure itself. Again, suitable soil conditions and the corresponding absence of boulders in the soil were an absolute prerequisite for employment of this method.[5.49]

Yet another procedure, not unrelated to the concept of floating foundations, that can be used on sites underlain by weak soil is the loading of the building site, before construction starts, so as to "precompress" the strata that would otherwise cause undesirable settlement. This can only be done, naturally, when there is full knowledge not only of the geology of these strata but also of the exact engineering

Figure 5.34 Geneva, Switzerland. The basement caisson for the Rive-Centre garage being sunk in place by controlled excavation. *(Courtesy of the Societe Anonym Conrad Zschokke, contractors, Geneva.)*

properties of the soils, obtained by modern soil mechanics techniques. Even the site of a new cathedral church, in Baltimore, Maryland, was so prepared prior to the start of building, but preloading is more often applied at unusual sites (such as the filling over of swamp land) and for special purposes.[5.50] A striking example of the latter is provided by the rehabilitation of a large wartime building at Port Newark, New Jersey, by the Port Authority of New York and New Jersey.

Built in 1941 by the U.S. Navy, the building (measuring 165 by 76 m) was essentially a structural steel frame supported on 25.5-m wooden piles. The Port Authority acquired the building in 1963 and wished to use it as a warehouse, but studies showed that the support of the floor was not adequate for this. Newark Bay, on which the building is located, is underlain by red shale bedrock over which there is a fairly uniform stratum of red clay 21.3 m thick. Over this is about 7.8 m of black organic silt, and on this the usual heterogeneous collection of miscellaneous fill material so often found around the shores of long-established harbors. At the site of the building, the fill consisted of cinders. Following much experience gained by the Port Authority in this area with normal preloading of outside areas, it was decided to apply the same procedure to the floor inside this building. The entire building was therefore filled to a depth of 3.6 m with soil brought in by trucks, giving an additional floor load of 6,350 kg per m^2. Left in place for 14 months, the fill was all removed by scrapers in January 1966, when the floor was found to have settled 0.43 m. A new floor was then built that, careful calculations suggested, might settle an additional 38 mm in the ensuing 5 years, a small amount that could readily be arranged for in the final floor design.[5.51]

Although the use of freezing of the water in water-bearing strata as an aid to construction will call for mention in the following chapter, since its most vital use is probably in connection with shaft and tunnel work, it should be mentioned briefly here since it is a construction procedure that can, in extreme cases and when economically justified, be applied also in the construction of difficult foundations in water-bearing ground. At Fleetwood, in northwest England, a small pump house and storm water overflow structure had to be constructed in difficult ground within sight of the sea. Problems with water became so troublesome that, almost as a last resort, the freezing process was applied and this enabled the work to be complete as designed.[5.52] The application of freezing to bad ground naturally requires skilled and experienced experts in this field; it is therefore an expensive operation, but that it is a method which can be used to good effect is warrant for this brief reminder.

Some of the most difficult of all foundation problems are encountered when, for one reason or another, existing buildings (and especially valuable old buildings) have to be "underpinned" to a firm foundation bed, being given a new foundation in effect and so a new lease of service. Although it is a highly specialized part of foundation engineering, it goes without saying that underpinning can be carried out only when subsurface conditions are known with absolute certainty and accuracy. The risks involved in interfering with existing foundations are far too great to permit of

Figure 5.35 Vancouver, British Columbia, Canada. Site of the Iona Island Sewage Treatment Plant of the Greater Vancouver Sewerage and Drainage District when preloaded with fill that would be eventually removed before construction in order to obviate estimated differential settlements of up to 1.2 m in the underlying soft silt and clay. *(Courtesy of Ripley, Klohn and Leonoff Ltd., consulting engineers, Vancouver, C. Leonoff, Executive Vice President.)*

any doubt whatsoever that the proposed underpinning operation cannot be carried out exactly as planned. What is involved is the "picking up" of loads on existing columns by some form of temporary expedient and their transfer to new and reliable foundations. The decay of wooden piling beneath buildings (see page 233) is one problem with foundations that can necessitate underpinning, but so also can progressive settlement that finally becomes so serious that it must be corrected.[5.53]

All visitors to Stockholm will know the outside appearance of the great Royal Palace located in what is known as the Old Town, immediately opposite the Grand Hotel on the inner harbor. The palace, built at different periods in the last two and a half centuries, with its wings founded on the site of an older palace that burned in 1697, is said to have 700 rooms. It has long been the residence of the Swedish Royal Family, but its two wings have suffered from serious settlement in the last half century, as much as 0.6 m. Some remedial work was done in the 1920s, but trouble continued, due possibly to the increased load of the concrete then placed, the heavier and increased traffic on roads adjacent to the palace, and the slowly dropping groundwater levels possibly associated in part with the known rise in the level of all of Scandinavia due to rebound following the last glacial period.

The two palace wings rest in part on the remains of the former building that burned. A timber raft, near the main building, and timber piles were used as foundation units, the mat resting on 3 to 6 m of miscellaneous fill. Beneath the fill is a thin stratum of clay with some sand, then a bed of compact gravel from 9 to 23 m thick overlying bedrock. Using the concrete mat placed beneath the building in the twenties as a working platform, the specialist contractor for the underpinning operation sank 29 cylinders through all these strata to bedrock. These were cleaned out, filled with concrete, and used as the new foundations for the two wings. This was difficult work, carried out in the confined quarters of the old stone-arch basement but was successfully completed. In the excavation of the old fill, quite a number of archeological items were discovered, such as a shoe from the sixteenth century and ceramic ovens, of unusual interest to the resident of the palace, King Gustav Adolf VI, himself a distinguished archeologist; all were passed to the Stockholm City Museum, where they may now been seen.[5.54]

5.15 GEOLOGICAL SIGNIFICANCE OF EXCAVATIONS

It is only rarely that items of real archeological interest will be found in excavations for foundations, even in the older lands of Europe, but every excavation reveals geological information that has never been previously available. In most cases, this will not have unusual geological significance, even though always of some interest, especially in showing whether preliminary investigations have been accurate. As in all geological studies in the field, however, one never knows! It is, therefore, desirable that certainly every major excavation, and all smaller excavations that reveal anything that seems to be unusual, should be examined by a geologist familiar with the local geology. It behooves the department of geology of every university throughout the world, therefore, to have at least one member of its staff alerted to the possibility that local excavations can provide for the procurement of new geological information. If approach is made for this scientific purpose to the appropriate authorities in the proper manner, there should be no objection to study of all exposures of interest, provided that no interference with construction operations is involved. It is by the accumulation of such information that local geology can be so steadily advanced to general public benefit, and especially to the advantage of all future local building.

There is a wealth of illustrative examples that could be cited from the literature of geology. A few must suffice. The stratigraphy of Pleistocene deposits can be studied only by examining successive exposures, caused either naturally along streams and rivers, or by the action of man in carrying out excavations for buildings, roads, and mines. Accurate knowledge of this stratigraphy is important not only scientifically but also for predicting of subsurface conditions in Pleistocene covered areas to assist with the planning of subsurface investigations, and for the correlation of the information obtained in such work. This is of unusual importance in the highly developed areas of northeastern North America. A splendid example of how this work has been advanced in Pennsylvania is given in a general report issued by the Bureau of Topographic and Geologic Survey, Department of Internal Affairs, of Pennsylvania. The authors, Drs. White, Totten, and Gross, have studied excavations all over northwestern Pennsylvania, notably in new interstate highway construction, expanded strip mining operations for coal, and in quarries for limestone. They have assembled their results in the form of a clearly written report, in maps and in sections, the combination of which is thought to be "the most extensive and complete three-dimensional picture of the glacial materials in any area of comparable size in the world." The availability of this material means that all those engaged on any foundation work in this part of the Commonwealth of Pennsylvania have immediately available an exact general guide to help them in their more-detailed studies. This report is a fine example of the reciprocal service of geology and engineering made publicly available.[5.55]

Preliminary investigations for the Quinnipiac River Bridge in Connecticut, across New Haven Harbor, yielded significant information even in advance of excavation. The engineers responsible for the necessary test borings noticed some organic matter in their samples coming from a depth of from 9 to 12 m below sea level. They passed specimens of this material to members of the U.S. Geological Survey who studied it with the aid of modern methods of investigation such as analysis of the pollen in the samples and dating by the carbon-14 method. When correlated with what was already known of local geology, this information confirmed that the land in the area of New Haven has been rising at the rate of about 1.8 mm per year due to postglacial uplift. This result correlated well with deductions from other geological information available for this part of the New England coast.[5.56]

Further up the New England coast lies the city of Boston, Massachusetts, which will call for repeated reference in this volume, if only because local engineers and geologists have cooperated there in such a remarkable way in recording information from almost all borings put down in the Boston area, and details of the geology encountered in civic engineering works, notably recent tunnels (see page 281). As this information has accumulated, it has been carefully studied in a number of ways, one of which may be mentioned. The local geology is somewhat complex, but in very general terms, the local bedrock is Devonian or Carboniferous in age (probably the latter) and consists under the city proper of argillite and sandstone with some conglomerate and volcanic rocks and of conglomerate with the argillite as a subsidiary constituent to the south of the city, all known as the Boston Bay group. In recent years, a number of cases have been reported of a soft whitish clayey material overlying the bedrock, quite unlike the normal rocks of the Boston Bay group. Dr. C. A. Kaye has studied this material and its occurrence and has reported that kaolinite is the principle mineral found in this strange material. Siderite also occurs in the iron-rich igneous rocks. These alteration products have been found as deep as 90 m beneath the upper surface of the bedrock (in tunnels). There is still doubt as to its origin— whether from weathering or as a result of hydrothermal action or even as the roots of an extensive covering of lateritic soils over this whole area in Tertiary times. Further work on this problem will benefit both the earth sciences and the practice of foundation engineering in the Boston area. The example is illustrative of what can be done in so many cities throughout the world.[5.57]

". . . and we can save 700 lira by not taking soil tests."

chapter six

Excavations Beneath Cities

This navigation begins at the foot of some hills, in which the duke's coals are dug, from whence a canal is cut through rocks, which day-light never enters. By this means large boats are hauled to the innermost parts of those hills (about a mile and a half underground), and being filled there with coals, are brought out by an easy current, which supplies the whole navigation, for the space of about ten miles. At the mouth of the cavern is erected a water-bellows, being the body of a tree, forming a hollow cylinder, standing upright; upon this a woden basin is fixed, in the form of a funnel which receives a current of water from the higher ground. This water falls into the cylinder and issues out of the bottom of it, but at the same time carries a quantity of air with it, which is forced into tin pipes, and forced to the innermost recesses of the coal-pits, where it issues out, as if from a pair of bellows, and rarifies the body of thick air, which would otherwise prevent the workmen from subsisting on the spot where the coals are dug.

From a small book, The History of Inland Navigation . . ., *published anonymously in 1766 but believed to have been written, or inspired, by James Brindley (1716–1772)*

From the very earliest days of history, man has used "holes in the ground" for his own purposes of living, refuge, and burial. The sibyls and nymphs of Roman mythology were known to inhabit caves. The Greek oracles at Delphi, at Corinth, and at Mount Cithaeron all used large natural cavities for their mystic purposes. The River Styx and the waters of Acheron disappeared into a series of caverns widely supposed to lead to the nether regions, probably the first recognition of the fact that in limestone regions it is not uncommon to find flowing streams using underground channels for a part of their courses. The caves of early history, and of prehistory, were usually in limestone country, caverns having been formed by the slow but steady solution of calcium carbonate by natural waters. This simple geological fact dictated the location of some of the very earliest human settlements when the ancestors of the men and women of today used caves for shelter.

Use of natural caverns by animals has been traced back to Pliocene time, but it was in caves that can be dated in the Pleistocene that flint instruments, clearly man-made, were first found together with the remains of animals. Cave dwellers are well recognized as one phase of prehistory not only in Europe but also in Brazil, in Pennsylvania, and even in Australia, to mention but a few locations. It is known that cavemen roamed widely over northern Europe, as far south as the Pyrenees and the Alps. Later came the ages of Neolithic man, and those who used bronze and iron, but all still making use of caves as shelters. Even in central Africa in modern times, David Livingstone found huge caves in which complete tribes would shelter themselves, their goods, and their cattle.

These brief notes, that merely touch upon one unusually interesting aspect of early history, serve well to introduce this chapter in which the uses that modern man makes of "holes in the ground" are to be treated. As wider use is made of deep excavations, and even of natural caverns, in and near cities, and even in place of cities, this is naturally regarded as something generally quite new. It is, rather, a return to a practice that in its essentials predates written history, even though the caveman's simple dwelling is a far cry from the great underground complexes that now exist in many countries as specially secure centers for critical operations. The advantage that caves present because of their uniform temperature and relative humidity must have been noticed by primitive men. This feature is well illustrated by the finding in 1947 of the Dead Sea Scrolls, in a cave by an Arab shepherd, still preserved after almost 2,000 years. These conditions may possibly have led to the development of caves beyond their mere use to the actual excavation of underground spaces specifically for human use, excavation possibly being started simply as extensions to the caves but ultimately going far beyond this, as all visitors to the ancient city of Petra see so clearly today.

Located in the desert part of Jordan about 480 km due east of Cairo, Petra is a phenomenal place even today, many centuries after it ceased to be an active city. It was very largely an underground city, its temples and halls hewn out of the local red sandstone that makes it such a colorful place. Geologically it is located in a great rock basin on the eastern side of the Wadi el-Araba, the great Rift Valley that runs from the Jordan depression to the Gulf of Aqaba. The country around had been traditionally the home of the Horites, who were cave dwellers, predecessors of the Edomites of the Old

Figure 6.1 Petra, Jordan. Ancient rock-cave dwellings, the scale of which can be seen from the human figures in the foreground. *(Photograph by W. and D. Glowacki, Winchester, Mass.)*

Testament. It is uncertain whether any specific reference to Petra can be found in the Bible, but it was certainly in use in the sixth century B.C. It developed into a major trading settlement, reaching the peak of its activity around the year A.D. 100, and lasting until the great Mohammedan conquest of 629–632. For over a thousand years, therefore, this "underground city" served the diverse purposes of its desert residents, becoming an important religious center early in the Christian Era. The appearance today of its temples and its carvings is a salutary reminder that modern man was not the first to think of gaining security by "going underground."[6.1]

Petra was not alone. The neighboring valley of the River Nile has long been regarded as one of the cradles of civilization. There, too, are to be found temples and other spaces for human use carved laboriously out of the solid rock. Probably the best known today are the Temples of Abu Simbel, if only because of the international effort that went into their preservation. Located 280 km upstream of the site of the (new) Aswan High Dam, the great carvings in the immense cliff of the local pink sandstone are so remarkable that they would probably have been long regarded as one of the wonders of the ancient world had they not been lost to sight until 1813, when they were rediscovered, almost completely buried in sand, by the Swiss explorer Burckhardt. Not only did they include the frequently illustrated four immense figures of Ramses II (20 m high), which date the carvings as being probably older than 1200 B.C., but the great temple is an excavation in the cliffside 16.2 by 17.4 m, with a corridor connecting it to an inner sanctuary, extending 60 m into the solid rock. The raising of this masterpiece to obviate its being flooded by the rising waters of the Nile, on completion of the High Dam, is one of the epics of modern foundation engineering, but the temples are mentioned here only to lend further confirmation to man's early use of underground shelter.[6.2]

The use of tunnels was a natural extension of the idea of using underground caverns for habitation and refuge. The occurrence of rivers that disappeared into buried limestone channels must have set ideas running in the heads of some early builders. In Malta, one may still see underground tunnels and gathering places hewn out of solid limestone 5,000 years ago, with flints that must have been brought to the island from the mainland. The Romans were tunnel builders of note. They used tunnels for drainage, for roads, and for water supply. The great tunnel at Lake Fucino, built as a drainage work, was driven through limestone for a distance of 5.6 km, with a cross section of roughly 1.8 by 3.0 m; it is said that 30,000 men were employed on its construction during a period of 11 years. Many similar examples could be given, but all would carry the same message—that the modern tunneler is following in a long tradition.[6.3]

As with most branches of technology and engineering, the Middle Ages saw little advance over what the Romans had done and, to a large extent, a cessation of major engineering work. Probably the main use of tunnels through these long centuries was for access—access to castles of refuge from concealed entrances, and exit from these fortresses as a means of escape. And tunnels are being used today for very similar purposes, although without the romantic glamour that attaches to the hidden passages of the past, the history of which would be a singularly interesting footnote to the history of engineering. With the coming of the Industrial Age, and the development of new means of transport, major tunneling again became necessary. Some of the earliest "modern" tunnels were for the passage of canals through hills that blocked the level routes that such waterways had to follow, some of these dating from the closing years of the eighteenth century. With the coming of railways, the great days of modern tunneling began. Many notable tunnels still in use today within city limits are now more than 100 years old; passing reference will be made to one or two of the more famous in the following pages.

It is of more than passing interest that one of the earliest tunnels of the Industrial Age, constructed for public water supply, is in the New World rather than the Old. Even though the records of its construction give only scanty information about the ground encountered, it is worthy of brief mention as one of the very earliest "city tunnels" of modern times. Very shortly after Benjamin Franklin made his percipient suggestion about the water supply of Philadelphia (see page 132), conditions became so bad that some action had to be taken to get good water to this growing city. After much debate, the scheme of Benjamin La Trobe (who described himself as "the only successful architect and engineer" in America at that time) was accepted and carried out in the year 1801. Water was taken from an intake on the Schuylkill River and conveyed a distance of 90 m through "a subterranean tunnel six feet in diameter . . . cut nearly the whole distance through granite rock." The water was then pumped up to near street level, on Chestnut Street, and conveyed by tunnel to another pumping station at Center Square, a distance of 1,320 m. This tunnel is known to have been built as a brick culvert, having probably been excavated through gravel, although no records have been found to determine this with certainty. It served with satisfaction until 1815, when a new water-supply project was initiated. Subsequent grading down of Chestnut Street removed some of the old tunnel, but that portion east of Seventeenth Street was put to new use to carry sewage toward the end of the century. Dams were built in its invert about the middle of each city block, and false inverts installed sloping each way from the dams to the cross north-and-south streets. It was encountered when excavations for the subway near the city hall were carried out in 1906. Although so little is known about the actual geology encountered by this pioneer tunnel, the men who built it were clearly not unlike tunnelers of today, for the records of its building that do still exist include this item: "Liquor, supplied to workmen, cost $898.44."[6.4]

Two construction operations that have probably never ceased down through the ages were the mining of ores of precious metals and the quarrying for building stone and other building materials. As will be related in the following chapter, many older quarries were actually mines, good stone being "followed underground," and mining methods very similar to those employed in metal mines used for its procurement. These manmade excavations were in many respects more desirable underground

Figure 6.2 Loire Valley, France. A meeting of the Grand Council of Les
Chevaliers de la Chantepleure in a limestone cave used for maturing wine.
(Courtesy of Artaud Freres, Nantes-Carquefou, France, and J. Tassie.)

spaces for human use than natural caverns. In addition, they were not restricted to
limestone areas, building stones and metallic ores being found in a wide variety of
geological formations. Accordingly, another line of historical inquiry is the use, down
the years, of abandoned mines or parts of mines for human activities. There are many
widely distributed examples, especially in Europe, still being used for a variety of
purposes, including the storage of wines while maturing. Probably the most unusual
and still remarkable examples of all are the quarries used for providing the building
stone (and the finishing plaster) for the buildings of Paris until Napoleon put a stop
to this underground quarrying. Since Paris will call for special mention in the next
chapter, this passing reference to the underground of Paris must suffice for now, even
as it serves so well to introduce the modern use of the same sort of underground
excavated space for urban purposes.

6.2 MODERN USE OF OLD MINES AND QUARRIES

Wherever there are unused mines or underground quarries conveniently located
adjacent to or even in city areas, their use for purposes other than for mining can
often prove to be economical. They should not be overlooked, therefore, in planning.
In time of war there has always been a demand for such "safe" space for storage.[6.5]

The Second World War saw great activity in this direction. The salt mines at Hungen, north of Frankfurt, were used by the Germans to store their choicest art treasures during the years of war, including the world-famous bust of Nefertiti, the beautiful Queen of Egypt. One hundred tonnes of treasures from the British Museum were stored, during the same period, in a disused tunnel near Aberystwyth in Wales, while the famous Elgin Marbles were stored in one of the London underground tunnels. In Poland the old salt mines at Wieliczka near Cracow are used permanently as a picture gallery. It is known that the mines from which the famous Bath Stone of England is obtained were put to good use as underground workshops. This was a wartime expedient, but in times of peace, the same mines have been used for growing mushrooms. The even temperature, good ventilation, steady relative humidity, and absence of sunlight combine to make the location ideal for mushroom culture. At one time, 5.2 hectares underground were used for this purpose, producing between 113,000 and 136,000 kg of mushrooms per year. The even temperature is of significance for much more sophisticated uses of underground mines. It was mentioned in connection with the temperature of groundwater but demands this further reference.

The thermal properties of the materials that make up the crust of the earth are such that, under the influence of varying daytime and nighttime temperatures, the temperature of the ground itself will vary in a daily cycle to a depth of only 0.3 m or slightly more. Below this, an annual variation will take place in accord with the annual variation of the average local daily air temperature, daily variations quickly disappearing. In Canada, where annual variations of temperature can range up to 65°C, the depth to which the annual temperature of the ground will vary by more than one degree will vary up to about 10 m. Below this, the temperature will remain sensibly constant throughout the year. It will increase very slowly with depth—about 1°C for every 81 m is a typical figure—due to the flow of heat to the surface from the interior of the earth, but this feature will rarely affect the use of underground space for urban purposes. The steady ground temperature will be close to but not identical with the local average annual air temperature.[6.6] It is this feature that makes the use of underground space, when otherwise convenient, so attractive since air conditioning becomes a very easy matter to arrange at little cost. It is a feature that is now being put to wide use, probably nowhere in the world on so extensive a scale as in the area of Kansas City, Missouri.

This important Midwest urban area is in the middle of a 225-km-wide belt of exposed Pennsylvanian beds. These are subdivided into a number of subgroups, one of which, the Kansas City group, is widely exposed in the vicinity of Kansas City. The group consists of alternating limestones and shales. Many rock escarpments in the area, up to 15 m high, expose different members of the group, quite the most important of which is the Bethany Falls limestone, an excellent building stone. From the closing years of the nineteenth century, quarrying, and eventually mining, of this and associated beds of limestone has steadily increased. The value of such nonmetallic mining is now estimated to be at least $25 million per year. The limestone has been used not only as building stone, but also for making lime and portland cement, for concrete aggregate, and for road construction. Although mined from the surface in early days, the Bethany Falls limestone in particular has now been mined for many years by underground quarrying, many of its exposures permitting of easy access from roads in the area with a minimum of preparatory work for approach to good faces of the rock.

The general method of mining has been to leave standing large pillars of rock to serve as roof supports. The generally level character of the beds results in level floors in the mined-out areas. Groundwater gave little trouble, being encountered only occasionally, so that these large underground areas were generally dry, with the usual constant temperature and steady relative humidity. The total thickness of the Bethany Falls limestone, of from 6 to 7.5 m, resulted in space that was almost ideal for underground operations. There are still about 15 active underground limestone-mining operations in the vicinity of Kansas City, excavating about 4 to 5 hectares each year. But it has been estimated that there are already 1,160 hectares of mined space beneath the area around the city, with 4.7 million m^2 of finished space available for warehousing and other purposes in 21 different mined areas.

Figure 6.3 Kansas City, Missouri. A view inside one of the disused limestone mining areas, showing the naturally level floor and competent rock roof. *(Photograph by Jerry D. Vineyard, courtesy of the Missouri Division of Geological Survey and Water Resources.)*

Figure 6.4 Kansas City, Missouri. One of the entrances to the old limestone mine workings, showing the rock formations involved, and one of the railway tracks that leads to areas now used for storage. *(Photograph by Jerry D. Vineyard, courtesy of the Missouri Division of Geological Survey and Water Resources.)*

     As far back as 1938, Mr. Amber N. Brunson, President, Brunson Instrument Company, in Kansas City, started plans for an underground facility to house his very delicate operations of manufacturing precision instruments . . . . He purchased [a] site and started mining out the space to his rigid requirements, selling the quarried limestone to help defray expenses on the overall development. Today his company is operating in an attractive, efficient plant, a marvel of ingenuity. . . .[6.7]

To this the author can testify, having had the privilege of visiting this pioneer undertaking.

     Today, most if not all of the limestone mining in Missouri is being carried out with eventual use of the mined-out space in mind. The pillars, instead of being left in place to no definite plan, are now geometrically spaced so as to give efficient cleared spaces. Floors are properly graded, and entrances are left with sufficient roof cover to give portals that are safe. So valuable is this space becoming that it has been quite seriously suggested "it might sometimes pay to quarry the rock and throw it in the river, if necessary, to make the mine safe for the future, because the value of the rock mined is but a small portion of the extended value of the space"—so rapidly have the economics of this mining operation changed. But limestone is still in needed in increasingly large quantities, and so underground space in Missouri generally will probably still come from suitable mined-out limestone quarries for some time yet to come.

Almost 60 hectares has now been put to use for industrial purposes in the Kansas City area alone. The J. G. Nicholls underground industrial park, 16 km from the city center, has an area of 4.8 hectares converted into office, manufacturing, and storage space for the individual uses of five tenants. The Epic Manufacturing Company finds underground conditions most suitable for its toolmaking business. Woodward,

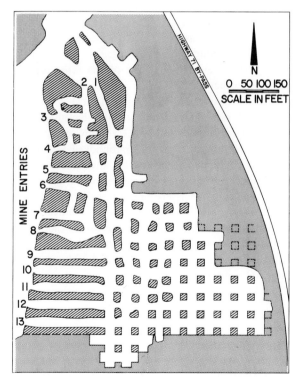

Figure 6.5 Kansas City, Missouri. Plan of old limestone mine workings, showing the random spacing of pillar supports in old workings but the regularly spaced pillars in areas mined with later use envisaged. *(Courtesy of the Missouri Division of Geological Survey and Water Resources, based on a diagram published in* Missouri Mineral News.)

Clyde, Sherard and Associates, consulting soil and foundation engineers, appropriately find the constant temperature and relative humidity conducive to accurate soil testing. Ventilation must naturally be provided and, with this, any necessary adjustment to air temperature and humidity. The plant necessary for this, however, involves but a fraction of both the capital and operating costs for what is required in a normal building. Rock-bolting to secure safe roof rock is occasionally necessary, but in the areas that have been well mined, little extra work is usually found to be necessary prior to the finishing of the space for use. Railroad spurs have been constructed into the inside of some of the areas used for warehousing, from conveniently located tracks of the Missouri Pacific and other railways. The Pixley Company of Independence, Missouri, has a total area of 413,000 m^2 of serviced underground space, with railroad service, now available for use, all excavated by removal of Bethany Falls limestone. Even larger—over 600,000 m^2—is the underground property of the Centropolis Crusher Company, similarly serviced and located on the Manchester Trafficway, two blocks from U.S. Highway 40. One of the other large developments has even been said to contain a clubhouse for underground trout fishermen.[6.8]

With such a fish story, possibly enough has been said to indicate the great utility provided by this vast area of underground mined-out space. It has been described in some detail because of its extent, even though use of the same type of underground areas is to be found in many other locations. It is a possibility to be kept in mind for the planning of future urban growth when local geological conditions are suitable. There are other uses to which old mines adjacent to cities have been put. Naturally not within city limits, but in some cases not too far from urban areas, abandoned salt mines have been used for the storage underground of petroleum products, just as natural gas fields when depleted can be used for the same purpose. This is a highly specialized exercise, always carried out by large petroleum producers in association with public authorities with all due safety precautions so that it does not warrant more than this brief recognition here. It is, however, further indication of the use to which old mines can be put. Even more unusual is the use in the Soviet Union of an abandoned salt mine near the township of Solotvino in Carpathia as a hospital for bronchial asthma sufferers. Patients spend between 7 and 12 hours a day in the converted mine at a depth of 202 m below ground. No medicines are used, but doctors are said to believe that the climate within the mine, coupled with remedial exercises, renders them unnecessary.[6.9]

6.3 LARGE UNDERGROUND EXCAVATIONS

The fact that the pioneer underground factory in the Kansas City area was specially excavated for this civilian use (even though the rock was sold commercially) suggests that major underground excavations may not, even today, be uneconomical when they are needed for special purposes and when rock conditions are suitable. Before attention is directed to tunnels, therefore, a brief account may usefully be given of

Figure 6.6 Wampum, Pennsylvania. Reception room for underground office and laboratory complex in old limestone workings. *(Courtesy of Medusa Portland Cement Co., K. C. Roberts, Director of Mineral Research.)*

one or two major examples of large underground spaces that have been specially excavated for their intended use. All appear to have been constructed with defense purposes in view, but the fact that many such underground urban areas are now in regular use suggests that the day may come when more peaceable purposes may be similarly served on a wide scale instead of only occasionally as at present. Most of the developed countries of the world probably have such underground shelter or work areas, but because of defense implications very little has been published about them beyond the occasional general reference that tells but little about the actual construction of the facilities. Sweden is a country often mentioned as having been very active in the provision of defense shelters for its citizens and underground centers for its civil defense and military workers. Some facts are known about recent Swedish underground works. Figure 6.7 indicates the large scale on which these facilities have been planned and built.

Under the revised Swedish Civil Defense Law of 1 July 1960, all communities of over 5,000 people must be equipped with properly designed "normal shelters." These are usually provided in basements and similar cellars; the legal requirement shows clearly the attention given to civil defense in this strategically located Scandinavian

Figure 6.7 Sweden. Swedish destroyers in a completely underground marine dock; the scale is given by the size of the man near the bow in the foreground. *(Courtesy of the General Director, Fortifikationsforvätningen, Stockholm, Sweden.)*

country. The 14 largest cities and certain important communes are exempted from this provision, but new buildings in the communities around these areas must have their normal shelters designed to take care of an overload of people. It is planned to move out 90 percent of the populations from these larger centers in case of emergency. The 10 percent of these urban populations required for controlling all emergency operations are to be accommodated in deep rock shelters. More than 100 of these unusual facilities have already been constructed at a cost running into tens of millions of dollars. These shelters must have a rock cover of at least 15 m, but some have as much as 30 m of rock above them. Quite a number of these excavations have been designed so that they can be put to use in peacetime so that the investment in them will not be wasted. Typical is the pumping installation for the water-supply system of Göteburg, on Sweden's southwestern coast.[6.10]

Much of the design work in connection with these excavations is related to planned resistance of the effect of bomb explosions; one general feature is the construction of free-standing concrete structures inside the rock excavations to serve as the spaces that will be occupied by people using the shelters. All design, however, is completely dependent upon the existence of satisfactory rock conditions at the site selected for strategic reasons. Not the least of the associated problems is the effect that major rock excavation work will have on the groundwater conditions in the rock around and above the resulting opening. Serious consideration was given to this and to similar problems in the proceedings of an International Symposium on Large Permanent Underground Openings held in Oslo, Norway, in September 1969. The fact that such an international meeting was held will confirm the growing importance of this increasingly frequent interference with the geology beneath cities.[6.11]

Of comparable underground installations in North America, the most notable of those that have been publicly described is undoubtedly the Command Combat Operations Center of the North American Air Defense Command (NORAD) near Colorado Springs, Colorado. Completed in 1962, this completely equipped underground installation is capable of accommodating a total staff of 700, with all services necessary for their living, such as water supply, power supply, and sewage disposal. Excavated almost completely in the local Pike's Peak granite, the center is located in Cheyenne Mountain, reached from the main road running south from Colorado Springs. The access road takes of to the west at Fort Carson, climbing steadily into the Front Range Mountains to the portals of the two access tunnels that are 360 m above the start of this 4-km road. Even the construction of these roads was a construction operation of note; naturally they had to be completed before excavation could start. Preliminary test borings had indicated that the rock was sound enough to permit the excavation of the large chambers necessary, but since excavation was to be in granite, it was known that close examination of the granite would be necessary as excavation progressed. The two approach tunnels are 789 m and 366 m long, respectively, 8.7 m wide, and 6.75 m high. Where the tunnels meet, the great complex of underground chambers starts, a typical excavation being 39 m long, 13.5 m wide, and 18 m high. Rock separation between chambers is as much as 30 m. Within the excavations, three-story steel "buildings," spring-mounted because of possible danger from blast shocks, were erected, and it is in these that the work of the center is done.

A geologist of the U.S. Corps of Engineers mapped the granite exposed as the access tunnels were excavated. This mapping revealed two major joint systems, and all indications were that they would persist into the large chambers. One of the joint systems was oriented in a direction parallel to the length of the largest chambers, the size of which prevented the use of any of the conventional means of roof support should this be found to be necessary. Accordingly, the direction of the chambers was reoriented to a more favorable direction, and excavation was completed as planned. Correspondingly, close geological observation of the excavation at one of the most vital intersections of two main chambers revealed in advance of its completion poor rock conditions. Highly weathered rock was encountered, as was close jointing extending in several directions, and this despite the 420 m of rock cover above. Various methods of dealing with this problem were considered, the final solution being the construction of a reinforced concrete dome at the base of the intersection chamber

Figure 6.8 Colorado. Construction of the NORAD underground command center in progress, the view showing the formwork and reinforcing steel for the reinforced concrete dome used at the major tunnel intersection. *(Courtesy of the Commanding Officer, North American Air Defense Command, Colorado.)*

and its jacking up into place below the imperfect rock roof, together with an integrated reinforced concrete lining to the chamber. These details of structural design are mentioned since they were developed during the course of the work based on the acute observation of the geology as exposed by excavation, a procedure that will call for repeated mention in this volume. Few examples could be so clearly illustrative of the need for constant vigilance in connection with subsurface conditions until excavation is complete.[6.12]

Brief reference should again be made to the fact that underground manmade excavations are now being specially designed and carried out for the storage of vital materials such as petroleum products, although only in the vicinity of cities rather than actually in urban areas. Especially notable is the storage installation for naval fuels at the great naval base of Pearl Harbor, Honolulu, where 20 cylindrical vaults were excavated in the local volcanic lava rock to hold steel storage cylinders 30 m in diameter and 75 m high.[6.13] Vast underground storage facilities were found elsewhere to have been built during the war years, one particular German installation having involved the removal of 5 million m³ of rock. These, however, were in days when normal economics did not apply. Wartime examples are thus briefly noted again, however, to emphasize that such underground spaces can easily be secured if local geology is appropriate, civil engineering design and construction procedures being now able to provide quite remarkable "holes in the ground" (to use once again the popular tag that has sometimes been applied to these really remarkable facilities).

Nowhere has this been better shown, probably, than in the steadily increasing number of underground powerhouses and pumping stations that form integral parts of hydroelectric projects all round the world. In Australia, all the main powerhouses for the great Snowy Mountains project are located deep underground, following most detailed preliminary geological investigations. Some of the largest examples of these hidden temples of power are in Canada. The main hall of the Kemano power station of the Aluminum Company of Canada, for example, is 342 m long, 24.6 m

Figure 6.9 Churchill Falls, Newfoundland-Labrador, Canada. Construction of the Churchill Falls underground water-power station in progress; the stainless steel ceiling has been erected and the excavation for the draft tubes may be seen, the man in the foreground showing the scale; 11 turbines and generators will eventually generate 7 million horsepower in this one station. *[Courtesy of the Churchill Falls (Labrador) Corporation Ltd., D. D. Willock, Director of Public Relations.]*

wide, and 41.7 m high—big enough to enclose a cathedral. Pride of place, however, must be given to the powerhouse at Churchill Falls, the controlling feature of the great hydroelectric project in Newfoundland-Labrador. Here the excavation for the generator hall is 46.2 m high, almost 300 m long, and 24.3 m wide. Even the underground transformer gallery is 256.8 m long, 15 m wide, and 11.7 m high. The successful excavation of these vast man-made caverns is absolutely dependent upon adequate preliminary investigation of the rock to be excavated, and of that all around the openings, the forming of which is an example of the art of tunneling on an unusually large scale.[6.14]

6.4 THE ART OF TUNNELING

The fact that great underground excavations such as these power stations can now be designed with every confidence in advance of construction is clear indication of the advanced state of the art of tunneling and of the possibility of predicting with reasonable accuracy underground geological conditions. Use of the word "art" to describe the operation of modern tunneling is a reminder that, if only because all such work is carried out in rock or soil, with all of nature's inevitable uncertainty, there can never be a "science" of tunneling. Experience and intuitive judgment in the face of subsurface conditions, as they are revealed day by day as a tunnel advances, will always be essential for successful tunnel work. It will be clearly evident that no tunneling should ever be contemplated without a most careful study of the probable subsurface conditions to be encountered, never forgetting the problems that groundwater can create. It may well be said that, important as geology is in all civil engineering work, there is no branch of any engineering work in which geology can be applied to better effect than as an absolutely essential aid to tunnel construction.

There must be few, if any, modern cities that do not have a variety of tunnels serving the needs of their citizens but generally out of mind and hidden from view beneath city streets. This was true even of some Roman cities. It is a common feature today of cities all round the world. All who know the city of London think instinctively of its famous tube railway system, the "UndergrounD" being one of the most remarkable of all subsurface railway tunnel systems. The subways of New York are similarly known by all visitors to the metropolis. Modern travelers by air to New York quickly become familiar with the convenience provided by the great vehicular tunnels beneath the East River and the Hudson River in giving such quick access to Manhattan. And those who still know the pleasure and convenience of train travel know that they pass through long tunnels in approaching one of New York's great rail terminals, again under the Hudson and East Rivers. Few who use the Pennsylvania Railroad tunnels under the East River in coming in to the Pennsylvania Station probably give a thought to the fact that they are using one of the true pioneer subaqueous tunnels of North America, the construction of which even today reads like an epic.

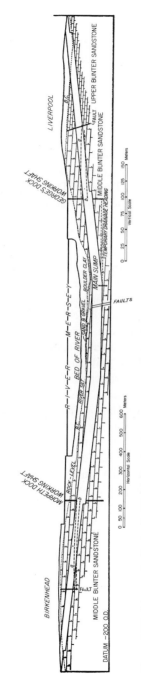

Figure 6.10 Liverpool, England. Geological section along the center line of the underwater section of the Queensway Vehicular Tunnel under the River Mersey, connecting Liverpool with Birkenhead, Cheshire; *a–a* a probable water level after pumping stopped; *b–b* water level under conditions of maximum pumping. *(Courtesy of the Liverpool Geological Society.)*

Other cities are well served also by tunnels. England's great port of Liverpool has its traffic greatly assisted by the largest of all subaqueous tunnels, the Mersey Tunnel connecting Liverpool with Birkenhead. Well over 3.2 km long and 13.2 m in internal diameter, its successful completion was due directly to accurate advance knowledge of the Bunter sandstone through which it was constructed. So useful has it proved that it has been duplicated with a second Mersey twin-tube vehicular tunnel, while an earlier railway tunnel still continues to serve in transporting passengers beneath the busy waters of the River Mersey.[6.15] The even busier port of Rotterdam in the Netherlands is similarly served by a modern vehicular tunnel constructed beneath the River Scheldt at one of its busiest sections. Many cities have their traffic flows aided by smaller vehicular tunnels through rocky hills that lie across the desirable routes for thruways. One thinks of the Fort Pitt Tunnel in Pittsburgh (shortly to be described), the Kingsway Tunnel in London, the tunnel at the end of the Jana Svermy Bridge in Prague, and many more. The portals of many of these tunnels within city limits have been attractively finished so as to be architecturally pleasing rather than being a disfigurement to the city. In fact, one sometimes gets the idea that tunnels have come to be on occasion a civic attraction. The suspicion sometimes arises that provision of a tunnel rather than a more mundane open cut was utilized as a prestige symbol. There is certainly one tunnel in northeastern North America that is said by those who know to have been demanded by civic authorities, even at a cost much in excess of what an open cut at the same location would have involved.

Far more numerous, although usually on a smaller scale within urban limits, are the tunnels that the public never sees—those that carry urban services such as water, sewage, electrical cables, and even (as at Niagara Falls) water under pressure for power generation. The 25.6-km labyrinth beneath Washington, D.C., of tunnels for heating purposes that serve buildings of the United States government achieved some unusual publicity at the end of 1970, this being probably the first time that most citizens realized that there was under their streets this modern equivalent of the sewers of Paris. Possibly the most remarkable of such service tunnels is the "Post Office Tube" in London, another tube railway 10.4 km long but only 2.7 m in diameter, in which small automatic trains operate regularly on a 60-cm-gauge track, conveying the mails between railway terminals and the main postal terminal. Sewer and water tunnels are frequently under construction in cities, either by actual tunneling below ground or by what is called the "cut-and-cover" method. The latter involves the excavation from the surface of a trench deep enough to reach to the invert level of the tunnel, the lining for which is then placed and immediately covered up, the ground being restored to its accustomed state. Never an easy construction operation, cut-and-cover work is a great deal easier to execute then actual tunneling, even though it may disrupt adjacent services while work is in progress. These are the two main ways in which tunnels are provided for urban use. There is one further special and quite unusual method that can be used for subaqueous tunnels; it will be described later in this chapter.

The same basic steps (continually modified) have marked tunnel construction from Roman times, through the primitive canal tunnels of the eighteenth century, to the progressively larger and more complex tunnels of today. The face of the tunnel must be drilled and blasted if in rock, or excavated with suitable tools if in soil; the excavation ("muck" to the tunneler) must then be removed from the face and taken out of the tunnel; when necessary, a lining of appropriate design and necessary strength is then placed within the excavated bore and the tunnel finished off for its intended use. If water is present at the level of the tunnel, it can provide real problems. It may be possible to drain it, even temporarily, as Robert Stephenson did in the case of the famous Kilsby Tunnel in England, but this will not usually be practicable in urban areas because of possible damage due to the lowering of the water table. In exceptional cases, for short sections only, it may be possible to freeze the water and so tunnel through the frozen mass of soil, rock, and ice.

The usual procedure, however, is to place suitable barriers in the tunnel and then to increase the air pressure in the working area, the increase in air pressure being sufficient to hold back the groundwater while tunneling proceeds. Easy to describe, this is probably the most difficult of all civil engineering operations to carry out successfully. Great risks have to be run. The danger of a disease called "bends" is always present for the workmen despite the most stringent safety precautions that always govern the use of "compressed-air work" (as it is called) in all urban areas. It should, therefore, be avoided if at all possible. This possibility will be evident only from a most detailed geological study of the ground around, above, and below the line of the proposed tunnel, as an example (on page 303) will demonstrate. An almost unsuspected danger with compressed air was experienced during the construction of the new Victoria line in London, the first tube railway to be constructed there for 30 years. At one location where compressed air was being used in the Woolwich and Reading water-bearing sands that lie beneath the London clay, it had the effect of forcing into a neighboring tunnel, also under construction, the air that had been trapped throughout geological time in the voids of the sand. This long-stagnant air was deficient in oxygen and could have led to fatalities, although fortunately it did not in this case.[6.16] The same phenomenon has been noted in other tunnels in Melbourne and Seattle, for example, where two excavations were being worked in close proximity, one under air and in porous material.

No apology need be offered for describing such a detail of construction practice since all such practice in tunnel work is so directly related to the exact state of the ground, to the geology of the strata being penetrated. This is equally true of the means by which access is gained to tunnels. In the case of tunnels in hilly country, access can often be gained by driving in small tunnels from appropriate levels on hillsides as far as the line of the main tunnel, then turning in both directions and driving the tunnel along its designed route. These access tunnels are known as *adits*. For a tunnel that is to pierce a hill from one side to the other, operations can start right on the tunnel line at either one or both portals. But in the case of most service tunnels in urban areas, neither of these simple starts is possible, and *shafts* have to be sunk from ground surface exactly on, or very close to, the center line of the tunnel, down to the proper level for the tunnel. From enlargements at the bottoms of such shafts, work can proceed in both directions. The shafts will be used for removal of the muck, for transferring survey lines down to the line of the tunnel, and for all access purposes.

Shaft construction is therefore an integral part of the tunneling process. It can often prove to be even more difficult than the building of the tunnel itself. The tunnel will be located, so far as is practicable, in geological strata that will be as good as possible for the actual tunneling. The shaft to reach the tunnel, however, has to penetrate all the strata lying between the ground surface and the tunnel invert level. These have to be taken as they come; they cannot be selected as can the material in which the tunnel will be driven. The presence of water-bearing beds on the line of the shaft but above the tunnel level can be particularly difficult. A variety of construction procedures is available for dealing with this situation, such as water-lowering immediately around the shaft with wellpoints, chemical consolidation of the ground just around the shaft, or freezing of the water in a cylinder around the shaft. Selection of the method of attack is the task of the tunnel engineers, but it can be made only on the basis of accurate knowledge of the geological formations that have to be penetrated, and their characteristics.

The nature of the ground will also influence the number of shafts that are to be put down, in many cases. Clearly, the more shafts the faster can tunnel work progress. But shaft sinking, and the provision of the necessary services at the shaft, is expensive, much more so if water-bearing ground is going to be encountered. Frequently, therefore, a single shaft will be used for quite long tunnels in urban areas, especially since this will disrupt street traffic to minimum extent. It is often quite surprising how much work can be carried out from a relatively few shafts. The 22.4-km Victoria tube line in London was constructed using only 51 shafts, all strategically located such as the one in the Green Park. To many Londoners, the only sign they saw of the Victoria line works was the raised roadway at Oxford Circus, and this soon came to be accepted as commonplace. Yet under this simple-looking cover a complete and complex station was reconstructed, and from the 51 shafts a vitally important dual-tube railway was constructed. Only when it was completed could normal access be gained to it from its end connections with other lines.[6.17]

Provision of a lining to a new tunnel is another important design that has to be made before work begins, although always subject to change when excavation has revealed what ground conditions really are, as distinct from those that were predicted. Again geology holds the key. If, for example, excavation is to be through shale, then possible slaking of the rock when exposed to air must be anticipated. All sewer tunnels excavated in the downtown section of Toronto, Canada, have to be sprayed with a cement mixture as soon as they are exposed to prevent air from weakening the shale. If so protected, the shale will stand for some time, but linings are naturally necessary. Linings are sometimes called for to reduce friction losses in tunnels in

Figure 6.11 Toronto, Ontario, Canada. Construction of the Toronto Mid-Town Interceptor Tunnel in progress in 1970; a surveying instrument for tunnel alignment is in the foreground; excavation is in shale, and the use of steel ribs, steel mesh with rock bolts, and surface grouting of the rock—all as protective measures—can be seen. *(Courtesy of the Department of Works, Engineering Division, Metropolitan Toronto, F. J. Horgan, Chief Engineer.)*

which water is to flow (as water or sewage), even though the rock may be competent enough to stand unlined on its own. Sometimes light linings such as sprayed cement or concrete mixes will suffice. In most cases of urban tunnels, however, some type of permanent lining will be necessary, if only, in the case of vehicular tunnels, for the sake of appearance. If rock conditions are such that pressure may be exerted on the lining, or if the tunnel is to be itself a pressure tunnel that will lead to forces being exerted on the soil or rock around, then the design of the lining becomes a somewhat complex exercise in structural design.

All these features of tunnel work—the provision, or not, of lining, the number of shafts and the nature of the ground they will penetrate, the possibility of the tunnel being wet, the nature of the material to be excavated and so the methods of excavation to be planned—are completely dependent upon the geological formations to be encountered. Preliminary subsurface investigations for tunnel work are therefore of essential importance. In the case of tunnels running below open country—tunnels that are parts of major water-power or water-supply schemes, for example—much can be done by expert examination of the surface geology if this is amenable to predictive interpretation. The routes of tunnels under cities, however, are usually covered at least in part by paved streets or buildings, and so such surface interpretative work cannot be done. Even when there is available a good collection of information about the local geology, such as will be described in Chap. 9, accurate test borings and sampling will still be an essential supplementary check.

No risks can be run in tunnel work; every possible certainty must attach to assumed conditions when contract arrangements are made for tunnel construction. This attention to preliminary studies is also essential in order that costs may be accurately calculated. Although construction economics do not call for frequent mention in this volume, they are always there in the background of all planning for urban development. By eliminating many uncertainties, preliminary and continuing study of the geology to be encountered on all civic works can contribute notably to economy in the carrying out of such developments. Nowhere is this more certain than in tunnel construction. Through the accumulated experience on tunnel work that has now been recorded, and much of it published, it is possible to calculate with reasonable accuracy in advance of construction what the cost of a completed tunnel will be. This is of great service in that consideration of the economics of alternative solutions that is so vital a part of the planning process. Even for preliminary studies of such alternatives there is now available most useful information on tunnel costs, a publication derived from the extensive studies made in connection with California's great water project being of special value.[6.18]

In view of the need that can even now be seen for a great increase in the use of tunnels in urban development, there has been much public discussion of and research into what is called "high-speed tunneling." All such studies are of interest and may possibly lead to useful results, but no matter what advances may be made in tunneling techniques—and they cannot depart from the basic elements noted on page 273— tunnel geology will still be the final determinant. Even with the most sophisticated equipment, bad ground will always be bad ground, requiring human judgment and human skills for its penetration that no machine can ever replace. Water problems, especially the unexpected ones, will continue to be the tunneler's nightmare and may even cause more trouble than usual if complex and expensive machines have to be protected in tunnel headings. This has already been demonstrated in the use of machines that are now in regular use for the actual boring out of straight tunnel runs when geological conditions are suitable. Commonly dubbed "moles," these ingenious modern machines are essentially large-scale boring machines that grind out the rock at the cutting face by means of a variety of types of cutting head. Initially used in connection with softer rocks such as shales, they have now been extended in their use to bore through limestones and in exceptional cases through the more easily excavated igneous rocks. Their use is bound to continue and to develop, and this will be a fruitful advance in tunneling, even though their use in no way eliminates the need for continual attention to geology, both before work commences and while it is in progress. In fact, it could be suggested that the need for accurate prediction of rock conditions is even more important when a mole is being used for excavation than when normal methods are to be used, if this did not involve attempting to surpass an already essential requirement.

Typical was the use of an American-built machine for a tailrace tunnel in Tasmania. This tunnel, 4,380 m long and 4.8 m in diameter, had to be driven on a straight line through reasonably homogeneous hard mudstone (a form of shale). Trouble was encountered with groundwater at one location, but this was overcome. The tunnel was completed with progress for the last half averaging 125.4 m per week

Figure 6.12 Winnipeg, Manitoba, Canada. A typical example of a utility tunnel serving a major city, this being the Winnipeg Aqueduct Branch II Tunnel under the Red River, after excavation but before the installation of the 167.6-cm diameter reinforced concrete pipe that constituted the aqueduct. Excavation was in limestone of the Ordovician Red River formation, water bearing as may be clearly seen, the concrete lining in the lower section being an attempt to control water inflow, later sealed off by grouting. *(Courtesy of the City of Winnipeg Water Works and Waste Disposal Division, and of F. W. Render.)*

(with three shifts at work), 166.2 m being excavated in one week. Dust was a problem, surprisingly, in the handling of the ground-up rock by conveyor belt into narrow-gauge cars that removed it from the tunnel.[6.19]

Beneath the streets of Chicago a mole has been successfully used for tunneling in the local dolomitic limestone. A storm sewer beneath the suburb of Alsip is 5.12 m in diameter. It was bored out using a tunneling machine with special cutting heads at a rate of 1.8 m per hour, as much as 41.7 m in one day, and an average penetration of 420 m per month.[6.20] At the other extreme is the use of a mole for excavating the unusually difficult subsoil of Mexico City, already mentioned in connection with foundations (see page 205). Here the working face would have been so weak as to render full-face boring impossible without the use of a special steel bulkhead that isolates the cutting face and holds it in place by means of a bentonite slurry kept under pressure.[6.21]

The art of tunneling is, therefore, one of the most unusual of the construction operations that are needed to develop the cities of today. As cities increase in size and the services provided to citizens are steadily extended, as traffic needs make inevitable the development of underground rapid-transit systems, and as earlier objections to "living underground" gradually disappear, it appears to be certain that tunnels will have an increasingly important part to play in the urban planning of the future. Their efficient use can be contemplated only when local geological conditions are known. Their construction can be safely and economically completed even beneath the most crowded and complex parts of cities if advance planning is well done and if construction is carried out by experienced tunnelers, all against a background of continuing attention to the subsurface conditions that have to be encountered. The use of machines such as moles will undoubtedly increase as more experience is gained with them, but only when subsurface conditions are suitable for this mechanical aid. And the maintenance of tunnels beneath city streets will always continue to be a matter requiring the highest priority, necessitating the preparation and proper use of most accurate records of all tunnels "as constructed." To illustrate the use of tunnels in cities, there are innumerable examples that could be cited, some world famous and already well recorded, others equally important, even if sometimes smaller in scale than some of the more famous city tunnels and not so well known. A small selection of these lesser-known tunnels will be presented to illustrate some aspects of the art of tunneling, with only passing reference to major tunnels the construction of which can be read about elsewhere.

6.5 TUNNELS FOR CIVIC SERVICES

The provision of water throughout the area of a large city has always required extensive underground works, and so water-supply tunnels and tunnels for water-distribution systems have occupied a leading place in major civil engineering works in urban areas for many decades. Both London and New York have major tunnels beneath their streets carrying water to distribution reservoirs. The supply of water to New York, as was noted on page 151, has required the construction of some of the longest major tunnels of the world. Correspondingly, the disposal of waste water, and storm water running off city streets, can be effected in all normal cities only by means of buried pipes. When large these become tunnels so that waste-water tunnels constitute another major group of civic subsurface works of wide extent and great interest. They will become of increasing importance as more and more cities give that proper attention to sewage treatment and disposal that is so imperative if the environment is to be protected. One feature of this significant development is the concept of regionalizing such services in the interest of economy and efficiency. In turn, this very sound development will lead to the need for unusually large tunnels beneath the streets of cities in order to handle the resulting combined discharges. Detroit, for example, has already started on a regional sewage plan. One of the first works required was a 45-km long intercept, or tunnel, and this is but a beginning.[6.22]

The famous sewers of Paris are a reminder from history of the service that such tunnels provide, even as they show—to all who have seen them or seen views of them—the size of tunnel that was required for these services in the early years of such a "modern" development. To illustrate what a medium-sized, modern, and well-served city requires, consider Edmonton, Alberta. Edmonton, now the sixth city of Canada, is the capital of the western province of Alberta. Located about latitude 54°N, it is commonly referred to as the "Gateway to the North," being an important trans-shipment point for traffic going to Canada's western Arctic. Its population of about half a million reside on both sides of the North Saskatchewan River. The University of Alberta, mentioned on page 197, lies south of the river, with the central and older part of the city to the north. Excellent civic services have been provided for this rapidly developing urban area, typified by the fact that beneath the city streets are now over 112 km of tunnels serving as sewers, from 1.2 to 4.8 m in diameter. Water is supplied through pipe mains, but even for this service 4 km of tunnel have had to be constructed. Beneath the city's surface lie Pleistocene sands and gravels, glacial till, and lake sediments overlying Cretaceous bedrock consisting of poorly consolidated shales and sandstone with some coal seams, heavily eroded in some locations by glacial action. Tunnels have therefore to be driven through a variety of materials, but the city has developed appropriate construction methods, the selection of which is determined by the strata to be penetrated, which are always investigated by preliminary studies. Typical is the regular use of an electrically driven mole (a machine described on page 276) capable of excavating tunnels up to 5.4 m diameter. Power is supplied by flexible cables fed down 60-cm-diameter holes drilled from the surface, at intervals of 150 m, in advance of the tunnel excavation. When the tunnel bore reaches one of these holes, a new cable is threaded down from the surface and serves as the supply line for the next 150 m. The vertical holes are later lined and used as manholes.[6.23]

A common feature of earlier sewer arrangements in cities located on rivers was to have sewage collected and discharged into the watercourses by sewers generally at right angles to the direction of flow. As sewage-treatment plants are steadily being installed by major cities, and other sanitary improvements made, one common feature is the building of major "interceptor" sewers parallel to rivers, picking up sewage from these feeder sewers and conveying it to a treatment plant on the river bank usually located downstream from the city area. Ottawa, capital city of Canada, constructed in the late sixties such a main collector in the form of a tunnel parallel to the Ottawa River. It is 9.6 km long, and its invert is generally about 19.5 m below ground level. Part was built through the local limestone and shale beds, but the eastern end, where the inside diameter is 2.4 m, was driven through the Leda clay. The pressure exerted upon the tunnel by this sensitive material was successfully measured. Tribute to the excellent tunneling methods employed, the tight lining installed, and the properties of the Leda clay was the absence of any settlement at the surface above the tunnel, although the local groundwater situation was disturbed at least temporarily.[6.24]

Somewhat similar, although driven through much more difficult ground conditions, was the East Branch Ohio River Interceptor Tunnel at Cincinnati, driven in 1958–1959. This 9.6-km sewer will pick up sanitary flow from downtown Cincinnati

Figure 6.13 Ottawa, Canada. Section of steel lining for main sewer tunnel erected in laboratory for the installation of earth-pressure instrumentation. *(Photograph by H. Schade, courtesy of DBR/NRC.)*

and from the hills to the east, conveying it to the New Mill Creek Sewage Treatment works. Ground conditions were known to be a mixture of river-deposited clays, silts, sand, and gravel, with a high water table that was responsive to all changes in the level of the adjacent Ohio River. Since the tunnel was at a relatively shallow but variable depth, the possibility of damage to the many structures under which it was to penetrate was fully appreciated. In advance of construction, all structures were photographed and existing damage recorded. Bench marks were established so that any settlements could be accurately measured. Tunneling had been decided upon in view of the commercial and industrial area through which the route of the sewer passed. Typical was the presence of a large steel gasholder with a deep water-filled pit, enclosed in brick-masonry walls to act as a seal, the walls penetrating to a depth below the invert of the tunnel and only 4.8 m from the center line of the sewer at the most critical point. The pit was emptied of water as a safety precaution, but no settlement of the holder occurred. Another critical section was where the tunnel had to pass the 100-year-old brick building of St. Anthony's Church. The route was actually changed to increase from 6.6 to 13.5 m the clearance between the tunnel and the tower and steeple of the church. Compressed air was used here and at other critical sections of the tunnel. Although about 2.5 cm of settlement developed in the ground near the church, the building itself showed no indication of any settlement. The tunnel was completed in the face of these most difficult conditions and through this critically important urban area with no serious troubles and no damage to structures. Even from this summary account, it will be clear that such a result was possible only in view of the singularly accurate advance information that was made available on all subsurface conditions, utilized by expert design engineers and contractors.[6.25]

The city of Boston provides excellent examples of tunnels for water supply, as well as for drainage and sewage, not only because of the notable construction projects involved in their building but for a further reason that will be described in the last section of this chapter. Metropolitan Boston is located around the deeply indented bay that forms the famous Boston harbor, with the Charles River coming in from the west, past Cambridge, and the Neponset River from the south. The local bedrock geology is most complex, but it has naturally been intensively studied so that its main features are well known. The main feature is what is locally known as Boston basin; this is marked on Fig. 6.14. The Boston beds that occupy this basin are generally divided into the Roxburgh conglomerate and the Cambridge argillite. To the north, the latter is in contact with the Lynn volcanic rocks. Over all these folded and jointed rocks lie the surface soil deposits with an interest all their own, as will be explained elsewhere in this volume. From Fig. 6.14 it will be seen that all the tunnels marked lie within the Boston basin, except for the Malden Tunnel that crosses its northern boundary. All the tunnels other than the Dorchester Bay Tunnel (built in the 1880s) were projects of the Metropolitan District Commission of the Commonwealth of Massachusetts, through its Construction Division. Geologists on the staff of the commission and special consultants were able to carry out the necessary

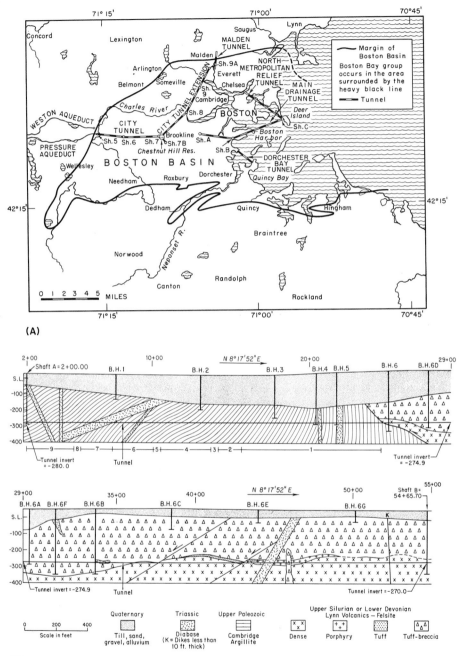

(A)

(B)

Quaternary   Triassic   Upper Paleozoic   Upper Silurian or Lower Devonian
Lynn Volcanics — Felsite

Till, sand,   Diabase   Cambridge   Dense   Porphyry   Tuff   Tuff-breccia
gravel, alluvium   (K = Dikes less than   Argillite
           10 ft. thick)

Figure 6.14 Boston, Massachusetts. *(a)* Index map showing the location of the principal tunnels in Boston and the outline of the Boston basin; *(b)* geological section along the Malden Tunnel showing relation of bore holes to geological structure and the fault discussed in the text. *(Courtesy of M. P. Billings and the Boston Society of Civil Engineers, from references 6.26 and 6.28.)*

282

preliminary investigations, including test borings into rock as necessary, so that all the recent tunnels were completed without undue difficulty, all by experienced contractors.

The Main Drainage Tunnel is 11.4 km long, for a large part of its length under the waters of the harbor. It was constructed between 1954 and 1959. It consists of two main headings connecting three shafts, two of which were used as main construction shafts. Between shaft *A* and shaft *B* the tunnel was 3 m in diameter; between shaft *B* and shaft *C*, 3.45 m in finished diameter. The full tunnel was lined with a concrete lining up to 60 cm in thickness so that the tunnels as excavated were slightly more than 3.6 m and 4.05 m in diameter, respectively. The rocks penetrated were the Cambridge argillite, which proved to be the most competent, requiring steel supports for only 11 percent of its exposure, and the Dorchester shale of the Roxbury formation, the least competent, requiring supports for 87 percent of its exposed length. A short stretch of conglomerate in the Dorchester formation was sound, the shales and argillites being the rocks that required almost continuous support. Much jointing and many minor faults were encountered, but these did not seriously influence the need for support.[6.26]

The City Tunnel Extension constructed between 1951 and 1956 is almost the same length as the Main Drainage Tunnel (11.4 km). It is also through solid bedrock for its entire length, its invert being between 30 and 117 m below mean low sea level, with ground level above the tunnel rising to 60 m above this datum. The tunnel had a finished diameter of 3 m but an excavated diameter of about 4.05 m. It conveys water from the Chestnut Hill Reservoir in western Boston to the southwestern part of Malden. The tunnel, located within the Boston basin, penetrated the same type of rocks as did the Main Drainage Tunnel, but they proved to be much better for tunneling, only 5.6 percent of the total length requiring steel supports; one-third of this was in weak shales. Another third was related to dikes, the remainder to shear zones at faults in the rocks, joints, and fractures. The tunnel cuts diagonally across one of the major folds within the Boston basin and so revealed geological information of much interest. One hundred and six faults were mapped, most of them with apparent displacements of only a few meters but with 17 cases of more than the height of the tunnel.[6.27]

The Malden Tunnel is the last to have been built, its construction taking place in 1957–1958. It is slightly less than 1.6 km long and forms part of the Spot Pond Brook Flood Control Project. Figure 6.14 will show why it was known in advance that the tunnel would pass through the northern boundary of the Boston basin. Since this was believed to be a major fault, bad driving was to be expected. The location of the contact was determined with reasonable accuracy by test borings and drilling, the results of which are shown in Fig. 6.14. Excavation proved the accuracy of the predictions, driving in the vicinity of the major fault—for the existence of the fault was clearly demonstrated when excavation got to the contact—being difficult. Fifty-two percent of the total length of tunnel required steel supports, all in the vicinity of the fault.

Figure 6.15 Boston, Massachusetts. Construction view in the City Tunnel looking east from main shaft, showing effect of the dip of rock strata on the tunneling operation. *(Courtesy of the Metropolitan District Commission, Construction Division, M. F. Cosgrove, Deputy Chief Engineer, and of M. P. Billings.)*

The actual contact of the Lynn felsite to the north and the Cambridge argillite to the south was tight on the west side of the tunnel but had a gouge-filled separation of about 2.5 cm on the east side. The effect of the faulting, however, had been to shear the rocks on both sides very seriously, with the result that a great deal of water was encountered, all of which could be attributed to the fractured condition of the rock. Pumping rates varied but reached an average of 5.5 million liters per day for February 1958, in contrast to the relatively dry state of the two other tunnels that have been described. Invert of the tunnel was 82.5 m below the local datum, land surface varying between 1.8 and 17.1 m above. The tunnel has a finished internal diameter of 3.75 m and was mainly driven from the southern of the two shafts at its ends.[6.28] Readers who have occasion to visit Boston may find interest in remembering these great bores that lie beneath the streets of the city and beneath its harbor, but they are quite typical of the tunnels that serve all cities of the modern world.

Water supply, sewage, drainage and flood control—these are the main services so greatly aided by modern tunneling beneath cities. There is one further major civic service that only rarely involves the use of tunnels, and that is the provision of power. Power will usually be brought to a city from distant water-power stations or be generated within or close to the city in thermal plants, transmission lines, and buried electrical cables transmitting the power to distribution substations. With increasing demands for power, there has been a steady increase in the voltage used for transmission over long-distance high-tension transmission lines. This is now being reflected in the voltages used for the interconnecting links between substations in major cities. So far has this development proceeded that cables are now being used for this purpose that must be artificially cooled. Merely burying such vital power links is not, therefore, sufficient. They must be placed in tunnels of such size that access can be gained to the cables for maintenance and for the operation of whatever system is used for cooling. Tunnels are called for, and already some notable examples have been built for this special purpose. A recent cable tunnel in England illustrates so well some of the considerations that must be looked into when subaqueous tunnels have to be constructed that it will be described in Sec. 6.9 rather than here, but it may then be recalled that it is an example of a type of service tunnel for which there will now be an increasing demand in major cities.

Only rarely does one find major water-power plants adjacent to cities, but there is one location that is a notable exception to this pattern—the cities of Niagara Falls in New York and in Ontario. These municipalities occupy an almost unique position so that what has been done for modern power development in their vicinity will hold few lessons for other cities. It is, however, of such general interest and shows so well what can be done in tunneling under a city that it will be very briefly described. In postwar years, two great new power stations were constructed, one on each side of the Niagara River gorge, in order to utilize more efficiently the fall of Niagara and the extra water made available by international agreement, in association with remedial works at and above the Falls. On the United States side, reinforced concrete conduits were constructed, somewhat to the west of the city, each equivalent in size to six double-track railroad tunnels. These convey the water to the United States powerhouse under ordinary flow but not under pressure. In order to construct them, rock cuts were excavated as deep as 45 m below the original ground-surface level.[6.29]

On the Canadian side, the Canadian share of water for the new powerhouse is conveyed immediately under the city of Niagara Falls in two pressure tunnels, each 13.5 m in finished diameter and 8.1 km long. Once past the city, the tunnels connect with massive shafts, through which the water comes up into the last 3.6 km of its journey, which is in open canal. The tunnels were most carefully located in relation to the local geology, which is well shown in Fig. 6.16, the strata selected for the tunnel location being expected to be competent rocks, as they proved to be in excavation. Even the canal was designed to take advantage of the local geology, its invert being located on the Grimsby sandstone for ease in construction and rising slowly as the bed of sandstone rose, its width being increased to compensate for the decreasing depth. (This was very clearly explained during construction on one of the best "public geological" displays that the author has seen.) Accurate measurements were taken during the construction of the tunnels. These showed that, in the first tunnel to be

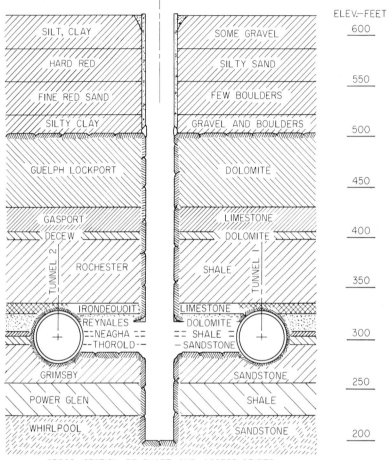

CROSS SECTION OF SHAFT AND ACCESS DRIFTS

Figure 6.16 Niagara Falls, Ontario, Canada. Geological section under Niagara Falls, Ontario, showing the location of the twin tunnels for the Sir Adam Beck water-power development near construction shaft no. 1. *(Courtesy of the Hydro Electric Power Commission of Ontario, H. A. Smith, Chief Engineer.)*

excavated, there was a movement inward of the rock on the central diameter of about 2.5 cm in the 180 days that elapsed before concreting. Due to the release of the confining effect of the surrounding rock, this "rebound" was as expected from theoretical considerations, and its rate confirmed that almost the maximum movement had then been experienced. In the parallel second tunnel, constructed some little time after the first, the corresponding movement was little more than one-quarter that experienced in the first tunnel, giving clear indication of the stress relief provided by the initial excavation. These technical details are mentioned in order to confirm yet again that, in dealing with rock (and soil), one is dealing with quite "normal" materials that will exhibit the ordinary behavior of structural materials under stress.[6.30]

6.6 TUNNELS FOR RAILWAYS

Railways appear to be going through a transitional phase in North America when considered as a means of passenger transport, even though they are still playing such a vital role in this field elsewhere throughout the world. There are many who consider that they will continue to provide an essential part of integrated passenger transportation systems. Their incorporation within cities of the future should not necessitate the heavy construction work that featured so much of urban railway construction in the nineteenth century. With good advance planning, railways can take their place in the cities of the future without the disruption of whole city areas that was so

Figure 6.17 Niagara Falls, Ontario, Canada. Billboard, with geological section in color, for the information of visitors to the Sir Adam Beck waterpower development during construction. *(Courtesy of the Hydro Electric Power Commission of Ontario, H. A. Smith, Chief Engineer.)*

often necessary in the great days of railway expansion. Railway tunnels may still be needed, therefore, in urban areas, but they should not loom so large as in the past, except for the provision of rapid mass-transit systems where it seems certain that they will have an increasingly vital part to play in the movement of urban populations. Railway tunnels of the past are often all too familiar, unlike the tunnels for services that have just been discussed. They call, therefore, for no extended reference so that attention will first be directed rather to some of the problems that geological conditions can create when existing tunnels have to be changed or are affected by later construction works nearby.

Those who have known the city of Montreal for some years will know how the area around what used to be called the Tunnel Station of Canadian National Railways has been transformed. Here in the center of the city was a major excavation, generally in rock, at the south end of the 4.8-km double-track rail tunnel that runs under the majestic Mount Royal, after which the city was named and around which it has been built. Occupied originally by a relatively small CNR station serving commuter traffic, this "hole" (as it was widely known) has been used to provide the spacious basement facilities of the great Place Ville Marie complex, one of the first major central-city development projects of North America. Rail services were rerouted, an older station abandoned, and a new Central Station serving all CNR trains to and from Montreal was constructed as a part of this great complex. As a preliminary to this multimillion dollar project, the southern end of the Mount Royal Tunnel had to be reconstructed. Although the tunnel itself is a double-track bore through the bedrock of Mount Royal, with an arched roof, the overburden naturally encountered at the two portals necessitated a change in design to two concrete roof arches supported by the tunnel walls and a central concrete wall.[6.31] To facilitate the new station arrangements, it was necessary to remove this central wall in the first 52.5 m of the tunnel, replacing the twin arches with a single concrete arch spanning between the tunnel walls. Immediately above the inner half of the section to be reconstructed was an exceptionally busy street, with its underground maze of sewers, conduits, and pipes, with large buildings (one a modern nine-story office building) on either side. The limestone bedrock was generally 9 m below ground level, the soil strata above it being first compact glacial till, then a layer of silt 1.8 to 2.4 m thick, followed by stiff brown clay. The silt was known to be a troublesome material, and since the water table was above the silt, any interference with it would have given rise to serious construction difficulties.

Every possible construction method that could safely be considered was reviewed, including the use of wellpoints to drain the soil strata, but all had to be discarded for practical reasons that need not now be detailed. Eventually it was decided that the only solution possible was to freeze the silt and clay, excavate the soil in its frozen state, and place the new concrete arch while the ground was still frozen. This meant occupation of the short stretch of street above the tunnel, but this was arranged with city authorities. Figure 6.18 shows the general arrangement, the freezing pipes being driven vertically downward from the surface well into the till, connected at the surface with

Figure 6.18 Montreal, Quebec, Canada. Freezing shallow ground above
the south portal of the Mount Royal Tunnel, Canadian National Railways,
during tunnel reconstruction. *(a)* View of the work from above showing
the piping installation for ground refrigeration *(photograph courtesy of
Canadian National Railways, R. J. Hansen, Chief Engineer). (b)* A view
showing proximity of buildings to the work, with the Queen Elizabeth
Hotel, St. James' Basilica, and the Sun Life Building in the background
(photograph by F. L. Peckover).

the necessary pipe network that was fed from a central refrigeration plant specially installed on the street for this purpose. The work was done in the winter (as is now regular practice in Canada), and the cold weather naturally aided the freezing operation; 1,528 m³ of clay and silt were frozen satisfactorily in 30 days. Excavation was carried out above the existing arches at a rate of a 45-cm advance per day, but all soil had to be drilled and blasted (since it was frozen) under controlled conditions since rail traffic continued to use the tracks below. The old arches were used as a working platform for the erection of the new arch when excavation was complete and removed only in the final stage of this unique operation.[6.32]

Freezing of soil is an expensive construction technique, but when geological conditions are so bad that any other solution is questionable, its use may prove to be truly economical, especially when time is considered. It has even been used on construction work for the London Underground, where construction is usually thought of as always being in the easily handled London clay. During the construction of the modern Victoria line, subsurface exploration showed that the upper half of the inclined tunnel for the access escalator at Tottenham Hale Station would have to be excavated through dense water-bearing sandy gravel that contained some cobbles. Few worse combinations can be imagined for excavation in confined quarters such as this station involved. The use of a chemical means of consolidating the gravel (another well-tried method) was first considered, but detailed test boring revealed the existence of lenses of silt within the gravel, material that would be questionable for chemical grouting. Freezing was therefore adopted as the method for consolidating the ground so that excavation could safely be carried out. A relatively new system using liquid nitrogen, instead of the more usual cold brine solution, was tried—with some initial misgivings but with complete success. The rate of freezing, so critical on this job, was retarded by the flow of the groundwater through the gravel, but eventually excavation could proceed, working a full face in the inclined tunnel. The time saved by the use of liquid nitrogen more than compensated for its increased cost.[6.33]

The London clay is a stiff, fissured, and overconsolidated Eocene clay. This is the correct geological-engineering description of the material that is of such importance to all subsurface work in London. The fact that it is of Eocene (geological) age shows that it is much older than the clays normally encountered in all the glaciated parts of the world. During the excavation of tunnels in the clay, when hand work is necessary the clay is cut off in large slices that have the consistency of a medium cheese. The slabs can be easily handled. The sight of these large pieces of this material being thrown so easily into mucking cars must always impress interested observers as about the easiest form of excavation possible. Its very advantages from the point of view of excavation, however, pose other problems when structures within the clay are disturbed. During the construction of the great Shell Building on the south shore of the River Thames in the center of London, for example, the presence of tube railways under the site added to normal construction difficulties.

The complex of buildings in this center is one of the largest of such aggregations of buildings in London, its site having an area of 3 hectares. Construction of a basement under the complete site is some indication of the extent of the project. Beneath the site of one of the main buildings, and lying very close to the location of the 20-story tower were the twin tubes of the Bakerloo Tube (as this part of the Underground is known), with the two tubes one above the other, the top one having only 1.5 m of clearance below the basement slab for the large building. Although the building load could have been carried on the clay, to avoid overstressing the tubes (and for other structural reasons) that part overlying the two Bakerloo tunnels was founded on cylinders, with belled-out bottoms, excavated in the clay to a depth well below the bottom tube and then filled with concrete suitably reinforced. There was the further danger that the tubes might be forced somewhat upward by the rebound of the clay when the deep excavation for the building was complete, again in the light of the characteristics of the clay. To guard against this, the excavation over the tubes was carried out in strips each 9 m long. The concrete foundation slab was placed in each strip as soon as it had been excavated and before the adjacent strips were excavated. As can be imagined, the tube tunnels were most carefully instrumented throughout the lengths that ran through the excavation. Through this instrumentation, in itself an unusual and most expert foundation study, the tubes were kept under constant surveillance. The job was completed without any disturbance to traffic in the tubes and with eventual movements so small as to be negligible.[6.34]

Construction of rapid-transit subways is now in progress or under consideration in many of the major cities of the world, clear indication of the planning attention that is being given to the essential movement of large numbers of people efficiently and with a minimum of pollution. It is axiomatic that the closer such railways can be to ground surface, the more convenient will they be and probably the more economical. This means, however, that the subsurface conditions to be encountered must be accepted rather than chosen, as would be the case with deep tunnels. In almost all

Figure 6.19 London, England. Photograph of a model of the foundations under the Shell Centre, on the south bank of the Thames, showing measures adopted to minimize interference with existing tube railway tunnels. *(Courtesy of the Editor,* Engineering News-Record.)

cases excavation will be in surficial deposits, possibly also in rock, this combined operation always presenting its own special difficulties on construction. A further factor is that, with location close to the surface, the cut-and-cover method of construction can sometimes be used even for the large excavations needed for such subways and provided that the necessary interference, at least temporary, with normal traffic can be cleared with civic authorities.

The first section of the Toronto Subway system has been selected as an example since it illustrates so well some aspects of cut-and-cover construction, and it had useful geological overtones. Now over 32 km long and steadily being expanded one short section at a time, the Toronto Transit Commission's subway system has featured cut-and-cover construction, open excavation on private right-of-way, and shield tunneling. Its first section was commenced in 1949 and completed three years later. Starting in the heart of downtown Toronto near the harbor shoreline on Lake Ontario, the first 3.2 km of this 7.4-km line was built through the downtown section by cut and cover. Prior to the completion of designs, a thorough study of all relevant geological information had been made. This showed that the portion parallel to the lake front and for a hundred meters or so up the main northern arm running under Yonge Street, the city's main downtown artery, the lower part of the dual-track reinforced concrete box structure would be founded in the Dundas shale, overlying which would be found a mixture of glacial till and glacial sands, gravels, silts, and clay. More detailed information was then obtained, based on this preliminary study, by means of a series of test borings and drilling along the right-of-way of the subway line. This involved some intricate locating of boreholes in busy city streets, but the excellent records of underground city services maintained by the city of Toronto (see Chap. 9) permitted this to be done with accuracy and certainty. One boring was located at the busiest intersection of the city in a 60-cm-square area bounded by a high-voltage electrical cable, a multicircuit telephone cable, and high-pressure gas and water lines. Later excavation showed that the casing for the boring was exactly in the center point of this small critical area. Some of the boreholes were fitted with porous casings, and levels of groundwater were secured for a period of well over a year.

When tenders were called from contractors for this first Canadian subway construction project, all this subsurface information (including groundwater records) was made available to all tenderers. The possibility of boulders being encountered in the glacial soils was clearly indicated in the contract documents; no large ones were actually encountered, but this was fortuitous as was also the absence of any major pockets of methane, another possibility in such deposits. When construction started, arrangements were made for a detailed survey of all soil and rock encountered; local geologists, coordinated through an advisory committee, were allowed to inspect critical sections as they were revealed. It will later be explained how unusually significant were the geological sections thus exposed. Here it will suffice to note that a complete suite of soil samples was taken at regular intervals (generally every 15 m) and lodged for safe keeping with the Royal Ontario Museum in Toronto. All subsurface conditions were found to be almost exactly as indicated on the contract drawings, from the careful preliminary investigations, and the work was finished on schedule and without any major difficulties. This pattern of most thorough preliminary subsurface investigations, and continuing attention to all geological conditions exposed by excavation, continues to mark all subway work of the Toronto Transit Commission, with consequent benefit to the contractors who carry out their work and to the commission, and with incidental benefits to the records of local geology.[6.35]

6.7 TUNNELS FOR HIGHWAYS

Tunnels for the improvement of road locations and so for the convenient use of road vehicles can almost be regarded today as the equivalent of the railway tunnels of the Victorian age. This can be said without any implications as to the future of major highways being carried into the centers of cities or without involvement in the difficult question as to the future of the automobile in city centers. Tunnels at critical locations, as will be seen from the few examples to be mentioned, can render great service. They are never easy to construct. They involve high construction costs. But the benefits they convey can often be shown to be worth far more than the financial costs. Their construction can be carried out efficiently and safely only on the basis of the most accurate predictions possible of the subsurface conditions to be encountered when ground is broken.

Readers will naturally be thinking of some vehicular tunnels they know in some of the larger cities with which they are acquainted. They can therefore imagine the surprise of the author when he found a fine example of a small vehicular tunnel through solid rock in the small and isolated settlement of Ketchican in the "panhandle" section of Alaska. This completely isolated town of 1,600 people, employed mainly in a local pulp mill and in fishing, is located amid magnificent scenery on a coastal strip that is so narrow that its single "main road" is carried in part on timber piles driven in the seabed, for which reason the road is built of heavy wooden plank. Even this device was insufficient to take care of the increasing traffic in the town, although it can circulate only in the town, and so a tunnel was planned to provide an extra lane of traffic at the most critical corner of the one main road. It was constructed in 1953-1954 without any real problems, being driven through a soft greenstone schist that was quite badly faulted and thus fractured, containing numerous quartz veins. Its appearance, with appropriate local decoration, is shown in Fig. 6.20.[6.36]

More in keeping with the general impression of modern vehicular tunnels are the twin Fort Pitt Tunnels in Pittsburgh. Part of the really remarkable redevelopment of the downtown section of this important industrial center was an entirely new highway exit across the Monongahela River, just upstream of its junction with the Allegheny River. A new high-level bridge provides the river crossing, but even before this was constructed a new route had to be provided through Mount Washington, a plateaulike area bounded by very steeply sloping escarpments roughly parallel to the river, rising about 10 m above river level, and about 1 km wide at the tunnel location. Bedrock consists of the widely distributed local Pennsylvanian beds that

Figure 6.20   Ketchican, Alaska. North portal of vehicular tunnel on the town's main street. *(Photograph by R. F. Legget.)*

include shales, indurated clays, siltstones, sandstones, and limestones with some coal, all in thin parallel strata slightly inclined to the horizontal. The exact location of the tunnels was fixed by highway and bridge locations, and so the strata penetrated had to be accepted rather than selected. Figure 6.21 is a cross section through Mount Washington on the line of the tunnels, from which it will be seen that the twin tubes penetrated strata of gray silt shale, gray indurated clay, and dark gray to carbonaceous silty shale. The tunnels are about 1,030 m long and are slightly unequal in length since, although they start at the south portal at the same level, the tunnel for north-bound traffic gradually rises above its twin to be 5.4 m higher at the north portal where the two roadways connect with the two decks of the new double-decked bridge. The tubes are 18 m apart on their center lines, each providing two 3.6-m roadways, their excavated width being 9.9 m at roadway level, the two connected by seven cross passages for maintenance and repair.

Construction was complicated more by logistics than by geology, although this was complex enough. Since the north portal was one-third of the way up the steeply sloping face of Mount Washington, with four well-used railroad tracks at the foot, close by the river, the tunnels had to be driven from the south end only. Here the available working area was severely restricted by the already constructed major highway

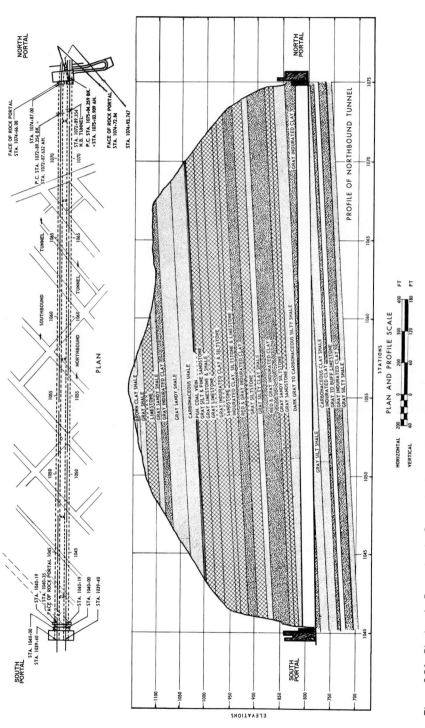

Figure 6.21 Pittsburgh, Pennsylvania. Generalized geological section along the northbound Fort Pitt Tunnel. *(Courtesy Michael Baker Jr., Inc., consulting engineers, Beaver, Pa., and A. C. Ackenheil.)*

Figure 6.22 Pittsburgh, Pennsylvania. Aerial view of the Fort Pitt Tunnels under construction, showing limited space available at the portals. *(Courtesy of the Sanborn Map Co., Inc., Pelham, N.Y.)*

that would eventually lead directly into the tunnel and by the steeply sloping southern escarpment. By using the area excavated at the southern portal to give good working faces from which to start tunneling, a total area of about 0.8 hectares was obtained. but this severe limitation necessitated meticulous "housekeeping" (as the layout, arrangement, and use of the working area at a construction job is always called). Of unusual interest was the arrangement made for "mucking" the tunnel. Blasted rock was removed by major trucks from the tunnel faces but not taken directly to the ultimate dumping area. It was dumped instead in the working area by the large equipment, there to be picked up by a subcontractor using much smaller trucking equipment that was allowed to use the local highways in accordance with traffic regulations and in which the muck was taken to the dump. The two headings were advanced together, the truck-mounted drilling equipment going back and forth between the two headings. In order to improve working conditions, as the north portal was approached, 15-cm-diameter horizontal drains at 15-m centers were drilled up to 150 m into the hillside at three elevations. Even so, the final excavation of the tunnels at this location and the associated excavation for the ventilation building involved intricate construction techniques and continuous observation in order to obviate the very real possibility of landslides in the soil mantle and weathered rock. Weathering of the bedrock was found to extend as deep as 9 m.[6.37]

Today, automobiles are driven through the two convenient and excellently finished tunnels probably with little if any thought given by their occupants to all the skills that combined to give Pittsburgh this convenient access to the south. This is, however, inevitable and understandable. Geologists and engineers gain their satisfaction from the knowledge of work well done, natural conditions adapted to the "use and convenience of man," experience broadened, and knowledge enhanced. There is one vehicular tunnel in California that has a history that should not be so quickly forgotten, certainly by all who carry any responsibility for the planning and execution of urban works, for it is an almost classical example of what can happen when adequate preliminary investigation of a tunnel site is *not* carried out. The tunnel was built in the mid-thirties, but because of all the trouble that developed during construction, its geology was not publicly described until 1950, when a notable paper was published containing a full description. All too seldom are such records of difficulties made available, even though they can be of such great value, often of more value than the simple record of a job on which no difficulties were encountered. The description of the "Geology of the Broadway Tunnel, Berkley Hills, California," a paper by Professor Ben M. Page, is therefore of unusual interest and value; the following brief summary is based upon it and, to some extent, quotes from it.[6.38]

The Broadway Tunnel was constructed on the outskirts of Oakland and Berkeley to improve road access to the east. It forms a section of California Highway 24 and was built as two parallel tunnels, about 900 m long and 11 m in excavated width. The highway district that was formed to plan and construct the tunnel employed a prominent geologist to make a preliminary survey of the tunnel route. His report was favorable and was mentioned in the contract specification but not officially included or quoted. The report was made available to tenderers by the district, which assumed no responsibility for the views it expressed. The contract was awarded to a combination of six experienced contractors, but, like all the other tenderers, they relied upon this geological report and did not make any investigations of their own. Apparently a small adit was excavated in advance of construction, but it penetrated only the rock removed for the portal works and so could have been of little assistance in showing what the tunnel rock would really be like. Before construction began, all those concerned believed that no timbering would be necessary, except near the portals and at local fault zones since this had been predicted on the basis of the preliminary geological examination. When, finally, pilot drifts had been completed from portal to portal, "it was evident that none of the ground could be left unsupported prior to placing the concrete lining. Not only were incredibly difficult tunnelling conditions encountered throughout the entire length of the tunnel but two bad cave-ins took place, despite all precautions, in one of which three men were unfortunately killed." After experiencing these troubles for two years, with 70 percent of the contract complete, the original contractors "rescinded their contract and unsuccessfully sued the highway district for $3,359,695.00." The tunnel was finally completed by other contractors and has been in successful use ever since.

The tunnels lie beneath the crest of the Berkeley Hills, approximately at right angles to the range. The southwest portal is in a canyon that, topographically, continues over the first part of the tunnel line. Subsequent geological studies have shown that this canyon "follows an ill-defined zone of weakness in which the rocks are highly fractured and soft altered dikes exist in great numbers." These conditions were experienced from the very start of construction. Little would now be gained by any detailed description of the really great difficulties that had to be overcome in excavating through the relatively young rocks of Pliocene and Miocene age that were encountered. They included mudstones, sandstones, and sandstones and conglomerates of almost bewildering variety. The Claremont formation was known, from an explosion that had taken place when an earlier tunnel had been constructed through it, to be highly bituminous in content to a dangerous extent. The contractors therefore took special precautions against possible explosions; fortunately, no serious trouble with explosive gases was encountered. A large number of diabase dikes were encountered and this further complicated tunnel excavation, as did also the existence of some sandstone dikes, the origin of which was but one of the interesting purely geological features of the excavation. So variable were the rock conditions that frequently the rock exposed at one face would be quite different from that at the other, only 30 m away. A detailed description of the rocks and driving conditions encountered will be found in Professor Page's paper, a reference to which should be kept handy by all those who may have occasion to have to justify the expenditure of money on essential preliminary subsurface exploration, especially for tunnels.

Sometimes bad rock conditions cannot be avoided, although the location of the Broadway Tunnel appears to have been at least questionable, but they can always be met with appropriate methods and equipment if predicted with reasonable accuracy. In great contrast to the experience just described was that gained on the construction of very similar twin highway tunnels on the outskirts of Monmouth near South Wales. An improved location for the Monmouth to Mitchell Troy section of one of the new British motorways (road A40) involved tunneling under Gibraltar Hill. The hill was known to consist generally of the Old Red Sandstone, dipping from 30° to almost vertically across the line of the tunnels.

This information came from a study of the memoir of the British Geological Survey describing the regional geology. It was supplemented by detailed study in the field of all outcrops and by the sinking of eight boreholes (even for just 180 m of tunnel). Excavation confirmed the accuracy of advance predictions arrived at in this way. The sandstone was found, through the eight boreholes, to be reasonably hard, but marls were also encountered varying down to a friable claylike material. Calcite veins were also encountered but no major faults. Extensive jointing indicated some minor faulting. Many of the joints carried groundwater and thus lubricated the small amounts of decomposed marl and clay. Maximum ground cover was about 30 m.[6.39]

Knowing that these were the rock conditions that would be met, the contractors designed a new type of "shield," a structural steel frame with an extended hood

Figure 6.23 Monmouth, England. Special shield constructed for the excavation of the Gibraltar Hill Tunnels in weak rock. *(Photograph courtesy of Howard Humphreys and Sons, Consulting Engineers, London, and D. A. Howells.)*

cover plate and forepoling steel fingers extending ahead of the supports. It is seen in Fig. 6.23, the basic simplicity of its design being clearly evident. Movable formwork for the concrete lining followed right behind the shield, which naturally protected all workers at the face, the folding supports for the formwork being designed to fit in with the shield framework. Using this shield, even in these poor rock conditions, as much as 2,300 m³ of rock was excavated in one week from the two tunnels. The paper describing this work gives cost details for this somewhat elaborate piece of special equipment that apparently proved economical even for such short tunnels.[6.40] The finished tunnels are shown in the chapter-opening photograph.

6.8 ACCESS TUNNELS

The passing reference made on page 257 to the use, especially in the Middle Ages, of tunnels to provide access to and exit from such romantic buildings as fortresses might have suggested that this use of tunnels was solely medieval. There are, however, numerous examples of modern tunnels used for similar purposes—not to serve castles but quite modern buildings and civic facilities. Unusual to the point that it is probably unique is the service given to the small Italian village of Ca di Landino, lying between the cities of Bologna and Firenze. The railway line between these two points is, perhaps, the most critical section of the vital Italian main line from Milan to Rome and Naples. Traversing the Appennines has always been difficult for railway location. Not until the late twenties was a really direct route provided by what is still the second longest railway tunnel in the world, generally known as the great Appennine Tunnel. It is 18,507.38 m long. Work on it started before the First World War but was seriously interrupted by the war and by postwar developments in Italy. Construction shafts had been put down, however, from near the little village that is located in the mountains almost exactly above the center of the tunnel. A large central chamber was excavated at the midpoint of the tunnel, large enough to accommodate two passing tracks, a signal box, a station building, and workshops. And 1,863 steps were constructed in one of the diagonal construction shafts to give access to the village above. Although the stop is not shown in public timetables, some trains do stop at this central underground station (Precendenze), and residents of the village can, if they wish, get home by climbing this unique access tunnel.[6.41]

Of rather more general interest is the access tunnel that was constructed as a part of the $4 million restoration and modernization program carried out in the late fifties at the 100-year-old Tennessee State Capital building in Nashville. Prior to the completion of the tunnel, a climb up 103 steps was necessary to reach the floor of the legislature. A new subbasement was constructed in which two elevators were provided for access to the main part of the building. The access tunnel was driven from street level beneath the venerable building to give direct access to the new elevator service. The tunnel was only 73.6 m long, but it had to be driven under the building through limestone. Drilling and blasting had naturally to be carried out with unusual care to avoid any damage to the building. Monitoring with seismographs was continuous, and this showed no noticeable vibration in the building, tribute indeed to the skill of the tunnelers. A safety door was installed across the tunnel entrance in order to prevent the sound of the blasts being heard down the main street of the city since the line of the tunnel faced right down the street. A concrete lining faced with marble was installed, giving a finished section 3.35 m high and 3 m wide for this modern equivalent of the old "mysterious hidden passage."[6.42]

6.9 SUBAQUEOUS TUNNELS

It requires but little imagination to appreciate that the most difficult tunnels of all in general practice are those that have to be constructed beneath water. Because so many cities are located on the shores of rivers, lakes, or the sea, it follows that many of the tunnels that serve cities have to be excavated beneath such bodies of water, with all the extra hazard that this involves. In some cases, a tunnel is the only possible solution to the particular problem that has to be met—as, for example, the tunnels to intake cribs in the Great Lakes from which some major lakeside cities obtain their water supplies. Again, there are many waterways that carry so much shipping that construction of a bridge crossing, for rail or roadway, is really not practicable or, if practicable, clearly not economical. Despite all the difficulties, therefore, the record of tunnels serving cities includes many notable examples and, surprisingly, some of the earliest major urban tunnels.

The first underwater tunnel ever to be completed still provides an epic chapter in the history of civil engineering. It runs under the River Thames at Wapping. Started in 1825, it was completed in 1843 after the surmounting of tremendous difficulties with most primitive equipment. Advice from early unnamed geologists of the day proved to be quite misleading, since solid clay was not found throughout the length of the tunnel as had been predicted. One of the many difficulties was encountering a low section of the bed of the Thames from which gravel had previously been dredged, a practice that will call for mention in the next chapter. The great engineer responsible for the conception and completion of the tunnel was Sir Marc Isambard Brunel. He was valiantly assisted for part of the work by his even more brilliant son, Isambard Kingdom Brunel, who was to achieve eminence later in a variety of fields, railway engineering and tunneling being one, the building of the noted steamship *Great Eastern* another. Originally used by foot passengers, the tunnel was purchased in 1866 by the East London Railway and with little difficulty was converted into a railway tunnel; as such, it continues in use today. So far removed from modern tunneling practice were the problems that had to be faced that little would be gained by any recital of them, although it must be noted that this was the first tunnel in which a shield was used. One of the many human interest stories of the tunnel construction, however, has great relevance today despite its amusing aspects.[6.43]

Brunel's great-granddaughter has told of his invariable practice of personally examining the soil being encountered by the miners at the working face every two hours, day and night. His wife must have insisted that he arrange for a pulley to be installed outside his bedroom window in the house he occupied close to the tunnel works. This was used by workmen who placed the regular soil samples in a basket and hauled it up to the window after ringing a bell to alert Brunel; he examined the sample, wrote down his instructions, and gave a signal for the return of the basket to the ground. For 4 years of the final stages of tunnel construction he followed this practice. It is small wonder that he and his wife continued to wake up automatically every two hours during the night for many months after the tunnel had been successfully completed. Today there are more convenient ways of keeping constant check on materials exposed in tunnels (and without disturbing wives), but attention to this matter such as it was given by Sir Marc Isambard Brunel is no less important today than it was with his pioneer tunnel.[6.44]

Another tunnel under the River Thames, far different from that at Wapping, may usefully be mentioned next since it represents the result of most careful consideration of the three main methods of constructing tunnels under waterways. They may be constructed at shallow depths beneath a river or a seabed, but this will almost always involve the use of compressed air in addition to the use of mechanical shields at the working faces. Alternatively, if they are located deep enough below the level of the bed, they may be excavated without the aid of compressed air, even though much water may have to be handled in the shaft-sinking and at the working faces. A third possibility that only modern construction techniques has made possible is the construction of the underwater part of a tunnel as precast tubes that can be built in convenient locations such as dry docks, floated into position, and sunk onto specially prepared trenches in the waterway bed.

All three methods were studied in connection with the construction of the first Thames Cable Tunnel, crossing under the River Thames from a large power station at Tilbury to Gravesend and designed to carry very-high-tension electrical cables as an alternative means of transmission to the use of an overhead crossing. The tunnel, 1,610 m long and generally 3 m in diameter, is enlarged at its end sections, adjacent to the two access shafts, to 4.26 m diameter. The selection of a tunnel crossing for this purpose, and the necessary arrangements for the cooling of the cables in the tunnel, are of great interest, but relevant here is the decision to construct the tunnel in open headings at a depth of about 24.4 m below the lowest elevation of the river bed. This obviated the necessity for using compressed air, since the entire tunnel was excavated through the Chalk, even though sinking of the two shafts was a difficult and costly business. This excellent example of modern tunneling has been admirably described in a succinct paper to which reference may most usefully be made by all who have to face the selection of a tunneling method for a underwater crossing. The advantages and disadvantages of working in compressed air are most helpfully and frankly discussed. Despite all the advances in modern preventive medicine, and in the regulations governing and the equipment permitting work under compressed air, danger to human lives is still involved. Avoidance of this danger was an important factor in the decision to drive this tunnel through the Chalk.

The two shafts of 6.1-m diameter had to be sunk to depths of 38 and 40 m, respectively. Most thorough preliminary subsurface investigation had shown the difficult strata that would have to be penetrated, the water table being relatively close to the surface. The north shaft was sunk by handling the water by pumping out of deep wells, recharging of water through additional "reverse wells" being necessary to maintain adequate groundwater levels in the vicinity of the shaft. By way of contrast, the south shaft was sunk by means of chemical treatment of the ground in advance of excavation. Both methods were successful; the written record provides much useful, comparative information. Of unusual interest was the fact that, when the upper surface of the Chalk was reached, it was found to be badly disintegrated to a depth of about 6 m. Difficult to handle, this disintegrated rock impeded progress, but no more than this. Geologically it was of interest since the disintegration was attributed to the existence of permafrost conditions during the last glacial period in Great Britain, as was discussed in Chap. 5 (see page 194).[6.45]

Despite the "glamour" that is sometimes popularly associated with compressed-air work, all experienced contractors know that it is a method to be used only as a last resort and then under stringent control, based upon the most meticulous investigation of the ground conditions to be encountered. As illustrating the efforts that contractors will make to avoid "using air," the case of the north shaft for the pressure tunnel that brings water to the city of Vancouver, British Columbia, under the First Narrows of Vancouver Harbor may be instanced. This remarkable supply of water, briefly noted on page 160, is conveyed under its own pressure below this beautiful harbor entrance in a 914-m-long, 2.28-m-diameter tunnel, excavated in solid rock at a depth of about 122 m below the ground surface. At its southern end, sandstone bedrock comes within a meter or so of the surface in the famous Stanley Park, where the shaft was to be located. On the northern side of the harbor, however, bedrock was reached at a depth of only 39.6 m below water level.

Test borings showed that below bed level at the shaft location there was a depth of about 30 m of tightly packed sand and gravel, washed down the steep creek beds from the higher reaches of which the water supply is obtained. No good samples were obtained for more than 30 m below water level. Boulders were encountered above rock level, the rock proving to be greatly weathered shale of an almost claylike consistency, eventually grading into firmer sandstone. The successful contractor solicited permission to sink the shaft in the form of a cylindrical concrete caisson, 7.3 m in diameter, in order to avoid using the compressed air originally intended. He offered to make a $50,000 reduction in his price if this was allowed, the shaft to be finished under air if his proposed method failed. It did not, but the sinking of the caisson shaft was indeed a "battle with nature." The first boulder to be removed, for example, after snagging by divers, weighed 5 tonnes; others were so tightly wedged together that they had to be blasted within the confined space inside the cylinder. The first bedrock was so soft that it was removed by an orange-peel bucket. To seal the bottom of the shaft a concrete seal had to be placed, but when, eventually, the shaft was pumped out it was found to be quite dry. Excavation then proceeded through the concrete seal and for 82.2 m, below, all in sandstone, without difficulty. Tunnel construction after this experience was relatively easy.[6.46]

From the many examples of modern tunnels for which compressed air had to be used, the second vehicular tunnel between Boston and East Boston has been selected. This was driven not in the rocks of the Boston basin but in the difficult soils that overlie the rock through which the water-supply and drainage tunnels were excavated. Its location in Boston is almost incidental since similar soil conditions can be encountered in many a seaboard location, but this particular tunnel illustrates in a somewhat singular way the value of preliminary geological information. The tunnel is 1,480 m long, with a finished diameter barely over 9 m. It was built in 1959–1961 at a cost of just over $29 million. It is the second tunnel to be built at this location. Dredging of the harbor bottom has decreased available cover, in view of the rather rigid limitations upon the elevation of the tunnel roadway. Accordingly, the contractor obtained permission to place a temporary heavy clay cover over the line of the tunnel in the harbor bottom, to a depth of 6 m, with the understanding that it would be removed when the tunnel was complete. Inevitably this meant the use of compressed air for the central section. Starting from the East Boston ventilation shaft, the first 457 m of tunnel was through stiff clay, glacial till, and boulders. As the tunnel approached the harbor line, the ground changed to soft clay, and so the remainder of the work was done under air.

Excavation was aided by means of the use of a large shield, with three working levels, clay knives with similar tools being used for actually taking the clay out. Close to the East Channel line under the harbor, very soft silt was encountered. This material proved to be so difficult to handle in the usual way that it was decided to advance the shield "blind," i.e., by forcing it into the soft silt that would then be forced ahead of or out from around the shield face, apart from a small quantity that was initially allowed to come into the working through one opening where it could be moved straight onto the muck-conveyor belt. Even this was eventually closed off. This critical operation worked well and was used as far as about the center line of the harbor. Here, as had been predicted from advance test borings, gravel and boulders were encountered for about 61 m, and so the pocket was opened again and mining of this harder material carried out through it. Then, also as shown by the preliminary investigations, soft silt was again encountered, and the "blind" shield penetration was resumed as far as the West Channel line, when the full face of the shield was opened up again and more normal excavation of the clay and till was resumed. As the contractor said, "the uncertainties involved in building a tunnel make it impossible to anticipate all the problems that will be encountered but detailed preliminary investigations will give some indication of the areas where difficulties will arise"—a statement to which his Boston Tunnel contract bears lively testimony.[6.47]

No account of modern vehicular tunnels, no matter how brief, would be complete without some mention of the Queens Midtown Tunnel in New York City, so well known to all travelers who come into New York by air, in view of the convenient access it gives to the East Side Airlines Terminal. The underwater section is just under 1,220 m long. The twin tubes are each 9.75 m in diameter. The best way of showing the ground conditions that had to be met in the driving of these twin tunnels is to direct the reader's attention to Fig. 6.24, which shows the most complex geology that featured the entire length of this project. Compressed air had naturally to be used, with pressures as high as 2.6 kg per cm^2, which is close to the limit that can be used with safety. At one location the heading showed 2.44 m of coal at the top, deposited long since in the river bed, then 2.74 m of sand, clay, gravel, and boulders well mixed, and then 2.44 m of sound and hard bedrock, a variation of material that was probably unique in the history of tunneling. But the work was satisfactorily completed without ever the face being "lost" and without any fatality due to "bends," the crippling disease that sometimes affects workers under compressed air. The author regards a visit he made to this job while it was under construction as one of the greatest privileges he has had in this field.[6.48]

Correspondingly, the record of the construction of the even longer tunnels under the River Mersey at the great British port of Liverpool constitutes a special chapter

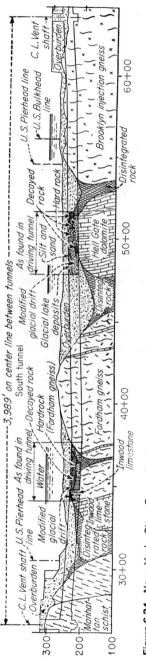

Figure 6.24 New York City. Generalized geological section across the East River along the line of the Queens Midtown Tunnel, showing the very variable subsurface conditions encountered. *(Courtesy of the Editor, Engineering News-Record.)*

305

Figure 6.25 Liverpool, England. West portals of the second Mersey Tunnel, the Kingsway, with one tunnel already in use and final construction operations proceeding in the second. *(Courtesy of Mott, Hay and Anderson, consulting engineers, London, G. S. Dodds, Senior Resident Engineer.)*

in the annals of tunneling. All have had to be over 3 km long, the first vehicular tunnel being 13.3 m in internal diameter. All have been excavated in the Bunter sandstone, a red sandstone of the Triassic system. All have benefitted in an unusual way from local geological studies. The original preglacial drainage at this locality was in the opposite direction to the present flow of the River Mersey. This was predicted by geologists, as was the almost certain existence of an old buried river valley beneath the present bed of the river, despite the fact that the first test borings put down had not shown this. Further borings did reveal this critical feature; tunnel location and tunneling methods were adjusted accordingly and these unusually large bores successfully completed.[6.49] Attention must now, however, be directed to the third and most unusual method of tunnel construction.

6.10 FLOATING TUNNELS INTO PLACE

Implicit in some of the foregoing accounts is the necessity for keeping the grade levels of underwater rail and vehicular tunnels as close as possible to the ground level at both ends, in order to minimize the necessary grades into and out of the tunnel. Inevitably, this means that the geological conditions to be encountered are those created by the most recent of geological processes, often the deposition of river sediments within the period of human history. Construction problems are an inevitable consequence, and in many locations they simply cannot be avoided. This combination of circumstances has led to the development within relatively recent years of the bold scheme of building the tunnel tubes as precast boxes "in the dry"—usually of concrete, but sometimes of steel. With their ends sealed, these huge tubes can then be floated into place over the tunnel line and sunk into position using appropriate water ballast. Connecting the adjacent tubes is an intricate construction operation, but there are now well-accepted methods of achieving these connections, as there are also of connecting the sunken tubes with approach tunnels, or cuttings, on the two banks. These are standard construction procedures, but the initial decision to use this method and the satisfactory founding of the tubes on the prepared beds in the trenches excavated for them both depend upon the usual essential accurate knowledge of the subsurface conditions not only along the tunnel line but along the lines of all possible alternative routes so that the necessary economic comparative studies can be made in advance of final design.

There is one area that has already become noteworthy by reason of the extensive use made there of sunken-tube tunnels in providing solutions to its unusually difficult traffic problems. This is the region around Hampton Roads in Chesapeake Bay, Virginia, including the city of Norfolk. The latest of this series of notable tunnels was the Second Elizabeth River Tunnel, opened for use in September 1962. This $23 million project involved the construction of a 1,275-m-long tunnel, from portal to portal, almost all of this length being built as a series of 12 precast concrete tubes floated into place, short approach sections to the two portals being constructed within cofferdams. The first phase of the necessary and extensive test-boring program was carried out in 1957. Borings were put down across the river at 152-m intervals, this being thought to be enough, in view of the relatively uniform local geological conditions. On shore, borings were spaced at 61-m intervals because of the known complexity of the shore deposits and the presence of meandering streams in the areas involved. Soon after the start of construction it was found that these spacings were not close enough. Such variations in ground conditions were experienced that a second phase of exploration was undertaken, combined with a detailed program of testing of the undisturbed soil samples obtained. Additional borings were also taken during the progress of construction for aid in dealing with specific local problems.

The soil profile thus determined along the tunnel route showed a thin layer of river silt underlain by gray silty clay; in turn it was underlain by a gray-green marl. The location of the tunnel placed its foundation mainly in the marl, except at the two ends, where the tubes had to rise to meet the two shore portal sections. All this subsurface information greatly facilitated design and construction so that a most satisfactory job was the result, but there were the inevitable problems. One of these was under one of the end tubes, when unsuitable organic material, not detected by the original borings, was found below the projected dredged line. This was solved by calculated overdredging, backfilling with sand, and consolidation of the sand with timber piles. The same thing was found under a necessary mole fill on the Norfolk side. Hydraulic fill was used to create this embankment and then compacted by a specialized vibration

Figure 6.26 Norfolk, Virginia. Prefabricated tunnel tube for the Second Elizabeth River Tunnel crossing from Norfolk to Portsmouth, Virginia; the massive tube is being outfitted with its interior concrete lining; the scale is given by the size of the two men near the right-hand tube. *(Courtesy of Parsons, Brinckerhoff, Quade and Douglas, Inc., consulting engineers, New York, W. H. Bruce, President.)*

method. Test borings were put down through the compacted fill in order to obtain samples for checking the degree of compaction (which was satisfactory).

Some of the borings penetrated through the fill and into the original ground. These revealed another pocket of organic silt running for about 53.2 m along the tunnel center line, a pocket so restricted in location that the test borings had not detected it since they just straddled its location. Tests on samples of this material showed it to be so weak that, when loaded, it would have produced a long-term settlement of about 15 cm, and this was not permissible. Fortunately, the construction schedule being followed permitted the use of a simple but elegant solution. The location was loaded with a 1.83-m-high surcharge of fill that was left in place for 5 months. Calculation showed that in this period the excess load would induce settlement about the same as the calculated long-term settlement under normal load. Rather more than the 15-cm settlement developed within the 5-month period before the extra fill had to be removed, and so the original plan was then proceeded with confidently.

Subsequent observations have shown no further settlement. This experience, so successfully overcome, has been described in some detail since it was caused by a feature that is never uncommon in marshy areas, the existence of small pockets of organic material limited in extent but still large enough to cause trouble if not detected.[6.50]

6.11 ROTTERDAM SUBWAY

All who know the modern city of Rotterdam in the Netherlands know what a delightful blending of the old and the new it now presents. Some of its older streets are typical of what one imagines the older towns of the Low Countries to be like. The new city center, however, is one of the finest of all examples of enlightened modern city planning, its broad streets lined by elegant modern buildings, with a shopping mall that must have led to more imitations than almost any other postwar example of urban development. Visitors with any sense of history know that this entire area has been completely rebuilt since the end of the Second World War, following its devastation by low-flying bombers at the start of the war as a result of heroic defiance of demands for an easy crossing of the Nieuwe Maas. Today this peaceful river is one of the busiest commercial waterways of the world, the port of Rotterdam being now the first port of the world, as it handles not only ocean shipping from the seven seas but also almost all the traffic coming down the Rhine, the Nieuwe Maas being one of the outlets of the great river to the sea. But the waterway has long been an impediment to passenger traffic to the central part of Rotterdam so that even though two bridges cross it, a notable vehicular tunnel beneath its waters was constructed in 1938-1942. There has now been opened the first section of a rapid-transit subway system, including another tunnel under the Nieuwe Maas that gives ready access to the business area, while not adding any vehicular traffic to the already crowded central section of the city. It provides the most remarkable of all uses of floating tubes for tunnel construction. The subsurface of Rotterdam must, however, be outlined in the first instance so that this remarkable construction operation can be the better appreciated.

The most important feature of the geology of Rotterdam is the existence at a depth of from 16 to 18 m below the local datum level, equal to average sea level, of a stratum of medium to coarse sand containing some gravel, a Pleistocene deposit brought down by the Rivers Rhine and Meuse. It is naturally water-bearing; pumping from it in recent years for air-conditioning and cooling installations in city buildings has been extensive. It extends to a depth of more than 40 m in the eastern part of the city, diminishing to about 30 m in the western area. Upon this excellent foundation bed all major buildings and structures in Rotterdam are founded with every confidence through the medium of piles. Above the sand is a stratum of alluvial clay about 1 m thick, followed by a layer of organic peat, and a final stratum of marine clay with a total thickness of about 2 m. Thence to the surface are a variety of shallow clay and peat deposits, with man-made fill naturally present to varying degrees. It is on these varied deposits that roadways and light buildings have to be founded. Since much of

Figure 6.27 Rotterdam, the Netherlands. Rotterdam subway under construction; construction scene near the city center, with the rebuilt center of the city in the background; the excavated trench between steel sheet piling can be seen, water-filled, and the yard for the fabrication of the tunnel sections to the right of center. *(Courtesy of G. Plantema, Director, Gemeentewerken, Rotterdam.)*

the outlying part of Rotterdam is of very recent development, the observant visitor can usually see some roadways being reconstructed as the slow settlement of the organic peat beneath them has to be offset by filling and rebuilding. The devices of sand drains and preloading are used to accelerate the process of consolidation already mentioned in Chap. 5. Because the general level of the city is below sea level, as with so much of the Netherlands, the Dutch dikes against the sea being justly world famous, the groundwater throughout the entire area of the city is close to ground level, never more than 2 m below the surface. Fortunately, it is reasonably constant in elevation, and so no difficulties are experienced with deterioration of the timber piles so widely used all over the city. But any deep excavations necessarily interfere very seriously with the water table. Herein lay the great problem to be faced in the building of the subway system.

All the rapid transit lines on the north side of the Nieuwe Maas, i.e., in the central part of the city, had to be constructed in tunnel. Once the line emerges to the south from the tunnel under the Maas, it becomes an elevated line and will so continue, with surface portions, as it is extended into the suburbs. Of the initial 7.6 km, 3.1 km had to be in tunnel, with the remaining 4.5 km on a prestressed reinforced concrete superstructure. Bottom level of the tunnel section had to be at about 11 m below ground level, the combined twin tunnels requiring a structural width for the tunnel of about 10 m. A tunnel of these general dimensions had to be constructed right through the central city area, close to many large buildings founded on piles, with its terminal adjacent to the new Central Railroad Station. Tunneling through the varied soil strata to be encountered would have been difficult and hazardous, especially with the high water table to be handled. Excavation of open trenches for construction by conventional cut-and-cover methods would have involved a massive pumping operation for each section of trench for a 5-year period and great disturbance of groundwater conditions around each trench, even with the most expert use of wellpoints and controlled pumping. The decision was therefore made, in order to avoid pumping, to build even these "inland" sections of the subway tunnel as precast concrete tubes and to float them into place right in the center of the city. This bold operation was

Figure 6.28 Rotterdam, the Netherlands. Another view of the Rotterdam subway under construction looking toward the main railway station and subway terminal; this view gives an idea of the scale of the works by comparison with the automobiles on adjacent streets. *(Courtesy of G. Plantema, Director, Gemeentewerken, Rotterdam.)*

successfully completed in 1967, and the first section of the subway was opened on 9 February of the following year.

The large tunnel sections were constructed in three "dry docks," two in the central city area and one on an island in the Maas about 5.6 km away. Two complete sections could be built in each dock at once. The inland sections measured 45 to 60 m long, 10 to 25 m wide, and 6 to 10 m deep. Sections for the river part of the tunnel, which was also built by sinking tubes, were 90 m long, 10 m wide, and 6 m high. Some of the inland sections had to be curved. They weighed up to 5,090 tonnes, but most fortunately this vast load could easily be carried by water. While the tubes were being built, trenches of the appropriate size were excavated within single rows of steel-sheet piling. Pumping was carried out only for the initial excavation. Installation of the necessary steel bracing was easily completed. The trenches were then allowed to fill up with water, excavation was completed with clam-shell buckets, and specially designed concrete piles were then driven from a floating pile driver all over the bottom of each trench to provide the bearing medium for transmitting the load of the tunnel section down to the underlying sand. At invervals, the great tubes were ballasted with water, their ends having been carefully sealed, and they were then floated along the excavated trench in sequence. When in final position, they were sunk into place and connected with the adjoining tubes by most ingenious sealing mechanisms. Fill was placed around them and on top, the steel piling was removed, and the street surfaces were restored so well that, even shortly after the work had been finished, it was difficult to imagine that sections of railway tunnel had indeed been floated into place along these self-same roadways.

Casual visitors to Rotterdam during the 5-year construction period may have thought to themselves that the Dutch people were enlivening the great city by a modern type of canal with somewhat unattractive steel sides. All visitors who knew anything about building, however, knew that they were looking at one of the boldest urban construction operations ever carried out. They must have shared the admiration felt by the author as he was privileged to follow the necessarily slow progress of this remarkable work during annual visits to Rotterdam during the period of construction. The project will long remain a classic example of fine engineering and excellent construction, taking advantage of unusual subsurface conditions that appear at first sight to be so unfavorable for tunnel construction. Details of the construction techniques employed, especially for the critical river crossing, have been made available in the literature of engineering by those responsible. All that need be said here, in addition, is that construction throughout Holland is complicated by subsurface and groundwater conditions not dissimilar to those in Rotterdam so that examples from Dutch urban developments could feature many sections of this volume. None can compare with the Rotterdam subway construction, however, so that it must be left as the supreme example of how some of the most difficult subsurface conditions beneath any major city have been successfully overcome—because they were known in advance with such certainty.[6.51]

6.12 RECORDS OF TUNNELS

In the practice of civil engineering and building, it is standard to have prepared at the conclusion of construction work a set of "as-constructed drawings." These will be the contract drawings from which the work was built but amended to take into account those minor changes in the structure that were found necessary during the course of construction. The exact level of the foundation and details of the foundation beds will be among the items shown on such records. The value of these final drawings can readily be imagined. They will always be consulted when any changes or additions and extensions have to be made to the structures in question. Frequently, and because they are of such vital importance, they are printed on special linen, in which form they may be expected to last indefinitely. Associated with these as-constructed drawings will be the corresponding written records of everything of significance in connection with the structure that may conceivably be needed in the future. Easy to overlook in the hurry of completing building work, these final records should always have high priority; their preparation often marks the real completion of the job.

With tunnels, the situation is somewhat different; it is for this reason that this engineering matter calls for a brief reference. Apart from the lining in those tunnels that have to be lined, tunnels themselves involve no "structure" of the usual sort that can so readily be shown on drawings. Yet their construction involves considerable interference with natural conditions, and their exact location must be known with certainty in case any other construction operations are to be carried out in their vicinity in later years. This is obvious, but it is remarkable how easy it is to overlook the absolute necessity for the preparation of as-constructed drawings for tunnels. There have been all too many cases in which difficulties have been experienced long after a tunnel has been constructed due to lack of good records of the tunnel as it was constructed, sometimes involving considerable extra cost for future work. There is at least one case in which lack of tunnel records had a tragic result. Even though it is probably a unique example, it may usefully be described briefly since it confirms so strikingly what has just been said.

A small railway tunnel in England known as the Clifton Hall Tunnel, located near Patricroft, Yorkshire, was opened in 1850. It was only 1,185 m long, straight in plan, lined in brick, used for mineral traffic on a branch line until the Second World War. Opened again for limited traffic in October 1947, it was regularly and carefully inspected in the best tradition of British Railways. On a morning in April 1953 the regular inspector noticed a small pile of brick rubble on the track and reported this immediately. Further inspection was made, showing that the brick lining at this point was under stress; corrective measures were immediately planned. Before they could be executed, however, the crown of the tunnel lining failed completely, precipitating a mass of wet sand and rubble into the tunnel. This would not have been serious in itself, since the tunnel was not then in use, but the debris came down an old construction shaft, previously unsuspected, extending up to the ground surface on which three houses had been built. They fell into the shaft and were completely destroyed, and five residents of two of the houses were killed.

A thorough public inquiry was held and the results published in a masterly and constructive report. No blame could be attached to any of those responsible for the tunnel, for the district engineer had no knowledge at all of the old shaft. All the old records in the office of the district engineer had been lost either through air raid damage or in a subsequent fire. What information could be found disclosed that eight shafts had been used to build this short tunnel, probably because of difficulties encountered in the water-bearing sand through which it had been driven. The inspecting officer had this to say:

> The loss of the tunnel records contributed materially to this accident, and the events leading up to it have shown only too clearly the danger that arises when vital knowledge is not readily available. The maintenance staff should know of the existence of old shafts and other features which may cause weaknesses but in many cases the only records are the original construction drawings which, with the growth in the number of documents to be preserved in district engineers' offices, may possibly be overlooked. . . . I recommend, therefore, that all tunnel records be reviewed and that any special features be brought to the notice of the maintenance and examining staff.[6.52]

This simple warning, based as it was on such a tragic occurrence, can well serve as a continuing guide to all who are responsible for the maintenance of tunnels beneath city streets.

6.13 TUNNELS AND GEOLOGY

All excavations necessarily provide a reciprocal relationship with geology. It should be, and today usually is, good practice to consult all possible geological information about the site of any work to be carried out in relation to urban development. When excavation is carried out, it reveals the adequacy of this preliminary information as the actual geological conditions underlying the construction site come into view. This is particularly true of tunnels. Since they penetrate well below the surface of the ground, sometimes at great depths below the surface, their excavation will reveal geological conditions that could not possibly be seen in any other way. Not only should this geology be recorded as a part of the permanent record of the tunnel, but it should be made available for study from the strictly public point of view. Information of scientific interest will always be obtained; sometimes the information will be of great value; occasionally, it will be unique. The geological departments of all universities should, therefore, always be on the alert for the prospective start of any tunneling in their area so that they can solicit permission to view the geology as revealed by the excavation. Larger organizations will have their own geological staffs who will be responsible for this recording of the tunnel geology. In the normal course of their scientific interchanges, they will be able to bring unusual features to the attention of specially interested geologists known to them. It is a professional responsibility to see that all such scientific information is made available generally, to the extent that is possible, for the advancement of the science and in the public interest.

There are, most happily, many records in the public domain that exemplify how tunnel geology can be thus recorded and scientifically evaluated. The great tunnels through the Alps yielded much information about the geological structure of this great mountain group that could not possibly have been obtained in other ways. Information gained in the London tube railway tunnels has added greatly to knowledge of the characteristics of the London Basin. The many great tunnels serving New York have been most faithfully recorded, with summary accounts of the geology published for all to see who are interested. What was, in some ways, the most difficult tunnel ever driven—the Tecolote Tunnel through the Santa Ynez Mountains near Santa Barbara, California, was geologically most interesting, its unusual geology being in large measure the cause of the tunneling difficulties. But the geology was faithfully recorded and described to the Geological Society of America. So the listing may continue. In the hope that they will inspire other geologists to "go and do likewise" and that they will assist in gaining the sympathetic support of civic authorities for such endeavors, a few cases will be described in some detail, selected—it must be stressed—from a large collection.

The water-supply and drainage tunnels of metropolitan Boston were selected for mention earlier so that they could again be referenced in this connection. The structure of the Boston basin has been intensively studied not only by members of the staff of the U.S. Geological Survey (one of whom, Dr. L. LaForge, wrote a masterly report upon it) but also by Professor Marland P. Billings of the Department of Geology at Harvard University. Dr. Billings has himself studied in detail the geology of these tunnels and has encouraged his students to do the same. The result has been a notable series of papers presented to the Boston Society of Civil Engineers, the oldest engineering society of the United States, and published in their journal. Although the geology of these tunnels was studied as excavation progressed, the most detailed mapping that Dr. Billings directed (with the cooperation of the staff of the Metropolitan District Commission) was done after the tunnel walls had been washed down just prior to the placing of the concrete lining. This involved intensive work during a short period, but methods of mapping were developed that made possible the recording of the complete tunnel sections to a scale of 20 ft to the inch. Copies of the resulting folios were placed in the custody of the Construction Division of the commission and with the Department of Geological Sciences of Harvard. Their permanent value can well be imagined and can indeed be studied by all, since, with the aid of ingenious graphical symbols, small-scale sections through the tunnels were included in the BSCE papers in which they were described.[6.53]

More than description was involved, however, for the study of the geology has revealed answers to long-standing questions about the geology of the Boston basin.

In the case of the City Tunnel Extension, the tunnel revealed "for the first time that the Roxbury and Cambridge Formations are actually facies of one another . . . [diagrams showing] that the Cambridge type of lithology inter-fingers with the Roxbury type of lithology . . . ." The explanation is that the Boston Bay group of sediments that became the present bedrock was deposited in a basin, the movements of water across which, in combination with a large deltaic formation, resulted in the variety of rock types in the two formations. More remarkable was the geology as revealed in the Malden Tunnel, for here the major fault, long suspected, between the Cambridge formation and the Lynn volcanic rocks to the north was clearly to be seen. It was naturally examined with unusual care and recorded in detail, confirming the deductions made from study of the geological structure of the basin. These Boston Tunnel papers can be commended without reservation as splendid examples of the sort of record that should be prepared and published for all major tunnels and for all those exhibiting unusual geological features.

Excavation of the first section of the Toronto Subway was similarly selected from the many cut-and-cover jobs that could have been described so that it could also be mentioned here. A symposium of four papers on the geology as revealed by the subway excavation was presented also to the Geological Society of America, which happened to hold its annual meeting in 1953, while the subway construction was in progress, in Toronto. Two general papers described the preliminary investigations and the continuing job study of geology and soil mechanics. A third paper described the Dundas shale as exposed in the bottom of the lower section of the excavation, this being disappointing in a way since no glacial striae were found on the rock surface as might have been expected, and no actual exposure of the Danforth-Humber contact was revealed. This negative result may have shown, alternatively, that there is no contact between the two faunal zones, the junction being a gradual one. A fourth paper discussed the correlation of the soils encountered in the excavation with the local Pleistocene geology. This happens to be world renowned in geological circles since the recent deposits contain some interglacial beds of unusual interest—soils that must have been laid down during periods of much warmer climate than the present, as shown so conclusively by the fossils they contain. Subway excavations in Toronto have therefore been followed with unusual interest by Pleistocene geologists, with the sympathetic interest and support of the Toronto Transit Commission through its general manager of subway construction, and a valuable group of papers in geological literature has resulted.[6.54]

A final example comes from Germany. It is a tale well known to many geologists, but because of its unusual human interest and geological significance, it may well be related again to bring this chapter to a close. One of the great German geologists of recent years was Dr. Hans Cloos. Just before his death he wrote a singularly moving autobiography entitled *Conversation with the Earth*, as translated into English by his brother, Dr. Ernst Cloos. Dr. Cloos was specially interested in the geology of the great valley of the Rhine, about which discussion had continued for many years.

An answer to the riddle of the Rhine graben would settle this great argument. So it was that Dr. Cloos heard with interest of the proposal to construct a short railway tunnel through the Lorettoberg in making a new approach to the railway station in the lovely city of Freiburg in the Black Forest near the Swiss border. He visited the tunnel works regularly as excavation progressed, the western portal starting in sandstone and the eastern in gneiss. The contact between the newer rocks of the Rhine Valley (the sandstone) and the ancient gneiss of the Black Forest and the Vosges might give the answer. In April 1929, Dr. Cloos was able to examine the completed excavation:

> There it was, right before my eyes . . . a furrow ran up the wall into the ceiling and down the other side, as neatly as it had been done with a knife . . . dipping 55° away into the Mountain and downward below the plain . . . . I took pencil and paper and drew as much of the three-dimensional picture as I could to reduce to lines and planes. For the wet spongy stone would not be there for long. It was to be sheathed in and only a little window left open through which posterity may catch a glimpse of the extraordinary phenomenon that I had been privileged to see.[6.55]

chapter seven
Materials of Cities

Wages of John Hobbys, mason, riding to the quarry of Upton and the quarry of Frene to pick out and prove good stones from the bad stones called cropstone, and marking and scrappling and proving the stones so picked out, so that the King shall not be deceived therein, at 6d. a day.

From an entry of 1442 in the Exch. K. R. Accounts regarding the building of Gloucester Castle[7.1]

All the materials used to create cities are derived from the earth. Metals have been obtained by the refining of ores mined from the ground. The trees that supply the wood that is used in such large quantities in almost all building operations can grow only in soil that provides the necessary nutriment and moisture. The asphalt so widely used in road construction may have come from natural asphaltic deposits or from the refining of crude oil obtained from far below ground surface. More obviously, building stone is a geological product used directly after being finished to necessary size and shape. The sand and lime used for mortar have equally obvious geological origins. The soil used for backfilling, for embankments, and for the subgrades of modern highways is another geological product that is used directly. So also are the materials used as aggregate for the manufacture of concrete whether they be natural mixtures of sand and gravel or specially crushed rock mixed with sand, either natural or specially prepared. And the cement that binds together the aggregate particles to make finished concrete without which no modern urban construction can even be imagined, is itself the product of the calcining of suitable mixtures of natural rock materials. Geology therefore lies behind the selection and use of all the materials that provide in combination the structures of cities, remotely so in the case of manufactured materials such as the metals but directly in the case of many so-called building materials.

The term "industrial minerals" is often applied to those naturally occurring materials that can be used directly, or with a minimum of processing, for building. Clay products, cement, lime, sand and gravel, and stone are the main groups usually indicated by this group name. Soil is not generally included since it is not a commercial product in the normal sense, being obtained, if at all possible, from the building site itself. When this is not possible, as for the construction of very large embankments or for earth dams, the selection and provision of the great quantities that may have to be used becomes an integral part of the construction operation, aided by direct application of the techniques of modern soil mechanics. But industrial minerals as such also involve vast quantities and thus considerable expenditures. Typical is the fact that in Canada, even though its mineral production is usually thought of in terms of uranium, gold, silver, nickel, or asbestos (its total production placing it as the third largest mineral

321

producer in the world, surpassed only by the United States and the Soviet Union), about 12 percent of the total annual production of all minerals is accounted for by the production of industrial minerals, almost all of which are used in building. The annual value of these materials is approximately $500 million.[7.2]

This figure is the more remarkable when it is recalled that the unit cost of all industrial minerals is relatively low in comparison with that of other materials. Manufactured products such as cement and lime naturally have unit costs somewhat similar to those for other products manufactured in large quantities, but sand and gravel, as the main example of industrial minerals used directly, can be purchased at the pit where it is produced for relatively low amounts per cubic yard. The qualifications are important. Large quantities have to be used in building, and so the *total* cost for sand and gravel supply can be high.

If the material has to be transported any appreciable distance from the originating pit to the building site, then transport costs can readily come to be even higher than the original purchase cost. This is true of other bulk materials used in building. The understandable result has been the development of sand and gravel pits, of quarries, and of rock-crushing plants as close to cities as possible, with consequences affecting directly the expansion of urban areas that are obvious but that will call for comment later in this chapter.

As was seen in Chap. 2, in earlier days, settlements that became cities were sometimes located because of the availability of good building materials. The examples of Malta, as selected by the Knights of Saint John, and Bath, as developed by the Romans, will be recalled. It is improbable that the supply of materials, other than water, has dictated the location of any permanent settlements in more recent centuries, but there have been numerous cases in which materials that had to be excavated were used for building in the same vicinity, even though this use was a byproduct of the main excavation. The example of Bath may possibly have crossed the mind of that inventive genius Isambard Kingdom Brunel when he came to excavate the famous Box Tunnel on the main line of the Great Western Railway between London and Bristol. Nearly 3.2 km long, it was by far the greatest railway tunnel to be attempted when construction started in 1836. Much trouble was experienced with groundwater, but it was successfully completed in June 1841 at the stupendous cost (for those days) of £6.5 million. Strata encountered were, in the main, clay, blue marl, and the Inferior oolite for about three-quarters of the length, and the Great oolite for the remainder. Most of the tunnel was lined, bricks being specially manufactured in a special plant located in a meadow to the east of the tunnel; 30 million bricks were made and hauled into the tunnel in 100 horse-drawn carts. (Candles had to be used for illumination, another reminder of the early stage in construction that this tunnel represented; 1 tonne of candles was consumed every week.)

Gunpowder was used for blasting, but the Bath Stone that had to be excavated was not too badly shattered. Much of it was salvaged by Brunel and used for the construction of the cottage estate that he developed at Swindon, 40 km from the tunnel, for the workmen in the locomotive shops established there. By 1846 this new town had a population of 5,000. The stone-built houses may still be seen; they have now been declared a "national monument," and so should long remain as an example of sensible frugality in the use of materials. It should be added that Brunel was solemnly warned against trying to build the Box Tunnel by one of the most eminent geologists of those early years, the great Dr. Buckland of Oxford. Even after the tunnel had been triumphantly opened, Buckland still warned that the unlined portion was dangerous and would certainly fall in owing to "the concussion of the atmosphere and the vibration caused by the trains." Brunel replied appropriately, albeit sarcastically, just as he had to the initial warning to which he had paid no more attention. Most fortunately, the liaison between geologists and engineers that Dr. Buckland did not appreciate is now a firmly established part of professional practice in civil engineering.[7.3]

Bath Stone is still being quarried almost 2,000 years after its use by the Romans. Box Hill, under which the famous tunnel is located, contains a labyrinth of tunnels and caverns from which the best stone has been "mined" through the centuries. There is even a siding leading off the main railway line at the tunnel into one of the many underground spaces that make this whole area so interesting and of such strategic importance. There are, for example, 97 km of interconnecting passages in the Box-Corsham area, only a part of which have been explored in recent years by members of the Cotham Caving Group, who have published an interesting account of their findings.[7.4] Only the Monk's Park Quarry is now worked, but it contains a supply of good stone estimated to last for another 200 years. Adjacent to it are some of the many underground areas used for defense purposes, and another that is Britain's sole H-bomb-proof security deposit, operated by a private company. The stone is now mined with modern electrically operated equipment and hauled to the surface up an inclined railway. But the art of the quarryman is still to be seen as one watches an expert foreman test the soundness of one of the large quarried blocks, suspended from a crane, before it is sent up to ground level for storage.[7.5]

From the many other early examples of this use of excavation for building purposes, in days when the costs of construction made this economical, there may be mentioned the great Lockwood Viaduct in Yorkshire, England, on the line from Huddersfield to Penistone of the (old) Lancashire and Yorkshire Railway. This was entirely constructed from 22,920 m^3 of the rock that had to be excavated to form the adjacent cutting at Berry Brow station. On the Southern Railway, immediately on its line to the Kent Coast to the south of London, is the long Penge Tunnel excavated through the London clay. A special brickmaking plant was established at one of the tunnel portals, and all the excavation was taken to this plant where it was molded and fired into building bricks that were then used for railway buildings and houses in the area around.[7.6] Long before this, the same economy of operation had sometimes featured canal building. The anonymous author of the old book (1760) from which the quotation at the head of Chap. 6 was taken (probably James Brindley), in

Figure 7.1 Huddersfield, England. The Lockwood Viaduct on British Railways showing the cutting, rock from which was used in the masonry of the viaduct. *(Courtesy of R.O. Harrison, Editor,* The Huddersfield Examiner.*)*

writing of the Duke of Bridgewater's Canal, one of the earliest in Great Britain, from Manchester to Runcorn near Liverpool, includes this footnote: "I must not omit to observe, that in digging the canal, a kind of sand or gravel was found, which after repeated experiments, was discovered to be lime; and so good a method of burning it was contrived, that it has been made to supply all occasions hitherto, which have been very great, and has saved many thousand pounds, as lime must have been brought thirty miles, if this discovery had not been made."[7.7] (The unusual punctuation is from the book; James Brindley was a practical man, unaccustomed to writing, and did not have the advantage of a modern editor.)

In the New World, the same attention to the economical use of materials features many early works. One of the most unusual examples was the development of local cement for grouting and mortar for the masonry work in the locks and dams of the Rideau Canal in eastern Canada. This lovely waterway, still in use but now for pleasure purposes, was built between 1826 and 1832 as a military waterway joining what is now the city of Ottawa with Kingston on Lake Ontario, its purpose being to provide part of an alternative route between Montreal and Kingston in case hostilities should again break out between the United States and England (Canada then being a colony). Initially, all the cement used was brought from England in casks, being the so-called Harwich cement. This name was used to describe an early form of cement made from septaria dredged from the sea bottom off the port of Harwich on England's east coast. Over 1 million tonnes of "cement stones" were dredged up by as many as 300 small boats to give this early high-class cement. Colonel By, the Royal Engineer officer who built the Rideau Canal, and his young assistant officers must have closely examined the area around the canal works, for they found on the opposite side of the Ottawa River to the entrance locks to the canal a limestone most suitable for calcining into cement. A kiln was established and cement manufactured that "proved a better water-cement than some obtained from the States, and far superior to the Harwich cement, which was nearly spoiled before it reached the canal." Lending special interest to this case is the fact that the Canada Cement Company still operates a cement plant taking limestone from what is believed to be the same location used so long ago, the great quarry now being slowly surrounded as the adjacent municipality of Hull steadily expands.[7.8]

It is only rarely that the same practice can be followed on modern construction projects, although all rock excavated from the Mount Royal Tunnel in Montreal in 1916 was crushed and used as ballast for CNR lines in Montreal, but the possibility is one that should not be forgotten, especially as sources of suitable building material get further and further away from urban building sites. An unusual but significant example is provided by the construction of a large modern hotel in Denver, Colorado. Test borings on the site disclosed the existence of a light-pink pea gravel at such a level that it would have to be excavated in order to provide the necessary space for the basements of the hotel. It was therefore used as the aggregate for the precast concrete panels with which the outer walls of this fine building are sheathed, the panels having been treated with acid after casting and then washed down to expose the attractive-colored gravel aggregate. It is doubtful if great economies were achieved by this use of excavated material, but it lends to this particular hotel unusual geological interest.[7.9] This is in great contrast with the corresponding geological interest provided by the world-famous Brown Palace Hotel in the same city, a massive sandstone building built in the closing years of the nineteenth century but naturally modernized within in recent years without any loss of its special atmosphere. The local red sandstone was not used for this building, for reasons that can now only be imagined and thus cannot be stated; all the stone for the Brown Palace is reported to have come halfway across the continent from Connecticut. These two extreme examples naturally are not typical, despite their interest. In almost all cases of urban building today, the supply of the necessary building materials is a straight matter of economic comparison between various sources of supply so that the geological aspects of the materials used in cities may be considered without specific reference to the geology of building sites.

There are, however, new problems in connection with the materials and cities to which brief attention will have to be directed. They relate to the disposal of materials after use. In olden days, when a building had to be demolished, it was only rarely that the rubble resulting from the demolition of the building was removed from the site. Examples have already been given of modern cities the street levels of which, in their older parts, are now a meter or more higher than the original natural ground level. Prague is a typical example; Warsaw, a very special case. Today this practice can only rarely be followed, and so the disposal of the debris provided by building demolition is an increasingly serious and costly problem. Correspondingly, as the demand for deeper and deeper basements and other underground spaces (such as for automobile parking garages) steadily increases, the disposal of the earth and rock materials so excavated becomes an increasingly difficult problem but one to which some cities are finding satisfactory answers. There is the further and most complex problem of disposing of the waste materials from cities, the solid wastes generally described as garbage and the semiliquid wastes from sewage-treatment plants. Any connection between geology and these problems might seem to be remote, but this is a superficial impression only, as will be demonstrated when the geology of garbage-disposal sites is considered in some detail. Indicative is the fact that the largest source of sediments now being deposited in the Atlantic Ocean along the east coast of the North American continent is not the sand and gravel brought down by one of the large rivers that feature the coast but the waste that is dumped into the sea from the New York metropolitan area.[7.10]

There is yet a further problem that may be appropriately considered briefly in this chapter—one that readers may have expected to have been concerned merely with the provision and use of building stone. This is the fact that sometimes cities have been located, unknowingly, right above valuable mineral resources. Water and petroleum provide special cases since they can be removed, under control, usually without serious effects upon the city above their natural location within the ground. But a mineral such as coal, for example, cannot normally be removed if it is in any way close to the surface without disruption of civic facilities. There are cases in which complete towns have had to be moved to new locations in order that the coal deposits beneath them might be worked and the coal removed. And there is one case in which coal was removed from far below surface level deliberately to induce settlement at the surface for an almost unique reason. This wide-ranging influence of the geological aspects of materials in the development and operation of cities is usually so unsuspected that this capsule summary has been provided at the outset of this chapter so that the individual features of the subject may be properly appreciated against the more general background. To the ancient but still vitally important subject of building stone, attention will first be directed.

7.2 BUILDING STONE

Aberdeen, on the east coast of Scotland, is known around the world as "the Granite City"—at least to all expatriate Scots and also to many geologists. Its famous quarries have provided splendid building stone not only for all its own main buildings but for buildings in many other cities, even as far away as San Francisco. But it is the use of fine gray granite for Aberdeen's own buildings that has given the city such a pleasing appearance so obvious as one walks its wide streets, an impression well conveyed by the nickname it has acquired. There are similar popular designations of cities related to the stone from which their major buildings have been constructed in many countries of the world. Kingston, Ontario, is a fine old Canadian town long known as the "Limestone City" (see page 101). Some readers may recall how this influence of building stone on the "atmosphere" of a city is reflected in the writings of John Ruskin, not only in *The Stones of Venice* but in other works, so that it is not surprising to find that this eminent writer of the Victorian age was himself keenly interested in geology.

Visitors to the campus of the University of Saskatchewan, in the Canadian prairie city of Saskatoon, are often attracted by the pleasing appearance of the well-proportioned older buildings of the university, all built from a buff-colored limestone. The use of this building stone, for all but a few of the more recent buildings, gives

Figure 7.2 Saskatoon, Saskatchewan, Canada. Buildings on the campus of the University of Saskatchewan, all constructed of local fieldstone. *(Courtesy of the University of Saskatchewan and J. J. Hamilton, Saskatoon.)*

to this campus an architectural unity that is generally appreciated by observant strangers when they first see the university. Those with any geological interests will naturally ask about the source of this building stone, especially if they know that the outcrops of bedrock nearest to the city are about 320 km away, in the northeast corner of the province of Saskatchewan, just south of the southern edge of the Precambrian Shield. The limestone, both dolomitic and calcareous, comes generally from an Ordovician formation known as the Red River formation, some from two allied Ordovician formations, and some from the Interlake formation, which is Silurian in age. These Palaeozoic rocks do outcrop in the location mentioned, but the building stone was not obtained from the outcrop. When early farmers started to clear the land around Saskatoon and to the northeast of the city, they found many boulders on the land. These were cleared in the usual manner and piled up to the extent that early farm equipment made possible. Those responsible for the first buildings at the university saw in these boulders an economical source of building stone. They were hauled to the building site and there worked by masons into the desired shapes for building purposes. Their origin was in what is called a *boulder train*, a collection of glacial erratics, scoured out from the underlying bedrock by glaciers and deposited from the glacial ice in a fanlike formation, the apex of which is approximately 40 km to the northeast of the city of Saskatoon.[7.11]

Not many cities have such a natural source of good building stone provided for them, but a little study will show quite unexpected resourcefulness on the part of the early builders of many cities. Dr. Clifford A. Kaye of the U.S. Geological Survey has given an interesting description of the development of building in the city of Boston, the geology of which he has studied so carefully:

> After the initial pioneer period of timber construction (about 1630–1670), earth materials were widely used for public and commercial buildings and for the more expensive town houses. For nearly 150 years, Boston was preeminently a red-brick city. Glacial marine clays were abundant in the area and brick-making was a natural consequence. The adaption of red brick to eighteenth century Georgian architecture resulted in that happy blend of colour and style known as Colonial Georgian . . . . In the mid-eighteenth century, a family of German stone dressers moved to Quincy and plied their trade for a few years. Enough stone was dressed to build King's Chapel (still standing) and the fine house of John Hancock . . . but after the Germans moved away, the city slipped back to brick . . . . In the early nineteenth century came almost four decades of splendid granite construction, Boston being transformed from a red-brick provincial city into a city of fine classical stone buildings matching—at least in the eyes of its loyal citizens—the great stone cities of Europe. This followed the decision of the committee responsible for the Bunker Hill monument to have a great stone obelisk as the monument. For economic reasons, the stone had to be quarried locally. The dark grey granite of nearby Quincy was found to be most suitable for building purposes and so stone quarrying was taken up seriously with such

satisfying results for Boston architecture. The Classical Revival style of architecture rapidly lost favour in mid-nineteenth century to be followed by a style based more on the architecture of the Middle Ages. Many fine churches in the newly filled Back Bay area are amongst the continuing buildings from this period. A search for a building stone of the appropriate texture and colour to satisfy this medievalism led to the discovery of the Roxbury conglomerate; quarries were opened up less than two miles away and a new phase of Boston building was aided by this second local building stone.[7.12]

There must be many comparable stories of great local interest regarding the uses made of local building stones by cities both ancient and modern, extending in time up to about the start of the twentieth century. With the excellent transportation facilities then available through national rail networks, building stones could be selected from

Figure 7.3 Boston, Massachusetts. Contrasting architectural styles based on local building materials; the brick building on the right is typical of eighteenth-century Boston; the customhouse on the left is one of the classical revival buildings constructed in 1850 using the local Quincy granite, one of the last buildings to use this stone; the columns consist of single shafts of granite, an indication of the advance in the art of quarrying and stone dressing in the preceding few decades. *(Photograph by C. A. Kaye, courtesy of the U.S. Geological Survey.)*

a wide variety and brought great distances for local use. At the same time, the use of structural steel and reinforced concrete frameworks was beginning its great advance that so revolutionized the whole concept of building design, an advance that still continues. Stone rapidly ceased to be the material used for bearing walls, as in older designs, building frames now providing the structural support for buildings Outer walls came to be a sheathing for the frames, providing protection from the weather and, in more recent buildings, the envelope for the containment of controlled interior climate. There was a time when some thought that the days of building stone were numbered, but its enduring qualities and the technological advances made by building-stone producers have combined to ensure its continued importance as a building material.

Massive masonry is still regularly used for monumental buildings and for the more ornamental parts of modern frame buildings, such as entrances. The main use of stone today, however, is in the form of cut stone or masoned stone, thin slabs of stone cut to close tolerances and used as a facing material for exterior walls or for special interior finishes. The most modern types of cutting machinery are now used for the shaping of cut stone, with elaborate controls in the largest plants, but the selection of the stones to be cut still depends upon the art of the quarryman. Since, in developed countries, the stone quarries still in use are the larger and older ones (small quarries developed for special jobs having usually become obsolete), the principal building stones in use today are the stones that are "tried and true," with many years of experience in their use now available. The significant place still occupied by these materials in modern building is indicated by the fact that there are now available standard specifications for use in the procurement of cut stone, either in the form of dimensioned slabs of stone or even in the form of "sandwich slabs" of stone combined, through the medium of special adhesives, with insulating material. Typical is Standard No. C568-67 of the American Society for Testing and Materials, a standard developed by a truly representative committee including representatives not only of stone producers but of stone users.[7.13] It is, therefore, entirely appropriate that this attention should be devoted to this long-standing building material, allied so closely as it is with the geology of the bedrock from which it comes.

Well-established producers of building stone have expert technical staffs ready to supply to those who need it the best available information on the properties and the proper use of the stones they sell. In newer countries such a service is not normally available. Brief note may therefore be made of some of the requirements that should be followed in the use of natural building stone. It is always advisable to use sedimentary rocks, such as limestones and sandstones, in settings that are parallel to their bedding planes. It is clearly essential that this orientation should be determined before rough stone is dressed. No matter how desirable it may be from the architectural point of view, sandstones and limestones should never be used in direct contact with one another. All mortar for use in masonry work should be kept as low in lime, and particularly in cement, as possible. The moisture properties of a new building stone should be determined most carefully. Many stones will have an appreciably high

Figure 7.4 Wichita, Kansas. Precast panels of sand-blasted texture-vein marble and reinforced concrete being set in place on the building of the American Savings Association, a new form of use for building stone. *(Courtesy of the Carthage Marble Co., C. T. Yarbrough, Vice President.)*

moisture content when first quarried; for this reason, many stones are not used until an appreciable time after quarrying, but they are naturally easier to work when freshly taken from the quarry. In the process of naturally drying out, the movement of water toward the surfaces of the stone will also draw dissolved salts to the surface, where they will accumulate as the water evaporates. Expanding to fill the pores in the outer surfaces of the stone, these salts in the course of time will give a tough outer "skin" that is so desirable a feature in resisting the deleterious effects of pollutants in the atmosphere. Without going any further into these practical matters, it can readily be seen that all of them depend upon the geological character of the stone. This must be determined with accuracy before any work is done in the development of a new quarry.

Figure 7.5 Portland, Dorsetshire, England. Typical limestone strata in the long-used Portland Stone quarry on the Isle of Portland. *(Courtesy of the Stone Firms Ltd., J. V. Borthwick, Managing Director.)*

Because building stone is a natural material, used directly as it is won from the ground, it is possible to correlate any potential new source of building stone with stones that have been in satisfactory use for many years, or even centuries, and even in other countries, provided that exposure conditions are to be similar. The accumulated experience that is available in older countries can, therefore, be turned to good effect in newer countries if proper geological correlation is made. Two of the oldest building stones still in wide use and so providing centuries of experience are the Bath and Portland Stones mentioned in Chap. 2 in connection with Roman settlements, their use probably going back even to pre-Roman times. Both are oolitic limestones of Jurassic age; they can therefore be dated geologically as being about 145,000,000 years old. The term "oolitic" indicates a texture of the rock not unlike fish roe, each little rounded particle visible to the naked eye, being an accumulation of calcium carbonate around a fragment of shell or grains of sand or silt. The Doulting stone used for the construction of and today for repairs to Wells Cathedral is similar. Now widely used in England as facing stone, in dimensioned cut form, these famous stones can provide invaluable experience in their use and exposure to a variety of atmospheric and climatic conditions. They still come from quarries in the same location as used by the Romans, the beds still mined in the same way although with modern equipment.[7.14]

In the case of the Portland quarry, for example, when the cap rock has been removed, a bed known as the Roach is first encountered. It gives a limestone with a pronounced shell formation and is much used for ashlar work. Then comes the thicker Whitbed, which gives a fine-grained evenly textured stone, that which is in most common use for building purposes. Finally comes the Basebed, which gives an equally useful stone with little shell texture so that it is widely used for decorative work. Much more could be said about these famous stones—about the widespread use of Portland Stone, for example, by Sir Christopher Wren in the rebuilding of London after the Great Fire of 1666—but the only further comment that can be made is about the distance of the quarries from London, where so much of the stone was (and still is) used in view of what was said earlier about the necessary use, in older times, of strictly local building stones. The explanation of this departure from normal practice is given by the fact that Portland Stone is quarried almost on the seashore so that it

Figure 7.6 Corsham, Wiltshire, England. Inclined tunnel and steps leading from the Monk's Park mine in which Bath Stone is still quarried, stone being hauled to the surface from the underground workings up this incline. *(Courtesy of the Stone Firms Ltd., J. V. Borthwick, Managing Director.)*

was possible to transport it to London very easily in sailing ships, London itself being a notable port.

There are, unfortunately, examples of bad weathering of building stone that will be known to most readers. Before any final judgment is made, however, the geological suitability of the stone for the use to which it was put should carefully be studied. Not only have location and local climate to be considered but even the details of the architectural design in which the stone has been incorporated. Much unsightly staining of cut stone used as wall facing, for example, is to be seen in many modern buildings. In some cases this can clearly be seen to be due to the omission of window sills and the associated "drips" that were developed by experience as desirable design details but that are frowned upon by some architects of today. The simplest form of weathering of exposed stone is that due to the physical action of wind and rain in actually eroding material from exposed surfaces. There is abundant evidence to show that this is in itself an extremely slow process. Exposed parapet copings of Portland Stone high up on the outside of St. Paul's Cathedral in London have been studied and found to have eroded only 13 mm in 250 years.[7.15]

Staining has been mentioned; it is sometimes classed as weathering but strictly speaking is usually only a change in appearance. In older cities where soft coal is still used as fuel, staining with soot can be most unsightly, but it is rarely serious. What is important and a feature of increasing seriousness in cities is the acid content of many urban atmospheres. If in an area of regular rainfall, this pollution can result in rain that is acidic; if this lies on ledges on the exterior of buildings, it can induce very serious deterioration. It has been found, for example, that the sulfuric acid content of soot-laden rainwater can be as high as 5 percent. Here is yet another even if a minor reason for strong support for the current attack on all phases of atmospheric pollution. Physical deterioration of exposed stonework through pitting or even slaking is the most serious type of weathering. It will always call for detailed investigation as soon as it has been detected, since the cause may be one of many. Fortunately, it is today experienced but rarely and so need not be discussed in detail. Internal movement of water is sometimes involved, associated with crystallization of salts brought to the surface, in effect an artificially induced version of the natural weathering that occurs when most stone is exposed to the air after quarrying.

It follows that the cleaning of exposed stonework, so often a part of civic rehabilitation measures, is something to be embarked upon with the greatest caution since irreparable damage can be done if the protective "skin" that exposure gives to many stones is destroyed. Before any cleaning is attempted, geological advice should be sought regarding the characteristics of the stone that is to be cleaned. Experience with the cleaning of this type of stone elsewhere should be sought out and, in every case, experimental cleaning done on some obscure area of the stone that will not result in disfigurement should it be decided to leave the stained or darkened stone just as it is. Cleaning with plain water at appropriate pressure is the easiest and safest method and can often effect good results. The use of sandblasting or of chemical cleaning agents must always be most carefully assessed before any work commences, lest far more harm be done than the beneficial results to appearance.

It is hoped that even this summary treatment of a subject that so obviously has such wide ramifications has indicated the special interest that building stones can provide to all who have any concern for the buildings they use. In Chap. 9, reference will be made to the information that is all too infrequently made available to visitors about the stones at which they look when they admire a building. This public geological interest is (at least to the author) so desirable a matter that, as a brief indication of what will be said later, three famous buildings will here be mentioned. The Capitol of the United States, dominating the Washington scene, includes within its structures a number of different kinds of building stone from a number of locations in the United States. The Senate and House of Representatives' wings are finished with marble that came from Lee, Massachusetts. They were built between 1855 and 1865. The East Front of the Center Building, built between 1958 and 1962, is finished in Georgia marble, the original wall, now an inside wall, having been of sandstone as is the West Front, dating from 1829, the stone being from Aquia Creek in Virginia. Interior stairways are of granite, but none of these building stones is marked as to their origin.[7.16]

Figure 7.7 Washington, D.C. The west front of the Capitol, the two wings being of white marble, the central section of sandstone, painted white to match the wings. *(Courtesy of G. M. White, Architect of the Capitol, and the Library of Congress.)*

The stones used for the building of the stately Parliament Buildings in Westminster, the Palace of Westminster being still the official name, are of such interest that at least two volumes have been written about them. The buildings so well known today include parts dating back to the year 1099, with additions built at various times during the intervening centuries. A disastrous fire in 1834 destroyed most of the old palace; the Commons Chamber and other parts were seriously damaged in air raids during the Second World War. Clipsham Stone has been used for most of the recent restoration work, this being yet another local variety of the Jurassic oolitic limestone of central England; it has been widely used for the building of Oxford's colleges. A variety of stones is to be found in Westminster Hall, even some from Caen; Bath Stone was used for some restoration about 1820. After the 1834 fire, four commissioners were appointed to select a suitable stone for the great job of reconstruction; William Smith, the "Father of English Geology," was one and the Director of the Geological Survey, Thomas de la Beche, another. After exhaustive study, they recommended the use of a dolomitic limestone from Anston, but within 20 years another commission had to be appointed to consider the "Decay of the Stone of the New Palace of Westminster." The fault appears to have been due to the absence of inspection of the stone used at the quarry; it was said that if only 15 percent of the original stone had been rejected, trouble would have been obviated. A very full report on the performance of stone at Westminster was published in 1926. Portland Stone was used for the postwar reconstruction of the Cloisters to St. Stephen's Chapel, with Caen Stone being used internally to match some of the older work. These notes merely touch upon this fascinating record of the use of so many of the leading building stones of England in these most famous buildings, a visit to which will probably always reveal some building in stone still in progress.[7.17]

Finally there may be mentioned the Parliament Buildings of Canada, located on a prominent hill overlooking the Ottawa River and forming the focal point of the Canadian capital. The East and West Blocks remain from the original group of three buildings built when Ottawa was little more than a village; the original Center Block, all but the famous Library, was destroyed by fire in 1916. Local Nepean sandstone was used for most of the original three buildings and for all rough stonework of the new Center Block with its fine Peace Tower. A sandstone from Ohio was used in the original buildings for dressings and pinnacles, together with a contrasting red sandstone from Potsdam in New York for all door and window trim. The Potsdam sandstone was not used for the new Center Block, but the Ohio sandstone was, as well as Tyndal limestone from Manitoba for all interior finish. Its high fossil content lends an unusual but attractive (and "very geological") appearance to the interior hallways.[7.18]

7.3 QUARRIES

Building stone must be quarried from the ground. The resulting excavations are often extensive and sometimes an impediment to urban planning if they have been located

Figure 7.8 Ottawa, Canada. Main entrance doorway to the East Block of the Parliament Buildings of Canada, built in 1860; three varieties of sandstone may be seen, and an ingenious use of fieldstone in the decorative panel above the door. *(Courtesy of Information Canada.)*

so close to a central city area that the growth of the city surrounds them. The Rubislaw Quarry in Aberdeen from which most of the famous Aberdeen granite has come is now in this position. It was opened by the Corporation of the City of Aberdeen in 1741 and so has been in continuous operation for well over 200 years, now for many years under private ownership. It is not therefore too surprising to find it hailed as the deepest quarry in the world, the working level being now 146 m below ground surface, or 55 m below sea level. It is 275 m long and 230 m wide, dimensions that are dwarfed by its great depth, as may be seen from Fig. 7.9, which shows also how urban development now surrounds this famous "hole in the ground." Over 6 million tonnes of the "Blue granite" from this quarry have now been used for the buildings of Aberdeen in the first instance and for buildings in every continent as well. It was used, for example, for the construction of John Rennie's first masterpiece, the Waterloo Bridge across the Thames in London (1811–1817). When this had to be replaced in the 1930s, part of the balustrade was presented by the owners, the London County Council, to the quarry company as a memento of well over a century of service. In the early years of this century as many as 60 men were employed as "sett makers," hand-cutting the granite into small cubes for use as roadway setts such as may still be seen in some older roads in Europe even today. All recent production has been for building purposes, but as this book goes to press the future of the great quarry is in doubt; its product will long be in use around the world.[7.19]

When quarries of this kind have to be abandoned within city limits, they pose difficult problems for urban planners. Rarely are they shallow enough to be used for normal building purposes. Filling is the obvious solution, but this is difficult to undertake in a satisfactory manner if future settlement of the finished surface is to be avoided. The area can be reclaimed, however, but the assistance of skilled professional advice is essential. Of extreme importance in all such cases is the recording in detail of the outlines of the final shape of the quarry and the nature of the fill used. This information can be of vital assistance in the future use of the filled site. It is improbable that new quarries for building stone will be opened up in the close vicinity of existing cities, but in newly developing areas they will still be needed. It is hardly necessary to record the desirability of so locating new quarries that they will not interfere with normal urban development, but the experiences with sand and gravel pits that will shortly be recorded is warrant for at least this passing reference. Dr. Asher Shadmon of Israel has put on record useful guides to the selection of new quarry sites based upon experience gained in locating an entirely new quarry for building stone of an unusual kind, that used for the construction of the new break-water in the new harbor at the ancient town of Ashdod some kilometers to the south of Tel Aviv, a town that was briefly mentioned in Chap. 4. He points out the necessity for attempting to estimate the needs for rock supply for many years to come, and the integration of this study with overall urban planning, before any final location is approved.[7.20]

There will be few locations where underground quarrying can be conducted so conveniently as in the Kansas City area of Missouri, as described in the last chapter. There is one location, however, where underground mining of limestone was carried out in a manner that has left a unique legacy of geological problems, this being the city of Paris. Even here the story must start with the Romans, for they had selected Paris as a convenient site for a settlement. With a technical skill that even today excites surprise, they discovered that beneath the geographically convenient site there were horizontal beds of rock that could supply good building stone. The entire city is underlain with almost horizontal beds of excellent limestone suitable for building and, beneath the limestone strata, a thick bed of gypsum. From the time of the Romans until the year 1813 practically all building in Paris was carried out using stone

Figure 7.9 Aberdeen, Scotland. Rubislaw quarry from which so much Aberdeen granite has come; the scale of the quarry is given by the houses around. *(Courtesy of B. W. Tawse, Deputy Chairman, Aberdeen Construction Group Ltd.)*

quarried from beneath the city streets. Toward the end of this long period, interior finish was of plaster also derived from the same unusually convenient local source. To begin with, access was gained to the limestone beds by driving in simple adits on the sloping ground where it was exposed. This operation was limited, however, with the result that much of the quarried stone was hoisted up into the center of the city through specially excavated shafts, some of which can be seen today. The limestone was regularly quarried from two levels and the gypsum from beneath the lower limestone quarry level. Parts of central Paris are, therefore, still underlain by three "tiers" of quarry workings. The limestone quarries were worked by leaving pillars of the rock in place to serve as supports for the excavated sections. Roof cover varied from as little as 2 m to a maximum of 35 m. With adequate cover, the quarries did not interfere with the normal life of the city, but when the cover decreased to its minimum value, dangers arose and collapses into the workings did occur.

These had become so serious by the latter part of the eighteenth century, when the quarries were being exploited to an increasing extent, that in 1777 a special commission was established to investigate the ancient workings and to make recommendations about their strengthening. This followed serious accidents in 1774 and 1776 in which a number of lives were lost. This commission was the precursor of l'Inspection Generale des Carrières de la Seine, established on 18 November 1810 and still responsible to this day for the supervision of all aspects of these underground workings, including the well-known catacombs of Paris. The latter were special workings in the limestone made to accommodate the bones from the cemeteries of Paris that were converted to other purposes in the eighteenth and nineteenth centuries, notably the Chantier des Innocents. Well known to tourists, the catacombs are identical in concept to the older limestone quarries. Within 3 years of the establishment of the inspectorate, an imperial decree was issued by Napoleon prohibiting any further use of this unique source of building stone and gypsum. From the year 1813 Paris has therefore had to obtain its building materials in more orthodox ways, but the quarries remain. In total, they cover an area of 835 hectares of limestone beneath Paris itself and 65 hectares of gypsum, representing about 10 percent of the area of the city. The total areas within the Department of the Seine, including the city, are 1,300 hectares of limestone, 263 hectares of gypsum, and 19 hectares of chalk workings.

All the workings were most accurately mapped by the inspectorate and these invaluable urban records have been kept up to date ever since. Now plotted in color on geological maps that show at a glance the excavations at the three levels, these records must be among the very earliest maps of urban geology ever to be prepared. So remarkable are these maps of the subsurface of Paris that, by special permission of the Inspecteur Général des Carrières, a portion of one of the maps has been reproduced as the end papers of this volume. Its strange but artistic beauty—which has real meaning—can be left to speak for itself. Inspection of all the workings has been carried out regularly throughout the 160-year history of the inspectorate. When it is found to be necessary, new roof supports are constructed. All new surface con-

Figure 7.10 Paris, France. Underpinning with hand-placed masonry in the old underground limestone quarries of Paris to support structure of the new autoroute H.6 in Paris at Rungis. *(Courtesy of M. Perricaudet, Adjoint á l'Inspecteur Général des Carrières, Paris.)*

struction above the workings must naturally be checked with the inspectorate and recorded with them. When deep foundations are involved, special concrete supports will be necessary within the old workings, and these must be completed before any normal construction can begin. Building of the Paris Metro posed unusual problems, but these were all readily solved and without difficulty because of the availability of the excellent underground records. The example chosen as an illustration shows very clearly the special masonry pillars ("underpinning" of a very special kind) that was necessary in the lower levels of the workings before the autoroute could be constructed at this location. It is hoped that the use of this illustration will demonstrate, if only because of its unusual character and its macabre association with the catacombs of Paris, the vital importance of accurate records of the subsurface of all cities, even though none may have the peculiar problem that led Paris to be a pioneer in this field so many years ago.[7.21]

7.4 BRICK AND TILE

When early man was unable to use caves for his shelter or to find convenient stone for simple buildings, he was forced into the use of other materials. Wood would naturally have been a first choice when available, and it is known that this versatile material served early man just as it serves the world today. When wood was not available, still other indigenous materials had to be used. The building of huts made of grass sods cut out of the lush prairie ground in the early days of settlement in western Canada, and the continuing use by the Eskimo of snow for the building of their ingenious and singularly efficient igloos, are modern examples of this enforced choice of building materials. Soil was the only material available for building purposes in many parts of the ancient world. Its use as a building material is probably as old as, if not indeed older than, the use of stone. One can imagine its being used at first merely as "mud," to be molded into small shelters in a manner not unlike the use of mud huts today in some primitive areas. The effect of the heat of the sun in drying soil that has been wetted would have given the idea of molding the soil into convenient forms before it was used in the body of a hut, and so the idea of sun-dried bricks can be traced back to the dawn of human history. By Roman times, sun-dried bricks of high quality were in regular use for building. Vitruvius, for example, has a complete chapter dealing with bricks in one of his famous *Ten Books on Architecture*. "They should be made in Spring or Autumn," he says, "so that they may dry uniformly. At Utica," he explains "in constructing walls they use brick only if it is dry and made five years previously, and approved as such by the authority of a magistrate"—surely one of the earliest examples of that extremely difficult control, the approval of building materials?[7.22]

It was but a step to the acceleration of the drying process by application of artificial heat and thence to the use of furnaces, once it was discovered that the effect of "burning" gave a greatly improved product, really a different material. Although early brickmaking in kilns was an empirical process based on gradually accumulating experience, brickmaking of today is a highly scientific procedure, using modern equipment for mixing the ingredients, for molding, pressing, or extruding the moist bricks, pipes, or other products, and then for firing them in specially designed kilns under rigid control, aided by well-established standards and standard test methods for evaluating the finished products. The range of burned-clay products will be well known, extending all the way from small decorative tiles to sewer pipes of the largest size in normal use.

Burned-clay brick and tile products, therefore, have come to be manufactured products that can be ordered "off the shelf" with a wide variety of properties, including color and surface texture, always manufactured to high and definite standards of quality. It is well to remember, however, that they are made directly from clay or shale that must be properly selected to give satisfactory products. Established brick and tile plants have their own developed supplies, but there are still many parts of the world where brickmaking is a local operation of limited capacity. The making of brick in simple plants gives promise of being one way in which the necessary building can economically be carried out in those rapidly developing parts of the world that are not yet heavily industrialized. Guides are available to the best selection of clays and shales for this purpose. Geology will be an essential guide to the probability of there being useful "brick clays" in areas being newly developed. The combination of geological information and technical guides to brickmaking should help to eliminate the long periods necessary in earlier days for the simple experimentation by which the possibility of local brickmaking had to be explored. Champlain, the founder of

Canada, for example, when deciding in 1611 on the location of his first tiny settlement on what is now the island of Montreal, found "many level stretches of very good potter's clay suitable for brick-making and building, which is a great convenience. I had a portion of it prepared, and built a wall . . . to see how it would last during the winter when the floods came down . . ." this being the start of building research in Canada.[7.23]

All travelers in India are reminded by every village they pass of the dominant place that brick plays in that vast country, almost every village having at least one simple brick plant. They have to use the soils immediately available. While some of these are clays that mold easily with water and burn hard at reasonably low temperatures, thus giving good bricks despite the simplicity of the manufacturing process, there are areas in which suitable clays are not available. Research work is therefore proceeding, in India and elsewhere, into alternative methods of brickmaking with local materials, such as sand-lime bricks or even concrete bricks. Now widely available in developed countries, these manufactured products are similar to fired-clay bricks in their uniformity and good quality. They, too, are made directly from naturally occurring materials, the availability of which will be especially strong in newly developing areas where economic considerations will be evident from study of the local geology. The temptation to locate new brickmaking plants as near as possible to the area of building will be so all-important. Even here, however, the probability of expansion of urban areas must be kept in mind. One has only to think of the local brick plant in almost every "hometown" that has had to be moved into the country

Figure 7.11 Cooksville, Ontario, Canada. Working face of a modern brick-clay-shale quarry. *(Courtesy of Domtar Construction Materials Ltd., J. Cochran, President, and W. M. Naish, Manager of Manufactured Clay Production.)*

as it was engulfed by urban sprawl to appreciate that preliminary consideration of the geological source of local building materials must be an essential part of all urban planning.

7.5 ROAD–MAKING MATERIALS

The importance of road construction in urban areas is sometimes overlooked. It is, for example, not generally appreciated that even in a country as large as Canada, second largest country in the world, about one-half of all the paved roads of the country are located within urban areas. The building of roads is therefore an important part of the building of cities. Good road construction has always been a hallmark of sound development. Telford's great work in building roads in the Highlands of Scotland in the early nineteenth century has been described as bringing an improvement "unequalled in the history of any people." The Romans were preeminent in this regard. At one time they had about 80,000 km of good roads in regular use. They paid special attention to the subgrades of their roads, a matter now regarded as of supreme importance. Typical of their construction methods was the use of a base course of sand upon which four separate layers of masonry were laid with the addition of a simple kind of concrete. In Italy, the top layer (the *summa crusta*) was usually constructed of lava cut into hexagonal shapes so carefully that the joints could scarcely be seen. The Romans always selected the hardest stone they could readily procure in each district served by their roads, just as did the Incas in their almost incredible road construction down the Andes in the northwestern part of South America. Passing through scenery as mountainous as it was beautiful and 6,500 km long and 7.6 m wide, the great road of the Incas excites admiration even today, for some of it is still in use. When built, parts of it were even paved with bitumen; here again there is little new under the sun.[7.24]

Among the road-making materials used regularly by the Romans was the waste from iron forges, especially the cinders from the forge fires. Roads so constructed were known as *viae ferriae*, a name that is said to be the origin of the French term *chemins ferrés* and almost certainly the origin of the English expression *road metal*. So recent have been the basic changes in road construction that there will be readers of this book who can recall hearing this old term actually in use. It derives from the use of crushed stone that dates from the start of modern road development in France and Great Britain in the early years of the nineteenth century. Thomas Telford and James Loudon McAdam (whose name is memorialized in "macadamized" roadways) were the two great British pioneers. Although differing in their ideas on roadway design, each in his own way had a thorough appreciation of the importance of geology in road planning and in the selection of natural materials for road-making.

The necessity for good wearing surfaces for city streets to resist the abrasion of steel-rimmed wheels and to give adhesion for horses, the universal source of motive power, led to the development of special pavements using both natural or manufactured materials in the form of granite setts or paving brick. Granite setts, usually 10-cm cubes, used to be one of the main products of all granite quarries, as in the case of the Rubislaw quarry. Although generally superseded, they may still be seen in use in the older parts of industrial cities and quite frequently, even on country roads, in the older parts of Europe, such as in central Bohemia. In Prague may also still be seen slices cut from large trees and trimmed to hexagonal shape forming the roadways of ancient courtyards—an early example of acoustical control. When naturally shaped hexagonal blocks were readily available, as from quarries in basalt, they were sometimes used directly, a practice that may still be seen in use today for the revetments along the banks of the Rhine, some of the hexagonal blocks so used coming from Czechoslovakia.

With the turn into the twentieth century came also the beginnings of great changes in traffic upon roads and streets, especially in cities, and a corresponding change in the previous somewhat empirical approach to the design and construction of roadways. It was in 1906 that the first "scientific" tests were made on soil, for example, technical papers upon advances in highway work beginning to appear about 1914. Following the years of the First World War, this development accelerated to such a degree that the interwar years saw what may truly be called a revolution in highway engineering. Soil was used as an engineering material. Drainage was recognized as of paramount importance in all road construction and maintenance. The cross sections through roadway surfaces and subgrades became examples of good structural design, selected for the wheel loads that they would have to carry. More recently, the same scientific procedures have been further extended to the design of runways and taxi strips for airports, "structures" (for such they are) capable of carrying safely in all types of weather such loads as the 355 tonnes of the modern "jumbo jets." Soil, carefully tested, mixed if necessary with small quantities of cement or other stabilizers, compacted to proper density, its state in the ground ensured by adequate drainage facilities, naturally remains as the main supporting material, transferring the wheel and other loads from the materials of the pavement to the underlying natural ground. For simple rural roads, the pavement itself may be constructed of stabilized soil or soil cement; oiled surfaces are also so used. For roads with heavier traffic the choice will be between an asphaltic so-called flexible-surface finish or one of concrete, with concrete of appropriate strength sometimes used beneath the actual wearing surface of a modified asphaltic mixture.

This summary outline of modern highway construction has been given in order to make clear the supreme importance of the three main materials—all directly of geological origin—soil, asphalt, and concrete. Since soil and concrete are so widely used in other ways, they will be treated in following sections. Asphalt will not generally be so familiar to others than engineers; it is a truly remarkable material. The word is properly used to describe solid or semisolid native bitumens and bitumens that are obtained by refining petroleum, which melt upon the application of heat and which consist of a mixture of hydrocarbons and their derivatives. A vast technology has been developed to serve all users of bitumens and bituminous mixtures, but it will have been noted that, whether obtained directly in nature or extracted from petroleum, asphalts are ultimately derived from geological formations. The naturally occurring asphalts are of unusual geological interest. Important deposits of pure bitumen are found near the Dead Sea and in the world-famous Asphalt Lake in Trinidad. Refined bitumens are obtained from a wide variety of crude petroleums. Of special geological interest also are the asphalt-bearing rocks that are found in many parts of the world and that may be used, after crushing, directly in highway work. Many of the streets of Paris have been paved with such material. From the numerous examples of its use in North America, the practice of the Texas Highway Department may be cited.

About 160 km west of the city of San Antonio is found a porous and highly fossiliferous limestone known as the Anacacho formation, a member of the Gulf series of Cretaceous rocks. The formation covers a wide area, but that part with the highest concentration of natural asphaltic content is found in southern Uvalde and Kinney Countries. In the 1890s asphalt was actually extracted from this rock for use in the paint and rubber industries. It was used, after crushing and screening, in the construction of streets and sidewalks in San Antonio as early as the turn of the century. It was put to wider use in highway construction for paving in 1912. This was the start of a gradual increase in its use in road work to such an extent that the Texas Highway Department has been using more than half a million tonnes of it every year since the early 1950s.

According to Dr. T. S. Patty, "the asphalt content of the presently mined lime-

Figure 7.12 Uvalde County, Texas. Rock-asphalt quarry and processing plant. *(Courtesy of White's Mines, C. Holloway, Sales Manager, San Antonio, and the Texas Highway Department.)*

stone ranges from less than 1% to about 14% ... [but] ... quarry operations coupled with plant practices are used to blend proper proportions of the 'lean' rock with the 'rich' to insure an asphalt content between 5 and 9% [by weight] for the commonly used asphaltic paving materials shipped for highway use from the Uvalde sources."[7.25] In order to activate the native asphalt in the limestone so as to render the mixture suitable for direct use, a flux oil, consisting of a nonvolatile oil containing about 26 percent of oil-produced asphalt, is used. So important has this source of material become that the highway department operates its own field-testing laboratory at the Uvalde rock-asphalt mines. Known reserves of this valuable "industrial mineral" are sufficient to last into the twenty-first century; it is anticipated that the material may well come to be substituted for other kinds of aggregate that are rapidly becoming exhausted in parts of Texas. Similar records are available for other areas that have the good fortune to have natural "rock-asphalt" deposits. In regional geological studies related to the urban planning of new towns, therefore, this is one mineral that should always be kept in mind by those responsible for the studies since it can be of such convenience as well as of great economic benefit.

7.6 SOIL

Enough has now been said about soil in a number of places in the foregoing text to indicate that, surprising though it may be to those not familiar with its use, soil is now treated in engineering and building just the same as any other material—capable of being accurately described, susceptible to accurate testing, and possessed of quite specific and definable properties that may be used in design with every confidence. The word "soil" is used by all engineers and by most geologists to indicate all the fragmented material found in the crust of the earth that is below the size of cobbles or boulders; i.e., it is the counterpart of solid rock. The two materials blend into each other, some stiff clays, for example, being but little different from soft shales, shale being indurated clay. These borderline materials will not often be encountered, however, so that there should be little misunderstanding whenever soil is mentioned in planning work. The topsoil of the agriculturalist is also included in the general term, even though agricultural soil scientists (pedologists) use the one word—soil—in their own literature in the restricted sense of describing the soil material close to the surface of the ground. There is an explanation of this semantic difficulty; it is related to translation from German and Russian in the early days of scientific soil study. Although it is regrettable, it should lead to no real difficulty since the context in which the word is used will always show whether it is being used in its original geological sense or with its modern restricted pedological meaning. In this volume it is naturally used in its original and all-embracing sense (see Fig. 3.15).

Not only is soil a basic material in all road construction, but it is also widely used as fill in the creation of embankments, in backfilling around finished structures, and even for providing part or all of the foundation beds beneath structures that cannot be founded directly on exposed rock surfaces. If poor soil is encountered on a site, or along the route of a road, it is now not at all unusual for the poor soil to be removed and be replaced with soil of a more appropriate character. In the construction of modern city streets, for example, old roadbeds may sometimes be seen being removed bodily and replaced with carefully compacted layers of sand upon which concrete will be placed to form the foundation for the road pavement. All these uses, and the many other ways in which soil is used today in engineering and building construction, are possible only because of the results of the scientific study of soil as a material. Dating, officially, only from 1936 (although individual investigators had done notable work before that time), soil mechanics—as this study is known—is now a well-established part of the practice of civil engineering. Clearly, soils can be properly studied *only* against a background knowledge of their geological origins so that soil mechanics is closely allied with engineering geology and the corresponding study of the mechanical properties of rocks. In combination, these modern scientific disciplines are happily known as *geotechnique*, a new name for what is really an old branch of science that, hopefully, will come into steadily wider use in this borderline field between geology and engineering. Naturally, no more than an introduction to the subject can be given in this book, but there are now available valuable guides for all who wish to study the subject further. All concerned with planning, however, should be generally familiar with what can now be done with soil in this application of scientific methods. A brief outline is here presented.

A good starting point is appreciation of the fact that all soil has its origin in solid rock. By chemical deterioration or by gradual erosion by physical means, rock can be broken up into small fragments, and this is where soil begins. As already noted, soils can be generally divided into those that are *residual* and those that have been *transported*. Transported soils may have originated in different ways, but they have reached the position they occupy today by being transported from their original position by wind, water, or ice. Residual soils in tropical areas may have been transported by running water from their original location as was mentioned, for example, in the description of the foundation bed conditions for Carlton Center in Johannesburg, South Africa (see page 212). Study of the local geology will give clear indication of the origin of almost all soils encountered in normal practice. In areas that have been glaciated, for example, residual soils will not normally be encountered at all. Glaciation in North America covered almost all of Canada (except part of the Yukon and most of the Queen Elizabeth Islands) and extended as far south as St. Louis in the United States. In Europe the southern limit of glaciation was irregular, but it extended almost to the borders of Switzerland and down the Danube valley almost to the Black Sea. Soils transported by and deposited from moving ice will be unsorted in particle size. Those transported by water will be uniform in particle size, or well sorted. Aeolian soils, as those that are transported by wind are known, will always be uniform in grading.

The distribution of particles of different sizes in a soil, its grading, is a first indicator of its type. *Gravel* is the name given to particles down to 2.0 mm in diameter, *sand* to grains down to about 0.1 mm in diameter, silt down to 0.002 mm in diameter, and clay-sized particles are those even smaller than that. Most soils will naturally be mixtures of particles of these different sizes, but in many soils one size predominates so that the soil will have the appropriate name as its main designation, qualified by reference to the minor constituent, e.g., a silty sand. Particle size by itself, however, may not tell very much about the character of a soil, certainly those made up of very fine particles. The mineralogy of the particles may prove to be, and in clays almost always is, of more importance than size. Even the minute particles of which clays are constituted are minerals, the "clay minerals" being now a well-accepted branch of mineral study. Mineral type can be determined by scientific tests in suitably equipped laboratories, but there is fortunately a rough method of making this determination. This is by studying the way in which the dried soil particles will behave in the presence of water, i.e., considering the plastic characteristics of a soil-water mixture. There are available simple tests that can be easily carried out in field laboratories to give the *plastic limit* and the *liquid limit* of soils, "index properties" that are simply expressed as percentages of water in relation to the weight of the dry soil particles. Soils can, therefore, be identified in the laboratory by simple and now standardized tests. Their strength properties can, in a similar way, be determined by testing samples in special testing machines in laboratories or even by testing them *in situ* by means of simple but ingenious field-testing tools. Some of these are used in the boreholes that are made for taking soil samples, an art that is now so well developed that so-called undisturbed samples can be tested with every confidence, just as if the natural soil in place was under test.

There is one property of soil that is of direct importance to those concerned with city development, the more specialized aspects (such as strength properties) being naturally in the province of the designing engineer. This is the natural density of a soil in place in the ground. This can be accurately measured. In almost all cases it will be the density of the soil particles packed in a relatively dense state. When soil is excavated and piled, as all gardeners know, it will occupy a greater volume than the hole from which it came, i.e., its density as piled is less than what it was in place. Correspondingly, and commonly experienced also, when soil is put back again into a hole from which it has been removed, it is difficult with ordinary procedures to get the soil as dense as it was before being moved. Some soil will be left over, and in the course of time the soil in the hole will slowly settle, leaving a depression at the surface. This phenomenon is all too common as evidenced by the "bumps" that are so frequently experienced when driving over backfilled trenches in city streets. With modern soil technology there is today no excuse for such poor practice. The compaction characteristics of all soils can be easily determined by simple tests. It is found that every soil has an "optimum moisture content," the amount of water (expressed as a percentage of the dry weight of the soil material) that it should contain to give its maximum density when compacted in place by appropriate methods.

These methods all rely on the placement of the soil in layers, thin enough so that they can be compacted to this maximum density with the available equipment. All readers will be familiar with the great "sheepsfoot rollers" so regularly seen working on new highway construction, being rolled backward and forward over newly placed soil. They are compacting the soil to its maximum density, the optimum moisture content being achieved by sprinkling water on the soil from large water-carrying trucks. In this relatively simple way soil can be placed in position so compacted that its density will not change with time. Settlement of the soil will not then take place, and so finished pavements can be placed with every confidence on top of even large embankments as soon as they have been brought to full height. In the same way, backfilling around buildings can be placed with the certainty of no unsightly settlement, when circumstances warrant the slight extra expenditure that the compaction process involves.

What is even more important, soil can be placed on the site of a proposed building to give a level foundation bed when natural ground conditions are uneven with every confidence of providing the required bearing capacity without undue or uneven settlement. The construction of some notable buildings, such as the extensive electromagnetic plant at Clinton, Tennessee, has been aided most satisfactorily by this simple construction procedure.[7.26] Finally, but most difficult to ensure because of the small size and multiplicity of the works involved, the backfilling of trenches *can* be carried out in any location with assurance that no subsequent settlement will occur at their surfaces. Suitable equipment for compacting soil even in the confined space of a narrow trench is now regularly available. The extra cost of backfilling soil in layers, with proper attention to its water content, is usually far more than repaid by the convenience provided and by the elimination of the need for repeated surfacing of the area above the trench.

In view of all the urban development work that is going to be done in the years ahead in the warmer areas of the world as newer countries develop their economies, with the inevitable consequence of greatly increased building activity, the importance of *tropical soils* is certain to increase. They have not been studied to the same extent as the soils of more temperate regions of the world, but already enough is known about their engineering properties to indicate that they will present unusual problems when in widespread use. The Road Research Laboratory of Great Britain has pioneered in much of this work with special reference to the use of the residual soils so frequently found in those areas that used to be grouped together as the British colonial territories. Difficulties arise mainly because of the mineralogical content of newly formed residual soils, many of the minerals found being transitional, in a way, between the minerals of the parent rock and the more stable minerals generally encountered in glacial soils. Typical is the fact that with some tropical soils freshly formed from the weathering of volcanic rocks, it is not possible to obtain in compaction tests the normal water-content-to-density relation. Some years ago, this fact led to serious difficulties in the construction of a large earth dam for a water-supply project in east Africa. Similar

Figure 7.13 Typical view of machine compaction of soil used for back-filling in trenches and, as in this example, adjacent to building walls. *(Courtesy of Wacker Canada Ltd., W. Schmaus, Executive Vice President.)*

problems are encountered in using the volcanic soils, locally known as "tiffs," for road construction in the island of St. Lucia. Other unusual properties are encountered with the soils of Hong Kong that are derived from the weathering of the local granite, which has already called for mention on several occasions earlier in this volume.[7.27]

These far-distant parts of the world are mentioned in order to emphasize the importance of residual soils in those parts of the world that are happily described as "developing." The same kinds of difficult soils are, however, encountered in many parts of the world that have already carried their development a long way. In the Hawaiian Islands, for example, weathering of the volcanic rocks of which the lovely islands are formed has extended in places to depths of over 30 m, the resulting formations of soil being variable and complex. The soil grains are found to be amorphous materials with little in the way of identifiable clay minerals present. The soils are unusually sensitive to disturbance from their natural condition *in situ*, their compaction characteristics (the importance of which has just been explained) being quite unusual. Throughout the southern parts of continental United States, residual soils are the invariable surface deposits. In the southeastern Piedmont, for example, deep residual soils derived from the weathering of the local gneisses, schists, and associated crystalline rocks in a warm humid climate are the only soils normally available for building purposes. They do consist very largely of the clay minerals but are so variable that they present their own special problems in use. Residual soils in general present so many interesting problems in their use that this can be but an introduction to them. All projects for urban development in areas featured by residual soils, and especially in the tropics, must be based on a thorough study of all the soil that will have to be used in building work, knowledge that can be obtained only as a result of an unusually extensive soil mechanics investigation, aided by meticulous mineralogical study.[7.28]

7.7 CONCRETE

Concrete is a most versatile construction material. It can be made by a child and used to make a tiny doorstep, but, on the other hand, over 7.6 million m^3 of high-class machine-mixed concrete have been used in a single structure, the Grand Coulee Dam on the Columbia River. Of all manufactured construction materials, its use is increasing most rapidly. This is no denigration of other invaluable materials such as steel and wood (to mention but two leading materials) but is rather a reflection of the adaptability of concrete to a variety of uses and to the fact that, unlike many other materials, it can be made with a minimum of equipment and under any sort of climatic conditions, using local materials for all but the essential cement content. It must be stressed that cement is only one of the constituents of concrete. This will be well known to all readers, despite the frequency of references in the popular press, and even in quite prestigious journals, to "cement sidewalks" or to "pouring cement foundations." Concrete is a carefully prepared mixture of cement, water, and aggregate, the water reacting with chemicals in the cement to convert them into other chemicals that have the property of setting hard after a period of time and so binding together the loose aggregate into one solid mass—the concrete that is today so familiar. The machinery for mixing the three ingredients used to be a familiar sight on all construction projects. Today, almost all concrete used in urban areas is mixed in central plants or in special trucks filled with the proper mixture at central batching plants and delivered to building sites ready to be placed in the forms. If it is of correct consistency it will be placed and not "poured" into the formwork that has previously been built to act as a mold. "Shuttering" is an alternative name for the wooden forms that must hold the concrete securely as it sets into its final solid state.

One of the great increases in specific uses of concrete has been in the form of "precast units," building elements such as complete wall sections that are manufactured under controlled factory conditions and delivered to the building site ready for placing in position. Many such precast units have also been "prestressed"; i.e., the steel reinforcing they contain has been ingeniously put under stress before or after placement of the concrete in order to increase the strength of the finished unit. It is in the use of steel reinforcing within concrete, in the form usually of bars but sometimes of fine wires or even wire mesh for roadway surfaces, that distinguishes the modern use of concrete from the use of a corresponding material in the earliest days of building. Much Roman building—including such majestic features as the great dome of the Pantheon—was carried out using *structura caementicia*. This was a concrete made from aggregate and pozzolana cement, which is made from volcanic ash. With an economy that can be admired today, the Romans often used as aggregate crushed tile and stone from their demolitions. That they knew how good concrete should be placed is shown by this extract from Pliny's *Natural History*: "Cisterns should be made of five parts of pure gravelly sand, two of the very strongest quicklime, and fragments of silex (lava) . . . when thus incorporated, the bottom and sides should be well beaten with iron rammers." The same effect is obtained today with vibrators that are in almost mandatory use for placing concrete in all constricted formwork.[7.29]

So well did Roman concrete last through the centuries in many locations that it was studied in the early days of modern building and exactly copied in some of the works executed before modern portland cement was invented in 1824 (the name indicating use by the inventor, Joseph Aspdin, of limestone from the famous quarries at Portland). John Smeaton, the first man to be called a civil engineer, for example, used a concrete copied in detail from Roman practice for the building of the first Eddystone Lighthouse. He even went so far as to secure a supply of pozzolana from original Roman sources in Italy in carrying out this epic piece of early construction.[7.30] The availability of manufactured cement made possible the great advances that are now so well known in the steadily increasing use of concrete. Cements with special properties, such as the sulfate-resisting cements mentioned in Chap. 4 (see page 137) and the high-early-strength cements, are now readily available, all manufactured to very high standards and tested before they are used on the job, so as to ensure their suitability for use. Supplies of good water must be available on all construction sites. With good aggregate available, concrete of excellent quality and indefinite durability can readily be procured today, as so many buildings and fine structures in every city demonstrate clearly. When concrete is mixed, placed, and cured under strict and expert control, remarkable results can be achieved, as in the high-density concrete that today features so many nuclear plants and that has to be of undoubted reliability. Really good concrete is so impervious to water that, if used in well-designed structures, it has no need of any extraneous waterproofing.

Against this background of what good concrete can do and does all around the world, there must be placed the admission that poor concrete is also sometimes to be found, even when reasonable control has been exercised in its use. From what has been said about good cement and good water it will be clear that trouble with concrete can almost always be traced to the aggregate that has been used. It is not often appreciated that the aggregate in concrete can amount to 70 percent by volume and almost 80 percent by weight of the finished mass of concrete. It is not a manufactured product like the cement but is usually a naturally occurring material selected by those responsible for construction and brought to the job directly from quarry or pit. Crushed rock with sand or naturally occurring sand and gravel are the almost universally used materials for concrete aggregate. The same materials are used also for other purposes. Their properties, so vital to the making of good concrete, are essentially geological in character. The quantities needed for construction are so great

Figure 7.14 Sydney, Australia. An example of the versatility of rein-forced concrete as a building material—the Sydney Opera House under construction (with the Sydney Bridge in the background). *(Photograph by R. F. Legget.)*

that the supply of these materials in modern cities has become a major problem. Their supply therefore constitutes one of the really vital geological problems related to urban development. They must each be considered in some detail.

7.8 CRUSHED ROCK

Solid rock that has been broken into fragments by crushing, blasting, or ripping is generally known as *crushed rock* and is widely used in building operations. Carefully crushed and graded rock is often used as coarse aggregate in concrete, needing the addition of sand with proper grading to complete the aggregate mixture. It is often used for fill in such locations as beneath concrete floors and around tile drains. In coarser form it can be used to form embankments or even large dams for the retention of water when incorporated in a design that includes also a water barrier. The direct relevance of geology to the location, removal, crushing, grading, and final use of crushed rock will be obvious. It is often a byproduct from rock-mining operations when cut stone is the principal objective. Rock-crushing plants are, therefore, a familiar sight in rock quarries and a familiar sound also, for the operation of rock crushers is inevitably a noisy and dusty procedure. The same problem therefore arises as with ordinary rock quarries that are so located as to impede urban development. Crushed rock is an almost essential material in building, and so the location of rock-crushing plants is a matter that cannot be overlooked in urban planning.

This will always be a particularly local problem, to be decided after a full review of all local circumstances. The possibility of placing rock-crushing installations underground should not be overlooked if the topography of the area being planned in any way provides an opportunity of so shielding what can be a nuisance, especially in heavily developed locations. This is not an idealistic suggestion. Underground crushing plants have been regularly used in mines and on some large construction projects to great advantage. For the construction of the Dworshak Dam in Idaho, for example, about 7.6 million m^3 of rock had to be quarried and crushed as aggregate for the 5 million m^3 of concrete contained in the dam and associated works. Location of good rock on the left abutment of the dam site would have meant a long and winding haul for a large fleet of trucks, had usual procedures been followed. Instead, the general contractor for the dam tunneled into the hillside beneath the quarry site at the normal working level and excavated a cavern 30 m high in which a large crushing plant was installed, quarry rock being fed to it down a 6-m-diameter shaft sunk from the floor of the quarry. Not only did the contractor realize a large saving of money, said to amount to $1 million, by this unorthodox approach, but construction scars upon the landscape were minimized. It is this feature of the Dworshak rock-crushing installation that makes it so significant for the smaller installations that will be needed to satisfy urban demands for this versatile and most useful material.[7.31]

As used for concrete aggregate, crushed rock must be clean and so will usually require washing; it must be durable, with reasonable uniformity in quality; and it must be properly graded for the purpose intended. There are, naturally, standard tests by which its grading and quality may readily be determined, but it will be at once obvious that all rocks cannot automatically be used as aggregate in concrete. This can be most frustrating, especially when construction work has to be carried out that involves at once much rock excavation and the mixing and placing of much concrete. In earlier days, before concrete technology had developed to its present advanced stage, rock excavated on a job was simply assumed to be satisfactory for making concrete. There were occasions when this practice led to very serious trouble. This had been mainly due to yet another characteristic that is essential for crushed-rock aggregate—it must not react chemically with the cement with which it is mixed. The alkali content of ordinary portland cement varies considerably, depending on the qualities of the natural materials from which the cement is made and upon the method of manufacture followed. The alkali content of high-alkali cements will react with certain types of rock. These include acidic and intermediate volcanic rocks and tuffs, cherts, and siliceous limestones. There are now available standard laboratory tests that can be used to detect such "unsound" aggregates (as they are known) prior to use and, so, to obviate the alkali-aggregate reaction that would result from their use. This reaction gives concrete that is, to say the least, unsightly due to fine cracks if not indeed actually unsound.[7.32]

Studies in Canada have shown that there are some aggregates that will react with high-alkali cements but that cannot be detected by the standard tests upon which reliance is so widely placed. The city of Kingston, Ontario, already referred to as the

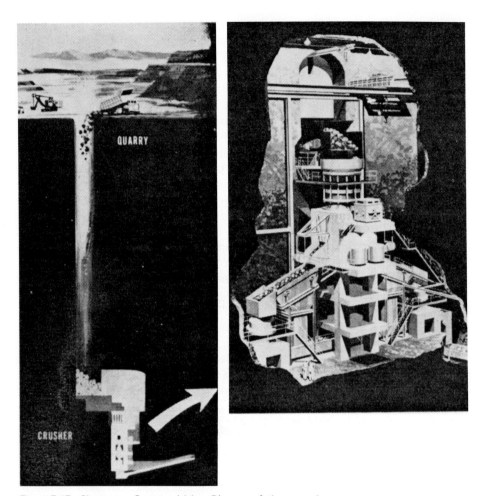

Figure 7.15 Clearwater County, Idaho. Diagram of the general arrangement of the underground rock-crushing plant for supplying aggregate for concrete in the Dworshak Dam; the crushing plant is a 10-story-high structure in an excavated cavern 30.5 m high. *(Courtesy of the Editor, Engineering News-Record.)*

"Limestone City" of Canada, rather naturally uses crushed limestone extensively as coarse aggregate for the concrete that is so widely used in the city and its surroundings. Many years ago, the author noticed the hairline cracking that distinguished the earlier concrete used in this area, but it was not until several years later that colleagues of his were able to study this problem in depth. It was then traced to the reaction of a localized stratum of dolomitic limestone. After very tedious chemical-detection work, an unusual reaction between the cement and some of the minor constituents of the limestone was determined, but no quick test has yet been developed that will indicate the danger of using this particular type of limestone. All that can be said is that dolomitic limestones should be selected for concrete aggregate with the greatest caution. A good guide is to study carefully the performance of concrete throughout the area in question. Making every allowance for concrete that has been improperly mixed, a wide-ranging survey will undoubtedly show if there are local rocks that have been used as aggregate without complete satisfaction. This has been done throughout the Canadian province of Nova Scotia, where aggregate trouble had not been generally suspected but was certainly found as a result of such a survey. The causes are still under investigation as this volume goes to press, but they appear to relate again to the ordinary use of high-alkili cement with certain local rock types.[7.33]

It will therefore be seen that crushed rock is not quite the simple and straightforward material that it might at first sight appear to be. It is an invaluable material, but, as with all other naturally occurring materials, it must be used with due caution and always only after an assessment of its geological characteristics. Even the process of crushing will vary, depending on the geological origin of the rock being crushed. It has been recorded that the jaws of a large rock crusher when used to crush granite lasted only 10 days before having to be renewed because of excessive wear, whereas

Figure 7.16 Kingston, Ontario, Canada. An example of crazing in concrete caused by alkali-aggregate reaction. *(Photograph by E. G. Swenson, courtesy of DBR/NRC.)*

exactly the same type of jaws lasted 7 years when crushing limestone.[7.34] Correspondingly, when rock has to be excavated rather than carefully quarried, methods and progress will vary greatly, depending not only on the type of rock involved but also upon its stratification and even upon its joint pattern. This is especially important on very large rock-excavation jobs when economy will be served if the excavated material can be used for some other purpose. The example of the Lockwood viaduct was mentioned earlier (page 323), when excavation from a neighboring deep cut was used as building stone. This was done at a time when labor costs were not what they are today. Its modern equivalent is shown by another example from the same region of Yorkshire, the coincidence being quite accidental, dependent upon the ability of engineers in Yorkshire to write up and have published accounts of their good work.

Near the city of Huddersfield some major road construction has recently been carried out under the supervision of the engineer and surveyor to the County Council of the West Riding of Yorkshire. The new Lancashire-Yorkshire Motorway, for the construction of which the West Riding County Council were agents for the British Ministry of Transport, connects the Great North Road up the east coast of England with the Stretford-Eccles Motorway (Road M62) in the west. Passing through the Pennines involved some very heavy engineering work, including rock cuts as much as 46 m deep and an embankment as high as 65 m. This very high embankment was adjacent to the city of Huddersfield, and so advantage of its construction was taken to use it as a rock-fill dam to impound water for the Huddersfield Water Undertaking. This most economical dual project was therefore under two engineering jurisdictions, that of the county for the excavation and all road work and that of consulting engineers for the impounding dam. For the latter use, broken or crushed rock had to have certain very specific properties in the way of density, durability, strength, and grading. On the other hand, excavation of the great quantity of rock from the roadway cutting would be desirably carried out using the heaviest equipment possible, if it could be done without blasting, and with strict limitation upon blasting if it were necessary. Accordingly, a very extensive field trial of both excavation (using different methods) and fill placement was carried out in 1964 at the site of the works in order to ensure that the rock could be successfully used and to obtain information that would permit of the preparation of an adequate specification for the main contract.

The trials were carried out at the western end of one of the deepest of the proposed cuttings that would have a maximum depth of 46 m. The trial embankment was constructed 1.2 km further to the west. The trial drilling and excavation was confined to the top 18 m of the cutting. The strata to be traversed by the new road form part of the Millstone Grit series of rocks, one of the great divisions of the carboniferous rocks of Great Britain. The trials were carried out in a sandstone known as the Midgley Grit, which is generally massive in character but with many open joints. The work was carried out on a day-labor basis by an experienced general contractor under unusually close supervision. Most careful records were taken of all aspects of the trials, even including cinephotography, from the results of which a sound film was

Figure 7.17 Huddersfield, Yorkshire, England. The Scammonden Dam and reservoir, with motorway M62 crossing the top of the dam, which is of rock fill with a clay core; when built it was the highest dam in England. *(Courtesy of W. M. Jollans, Engineer and Manager, Waterworks Department, City of Huddersfield.)*

made for displaying to contractors when they came to tender on the main contract. The jointing in the rock permitted the use of massive rippers, hauled by 385-hp tractors, but the resulting grading of excavated rock was not satisfactory. Multiple-row and single-row drilling and blasting were tried using a variety of explosives. Corresponding variations were used in the deposition of the broken rock in the test embankment and for its compaction in place.

Laboratory tests were run on samples of the excavated rock using standard and special tests. These showed that the rock was not suitable for coating with tar or bitumen, that it could be used as aggregate for concrete of specified low compressive strength only, and that the rock was not acceptable for use as a subbase in road construction but that it could be used up to within 15.2 cm of the surface of the subbase. The results of the major field trials cannot usefully be summarized, but they are clearly set out in the excellent paper that was published soon after these trials were carried out. This reference can be recommended for careful study to all who have to face similar problems in the use of large quantities of excavated rock for embankment construction, or indeed for any purpose other than dumping to waste.[7.35]

It should be added, to avoid any misunderstanding, that it is only very rarely in the conduct of civil engineering work that full-scale trials of this kind have to be carried out. The process of design based upon the accumulated experience of the profession and the steady development of sound theoretical methods is so far advanced that, when materials are under the control of the design engineer, a project can be designed completely in the design office with certainty that when constructed it will perform as intended. When dealing with the ground, however, the materials are not under the control of the designer; he has to accept what is found and "make the best of it." This is why foundation engineering will always remain an *art*, depending on experience and the ability to assess right on the job the best way of dealing with soil and rock conditions as revealed by preliminary investigation. Correspondingly, when large quantities of material have to be excavated, most careful assessment of the results of preliminary investigations is essential, and, when necessary, as in this case from Huddersfield, actual full-scale trials must be carried out to remove all uncertainty.

7.9 SAND AND GRAVEL

Crushed rock was dealt with first, as providing aggregate for concrete, since in many parts of the world there is no good supply of sand and gravel for this purpose. Rock has then to be crushed and blended with sand of suitable grading, or even with fine rock crushings, to provide the main content of all the concrete used. This practice will have to be used to a steadily increasing degree as natural deposits of sand and gravel in areas that have provided this naturally mixed aggregate are gradually used up. "Manitoba is Running Out of Gravel for Roads" was a headline in a most reputable newspaper as early as 1963—and this in a province of Canada that has only just celebrated its centenary and which was glaciated in Pleistocene time so that it is blessed with the normal sands and gravels derived from glacial deposits. Many readers will have seen similar announcements regarding their own regions. All such statements are a reflection of the quite remarkable rate at which available sand and gravel deposits are being used up in rapidly developing parts of the world. The word "available" is of key importance. Sand and gravel constitute a material that is heavy to transport in the quantities in which it is normally used so that, just as for crushed rock, transport costs are usually the basic determinant in the use of any suitable deposit of sand and gravel.

To illustrate the importance that sand and gravel have come to have in the building world, it may first be noted that something over 1 billion tonnes are produced annually in the United States. This figure is so astronomical that it will be meaningless to many readers. It can better be expressed by saying that the average consumption of sand and gravel in the United States rose from about 2.5 tonnes per capita in 1950 to a little less than 5 tonnes in 1965, being now well over 5 tonnes in 1970 for every man, woman, and child. The mythical "man on the street" would naturally be inclined to reply, when faced with this figure expressed in this way, that he does not use any sand or gravel. Dr. Charles Withington of the U.S. Geological Survey has used some figures that should show the average citizen how well he is served by this material. After observing that when sand and gravel is used as aggregate with asphaltic mixes or concrete, 95 percent of asphalt and 75 percent of concrete consists of the aggregate, i.e., sand and gravel, he points out that between 50 and 100 tonnes of sand and gravel will be used in the construction of an ordinary residence. For a group of 10 houses and the short street to serve them in a new housing development, as much as just over 400 tonnes of sand and gravel will be needed.[7.36]

Figure 7.18 Niagara district, Ontario, Canada. Typical sand and gravel pit in glacial soil deposits. *(Courtesy of D. F. Hewitt, Chief, Industrial Minerals Section, Ontario Department of Mines and Northern Affairs.)*

It is no small wonder that almost all large cities are facing real problems in connection with supplies of sand and gravel. Search for new deposits is a major occupation of bodies such as state geological surveys, and the deposits must be reasonably accessible. The author knows several wonderful deposits of magnificent sand and gravel in the high Arctic of Canada. If located near New York City, which, it has been estimated, will need 710 million tonnes in the year 2000, these deposits would be worth millions. As it is, they lie untouched beneath Arctic skies, useful only as adding some interest to an otherwise rather bleak landscape.

In order to use figures that will be meaningful in giving a good general impression of what is happening to the supplies of sand and gravel, southern Ontario will be considered, if only because it is the area whose geology is most familiar to the author. A further reason is that the Department of Mines of Ontario has published an excellent report by two geologists on the sand and gravel resources of this area, a report that is a model of its kind.[7.37] Similar reports are now available for most regions; readers are urged to inquire about the availability of similar reports for their own areas. These will always be found to be interesting documents, usually providing a good introduction to the Pleistocene geology of the regions involved.

Southern Ontario is that part of the province lying between the Quebec border (about 48 km west of Montreal) and Windsor on the Detroit River. It includes the Toronto-Hamilton industrial complex. Roughly 800 km from east to west and never more than 160 km wide, the area includes rather more than one-quarter of the total population of Canada. Its geology is most favorable for the finding of sand and gravel. The entire area has been glaciated so that eskers, kames, deltas, spillways, and old beaches all contribute excellent deposits. As in other areas, production has been increasing in postwar years. Table 7.1 shows the overall figures.

TABLE 7.1

Production of Aggregate (Crushed Rock, Sand, and Gravel)
and of Sand and Gravel in Southern Ontario*

		Total Aggregate		Sand and Gravel	
Year	Population	Tonnes	Tonnes Per Capita	Tonnes	Tonnes Per Capita
1945	4,000,000	13,633,954	3.41	10,613,703	2.65
1950	4,471,000	36,570,200	8.19	30,599,754	6.85
1955	5,266,000	65,254,840	12.40	52,311,876	9.95
1960	6,111,000	97,129,004	15.85	78,903,401	12.90
1965	6,788,000	115,035,315	17.00	89,981,718	13.25
1970 (est.)	7,637,000	112,776,000	15.30	86,360,000	11.12

*Reproduced by permission of the Ontario Department of Mines and Northern Affairs, D. F. Hewitt, Chief, Industrial Minerals Section.

Roughly one-half of this vast production comes from privately operated pits, roughly one-half from direct production by the provincial Department of Highways, individual counties, and townships (mainly for road work), with a small amount coming from dredging in lakes and rivers by 12 operators. Of the approximately 350 private producers, one-half are small operators of individual pits, one-quarter have production amounting to as much as $100,000 annually, about one-eighth have an annual production of between $100,000 and $300,000, and about 25 are really large operators. This is a pattern that will be found to be similar to that in other comparable areas. It can be seen that, since the pits are well distributed throughout the area, southern Ontario is well served with producers of sand and gravel. Yet despite this, supplies for the Toronto metropolitan district have had to be brought from as far away as 96 km to the east and to the west already for more than 10 years. This, too, will be found to be a familiar pattern and points directly to the serious problem that already exists, throughout North America, of providing adequate sand and gravel for urban areas.

The purpose for which sand, or gravel, or both, is to be used must naturally be known before supplies can be tested for suitability. Principal uses, in Ontario but in general elsewhere as well, are for road-making, either directly for rural roads or mixed with asphalt, for use as concrete aggregate, as aggregate for making concrete blocks, for railway ballast, for providing sand for mortar and plaster ("brick sand" as commonly expressed), and as backfill in mines when regulations or normal safety procedures demand that mined-out spaces be filled up again. High-grade sands are also used for such specialized purposes as abrasives and glassmaking and as filtering media. For all these uses there are available standard tests to which sand and gravel must be subjected before they can be passed for use. Cleanliness is a prime requirement for most uses and in particular freedom from organic materials, this being of special importance in concrete work. Soundness under ordinary conditions of use and exposure is another essential property that can be readily tested. The ability to adhere to bituminous coatings is naturally vital for material that is to be used in asphalt mixes. Correspondingly, freedom from all materials that might possibly react with the alkali contents of cements is essential for all material to be used as concrete aggregate, just as it is for crushed rock. None of these desirable properties can be assumed, even if the geological origin of the particular deposit is known with reasonable certainty. Tests must be run not only initially but regularly as the sand and gravel is used, this control testing being a regular feature of construction work, often carried out in special field laboratories.[7.38]

Overriding all these requirements is the necessity for the sand, the gravel, or the sand and gravel mixture to have the desired grading, i.e., the proper distribution of particles of different sizes. Regular testing is again an essential and continuing operation, using standard-sized sieves for all particles above the size of silt and special laboratory techniques for determining smaller-sized particles if this is necessary. Usually, however, very fine material will not be required, being one of the items to be removed by washing. A washing plant is, therefore, frequently an essential part of the installation at a pit, as are also the screening and handling mechanisms by which the material can be subdivided into different sizes and different graded mixes.

Figure 7.19 Stouffville, Ontario, Canada. Typical modern plant for crushing, washing, and screening of sand and gravel. *(Courtesy of the Consolidated Sand and Gravel Co., Ltd., Toronto, L. J. Chapman, Chief Geologist.)*

Ordinary washing with water will not normally remove some of the extraneous materials often found in gravel and that can have deleterious effects if not eliminated. The main undesirable impurities—again in Ontario but also in very general experience —are siltstone, shale, and chert.

At first sight it might be thought impossible to separate out small fragments of these materials from the large volumes that have to be handled from any ordinary pit. The problem is a common one in the mining industry. Ingenious use has been made of the regular method of separation used with ores for the beneficiation of gravels. First tried by engineers of the Royal Canadian Air Force in construction of a new runway at Rivers, Manitoba, "heavy media separation" (HMS, as the process is known) has now come to be used widely, one of the first installations in the United States being a floating plant on the Ohio River (1952). In the work at Rivers in 1947, fragments of shale occurred in the local gravel, with deleterious effect upon concrete. The nearest alternative source was 265 km away; the use of this would have added $3.00 per m^2 of runway. After laboratory tests had proved that the use of HMS was practicable, a full-scale installation was developed and operated successfully for less than half the cost of bringing in the alternative gravel. The method is based on the varying specific gravity of the gravel particles. By placing them in a liquid of a specific gravity intermediate between that of the impurities to be removed and that of the principal constituent of the gravel, those that are heavier than the liquid will sink, those that are lighter will float, and so separation becomes easy.[7.39]

Sands and gravels even if they do contain impurities can, therefore, readily be processed into materials entirely suitable for the diverse purposes to which they may be put. As already indicated, they may be found in a number of the physical features left on a landscape following glacial action. They are also to be found in all beaches, those of the present day and those of earlier days that may now be at high elevations due to uplift of the land. They come also from the beds of rivers and lakes into which they have been transported from the upland in one of the ordinary processes of physical geology. In some parts of the world, this underwater source is of the greatest importance. Probably nowhere is it of more importance than along the River Rhine, in the upper reaches of which is one of the greatest collections of "underwater gravel pits" in the world, as all travelers on this great river can see so clearly. It has been said jocularly that "half the sand and gravel for Europe comes from the Rhine." Although this must be an exaggeration, the sight of the constant stream of 1,000-tonne barges filled with clean sand and gravel that one passes when sailing up the Rhine is a wonderfully impressive sight. The fact that well over 1 million tonnes have been handled in 1 year through the Ruhr port of Duisburg alone is some indication of the extent of this particular example of sand and gravel production. Dredging from the river channel itself amounted to over 1 billion tonnes in 1967, much of this sand and gravel that was sold for industrial use.[7.40]

The same source of sand and gravel is available on most of the major rivers of Europe and North America, although to nothing like the same extent. Visitors to the rebuilt city of Warsaw in Poland can see large dredgers at work on the Vistula River right in the center of the city. One of the most unusual examples and yet one that is of special interest geologically is the provision of good material for fill purposes at the eastern entrance to the harbor of Toronto. Figure 7.21 is a simple sketch plan of

Figure 7.20 River Rhine, West Germany. Typical sand and gravel plant for processing material dredged from the River Rhine. *(Photograph by R. F. Legget.)*

this remarkable inland harbor, completely protected by the Toronto Islands, which are actually (in geological language) a "compound recurved spit," the entire peninsula—as it was originally—having been formed and now being nourished by soil that is eroded by wave action from the Scarborough Bluffs some kilometers to the east. The *littoral drift* that features this part of the northern shore of Lake Ontario is from east to west. As the cliffs are eroded, the material so washed down is water-sorted, the coarser material moving in a regular way along the shore until it meets the outflow of the River Don, near to what is now the center of Toronto. This originally deflected the drift out from shore, with the resulting formation of the islands. The drift still continues and is well appreciated by local engineers and contractors. It has been estimated that about 300,000 m³ are eroded each year from the cliffs, about 10 percent of which is the coarse sand that has gradually built up the islands. The remainder is swept along the bed of Lake Ontario. Dredging this material has regularly been carried out off the eastern entrance, over 10 million tonnes of sand having been obtained in this way within a 22-year period. As with other underwater sources of sand and gravel, this supply is self-replenishing, and it is washed clean by its movement in the lake.[7.41]

7.10 SAND AND GRAVEL PITS

The search for new sources of sand and gravel continues unabated in most parts of the world around great metropolitan areas as well as in countries that are in the early stages of developing their cities. Geology is the starting point. Against a general background provided by the overall local geology, detailed field studies must be made to locate possible sources, followed by test drilling and sampling when sand and gravel have been located. For preliminary studies over wide areas, study of aerial photographs is an excellent aid. Even geophysical methods have been enlisted in the search. With these exploratory efforts the urban planner will not normally be directly concerned, but one recent special study may be briefly mentioned, if only to emphasize the coming critical situation that major cities in the northeastern part of North America will have to face.

In 1964 the U.S. Corps of Engineers conducted a sand-resources survey along the New Jersey coast between the 4.5-m and 30-m water depths on what is known as the Continental Shelf; 2,660 km of seismic refraction survey were undertaken, and 198 cores of the sediments encountered in the survey were obtained. Sand from the sea can be used for fill purposes directly and for renourishing beaches that have been eroded. Between Sandy Hook and Cape May a quantity of 2.15 billion m³ of recoverable sand and gravel was located in this way. The survey was concentrated upon five segments—Sandy Hook, Manasquan, Barnegat, Egg Harbor, and Cape May, all names that will be familiar to those who have occasion to visit Atlantic City either for business or pleasure. Typical of the results was the finding of over 1.8 billion tonnes in an area of 88,000 hectares off Cape May. It must be noted that this was just a

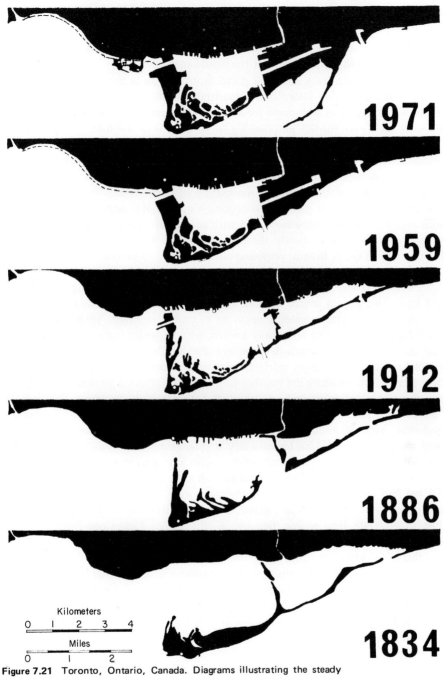

1971

1959

1912

1886

Kilometers
0 1 2 3 4

Miles
0 1 2

1834

Figure 7.21 Toronto, Ontario, Canada. Diagrams illustrating the steady development of Toronto harbor and its fortunate association with Toronto Island; the direction of the littoral drift that has formed the island is from right to left. A view of the new breakwater is given in Fig. 7.25. *(Courtesy of the Toronto Harbour Commissioners, J. H. Jones, Chief Engineer.)*

survey; much study would be necessary before any large quantities could be safely dredged so close to a coast line, but the significance of the survey will be obvious.[7.42]

In Europe, dredging sand and gravel from the sea is already being carried out on a steadily increasing scale. The Netherlands, having almost no exposed bedrock, has to rely upon sand and gravel for all concrete aggregate; about 12 million tonnes are used each year for this purpose. Up to 10 percent of the total is imported from Germany, most of the rest is dredged from large Dutch rivers, and now something over 300,000 tonnes are being obtained from the sea. These figures were given in one of the papers presented at a conference on "Sea-dredged Aggregate for Concrete" arranged by the Sand and Gravel Association of Great Britain in December 1968. The proceedings of this gathering constitute a most useful guide to present thinking with regard to the problems associated with the use of material dredged from the sea, even as they indicate so clearly the importance that this source of sand and gravel has assumed in Great Britain, providing already about 10 percent of the total British consumption.[7.43]

Excluding the special procurement of sand and gravel by dredging from rivers and lakes, the general source of these materials is from excavations made in ground that consists of suitable material once the topsoil is removed. Three aspects of the resulting pits, as they are universally known, are of relevant importance—determining that land set aside for urban development does not have good deposits of sand and gravel beneath it that might safely be removed before building commences, control over pits that are in active use but that come to be surrounded by urban development, and the rehabilitation or reuse of pits that have ceased to be active. The first is an "obvious" requirement of land planning, but all too often in the past it has been neglected, with the result that there are, literally, millions of dollars worth of good sand and gravel now hidden beneath city streets, never to be available for use. This is one case when it would not be advisable to give any specific example; readers can be left to consider their own local situations with a view to noting cases where planning has not had this essential geological emphasis, with the result of lost convenience in using local sources of sand and gravel quite apart from the monetary loss involved. Just to illustrate how serious this loss is, the author knows one North American city in which there are said to be over 500 million tonnes of sand and gravel within a radius of 24 km of the civic center that are now forever inaccessible. Planning land use, therefore, *must* take into account possible sources of sand and gravel. When located it will be necessary to consider the economics of the particular situation to see if it will be socially desirable to utilize the deposit in advance of utilization of the land for building purposes. It will be seen later that this can often be done not only with no disadvantage to development but sometimes to the great advantage of good site planning.

The problem of controlling the operation of existing pits, whether for sand and gravel, for brick clay, or for crushed stone, is always difficult since nobody ever thought of urban development extending as far as the pit location. In some cases, outright purchase is the only solution; even though costly in the first instance, this is economically viable in view of the certain increase of property values once the pit disappears. In cases where available supply of material is within sight of exhaustion, arrangements can usually be made to arrange development of the surrounding land so that the area occupied by the pit can be integrated into the overall plan when the pit is finally closed and its area becomes available for other use. While continuing to operate, however, the pit may be required to observe certain minimum requirements consistent with public convenience, as also must other pits that must continue to operate for some appreciable time, even though surrounded by developed land. Legislators are still grappling with the legal difficulties of ensuring such convenience in operation without putting the operators to undue hardship. Similar problems have to be faced in connection with the opening up of new pits near developed areas. And in all cases, an overriding consideration (now happily being recognized) is the preservation of natural beauty around the pit site and the elimination of that ugly scarring of the landscape that so frequently accompanied sand and gravel procurement in the past. It is so easy to consider straight prohibition of new pits, but this is often economically undesirable from the public's point of view. The extra cost of transporting sand and gravel, and crushed rock, simply cannot be overlooked in these days of high costs; 32 km of hauling can add as much as 50 percent to the cost of sand and gravel as purchased at a pit. To the extent that is possible, such economic waste must be avoided.

It follows that the nearer pits can be to the location of building the better from the economical point of view, even though this carries with it, today, the almost mandatory requirement of orderly development and rehabilitation of used portions of pits and of complete pits when exhausted. Major pit operators need no legislation to enforce good pit operation. Many are finding that by good pit planning and regular rehabilitation of used pit areas, the extra expenditure is self-liquidating because of easier handling of material. Legislation, however, is always necessary for the less-enlightened operators. It is coming to be common practice to insist that $300 per acre be set aside by owners for rehabilitation work, although in one Canadian province the sum of $500 is required. Different methods are followed for ensuring that this money is available for the purpose indicated. A growing amount of useful information is available as to the precautions that should be taken in pit operation and about desirable rehabilitation measures. Indicative of the interest now being taken by enlightened owners in this social-technical problem of rehabilitation are publications of the National Sand and Gravel Association, one good example being a brochure entitled *Land Use Planning and the Sand and Gravel Producer,* by V.P. Ahearn.[7.44] Typical of the excellent guides now available from public bodies is *"A Guide to Site Development and Rehabilitation of Pits and Quarries,"* by A. A. Bauer, published by the Ontario Department of Mines—a well-illustrated and singularly constructive guide containing enough examples from practice to be suitable for use in a wide variety of topographic and geological situations.[7.45]

It is not often that the development of a pit can actually effect an improvement in land use, but there are cases where this has proved to be the case. Typical is the example of

> a college in an eastern state [that] wanted to expand, but found the way blocked by a large limestone hill. A local mineral firm offered to remove the hill for the limestone that it contained. Geologists assisted in locating the deposit and explosives experts advised the quarrymen on methods of breaking the stone with minimum blast damage and noise problems. When the work was completed, the college had an ideal site for expansion and the quarrying company profited from the sale of stone. The city reaped double benefits—a larger college and a ready supply of growth materials.[7.46]

Possibilities such as this should always be kept in mind in initial land planning since the case is not an isolated one. More usual, however, is the case when a quarry or pit has been taken out of production and has to be integrated with the planning of the land around. Filling is the first thought that comes to mind, but in many cases the leveled area provided by a quarry or pit floor can be put to good use as it is, if not too deep, by careful planning that takes advantage of the excavation that has been made to obviate any further excavation. Storage space can thus be provided at minimum cost. Parking garages for automobiles can sometimes be fitted in to the excavations resulting from sand and gravel operations. Modern shopping centers often need deep underground spaces for their circulation systems. There are, indeed, limitless possibilities for using abandoned pits effectively and economically. The working areas will frequently indicate a change in strata: in the operation of the pit some leveling of the floor may have been done with fill material, or parts of a pit may have already been used for fill disposal. Subsurface exploration, therefore, must be carried out always with the very greatest care.

This was well shown in the planning and building of the Denver Coliseum constructed in the early fifties. This great building covers an area of about 137 by 90 m and serves not only as a civic amphitheater and convention hall but also as an arena for the annual International Stock Show. It had therefore to be located as near as possible to the existing stockyards; this indicated an area of relatively flat land at the intersection of 46th Avenue (now Interstate Highway 70) and 44th Street. This land is on the west slope of the valley of the North Platte River, the geological history of which suggested that the site would be underlain by fairly loose fine sands, overlying heterogeneous gravel deposits, with soft shale as the bedrock. The gravels had been extracted from pits over a part of the site but not within half a century of the time of building. This was shown by the remains of a long-abandoned smelter on the floor of the pit. Old residents around the area thought that slag from the smelter would be found among the fill that had been deposited in parts of the old pit. Most of the fill material, however, had been sand, straw, and manure from the stockyards, but there was no information at all as to its extent. Auger borings were put down in an attempt to determine subsurface conditions, and a few test pits were dug; very little slag was found either in this way or in later more refined investigations. In order to facilitate traffic arrangements, it was desirable to locate the building as far west as possible, i.e., in the direction of the presumed edge of the gravel pit. A location was selected tentatively, but a more thorough subsoil investigation was carried out before the design was completed.

So many obstructions had been encountered in trying to put down auger borings that it was clear that conventional methods of boring and sampling would not be possible. Accordingly, another tool of the foundation engineer was put to good use, this being a 64-mm-diameter penetrometer. This is a conically headed point suitably supported by strong pipe and driven into the ground by a 160-kg hammer dropping (in this case) 60 cm, the penetration being carefully measured so that the penetration resistance can be determined. About 80 soundings were made in this way. As the drilling crew gained experience, it was possible to detect with accuracy the interface between

Figure 7.22 Denver, Colorado. Denver Coliseum, showing the general area in which it was so carefully located. *(Courtesy of F. Handy, Boulder, and the Denver Convention and Visitors Bureau.)*

fill and the natural ground (sand and gravel) and also the surface of the shale. Special care was taken at the pit end of the proposed site. Samples were taken at three locations and correlated with penetrometer results. When all the results were studied, it was clear that the original location would be too close to the pit and so would have had an inordinate depth of fill under it at that end. The whole structure was therefore moved 15.2 m to the east on the design plans and successfully constructed on this carefully selected site.[7.47] It has since served with complete satisfaction, as visitors to Denver will know. They will also know what excellent parking facilities adjoin this immense building, but few will realize (except local geologists) that the parking lot itself is mainly the bottom of the old sand and gravel pit used so many years ago. This is what was done with a big building on a large site, but the same careful approach, with a realization of the necessity for most detailed subsurface investigation, can lead to convenient and economic use of many small abandoned pits.

7.11 LIGHTWEIGHT AGGREGATE

In modern concrete practice, it is sometimes desirable to produce concrete with aggregate lighter than the usual crushed rock or gravel. Lightweight concrete is of special importance in tropical areas since it can be produced with desirable insulating properties; it also can give improved acoustical isolation. In ordinary practice, its use will reduce the dead weight of concrete structure so that its increased cost can be weighed against possible savings in design. Materials used to produce such special concretes are naturally of geological origins. One important group of lightweight materials is those rocks found in relation to volcanoes—pumice, tuffs, and some lavas. Pumice was used by the Romans, who had large supplies upon which to draw; their use of lightweight "concrete" for some of their great domes was notable. Only very rarely will these materials be found adjacent to a modern city so that, if used, they will have to be imported.

A second group of lightweight aggregate materials is provided by some by-products of industry. Cinders are sometimes used, especially in the manufacture of concrete blocks; they must naturally be washed free of all acid content. More common is the use of slag from steel works that has been specially processed by one of the proprietory methods now available so that it becomes "foamed slag," an excellent material for this purpose. Of the same type is expanded vermiculite, a form of mica that, when properly processed, can be blown up to much greater size and so much lighter weight than its normal form. Vermiculite and perlite (a similar mineral) when expanded in this way will give the lightest of all concretes; they are also used for mixing with plaster and provide plaster with most desirable properties.

Even more significant from the geological standpoint is yet a third group of materials used for making lightweight concrete, these being what are known as "bloated clays." There are many naturally occurring clays that possess the property of bloating when heated to a high temperature under suitable conditions. Clays that bloat must contain a combination of fluxes that will produce a viscous glass when heated almost to melting point. They must also contain minerals that will release a gas or gases at this temperature. The gases will be trapped in the viscous glasslike material and so expand it rapidly, this expanded shape being retained when the material cools. Most bloated clays are heated in rotary kilns, up to 48.6 m long and up to 3 m in diameter. Detailed study of Texas clays has shown that the principal characteristic of clay that will cause one clay to bloat while another will not is the mineral content, with the acidic property (its pH) of clays also being important. For clays in this region the property of bloating can now be predicted, from clay analysis, with a 90-percent degree of accuracy. Generally it was found in Texas that clays with less than 30 percent kaolinite, more than 10 percent illite, and between 20 and 90 percent of montmorillonite would be good "bloaters."[7.48] Similar studies have been made in other areas, but much research into this interesting, and most useful, characteristic of clays is continuing in many laboratories. It will be seen how important this particular lightweight aggregate can be, in view of the widespread extent of clay deposits. In preliminary studies of entirely new areas that are to be developed for building, especially in regions where normal aggregates are in short supply, the bloating properties of the local clays should always be investigated. Sintering and ordinary calcining are other heating processes that can be applied to clays in order to produce rocklike substances. Clay burned *in situ* has even been used for road construction in Australia.

7.12 SOME OTHER MATERIALS

There are a number of other naturally occurring materials—industrial minerals—that are used in building and that might be found in an area of new land that is to be planned for urban development. Most of them are used in much smaller quantities than the materials already mentioned, although two—lime and gypsum—stand high in most national lists of industrial mineral production. Gypsum occurs in nature usually as a sound and solid rock, some of the finest North American deposits occurring in the far north of Cape Breton Island in Nova Scotia. It must be heated to drive off chemically included water; the result is the material widely known as "plaster of paris," a name readily explained if the occurrence of beds of gypsum beneath the city of Paris be recalled. This provides the basis for all plaster, still a vital material for the interior finish of buildings, despite all the advances in alternative methods.

Lime has for centuries been a material in wide use not only for building but for use in agriculture for the "dressing" of acidic soils. It consists of pure calcium oxide, but it does not occur as such in nature. It must be made by calcining calcium carbonate, usually in the form of a suitably pure limestone. Lime kilns, in which the heating of the limestone is carried out, must be among the oldest examples of "industrial furnaces" in existence. In many parts of the world, the remains of old lime kilns provide a happy hunting ground for the industrial archeologist. One interesting variety is to be found, always now in ruins, in the county of Hertfordshire in England where kilns were regularly built into steep hillsides so that they could be fed at the top from ground surface, an early example of economy in labor force that even today can command respect.[7.49] But the Romans probably did the same thing, so advanced were they in the use of lime for mortar in their great buildings. Interesting studies of Roman mortars have been made in Great Britain that show that good lime was used, as was sand that had clearly been graded in some way into an appropriate range of sizes. Red brick dust is also found, showing how economical of building materials the Romans were. In one particular period during the Roman occupation of Britain, they even mixed crushed red tile in small fragments with the other constituents to make a coarse mortar. They had good advice on these matters since Vitruvius, writing just before the dawn of the Christian Era, has some still sound comments to make of mortar, and indeed on the slaking of lime, in his *Ten Books on Architecture*. It is slaked lime, i.e., quicklime that has been slaked with water, that is used for mortar and other building purposes, the actual process of slaking still being very much of an art, to judge by the personal care that many masons will still take in preparing their own lime for mortar.

Limestone was mentioned as the main source of lime, but it is not the only one. The Texas Highway Department, and other agencies in the Lone Star State, use oyster shells. This always sounds like a joke when first mentioned, but it is a very serious reference to an interesting use of one of the unusual evidences of marine life in past geological ages. Extensive deposits of oyster shells are found on old beaches in a number of parts of the world, in Alberta, Canada, for example, as well as in Texas in North America. The shells are relatively pure calcium carbonate and so can be used for the production of lime and also cement. In Alberta there is even an Alberta Oyster Shell Company that supplies crushed oyster shells for chicken feed as well as for other purposes. But a reference to chicken feed is perhaps an indication that this review of the materials used from the earth in the building of modern cities should come to a halt.

DISPOSAL OF MATERIALS

7.13 RUBBLE AND EXCAVATION

Not only are large quantities of material needed for the construction of cities, but appreciable quantities of unwanted material have to be disposed of in the course of normal operation and development. When buildings have to be demolished to make way for more modern structures, the materials of which they are built must be put somewhere. When excavations have to be made to provide for underground space, the soil and rock so removed must be disposed of safely and economically. These might appear to be strictly engineering matters, but when thought is given to the fact that all such material has got to be placed somewhere on the ground, then the possible connection with geology may become apparent. This is really a case of man being a geological agent, providing material instead of taking it out of the ground, which is his more usual role. Brief mention of some effects of the disposal of building material from cities therefore appears to be warranted even before consideration is given to the more serious problem of disposing of waste material.

The demolition of buildings either by fire, by flood, or by the deliberate action of man has gone on ever since the first groups of buildings were used for habitation. Only when collections of buildings large enough to be called cities gradually came into being did the particular problem of disposal loom large. The Great Fire of London in 1666 may be mentioned as an example of a catastrophe that led to the loss of a very large part of a medieval city. Starting in a baker's shop in Pudding Lane, it raged for four days, destroying 13,200 houses, 87 churches including St. Paul's Cathedral, and involving 400 streets. Most of the buildings were damaged beyond any hope of repair and so had to be demolished. With the transport facilities then available, it was impossible to remove all the resulting rubble, and so much was left in place after being suitably broken up and leveled off. The uppermost "geological" stratum today, therefore, under much of the old city of London derives from this time. Now often called "made ground," deposits of this sort are to be found beneath many parts of all the older cities of the world. These layers of made ground are always well known to those responsible for building in the cities concerned and so are usually anticipated in subsurface exploration. They can form a good solid foundation bed for lighter buildings, but, equally, they can complicate excavation when foundations for larger buildings have to be carried to greater depths. Exactly the same thing, although not to the same extent, is to be found beneath the older cities of the New World so that one of the aspects of the subsurface of all cities that must always be kept in mind is the possibility of a bed of made ground lying above the original ground surface.

There is one city of the world that is unique in this respect, and so it must be mentioned, tragic as are still the implications of its special subsurface problem. Warsaw, ancient capital of Poland, lies at the intersection of two of the oldest trade routes of Europe. Although the date of its founding is not known, it was already the capital of the Duchy of Mazovia in the fourteenth century. In 1939 it was therefore one of the truly historic cities of Europe, as well as a thoroughly modern commercial center with a population of about 1,300,000. It was the first city to suffer from bombing in the Second World War; its role is now a part of history. On 11 October 1944 a written order was issued by the Governor of the Warsaw District on direct orders from Hitler that "Warsaw shall be pacified i.e. razed to the ground while the war lasts . . . ," and razed it was, in a way never previously seen in the world, special demolition units even being assigned the task of destroying historical buildings, libraries, etc. In January 1945 all that remained of its prewar population was a mere 160,000 of whom 150,000 existed on the right bank of the Vistula River.[7.50] The entire city was a mass of rubble, estimated to amount to 20 million m^3. Most of the buildings that could

Figure 7.23 Warsaw, Poland. Dredging for sand and gravel in the Vistula River close to the center of the city, material that was used in the tremendous rebuilding job shown in Fig. 5.23. *(Photograph by R. F. Legget.)*

be rebuilt were, naturally, the older buildings. Today, the city is again a fine modern commercial center with a population of over 1,200,000, with its historic Old City looking just as it did in prewar days, even though it is actually a re-creation, the story of which is one of the epics of urban rebuilding. As one listens to the wonderful record of the great rebuilding operations of the city proper, one is told, with a somewhat deprecating smile, that of course the whole city is today 1½ m higher than it was before the war, with the added comment "You don't think that we could have moved *all* that rubble do you?" Some was moved—to form, for example, the great sloping banks that now constitute a large part of the great sports arena of the city. Most of old Warsaw, however, remained where it fell, and upon it has been built the modern city, with its broad streets, its multistoried buildings, its services, and its efficient transportation system.

   The problem of disposing of material from excavations is much more general, much more serious, than disposing of rubble, and one that is steadily increasing in complexity as cities grow larger and available sites for the easy dumping of material diminish in number and size. It is a problem governed to a large extent by economics, due especially to the high cost of trucking. In earlier days, a simple solution was to find an unused area of land, an old quarry or even an unused ravine, and merely end-dump the rock or soil into it from trucks. Uncontrolled dumping of this kind led to much trouble. In one city that has the good fortune to have many lovely ravines around it, many natural beauty spots were thus lost to public use. What was a real problem for a time was the occurrence of slides of this dumped material due to instability of the steep slopes, but this is a situation that would not normally arise today with public control over so many dumping operations. End-dumping on private ground is still widely practiced, however; owners see an easy and cheap method of obtaining what they consider to be good building lots as depressions are filled in and level areas developed. As already explained, however, unless fill is properly placed, in layers and compacted, there may be continued settlement of land so formed due to the slow natural compaction of the fill quite apart from any settlement that the load it induces may cause on any underlying weak soils. A first requirement for the disposal of fill is, therefore and as usual, accurate knowledge of the subsurface conditions. The need for accurate records of original surface levels has been explained.

It has been a combination of factors that has led many cities to consider the proper use of excavated material since it is often desirable fill conveniently available to downtown areas with their extremely high land costs. The procurement of 9.5

Figure 7.24 New York City. New ground being formed on the shore of Manhattan Island by the use of excavated material from the site of the World Trade Center, as seen in Fig. 5.31. *(Courtesy of the Port Authority of New York and New Jersey, M. S. Kapp, Chief Engineer.)*

Figure 7.25 Toronto, Ontario, Canada. New breakwater under construction for the enlargement of Toronto harbor, as shown in Fig. 7.21, the breakwater being built of excavation and other suitable waste material from the city. *(Courtesy of the Toronto Harbour Commissioners, J. H. Jones, Chief Engineer.)*

hectares of new land at the tip of Manhattan Island was described in Chap. 5 (page 242), and this is a practice that is being followed elsewhere. The city of Milwaukee, for example, has reclaimed 15 hectares from Lake Michigan, most conveniently located close to its downtown area, and this will be used for harbor and marina developments. It is not surprising to find that, always excepting the special case of the Netherlands, Japan probably leads the world in the creation in this way of new land for cities. A national program of reclaiming no less than 47,000 hectares around its major ports at an estimated cost of $7 billion was announced in 1970. Much of this will probably be material pumped from the adjacent seabed, but for many years Japan, with its desperate shortage of land, has been using also its urban waste materials for filling. As but one example, two areas in Tokyo harbor at Kawasaki were filled between 1957 and 1963 with 24 million m³ of soil, most of its hydraulically placed by pumping but with the upper 1-m thickness provided from excavated material, ash, and slag, giving a total area of 3.8 million m². And this was but the start of a major filling program at this location.[7.51]

An alternative use of excavated material is being followed by the city of Toronto. Its existing harbor (shown in Fig. 7.21) is incapable of any further extension within the wonderfully sheltered Toronto Bay, and so plans have been developed for a new section of the harbor to the east of the present area. It must be out in the open water of Lake Ontario, and so protection is essential. A new breakwater has been planned that will be 4,920 m long when completed, giving an eventual increase in harbor capacity of two-thirds. As a result of long-term advance planning, the new breakwater is being constructed rather more slowly than is usually the case but is costing the public practically nothing. It is being constructed entirely of fill from excavations in the central part of this rapidly growing city. Contractors are not charged for the privilege of dumping, and so they save in their operations by the relatively short haul out to the breakwater. The Harbour Commission has to operate a bulldozing operation for control of the fill, but this is estimated to cost not more than $50,000 for the entire job, which will eventually contain about 13 million m^3 of material—all obtained conveniently and for nothing. Even a large consignment of French wines was contributed to the breakwater by the Liquor Control Board of Ontario, as fill, but only because it had been accidentally frozen and so was unfit for the palates of their customers. Blocks of concrete and rock are not used for the breakwater but are broken up and crushed in a special installation from which a steady supply of crushed rock for surfacing harbor roads is obtained. Geology helps, for the locally excavated glacial soils and shale bedrock are suitable materials for this unusual use, and the bottom of Lake Ontario, formed of the same materials, provides an excellent foundation bed. There must be many cities that could use their valuable materials from excavations in similar constructive ways, with no disfigurement of the landscape and to public economic benefit, but only as a result of careful advance planning and provided that the local geology ensures material that is suitable and locations for its disposal that can be used safely. The relatively small expenditure needed for the necessary subsurface investigation can pay dividends many times over, even for this unusual phase of modern urban development.[7.52]

7.14 DISPOSAL OF DOMESTIC WASTE

It was mentioned at the outset of this section that probably the greatest source of sediment now being discharged into the Atlantic Ocean from the North American continent is the solid wastes from the New York metropolitan area. Any further need to justify reference to such an apparently nongeological subject as waste disposal will probably be unnecessary. Waste disposal has been one of the hidden problems of city administration for far too long. It is now being recognized for what it is—an essential civic service that must be carried out as economically as possible but without disfiguring the landscape or causing any harmful effects to the environment in which it is deposited.

The extent of the problem is but rarely realized. Recent estimates by the U.S. Public Health Service suggest that the total amount of household, commercial, and municipal wastes in the United States in 1 year as the sixties came to a close was more than 250 million tonnes. To this must be added an estimate of more than 550 million tonnes of agricultural wastes generally disposed of on farms; more than 1.5 billion tons of animal wastes, including slaughterhouse paunch, manure, and pen sweepings; and more than 1.1 billion tonnes of wastes from the mineral industry, waste such as mine tailings. This impressive total of more than 3.5 billion tonnes of solid wastes from the United States in 1 year is estimated to cost $4.5 billion annually for collection and disposal.[7.53] When thought be given to wastes not included in this main list, it can be seen that the total given is probably an underestimate. It is rapidly increasing year by year. One of the most recent reasons for unusual increase is the severe restrictions now being imposed by major cities on the use of private domestic incinerators (such as in apartment buildings) in the interest of reducing air pollution. Every such incinerator that goes out of use, for the very best of reasons, adds still more to the waste disposal problem. And much of the domestic waste, the result of the "affluent society," is material that will not quickly disintegrate—every year in the United States alone, 7 million automobiles, 50 billion cans, and 30 billion bottles and jars to mention just the leading items. And of the $4.5 billion dollars spent in dealing with this critical problem, 80 percent is spent for trucking from collecting point to the disposal location. This is where geology comes in.

Considering merely the domestic and commercial rubbish generally described as "garbage," most of this is hauled away to dumps. The average citizen sees the garbage truck take his waste away and probably gives no more thought to what happens to it. This is probably the underlying reason why so relatively few major cities have yet equipped themselves with modern incinerator plants for the combustion of all the garbage that will burn. These plants involve heavy capital expenditure, even though an economical civic investment, and taxpayers dislike such "hidden investments." It is essential that this reluctance be overcome. Possibly the modern and efficient plant now being built by the city of Montreal may act as a catalyst to other civic action.[7.54] Even when incinerators are used, however, they too have residues to be disposed of, even though it is not so bulky or objectionable as ordinary unburned garbage. Where can such materials be dumped? The old village garbage dump has often been the butt of much dubious humor, but many city garbage disposal areas do not qualify for any better treatment. In 1968, the U.S. Public Health Service conducted a National Survey of Solid Waste Practices, examining 6,000 typical "land disposal sites." Of this total, only 6 percent could be classed as "sanitary land fills." Less than 14 percent were covered daily; 41 percent got no cover at all. Of this large sample, 75 percent had an unacceptable appearance and some form of open burning. And the survey did not reveal how many of these sites had fouled their environment because of penetration of the leachate into the local groundwater system. The term "leachate" (which should be familiar to all geologists) indicates the water, generally rain, that has contact with garbage dumps and runs off them, having picked up any soluble materials with which it has been in contact, undesirable though they may be.[7.55]

A typical example is provided by the town of Alton, Missouri, located in the attractive Ozark country, distinguished for its large karst springs. The town used a most convenient feature for disposing of the town garbage, a 15.2-m-deep sinkhole that is normally quite dry. (Most of the town's refuse is now dumped at another location, but the sinkhole was still in partial use in 1969.) During the winter and spring of 1969, the sinkhole filled with approximately 9.1 m of water. Before it drained dry again, the U.S. Forest Service, as a part of their study of sinkholes in the Ozarks, had injected some fluorescein dye into the water. It was estimated that 230,000 liters of dyed water disappeared into the underlying groundwater system. Between 2½ and 3 months later, the dye appeared in the water of Morgan Spring, located 25 km away, although it did not appear in the Blue Spring, which is only 400 m away from the Morgan Spring, illustrating the complexity of underground flow in this type of country. This is no isolated case, even though small in magnitude with no serious results caused by the leachate. It is mentioned, however, to illustrate how far-reaching can be the effects of leachate from a garbage dump if the local geology is not first studied in order to ensure that dumping can be carried out safely. How many of the tens of thousands of garbage dumps in North America have been developed on geologically suitable sites? Rhetorical though the question is, it points to the necessity of having geological examinations made of *all* sites used for dumping before *any* disposal is permitted, a practice that is now being followed by an increasing number of regulatory agencies.

Such good progress is now being made at the development of truly sanitary landfills on geologically acceptable sites that it may be invidious to mention specific agencies. Typical, however, has been the work of the Illinois State Geological Survey Division in studying and reporting upon geologically acceptable disposal sites in its state. The Missouri Division of Geological Survey and Water Resources is actively engaged in similar work in its area, as are other state surveys. In the state of Pennsylvania the State Department of Health is carrying out this work through its Bureau of Sanitary Engineering, which has its own geological staff. As early as 1963 this department appointed its first geologist, in connection with groundwater-pollution abatement; although he assisted with other problems, the geological work of the department soon necessitated additions to the geological staff. In 1968 legislation was passed that gave the department authority to require permits for all sanitary landfills in the State. Between 1968 and 1971, geologists examined over 300 existing landfills in addition to studying proposed sites for new disposal areas. Regulations that are now mandatory, adopted in November 1969 and since amended, require that a report on the soil, geology, and groundwater characteristics of a site must be provided and approved before a permit will be issued. They also specify the minimum test-boring program at a site that is acceptable and the type of cover material that shall be used; geohydrological requirements are also clearly set out in the regulations, as are the necessary provision of all-weather access roads.[7.56] Geology, therefore, is at last playing an essential role in this vital if somewhat mundane civic service.

The availability of suitable sites adjacent to developed city areas is naturally becoming an increasingly serious problem, if only because of the high cost of trucking. Some very large municipalities that have still not got incinerators for their rubbish

Figure 7.26 Portsmouth, Hampshire, England. New disposal area in Portsmouth harbor; an aerial view showing construction of embankments to enclose areas to be reclaimed and new road construction in the distance; the white area (on the left) is where the Chalk is being excavated for the new autoroute M27, the material excavated being moved by belt conveyor to serve as foundation material at a new building site. *(Courtesy of J. C. Cotton, City Engineer, Portsmouth.)*

disposal are even turning to the use of rail haul for their garbage. This gives good business to the railways and involves no large capital expenditure on the part of the city. But disposal sites have still to be found, even though "out of sight and out of mind" in so far as the city dweller is concerned. In one case, rail-transported rubbish is being used as fill for abandoned strip mines; in another, a desert location is being proposed. One problem is common to all disposal projects, even if carried out (as all should be) in conformity with the best principles of sanitary landfill, principles that need not be detailed here but that include elimination of all nuisance, proper cover, and no burning. This is the inevitable generation of methane gas through the decomposition of organic rubbish. The dangers that this creates were mentioned when discussing foundations that have to be built over filled ground, but this is a practice that should be severely restricted. Accordingly, careful planning is always necessary in the selection of areas as disposal sites so that they can be put to good use, when completely filled, graded, and landscaped, for such purposes as parks and other open areas in which the presence of methane will not be objectionable.

In Great Britain, municipal officials have no opportunity of sending their garbage off into the desert in the hope that it can be forgotten. They have to adopt other methods. On the south coast stands the city of Portsmouth. An area of 164 hectares of Portsmouth harbor, long known as Paulsgrove Lake situated between the mainland and Hornsea Island, has now been enclosed from the sea by the construction of relatively simple embankments made of Chalk excavated from a nearby hill. Refuse is now being dumped under controlled conditions within this large area. It is estimated that it will hold more than 2.25 million tonnes, but plans are already being developed for an incinerator plant that will be in operation when the area is about half full. The residue from the incineration process will be so much less bulky that the life of the area for disposal will be increased from the original estimate of 20 years to perhaps 50 years. In addition to providing 161 hectares of new land, this disposal site will also provide new road access to Portsmouth. This was a part of the initial planning that naturally included a careful program of subsurface exploration to ensure that the site was quite suitable. The results of advance predictions based on the geological survey that was first made were confirmed by 28 test borings and 4 probes. Very recent marine deposits formed the surface, overlying earlier alluvium and then the Upper Cretaceous Chalk.[7.57]

Figure 7.27 Liverpool, Lancashire, England. Otterspool esplanade, the new sea wall having created an area that was used for disposal of domestic wastes and then finished off as this pleasant park; the view is taken looking north toward the mouth of the River Mersey, the cranes in the background being at ship-building yards in Birkenhead. *(Courtesy of I. T. Cucksey, Chief Engineer, Engineering Division, Department of Transportation and Basic Services, City of Liverpool.)*

The same practice, on a more limited scale, was started in 1932 by the city of Liverpool, England's major port on the River Mersey. At a location with the delightful name of Otterspool, to the south of the city, 17.3 hectares were enclosed by a seawall, and embankments were made from the sandstone rock excavated from the first Mersey Tunnel. Some years after tipping was finished, the area had been converted into a waterside park with good landscaping, including gardens and a waterfront promenade. In 1955 a further 28.2 hectares were reclaimed in a similar way, and here it was estimated that 6.1 million m^3 could be deposited.[7.58] Across the Irish Sea, the port of Dublin in Eire (Ireland) has been regularly reclaiming 6 to 8 hectares a year using domestic refuse and excavated material under controlled tipping. Suitable embankments are first built. Dumped material is compacted by the simple means of dropping a 3-tonne weight from heights up to 6.1 m. After compaction, a gravel top is added, and this new land is used for any loading up to 5.47 kg per m^2.[7.59]

There are, therefore, solutions to this most pressing problem, but they involve sound long-term planning and an acceptance before any plans are finalized. The crowded nature of Japan's cities suggests that here, too, the problem must be pressing. It is, and there are some lessons to be learned from the Japanese attack on the problem. Eighty percent of all the solid waste of Tokyo is burned in incinerators. Even so, this generates large quantities of burned waste that, together with the 6,800 tonnes daily that are not burned, is used for fill in areas controlled just as have been described. Power is even generated from the incinerators, the 2,400 kilowatts of byproduct power being used for refuse plant operation. The extensive reclamation of new land already mentioned (page 378) is in part being filled with refuse and incinerator waste. Dream Island in Tokyo Bay, an enclosed area of 45.3 hectares, has been formed entirely in this way, solid waste, incinerator residue, and clean fill being placed in alternate layers. It will be used as a public park and for the site of another incinerator. One commercial development in Japan has attracted worldwide attention and possibly points the way to future attacks on the garbage problem. The Tezuka Kosan Company has developed a satisfactory process for compressing garbage under unusually high pressures, forming rock-hard blocks. Wire mesh is used to contain the rubbish at the start of the process. After being compressed under a force of more than 2,400 tonnes, the finished blocks are dipped in hot asphalt and can then be used for a variety of purposes, such as forming simple embankment walls. The high pressures used are said to prevent rotting and the formation of methane. Perhaps most importantly, a "waste" material is being turned to constructive use, as it is, of course, when properly used for desirable filling. This economy of material is something that will become increasingly vital.[7.60]

A small start in this direction has been made in seeking uses for the glass in glass bottles that are classified as "waste." In both the United States and Canada, highway authorities have been willing to experiment with the use of crushed glass bottles for road construction—in effect using it as a man-made geological material. In 1970, 125 tonnes were used as a subbase for a short section of Interstate Highway

No. 75 at Toledo, Ohio, the necessary processing costs being found to be about the same, in total, as for gravel. In Ontario, the Glass Container Council of Canada has assisted with experimental use of broken glass as aggregate in asphalt paving material. One West Coast brewer in the United States has crushed beer bottles to make an experimental paving material called "glasphalt" that was used to pave a parking lot. It has even been proposed that crushed glass bottles be used to replace the beach

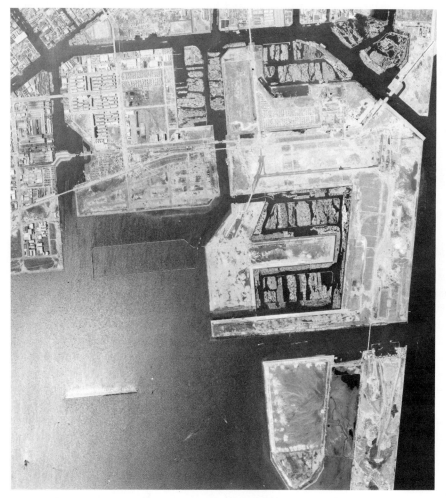

Figure 7.28 Tokyo, Japan. Reclamation of land in the harbor of Tokyo in active progress using fill material from the city; an aerial view that shows completed reclamation and also filling in progress. *(Courtesy of the Director, Geographical Survey Institute of the Ministry of Construction, and K. Kamimura of the Ministry's Building Research Institute.)*

sand that is washed away each year.[7.61] These are still experimental projects; as always when exposure to the elements is involved, it will take a number of years before any certainty can be attached to initial experimental results.

In a corresponding way, the burned residue of sewage sludge is being tried out as the equivalent of soil. Disposal of this semisolid residue from the treatment of sewage in municipal plants is a civic problem even less well realized than the disposal of garbage. Sewage-treatment plants are now being constructed in ever-increasing numbers in delayed response to the demand for a reduction in the pollution of waterways. They result in an effluent that is of such quality that it can be discharged safely into running water or lakes, but there remains in the plant, for disposal in some other way, the sludge that collects in the treatment tanks. Burning it is one way of disposing of the sludge since it does contain combustible material. In seaboard cities, dumping it in the sea is an alternative way of getting rid of it. It is sludge from New York's sewage plants that forms an appreciable part of the waste materials mentioned at the outset of this section. In recent years an average of 150,000 m^3 a year have been deposited in a specially assigned location near the head of the Hudson Canyon in the Continental Shelf, about 48.3 km out to sea. The effect of this material, with its organic content, on marine organisms is not yet known with any certainty. Possibly the best known of all methods of disposing of sewage sludge is that practiced, now for many years, by the city of Milwaukee in the preparation of their well-known fertilizer "Milorganite."

7.14 DISPOSAL OF INDUSTRIAL WASTES

Similar problems to those of municipalities in getting rid of their waste are faced by many industries. Minor wastes can be handled similar to the domestic wastes of cities. Liquid wastes have, all too often, been discharged into neighboring watercourses, often with serious effects. The public conscience has at last been aroused over this whole matter of pollution so that support is coming from the public sector for those industries that have always taken a serious view of their responsibilities in this matter. Disposal of solid wastes from industry is often a difficult and costly matter. It is something that industries have to include as a part of their overall operations. Much research has been done in finding better ways of using wastes; today this search for economic solutions to the "waste problem" is being intensified. In some cases, such as the sludge obtained from the refining of bauxite for the manufacture of aluminum, there is no solution at present other than to provide storage ponds in which the sludge can settle out from the water with which it is processed. Satisfactory methods of providing this storage have been developed, costly though they can be.

Geology is implicit in the provision of all sites for such disposal purposes, as is always the case, but the somewhat unusual geological implications of this subject relate to the materials that can be made from some industrial waste products. In the manufacture of steel, for example, there are large quantities of slag to be disposed of.

The use of treated slag as a concrete aggregate has been mentioned (page 372), but it is also widely used as fill when its high specific gravity is no disadvantage. As with natural materials used directly for fill, knowledge of the properties of slag proposed for fill is essential before its approval for use. It has been found, for example, that certain types of slag from the open-hearth system of steelmaking have the undesirable property of expanding in the course of time. If placed under a building, such material can cause very serious trouble, due to this expansion, as some cases on record have shown.[7.62]

Correspondingly, the large quantities of fly ash that derive from the operation of fuel-fired large steam-power stations present a massive problem of disposal so that extensive research programs are under way in many countries in seeking uses of this interesting material, another man-made geological product. It is being used as fill in old mine workings, as a filler with bituminous mixtures, as a constituent of stabilized soil mixtures, for the manufacture of bricks, as a medium for water treatment, especially in neutralizing acidic soils, and in concrete. It is mentioned here, if only to indicate that, as man in the vicinity of cities uses up naturally provided materials such as sand and gravel, at the same time he is producing new materials some of which may in the course of time be used as substitutes for the natural materials supplies of which have been exhausted.

The quantities of fly ash that are today being produced are immense. British Railways have built four complete special trains merely for transporting fly ash from just three steam-power stations in the English Midlands to the Fletton area. Here the ash is being used to fill up worked-out clay pits and an old reservoir in a major land rehabilitation project that is estimated to last for 35 years. Each train carries more than 1,000 tonnes; it is unloaded at a specially built station under pressure, mixed with water, and pumped to the disposal area. The self-contained trains operate on a regular round-trip basis day in and day out and have to handle more than 1 million tonnes of fly ash every year. Landscaping of the rehabilitated area is being very carefully carried out, following necessary geological studies. The scheme is a model of what such projects can be.[7.63]

They are badly needed in so many parts of the world where the landscape has been disfigured either by massive excavation (as for coal or iron ore obtained from open pits) or for other types of ore that have been handled hydraulically. California faces unusual problems from this cause, stemming from the hydraulic placer mining for gold carried out in years before 1884 when the U.S. Circuit Court of Appeals prohibited uncontrolled deposition of hydraulic-mining debris. Despite the years between, such debris has been responsible for reducing the capacity of reservoirs such as that behind the Combei Dam by as much as 125 hectare-m. Dredging gold-bearing gravels has been carried out more recently on almost every gold-bearing river in northern California. Some of the dredged tailings were used in the construction of the great Oroville earth dam. An extensive research program has been initiated seeking ways of manufacturing building materials from this old waste material, and some success has been achieved.[7.64] Again, therefore, man is using products once regarded as useless waste to develop materials that can aid in the growth of his cities without using up any more natural materials.

MATERIAL BENEATH CITIES

7.15   WATER, GAS, AND OIL

The main heading may remind some readers of schoolboy stories of gold ore being found under sidewalks that were therefore ripped up with hair-raising results. That sort of thing probably did happen in some of the early mining towns, but one could hardly say that they were planned communities. On the other hand, many early settlements were sited so as to take advantage of good water supply from wells or springs right at the location used for building. Such supplies were an indication of a high water table beneath the settlement. As groundwater was drawn upon to an increasing extent, the springs would disappear, the water in the wells would fall lower and lower until pumping had to be resorted to. This was such a natural sequence of events that rarely, in earlier days, did authorities stop to question the wisdom of the proceeding, the general assumption of the earth's crust as something solid and immovable being widely prevalent, as it is even today. Unfortunately, assuredly in this connection, it is not so. Around the world there are all too many urban areas that have suffered from serious ground settlement due to overpumping of water from beneath them.

With the discovery of natural gas and petroleum available for man's use by pumping from the ground, sometimes at great depths, the same thing has happened when these valuable materials were traced beneath urban areas. All visitors to the Los Angeles—Long Beach area of California will be familiar with the sight of pumping plants steadily operating without any apparent supervision. They will not normally observe the ground settlement that has taken place in the Long Beach area. These settlements can properly be classed as geological hazards and so will be considered in the following chapter. The widespread abstraction of these fluids from beneath cities points the way, however, to the occasional abstraction of solid materials.

7.16   COAL BENEATH CITIES

In coal-bearing regions, coal beds are often of great areal extent. Urban settlements have naturally been formed adjacent to coal mines, and so it has been inevitable that, in some parts of the world, there should be ground settlements in cities, due to the abstraction of coal from beneath the ground where the overlying strata were not strong enough to provide a stable roof over the workings. The same thing is true of salt deposits and, in extremely rare cases, of other minerals. These problems will

Figure 7.29 Most, Czechoslovakia. The ancient church at Most being prepared for moving to its new location to release the underlying brown coal beds for development. *(Courtesy of Transfera, Prague, and J. Skopek.)*

also be considered in the next chapter. There are, however, two other features of coal removal from beneath the sites of cities that properly call for mention here since the controlled removal of material is involved; they bring this wide-ranging treatment of materials and cities to a fitting close.

To the east and northeast of Prague in the lovely land of central Bohemia are some of the most important and valuable brown coal deposits of Europe. Only in relatively recent years have these vast beds of coal been worked extensively. They lie close to the surface and so can readily be worked by surface mining. In one pit that the author has seen, coal is brought right out of the pit by belt conveyor to a screening plant and thence directly into the bunkers of a large steam-power plant located on the edge of the mine. The deposits are, therefore, being worked efficiently, but overall planning has been hampered by the fact that small villages and some fairly large towns were sited, very many years (if not centuries) ago, right on top of these valuable coal beds. Some of the larger towns had to be moved. Buildings that could profitably be replaced by more modern buildings were destroyed when their replacements were ready, but historical buildings were preserved to the extent that was possible. This movement of complete towns and displacement of rural settlements in the interests of winning coal is, as can be imagined, a fascinating chapter in the history of European mining, with the complex local geology the root cause of all the disruptions.

Only one case can be mentioned from the many interesting byproducts of this accident of geology, as it may well be called. In the largest of the brown coal areas, about 70 km to the northeast of Prague, lies the thirteenth-century town of Most. Covering an area of 390 hectares, with a population of 54,000, Most sits right on top of a lignite bed 27.3 m thick that contains 90 million tonnes of high-quality brown coal only 1.5 to 15.2 m beneath the narrow streets of the old town. Moving it is clearly essential. Modern apartment blocks in the New Most, about 3.2 km away, are providing more modern accommodation (even though not so picturesque) for the town's inhabitants. A central point of the old town has been the sixteenth-century Gothic Church of the Ascension. Its singularly beautiful interior has three naves; it is 59.3 m long, 26.4 m wide, and 31.3 m high. Its total weight is estimated to be more than 12,000 tonnes. The Czechoslovakian Government decided that this beautiful church must be saved, even though the masonry of the adjoining bell tower is too badly fractured to make moving it practicable. The church itself, however, is to be carefully "caged," or reinforced with a steel framework, before moving and after it has been underpinned to new supports. When secure in this temporary frame, it will be moved 870 m and downhill by 10.5 m to a newly prepared site. Even the move will be complicated by old mine workings, a 152-m stretch of the route being over old mine shafts that have to be specially backfilled and strengthened. It is hoped to complete the move in the year 1975.[7.65]

Finally there may be mentioned the most remarkable case of the interrelation of geology with city development known to the author, a case that he has had the privilege of observing at first hand so that, incredible though it may appear to be to some readers, it can be presented with full assurance that geology was used in this way. The city of Duisburg is the main port for the Ruhr of West Germany. It is the main inland port on the Rhine and is said to be the largest inland port in the world. It dates back to the fourteenth century and so has been a busy river town and city for six centuries. Its postwar traffic has exceeded 20 million tonnes in one year. It is located about 130 km from the mouth of the Rhine and stands at the junction of the Ruhr River and the Rhine-Herne Canal with the Rhine. Progressive straightening and improvement of the Rhine in the interests of more efficient navigation have had the inevitable effect of lowering the normal level of the river. This lowering has amounted to as much as 2 m at Duisburg since 1900. The effect of this on the many miles of wharves in Duisburg harbor, well equipped for the handling of coal, iron ore, and miscellaneous cargoes, can well be imagined. The future of the port was in real jeopardy.

The existence of valuable coal seams beneath this great industrial city was well known. Even though the main seams were located at great depths below the surface (the lowest about 600 m down), mining of the coal had been prohibited for many years. The coal beds are generally horizontal. Much experience had been gained in extracting the coal from them in the area all around Duisburg. It was finally decided by Harbour Director Herman Bumm to embark on a special program of progressive mining of the seams under the harbor area, deliberately with the intent of causing settlement of the whole area, which would, therefore, compensate for the drop in the water level alongside the busy wharves. And this bold program was carried out by expert miners, under constant control, without any interference with the operation

Figure 7.30 Duisburg, West Germany. The northwest part of Duisburg harbor after the lowering of the main section of the harbor; the slight slope to the concrete structure on the wharf is the only visible evidence of the differential settlement due to underground faulting. *(Photograph by R. F. Legget.)*

of the harbor, or the many industrial plants and power stations located all over the great basin-shaped area that was lowered. The entire harbor area had been lowered by an amount of 1.75 m when the mining had to be stopped due to increasing complexities in the underground geological structure, caused by extensive faulting. But the main objective had been achieved; good water depths were restored to the harbor, and more than 12 million tonnes of high-grade coal were obtained as a byproduct of what is probably the boldest geological engineering undertaking ever carried out beneath the streets and the waterways of a great modern city.[7.66]

chapter eight
Geological Hazards and Cities

What plagues and what portents, what mutiny,
What raging of the sea, shaking of the earth,
Commotion in the winds, frights, changes, horrors,
Divert and crack, rend and deracinate
The unity and married calm of states
. . . .

Take but degree away, untune that string,
And, hark, what discord follows! each thing meets
In mere oppugnancy: the bounded waters
Should lift their bosoms higher than the shores,
And make a sop of all this solid globe:

Ulysses in Troilus and Cressida
act I, scene iii
William Shakespeare
(1564–1616)

The controlled lowering at Duisburg is a useful reminder that the "solid earth" is not always the fixed and immutable platform for human activity so often and so generally imagined. Not only are the materials of which it consists susceptible to stress and strain, as are all structural materials, but the physical processes that have given the surface of the earth its present form are still at work. Slowly and usually imperceptibly the action of wind and water and ice is wearing down the higher parts of the lithosphere and moving the products of such "weathering" downhill, down the beds of streams into rivers, down rivers to lakes and eventually to the sea. Those who have been priviledged to see one or another of the great deltas of the world need no reminder of this continual geological action in wearing away the surface of the earth and transporting the debris down to the sea. All who have stood on the shore of the sea, or even of a large lake, and heard the waves grinding the shingle of the beach or seen the ever-moving water with its ebb and flow moving sand backward and forward— they know that geological processes are indeed dynamic.

More dramatic, although seen only by few, is the mass movement of soil caused by a landslide, a disturbing sight even when the slide does no damage to developed property. Equally significant are the streams of boulders that can be seen in many a narrow defile in mountainous country, well established in dry stream beds throughout the year but silent reminders of the transporting power of ice and water that has brought them to their present location during high spring-flood flows. These mass movements have their "models" too, as anyone can see who will take time to watch a bank of soil during a heavy rainstorm, the running water picking up grains of soil and moving them down the face, often into miniature deltas at the foot of the slope. Innumerable are the examples that can be seen by the observant eye, all reminders of the dynamism of nature, even of its inanimate surface materials.

The beauty of Niagara Falls is world famous and rightly so, as all visitors to the Falls will agree. A glance at the American Falls will show the great pile of huge blocks of rock that provide such vivid evidence of the erosion of the lip of the Falls. Those who have any knowledge of the geological structure of the rock exposed in this magnificent gorge will know that the same sort of erosion has been going on, but at a vastly greater rate, beneath the majestic Canadian, or Horseshoe, Falls, the difference being that the deep pool into which this cataract tumbles completely hides the blocks of rock, the falling of which cause a recession of the lip at a rate of about 1 m per year. A recent study of the American Falls has provided a useful reminder of the recession of these great Falls ever since the day on which they were first seen by Father Hennepin in 1678. Figure 8.1 shows in a simple sketch something of this remarkable example of the results of the erosive forces that are at work all over the earth's surface.

In the planning and developing of cities, therefore, not only must the geological conditions beneath the city and all areas intended for development be known with certainty, but the possibility of disturbance of the surface must also be considered, with the aid of appropriate geological advice. These *geological hazards*, as they may be called, will be rare in their occurrence, but they must be considered as possibilities in all urban planning, not in any alarmist manner but rather as a precaution that may have most beneficial results as examples will show. In many cases, such as earthquakes, the causes of earth movements will be natural, causes that must be accepted with their inevitable consequences, even though anticipation of the possibility of such movements will usually permit some precautionary planning. In other cases, the works of man may have served to intensify the degree of natural geological hazards, the increase in the severity of floods often being clearly influenced by human activities

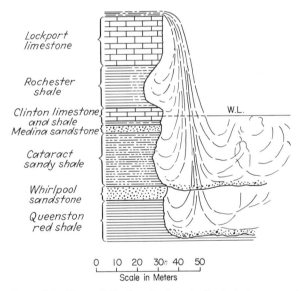

Figure 8.1   Niagara Falls, Ontario, Canada. Geological cross section through Niagara Falls, showing the alternation of rock strata that assists erosion of the lip of the Falls. *(Courtesy of the Director, Geological Survey of Canada.)*

in catchment areas. In a few cases, hazards that must still be classed, for convenience, as geological are almost entirely man-made, even though a natural occurrence such as a heavy rainstorm may act as the final trigger. The collapse of coal tips, with that at Aberfan being the most tragic and most notable, are in this category.

In this chapter the main groups of geological hazards will therefore be reviewed—briefly but with adequate references to sources of additional information. Brevity is essential not only because entire volumes have been devoted to treatments of even individual groups of the hazards to be discussed but also because any treatment in depth might distort the overall view that this volume essays to present of the intricate interrelation of geology with the planning, building, and development of cities. A few hazards must be considered as possibilities in all urban areas. As will be seen, a few regions in the world present special problems with regard to one major group of hazards, such as earthquakes. In the overview, however, the incidence of hazards in urban development is very limited in comparison with the constructive uses of geology such as have been discussed in the immediately preceding chapters.

If trouble does occur, however, due to geological hazards, human lives are inevitably involved. This immediately places the disaster—and this is not too strong a word to use for many of the consequences of the events with which this chapter deals—in a very special category. With human lives at stake, and many lives in view of the congregation of people that is an essential part of urban development, every possible effort must be exerted in taking all necessary and desirable precautionary measures. It is here that geology has so vital a role to play. When one considers, as can so easily be done, cases in which available geological advice was not used in advance of a catastrophe, advice that would have saved human lives, the urgency of developing public appreciation and especially professional understanding of the importance of geology in all aspects of urban growth becomes so obvious that mere words—such as these—seem to be inadequate in making the urgency crystal clear.

It is hoped that the selection of the examples that now follow will serve to demonstrate that, although geological hazards must be contemplated as possibilities in all cities, their worst effects can be minimized by advance recognition of their possibility and by ensuring that urban planning is always carried out in full recognition of these possibilities, using geological and engineering advice to ensure the best possible planning and building in the face of all local circumstances. As the scramble for good building land around cities becomes more intense, under inevitable population pressures, there will be increasing attempts to develop land that is geologically unsuitable even though superficially satisfactory. There is probably no branch of engineering geology that can have such socially beneficial results as the application of geological knowledge in pointing out to planners, engineers, and architects the hazards that the use of such building sites may present. It is fervently to be hoped that those who are responsible for the decision making in all urban development will give steadily increasing attention to such geological advice in order to ensure the safety of cities as well as their desirable amenity.

8.2 VOLCANIC ACTION

The most obvious and most commonly appreciated evidence of the occasional instability of the earth's crust is the occurrence of volcanoes—the eruption of existing volcanoes, but even more so the infrequent formation of entirely new volcanoes. Destruction of the ancient city of Herculaneum by the eruption of Mount Vesuvius in 79 A.D. is now well known, following the discovery of the ruins in 1748 and the wide publicity given in words and pictures to the remarkable excavations that have revealed so much of the buildings and streets of the old city. Vesuvius and Stromboli in Italy, Hekla in Iceland, and Mont Pelée in Martinique are the most notable of the volcanoes that have built up cones around the vents in the earth's surface through which molten lava has been emitted from the molten magma beneath the crust. Mont Pelée was in violent eruption in 1902 when the town of St. Pierre was completely destroyed. Another tremendous natural explosion of recent times was the eruption of Krakatoa in the Strait of Sunda, Indonesia, in 1883. The volcano of Paricutin in Mexico, which started in level farm land in 1943, is of the same conical type (see Fig. 8.2), whereas the new Icelandic volcano, Surtsey, started by emission of lava beneath the sea from a long fissure rift. The fact that the Hawaiian Islands are the eroded tops of volcanoes rising from the depths of the Pacific Ocean is well known and is evidenced by the generally mild activity of the still active peaks.

This short list includes the best known of the relatively few volcanoes that have been active in recent times. Their existence is so well known that their influence on any urban development in their vicinity can be taken for granted. Equally limited in distribution today are those areas in which hot water and associated gases, including steam, escape from the crust of the earth through cracks or hot springs. The ways in which this supply of subterranean heat can be harnessed for public use were touched upon in Chap. 4, the city of Reykjavik in Iceland being preeminent in this connection. Here a minor form of volcanism is being turned to good effect.

Engineers in Italy can never forget the influence of volcanic action in their country, as was recently demonstrated by a sudden rise in the ground level in the city of Pozzuoli, well known at least by name as the location from which pozzolana was first obtained in quantity by Roman builders. The movement started in 1969, and within 6 months the ground had risen in places as much as 0.7 m, continuing to rise at the rate of about 10 mm per day. It is believed that underground movement of molten lava, the area being very close to Mount Vesuvius, is the cause of this reversal of the usual form of ground movement to trouble cities, settlements being almost the only kind of movement normally encountered. By the spring of 1970, the Italian Ministry of Public Works had ordered 9,000 of the city's 65,000 residents to evacuate their homes. A new city is being built at a cost in excess of $12 million to house the displaced townsfolk. This most unusual movement may also be responsible in part for serious ground movements that have affected an area close to the adjacent city of Naples. Serious subsidences have taken place, with accompanying slides and even opening up of cracks in the earth's surface, with consequent damage to property.

Figure 8.2 Parícutin, Mexico. The new volcano at Parícutin that first appeared as a small eruption in 1943, a reminder of what exists beneath the surface of the earth. *(Courtesy of the Departamento de Turismo, Mexico, D.F.)*

Heavy rains in the fall of 1969 are believed to have been a contributing factor, causing the infiltration of groundwater into a geological unstable area, but the subterranean volcanic action is thought to be at least partially responsible.[8.1] The world as a whole is fortunate in that such evidence of the instability of the thin crust on which the welfare of the entire world depends are so very limited.

8.3 GEOLOGICALLY ACTIVE FAULTS

Mention of "cracks in the ground" may strike some readers as somewhat unusual, until they recall what has already been said about geological faults. In almost all bedrock, as it is exposed at the earth's surface, some evidence of faulting will be found, an indication of the stresses to which the rock has been subject in far-gone geological ages, stresses that have induced strains so great that failure of the solid material resulted, with consequent movement on the fault plane, or shear plane as it is sometimes and quite accurately described. This movement, the "throw" of the fault, may extend several kilometers but will vary from such vast distances down to a few millimeters. Faulting is also to be seen even in deposits of soil, but the movements here are almost always small, the faulting being relatively recent in geological terms. The study of

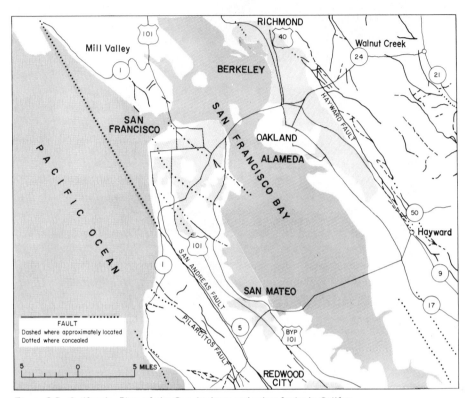

Figure 8.3   California. Plan of the San Andreas and other faults in California. *(Courtesy of the Director, U.S. Geological Survey, from reference 8.2, the map being based on the Geological Map of California of the California Division of Mines and Geology.)*

fault movements enables geologists to build up a picture of the history of the bedrock in which they occur, and its relationship with adjoining rocks, as does also the detailed study of the solid material that will often be found to be filling what were originally open cracks in the bedrock. These veins, frequently of quartz, add their own interest to many exposures of bedrock. Even the veins may be faulted, clear evidence of earth movement *after* the veins had been filled with molten rock and all had cooled into its present form.

Faults can be of great importance in engineering works if the rock on one or both sides of the fault plane has been shattered, as it often is in the case of major faults. If undetected by preliminary investigations, this fractured material can cause real trouble in excavation, either in the open or in tunnels. The faults themselves are usually quite stable, with no movement now occurring along the fault plane—but not always. Some faults are still "active," with movement of the bedrock on one side or the other (or both) still taking place, albeit slowly. Their existence constitutes another form of geological hazard and one that is again related to the stresses exerted on the crust by the underlying magma, even though this will never be evident. Fortunately, such geologically active faults are not commonly encountered, but they must be anticipated. When faults are encountered in excavations, and especially in tunnels, special precautions must be taken (with appropriate instrumentation) to determine whether the faults are as inactive as they will always appear to be. If any movement at all is detected, then unusual arrangements will have to be made to compensate for any future movements in the design of the structure, be it tunnel lining or foundation.

Probably the most famous, the best known, and the most intensively studied active fault is the San Andreas fault of California. It is the master fault of a great network of faults in the coastal plain of California, indicative of extensive earth movements here many eons ago. The San Andreas fault extends on land for a total distance of about 1,000 km until it runs into the sea off the northern coast of California. It extends deep into the earth a distance of at least 32 km. The total accumulated displacement along the fault may be as much as 550 km. And this movement continues, at a rate of about 5 cm per year as disclosed by precise surveying techniques. If the fault has been similarly active during 100 million years of existence, a displacement of over 500 km is quite understandable. The movement is so slow that many residents of California who live close to the fault are not even aware of its existence. During the 1906 San Francisco earthquake, however, a movement of more than 1 m (6 m being the maximum) occurred, as was shown by the distortion of roads and structures that crossed the fault; in each case the ground to the west of the fault moved relatively northward.[8.2]

It is earth movements along faults that cause, or are evidenced by, the occurrence of earthquakes. It is, however, somewhat surprising to find that although a number of earthquakes in historical times can be related to movements along the San Andreas fault, they have never been repeated at the same location, with two possible exceptions. Figure 8.3 shows generally the location of the great fault, and it will be seen that it passes immediately to the south of the great concentration of population around the city of San Francisco and within a few kilometers of the San Francisco Airport. Its location is known with accuracy; it has been photographed from a high-flying jet aircraft using side-scanning radar in a manner that gives promise for the detection of other faults in other areas using this modern technique. There is today, therefore, no possible excuse for any structure that would be damaged by excessive movement being built across the fault, as has happened in the past. Roads must naturally cross the fault, but if movement does occur here it can readily be corrected. Difficult though its location is from the point of view of urban development, the San Andreas fault is most conveniently located for geological study. It is, therefore, being intensively studied, just as it has been under careful observation for many years; it still presents many unresolved scientific questions, the solutions to which will certainly aid in

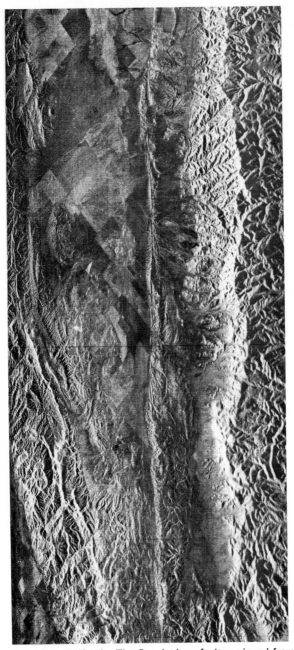

Figure 8.4 California. The San Andreas fault as viewed from a height of 20 km through the medium of side-scanning radar. *(Courtesy of the Westinghouse Electric Corporation, M. B. Crowe, Defense Products Division and C. F. Withington.)*

determining the best way to deal with such geological features when they are encountered in other areas.

One of the subsidiary faults in California, running roughly parallel with the San Andreas fault, is that which passes through Oakland and Berkeley on the eastern side of San Francisco Bay. It is related to the earthquake of 1836 and to the well-known Hayward earthquake of 1868. Some structures and railways had been built across the fault as early as 1866, and so it was possible to determine the fault slippage that then took place. Detailed studies of recent movements have been carried out in the Niles district of Fremont, located almost at the south end of San Francisco Bay. The evidence suggests that most of the recent movement took place between 1949 and 1957 and that no appreciable movements have taken place since then. Six sets of railway tracks cross the fault near Fremont almost at right angles and so serve, although not by design, as excellent indicators of movement. They are built over the low-gradient alluvial fan of Alameda Creek, a surface underlain by over 90 m of sand, gravel, and clay. Movements are, therefore, modified by this soil cover, and good maintenance of the tracks naturally conceals the long-term movements. Surveys suggest, however, that the oldest sets of tracks, built about 1910, have suffered a total displacement of 21 cm. An average movement of 4 mm per year has been recently reported, but a much greater rate seems to have taken place for relatively short periods. Railway personnel have reported as much as 4 cm in a period of 2 or 3 days. The zone of deformation on the railway tracks is from 6 to 24 m wide, another result of the shielding given by the soil overburden.[8.3]

Small though these movements are, their accumulated effect could naturally be serious, even though with good maintenance on such works as these railway tracks, no untoward results have ever developed. The fact that such movements can take place, however, is the reason for giving these very practical details so that the geological attention to faults in studies of urban land development can be appreciated in its proper context. Few active faults will normally be found in urban areas, but their possibility must never be forgotten and every effort must be made, in advance planning, to ensure that encountered faults are known with certainty to be inactive.

8.4   EARTHQUAKES

Earthquakes are among the most terrible and devastating of all natural phenomena to affect the surface of the earth and so the lives of people. The whole world was shocked at the loss of over 50,000 lives in the Peruvian earthquake of 31 May 1970. This was of the same order of magnitude as the first major earthquake in modern times, that which devastated the city of Lisbon in Portugal in 1755 and claimed about the same number of lives. The 1908 earthquake in Sicily probably caused a death toll of 75,000, while that which took place in Japan in 1923 had the terrible result of killing more than 140,000 citizens. The city of Tokyo sustained most of the physical damage, which was estimated to amount to $3 billion, but this was secondary to the tragic curtailment of so many human lives. China is reported to have had more than 10,000 earthquakes in the last 3,000 years, 530 of them causing real disasters, the worst being in the province of Kansu in 1556, killing 800,000 people. If earthquakes do occur with cities near to or at the center of their intensity, buildings will inevitably be destroyed, with possible loss of life. They constitute, therefore, one of the most serious of all geological hazards to urban development.

The association of the 1906 San Francisco earthquake with the San Andreas fault has just been noted. Earthquakes—and the name is accurately descriptive—are the result of a sudden release of stress in the earth's crust. If stress is thus released, fracture of the crust is inevitable. In some cases, this will take place along existing faults that are suitably located. In other cases, new fractures will occur in the ground, creating new faults that will often become prominent local features if vertical movement takes place on either side of them, as it often does. The causes of the stresses that are relieved by earthquakes are complex, but changes in the loading of the surface by erosion in one locality and deposition in another, those simple processes noted at the outset of this chapter, are certainly involved. The release of stress may be looked upon as a readjustment of the earth's crust, and it will take place wherever geological conditions are suitable.

Earthquakes have been known since the dawn of history. In earlier days they were often the subject of myths, with a variety of explanations that are now amusing but that represented the gropings of early man to explain the phenomena that so terrified him. The Lisbon earthquake is the first one of which any really scientific description exists. Robert Mallet presented the first scientific explanation of earthquakes in his account of the Neapolitan earthquake of 1857. This led to the development of an instrument that would measure the magnitude of earthquake shocks, the *seismograph*, records from many of which will be quoted in any account of an earthquake today. This marked the beginning of the science of *seismology*, now pursued all over the world—with every earthquake shock, even though it does not actually result in any physical disruption of the earth's crust, measured in many places and studied by comparative analysis of the records, which constitutes a fine example of international scientific cooperation.[8.4]

Because of their dramatic effects, earthquakes are now always well publicized. Many readers will recall the earthquake in Chile in 1960. The next major disaster was that in Skopje, Yugoslavia, on 26 July 1963, when an earthquake of great intensity demolished most of the city. The center of the earthquake action, the *epicenter* in scientific terms, was between 6 and 10 km northwest of the city, which therefore felt almost the full force of the vibrations set up by this sudden geological disturbance. About 2,000 people lost their lives; about 85 percent of the city's population were left homeless. The city had grown very rapidly between 1949 and the time that disaster struck, with the result that the unreinforced multistory masonry buildings that had been used to provide much needed accommodation suffered severe damage.[8.5] In

1967 an earthquake of only moderate intensity occurred about 48 km east of Caracas, Venezuela, but close enough to cause considerable damage in this rapidly growing city. The loss of life was limited to an estimated total of 277, about 200 of whom were killed by the complete collapse of five buildings. Of the thousand multistory buildings then in use in Caracas, ranging in height from 10 to 30 stories, 180 suffered serious damage. The structural results of this earthquake were therefore studied in detail, as is now done for all major earthquakes, and the results have been published in a series of notable and useful reports.[8.6]

North America is not immune from these geological hazards. The San Francisco earthquake of 1906 has already been mentioned. In more recent years, there were two 'quakes of moderate intensity in Churchill County, Nevada, on 16 December 1954, fortunately not close to any large city but serious enough to be felt in six states. Surface fault displacements occurred throughout a zone 32 by 96 km, as much as 6 m vertical displacement occurring, with lateral movement along faults of as much as 3.6 m.[8.7] On 17 August 1959 the well-known Hebgen Lake earthquake took place in Montana, well known because of the human-interest stories that came from the

Figure 8.5 Caracas, Venezuela. Wreckage of the San Jose building by the earthquake of 1967, typical of the widespread damage done in the city. *(Courtesy of* El National, *Caracas, and H. J. Degenkolb, San Francisco.)*

Figure 8.6 Hebgen Montana. Visitors viewing the commemorative plaque at Hegben Lake, formed by the earthquake of 1959, after the dedication ceremony on 17 August 1970. *(Courtesy of the U.S. Forest Service.)*

site, in view of the presence nearby of many campers, and of the formation of a new lake by a fall of 33 million m³ of rock into the gorge that was most affected. Again, fortunately, no cities were involved, but the inevitable movement along a fault took place, fortunately paralleling an existing small dam, a vertical movement of 4.5 m that can still be seen today.[8.8]

Lest it be thought that all North American earthquakes take place in the western part of the continent, it may be pointed out that one of the most potentially active seismic areas of the continent is the St. Lawrence Valley and adjoining parts of New England, Ontario, and Quebec. There is a long record of earthquake activity in this region, fortunately with no serious 'quakes having taken place in very recent times. On 28 February 1925, however, an earthquake of relatively low intensity took place and affected a surprisingly wide area, centered in the region of Quebec City where serious damage was done to heavy reinforced concrete columns supporting a large grain elevator. Most fortunately, no lives were lost directly, but there were several deaths due to associated shock. On 2 May 1944 a small earthquake occurred west of Montreal, its epicenter not far from the seaway city of Cornwall, Ontario. The author was in Cornwall on the day following the earthquake and examined the damage done by this minor earth shaking; it amounted to about $1 million. No lives were lost, again fortunately and almost miraculously, due to the late hour at which the disaster took place; had it been earlier in the day the collapse of many chimneys and parapets would almost certainly have caused a number of deaths, many of them children since school buildings were affected.[8.9]

The same fortuitous timing led to the very small loss of life in the most recent of all earthquakes in North America, that which took place at 5:36 P.M. on Good Friday, 27 March 1964, at Anchorage, Alaska. It released twice as much energy as the 1906 San Francisco earthquake, and it was felt over an area of 130 million hectares. It left 114 people dead or missing, but had it taken place on an ordinary business working day, or even earlier in the day on that Good Friday, the possible loss of life is disturbing even to consider. It was estimated that it would take the better part of a billion dollars to rehabilitate the damaged public and private property. Uplift and subsidence affected an area of at least 9 million hectares, these vast earth movements taking place about a well-defined zone that can be regarded as a "hinge." To the east of the hinge zone, land levels went up as much as 2.25 m, while to the west, subsidence of as much as 1.62 m took place. In the country around, thousands of avalanches were triggered, as were massive rockslides. One rockslide occurred 217 km away from the epicenter, at the southern tip of Kayak Island, and unfortunately killed a Coast Guardsman stationed at the Cape St. Elias Lighthouse.[8.10]

The Alaska Railroad was violently disrupted, most of the bridges on the affected 300-km stretch being seriously damaged. Of unusual importance were the deep-seated landslides that took place along the adjacent coasts, taking out much of the waterfront property at the cities of Valdez and Seward. At Valdez a 10,815-ton vessel was being unloaded at the docks, which were accordingly crowded with people. As soon as the tremors started, the entire dock area began to sink into the sea; 30 lives were lost. At the town of Homer, 256 km southeast of the epicenter, the small harbor dis-

Figure 8.7 Anchorage, Alaska. Building subsidence due to the Fourth Avenue slide caused by the Good Friday 1964 Alaska earthquake. *(Courtesy of the Director, U.S. Geological Survey.)*

appeared into a funnel-shaped pool, as it was described by a witness. An area on a sand bar extending out from the town has subsided from 1.2 to 1.8 m, most of this being due to the consolidation of a 140-m-thick stratum of alluvium by as much as 75 cm, and the further settlement of the underlying bedrock by about 60 cm. But the effects of the earthquake were felt far beyond Alaska. Incredible though it may seem, the water level in wells to which automatic level recorders had been fitted in both Winnipeg and even in Ottawa, Canada, 3,000 and 5,000 km away, respectively, from the epicenter, showed violent oscillations 6 and 8 minutes after the first shock took place at Anchorage.[8.11]

Many pages could be filled with similar summary notes on just the main features of this great earthquake, but enough has been said to show that it was truly a remarkable natural phenomenon. It has been studied in great detail, probably in far more detail than any previous occurrence of this kind. The results have been published in many notable papers and reports, to which readers who wish more information may be directed. A few words more must be said, however, about the effect of the earthquake on the city of Anchorage. Damage estimated at $200 million was caused, including the destruction of 215 residences and severe damage to 157 commercial properties in this leading Alaskan city. Nine people lost their lives. Most of the casualties and the most serious damage resulted from some serious landslides triggered by the earthquake, at Turnagain Heights, L Street, and 14th Avenue. Each of these areas is underlain by a gray silty clay, with some lenses of sand, well known locally as the "Bootlegger Cove clay."

Geologists on the staff of the U.S. Geological Survey had studied the geology of the Anchorage area in 1949. A preliminary report on this work and a map were made available in 1950. The final printed report was published in 1959 as "Geological Survey Bulletin No. 1093." This valuable report was therefore publicly available for use 4 years before the earthquake took place. The Bootlegger Cove clay is described in the report and delineated in its extent. Its physical properties were described, and conditions under which landslides could be activated in the clay are described under a section dealing with slumps and flows. Local engineers used this report in their soil and site investigations in the Anchorage area. The Alaska Road Commission and the Alaskan Department of Highways both used the report, but for a variety of reasons it was not used as a background for planning in Anchorage: "The planning department was relatively new and its early problems concerned more pressing matters. The report is a general treatment and did not zone or classify the ground except by geologic map units. The map is not a document the planners can use directly without interpretation by a geologist. There were no geologists on the planning staff."[8.12] The fact remains that the report was publicly available but apparently was not used in the planning of this rapidly developing city. It is idle to speculate what its use in planning might have done, since the damage by the earthquake has taken place and cannot be undone. USGS Report No. 1093 has already taken its special place in the literature of urban geology not only as a record of fine work on the geology of an important urban area

Figure 8.8 Anchorage, Alaska. Damage in the Turnagain Heights area due to major sliding caused by the Good Friday 1964 Alaska earthquake. *(Courtesy of the Director, U.S. Geological Survey.)*

but also as a report that should have been better known beyond purely geological circles. Its relevance to the message of this volume will be obvious.[8.13]

Earthquakes will continue to take place; they cannot be stopped. Cities will still be built and existing cities further developed in regions in which it is known that earthquakes can occur. What can be done? Fortunately, a great deal even now, with the prospect of further significant advance in precautionary measures. Figure 8.9 shows the occurrence of earthquakes throughout the world in the year 1970. The pattern, which is generally similar every year, is a striking one, with the greatest concentrations of earthquakes located all round the rim of the Pacific Ocean and in the eastern Mediterranean. There is interesting geological significance in this distribution. Study of the records accumulated over many years shows that there are certain well-defined areas in which the occurrence of 'quakes is more probable than in others. If the science of statistical analysis is then applied to such accumulated records, the probability of an earthquake's happening in any location during any given number of years can be established.

One of the more recent of such compilations is the "Seismic Map of Canada" prepared for use with the 1970 (5th) edition of Canada's National Building Code.

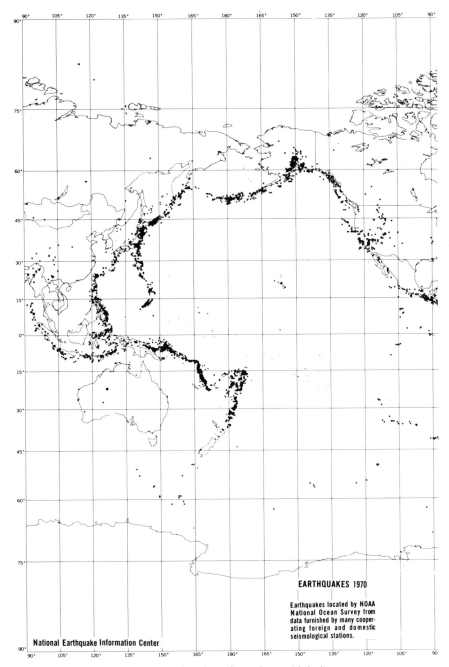

Figure 8.9 Map showing major earthquakes throughout the world during 1970. *(Courtesy of the National Earthquake Information Center, National Oceanic and Atmospheric Administration.)*

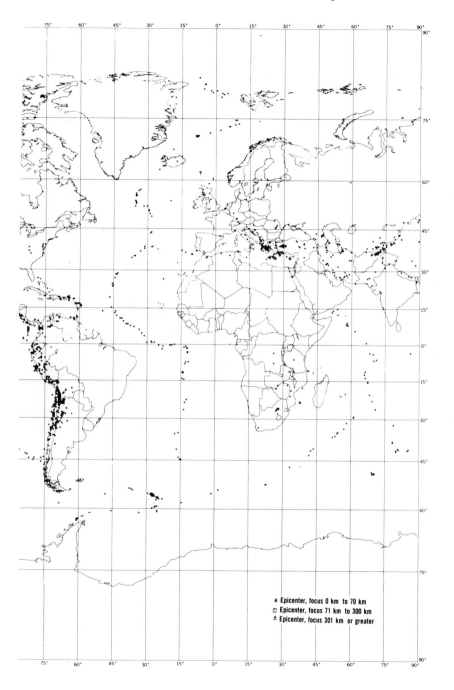

* Epicenter, focus 0 km to 70 km
▫ Epicenter, focus 71 km to 300 km
△ Epicenter, focus 301 km or greater

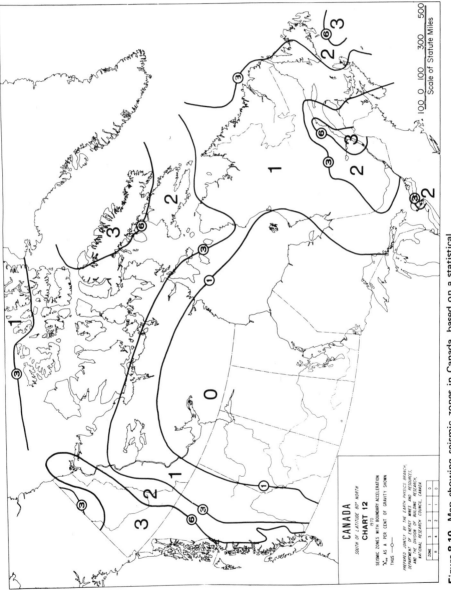

Figure 8.10 Map showing seismic zones in Canada, based on a statistical study of earthquake records, as used with the National Building Code of Canada, 1970. *(Courtesy of the National Research Council of Canada. Associate Committee on the National Building Code.)*

It is reproduced as Figure 8.10. It will be seen that the whole country is divided into four different-numbered zones. Zone 0 indicates those parts of the country in which no earthquakes are to be expected. Zones 1 to 3 are areas with increasing probability of earthquakes occurring, with corresponding increasing probability of damage being experienced if an earthquake should occur. The map was prepared by scientists of the Canadian Department of Energy, Mines and Resources, with advice from a national committee of experts, and in association with officers of the National Research Council of Canada. The record of every earthquake that has ever happened in Canada and of which there is any written record was carefully examined; the first one dates from 1545. When all the records had been assembled, a computer study of a suitable sample was made to determine the probability of earthquakes occurring at selected locations once in 100 years. From the results of this extensive analysis, the seismic map was prepared. A "seismic regionalization factor" has been developed for each of the three zones of possible activity. The values of this factor for all the main municipalities of Canada are given in one of the technical supplements to the Canadian Code. They are thus available for use by all responsible for the design of buildings and other structures throughout the Dominion. The values are inserted in the formulas that must be used to allow for earthquake loads in structural design, and they can be relied upon as being as accurate as is possible, based on the records of actual earthquakes of the last 300 years.[8.14]

There is another factor that must be used in building design, this being what is called the "foundation factor." Experience throughout the world has shown that much more damage is caused to structures by earthquake shocks when they are founded on soil than when they are directly in contact with firm bedrock. An expert Japanese committee has suggested, based on the extensive experience that the Japanese have unfortunately accumulated in view of the long history of earthquake shocks in their country, that the effect of differing ground conditions can be expressed by the following factors:[8.15]

Marshy land 1.5

Alluvial ground 1.0

Diluvial (older and more consolidated) ground 0.7

Tertiary rock 0.4

There is still much uncertainty about the actual values that can be attached to different sorts of ground, even though the major difference between soil and rock is well attested. This is one of the many matters under investigation by seismologists and allied workers in all those countries that suffer regularly from earthquake shocks. The Canadian Code, noted above, uses the factors of 1.5 for "soils [of] low dynamic shear modulus such as highly compressible soils" and a value of 1.0 for all other soils.

Accordingly, there are helpful guides available for all who are charged with decision-making in relation to urban planning. By consulting the appropriate authority, it can readily be found for most countries whether the proposed location is in a potentially seismic area. In those countries that have developed their building regulations to the extent that has been done in North America, an indication can be obtained of the probable severity of any earthquake that might occur. Through the powerful medium of building regulations, allowance for earthquake loads can be required in accordance with such predictions of probable seismic action. This means increased cost for the extra structural measures for ensuring adequate resistance to earthquake loads, but with human lives at stake there is usually little question as to the desirability of such extra design provisions, although the degree of earthquake-resistant design to be adopted may be a matter for discussion. There is, however, no doubt that buildings can now be made reasonably safe against all earthquake shocks normally to be expected in any area. Experience with such properly designed buildings in all the recent earthquakes (such as those already mentioned) has clearly demonstrated this.

Beyond this, however, and as the example of Anchorage makes so clear, building in seismic regions on areas underlain by the soils that are sensitive in any way is something that requires the most expert geological and engineering advice before any planning decisions are made. The techniques now available through soil mechanics enable the properties of any soil to be accurately determined, on the basis of "undisturbed samples" (as they are tautologically described) carefully obtained from the ground, preserved in their natural condition, and tested under controlled conditions in a laboratory. With the information given by such tests, coupled with expert geological knowledge of the site in question, decisions can be made with reasonable certainty as to what can be safely built and what should be avoided. It is not necessary to go into details of engineering design, but it may be mentioned that the use of floating-raft foundations, for example, has been found to be satisfactory even on poor ground subjected to earthquake shocks.

If, therefore, those responsible for urban development will make use of the information that is available to them, building in seismic areas can be carried out with the assurance of reasonable safety. Where solid rock is available as the foundation bed, problems are restricted to those of allowing for earthquake loads in structural design. Where soil has to be used, extra precautions will be necessary; and where sensitive soils exist, the most expert advice possible is essential. To all this may now be added the prospect that it may be possible, in years to come, to predict when earthquakes are going to occur. One of the most extensive current research programs in the whole geotechnical field is that which has been mounted to explore the possibility of earthquake prediction. The subject is extremely complicated, but the possibilities can be visualized by considering that the stresses relieved when an earthquake does take place have not suddenly come into being, the earthquake being only the final and catastrophic step in what must be a gradual buildup of stress.

On a smaller scale, some progress has been made in detecting stresses in rock in mines, the stresses that cause what are known in mining as "rock bursts." Similar techniques have been applied to detection in advance of failures in rock excavation, a vital matter in the maintenance of safety on construction. The device that is used is a very sensitive listening instrument that picks up the minute sounds that may be developed by the microseisms and magnifies them as much as 2.5 million times. Extension of this idea is a possibility, but even if earthquakes could be predicted, the necessity for sound structural design in all seismic areas would still be paramount, as would also most careful attention to all the geological aspects of building sites.[8.16] New problems would be created in the social field since any prediction of an earthquake would immediately necessitate consideration of evacuation of all buildings not designed to withstand earthquake loads. Fortunately, perhaps, this is a problem that is still in the future.

8.5 TSUNAMIS

Figure 8.9 shows that earthquakes, quite naturally, occur beneath the sea as well as on dry land. Earthquakes on land and near sea coasts will inevitably affect the solid ground beneath the sea within the radius of influence from their epicenters. Underwater disturbances may create severe upheavals of the sea water in the vicinity, and these will form great surface waves. These are known by the Japanese name *tsunami*, a much more accurate title than the name "tidal wave" that one still sometimes hears. Quite unlike the ordinary waves on the ocean, tsunamis may extend for 160 km in width and be as much as 1,000 km from crest to crest. In the deep waters of the Pacific Ocean they can travel at the amazing speed of 800 km per hour. Since they may be from 6 to 18 m in height, their devastating effect when they hit a shoreline is difficult to imagine. But it has been observed by skilled scientific observers, and so a good deal is known about their action.

The tsunamis caused by the Good Friday Alaskan earthquake struck all the adjoining coastline of Alaska with destructive force. They were recorded on tide gauges as far away as Japan, Hawaii, and southern California. But the tsunami created by the eruption of Krakatoa in Indonesia in 1883 raced across the Pacific and created heavy seas even as far away as San Francisco They are much more common in the Pacific Ocean than elsewhere, very seldom occurring in the Atlantic Ocean. Japan has been subjected to 15 destructive tsunamis since 1596, 8 of them being disastrous. The Hawaiian Islands are subjected to a serious tsunami about once every 25 years. A particularly bad one struck the Islands in 1946; it was fortunately observed by a number of scientists and led directly to a study of the possibility of detecting tsunamis in advance of their reaching a coastline. An ingenious instrument was developed by an officer of the U.S. Coast and Geodetic Survey, and a warning system centered in Honolulu was established to correlate the results obtained from the instruments that have now been installed at critical Pacific locations. There have been 15 tsunamis in the Pacific since 1946 but only 1 (in 1952) of any serious magnitude. The warning system worked well. Not a life was lost, and damage in the Hawaiian Islands amounted to only about $800,000. It has been stated, "there is little doubt that the warning system saved lives and reduced the damage."[8.17]

As with earthquakes, however, tsunamis will continue to occur; they cannot be stopped, even though they may be detected in advance. As was shown in 1952, this can lead to the saving of lives, but if property is built too close to shorelines that may be subject to the pounding that tsunamis can give, nothing can save fixed property from the inexorable force of the sea. Urban development close to shorelines on any Pacific coast must, therefore, be considered in relation to the possibility of damage by tsunamis. If this is a probability, buildings must be firmly anchored to the ground or raised above it, if indeed, they have to be placed close to the shoreline and cannot be relocated on higher ground. One of the most percipient questions that the author ever received in the course of his work in directing Building Research in Canada was about the possibility of tsunamis in the Atlantic Ocean from a planner in Newfoundland, charged with responsibility for developing the new fishing villages that have been created in "the oldest Dominion" by the amalgamation of isolated small groups of fishermen's homes. This intriguing social operation often meant floating complete houses across some of the many bays that feature the rockbound coast of the island to a carefully selected site for a new village. Few records of tsunamis in the Atlantic were traced, the most serious having been that caused by the Lisbon earthquake of 1 November 1755, the waves following which persisted for about a week and reached as far as England. But despite this, buildings in the new villages of Newfoundland are being located so that all buildings are well above high-tide level.

8.6   FLOODS

The sea can cause trouble to urban communities located on seacoasts quite apart from the rare occurrence of tsunamis. Combinations of high spring tides and violent winds can combine to cause phenomenal high-water levels that, coupled with the waves created by the high winds, can lead to disaster conditions. As this book was in preparation, the eastern side of the great delta of the Ganges, in Eastern Pakistan, was devastated on 12 November 1970 by just such a combination of typhoon winds and high tides. The catastrophe may prove to be the most serious disaster of its kind in history. Early estimates placed the number of dead at over a million, but the full extent of the tragedy is still not known. Anyone who has flown over this heavily populated, flat-lying area, intersected by the seemingly innumerable channels into which the great river divides, will long carry in their minds the thought of what the disaster must have meant to those living on their little farms on the many islands, with no possibility of escape in the face of such mighty natural forces. And the use of such areas for settlement can really only be understood by those who have seen what the concentration of population in the Indian subcontinent means in human terms.

Figure 8.11 Hilo, Hawaii. Damage done to residential buildings by the tsunami of 1 April 1946. *(Photographer unknown; courtesy of G. A. Macdonald, University of Hawaii.)*

Similar combinations of extremes of natural occurrences in other parts of the world can usually be predicted and necessary precautionary measures taken. Throughout North America, citizens are now used to reading reports of hurricanes forming over the Caribbean (if only because of the chauvinistic use of women's names to identify them), with disaster warnings issued well in advance by the responsible authorities to all who live in the coastal areas that may be affected. Evacuations are now accepted as essential under extreme conditions. For example, 150,000 people were evacuated from the delta area in Louisiana in 1965 because of the onslaught of "Hurricane Betsy." The evacuation is said to have probably saved 50,000 lives, since the whole area was completely inundated. These unusual combinations are not limited to tropical areas, even though it is in such areas that hurricanes develop. The North Sea has an unenviable reputation for bad storm conditions, and these have combined with high spring tides to wreak disaster on European coasts. History records one such tragedy in the year 1421, but the much worse inundation that occurred on 1 February 1953 will never be forgotten by those on the southeast coast on England and, more particularly, those in the coastal area of the Netherlands who lived through that critical period; 133 Dutch villages were seriously damaged and 1,800 people died. Damage was estimated to be at least $400 million. Dikes were breached and seawalls on the coasts of England badly damaged. Reacting with characteristic courage, the Dutch people passed legislation within 20 days of the flood, initiating the great delta scheme that has been under construction since that time and that will ultimately benefit the whole of this most interesting country.[8.18]

Planning in coastal areas for urban development must, therefore, take into account not only the local geology but also the relation of local landforms to the possibility of inundation by the sea under extreme combinations such as have been mentioned so briefly. Rare though these be, there is now reasonable expectation that warnings of their incidence can be given in sufficient time to prevent loss of life. If proper precautions are taken in planning and design, damage to property can also be minimized. There are other catastrophic floods, however, that may occur without any possibility of warning; exceptional though they be, they call for brief mention. These are floods on rivers, or even smaller streams, due to the interference with normal flow of the river either by natural causes or through accident. The most terrible of recent examples was the overtopping of the Vaiont Dam in northern Italy on 9 October 1963, with the devastating loss of almost 3,000 lives and inestimable damage. The flood

Figure 8.12 Harwich, Essex, England. An indication of the havoc caused by the North Sea flood of 1 February 1953, the photograph showing the level of the sea. A Royal Navy diver is about to descend in order to find a manhole through which drainage would be assisted when the cover was removed. *(Courtesy of Fox Photos, London.)*

was due to the sudden sliding into the reservoir above the dam of 237 million m³ of rock and earth, the resulting huge wave causing the flood that poured over the crest of the dam and into the valley below. No urban planning could possibly have foreseen such an eventuality since it was an event that probably should never have happened and, it may be hoped, will never happen again, especially in view of the lessons that are still being learned as a result of the extensive studies of this geological disaster.[8.19]

Floods of a not dissimilar kind can occur without the intervention of any man-made dam. In northern India a great fall of rock took place in 1893 in the narrow valley of the Birehiganga River, a tributary of the Ganges, blocking the flow of the normally small stream and so creating an artificial reservoir. When visited by the district surveyor, the fall was found to have created a rock-fill dam 300 m high. The British superintending engineer had a telegraph line put in so that due warning could be given before the dam was overtopped; other precautionary measures were also taken. On 25 August 1894, almost 1 year later, the first trickle of water came over the top of this vast dam; the flood followed. A rush of 283 million m³ of water poured down the small valley and into the larger valleys below, but no lives were lost due to the precautions taken, apart only from a fakir and his family who were killed by a collapse in the face of the remaining barrier when they returned to their home from which they had previously been unwillingly and forcibly removed.[8.20] A similar rockfall occurred in 1964 on the Zeravshan River in the Uzbek S.S.R. of the Soviet Union, creating a rock dam 200 m high and 400 m wide that also began immediately to retain water. In this case, the site was accessible and so Soviet engineers were able to move in construction equipment and blast and excavate a spillway directly through the slide. In this way, all danger to the ancient city of Samarkand, 160 km downstream, was removed.[8.21]

Much more serious are the floods that result from the sudden failure of glaciers that are retaining water in glacial lakes. The failure may take place in a number of ways, but melting of critically located ice is usually one cause. The resulting floods are naturally intense, bringing not only water and ice but all the loose material that lies in their way. The name *lahar* has been coined to describe these most serious phenomena; it is a name that should be known and understood by all concerned with any urban development in the foothills below glacier-covered mountains. One of the most tragic examples was that in New Zealand on Christmas Eve (high summer in the Antipodes) on the Whangaehue River in the North Island. The lahar destroyed a railway bridge in the darkness of night. Before any warning could be given, an express passenger train filled with holidaying passengers plunged into the river bed, with the loss of 151 lives.[8.22] Even more serious was the mud-water avalanche that took place on 10 January 1962, due to failure of a glacier on Peru's highest mountain, devastating the high Huaylas Valley in the Andes, destroying several villages, and taking over 4,000 lives. An even worse disaster took place on 13 December 1941 in the valley of the Rio Paria, killing probably 7,000 people and destroying much of the old Spanish colonial city of Huaraz.[8.23]

Peru has now established the Corporación Peruana del Santa, with its head-quarters at Carhuaz. Annual surveys of glacial lakes are undertaken, and any known hazardous conditions are carefully investigated and if possible ameliorated before any real danger develops. Dynamiting the exits from glacial lakes and even tunneling to lower the level of critical lakes are two measures already used. In New Zealand, a fully instrumented warning tower has been installed above the bridge site so that a recurrence of the Tangiwai bridge disaster can never recur. It can be seen, therefore, that when geological hazards even as serious and unpredictable as these are recognized, measures can be taken to provide warning to all those living below the danger zones so that the necessary precautionary measures can be taken. Fortunately, such areas are rare throughout the world, but they warrant this attention here since they demonstrate so vividly the fact that geological conditions are not permanent and static but dynamic, a fact that must never be forgotten in all urban planning. The occurrence of what will have to be called, in this context, "normal floods" is further evidence, even though less dramatic. Such river floods were dealt with in Chap. 4 since they do constitute a part of the hydrogeological picture of urban areas, but, as was then made clear, they can cause much human misery and great property damage. They are, indeed, geological hazards of serious consequence. Consideration of the probability of flooding along all watercourses within planning areas is one prime essential of terrain evaluation. This is true if water alone is involved. Some floods, however, will bring down soil and rock as well; the "mud runs" so created next demand attention.

8.7 MUDFLOWS

The fact that rivers in flood can carry large amounts of sediment is common knowledge, if only because of the frequent references to the "Nile flood" and the well-known annual deposition of fertile silt on the flat alluvial farm lands of the Nile Valley, annual at least until the construction of the new great dam at Aswan. Pictures of the devastation of the beautiful city of Florence and many of its art treasures by the disastrous flood on the River Arno in November 1966 will be vivid recollections for all art lovers. Many readers may have had personal experiences of the mess that can so quickly be caused by mud deposited by flood waters where it is not wanted. All these occurrences are reminders of the transporting power of running water and of the fact that this movement by water of soil and rock is an important part of the geological cycle. There are some parts of the world where such mass movements of solid material occur regularly, and not in the orderly and controlled way featured for so many centuries in the Nile Valley. In India and in South America *mud runs*, as these mass movements are usually called, are of common occurrence. So common are they in certain parts of South America that they have been given the local name of *huaicos*. If they take place in open country they may do little harm, but if they encounter in their path any obstructions such as bridge piers or other man-made works, real trouble may result. If they flow as far as developed urban areas the damage they cause may be considerable.

Figure 8.13 Putnam, Connecticut. Aerial view of the damage caused by the Quinebaug River in August 1955 following unusually heavy rainfall; the normal river channel is to be seen in the lower left corner. *(Courtesy of the Editor*, Providence Journal-Bulletin.*)*

There must naturally be a convenient source of disintegrated rock or soil to be moved, and so mud runs are usually encountered in hilly or mountainous country. Landslides, large and small, are a potent source of "mud," especially if they block the normal flow down watercourses. In July 1953 a remarkable mud run took place 64 km to the northwest of Needles, California, following a series of small landslides near the Von Trigger Spring. Streams fed by the heavy rainfall carried material from the toes of the slides out of the Lanfair Valley and downstream beyond the Von Trigger Spring for a total distance of at least 72 km. Although not observed, it is believed that the mud run extended as far as Cadiz Dry Lake, which would have meant a total travel of almost 100 km.[8.24] This case is mentioned, even though no damage to cities was involved, to indicate how far mud runs can extend at times of high flood. In Japan, the local volcanic soils provide in many places ideal material for mud runs. The Nirasaki mudflow is a well-known feature extending from the slopes of the volcano Yatsuga-take to the town of Nirasaki, a distance of 20 km, and it is regularly replenished in times of high rainfall.[8.25]

Fortunately, most mudflows take place far from cities, but when they do strike urban areas, a scene such as that shown in Fig. 8.13 can result. Extraordinary rainfall in August 1955 caused severe flooding on the Quinebaug River. It flows through the town on Putnam and normally is channeled under the railway tracks, here seen, through a small bridge. The flood of 1955 overflowed the main normal channel eroding a 7.6-m bank of sand and gravel as it did so, with the results that are so graphically shown in this view. It must be emphasized that this flood was the result of quite phenomenal rainfall of an intensity that will be experienced possibly once in a century. With steadily accumulating rainfall records and advances in the science of meteorology, there has been great advance in estimating with some degree of certainty the probability of rainfall beyond a certain amount occurring within a stated number of years. Planning must then take account of all the geological features through which streams and rivers flow, upstream of urban areas, in order to assess possible damage should such unusual rainfall ever occur. Decisions then have to be made on the basis of engineering economics as to what expenditures for remedial works are warranted if there is danger of damage, during high floods, from potential mud runs.

Figure 8.14 Whitehorse, Yukon Territory, Canada. Mud run due to erosion of escarpment in background, following disturbance of natural vegetation. *(Photograph by R. F. Legget.)*

and in the region of the St. Lawrence and Ottawa Valleys in eastern Canada. Many examples in recent years have been studied intensively and recorded in geotechnical literature.

Of special interest in this context is the existence of a small village municipality in the province of Quebec with the significant name of *Les Éboulements* (one of the French words for landslides). Located 104 km downstream from Quebec City in the broadening section of the St. Lawrence River, it is located on the consolidated fan caused by one of these flow slides of long ago. Some terrible examples were recorded in early Scandinavian and Canadian history, slides such as that at Notre Dame de la Salette (on the Liévre River near Ottawa) that took 33 lives and removed 2.4 hectares of land. In more recent years, and affecting a prosperous small city, the slide at Nicolet, Quebec, on the Nicolet River, was serious and could have been much more so had it not stopped providentially just before undermining the local cathedral. It took place on 12 November 1955, just before noon, and in a very few minutes a volume of about 165,000 m^3 had flowed out from what had been a solid bank into the Nicolet River. Three lives were unfortunately lost; damage was estimated at several million dollars.[8.27]

Just after the foregoing words had been written, another terrible landslide in the Leda clay took place at St. Jean-Vianney in the Lake St. John district of Quebec. Shortly after 10 P.M. on 4 May 1971 a major slide took place on the bank

Figure 8.17 Portland, Oregon. Small landslide caused by unusually heavy rains in a steeply sloping residential area of Portland. *(Courtesy of the Editor, the* Oregonian, *Portland, Oregon, and W. H. Stuart.)*

Figure 8.18   Les Éboulements, Quebec, Canada. A village called by one of the French words for "landslide" situated on the stable fan created long ago by a major slide. *(Photograph by C. B. Crawford.)*

of the Rivière aux Vases, involving some houses in a recent residential development. It is estimated that about 6.9 million m³ moved during the slide from an area of 268,000 m². Unfortunately, the slide carried 40 homes to destruction and 31 persons to their deaths. The slide appears to have taken place within the crater of a much larger slide of the same type that took place about 500 years ago. A preliminary report has been published; the final report of the extensive investigation that is naturally being made will be a most valuable geotechnical document.[8.28]

Although fortunately localized within those areas underlain by sensitive clays, these flow slides are mentioned not only because of their special character but because they illustrate well an important aspect of slide detection. Of the slides mentioned, two started from purely natural causes with no human intervention. The exact cause of the Nicolet slide has never been accurately determined, although natural erosion of the river bank must have been involved; some local construction activity may have triggered it off. It can be seen, therefore, that there are landslides that occur quite naturally. They have been occurring for centuries in recent sediments and back through geological time in older formations. There are in addition slides that are caused or at least started by human activities. Many natural slides are of tremendous extent. Many have occurred so long ago that they have become completely concealed by subsequent growth of vegetation, by the plowing and farming of their surfaces, and in other ways involving human activity. Accordingly, it is very difficult and often quite impossible to detect old slides from the ground, and yet their existence may be of unusual importance in planning for land use.

Fortunately, the techniques now available through aerial photography have provided a quick and reasonably certain method of seeing where these old landslides have taken place. By examining aerial photographs, preferably stereoscopically, a very large number of old, previously unsuspected landslides have been found in the St. Lawrence Valley region of Canada and in Norway and Sweden. Figure 8.20 shows one example that is located close to the boundaries of the city of Ottawa. Although

Figure 8.19 St. Jean-Vianney, Quebec, Canada. View from a helicopter shortly after the disastrous landslide at St. Jean-Vianney on 7 May 1971, in the Lake St. John district, as a result of which 31 lives were lost; the "flow" character of the slide is clear. *(Courtesy of the Department of National Defense, Canada.)*

not more than 1.6 km from the office used by the author for many years, neither he nor any of his colleagues had ever suspected its existence until they first saw this aerial photograph, so completely had nature shielded with vegetation this disruption of several centuries ago. Subsequent studies of the slope in which the slide occurred revealed the old land surface so that it was possible to measure and analyze the slope stability.

Examination of aerial photographs of land that is to be used for urban development is essential, therefore, with the specific objective of seeing if there is any evidence of old landslides. Examination of the site itself is equally essential. Trees that are sloping instead of vertical, especially if their trunks show a change in curvature, are a sure sign of recent movements. Unusual scarps may betray old sliding planes. In extreme cases, such as the famous Folkstone Warren on the south coast of England, a mere glance at the great escarpment will show the rents caused by the succession of serious slides in this location, now well stabilized by extensive drainage and other remedial works carried out mainly in connection with the important railway line that runs at the foot of the cliffs. More usually, however, all signs of earlier and older slides will be so shielded that only careful geological study will reveal them. Often it will be only after actual test drilling or test excavation that the old slide planes will be located accurately; but if they are there, this becomes absolutely essential before any land-use planning can be done. Here is where detailed geological surveying of all the area involved, and beyond it to the extent that is necessary, is the only way in which certainty can be achieved as to the suitability of a site, and economy developed in the planning of the detailed exploration of the site by test drilling, all holes being located in relation to geological findings.

The idea of what appears to be solid ground being actually the surface of an old landslide may be so novel to some readers that it might be helpful if some examples were described and illustrated. Space limitations make this impossible, but it may at least be mentioned that many such old slides have now been studied so carefully that it is possible to date the occurrence of the slide quite accurately even as long ago as 10,000 years. (This is done through the aid of carbon-dating fragments of organic matter that may be found at the old slide surface.) In the Upper Ohio Valley, for example, a number of old slides were discovered initially when they were intercepted by excavation for roads and other civic services; they were found to date at between 9,000 and 10,000 years before the present time. Some old slides in southern California have been found to be about 17,000 years old. These, however, are very young slides as compared with those found in older geological formations. In the Cretaceous areas of Czechoslovakia, for example, massive landslides have been discovered by detailed geological work in areas in which solid rock overlies ancient clays. Immense blocks of sandstone and limestone, blocks so large that nobody would suspect that they are today anything but the local bedrock in place, can sink into underlying clays or marls at phenomenally slow rates, leading to a geological condition that is potentially unstable. Czechoslovakia is a lovely land with more than its fair share of landslides,

Figure 8.20 Ottawa, Canada. Stereoscopic twin views of an ancient land-slide in Leda clay that was detected only after examination of this aerial view, since surface signs have been obscured by vegetation and land culti-vation. *(Courtesy of the city of Ottawa and the National Capital Com-mission, Ottawa.)*

especially in the Carpathians of Slovakia. So important are these land movements that some years ago a survey resulted in no less than 9,100 being registered. Results of these extensive studies have been published, and in English, one of the most notable books on landslides being by Drs. Zaruba and Mencl, of Czechoslovakia.[8.29]

The existence of many landslides, large and small, new and old, in almost all parts of the world testifies to their importance as a part of the normal geological cycle. They show also that landslides may be triggered by purely natural events such as unusually heavy rainfall, the erosion of river banks, or the vibrations created by earthquakes. More important from the point of view of urban development, however, are the slides caused by man's activities. In earlier days, these were not well understood (despite the work of pioneers such as Collin), but today, professional advice is everywhere available to assist with the prevention of landslides, if only those concerned with urban development are alerted to their possibility. Many varieties of human activity can cause slides, possibly the most unusual case on record being from France. Near Menton, market gardens were developed for the growing of carnations. Local farmers uprooted so many of the olive trees that previously had been the major local vegetation that the stabilizing effect of the deep tree roots was disturbed and some serious landslides developed, with some loss of life.

In the early days of irrigation, when some of those who gladly fed irrigation water onto arid land did not stop to ask where the water went, very serious slides occurred when the water finally appeared on slopes below, disturbing local groundwater conditions and slope stability. Slides of vast extent in the valley of the Thomson River in British Columbia were attributed to this cause. It points to the vital importance of water in all considerations of slope stability. Any change in groundwater conditions in the vicinity of steeply sloping ground must be regarded with suspicion and a study made before the change is made as to its probable effect. Shrinkage cracks that develop in dry weather can lead to serious slides when later rains can fill the cracks. More usually, however, it is an increase in groundwater flow or a rise in the water table that can lead indirectly to such serious results.

Even more obvious as a cause of slides is the carrying out of excavation unwisely or in ground the complete geological structure of which is not known as fully as it should be when excavation commences. With the advance there has been in recent years in both geological and geotechnical investigations, the chance of such slides occurring is steadily diminishing. Geology being what it is, there will always remain the chance of the unexpected, but landslides due to construction work in urban development should become conspicuous by their infrequency in the foreseeable future. The possibility of such slides is obvious. Engineers, with the geological advice now available to them, should be able so to design and construct urban works that danger from landslides should be negligible. This introduction to landslides may, therefore, finish not with an obvious example but with a brief description of one of the most remarkable landslides on record.

Handlova is an important coal mining town in central Slovakia. It is bordered on the south by the small Handlova River, beyond which there is most pleasant, well-treed pasture land sloping upward from the river bank. In the town is a large power station, fired with brown coal and therefore emitting much fly ash. Prevailing winds carried the ash to the south, and so the character of the grazing land was gradually changed by the surface layer of ash that slowly accumulated. In some parts, grazing had to be given up and the land was plowed. This immediately allowed rain to percolate into the surface. This percolation disturbed the very delicate groundwater condition that existed beneath the sloping ground. Handlova was subject to unusually high rainfall in the year 1960 (1,045 mm as compared with the long-term average of 689 mm). The combination of all these circumstances, leading to a rise in the water table beneath the

Figure 8.21 Handlova, Czechoslovakia. Two views of the major landslide described in the text showing *(a)* progressive growth of the scarp of the slide due to movement at the toe and *(b)* the first indication of ground displacement at the head of the slide. *(Photographs by Q. Zaruba, Prague.)*

pasture land coupled with the geological conditions, led to a start of earth movement early in December 1960. Accurate measurements were initiated by 22 December; at one point a movement of almost 150 m had taken place within a month. And a volume of about 20 million m³ of clay, clayey silts, and rock debris was moving downhill, threatening to engulf the town.

The slide was very quickly brought under control by a splendid example of team work, with the result that by the end of January 1961 most of the movement had been greatly reduced, but not before 150 houses had been destroyed by the inexorable movement of this huge mass of soil. Drainage was the key to the control measures, as it is so commonly in all landslide remedial works. Today the great hill to the south of Handlova is again stable, the soil resting but not now moving on the underlying argillaceous shale rock that was so easily "lubricated" by the excess groundwater. To sit on its grassy slopes, as the author has been privileged to do, and to look at the town below, which could so easily have been so seriously damaged, and all because of fly ash interfering with sheep grazing, is to be very forcibly reminded of the dual importance of clean air and slope drainage. Flow from the drainage tunnels and pipes that were so hastily installed is now quite small, so limited that one has to have a very real appreciation of the mechanics of soil movement to appreciate what that small quantity of water meant before it was thus extracted from the soil through which it flows.[8.30]

The Handlova slide emphasizes the importance of drainage as a means of slide control, a subject that must be briefly noted since slides do still occur despite all the knowledge that is now available (but not always used) that can lead to their avoidance. Landslide control is naturally work that can be undertaken only on the

Figure 8.22 Handlova, Czechoslovakia. Damage to building by the movement at the toe of the Handlova slide. *(Photograph by Q. Zaruba, Prague.)*

between the lower portal and the Carboniferous limestone of the cliff. This limestone consists of thick beds of heavily jointed rock separated generally by thin layers of red clay, probably derived from rock weathering. The beds dip roughly parallel to the face of the gorge at an angle of 33°. A full-scale investigation was launched.

Test drilling confirmed the existence of a bed of clay about 1.5 m thick, first seen when a retaining wall near the portal was removed at the start of the rehabilitation work. It seemed clear that very large blocks of the limestone were tending to slide downhill on this clay surface. Test boreholes revealed that the groundwater was standing 1.2 m above the top of the clay layer, whereas the underlying limestone was dry, water draining into it even down the small test holes. After careful analysis had been made, it was decided to put down six gravel-filled boreholes as far as the under-lying limestone in order to act as permanent drains, thus keeping the top of the clay stratum reasonably dry. In addition, strengthening of the tunnel portal and an associated retaining wall and tying them by steel rods to the limestone bedrock was also carried out in case any further movement did tend to develop. It seemed clear that the disused tunnel had been acting as a drain for water moving through the upper limestone along the upper surface of the clay stratum since borings showed no water above the clay some distance from the tunnel. That the tunnel was disused may have concealed for some time any change in drainage conditions within the tunnel. The remedial measures were effective, and no further work has had to be done to maintain the stability of this particularly important section of the wall of the Avon Gorge.[8.37] The lessons are again so obvious as to need no detailed recital, but the existence of the disused tunnel provides yet another warning as to the absolute necessity of regular inspections of all works in urban areas that interfere or have interfered with natural conditions.

8.11 SLIPS IN REFUSE BANKS

The disposal of waste material was seen, in Chap. 7, to be a problem of steadily increasing magnitude. Waste from mines has long been deposited in large piles adjacent to mines, often to the disfigurement of the local landscape—a matter at last receiving attention from local authorities and mining companies. In some cases, slips have occurred in the sloping sides of these small man-made mountains, sometimes with disastrous results. The Aberfan disaster in South Wales will still be hauntingly familiar to all readers; it was essentially a geological failure. Slips in refuse banks often are and so warrant inclusion in this review of the hazards that geology can create in urban areas.

It was at 9 A.M. on the foggy morning of 21 October 1966 that the No. 7 tip above the village of Aberfan failed and created a flowslide that rushed down the valleyside at a speed of nearly 32 km per hour, engulfing a farm house, destroying the village school, and finally wrecking some homes in the village. In all, 144 people died, of whom 116 were children. As is always the case in such circumstances, a most complete public inquiry was held by the British Government, the inquiry tribunal consisting of a learned judge supported by a prominent civil engineer, an expert in geotechnical work. Their published report is a masterly document. It is accompanied by two companion volumes in which are printed eight detailed technical reports, covering every aspect of the disaster, naturally including the geology of the tip site, which was of critical importance.[8.38] Tragic though the disaster was, it has led to this constructive result, as major accidents properly investigated and reported upon always should. There is now available for all time a complete review of this particular accident and its background. The event directed attention around the world to this particular hazard, again with constructive results, one of which will be detailed below. The fact that this section is included in this chapter is probably one of the many minor indirect results of the tragedy because in the past it has been all too easy to neglect the hazards that spoil dumps can present, despite a long history of serious accidents that they have caused.

This neglect was brought out at the Aberfan inquiry when attention was directed to a paper entitled "The Stability of Colliery Soilbanks," written by a mining engineer and geologist of wide experience, G. L. Watkins, and published in the (British) journal *Colliery Engineering* in November 1959, 7 years before the Aberfan disaster, but apparently not taken to heart. In the third and fourth lines of the paper, Mr. Watkins says: ". . . to discuss the stability of colliery soilbanks, especially since in wet weather many slips have occurred."[8.39] It is, of course, always easy to be "wise after the event." It will never be known whether a reading of this paper by anyone connected with the Aberfan tip might have alerted him to the potential danger, but the existence of the paper is a telling reminder of the availability of almost limitless information, to be found and used by those who look for it. This is as true of geological matters as of any other field of science or engineering. The references at the end of this volume are but an introduction to printed geological information. It is hoped that they will lead some readers to explore for themselves some of the literature of applied geology and so become aware of the help they can receive from printed sources—never the substitute for personal contact and individual expert advice but at least an introduction. Mr. Watkins' paper was reprinted in November 1966, exactly 6 years later, in full, in the same journal in which it had originally appeared. The fact that this is the only case in all his wide reading that the author has ever seen of a paper being reprinted completely well illustrates the importance that was attached to it at the time of the Aberfan inquiry and supports the intent of the foregoing comments.

Since "Aberfan" will never happen again, it is to be hoped, it would not be profitable to repeat all the details, not even of the local geology, which was somewhat complex. It may be useful, however, merely to record that the Merthyr Vale Colliery, from which the material in the tip came, first produced coal in 1875. A number of tips were created for disposal of the colliery waste, all close to Aberfan. In 1944 a considerable slip occurred in No. 4 tip, and a large part of the tip traveled 480 m down the mountainside toward the village. The No. 7 tip, the one that failed, was started in

1958. Its height in 1966 was estimated to be 60 m from tip to toe. The tipping point was 156 m above the village and about 600 m away from the nearest house. Once the slide started it developed into a flowslide, not unlike those in sensitive clays mentioned on page 426) One of the contributing factors appeared almost certainly to have been artesian water from the underlying jointed Brithdir sandstone. The importance of geology in this investigation is shown by the fact that two of the eight official technical reports, now published, are by geologists; the companion geotechnical reports naturally touched upon the local geology.

Geologists, therefore, have naturally been involved with the inquiries into the stability of mine tips, especially at coal mines, that have been carried out in other countries, following the Aberfan disaster. In the United States, the U.S. Geological Survey undertook such an inquiry. The results were reported by Dr. William E. Davies in 1967 in a paper that is so important that nothing better could be done here than to quote in full from the author's own summary:

> Following the disaster at Aberfan, Wales, 60 waste banks were studied in the bituminous region of Virginia, West Virginia, and Kentucky. The banks occur as long mounds and ridges both across valleys and on their flanks, as isolated cones and ridges on flat ground, and as flat valley fills. The banks are as much as 800 ft. high and 1 mile long. Some are used as dams to contain settling ponds for wash water from coal processing plants. The banks consist primarily of coal, shale, and sandstone initially of cobble and boulder size, but the material is broken in dumping and quickly slakes to plates and chips as much as ½ inch across. Of an estimated 1500 banks in the 3 states, 600 are on fire or have burned, converting the waste to red dog, a weakly fused mass of angular blocks and coarse platy ash. Many of the banks are subject to failure from a variety of causes: slippage along shear planes within the bank, saturation of materials by heavy rains, explosion of burning banks, overloading of foundations beneath banks, overtopping and washout of banks that dam valleys, rock and soil slides on valley walls and hillsides breaking through banks, deep gullying, and excavation of toes of banks. In the last 40 years in the 3 states there have been 9 refuse bank failures claiming at least 25 lives; of the 60 banks examined, 38 now show signs of instability.[8.40]

8.12 AVALANCHES

Another geological hazard is due to the sliding down mountain sides of yet another material, snow. The word "avalanche" has already been used in its broadened sense to describe the descent of groups of rocks, but the name was originally restricted to the description of sudden descents of masses of snow down steep natural slopes. Avalanches can happen only in mountainous country and might, therefore, appear to have little to do with urban development. But with the steady encroachment of tourist resorts into mountain fastnesses, and the continual search for new mineral deposits in mountainous country, urban planning for such developments cannot neglect the danger of avalanches. The destruction of a new mining camp in the mountains of British Columbia in 1965, with the loss of 26 lives, and the tragic accidents to ski resorts in France and Switzerland during the winter of 1969–1970, despite their advanced protective services, were grim reminders of the toll to be paid if avalanches cannot be controlled. Fortunately, their occurrence is restricted to areas with very steep slopes that are subjected to heavy snowfall, but they certainly warrant this brief reference if this volume is to serve adequately to show how many and varied are the aspects of geology that must be considered in urban development in its wide range of service around the world.

History has its own grim reminders of the havoc that avalanches can cause to human settlements, such as the virtual destruction of the village of Leukebad in Switzerland in 1718, with the loss of 52 lives, and the destruction of many buildings even in the well-known and beautifully situated town of Davos on 23 December 1919, with the loss of several lives. One is forced to conclude that avalanches were then regarded as "acts of God" that just had to be accepted as they were, presumably, in the maintenance of the Canadian Pacific Railway through Rogers Pass in the Selkirk Mountains of British Columbia. Here they became so serious a problem that the 8-km Connaught Tunnel was completed in 1916 to provide a new route for the railway. The pass was left to revert to its original wild state—until it came to be used, in the late fifties, for the Trans-Canada Highway. It was then possible to plan avalanche control well ahead of the building of the highway, a research officer living in the pass through three preceding winters and measuring every avalanche as it occurred, with consequent on-the-spot defense-work planning.[8.41] This followed from a visit that the author was privileged to pay in 1946 to the Swiss Snow and Avalanche Research Center high up on the Pasern above Davos in eastern Switzerland. This famous station was a pioneer in this scientific approach to avalanches, having been established in 1936. Th⁓ director and his staff have shared fully their experience with others interested around the world, and especially in North America. Interestingly, the station was established by and still comes under the direction of the Swiss Forestry Department since avalanches have done so much damage to the reforestation of which Switzerland is so justly proud, even though the station's activities cover protection against avalanches for all types of property and, above all, for human lives, especially skiers.

Although the first study of works for protection against avalanches appears to have been carried out as early as 1880, such efforts were personal and spasmodic until after the years of the First World War. The first classification of avalanches—and there are many varieties—appears to have been that of E. C. Richardson in 1909 in a book on skiing. Thereafter it was the skiers who led the way toward the truly scientific study of these winter hazards, in Germany, Austria, Switzerland, and in England. Publication in 1936 of *Snow Structure and Ski Fields* by Gerald Seligman, founder and honorary president of the Glaciological Society and of its excellent journal, marked a real turning point. Today the mechanisms of avalanche flow are well

Figure 8.27 Andermatt, Switzerland. Destruction of the Hotel Drei König due to the avalanche seen in the photograph, in January 1951. Goethe stayed in this famous hotel when on his way to Italy. *(Courtesy of M. de Quervain, Director, Swiss Institute for Snow and Avalanche Research, Davos.)*

understood; the climatic and terrain factors that can combine to create incipient avalanches are known; field observations at any prospective building site, carried out through at least one or two winters (but preferably more) will indicate locations in which defense works are desirable.

Defenses against avalanches include not only snowsheds, effective but expensive, but also the use of mounds of soil and rock to deflect the flow of avalanches from critical places and the deliberate initiation of avalanches by mortar gunfire from carefully selected gun emplacements. All three methods are used for the Rogers Pass section of the Trans-Canada Highway. This major road has not been closed for more than an hour or two (usually after controlled gun firing) since it was opened in 1962, despite annual snowfalls as high as 15.5 m. It is mentioned only to show that avalanches can now be controlled, even under extreme conditions, although there can never be any absolute certainty about the incidence of avalanches, so many are the factors that can very quickly combine to create a hazardous situation. Constant vigilance is therefore necessary, with regular patrols by expert observers in areas where people are to be (such as skiers). Urban planners concerned with any mountain site must not forget the possibility of this hazard, faint though it may seem to be.

8.13   SINKHOLES

In earlier chapters, several references were made to sinkholes. The name was not then explained since it is self-explanatory to a degree, but it may now be noted that in geology the term is applied to any marked localized depression in the surface of the ground that has obviously been caused by removal of underlying material. Sinkholes are usually roughly circular in plan but not necessarily so. They may range from small holes 0.3 or 0.6 m in diameter to large depressions 100 m or more in diameter. They are usually the result of solution of underlying limestone, but again not necessarily so. The large depression now occupied by Crater Lake in Saskatchewan, about 32 km south of Yorkton, is thought to be due to solution of underlying salt beds; other sinkholes due to this cause are a feature of the Canadian west.[8.42] Usually, however, it is the slow solution of limestone by acidic water that eventually results in holes that evidence themselves at the surface, either directly or by the collapse of the soil or other material above the cavity. The slowness of this action must be emphasized, especially since the dissolving water is usually rainfall, with its minute content of carbon dioxide turning it into a very weak acid. It has been estimated, for example, that the rainfall in Kentucky (where many sinkholes are found) will dissolve a layer of limestone 1-cm thick in a period of 66 years.[8.43]

Sinkholes are a common feature of the landscape in many regions throughout the world in which limestone or dolomite is the local bedrock. Parts of Spain are characterized by sinkholes, some due to the solution of gypsum and the consequent collapse of overlying soil. Readers who saw either of the 1970 films *Patton* or *Cromwell* might find it hard to realize that they were both filmed (almost simultaneously) on the Urabasa Plain in Spain. One of the operational difficulties of the respective directors was the occasional disappearance of tanks (*Patton*) or horses (*Cromwell*) into the "underground caves," as they were described, new sinkholes in this context.[8.44] In England, the county of Cheshire is distinguished in its landscape by "meres," small shallow lakes, yet another evidence of sinkholes, in this case due to the removal of the underlying salt about which more will be said later. In Jamaica, there is a part of the lovely island that is called "the Cockpit Country" because of the sinkholes in the local white limestone, some as much as 150 km deep. And in many parts of the United States, more particularly toward the south, there are great areas in which sinkholes are either evident or are a potential hazard to development. All the project sites located on carbonate rocks in the area served by the Tennessee Valley Authority, for example, have solution cavities, the first phase of sinkhole formation, as one of the characteristic features of the subsurface. In all limestone and dolomitic areas, therefore, site exploration must be conducted on the assumption that sinkholes may be present, every effort being made to determine the soundness and continuity of bedrock near the surface.

Because of their mode of formation, natural sinkholes (as distinct from those caused by human activity below ground) will be irregular in occurrence. The solution channels in carbonate rocks may start out along joint planes but thereafter develop in quite heterogeneous fashion. There can be no certainty, therefore, about the absence of sinkholes on building sites in "sinkhole country." The only practicable solution, after preliminary-site studies, is to sink a test hole at the site of every important column or load-bearing member—a costly procedure at first sight but a most desirable "insurance procedure." One has only to think of such an accident as occurred in Akron, Ohio, in 1969 when the collapse of part of the roof of a 6-year old department store caused one death and injuries to 10 people, the collapse being attributed to settlement of one column that had been founded over an undetected sinkhole, to realize how essential is such detailed subsurface investigation if there is any possibility at all of sinkholes beneath a building site.[8.45] The extent of underground solution channels in limestone was shown by the careful study made of subsurface conditions at the site of a new paper mill for the Bowater Company at Calhoun, Tennessee. Knox dolomite was the underlying bedrock. In some places 10 percent of the rock by volume had been dissolved away by percolating waters. Cavities were found to extend to depths of more than 60 m below the level of the adjacent Hiwassee River.[8.46] Many more examples could be cited to show that buildings and other structures can be safely and economically founded on carbonate rocks, despite solution channels and the sinkholes that evidence these at the surface, if adequate subsurface investigations are first carried out, planned in detail in cooperation with detailed study of the local geology.

Although they can cause difficulties in some aspects of urban development, and especially in foundation design and construction, sinkholes can often be turned to good effect. The fact that the solution channels in carbonate rocks that lead to the formation of surface sinkholes are caused by the flow of water indicates that there must be some underground outlet for the water that moves through the rock. An example was given in the last chapter (page 381) when reference was made to a sinkhole used for garbage disposal. If the local geology is studied carefully and the underground course of percolating water determined with accuracy, sinkholes may provide a convenient means of disposing of surface waters. This can be done with safety and assurance only with the information that geological study can give. When underground conditions are known with certainty, however, excellent drainage systems can be developed by leading surface drainage through appropriately designed channels to one or more sinkholes, the sides of which must naturally be finished off properly to ensure their stability and successful performance when drainage water comes pouring into them.

The city of Springfield, Missouri, has used this system in a number of locations, turning a "geological hazard" into a civic convenience.[8.47] The airport at Bowling

Green, Kentucky, is completely drained in this way, all drainage ditches leading to selected sinkholes that were incorporated into the drainage system by appropriate design.[8.48] In road construction in southern England, there have been a number of cases when surface drainage both permanent and temporary has made use of the "swallow holes" or "soak holes" that exist in the Chalk bedrock that has called for such frequent reference. Being also a carbonate rock, it is sometimes featured by solution cavities and channels, disappearing streams being one of the more interesting evidences of this.[8.49] The regular use of sinkholes for drainage purposes is naturally for the conduct of surface waters only, waters that will not contaminate either the groundwater with which they may come into contact or the streamflow into which they will eventually discharge after their underground journey. It is not surprising to find that, in the past and before modern sanitary controls, the existence of convenient subterranean cavities provided an open invitation to economically minded persons and organizations to dispose of their sewage and other waste waters.[8.50]

All the sinkholes so far discussed were natural occurrences, either actual sinkholes on the surface or hidden cavities that caved in and became sinkholes when the surface soil was disturbed. Occasionally, sinkholes can be caused by man's interference with subsurface conditions. Many will have seen small holes in the surface of the ground caused by tunneling or by mining too close to the surface. These are usually minor manifestations of human activity. More usually, and because most mining takes place far below the surface, any ground disturbance from this cause will be a general settlement of the ground surface, as at Duisburg. Similarly, and as will shortly be seen, the pumping of water from the ground may cause widespread settlement, but if local geological conditions include hidden cavities then sinkholes may result. A well-recorded case happened at Hershey, Pennsylvania, 14.4 km east of Harrisburg near the plant of the Hershey Chocolate Company. A neighboring quarry from which high-calcium Annville limestone was obtained was kept dry by a continuous pumping program. The rate of pumping was suddenly doubled in May 1949. Groundwater levels were immediately affected in an area of about 2,600 hectares, including the site of the chocolate company's plant. Over 100 sinkholes appeared, some of them cauisng serious trouble. Groundwater-recharging operations were then started. Although these restored groundwater levels to some extent, they also increased the pumping load of the quarry company. Legal action followed but the recharging was not stopped. The quarry company therefore started a program of grouting around their operating site, and something like the original conditions were restored.[8.51] The case well illustrates the complete interdependence of groundwater conditions over a considerable area when ground conditions permit free underground flow.

Far more serious, since human lives were involved, is an example from South Africa. Johannesburg has already been mentioned. This great city, founded and developed in connection with the world-famous local gold mining, has seen the location of active mining change from within city limits to new mines to the west of the city. As mining has followed the gold-bearing reefs, operations have had to go deeper, and since the ground is water-bearing, pumping has had to be extended. In 1960 a major dewatering program was initiated in the Far West Rand mining district some 65 km to the west of the city. A thick bed of Transvaal dolomite and dolomitic limestone (up to 1,000 m thick) overlies the Witerwatersrand gold-bearing beds. Thick vertical syenite dikes cut across the dolomite and divide the great bed into compartments, one of which, the Oberholzer, is at the center of the new mining area. Large springs flowed in the vicinity of these dikes prior to 1960, but the big pumping program soon dried these up and then started to lower the entire water table in the compartment. Between 1962 and 1966 eight sinkholes larger than 50 m in diameter and deeper than 30 m had appeared, together with many smaller ones. In December 1962 a large sinkhole suddenly developed under the crushing plant adjacent to one of the mining shafts; the whole plant disappeared and 29 lives were lost. In August 1964 a similar occurrence took the lives of five people as their home dropped 30 m into another suddenly developed sinkhole. The mechanism by which these catastrophic holes develop is not fully understood, but it seems clearly to be related to the prior existence of caverns in the dolomite, the roofs of which are in unstable equilibrium to such an extent that the lowering of groundwater changes the ground conditions sufficiently to reduce the support necessary for the roofs, which then collapse with such dire results as are here summarized.[8.52]

Naturally a great deal of investigation has been carried out into these occur-

Figure 8.28 Johannesburg, South Africa. Sinkholes that developed suddenly in the West Reef area, after deep pumping had started for mine drainage. *(Photograph by R. F. Legget.)*

rences, which again emphasizes the vital importance of any interference with natural groundwater conditions. It is improbable that there will ever be a duplicate case to this one near Johannesburg, but the existence of caverns in carbonate rocks close to the surface, even though unsuspected, that has so clearly a close association with the sinkholes that have there been formed, is—on the contrary—a worldwide feature. Test drilling for individual building sites has been mentioned as a desirable precautionary measure. This is clearly impractical for anything more than relatively small individual sites. It may, therefore, be useful to mention that there appear to be real possibilities for locating such hidden cavities close to the ground surface by the employment of remote sensing techniques. These were touched upon in Chap. 3, and it was there indicated that they present promising potential in a number of directions for assisting with geological survey work. Detection of subsurface caverns is one of these directions. The use of microwave radiometers for determining the thickness of dust on the surface of the moon was investigated in 1965, and this led to the idea that this technique might be used for subsurface investigation on a wider scale. An experimental survey was therefore conducted in an area near Cool, California, to see if the existence of hidden caverns in the local Calaveras limestone could be detected in this way. The necessary equipment was housed in a mobile laboratory and on a 1½-ton flatbed truck, all the work being carried out adjacent to an existing highway. Soil cover varied from 3.6 to 18 m. No locations of any cavities were known when the survey started, but the microwave radiometer results were checked later, and in almost every case they had correctly detected caverns. The significance of this work is considerable, for it gives promise of detection of a serious geological hazard with certainty and at low cost.[8.53]

8.14 SUBSIDENCE DUE TO MINING

Most of the geological hazards so far discussed, with the exception of slides of waste tips, have been natural occurrences. Consideration of subsidence of the ground due to mining activity leads into consideration of hazards that are generally man-made, even though they are still geological in character. All, whether natural or man-made, are reminders that the crust of the earth is made up of materials that behave in the same way as the materials commonly used by man. They have no mystical properties and so will fail if overloaded, will move downhill under the action of gravity if free, and may be considerably influenced by the presence of water. The results of man's mining operations provide all too many examples to confirm these suggestions. A great deal of mining has always taken place in igneous rocks—"hard rock," as it is commonly called. If mining excavations are not too large, such rocks are competent enough to support themselves without trouble. Correspondingly, a good deal of mining today is carried out deep beneath the surface of the ground, so deep that excavations have no influence at all on the ground surface. For more shallow mining operations, especially in the less competent rocks, there are today in most of the developed countries of the world official regulations as to how such work may be carried out, the regulations serving as social controls designed to minimize damage to surface property in all normal cases. Typical is the requirement in some areas that all excavations must be backfilled with inert material after ore has been removed, this being one of the ways in which large quantities of sand and gravel are now being used up. In some mines it is possible to use the mine waste material for this purpose, thus solving two problems simultaneously.

Mining was not always so carefully conducted as it is, in general, today. Accordingly, there are on record many serious accidents due to the subsidence of the ground above mining cavities. Some of these have merely created depressions in open ground; others have led to the formation of small shallow lakes. Some, however, have occurred in urban areas, with consequent damage to buildings and sometimes with loss of human lives. Somewhat unusual was the loss of a steam locomotive that was working on the (old) Furness Railway of England in September 1892. While wagons were being shunted in a freight yard, the ground suddenly opened up and the engine disappeared into the hole, the driver just having time to escape. Although the tender was hauled out, the locomotive itself disappeared into the old coal workings that caused this disturbance; it is believed to be now about 60 m below the surface.[8.54] This was probably a unique case, but damage to ordinary property has been widespread, especially in coal-mining areas. As recently as 1968, for example, serious property damage took place in the borough of Ashley, 6.4 km south of Wilkes-Barre, Pennsylvania, streets, bridges, water and gas lines, homes, and churches being affected in various ways. Legal action came before the courts in 1970.[8.55]

Wherever there exist old mine workings at relatively shallow depths beneath the ground, the possibility of danger exists. Subsidence may take place suddenly as a result, for example, of slow but steady erosion of material in the workings by groundwater. Operations on the ground surface can sometimes affect the stability of these underground openings. The construction of foundations for new structures over mined areas is a matter that always requires unusual care in site investigation. The greatest caution must be observed, therefore, in urban development in any area below which mining is known to have taken place.

The district around the city of Pittsburgh, Pennsylvania, may be cited as an example, typical but not at all unusual. A score of urban areas could be used in the same way to illustrate some of the problems. Coal was first mined in Pittsburgh in 1759 by British soldiers on Mount Washington overlooking Fort Pitt, site of the present city. Those who know this busy center will know also that the area around is hilly, the flood-plain elevation being about 200 m above sea level, the tops of the surrounding hills about 360 m above the same datum. The main coal seam, named the Pittsburgh, is at the bottom of the local Monongahela formation, but it has been eroded, in the past, over one-third of the area. Other seams are also mined locally from as much as 180 m below the surface. The Pittsburgh seam outcrops on hilltops in the city area but then, because of the dip of the beds, goes to depths of over 190 m to the south of the city. It has been extensively mined, rights to mine it being originally purchased with waivers against all surface damage. Starting in 1957, one company, recognizing the social implications of their operations, guaranteed surface safety from subsidence if approximately 50 percent of the coal under a private property was purchased by the home owner and left in place. This practice has been extended. In one 10-year period, one company that had made such a guarantee provided support for 635 homes and had to repair only 2 percent of the total. In 1966 there was enacted the Bituminous Mine Subsidence and Land Conservation Act of the Commonwealth of Pennsylvania, which is designed to prevent undermining that would damage public buildings or noncommercial property. There has been accumulated in the Pittsburgh area, therefore, a large volume of experience with a wide variety of subsidence problems. Much of this has been placed on the record and is now available for the guidance of others facing similar problems.[8.56]

Accurate knowledge of all subsurface conditions and especially the extent of old mine workings is a starting point for all new use of land in this area. Plans of mine workings are helpful, if available, but this is not always the case with the older mines. Ingenious methods have been developed for examining old workings if they cannot actually be visited and surveyed directly. One method has been to drill from the surface 15-cm-diameter holes into the mine workings, then lowering a special rotating "borehole camera" down the hole that, with appropriate fittings, can be operated from the surface to photograph the area around the bottom of the hole. In this, and other ways, it is possible even today to prepare good maps of the outline of old workings and then to relate these to the locations proposed for new structures. When this was done for a proposed new school, for example, it was found that safer foundation conditions would be obtained if the building were moved about 240 m from the site originally proposed. Arrangements were made with the local authorities to exchange the original site for a new one at the correct location, parkland being involved, so that the school was finally built with 19.8 m of rock between the foundation and the mined-out Pittsburgh coal seam, 70 percent of which still remains in place and will not be touched.[8.57]

When sites cannot be changed, then other methods to avoid subsidence must be used. They are necessarily expensive since new supports may have to be provided deep below the surface to take the place of the support originally given by the coal when in place. Various engineering methods can be used to achieve this result, starting with the construction of solid concrete piers or even walls directly beneath the foundation locations for the structure to be erected above. Alternatives include varieties of grouting the ground, in some cases sand and gravel being introduced into the old workings and then grouted up into a solid and load-bearing mass. Precautions such as these require engineering judgement for their selection and use, but this can be exercised only on the basis of complete geological information about the subsurface conditions. In some areas it is necessary to consider such provisions for worked-out coal seams as deep as 45 m, but the necessity for subsurface rehabilitation work will

Figure 8.29 Pittsburgh, Pennsylvania. Photograph taken with a borehole camera showing aggregate filling of an old coal working in contact with the roof of the old excavation. *(Courtesy of General Analytics Inc., R. E. Gray, Vice President, Pittsburgh.)*

vary considerably, depending on local geological formations. An alternative procedure, if the danger of subsidence is remote, is to include in the building design provisions for jacking it back into place if settlement does take place after construction.

This has been done in some cases in Pennsylvania, but it has become a common practice in the Midlands of England where large areas are underlain by old coal workings. The very simple device of founding large tanks on three supports instead of the usual four has been used in some places. The Nottinghamshire County Council pioneered with a simple design for light school buildings that included in the structural steel frameworks adjustable joints that could be used after the buildings were in use to make quite appreciable changes in line and elevation should subsidence take place beneath the building. A three-story school building constructed as an articulated steel frame using this "Clasp" system was almost complete when coal mining beneath it caused a differential settlement, from one end of its 51-m-long concrete basement slab to the other, of over 30 cm. Located at Heanor in Derbyshire, England, the school was built over the valuable Piper coal seam that was worked out in the summer of 1963, with a maximum settlement of an existing school building of 0.93 m. The new building was designed with settlement in view. The concrete base slab was articulated in two sections, 15 m and 36 m long, respectively, and 12 m wide. One end settled 52 cm and the other 16.5 cm. All joints, including that in the roof, worked as intended and "no damage which would have rendered the building unfit for use had it been completed" resulted.[8.58] Such provisions suffice, of course, for small subsidences only, but local experience, and knowledge of all underground conditions

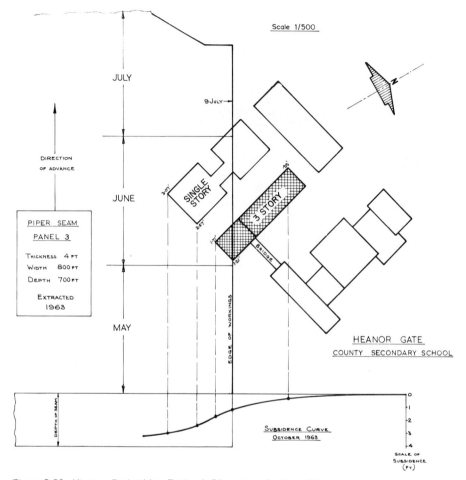

Scale 1/500

JULY

9 JULY

DIRECTION
OF ADVANCE

JUNE

SINGLE STORY

3 STORY

BRIDGE

PIPER SEAM

PANEL 3

THICKNESS 4 FT
WIDTH 800 FT
DEPTH 700 FT

EXTRACTED
1963

MAY

EDGE OF WORKINGS

HEANOR GATE
COUNTY SECONDARY SCHOOL

DEPTH OF SEAM

SUBSIDENCE CURVE
OCTOBER 1963

0
-1
-2
-3
-4

SCALE OF
SUBSIDENCE
(FT)

Figure 8.30 Heanor, Derbyshire, England. Diagrammatic plan of location of "Clasp" school building with articulated foundation slab, in relation to coal workings. *(Courtesy of F. W. L. Heathcote and the Institution of Civil Engineers; from reference 8.58.)*

and not least the geology, will serve as a sound guide to the adoption of such design features.

What has given new urgency to this problem in coal-mining areas is the trend toward the construction of high multistory buildings with their increased foundation loadings. Again, this is a worldwide movement, and so the special problem of founding such tall buildings over old coal workings has received much attention. An unusually comprehensive review of the matter has been published in Great Britain.[8.59] This excellent paper points out that there were (when it was written) probably 400 to 600 multistory buildings being constructed in the United Kingdom each year, of which possibly one-third are being built in areas that overlie the famous Coal Measures that provided one of the foundations for Britain's industrial eminence in the earlier part of the Industrial Age. It is further observed that the foundation loads imposed on the underlying foundation beds by these large buildings are similar to those imposed by many high dams. The paper, to which reference should be made by all who have to face similar problems, confirms what has already here been said about the vital necessity for accurate subsurface information, the detailed investigations of the old mine workings beneath any building site, and the careful selection of the exact location of buildings based on the study of this information. Many cases are described. A group of three multistory blocks in Leeds, for example, was relocated and reoriented by varying amounts to avoid two old mine shafts and a third possible shaft, as well as to fit better to the two underlying coal seams, one of which had been worked out and one of which was still untouched.

A particularly difficult problem had to be faced in connection with the erection of a 16-story block of 126 flats for the County Borough of Gateshead in northeast

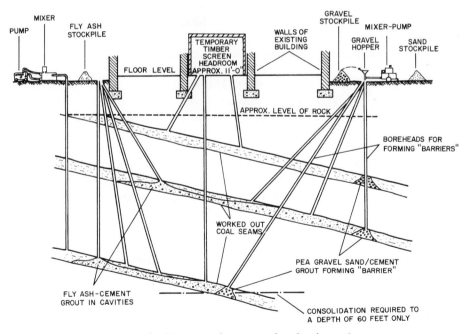

Figure 8.31   Kirkaldy, Scotland. Diagrammatic cross section showing coal seams and construction plant and injection boreholes used for filling up old mine workings in order to stabilize the building site above. *(Courtesy of Wimpey Laboratories Ltd., D. G. Price, London.)*

England. It was known that the gently sloping site was underlain by glacial till on top of nearly horizontal strata of productive Coal Measures. Mine records were available only for coal workings below a depth of 90 m. It was not known if the upper coal seams had been worked in much earlier days. A test borehole revealed six coal seams in the upper 90 m, three of which appeared to have been worked from the cavities encountered in drilling; shallow workings were also found under part of the site. Cavities 90 to 120 cm high were found by further drilling, but some had collapsed and were now filled with loosely packed debris fallen from the roof. It was decided after most careful study to consolidate the shallow workings and the top one of these old seams, the other two being at depths of 45 and 72 m, respectively. To do this, holes were drilled around the perimeter of the site and grouted up to provide an enclosing dam within which the remainder of the grouting could then proceed. Pressures up to 15.5 kg per cm^2 had to be used but assurance was gained that the upper 18 m of rock under the building foundation had been well consolidated. A rigid concrete-raft foundation under the complete building block was decided upon. Arrangements were included in the structural design for some jacking in the future if, despite all the precautions, subsidence of the supporting ground still took place. These details are thus briefly recorded to indicate that, even on a most difficult site with normally inaccessible worked-out coal seams now rubble-filled, it is possible with modern engineering and construction techniques to achieve a sound design for a 16-story building, provided, as always, that due attention is given to obtaining, in the first place, an accurate picture of the exact condition of the geological conditions beneath the site.

Attention has so far been concentrated upon subsidence due to the mining of coal, but the same phenomena are associated with other shallow mining activities such as the extraction of common salt. Although not so widespread in urban areas as that due to coal mining in recent centuries, subsidence due to extraction of salt from the ground is probably much more extensive in nature, if only because salt is soluble in water and so can be eroded even from its natural underground beds by steady percolation of groundwater. [A typical example was noted at the outset of Sec. 8.13, Sinkholes (page 448).] Salt is not so strong a material as coal, and so subsidence can take place at the surface, even though pillars of salt have been left as supports in mined-out areas. The plastic flow of such pillars of salt has been reported in salt mines in Kansas. Removal of salt by solution is widely practiced and is clearly a basically simple procedure and therefore undoubtedly economical. It cannot, however, be controlled in extent to the same degree as solid mining, with consequent possible uncontrolled subsidence. Some years ago serious subsidence developed very suddenly in Windsor, Ontario, where salt has long been obtained from the extensive beds underlying this part of southern Ontario and adjacent Michigan. Salt is extracted by pumping, the brine going directly to an adjacent chemical works. It was thought that the subsidence was due to collapse of old unused salt workings at the 270-m level, but whatever the cause, a hole measuring about 150 by 110 m and about 8.1 m deep suddenly opened up and filled with water from the workings below. Two buildings were lost and much material damage was done.[8.60]

One of the most famous of all salt deposits is that in the county of Cheshire, England, since it was in use even in pre-Roman times when the local salt springs were a source of salt for human use. The Romans introduced the more efficient process of evaporation from lead pans. There follows an unbroken period of almost 2,000 years of use of this valuable natural resource. The extent of its use is shown by records of shipments of "white salt" rising from 17,900 tonnes in 1759 to 41,000 tonnes by 1782. By the year 1820, as much as 190,000 tonnes were being delivered by barge to the nearby port of Liverpool for further shipment. The actual mining of the salt followed the discovery of beds of salt during test drilling for coal carried out as early as 1676 "in the liberties of Wm. Mayberry." It is not, therefore, surprising to find that a volume of no less than 1206 pages on *Salt in Cheshire* was published in 1915. Nor is it surprising to find that throughout the area of Cheshire overlying the salt deposits there is a wide variety of evidence of land subsidence, of which the Cheshire Meres (page 448) are but one example. There are two main beds, the upper one generally mined through shafts, the lower by the pumping process. When old mines collapse, funnel-shaped holes normally form, but the pumping gives generally no such localized subsidence. In more recent years, quite naturally, scientific methods have been applied to the control of all mining and especially of pumping. By maintaining accurate records and leaving concentrated brine in position in the salt beds when necessary, subsidence can be controlled within limits.[8.61]

Even gold mining has to be considered in relation to ground subsidence in some areas. Johannesburg has already been mentioned in connection with the recent change to deep mining for its famous gold ore. In earlier days, this was found almost at the surface and within the limits of what is now the great modern city. The old workings have long since been unused but they are still there. They necessitate severe restriction of modern building in a great wide strip of land (the old reef) running through the city from east to west immediately to the south of the main city center. Ground movements still take place, and so this area has limited capability of development. It was, however, ideally located for road construction when a great system of freeways was planned in the early sixties. Land for the east-west freeway, most conveniently located (as can be imagined) to serve central Johannesburg, was acquired at relatively low cost. From the planning point of view this was all to the good, but the design and construction of this modern highway presented most unusual problems. Ground movements over the old workings had to be included as definite possibilities, and yet a wide overhead modern highway had to be constructed with certainty of performance. Adding to the complications is the fact that some gold still remains in some of the old shallow workings. Although uneconomic to remove now, it must be left available for removal in case the price of gold should go up! The engineers responsible were able to lay down limits of movements to be allowed for in design, with the promise of strict control over any future mining, but these are considerable: a 5-cm change in

Figure 8.32 Johannesburg, South Africa. Construction of major bypass highway through the city of Johannesburg, the route following old gold reef workings; a photograph taken at the junction of the fixed viaduct and that part, for which the piers have just been started, founded upon piers with adjustable bearings to take account of any future ground settlements. *(Photograph by R. F. Legget.)*

grade in 30 m, longitudinal movements of up to 95 mm in 30 m in any individual span, and a maximum cumulative movement of 25 cm in a group of spans. The engineering solution is one of the greatest interest—the supporting piers, which weigh as much as 600 tonnes, are so mounted on bearings that, if and when necessary, they can be jacked either vertically or horizontally to compensate for any ground movement that may displace them. Few of the motorists who now use this fine highway can ever realize upon what an unusual structure they are riding.[8.62]

This unusual example from Johannesburg of the way in which the possibility of ground subsidence in mining areas can be satisfactorily countered in structural design is a useful reminder of the fact that it is not only buildings that are affected by ground subsidence, when it does take place, but all man-made structures. Bridges are especially vulnerable to differential settlement of the piers and abutments that support them. Accordingly, if new bridges have to be constructed in areas where mining subsidence is a possibility, due allowance for this must be made in the basic assumptions used in preparing the design of such structures. Typical was the requirement in the design of the new bridge carrying Britain's great Highway M1 over the River Calder adjacent to the city of Wakefield in Yorkshire. This area is still subject to subsidence as a result of earlier coal mining. The design of the bridge had therefore to allow for a differential settlement of no less than 45.7 cm and a possible total settlement of 1.2 m. Since the bridge crosses the river on a skew of 40°, is on a sharp horizontal curve in the road, and has a gradient of 1 in 248, it was a most unusual example of fine structural design. The solution to the settlement problem was to make a separate structure for each roadway, each of these main spans being just over 72 m long, and each a simply supported beam (with cantilever extensions to the abutments) resting on a three-point bearing system and designed as a hollow reinforced concrete box girder.[8.63] Similar design requirements can be laid down, on the basis of accurate knowledge of local subsurface conditions, for all the many other types of structures that are needed in urban areas.

In summary, if subsidence due to mining operations of the past is a possibility in any area to be developed for urban purposes, study must be made of the probable extent of any subsidence that may occur. Special requirements for the design of all structures can then be prepared and designs completed with every certainty of satis-factory performance of the structures when completed, provided that adequate maintenance and inspection is afforded. If there is any doubt as to the possible existence of old mine workings under any area to be developed, every possible source of information must be followed up to determine whether old workings do exist or not. Preliminary-site investigations must be planned and executed with this possibility in view as one underground feature to be watched for. In new areas, and for new cities, the possible existence of valuable ores, coal, or sand and gravel must be deter-mined in advance of any detailed planning. Once the local geology is known and the exact location of any mineral deposits has been determined with accuracy, then study can be made about their extraction. If the deposits are close to the surface it may be possible to extract them before the area is used for building. If they are at shallow depths but not available by surface working, then regulations can be drawn up in advance governing their future extraction so that surface subsidence will be under strict control at all times. There are many fine examples of such regulations that can be drawn upon for guidance, those of the Dortmund Board of Mines (West Germany) being an excellent example. If mining is to be deep below the ground, it will be possible to determine in advance with reasonable certainty what chance there is of any future subsidence and provision made accordingly in the urban planning process. Correspondingly, the shafts necessary for deep workings can be located in advance so as to fit with the overall plan.

8.15 SUBSIDENCE DUE TO PUMPING

The name "mining" connotes to most readers the concept of extracting solid material, ore, from beneath the ground. The same word can, however, be applied literally to the corresponding extraction of fluids from the ground, fluids that are of great value in themselves. The extraction of common salt sometimes as a solid material but often in solution as brine is a link between the two varieties of mining. It is convenient, however, and in keeping with normal usage to consider separately the extraction from the ground of fluids—mainly water, petroleum, and natural gas. The occurrence and use of groundwater has been fully discussed in Chap. 4, wherein the vital importance of this source of water for domestic and industrial use was made clear. Petroleum and natural gas were formed when organic material was buried in marine muds and slowly changed into natural hydrocarbons as far back in geological time as 600 million years ago, and from that time on up to the present. The process of change must have taken thousands of years, but eventually the liquid and gaseous products of the change moved in the porous rocks that had been formed and accumulated in "traps" that were the result of local geological formations. These are the reservoirs in which petroleum products are found today. So worldwide is the search for new sources of oil and gas and so demanding are the steadily increasing uses of these versatile natural fuels that exploration for petroleum is undoubtedly providing the greatest single application of geology that has ever been seen. When a new "field" is discovered, this is "news" of significant popular appeal. Extraction of gas and oil from the ground are therefore well known even in nongeological circles and are probably never questioned as anything other than a "good thing," with little if any thought ever given to the effect of pumping such large quantities of fluid out of the ground, except by those who happen to live above an oil field that is causing ground subsidence.

The winning of water, oil, and gas from beneath the crust of the earth is naturally a good thing, but in some areas it carries with it the penalty of land subsidence. Unlike subsidence caused by the mining of solid materials, subsidence caused by the withdrawal of fluids will rarely be sudden but will always be so slow as to be imperceptible under ordinary observation. It will usually cover so wide an area that even when extensive subsidence has been caused it will grade so gradually toward the undisturbed ground as to be difficult to appreciate unless there is some man-made structure to act as a telltale. When it is realized that in one well-known case subsidence from this cause has reached a distance of 7.8 m, at the center of an area of 5,200 hectares, all of which has been affected to varying degree, then it will be realized that this is probably a more serious problem than the better-known subsidences due to the mining of solid materials. It is a problem now of current importance in many parts of the world. Inevitably it will continue to be so, probably becoming even more serious than it is already, in view of the increasing demand for water and the never-ceasing hunt for new sources of gas and oil. It is, therefore, a matter of the very greatest importance in connection with all urban development if there is to be any pumping from underground sources anywhere near the area planned for building.

Once the matter is mentioned, the basic mechanism of subsidence can be imagined in general terms, even though the detailed analysis of some examples is complex indeed. Material is being abstracted from beneath the crust. If the fluids merely filled the open pores of porous rocks or soils at ordinary pressures, then abstraction of the fluids should cause no essential change in volume. If, however, there is any free fluid held in the ground under pressure until released by the drill hole or by pumping, then the possibility of underground movements can be readily visualized. The ground will tend to adjust itself to such changes of pressure just as it will because of any other change in applied stress. If, in addition, this underground pressure has been supporting claylike soils, its release may permit such a redistribution of underground stresses that the clay will begin to consolidate, with consequent decrease in volume. In these, and other ways, very slow movements of soil and rock can take place after considerable changes in the volume and pressure of entrapped fluids. If the local geological conditions are appropriate, these changes can show at the surface by a general but very slow subsidence.

The pumping of groundwater to supply a part of the demands of the population of London was mentioned in Chap. 4, as was the existence of the great stratum of London clay beneath the great city. The result has been exactly such a general ground subsidence as is here outlined, even though very few Londoners would probably believe that this has taken place. Precise leveling in London has permitted accurate assessments to be made of the relatively small settlements that have taken place. The latest estimate of maximum settlement since 1865 is 2.14 cm, occurring near Hyde Park, decreasing to almost negligible amounts at the Crystal Palace in the south and the Brent reservoir in the north. There has been, inevitably, a corresponding drop in the level of the water table beneath the city, this being an indicator of the cause of the subsidence. The drop started about 1820 when the head of artesian water was as much as 9 m above sea level; today it has dropped in places to as low as 90 m below the same datum.

This pattern is to be found repeated all round the world—a natural supply of groundwater beneath the site of a city, a start at pumping to use this natural source of essential water, overpumping (and there is no other term that can be used) leading to serious lowering of the original water table and the destruction of artesian conditions (if they existed to begin with), with increased pumping costs, possibly contamination from sea water if in coastal locations, and—of concern here—subsidence of the overlying land surface if the underlying geological conditions are conducive to this. Fortunately, there are still some exceptions where the water table has remained, or been kept, sensibly constant. Winnipeg is one such example (see page 144). The exceptions are all too few, however, for there are almost innumerable examples of cities, large and small, that have had a "groundwater story" such as is summarized above, naturally with occasional variations but in essentials just as described. It would be a tedious recital if even the principal examples were to be outlined. Fortunately there are good references where these sad stories may be read and studied with profit.[8.64] A few selected examples will be presented in summary so that readers may see how serious this problem can become.

Mexico City calls for pride of place in even so brief a recital as this. Inevitably this famous city was mentioned in Chap. 5 since the phenomenal ground subsidence that has occurred there has had a profound influence on the performance of buildings and on the development of foundation designs for the local foundation bed conditions. Here it may be explained rather more fully that Mexico City lies in the west-central part of the Valley of Mexico, a closed basin at a general elevation of about 2,500 m above the sea, surrounded by high mountains. The relatively flat part of the valley, including the site of the city, is underlain by alluvial deposits, but beneath these is a most complex geological structure dating from the end of the Cretaceous period when deformation of the local limestone was accompanied by great volcanic action, action that has continued at a decreasing rate almost to the present. Even as recently as 2,000 years ago, a basaltic lava flow drove the inhabitants from the valley. Subsoil therefore includes soft fine-grained deposits of volcanic ash and water-transported sediments, as well as sand and gravel with interbedded clayey silt. The latter constitute a splendid aquifer right beneath the city; it was natural that as the city grew so should pumping of water from this convenient source. The overlying beds of silts and clays are, however, highly compressible and so are susceptible to any change in moisture content. The inevitable result was that with the pumping from the deep aquifer came also serious subsidence at the ground surface. Demands from an increase in population from half a million in 1895 to 1 million in 1922, and to 5 million in 1960, led to a corresponding decrease in the pressure in the aquifer, originally artesian. The heavy stone buildings of the original Aztecs and later of the Spaniards naturally caused some early settlements due to the weak character of some of the underlying soils (despite the use by the Aztecs of deep pillars as foundations), but general ground subsidence seems to have started at the end of the last century.

Records taken on four bench marks in the center of the city show a general subsidence of about 1.5 m between 1900 and 1940, but then a rapid increase, with total settlement of the general ground level of as much as 7 m by 1960. All observant visitors to this interesting city can see evidence of the subsidence in older buildings and, more dramatically, by the protrusion of old well casings originally flush with the surface but now sticking up by as much as 6 m into the air. The skill with which Mexican engineers can deal with the unusual local geological conditions in their foundation designs was well shown in Chap. 5. It remains to note that water is now brought into the city in order to reduce the pumping of groundwater, now most strictly controlled. Recharge wells are being installed and other conservation measures taken. The ground subsidence must remain, but the further development of the city will continue without the same problems that this has caused in the past now that the subsurface conditions are so fully appreciated and understood.

Figure 8.33 Mexico City, Mexico. A well casing the top of which was once at ground level, illustrating dramatically the 6 m of ground settlement that has taken place here; the group are visiting members of ASTM Committee D 18 on Soils for Engineering Purposes. *(Courtesy of C. B. Crawford.)*

In Japan, on the island of Honshu, serious ground subsidence has taken place as a result of pumping of groundwater at Tokyo, Nagoya, and Osaka, to mention three important cities. In Osaka the subsidence is attributed to the consolidation of an alluvial clay stratum 30 m thick. Between 1885 and 1928, when pumping was much less than in more recent years, subsidence was from 6 to 13 mm per year. Since then, however, pumping has increased concurrently with population, with the result that as much as about 3 m of subsidence has taken place in some areas. If there be any skeptical students of this general phenomenon, they may be convinced

Year

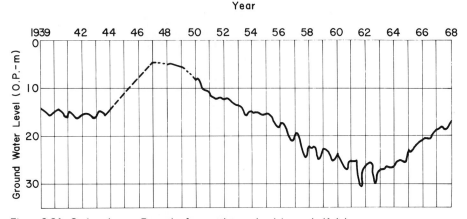

Figure 8.34 Osaka, Japan. Record of groundwater level beneath Kujoh Park, showing the effect of wartime interference with pumping during 1944-1948. *(Courtesy of S. Marayama: fig. 1.2.2 from his paper on land subsidence in Osaka in* Proc. Tokyo Symposium on Land Subsidence, Sept. 1969, 1, 105; *and of the International Association of Scientific Hydrology and UNESCO.)*

by the fact that ground subsidence at Osaka practically stopped in 1944-1945 when the city was being subjected to very heavy bombing in the closing stages of the Second World War and pumping correspondingly stopped. Tokyo experienced the same temporary lull in the record of its ground subsidence for the same reason during its wartime ordeal of bombing.

In North America, there are many examples to be cited from California caused by the pumping of both water and oil. The case mentioned so briefly at the outset of this section, with subsidence up to 7.8 m, is the area within the city of Long Beach overlying the Wilmington oil field; the harbor area of Los Angeles is also affected. There are port facilities, industrial facilities, a major naval shipyard, and many other important structures in the area of subsidence, and so the practical engineering problems consequent upon this subsidence can well be imagined. Extensive corrective measures were started in 1958, involving the repressurizing of the oil zones from the surface, and have halted the subsidence in much of the area. It remains as a truly remarkable example of what extraction of fluids from the ground can do to a heavily built-up area.[8.65]

It was the withdrawal of oil, gas (at an initial pressure of 70.3 kg per cm^2), and water from the Goose Creek oil field in Texas that led to the first case of ground subsidence from this cause that appears to have been described in the literature. The area affected was about 4 km long by 3 km wide, and subsidence amounted in 1925 to more than 0.9 m. The area affected conformed with the area being tapped by the producing wells. Because of the subsidence some land was flooded permanently. The state of Texas claimed title to this submerged land, but the courts did not sustain this claim on the ground that the subsidence was caused by an act of man.[8.66] Serious land subsidence has taken place at other oil fields such as those around Lake Maracaibo in Venezuela, with settlements of as much as 3.3 m between 1926 and 1954 recorded in one location.[8.67] In the Po delta of Italy, subsidence of deltaic lands has taken place due to the extraction of methane gas. Even more serious is the situation in the city of Niigata, Japan, where serious ground subsidence has taken place due to the withdrawal of methane gas and groundwater. The city is located on the coast so that protection from flooding by the sea presents special problems. A large chemical industry has grown up around the availability of the methane, and so intensive study of the situation has naturally been carried out. Repressuring of the strata affected is being carried out through wells.[8.68]

So the record can continue. One further example will be described briefly, this being the area around the modern city of Houston, Texas, the author having had the privilege of being one of a small group conducted around the city to examine the subsidence by an incomparable guide, the late Paul Weaver, a distinguished local geologist. The pumping of oil, gas, and water from beneath this rapidly developing

Figure 8.35 Long Beach, California. View inside the U.S. Naval Dockyard at Long Beach, showing the retaining wall necessary, as a result of the local ground subsidence, to keep out the sea. *(Courtesy of the Commandant, U.S. Naval Dockyard, Long Beach, California.)*

area had affected (even by 1962) an area of almost 180,000 hectares, with subsidence of at least 30 cm, maximum settlements exceeding 0.9 m, the area including not only the city of Houston but also the communities of Pasadena, Baytown, and Bellaire. The area is underlain by the Beaumont clay, mentioned in connection with the settlement studies carried out on the San Jacinto Monument, which is within the area of general subsidence. An unusual feature is the evidence of faults at the surface, faults in the underlying oil-field strata that show themselves by differential subsidence at the surface. Sudden changes in elevation of as much as 60 cm were evident along some of the roads used during the inspection trip Asphaltic roadway surfaces had performed well under these unusual distortions, but road maintenance was naturally a problem. Among the many local problems reportedly caused by the subsidence was the fracture of a natural gas supply line to an industrial plant, fortunately on a Sunday afternoon so that no lives were lost. This incident must not be magnified, but it does illustrate the urban problems that follow subsidences such as have been herein so briefly summarized. The faults in the Houston area are particularly troublesome; local practice in laying sewers across known fault lines has been to use twin pipes, the active sewer pipe being placed within a larger pipe for a distance of 150 m across the line of the fault as a precautionary measure.[8.69]

It must be emphasized that overpumping of groundwater does not necessarily cause ground subsidence in the area above. This will happen only if the local geological conditions are such that strata exist that will be affected by the withdrawal of fluids from the ground in their vicinity. Although normally these strata will be soils, and especially clays, withdrawal of fluids from rock strata that act as aquifers can have exactly the same effect since the groundwater conditions in all overlying strata will be so seriously affected. Precise leveling (by which most of these subsidences have been detected in the first instance) within the city of Savannah, Georgia, has revealed subsidence of as much as 10 cm that can be directly attributed to a great increase in pumping groundwater from the Ocala limestone and associated limestones of Eocene age that underlie the city.[8.70] In Memphis, Tennessee, on the other hand, a decline in the artesian head of more than 30 m within confined aquifers also of Eocene age does not appear to have resulted in any appreciable subsidence of the overlying ground. This is not to defend overpumping, since groundwater resources should always be conserved to the extent that is possible, through controlled pumping and recharging when necessary, but rather is meant to emphasize that the use of groundwater, even with excessive drawdowns, does not necessarily mean trouble with ground subsidence. The possibility always exists, however, and can be determined in its probability only by detailed study of the relevant geology and hydrogeology. If pumping of groundwater is used as a water-supply system, drawing from beneath an urban area, every effort must be made to check regularly on local ground levels to ensure that preliminary geological predictions are correct. Limitations upon such pumping, although superficially annoying, can have a multiple beneficial result not only in limiting the danger of subsidence but by conserving groundwater, eliminating danger of contamination of the supply in coastal locations, and even (in some cases) of maintaining satisfactory foundation bed conditions.

8.16 SUBSIDENCE DUE TO SOILS

In many parts of the world an unusual type of soil is encountered that is generally called *loess*. This is very fine grained (its particles generally in the silt range of sizes) and usually white or pale yellow in color. It is a transported soil, the particles having been carried into their present position by wind action. Loess is therefore one of the relatively rare aeolian soil types. It is often found exposed with almost vertical faces, usually in areas of low rainfall. Microscopic examination shows the soil particles to consist generally of fresh minerals such as quartz, feldspar, calcite, or mica but with other material acting as a binder so that the soil when dry has a relatively hard texture. The clay mineral montmorillonite is one such binding material; calcium carbonate is also found in some types of loess. This binder can give loessal soils considerable dry strength, sufficient to sustain the overburden of 100 m or more of dry soil. Why, then, have they to be mentioned as a geological hazard? Because, although so satisfactory when dry, they will usually lose much of their strength when water is applied to them. The addition of water generally destroys the binding action of whatever has been holding the individual grains together, and the internal soil structure will, literally, collapse. The previous open texture of the soil mass will be destroyed as the water breaks the bond between adjacent grains and then facilitates their moving

Figure 8.36 Kamloops area, British Columbia, Canada. Damage to a building due to foundation settlement caused by collapse of loessal soil beneath due to uncontrolled drainage. *(Photograph by R. M. Hardy, Consulting Engineer, Edmonton.)*

together. Even with loess in place, the addition of water to the surface will so destroy the strength of the soil that progressive collapse will take place, possibly leading to considerable settlement of the surface, in one recorded case to a depth of as much as 10 percent of the depth of the original dry stratum of soil. If such subsidence is not anticipated, its effect can be serious on any structures that may have been built on the dry soil.

Lest this appear to be a very remote and insignificant "hazard," it may be mentioned that a group of 15 buildings constructed on loess in the Kamloops area of British Columbia (where average annual rainfall is only 25 cm) all showed signs of foundation settlement due to this cause.[8.71] Individual examples of sudden collapse after water has been accidentally poured onto a loessal foundation soil are legion in the dry areas where it is encountered. Even watering of gardens can be hazardous. As early as 1915 trouble due to this reason had been encountered in a new pumping plant in the San Joaquin Valley, 64 km from Fresno. Some 52,000 hectares of land in this valley that are now being irrigated are subsiding due to change in character of the underlying loess. Settlements of 0.9 to 1.8 m are common; as much as 4.5 m has been recorded. An Inter-Agency Committee on Land Subsidence in the San Joaquin Valley was established in 1954; the report that it has issued is a valuable guide to all who have to deal with this particular hazard.[8.72]

It is therefore possible to determine in advance, by means of proper field and laboratory tests, what the "hydrocompaction" (as the change in loessal character is now called) will be. When necessary, hydrocompaction can be carried out in advance of construction so as to obviate any possibility of future subsidence. This has had to be done for irrigation canals that run through loessal country. Correspondingly, if excavations, such as for road cuts, have to be made through loess, it is essential that the side slopes be left as steep as possible so that rain will not penetrate into the soil. In addition to its limited occurrence in California and British Columbia, loess is found in large areas in the states of Washington and Wyoming. The most extensive North American deposits, however, are in the Missouri and Mississippi River Valleys. It has worldwide distribution, some of the most extensive deposits being in China, the name "Yellow River" coming from the yellow color given to the flowing water by loess that has been eroded.

The term "hydrocompaction" is a contribution from geology that uses the word "compaction" in the geological sense. It was explained earlier (page 347) that, unfortunately, there has not always been agreement as to the meaning of the same technical word in different scientific disciplines. Compaction to the engineer means the compaction of loose soil by the action of mechanical equipment such as sheepsfoot rollers (or should one say sheepsfeet rollers?—another technical semantic conundrum). In view of this duality of meaning and to obviate any possible mis-understanding, it may be useful to mention again that all loads placed on the surface of a soil mass will cause some consolidation or settlement. With light loads, and even with heavy loads on granular soils, this settlement will not be large, but with heavy loads on clay soils the amount of settlement can be considerable. It is, however, a phenomenon quite different from the subsidence of the ground itself that has been discussed in this and the preceding sections.

Consolidation of clay soils under load can be predicted with reasonable accuracy on the basis of test results in the laboratory upon undisturbed samples of the soil taken from beneath the site to be loaded. By selection of appropriate design procedures, such as are described in Chap. 5, it is possible to control this settlement and even to eliminate it for all practical purposes by using a floating foundation design. Even without this procedure, however, by careful selection of foundation designs and conservative proportioning of the sizes of foundation units, it is possible to predetermine such settlements within rigid limits. Foundations for the elaborate antennas now used with the more sophisticated types of radar establishment must be held to very close limits. A recent case of a large steel bowl-like structure, founded on a circular concrete foundation 35.4 m in diameter, the foundation beds being coral fragments similar to a gravely sand. Differential settlement across the diameter had to be controlled to within 0.75 mm under operating conditions, and this was successfully achieved.[8.73] Settlement of structures on clay (or any other) soils is not, therefore, any "hazard" at all today, even though in times now long past, when the scientific study of soils was almost unknown, the erection of large and heavy structures on soft clays could almost be classed as a hazard, as all too many early examples showed.

8.17 SWELLING SOILS AND ROCK

Although many of the problems that arise with man's use of the surface of the earth for his many purposes are caused by subsidence of the surface, there are occasional occurrences of the reverse procedure, some soils and even rock rising above its normal position and so earning the epithet of "swelling." Frost heaving in poorly constructed roads will be familiar to all who live in northern regions. This phenomenon is now well understood and can be completely eliminated in modern road design, as so many major highways in areas with cold winters now demonstrate every year. It is not this type of swelling that is referred to here but the occurrence of actual volume change in soil (and rock) rather than the growth of ice formations that evidences itself in the frost heaving of overlying soil. In some warmer areas, such as parts of Texas, Israel, and South Africa, trouble is sometimes encountered over clay soils that have become dessicated to considerable depths (as much as 6 m) and that are then affected by the presence of water in some form. This may be by the slow percolation of infrequent rain or by a slow change in the water table below the depth of dessication. Water will be absorbed by the clay through the cracks that have given it an open texture. If the clay minerals present readily absorb water, with corresponding increase in volume (as will commonly be the case), then the clay will swell, the cracks will seal up, and the surface will rise. The same phenomenon will, in some cases, follow the covering up of such soils, as by a road pavement or the foundation slab of a building. Evaporation of such water as is present will be prevented; the moisture content of the clay will increase very slowly and eventually heaving of the surface will result, probably irrespective of the weight of the slab or building, so great are the swelling pressures than can be developed in some soils.[8.74]

The processes outlined are complex; much has yet to be learned about some of the more extreme examples of this type of swelling. Research into the associated problems is proceeding in several of the countries in which this particular hazard has to be faced. Swelling soils that may cause trouble can now be readily recognized by preliminary testing. Their presence may also be indicated in built-up areas by local evidence of heaving. Necessary precautions in design can then be taken. Particularly troublesome are claystones and clayey shales that contain montmorillonite, as found in some of the Cretaceous and Tertiary rocks of Czechoslovakia. Swelling of the clay strata will lead to the formation of tensile cracks in the shale layers, even though these are quite stiff. Weakening of the shale will follow due to the access that water now has to the insides of the layers, and it may change in character into a fissured clay, with corresponding loss in overall strength. Mencl has reported a slide caused in this way that did not take place until 10 months after the excavation into which it slid had been carried out.[8.75]

From this last example, it will be gathered that the occurrence of fissured clays is not restricted to warmer areas, as are almost all so-called swelling clays. They are, on the contrary, widespread. They are found, somewhat naturally, generally among those clays that are geologically so old that they may have been subjected to earth movements in the geological past. The Upper Lias clay of England is of Lower Jurassic age and thus was formed about 150 million years ago. It is so commonly thought that all clays are of very recent origin that this reference to the Upper Lias clay will have a double value if it serves also as a reminder that the same processes to be seen today, of erosion-transportation-deposition, have been operating all through geological time. Although in the course of this time, sand deposits have usually been changed into sandstones and clays into shales or claystones, soils will still be found that have not been so transformed into rocklike substances. The fissured character of many of these older clays must, therefore, be recognized especially since laboratory tests upon the most carefully obtained samples may still fail to indicate the weaknesses that the fissures can induce. There is probably no part of soil mechanics that is so completely dependent upon geological assessment of soil samples as the study of fissured clays. Chandler has reported upon a study of a recent landslide (on a slope of only 9°) in the Upper Lias in the county of Rutlandshire, the slope that was investigated being close to the generally observed angle for the stability of this material in the East Midlands of England.[8.76] Further to the south, near Sevenoaks in the county of Kent, a bad slide took place some years ago in a railway cutting that had been stable for 80 years. This was in the Weald clay, which is of Lower Cretaceous age but also fissured.[8.77] The instability is usually the result of water action in the fissures, the slow swelling evidencing itself in these somewhat disconcerting ways. Fissured clays, therefore, if they are present, are materials that preliminary geological reports on sites intended for development can well highlight.

Swelling rocks might appear to be a contradiction in terms, but if the singular word is used then it does describe some infrequent but well-recognizable phenomena. Again, as with soils, the effects of frost action may first be eliminated. In the far north large blocks of rock may occasionally be seen forced out of their natural position in the ground by the effect of ice action in their joint system. There are "growing rocks" of this type near the (old) military establishment at the port of Churchill, on Hudson Bay in northern Manitoba, Canada. If, however, the excavation of overlying rock has the effect of releasing pressure previously confined in the rock now exposed, the release will occasionally evidence itself by a general upward movement of the rock still in place. This phenomenon was mentioned in Chap. 5 in connection with the excavations necessary for foundations of structures; the examples then given were all of overconsolidated shales. The matter is mentioned here again since it is a minor geological hazard that can occur with any excavation, whether for foundations or not, and it is not confined to shale, although it is with this type of rock that it is most frequently encountered. It is not unknown in quarrying operations. An example was noticed in 1969 in a limestone quarry in Missouri in which a 1.2-m-thick bed of competent Salem limestone fractured as it buckled (one night), rising almost 60 cm and cracking for a length of 90 m. The limestone rock at the bottom of the deep canal for the new power station at Niagara, New York, mentioned on page 285, gave evidence of similar rock heaving. It is, therefore, a perfectly natural result of releasing internal stresses in rock and so can usually be anticipated. The fact that such occurrences do occasionally happen is yet another useful reminder

Figure 8.37 St. Louis County, Missouri. "Pressure ridge" that developed overnight in a competent bed of Salem limestone in the base of this quarry, thought to have been due to the release of overburden pressure through quarrying operation. *(Photograph by E. E. Lutzen, courtesy of J. Williams and the Missouri Division of Geological Survey and Water Resources.)*

of the perfectly normal nature of the earth's crust, its constituent materials behaving exactly as do other materials and so having to be treated with exactly the same respect.

8.18 PROBLEMS WITH GAS

Problems with methane gas as encountered in fills composed of refuse have already been mentioned, as has the infrequent possibility of encountering this gas with ground-water due to decomposition of buried natural organic material. It is a particularly insidious gas since it has no smell, but it can form a highly explosive mixture with varying percentages of air (oxygen) while being lethal to human beings at much lower concentrations than would be explosive. Fortunately, there are instrumental means of detecting the gas and these should always be employed if there is any possibility of its being encountered in underground workings, local geological conditions being a useful guide as was mentioned when the Toronto subway excavation was described on page 292. Because of the hazards involved, and even though these further possibilities are fortunately most remote, brief mention will be made of yet another way in which methane can cause trouble and even tragedy.

When a dam is built and a reservoir thus formed, any naturally occurring organic material in the ground that is flooded by the rising waters will also be submerged. It is possible for this to decay as a normal natural process, but the methane cannot now escape. It is thought that it is possible for methane, under the great pressure that can exist at the bottom of a deep reservoir, to be dissolved in the water at the bottom. This may well stay there if convection currents do not move it. This bottom water may, however, be drawn out of the reservoir by the conduits leading either to powerhouse or floodway. In either case, its pressure will be very suddenly released and the methane can then escape. If it is free to dissipate in the air, no harm will result, but if trapped in an enclosed space, such as a tunnel, with air present, an explosive mixture can be formed that, if undetected, could accidentally be ignited. This recital might seem to be a purely theoretical discussion, but it would appear that exactly this process did take place at the Furnas hydroelectric project in Brazil in 1963. An explosion did occur in an outlet tunnel, doing considerable damage and providing almost insuperable construction problems in rectifying the damage. Later two lives were lost by the men accidentally inhaling methane in the tunnel. In the best tradition of civil engineering practice this whole disaster was described to the Institution of Civil Engineers. Discussion of the paper by Drs. MacGregor and Lyra revealed other instances of the same sort of explosion on civil engineering works.[8.78] It was later found that the same thing had been encountered in the U.S.S.R. Methane gas was noticed, for example, on the Kama dam 4 years after the filling of its great reservoir had started and also at three other important hydroelectric stations, fortunately, it is believed, before any accident took place. It has been encountered in tunnel work in Romania. Methane was also found, in some of the Soviet examples and in other cases, in open excavations being carried out at depth in solid rock. No chances can be taken with this dangerous gas; constant vigilance is necessary on all construction work where it might conceivably be encountered.[8.79]

Even more remarkable was a case in Florida in late 1969, believed to be the first of its kind but presenting strange implications, when 32 explosions took place in some precast prestressed reinforced hollow concrete piles that had been driven into place for the new Buckman Bridge near Jacksonville. The contractor carried out the work exactly as required but, as was normal custom up to that time, did not remove the cardboard forms from the inside of the hollow piles. Water got into the piles by wave action before the piles were capped. The court ruled that the plans for the bridge had failed to call for venting of the hollow piles, bacteria in the water had reacted with the cardboard of the inner forms, and the explosions resulted. And the bacteria? They were found to be due to pollution of the river water. It may well be said that this is not a geological hazard, but if water, probably the main geological material of the earth's crust, can be so polluted as to cause an accident like this, geologists can feel just as responsible as all other citizens, if not more so.[8.80]

8.19 HIGH-VOLTAGE DIRECT-CURRENT TRANSMISSION

Although the previous reference to problems encountered with gas may have seemed to some readers, at first sight, to be farfetched, reference to a new form of transmission for electrical energy will appear to be quite uncalled for. It is well known that almost all electrical power that is generated at some distance from cities—as in distant hydroelectric stations—is conveyed by means of high-tension transmission lines, as alternating current (ac). The voltages employed for these lines have been increasing steadily, now having reached the surprising figure of 735,000 volts, as for the lines that now connect the great Churchill Falls powerhouse in Newfoundland-Labrador with the electrical distribution system in the province of Quebec. As an alternative to these high-tension ac lines, electrical engineers have turned to the possibilities presented by transmission of power as direct current (dc), a practice that was used to a limited degree in the earliest days of electrical power generation, as for one of the first lines from Niagara Falls. Instead of using a multiple wire system, long-distance dc transmission involves the use of single-cable (monopolar) transmission with continuous return using the ground or the sea. The few systems already in use are using sea return exclusively, apart from a 500-km line in New Zealand that conveys power from the Benmore hydroelectric power station on the South Island across the Cook Strait to the Hayward terminal on the North Island. Since the molten core of the earth is a very good conductor of electricity, it has been assumed that, in such dc transmission of power, the return current would go down to the core and travel in it, only a very small part going through the crust of the earth. Intensive study is being made of the possibilities and problems presented by ground return, especially in California and particularly since the use of the ground in this way "introduces the possibility of hazards to underground pipelines or other metallic structures subject to electrolytic corrosion."

The relevance of geology to this challenging new technical development will now be obvious, for it is the geology of the earth's crust between the two ends of any dc transmission line, and in the area surrounding the route of the proposed line, that will determine the proportion of the return current that will travel through the crust. The subject is naturally most complex, but already a number of helpful reports of research conducted so far have been published. Quoting from one of these authoritative documents: "The crust is extremely heterogeneous and on the continents its near-surface parts are characterized by skeins of low to moderate-resistivity materials over large regions. Where such networks are present, they are likely to be preferred by currents traveling between grounded electrodes, as contrasted with much deeper paths involving parts of the lower crust, mantle, and core."[8.81] After noting that "in Southern California, current concentration paths in saline basins and interconnecting channels are intimately associated with the present expression of the ancient Pleistocene drainage," the report goes on to observe "the injection of DC currents at relatively low levels [in field tests] . . . produced current flows on pipelines at great distances from the electrodes as might be indicated from present study of the geology involved." Since it appears that dc transmission of power is going to be given serious consideration in several parts of the world, in order to serve great urban areas with the power they need, it appears desirable to include this brief reference to the significant importance of geological studies in connection with any such installations. The electrical authorities responsible will certainly have given full consideration to all the relevant geological aspects before any project is officially proposed. It is desirable, however, that those responsible for the planning and development of urban areas, with their gas and water supply lines and other buried utilities, should at least be cognizant of the importance of geological considerations in this challenging new field of electrical technology.

8.20 COASTAL PROBLEMS

In contrast with most of the geological hazards so far discussed, those related to building on the coasts of sea or lakes are obvious to all. The ceaseless movement of the waters, the obvious processes of erosion and deposition, the wildness of storms, and (on sea coasts) the cyclical effects of tides—all are reminders of the dynamic forces of nature that are ceaselessly tending to change the face of the earth. Residents of continental areas, unless they live on the coasts of very large lakes, will not have such reminders, but all who have stood on an ocean beach must have felt not only the fascination of the sea but the potential of the forces that it displays even when moving under the influence of waves and tides. Those who live on islands need no such reminders, for the influence of the sea is felt far inland, if only through offshore and onshore winds. It may not be generally realized that there is nowhere in the

British Isles that is more than 112 km from the sea coast, a good indication of how even relatively large islands are influenced by maritime conditions.

The tides are one of the most remarkable phenomena on sea coasts. The combined influence of sun and moon causes on almost all coastlines this dual variation in the level of the sea every 24 hours and 50 minutes, the 50 minutes causing complications in nautical operations. Tides range all the way from the 16.2-m difference in level between high and low spring tides at the head of Minas Basin in Nova Scotia to several centimeters. One of the most surprising variations is between the Bay of Fundy tides and the tides around Boston, a range of only 0.3 m being the tide at Nantucket, and this only 640 km away from the highest tidal range in the world. Ocean currents similarly have their own fascination, such as the constant surface flow from the Atlantic into the Mediterranean and the corresponding reverse flow deep beneath the surface. It is low tide, however, that serves to remind observers of "the land beneath the sea" that is so seldom even thought about. The surface of the crust does extend, however, from continent to continent under the seas. It is found at relatively shallow depths on what is known as the Continental Shelf that forms the seabed off almost all coasts, wide in some places, relatively narrow in others. It is on the shelf that the great platforms that support drilling rigs, now becoming so familiar in pictures, are founded. It is on the shelf that the experimental submersible "homes" have come to rest that have been so well publicized but that do not, yet, provide any possible solution to the increasing demands for more "living space." The bed of the sea does perform one function that aids city life, however, this being the support of transoceanic cables that are still so vital a communication link, despite all the advances of radio. As these cables plunge down to the midocean depths off the Continental Shelf, they are sometimes interfered with and even broken by the great underwater "landslides" (or turbidity currents, as they are often called in technical literature) that may be triggered on these slopes by shocks such as those due to earthquakes.

In earlier times, when water transportation was all-important, it was natural to locate settlements on sea coasts, the shores of lakes, or the banks of rivers. Although the original imperative has gone, water transport of freight is still so important that new ports continue to come into being in response to the demands of international commerce. Vizagapatam in India is now a major ocean port that came into being only in the earlier part of the present century, as did Takaradi in what is now the new country of Ghana. More recently this country has developed yet another new port at Tema. In Israel, the crowded conditions at the port of Haifa necessitated increased port facilities, especially for the export of citrus fruit, and so another entirely new port has been created at the ancient city of Ashdod just to the south of Tel Aviv. On the Great Lakes a new shipping port was built on Lake Superior in the fifties for the shipping of low-grade iron ore; Taconite harbor is now a busy operating facility. Shipment of iron ore up to the Great Lakes and to Europe from the remarkable deposits in Newfoundland-Labrador was responsible for the development of a new port and new city at Seven Islands, Quebec, on the north shore of the Gulf of St. Lawrence. Nature has here provided a splendid enclosed bay giving full protection from storms. There had been a small settlement on Seven Islands Bay for many years. When the author first visited it in 1937 it had a population of no more than 150, with visiting Indian bands for short periods in high summer; today, it is a thriving city with a population of over 15,000. These figures are mentioned as yet a further reminder of the growth of cities.

In all these cases, development of the urban community associated with the port had to follow the selection of the site of the port itself from considerations in what is called dock and harbor (or maritime) engineering, an important branch of civil engineering. The problems to be faced by the civil engineer in undertaking the complex decision-making that precedes port development are not a part of the subject matter of this volume, interesting though they be. To a large degree, the development of associated towns and all other coastal communities is governed by the same planning considerations as govern the development of towns on any normal site. There are, however, three special geological hazards that may be encountered and that therefore call for brief mention. These are the possible danger of shore erosion, the corresponding risk of accumulating littoral drift, and the occasional necessity of controlling the spread and the movement of sand dunes. Shore protection works for the preservation of property that must be developed in close proximity to either sea or lake can now be designed in advance of overall development with reasonable certainty, often with the ingenious aid of small-scale hydraulic models in which the action of moving water on a scale model of the site can be studied in the laboratory. Unlike other engineering designs, however, proposed works of this kind, in contact with the dynamic forces of nature to an unusual degree, must be very closely observed after they have been constructed and continuously thereafter. It is impossible to duplicate in a laboratory model all the natural factors that may influence a shoreline site. Nature has a remarkable way of balancing its operations. Any interference, therefore, with natural processes, destructive as they may appear to be (such as shore erosion) may have unexpected effects elsewhere in the course of time.

This is well illustrated by the phenomenon of littoral drift, which has already called for mention on earlier occasions (see pages 31 and 366). It is the constant movement of eroded material along the shore of sea or lake under the action of wind and waves and always in the same direction. If anything is done to interfere with this movement, drift (usually sand but sometimes gravel or shingle) will be trapped by the obstruction and will go on accumulating. On the other side of the obstruction, since supply of drift has been cut off, the moving waters will often start eroding what had previously been quite stable beaches, sometimes with disastrous results to local amenities. This is no theoretical matter, in view of the steadily increasing numbers of marinas now being built adjacent to urban areas, all needing protection for the pleasure boats they harbor and yet access also to sea or lake. It is so tempting to cut

Figure 8.38 Palm Beach, Florida. Sand bypassing installation at the entrance to Palm Beach harbor, the pumping plant transferring sand brought from the right by littoral drift across the entrance to the beach on the left-hand side (off the photograph). *(Courtesy of the Divisional Engineer, U.S. Corps of Engineers, Jacksonville, Florida, and G. C. Brown, Public Affairs Officer.)*

through natural barriers to enclosed protected waters in order to get convenient access to open water without stopping to consider what this new construction might do. Along the coast of Florida are several examples of this geological hazard "in operation." To mention any one example might be invidious, so let it just be said that beaches have been impoverished of sand due to the construction of such access waterways, and the maintenance of some of the waterways has been difficult because of the accumulation of drift. Since the drift cannot be stopped, sand-pumping or bypassing plants have had to be installed to take the place of Nature, so to speak. in getting the sand across the new waterway openings so that it can continue its steady movement along the coast on the other side.[8.82]

Littoral drift is a widespread phenomenon on many coasts around the world and on the shores of large lakes (especially the Great Lakes), but, fortunately, drifting sand and sand dunes are much more restricted. Where they are encountered, however, they constitute a real hazard. The shores of the Bay of Biscay provide one of the classical areas for sand-dune movement, there being one area in which sand dunes have been moving for two centuries at the rate of over 24 m per year. This has necessitated two separate reconstructions of the local church. In other locations, such as Monterey Bay in California, extensive sand dunes have become relatively stable, permitting attempts at their rehabilitation by appropriate seeding. Botanical studies have now produced grasses and low bushes that can be used for this purpose with reasonable certainty of success. Although mechanical means can be used with some success in sand stabilization work, it really requires the matting that the roots of vegetation will give to provide sufficient stability for any permanent solution. An interesting procedure was observed by the author during a visit in 1964 to the new port of Ashdod in Israel, then being developed. Apartment buildings had been constructed to provide some of the necessary residential accommodation adjacent to the new harbor. Instead of being located on pleasant, irrigated, grass-covered land some little distance inland, the new buildings had been constructed on exposed sand at a location closer to the harbor works. Fertile land is so valuable in this virile new country that it was decided that it could not be used up in this way, and, so the author was told, it was hoped that the residents of the new buildings would themselves be encouraged to develop gardens around their new homes thus combining rehabilitation of sand dunes with the amenities and pleasures of gardening—a very sound piece of planning.

All three of these coastal geological hazards are, somewhat naturally, encountered on the shores of lakes as well as on sea coasts. In many instances shores around the Great Lakes are indistinguishable from similar marine features, apart only from the freshness of the water in contrast to the saline content of the sea. Protection of coastal areas is, perhaps, a more obvious problem on the Great Lakes, in certain regions, since they have been so heavily developed for urban purposes. The protective measures are the same in both types of location, the natural forces to be controlled identical. One example can suffice to show what can be done despite all the difficulties of successfully controlling these hazards. South of the city of Milwaukee but now within the limits of this great city is a pleasant public park, Sheridan Park, within the (old) limits of the city of Cudahy. It abuts on Lake Michigan at the top of a steep bluff about 30 m high, a prominent feature of the local topography along this stretch of the lake. Erosion of this sand and clay bank, aided by the effects of drainage from the urban areas behind the bluffs, had been proceeding at a rate of as much as 60 cm per year when remedial measures were taken in 1933. Eleven groins, at right angles to the shore, were then constructed. They were unusual in being built of precast concrete units anchored together and formed into trestlelike structures that did not completely block the littoral drift along the shore, being, in effect, permeable groins.[8.83] In 1970 the author was able to visit this interesting installation, almost 40 years after it had been built. All the groins were in good shape and the rehabilitation of the shoreline was truly remarkable. The beach had built up, the erosion of the bank had been stopped, and a good growth of vegetal cover extended up the bluff for the full width of the stretch of coast protected by the groins while erosion was still continuing on adjoining beaches.

It is possible, therefore, to control these shoreline geological hazards by means

Figure 8.39 Milwaukee, Wisconsin. Permeable groins in front of Sheridan Park, Cudahy, showing their effect after 40 years of service; the contrast with the continued erosion of the adjoining unprotected shoreline is marked. *(Photograph by G. J. Gaensler, courtesy of the Milwaukee Public Museum and of W. G. Murphy, Marquette University.)*

of carefully designed and well-constructed engineering works. It cannot be emphasized too strongly, however, that all such protection works must be designed in full appreciation of the geological processes that are thus to be controlled. Unusually careful preliminary work is, therefore, quite essential. Engineering records of the past contain all too many cases of protection works that did not perform as planned because either they were attempting the impossible or they had been designed in conflict with the geological processes they were intended to control instead of in conformity with them. Little would be gained by recounting in detail any such examples since so much more is known today about this branch of civil engineering and so much more accurate methods are available for preliminary studies. Even the radioactive content of some littoral drift has been used to study its movement along the coast. On the Californian coast between Russian River and Point San Pedro there are several places where rivers flowing through thorium-rich granite outcrops deposit at their mouths sand containing this naturally radioactive material. At other places the granite outcrops along the coast and normal erosion have the same ultimate result. By careful sampling along the coast, and analysis of the samples obtained by modern laboratory techniques, the source and direction of the littoral drift have been determined with reasonable accuracy.[8.84] This example illustrates well how modern geological methods of investigation can successfully be applied to a very practical problem, one geological in character but requiring sound engineering for its control—a combination that has been reflected in so many of the examples in this volume, indicative of the way in which geology affects almost all parts of the physical development of cities.

8.21 CHANGING SEA LEVEL

The sight of a long sandy beach at low spring tide was noted as an interesting reminder of the land beneath the sea, to use again a phrase that is now common in geology as submarine geological studies advance at a rapid pace as a part of the worldwide attention now being devoted to the oceans. The same experience can also serve to remind the thoughtful observer of the dependence of all shoreline property upon the "unchanging level of the sea." "Unchanging" is here a strictly relative term. In terms of the few years normally considered in human affairs, mean sea level can be regarded as steady, but this volume deals with geology, and in terms of geological time the situation is very different. The life of cities far exceeds the normal human span of years, and so this chapter would not be complete without some attention to this long-term "hazard." On a number of the preceding pages mention has been made of old beach deposits, sand and gravel beds now far inland that clearly must have been deposited originally in water. Studies of local geology will frequently reveal topographical features that look like—and probably are—beaches of the sea or of a lake now at an elevation much above the nearest water. Around the north shore of Lake Superior, for example, there are many places where a succession of such "raised beaches" may very easily be seen. These geological features are a first indication that the relative levels of land and sea or lake today differ considerably from what they have been in the past. There is abundant and incontrovertible evidence that this has indeed been the case throughout the world. As with other geological changes, the relative movement of the two has not stopped, but the change in relative levels is fortunately so slow that it is only by most careful instrumental observations that it can be determined.

The coasts of Italy once again provide evidence of unusual interest. To the west of Naples at the ancient city of Pozzuoli there stand today the ruins of the temple of Serapis. Surprisingly, the floor of the temple is now beneath the waters of the sea, and so the few remaining columns stand on a watery base. Close examination of the columns will show that they are marked up to a height of 6 m above present sea level with small holes. These will be found to be the holes bored by a type of clam that can penetrate marble. Similar clams are found in adjacent bluffs to a height of 7 m above present sea level. They are a marine organism and so must have been alive in the sea when they did their boring into the columns. The only explanation that fits these facts is that the ground on which the temple was built must have subsided after the temple was built to such a depth as would have permitted the clams to do their boring at the height up the columns that can be seen today. Thereafter the level of the land, relative to the sea, must have risen again but not to its original elevation. There is some evidence to show that part of this uplift took place about the year 1500. The fact that similar evidence of changing relative levels is not found on all other coasts shows that this must have been a local phenomenon, but it was not an isolated occurrence since in the Mediterranean there have been discoveries of ancient cities now hidden beneath the sea, providing a fertile exploration area for scuba divers. The Temple of Serapis is of special interest since it was first described by Sir Charles Lyell in his famous *Principles of Geology*, first published in 1828, the first textbook on geology as it is known today and a precursor of the work of Charles Darwin, who always paid tribute to the contributions made to his thinking by Lyell. It is a book well worth reading today.

Evidence of a more general character is to be found in the New World. Diving has revealed the existence of a forest of at least 1,000 trees on the seabed off Panama City, Florida, at a depth of 18 m. The trees stand in a sandy bottom deposit; their trunks have been worn away, but as measured at the level of the sand a typical trunk is 20 cm in diameter. Radiocarbon dating has indicated an age of about 36,500 years before the present time; samples of a peat deposit associated with the trees

Figure 8.40 Pozzuoli, Italy. Ruins of the Temple of Serapis showing clearly the marks of marine-clam borings on the columns, indicating water levels previously much higher than at present; the temple must have been built when ground level was higher than at present relative to sea level. *(Courtesy of il Directore Generale, Ente Nazionale Italiano per il Turismo, Rome.)*

gives a corresponding age of 40,000 years.[8.85] This example, which has been studied in some detail (by diving), leaves no doubt but that the sea level today must be a good deal higher than it was tens of thousands of years ago, i.e., still in the recent glacial period. Evidence of a different sort but equally convincing is to be found in many raised beaches. In the Canadian Arctic, for example, there are to be seen on the east side of Pelly Bay three raised beaches, all of which have yielded sample of organic material that has been accurately dated. This study shows that the beaches have the following ages in years before the present (BP):

First:	52.5 m above present sea level formed at 7,160 BP
Second:	87 m above present sea level formed at 7,880 BP
Third:	162 m above present sea level formed at 8,370 BP

A little simple arithmetic will show that, to begin with, the sea was rising relative to the land at a rate of 17.5 cm per year, the rise slowing up to about 5 cm per year.[8.86]

These examples are given first since the bald statement that the level of the sea has risen about 100 m since the end of the last glacial period might appear to some readers to be a piece of science fiction. When it is remembered, however, that the ice cover in North America was perhaps 3,000 m thick at its maximum, extending from the far north to as far south as St. Louis, the water released as it melted must have had a profound effect upon the sea. Evidence from around the world, similar to the last two examples noted, shows that it certainly did. Not only did the volume of water in the sea increase due to the melting of the ice mass, but the land itself rose as the tremendous load of ice was removed from it, the rise naturally varying with the previous superimposed weight. And this process is still going on. This is the significant aspect in the present context of this excursion into geological theory.

It has been estimated, for example, that if all the ice in Antarctica and in Greenland that can be seen today were to melt due to amelioration of world climate, the level of the sea would rise at least an additional 70 m. Fortunately, the time scale of geological change is such that this eventuality can be regarded today with scientific interest but with no immediate concern. On the other hand, there is now available evidence obtained from careful study of the readings of accurate tidal-level gauges throughout the world that shows that the crust of the earth is still rising very slowly in those areas that carried the greatest loads of ice something like 11,000 years ago. There is in Amsterdam in the Netherlands a famous tidal gauge for which records are available since the year 1682. The records from this and other old-established gauges leave no doubt about the rise, especially around the Baltic. At Scandinavian ports, for example, rise of the land relative to the sea within recent time can be measured in centimeters. The most remarkable rises however, are found in the north of Canada, along the Arctic coast and more particularly in Hudson Bay. Tidal records there show that at the northern port of Churchill, Manitoba, the land is still rising at a rate of almost 25 mm per year. Because Hudson Bay is a relatively shallow body of water, it is possible to imagine the bed of the bay becoming dry land since extrapolation of the records already obtained of the rise of ground level in this vast region indicates a probable ultimate total rise of more than the depth of the bay.[8.87]

These changes in the level of the land, even on Hudson Bay, are still very small, even though within the next century the status of Churchill as a port is probably going to be affected, just as have been some of the smaller fishing harbors in Scandinavia already. It must also be remembered, however, that just as the regions once loaded with ice are still rising, so other parts of the crust are correspondingly sinking by small amounts. The eastern coast of North America, for example, starting in Nova Scotia and extending into the Gulf of Mexico, as well as many parts of the shores of the Mediterranean, show an annual subsidence of up to 2.5 mm per year. Again, the changes are so small as to be insignificant for all practical purposes, but they present one further prospect for the future. If the Great Lakes be considered, it will be realized that they lie between the region of maximum rise in ground level and the small subsidence of ground levels along the coast. There is, therefore, in progress a slow warping of the levels of the land around the lakes. This was first noticed as early as 1853 and has been studied carefully since 1894, water levels in the lakes being available from 1860. It is possible, therefore, to extrapolate from the records already obtained to show what are the changes that are actually occurring. Maximum calculated movement is on the north shore of Lake Superior, the amount being 0.53 m per century, decreasing to 30 cm at Sault Ste. Marie, 15 cm at the north end of Green Bay, and zero at Lake Erie. Within the century, therefore, harbors on Lake Superior will almost certainly be affected. Taking a longer-range view, it has been calculated that within the next 3,000 years, due to this warping of the continent, Lake Michigan will drain into the Mississippi River instead of into the St. Lawrence Valley, just as it did in glacial times. This will create problems for the International Joint Commission of that time, but since it is somewhat remote from the problems faced by the planner of the cities of today, this brief reference to one of the predictions of geology may well serve to bring this recital of geological hazards to a fitting close.

8.22 CONCLUSION

When thus grouped together for convenience in this one chapter, this score of geological hazards that may affect cities might almost seem to be a geological "chamber of horrors." Attention must therefore be directed to the fact that the five preceding chapters all dealt with the constructive applications of geology in the work of planning and developing urban areas. This overview will restore the perspective in which the foregoing review of hazards must be viewed. Balance will be further restored if it be recalled that these are hazards that only *may* occur. Some can only possibly occur in certain specific parts of the world. Some are of man's own making and so can be prevented by proper design, incorporating all possible precautionary measures. Others, such as coastal erosion, are perfectly normal geological phenomena that have to be accepted as a part of the natural order but that can be controlled by appropriate engineering works. They are all, however, hazards that have happened and that have affected cities. They must, therefore, be kept in mind in all urban planning, their possibility being considered in preliminary investigations until it can be eliminated with certainty.

For ease in description, the respective hazards have each been described separately. It will be appreciated, however, that some are closely associated. Earthquakes, for example, are usually linked with the presence of geological faults. When they do happen, they tend to trigger off landslides on any slopes that are susceptible to such earth movements. It may be helpful to conclude with a brief account of one serious disaster that appeared to involve the combination of several of the hazards discussed. Within the limits of Los Angeles, an earth dam 69.6 m high and 195 m long and containing 650,000 m^3 of soil was constructed to provide what came to be known as the Baldwin Hills Reservoir for the storage of water coming to the city from the Owens River and Colorado River aqueducts. The site used was convenient for supplying a rapidly growing residential area in southwest Los Angeles. Construction started in 1947 and was completed in 1951. Excavation revealed a zone of Late Pleistocene or Recent normal faults, with a displacement of 18 m, that were believed to be a part of the active Inglewood fault system. The gate tower was relocated to avoid this fault zone. The dam was naturally operated with the greatest care and kept under constant supervision, with special inspections made regularly. One such inspection was made on 3 April 1963, but on Saturday afternoon 14 December of the same year the dam failed, releasing most of the water stored in the reservoir in a disastrous flood. Leakage that started late on the Saturday morning enabled the authorities to issue warnings. With the efficient aid of the Los Angeles Police Department, using men on motorcycles, in cars, helicopters, with bullhorns to alert all residents, a mass evacuation from the area below the dam was made, but despite these efforts five persons were drowned, some trapped in automobiles. Naturally great property damage was done, estimates ranging to more than $10 million. In the ensuing legal actions, the city of Los Angeles, on its own behalf and for the Los Angeles Department of Water and Power, brought suit against a group of important oil companies, contending that the extraction of petroleum, water, and natural gas from the ground at the Inglewood oil field near the reservoir caused land subsidence that triggered the collapse of the dam, the design and construction of which were not called into question. The total claimed was $25.8 million. The matter was settled out of court for a total amount to be paid to the city of $3.875 million. Extensive studies of the dam failure were made, naturally, and these revealed—if nothing else—how complex were the geological questions that were raised by the accident.[8.88]

Figure 8.41 Los Angeles, California. The Baldwin Hills Reservoir after it had been emptied following the failure of the earth dam, the breach in which can be clearly seen, as can the adjacent residential area. *(Courtesy of R. V. Phillips, Chief Engineer of Waterworks, Department of Water and Power, Los Angeles.)*

Accidents do happen, despite all precautions, once man interferes with the normal condition of the crust of the earth. Accidents in mines are, for example, all too familiar. Even some of these affect the developments with which this volume is concerned. An old mine fire, for example, threatened at one time the safety of the famous Pennsylvania Turnpike until brought under control. Fire in the Jharia coalfield of India actually caused collapse of houses in the town of Jharia, this being an extension of underground fires that have burned for 30 years. The record seems never-ending but it shows how much work has still to be done in learning to use the crust of the earth safely and well for man's convenience. It demonstrates also how completely dependent are the works of man upon the geology of the sites on which they are built and of the region around. And it points to the essential need for civic authorities to know all about the subsurface of their cities and of the areas around into which they can expand. To this vital municipal service attention will now be directed.

chapter nine

What Every City Should Do

It does seem to me strange, to use the mildest word, that people whose destiny it is to live, even for a few short years, on this planet which we call the earth, and who do not at all intend to live on it as hermits, shutting themselves up in cells, and looking upon death as an escape and a deliverance, but intend to live as comfortably and wholesomely as they can, they and their children after them—it seems strange, I say, that such people should in general be so careless about the constitution of this same planet, and of the laws and facts on which depends, not merely their comfort and their wealth, but their health and their very lives, and the health of their children and descendents.

Charles Kingsley[9.1]

These words appear in the introduction to a small book entitled *Town Geology*. The Victorian style of writing betrays the fact that they were not written yesterday. The book was published in London, England, in the year 1877, almost a century ago. The writer was a celebrated Episcopal churchman who was well known to an earlier generation of children and young people as the author of a succession of popular books, including *Westward Ho!* and that minor classic *The Water Babies*. He was also a very popular lecturer. The rare book from which the quotation is taken is a printed record of a series of lectures delivered in 1871 in the city of Chester, mentioned earlier in this book, to young men meeting under the auspices of the Chester Natural History Society.

These bibliographical details are given since the words have such relevance today, 100 years after they were first voiced to what must have been a keen audience, for Kingsley describes his association with the society as "some of the most pleasant passages of my life." His lectures deal with such topics as "The Soil in the Field," "The Stones in the Wall," and "The Slates on the Roof," all delightfully phrased expositions of the elements of geology based upon consideration of the things of everyday, and in particular upon the influence of geology on the building of cities. The message of this book is therefore not a new one, but, like so many other things in life, it has to be learned anew and given fresh emphasis under the changed conditions of today.

There were others who saw the importance of geology to urban development in years now long ago. A paper was presented, for example, to the Royal Society of Canada in the year 1900 by Dr. Henry M. Ami entitled "On the Geology of the Major Cities of Canada" in which these words appear: "The larger cities of our Dominion, as well as those of other countries, are the centres of work and research in the pathways of science and economics. . . . What the drill has to penetrate in any one of our larger centres of activity in Canada. . . is a question not only of interest but also of economic value." There follows a clearly written review of the importance of geology to the development of cities, with notes on the geology of five leading cities of Canada at that time—Saint John, Montreal, Ottawa, Quebec, and Toronto. It is an indication of the way in which Canadian cities have grown that Vancouver and Winnipeg–third and fourth largest cities of the Canada of today–did not then warrant mention, and this only 70 years ago.[9.2] The Vancouver of today is shown in the photograph on page 161.

One could doubtless find other percipient statements in books and papers now long since forgotten, conveying similar indications as to the importance of geology in urban development. But the warnings were not heeded. The growth of modern cities has proceeded in general without any *public* appreciation of the importance of geology. There have always been a few notable exceptions, but they remain exceptions to the main course of municipal development. Private appreciation of geology, and subsurface conditions generally, has become well established. No major building, no tunnel work, and assuredly no large civil engineering works would today even be considered in the final stages of planning without reasonably certain knowledge of subsurface conditions. The growth of studies of soil mechanics and foundation engineering has been largely responsible for this advance. Owners can now readily see the economic value– in an insurance sense–of relatively small expenditures on preliminary subsurface investigations in order to obtain assurance that the proposed project can indeed be built. The gap that still exists, so unfortunately, is between this private procurement and use of geological information and the public appreciation and availability of this information for urban areas as a whole, as an aid to building, and as an essential prerequisite of all urban planning.

One of the factors probably responsible for this gap is the fact that every foundation study is a unique investigation. In the preceding chapters, over 300 cities in more than 40 countries have been mentioned, some briefly, some at length, but all illustrating some phase of geology in its relation to urban development. The geological conditions in every one of these cities, as also in every other city throughout the world that has not been mentioned, are unique to that area. They may be similar to those beneath adjacent urban communities, but they will never be the same. Not only is this true with regard to entire urban areas, it is equally true with regard to the geological conditions under individual building sites. Here the similarity between adjoining sites can be close, but it can be stated without qualification that they will never be exactly the same. Variations in groundwater conditions alone are often sufficient to present varying problems with excavation carried out on adjacent sites. Soil conditions, as so many preceding examples have made clear, are never certain. Appreciable variations can take place in a distance of 1 or 2 m alike in residual soils (as at Hong Kong) or in transported soils (as at Toronto). Distribution of joints and faults in solid rock is always heterogeneous; this one fact alone is sufficient to demand the closest attention to all rock conditions encountered in civic works, no matter how uniform the rock may appear to be superficially. Even with such an apparently uniform material as the blue clay beneath Chicago, laboratory measurements of the strength of the clay in samples taken within 1 or 2 m of one another show variations of as much as from below 2.2 to above 17.5 tonnes per m^2. Every building site, therefore, presents a special set of underground conditions that must be known with certainty before work commences.

Because of this unavoidable variety in geological conditions there can never be the same type of universal guides to design and construction as exist, for example, in the field of structural engineering. When a structural steel framework or one of reinforced concrete has to be designed for a major new building, there are available in every country some type of national codes for design, indicating the way in which the different members of the framework must be proportioned and connected. Structural design can therefore be carried out in offices far removed from the building site, and this is usually the case, with the resulting design recorded in plans and specifications that can be studied anywhere. Contractors in different cities can prepare tenders for their estimated costs with all reasonable certainty, knowing that, upon the foundation provided, the framework—as also all other parts of building superstructures—can be constructed exactly as shown by the designer. It is because of this process that, for example, a multistory steel-framed skyscraper can be erected on a building site surrounded by busy streets allowing for no possible storage of materials. With exact scheduling, based on the firm contract design, steel beams and columns can be delivered to the site exactly at the time, and in the order required, to be hoisted directly into place. Correspondingly, and in keeping with the quickening pace of construction, more and more building and bridge components can be made in factories and brought complete to building sites, merely to be set in place and connected up with the rest of the structure.

With foundations, and all other subsurface works for city development, the situation is different. There are naturally general code requirements available as guides to the designer, but they can only be very general in nature, telling what may be done with different varieties of subsurface conditions. Building codes will give, for example, typical bearing values for the load that can be safely applied from structures onto different kinds of foundation bed materials. These general values are always, and inevitably, on the low side. Their use is usually qualified by the requirement that, for structures above a certain size, subsurface investigations must be carried out and proper engineering determinations made of the safe bearing values that can be applied to the material that actually exists under the site of the proposed structure. As was explained in Chap. 5 (see Fig. 5.4), even this can be done with assurance only if subsurface conditions beneath the site are known with reasonable certainty to a depth of at least twice the width of the structure. When excavation starts, every step in its prosecution must be watched by those expert in such work since usually some slight indication will be given of any coming uncertainty so that precautionary measures can be arranged. Only when the excavation has been completed, and the foundation structure installed, can there be any relaxation of attention to every detail of this disturbance of the natural ground. In the case of tunnel work, ground conditions at each borehole that has been put down along the route of the proposed work will be known with reasonable certainty. Conditions between each pair of holes can be and must be assumed for purposes of preparing necessary lining designs and the necessary contract documents upon which contractors can base their tenders. But nothing can be certain until the excavation is actually carried out.

Foundation engineering and all other allied subsurface engineering is therefore an art, in the true sense of that word, depending for its successful completion upon a combination of sound technical knowledge, wide experience with actual subsurface conditions, and good judgment. It can never be a science, even though vitally aided by what the sciences can offer in assistance. It is one branch of engineering that will never be taken over by the computer. The ability to make instant decisions at the bottom of difficult excavations, or within the cofferdam for a bridge pier, when unexpected problems reveal themselves—this is not something that can be expressed mathematically or solved by a machine but must be the conscious and prompt decision of a person of wide experience and good judgment. Factual information and the skills given by study of the sciences can naturally assist; they are indeed quite essential. And of all the sciences to be applied in these adventures with the ground, geology is preeminent.

It is true that no two examples of foundation conditions will ever be identical, but they can be similar. In any one area, the characteristics of the different rock and soil types that are normally encountered within the area will gradually become known. Groundwater levels under adjoining sites, in particular, although they may differ, are intimately connected, as many examples have made clear. Even the variations in subsurface conditions to be expected on any one site will usually follow a local pattern. Accordingly, the detailed exploration of any one building site in urban areas can be greatly assisted by knowledge of the corresponding information that has previously been obtained for adjoining or adjacent sites. In exploring the material to be encountered along the route of a new tunnel, the necessary test-boring program can be immeasurably aided by the information that a study of all existing test holes along the proposed route, or near to it, will yield. In every case of work to be carried out beneath the surface in urban areas, convenience can be served and real economy achieved if access can be had to existing subsurface information for the city as a whole in the first instance, and then for the area around or adjacent to the site of the proposed work as more detailed studies proceed. This is of special importance in completely built-up urban areas where no possibility exists of seeing even surface conditions on adjoining sites prior to subsurface exploration at a new building site. There is clearly much to be gained and nothing at all to be lost by having such subsurface information available for general public consultation.

In view of this, one would imagine that a normal civic service would be the provision of this information in convenient form for the benefit of all urban planning, new building, and new construction within the municipal area. Unfortunately, this is not usually found to be the case. Some information of this kind is available for most cities, although usually to a very limited degree and often through other than official municipal sources. The information that is necessary will always start with that general picture of the local geology that was seen in Chap. 3 to be so essential for planning purposes. The wheel has therefore turned full circle, for here, at the conclusion of this volume, the vital need for full information on local geological conditions appears again as an urgent demand upon civic services. For all urban and regional planning, just as for assisting with construction, it is essential that all cities should have publicly available the best possible information upon geological conditions beneath and around their municipal area. How can this best be provided?

9.2 LOCAL GEOLOGICAL INFORMATION

In every city, large and small, there is one division of the municipal administration responsible for the carrying out of public works. In larger cities, there may be separate administrations for water supply and for sewerage and sewage-treatment services, but they must naturally work very closely with the public works authority. Names of senior officials will naturally differ. In some cities a *commissioner of works* is responsible for the administration of all such services. The long-established title of *city engineer* is still very widely used for the official directly responsible for all civic works. It is sometimes used for the municipal officer who is charged with the responsibility for all the physical aspects of city development including planning. Alternatively, the *chief of the planning office* may report to a commissioner of works. Correspondingly, the exact position in the municipal organization of the officer responsible for all building inspection and the issue of building permits varies considerably. In smaller cities he may be called the *building inspector*; in larger cities, the *building commissioner*. In almost all cases, however, this important officer will be responsible to a senior official, such as the commissioner of works in larger municipalities.

The main functions of the offices mentioned here so briefly must be appreciated. The city engineer will usually be responsible for the execution, directly or by contract, of all public works for which the municipality is directly responsible, such as roadways, bridges, parks, and civic buildings. He may also be in charge of waterworks and drainage and sewage works, although, as noted, these may possibly come under a separate administration closely allied with his office. He will be responsible usually for all land survey work within the municipality and, in association with his legal colleagues, for the supervision of the subdivision of private land for which the most meticulous records must be kept. The *building official* will be responsible for examining all plans of proposed buildings and for issuing permits for the erection of these buildings when plans are approved. His staff will inspect all new building construction to ensure that it conforms with the approved plans, and eventually, when a project is complete, he will issue an *occupancy permit* that officially authorizes the building to be used for the purpose intended. The *chief of the planning office* will usually be removed from such day-to-day operations but will be concerned with overall studies, estimates, and proposals for the further development of the city and for the reconstruction of those parts that are found to be in need of redevelopment.

All these officials, in the ordinary course of their respective duties, will have regular need of information about subsurface conditions beneath parts of the city or of its undeveloped land. For specific works, they will be obliged to make detailed site studies directly, by contract, or through the medium of consultants acting as their agents. It is, therefore, as much to their benefit as to that of private builders and developers to have available all possible information to facilitate this subsurface exploration work and to make it more efficient and economical. One can readily justify close attention to this service, and the expenditure of some funds upon it, merely from the point of view of benefit to municipalities themselves. When to this municipal need is added the great service that such information can give to all private builders, service that is thus given indirectly to the municipality itself, the eminent desirability of arranging to have this information available as a civic service becomes incontrovertible.

The fact that the city must approve all new building projects within its boundaries gives it direct access to the foundation bed information that must be available for every building. The carrying out of civic works, and especially those that extend over considerable distances within city limits, such as roadways and tunnels for water, drainage, and sewage, makes the city itself an automatic provider of much detailed subsurface information that is in the public domain and so should be available for public use if it can be of service—as indeed it can. Accordingly, from every point of view, it is clear that it should be the responsibility of every city to make suitable arrangements for having all the information on its subsurface conditions assembled for public use in a convenient manner and in a convenient location. For convenience in further discussion, and since it is so closely linked with the work of his office, it will be assumed that the locale for this information is in the office of the city engineer.

It will be obvious that the term "city engineer" is here being used in a quite general sense to indicate the senior civic official, no matter what his official title may be, who is responsible for civic works and so for survey controls. The logic of locating the municipal records of subsurface conditions in this office needs only little justification, but it may be pointed out that there is a direct parallel between maintaining public records of what is below the surface of the ground and of the subdivision of the ground surface in relation to land ownership. There are differences, naturally, the more important of which will be shortly discussed, but just as nobody would question the propriety of "going to city hall" (to use the popular phrase) to consult land survey records, so should the day soon come when there is the same instinctive public approach to information about subsurface conditions.

Once it has been decided to institute such a service—and what is here written will be based on the assumption that no such service exists initially—two essentials must be recognized. The service must have the interest and active support of the city engineer himself, and it must be made the direct responsibility of one appropriate officer. In small cities, the service should not require the full-time service of a professional officer once it has been established and organized; clerical help with professional supervision should suffice. In larger cities, it will be a full-time job for at least one officer; but even in the larger cities, if it is well organized and supported by all necessary office aids, the provision of a complete service should not be a costly item either in direct expenditure or in the manpower necessary for its operation. Since the records to be maintained will be on paper, space requirements should also be quite modest.

Geological maps of the area that includes the city will provide an essential starting point. These will be available, usually to quite a small scale, either from the national, state, or provincial geological survey. They will give the broad geological background against which the detailed records must be viewed. The existence of a city, in many cases, will have attracted the attention of geologists to geological features of the immediately surrounding area. Search should, therefore, be made for the existence of any geological papers or reports that deal with any aspect of the local geology. The information thus obtained will naturally be general in nature. It is merely the framework for the assembling of every piece of detailed information that can be obtained about geological conditions at specific locations.

The contrast with the approach outlined in Chap. 3 will be noted. For planning purposes, the overall general view of the geological character of the terrain to be planned is the first and essential requirement. As planning proceeds, the need for more detailed geological information about separate parts of the planning area will be necessary, the requirement going from the general to the more particular as work proceeds but rarely involving detailed knowledge of the exact subsurface conditions at any specific site. In considering the operating demands of a growing city, the need starts—so to speak—at the other end, with a requirement for detailed geological information at specific sites. When this information is assembled with like information from adjoining sites, a more general picture is obtained. As this process is extended to cover whole sections of a city, a regional concept of the subsurface conditions will gradually evolve. The combination of these more general approaches will eventually present an overall picture of the geology of the entire area, naturally correlated with the general geological pattern obtained from normal small-scale geological maps.

The meeting place of the two procedures will be the engineering-geological map of every urban area that should be available. The character of these specialist maps was discussed in Chap. 3. They show the local geology but show also its relevance to the normal engineering problems that have to be dealt with in urban development. Although engineering-geological maps of a general character can be prepared on the basis of regional assessments of topography and the soil and rock types to be encountered, more detailed and accurate maps of this kind can be produced only on the basis of the patient and methodical assembly of specific information based on actual experience with the rocks and soils locally encountered. A most important byproduct, therefore, of the collection of detailed local geological information such as is herein suggested is the ultimate development of good engineering-geological maps for the city in question and, by extrapolation, for the contiguous area. When accurate maps like this are available, then the task of the planner becomes easier and more efficient. This really vital and essential aid to future planning around, and within, a city is an additional benefit to be gained from the acceptance by a city of the responsibility for collecting and making conveniently available the records of its entire subsurface. Although the resulting maps can be such a great aid in planning work, it must be emphasized here that they can never take the place of expert and professional advice on the subsurface conditions to be encountered at specific sites of new foundations or tunnels or of any other construction within the city. They can be a most useful aid; they will assist greatly in the planning of detailed subsurface investigations at specific sites; and they can ensure real economy in all such work if they are properly used. But they remain as essential aids and can never replace that sound professional advice that is always so essential for construction work below the surface of the ground.

9.3 LOCAL SUBSURFACE RECORDS

What is the subsurface information that can be obtained at any specific site within a city? First is the geological profile from the surface down as far as exploration can be carried, showing the different strata of soil and rock that are encountered. Once this succession of strata is known, then it is desirable and often essential to obtain samples of the characteristic types of soil and rock so that these can be tested in a suitable laboratory and their engineering properties determined. The moisture content of soil samples is of extreme importance in the case of fine-grained soils, and this is a reminder of the importance of the third type of information, that relating to groundwater conditions at the site. Groundwater will be present somewhere at every site. It may be encountered only in very deep borings, but in many urban areas it can be surprisingly close to the surface. It must always be remembered that in most locations the level of the water table will vary throughout the 12 months of every year, often in response to annual climatic variations. If at all possible, therefore, arrangements must be made to measure and record the variation in the position of the water table throughout at least one complete 12-month period. The maximum and the minimum possible levels of groundwater can often be of the greatest importance. The variation from one to the other may be unsuspected if a single reading of the water table elevation is taken and assumed to be constant.

On sites where new structures such as buildings and bridges are to be erected and along the routes to be followed by such engineering works as highways or tunnels, test borings will be put down by expert crews for the purpose of obtaining this information. This is now a regular part of civil engineering practice; excellent equipment is available for boring in soil to great depths, for obtaining what are called *undisturbed samples* of soil that are quickly sealed at the surface to conserve their moisture content at its natural value, for drilling to corresponding depths in rock, and for retrieving the cores of rock from such holes. *Casings* are the steel pipes inserted in holes through soil in order to maintain the sides of the hole for further penetration. Although usually pulled out of the ground as a normal economic measure, it is common practice to leave casings in selected holes, suitably capped at the top, for observation of the variation in groundwater levels. Casings for this purpose are usually perforated at their lower sections, and even surrounded with copper-wire mesh in fine-grained soils, to ensure no interference with measurement of the variation of groundwater in the surrounding soil and not merely just in the restricted pipe. There are available standard procedures for recording the variation in strata penetrated by the test holes and the groundwater levels encountered, for identifying soil samples and cores, and for storing these when examined and tested.

All this information is usually recorded in an overall report for each subsurface exploration job. If well prepared, such a report will commence with a general account of the local geology, but the main part will be concerned with the details of the subsurface conditions at the particular site in question. The report will be used by the consulting engineers and architects for determining final plans for the structure they are to design. The more detailed contents, such as the results of laboratory tests upon the soil samples, will be used for the detailed design of the foundation structure. Thereafter the report will usually be stored away until needed for some other purpose, its only other use frequently being to refute the claims from contractors for extra payment for excavation that so often feature difficult construction jobs.

Once construction starts, excavation will be one of the first major activities to be undertaken in the case of bridges or buildings; the sinking of the necessary shafts will be the corresponding initial phase of tunnel work. Here the predictions made on the basis of the test borings will be proved or, in unusual cases, disproved. Every step in excavation must be observed carefully, not only by the contractor to make sure that his methods are working satisfactorily and safely, but also by the engineer or architect (naturally through their representatives on the job) to ensure that the material on which the structure is to be founded, or the rock and soil through which the tunnel is being driven, is exactly as it was assumed to be in design. For the latter reason, all such observations of rock and soil exposed in excavation must be recorded, often with the camera as well as through written notes. Additional samples may be taken if this ever appears to be necessary. Groundwater conditions will be under constant review since any sudden change in its level can interfere seriously with construction operations.

When the finally prepared foundation bed has been approved, when the tunnel excavation has been cleaned down (washed down if in rock), inspected, and approved, the contractor can commence the installation of the foundation structure or tunnel lining. Once concrete is in place, the foundation bed and exposed bore of the tunnel will never be seen again. The records that are made of the actual ground conditions as they were just before being covered up are therefore of unique value. They are commonly transferred to what are called *as-constructed drawings*, and these then constitute for all time the record of the subsurface conditions that were so briefly exposed to view. These records and associated photographs all too soon become of limited

Figure 9.1 Toronto, Ontario, Canada. Two very similar apartment buildings, that on the right founded on bedrock through concrete caissons and
that, on the left founded on a concrete raft, bearing on the glacial soil
overlying the rock, the difference in foundation designs having been decided
upon because of differences in the subsurface geology revealed by accurate
preliminary geotechnical investigations. *(Courtesy of W. A. Trow, consulting geotechnical engineer, Toronto.)*

interest as designers and contractors go on to other projects, provided the owner of
the structure is satisfied with its performance. They will be filed away, available for
reference if and when necessary, to be used again, in all probability, only if alterations
or additions are to be made to the structure.

There must be a wealth of information of this sort in every modern city, carefully
prepared, used for its initial purpose, but now filed away and inaccessible to all but a
few. This holds for both preliminary information on site explorations and subsurface
information obtained during the course of construction. And yet this same informa-

tion could be generally so useful if made available for public use. When assembled and correlated, it will add its quota to the overall picture of the local subsurface conditions beneath the city and make its own contribution to knowledge of the local geology. If any of the hazards described in Chap. 8 have to be faced in the area concerned, this sharing of subsurface information is a vital first step in guarding against them. Every city will have available the subsurface records from its own construction projects. Many cities have exerted great efforts in correlating these and in using them to best advantage in the planning of underground exploration work for their own future construction projects. Except in those countries in which the city or state government controls all construction and where the sharing of this information is mandatory, the geological records available from civic works alone will inevitably give only a partial picture of subsurface conditions. How can a city manage to procure, in the public interest, the additional records that can be so valuable in this way?

As in all problems of communicating information, it must be remembered that communication is a two-way operation. There must be those who provide information but also those who receive it and who know what to do with it and how best it can be put to use. Accordingly, a first requirement is that the office of the city engineer shall be ready with staff and the necessary organization and office equipment for the receipt of reports on subsurface condition, once they are solicited. Correspondingly, it will be essential that, as soon as possible, arrangements should be made, by a display of maps or the issue of simple preliminary publications, to show those who contribute information that what they have provided is being put to good use. When all such arrangements have been planned, and the responsible staff are ready, then a public appeal for the contribution or loan of all existing reports on underground conditions can be made, desirably with the highest possible endorsement from civic and professional authorities.

It will be clear that voluntary contributions will normally be the only means whereby existing information about borehole programs or excavations can be obtained. The need for such information will have to be carefully explained and interest developed in the public service that will be provided by the resulting assembly of information. An appeal on these lines to the professions involved, those of engineering and architecture in particular, should meet with a favorable response since it fits so well with that truly professional outlook in which the public interest is always paramount. Accordingly, the appeal will probably be the more fruitful if the active interest of professional organizations in the city can be obtained and their support ensured, as well as that of the more general type of organization that may also have an interest in the matter such as local groups of contractors, often found as excellent local construction associations. Even with such support, it will be impossible to tap all available sources of information without personal contact. Construction in all parts of the world is today such an active calling that it is extremely difficult for those involved in construction to donate time and effort to such seemingly peripheral activities as "digging out old records," as this effort will appear to be. It will be necessary therefore to make personal contact with the offices and organizations that are known to have such records in order to win many of them for public use. In the case of older buildings, records will usually be in the custody of the owners so that many trails will have to be followed before such records are unearthed, always starting, however, in the offices of professional designers.

For new construction the situation is naturally different. Drilling operations can be seen in action. Excavations can be inspected—as they are, today, by many interested citizens through the viewpoints now commonly provided for "sidewalk superintendents." The records are therefore current documents and should be all the more easy to obtain. If there is some appropriate way in which the provision of this information can be made a requirement without placing any undue burden on owners or designers, then general convenience would be served. This is the situation with regard to the vast amount of drilling that is done in the search for gas and oil. Drill holes for this purpose are on a very different scale to those normally used for foundation work, but the principles employed are just the same. Record is taken of the soil strata penetrated, and then of the underlying rock strata, cores of the rock and (sometimes) samples of the soil being obtained. This is done even for the deepest holes, there being now one hole drilled to a depth of about 8 km in Louisiana, before it was abandoned. In almost every state and province in North America, and in most other countries in which oil and gas have been found, it is today a legal requirement that the record of the strata penetrated be recorded with appropriate public authorities for eventual public use, although there is often a preliminary period during which the privacy of the information is guaranteed.

This system of recording the subsurface information obtained when exploring for oil and gas has worked well, with no real interference with the great industry involved but with absolutely invaluable assistance to the understanding of the complex geology of the regions in which natural petroleum products are found. This has been to the benefit not only of the companies immediately concerned but also to the public. It may be said that this is a special case, but something approaching this practice is found in connection with the corresponding, but much shallower, drilling in the search for water. The practice is not yet so widespread in this field, but there are a number of states and at least two provinces in which water-well drillers must also record with the appropriate state and provincial authorities the logs of the holes they put down. As the search for groundwater is intensified, with the steadily increasing demand for potable water, it can be confidently anticipated that the practice of requiring the registration of all water-well logs with public authorities will be extended. It is, therefore, not too difficult to imagine the same procedure being followed in connection with test holes put down for ground exploration for construction work. In a general way, this might be difficult to implement because of the limited scale of such operations and the fact that they are carried out all over the continent. If the concept be restricted to test borings put down in cities, however, then the prospect becomes immediately a perfectly practicable proposition. This idea, therefore, exists as a distinct possibility for the future, but its implementation can be anticipated only when the general idea of having such an information service in every city has been accepted as an essential civic responsibility.

There is already available in most cities, however, another way of achieving the same result that is immediately available for use. It was explained earlier that the building official of every city has the responsibility for issuing permits for building, without which construction may not start. Correspondingly, when a building is finished, the same official will issue an occupancy permit, without which the building cannot legally be put into use. It would be a relatively easy matter to require that, before a building permit is issued, the owner or his representative must file with the building official a record of the subsurface exploration that was carried out for the building or structure in question. This is not at all a "revolutionary" suggestion, for it would merely be formalizing what is done already, at least to some extent. The building official must issue the building permit on the basis of the final contract plans for the structure. He must examine and approve these before issuing the permit. These drawings almost always show at least the logs of the main test borings and often much other subsurface information obtained as a result of the underground exploration program. The records are, therefore, already given to the building official, although not as separate documents and in a way that makes them appear as subsidiary to the main purpose of the plans, which is to show the structure that is to be built. It would merely make the subsurface information more convenient for use if it were to be submitted, with the contract drawings, as a quite separate submission that can then be passed on to the officer in charge of the city's subsurface collection of records.

In a corresponding way, occupancy permits are issued only after a final inspection of the building that will, naturally, have been under the general surveillance of the building official during the entire course of construction. In some building regulations it is stipulated that the building official must inspect and approve the foundation bed before any part of the foundation structure is placed in position. This will also be done by the representative of the designing engineer. The building official will, therefore, have seen all the excavation carried out and been enabled, if he so wishes, to examine in detail the materials encountered in excavation. There is, therefore, nothing "secret" about the final record that is prepared of the details of the foundation beds on which the finished structure rests so that the submission of a record of it to the civic authorities is merely a recording of what has been seen, even though— again—it can be of such very great use as a public rather than as a private record. Legislation would be required to ensure that subsurface records were thus given to the city at the time of the issue of building and occupancy permits, but this would be legislation within the competence of the city council to enact in almost all cases. Since it would be in the public interest with no detriment to private interests, it should not be difficult to achieve, once the need for such a public service has been generally recognized.

All information so obtained will have to be carefully coded, indexed, and filed in the office of the city engineer. The detailed information must be transferred to suitable maps. These maps will be available for other civic purposes, including land subdivision, so that the accurate location of all boreholes should be a matter of no difficulty. The three-dimensional aspect of the subsurface will always be kept in mind. In due course, cross sections through various parts of the city can be prepared. In conjunction with surface maps, these will begin to give the solid picture of the structure of the city's subsurface. Photographs will provide a helpful supplement to the graphical records. As numerous examples in practice have shown, the use of models can be a most useful supplement to drawings and photographs. They can be especially useful to those who have difficulty in appreciating the three-dimensional aspect of subsurface conditions. It is not suggested that the city itself should always go to the expense of preparing such models, unless they are necessary for the carrying out of civic works, but the city can be the custodian of subsurface models prepared to assist with the design of specific structures and then not wanted, and usually discarded, after such use. In attempting to get an illustration for this volume of a particularly interesting subsurface model of an unusually difficult and important building foundation, the author found that even within the space of the 10 years since construction, this particular model had disappeared and could not be traced. If such models were deposited with the city engineer, they will always be available for such further public service.

Once such a service as has been sketched here has been started, it will probably be surprising what additional information will be found. The use of archival material was mentioned on page 195. Local archives should, therefore, be consulted about what older material they may have that can be added to the city's store, when time permits. Useful information may be found with private citizens or independent consultants. The author knows of one consulting engineering office in which the small staff was kept busy during the bad days of the early thirties, as a means of keeping the nucleus of this fine organization together, in hunting up and plotting all the old records that could be found in their city showing original courses of the small watercourses that used to run into the larger ravines that still make this particular city so picturesque today. Quite apart from the salutary effect that work on this map had at the time, its value has been immeasurable in the assistance it has rendered in connection with local subsurface works, and especially in the planning of test-boring programs, by the clear indication it gives of the location of these old natural valleys now hidden beneath city streets. In almost every city there will be miscellaneous information of this kind about old ground surfaces or earlier excavations that, when assembled with modern records, can make a real contribution to the overall picture of the city's subsurface.

The program of collecting and coordinating local geological information that has here been sketched shows what every city can do with little effort and with a minimum of expenditure, expenditure that will be many times repaid by the practical use that can be made of the resulting records. In the opinion of the author, it is *what every city should do* just as soon as possible, in view of the rapid growth of almost all cities that was indicated at the outset of this volume. Many cities have made a good start, in various ways and through various agencies, at what is here suggested. Some examples will shortly be given. The program that has been described is what might be called the ideal approach, entirely practical though it be in application. In France (as will be seen shortly) a good start toward the ideal has already been made. If, therefore, one can look ahead a few years, it is possible to imagine all such city record systems interrelated and tied in with the national systems of geological information in which records of boreholes and their exact locations can be stored and retrieved when needed from a centrally located computer establishment.

Figure 9.2 illustrates what the necessary tabulation of subsurface information looks like when arranged for storing in an RAX (remote control access) system. This form was developed by Professor R. H. Grice of McGill University initially for local use in Montreal, but it is capable of development for wider use.[9.3] The province of Quebec through its Department of Natural Resources has developed a convenient system for storing and retrieving field information. Canada is building a national index for all geological data assembled on a national scale.[9.4] Geofond in Czechoslovakia has also made wide use of data-handling methods. If, as these methods develop, international agreement as to systems of recording can be achieved, the public interest will be well served indeed. Earnest efforts are being made in this direction.

9.4 GEOLOGICAL INTEREST IN LOCAL RECORDS

All that has been said so far has related to building and engineering work—the procurement of the records, their collation and filing in the office of the city engineer, and the use of these assembled records for the planning of future works within the city. It cannot be emphasized too strongly that even the best of such collections of records is still not geology. The records are naturally essential pieces of information, like the individual bricks in a building. It is only when they have all been correlated and assessed against what is known of the local geology that their contribution to geological knowledge can be realized. This is a task that requires experience in geology, and more particularly with the local geological conditions around a city, for its effective prosecution. Accordingly, the help of local geologists is not only desirable if such collections of subsurface records are to be fully utilized, it is quite essential.

If there is a university in or near the city, it will almost certainly have a department of geology as one of its basic science departments. Despite the wide coverage of academic geology, there is almost certain to be at least one or two members of the

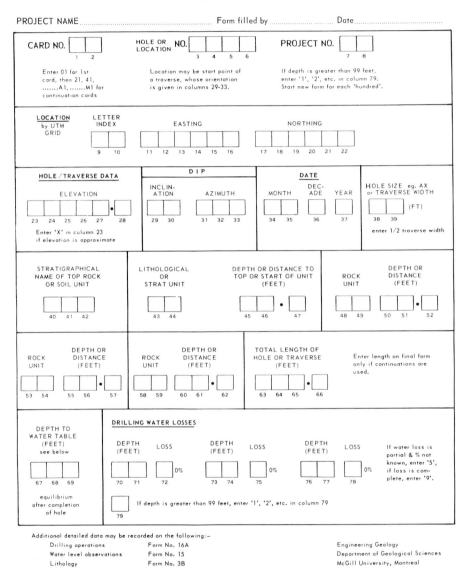

Figure 9.2 Master form for use in recording borehole records so that they may be stored in a computer system. *(Courtesy of R. H. Grice, McGill University, and the National Research Council of Canada.)*

staff who have interest in local ground conditions. In larger cities, there will usually be professional engineering geologists. If there is a museum in the city, it may also be expected to have someone with geological interest on its staff. Now that, at long last, the earth sciences are finally being recognized as essential subjects for high school curricula, there may be found high school teachers trained in geology who would welcome any association with records of the local subsurface. State and provincial governments all have divisions that are concerned with mining, and in these days this includes the mining of industrial minerals. These organizations, sometimes departments of mines, sometimes geological surveys, sometimes both, will frequently be found to have a lively interest in the geology beneath cities, with staff members having experience in this field of work. National geological surveys will also be found to be appreciative of the importance of urban geology and may, indeed, have staff members actually engaged on this type of work in specially selected municipal areas. National and state or provincial research organizations may also be found to have similar interest, either through geotechnical interests or involvement in assessments of industrial minerals. Finally, there is always the possibility that there may be private citizens who have a personal interest in the local geology, the "expert amateurs" who contribute so much to the scientific and cultural life of modern communities and whose interests and skills are all too often not widely appreciated.

In all cities, therefore, there should be a broad spectrum of interested geologists whose experience can be drawn upon for guidance in the development of the city's underground records and in ensuring that these are well known and are used by others than the engineers and contractors for whose primary interest they have been assembled. This can most usefully be done by the appointment of an advisory geological (or geotechnical) committee of geologists, engineers, and others interested to assist the city engineer with this special responsibility. The word "advisory" is essential to indicate clearly to the committee what its function is and to remove all possible misunderstanding as to its relation to normal civic administration. A group of this sort would not have to be called upon to meet very often, once it had been introduced to its task and had seen the information already assembled by the city. It could review the state of the records from time to time, be advised of any unusual conditions encountered either in boreholes or in excavation, and keep a watching eye, so to speak, on the gradually unfolding picture of the local geology presented by the accumulated records. Above all, however, it would be the means of ensuring that the records were maintained and developed in close association with the main features of the local geology.

The dual nature of this communication process will again be evident. An advisory committee of geologists and others interested would not only be able to advise the city engineer on the development of his record collection, with special reference to the local geology, but the members would be able to see how the records are aiding the developing pattern of knowledge regarding the local subsurface, often with regard to their own special scientific interests. Through the regular contacts that such a committee would provide with local excavation and tunneling work, members would know when any exposure of special geological interest was to become available. Arrangements could then be made, through the committee, for controlled visits of authorized persons to the work in question. Provided that such visits are arranged properly with the appropriate authorities, and that all visitors observe the necessary requirements on such visits (such as the invariable wearing of hard hats), there will usually be no difficulty in obtaining the necessary permission. The personal benefits thus to be gained need no elaboration. Nothing can replace the impression gained by actually standing in an excavation or tunnel and seeing in place the rock or soil that has previously had to be studied only by "remote control," such as through the medium of boring, sampling, or geophysical exploration. Block samples can be obtained, with permission, that will permit unique laboratory studies. If fossiliferous beds are encountered, specimens can sometimes be obtained that would never be available again.

This is no theoretical picture that has been painted. There have been many examples of such cooperation in advisory work, with most beneficial results. Reference to page 292 will show there a mention of an advisory committee established in connection with the geology that was exposed by the excavation of the Toronto subway. Its membership included men from the University of Toronto, the Royal Ontario Museum, the Ontario Department of Mines, the Ontario Research Foundation, the National Research Council, and the Toronto Transportation Commission (as it then was). Since the author was a member, he can testify to the usefulness of the discussions. It was a result of the deliberations of the committee that the commission was asked to donate the soil samples taken at 15-m intervals up the first (downtown) section of the subway to the Royal Ontario Museum, where they may now be inspected by anyone interested. The committee facilitated visits by interested geologists to the subway excavation. More than this, its existence helped to develop an appreciation of the importance of the geological profiles revealed by the subway excavation that has continued through all the extensions of the original section of this fine example of an urban rapid-transit system.

It is true that this was a committee advisory to a commission rather than directly to a city, but since the commission is a municipal enterprise and the cost of the subway was far above the total annual budget of many cities, the example is relevant. The committee's function was purely advisory, its findings being recommendations to the commission and to other bodies. In no way did it replace the professional work of those directly engaged on the TTC staff or as its consultants. It is thought that the work of the committee probably assisted this professional work, indirectly, but it in no way interfered with it. The committee had no executive responsibility at all, its operations depending on the keen interest and goodwill of its members. The subway construction could have proceeded almost as well without it, but it is doubtful if the fine series of resulting geological papers, which have added so much to knowledge of the geology of the Toronto region, would have appeared had there not been the stimulus that the advisory committee provided.

9.5 UNDERGROUND UTILITY RECORDS

Despite the example from practice that has just been given, perhaps some readers may still consider that this concept of a civic service in collecting, recording, and coordinating subsurface records is a rather theoretical concept. There is a close parallel in the records that have to be maintained of the various utility services that must be buried beneath city streets. Figure 9.3 is a good reminder of what can be uncovered when street surfacings are removed. Water mains must be installed under

Figure 9.3 New York City. Typical view of utility services revealed by excavation in the older streets of the city. *(Courtesy of J. J. Kassner, J. J. Kassner and Co., Inc., consulting engineers, New York.)*

every street of a modern city, as must also sewers, large and small. As the amenity of modern North American cities is steadily enhanced, "wires" must be taken off supporting poles and put underground in some way that is quite mysterious to the man on the street, except that he knows that it is a costly exercise. Telephone and power cables, therefore, are additional services that must be fitted into the limited space beneath urban roadways. Natural gas supply is now common to many cities, taking the place of the old town-gas supplies that are still to be found in some places. Underground pipes are the essential conveyors of this useful service. It is to be noted that each of these services is usually provided by a different organization. The list already given is still only a partial indication of the complexity of utility services that serve so well the needs of modern urban areas.

New York City constructed a new police headquarters building in the late sixties on a crowded site in lower Manhattan. The site involved the closing of sections of two streets, and so utilities were interfered with beyond those normally recorded between street lines. The consulting engineers for the relocation of these services started with a study of old records, finding that the site had been a portion of a collecting pond as early as 1783, into which a marshy area around had drained. The first sewer had been built across the site in 1847, followed by others in 1856, 1861, 1893, and 1910. Forty-four test pits had to be sunk in order to check on the buried utilities that were going to be affected. In the end, it was found that no less than 20

Figure 9.4 Toronto, Ontario, Canada. Utility services as revealed when the major city intersection of Queen and Yonge Streets was excavated in connection with the building of the first section of Toronto's subway, all services being found in the positions shown in the city's master plan of utilities. *(Courtesy of the Toronto Transit Commission, and W. H. Paterson, General Manager of Subway Construction.)*

different agencies had to be consulted, and their underground services correlated, before the site could be used for the new building. In addition to city and other agencies responsible for the utilities already mentioned (water, sewers, electric power, telephones, and gas), there were buried services for telegraphs, traffic signals, fire alarms and communications, police communications, and cable TV. There could have been more, such as tunnels for different purposes, including rapid transit and steam supply from central plants.[9.5]

This example is, admittedly, a rather special one since it involved services that were installed long before the era of modern and accurate subsurface utility records and below a site that, by North American standards, had been built on for a very long time. It serves to illustrate clearly, however, the problem faced by city authorities whenever major changes to underground services or important changes to roadway location or construction have to be made. The widespread public demand all over North America for the removal of disfiguring overhead wires makes the problem a pressing one. All readers will be familiar with the irritation caused by the tearing up of street surfaces, rerouting of automobile traffic at such times being one of the nightmares of a traffic department. The jibes about one division of the city not knowing what another division is doing are commonplace, even though thoughtful citizens must know that, despite the occasional duplication of street disruption, there lies behind all such work the most careful planning. Since so many agencies are involved, how can such work be properly coordinated? By exactly such a system as has been described as desirable for urban records of geological conditions beneath a city, the two cases being quite parallel but with the difference that utility services are generally confined to the routes of roads and streets, are most complex, and are always relatively close to the surface of the ground.

In almost every modern city there is today a well-established system for coordinating all buried utilities and for maintaining the most accurate records of their nature and location. This is achieved in a variety of ways, but essentially it is a sharing of information for mutual benefit, with one agency completely responsible for the maintenance of the essential underground records, even though all cooperating agencies will have copies. In the city of Philadelphia, for example, this coordinating function is carried out by the Board of Review, a working group coming under the City Planning Commission. The board consists of representatives of all utilities, the city Engineering Department, and the Federal Housing Authority. It meets twice a month and reviews all subdivision plans and proposed legislation affecting streets and highways. As plans approach the stage of implementation, all utility companies must gain clearance for the installation of their underground installations from the Municipal Board of Highway Supervisors. This board also meets semimonthly (an indication of the activity in this field). It maintains plans, drawn to a scale of 1 in. to 20 ft, showing the location and size of all underground utilities beneath city streets, including naturally the location of all manholes. This board acts as the coordinator, calling the attention of the

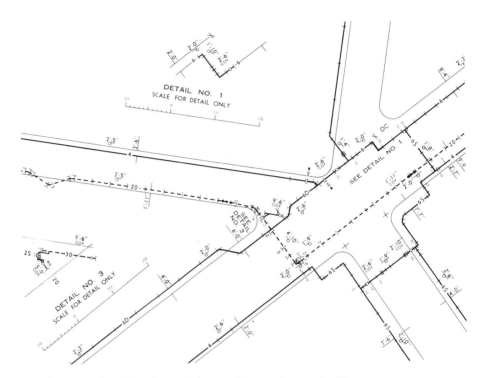

Figure 9.5 A small section of a typical map of one underground utility such as are maintained by most large cities for all utilities, jointly. *(Courtesy of H. C. Missimer, Philadelphia.)*

utilities to any plans for underground services that conflict. As an indication of the cooperation that develops in this sort of public service, in a period of over 40 years, the board has never had to act as an arbitrator between utilities wanting to place underground services in the same location.[9.6]

This example from the fourth largest city, and one of the oldest cities, of the United States shows what can be done to deal with what might at first sight appear to be an insuperable problem. The essentials of all such schemes are a complete sharing among all interested agencies of all information regarding underground services; the prompt recording of these on large-scale maps, the responsibility for the preparation of which rests definitely with one agency; if necessary, a sharing of costs for this service; and a spirit of cooperation so that each utility may provide its stated service efficiently and without interfering with parallel services. A general pattern for achieving these ends is to have a joint city-utilities committee with a rotating chairmanship, if only to indicate the complete cooperation on the part of all participants. All interested agencies must naturally be represented; the city will usually assume responsibility for the preparation of the record maps. These must naturally always be available for consultation by any agency and, indeed, by the public also. They can be of extreme value when bad fires occur in crowded downtown areas in particular and when other emergencies arise.

This is the system followed by the city of Ottawa, a city that has not yet reached a population of half a million. All construction carried out on streets within the city, except only for emergency measures, must be discussed and approved by the Underground Public Utilities Coordinating Committee. Nine agencies including the city and regional governments, are represented on the committee, the chairmanship of which rotates on an annual basis. The committee is responsible for the Central Registry of Utilities, which is operated by the city engineer for the committee at an annual cost of about $70,000 that is shared by the participants on an agreed-to basis.[9.7] The city of Toronto follows a similar system. Maps of underground utilities, prepared under authority of a joint committee, were used in the test-boring program that was mentioned on page 292. The accuracy of the maps was well demonstrated to the author when he stood with the drillers as they put down the critical hole mentioned on page 292. If such satisfactory results can be obtained by the central maintenance of records of buried utilities beneath city streets, records always available for public inspection, why cannot equally satisfactory results be obtained with records of subsurface geological information, certainly of equal importance in the development of cities?

9.6 SOME EXAMPLES

If any one city were chosen as an example and its geological subsurface records system described in any detail, invidious comparisons would be inevitable since so many cities have made a start in the direction already indicated, in various ways and through the medium of various agencies. If, on the other hand, brief details of a number of city underground information services were to be given, thus avoiding this danger of invidious comparison, the result would be a tedious recital of limited interest. As an alternative, a few major cities have been selected, each of which illustrates one of the aspects of this important civic service that have been discussed. Descriptions must necessarily be brief, but references are given so that further inquiry can be made by those who are specially interested in any one locality.

Boston, Massachusetts

The geology of the Boston district was touched upon when describing the foundation of the city (page 38) and later on in discussion of the use made of the exposure of rock in some of the city's major tunnels. It has been said, "Boston has probably been more completely probed, drilled, cored and investigated than any other American city." This reputation may well be regarded as a mark of geological distinction. The significance of these studies is shown by the fact that in the first issue of the

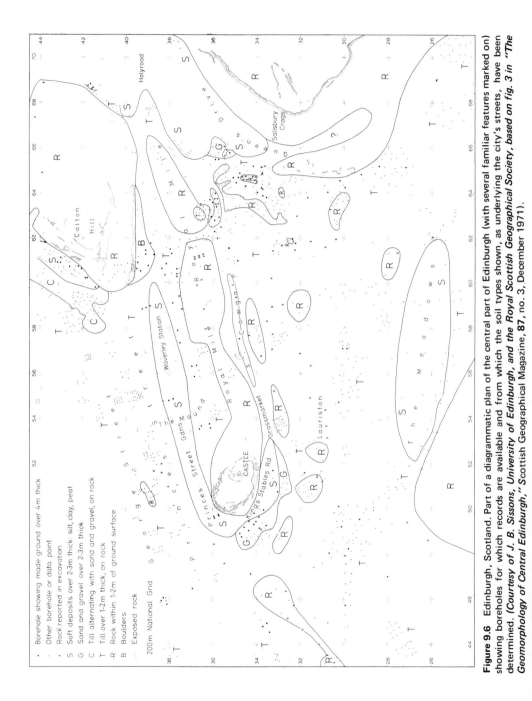

Figure 9.6 Edinburgh, Scotland. Part of a diagrammatic plan of the central part of Edinburgh (with several familiar features marked on) showing boreholes for which records are available and from which the soil types shown, as underlying the city's streets, have been determined. *(Courtesy of J. B. Sissons, University of Edinburgh, and the Royal Scottish Geographical Society, based on fig. 3 in "The Geomorphology of Central Edinburgh," Scottish Geographical Magazine, 87, no. 3, December 1971).*

first volume of the now well-known *Journal of the Boston Society of Civil Engineers*, published in January 1914, there appears a paper on "Boston Foundations," by J. R. Worcester, a noted engineer of that time.[9.8] It recorded details of some of the test borings already put down within the city of Boston. This was the start of a remarkable policy of publishing borehole records followed by this oldest of engineering societies in the United States.

A Committee on Subsoils of Boston was established in 1920; it published its first report in the society's journal for September 1931, and then stated its purpose as "to gather data regarding the character of the subsoils in Boston and adjacent areas, and to present it to the society in such form as to add to the general knowledge and to make it available for reference to any who may wish to get a clear idea of the geological construction of this city."[9.9] In the same report the committee stated that it "has also made a study of definition of various soils to be used for foundation purposes in our locality and desires to make constructive changes. . . ." It is not without significance that Dr. Terzaghi, founder of the science of soil mechanics, started his great work in North America in the Boston area (at MIT in adjacent Cambridge) and continued his great contributions while on the staff of Harvard University, making his home at Winchester, another of the communities adjacent to Boston. There has been, therefore, a long tradition of attention to soil and foundation conditions in the Boston area, a tradition still being followed today through cooperation between practicing engineers, experts in soil mechanics, geophysicists, and geologists.

Extensive compilations of boring records were published in the same journal in September 1931, with the committee's first report, and again in 1949, 1950, and 1951. The committee picked up its work again in 1967 and published (with financial support from about 50 contributors) another extensive set of records in 1969. In this last report they were assisted by the U.S. Geological Survey through Dr. Clifford Kaye, who has been engaged for some years on a detailed study of the geology of the Boston Area, as one of about a dozen urban areas selected for such intensive study by the Engineering Geology Branch of the Survey. All subsurface records are being critically examined; some are naturally found to be of doubtful value, but the records of over 10,000 borings were used for the preparation of the first USGS map of the area, covering 3,885 hectares. In addition to the more general maps, which were also used by the BSCE Committee, the Survey is preparing more detailed maps to a scale of 1:6,000. Each map will really consist of several sheets, showing, respectively, the underlying bedrock, the older glacial drift deposits, the two main clay strata, and more recent deposits of sand, gravel, and postglacial estuarine deposits. Results of soil tests will be associated with the maps so as to give the most complete picture possible of the local geological conditions. As is so often the case, the work has already yielded unexpected byproducts, in that (old) "culverts to drain swamps and springs, and wharf-like structures at the old shore line, have been unearthed and recorded in the course of geologic mapping [adding] . . . yet another chapter to the already rich historical records of Boston."[9.10]

London, England

Because the city of London has a continuous history going back to Roman times, with some examples of Roman building still to be seen, it might be thought that here is a city for which modern subsurface records would be few and far between. Exactly the reverse is the case, the subsurface of London being as well known as that of any other large city, its subsurface records so conveniently published that they can well serve as another example to be considered and possibly copied if local circumstances are suitable. London is fortunate in always having been the location of the head-quarters of the Geological Survey of England, now the Institute of Geological Sciences. Under the terms of the Mining Industry Act of 1926 and the Water Act of 1945, advance notice has had to be given to the Survey before any boreholes could be put down or shafts for mining started; complete records must be lodged with the Survey, and free access to the boring or mining operations granted to officers of the Survey. Although there is not yet any corresponding legislation with regard to test borings for building purposes, the same satisfactory result is generally obtained on a voluntary basis, supported as this cooperation has been by official commendation from the Ministry of Housing and Local Government in 1962.

The notice circulated to all local authorities (municipalities), joint water boards, and statutory water companies in England and Wales, on 6 April 1962, over the signature of the Assistant Secretary to the Ministry (J. Catlow), is so concise a statement of the desirability of such a service as is herein being discussed that it may usefully be quoted *in extenso* (Crown Copyright: reproduced by permission of the Ministry):

> The Minister thinks that local authorities and statutory water undertakers will often be able to provide information [for assisting the Geological Survey] from trial boreholes sunk in connection with the larger building projects which they undertake, such as tall flats, schools, town halls, swimming baths, mineral investigations and, in the case of water undertakings, dams and impounding reservoirs. The information sought by the Geological Survey is: (i) an exact 6" plan-reference showing the site or sites of the boreholes; (ii) details and depth of deposits encountered in the boreholes; (iii) date of the borehole. The Survey would welcome notification of any borehole in progress and, on occasion, permission for their officers to examine material brought up. If they are able to help with geological interpretation of any particular borehole, they would be willing to do so. The Minister asks local authorities and water undertakers to assist the Geological Survey to the fullest extent in this matter. In providing information about strata encountered in boreholes they will be helping to add to the value of advice given by the Survey."[9.11]

What a fine public service it would be if every "senior government" could issue a similar request.

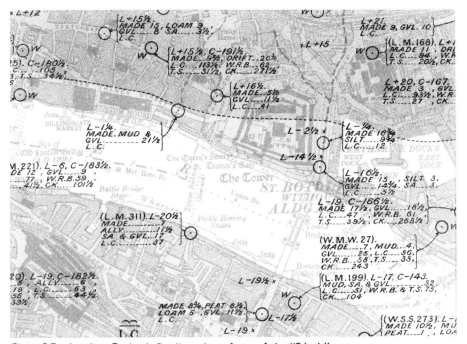

Figure 9.7 London, England. Small section of one of the "6-inch" map sheets covering Greater London, with boreholes marked on and using the following notations: *L* - height or depth in feet of London clay (surface) above or below ordnance datum; *W* - depth in feet of Woolwich and Reading beds (surface) below ordnance datum; *C* - depth in feet of Chalk (surface) below ordnance datum; together with other recognizable abbreviations, the top set of letters usually being an identification of source of the information. *(Courtesy of the Director, Institute of Geological Sciences, London.)*

The result of utilizing all the records obtained in this way, under the terms of the two acts noted and by voluntary submission, has been an accumulation for the London area of well over 10,000 well and borehole records. Some of these have been used by the authors of the many notable geological reports issued by the Survey on different aspects of the geology of the London area. They have also been plotted on a remarkable series of 42 maps, first issued in the thirties, covering about 63,000 hectares, each map being the convenient size of 45 by 30 cm, and all drawn to a scale of 6 in. to 1 mile (or about 1:10,000). The location of each borehole is shown, and for each borehole the levels of the surfaces of the London clay and the Chalk relative to Ordnance Datum, as well as depths of overlying materials such as made ground, sand, and gravel. For each location, it is therefore possible to obtain the depth to the surface of the Chalk, the thickness of the London clay, and the amount of overlying material that will be encountered in any excavation work undertaken in the Greater London area. "Blue lines are used to indicate the approximate courses of the smaller streams and 'Old Rivers' of London which in many cases are built over or otherwise hidden from sight. Serious trouble has been caused in the foundations of buildings, in sewers, drains etc., by such streams and their alluvial deposits, and for these reasons it has been thought necessary to indicate their distribution." This is part of the general guidance and advice given on the maps themselves and in an accompanying explanatory leaflet.[9.12] The fact that so many records and associated information have been contributed voluntarily to the Survey by those who have used the Survey's facilities for the pooling of records and for inquiries on geological advice is, clearly, the best of all tributes to the excellent service that has thus been provided for all who have to build in the Greater London area.

Zurich, Switzerland

All the main cities of Switzerland now maintain central files of information on the subsurface conditions beneath their streets, following the early lead of the city of Zurich. In the late thirties a start was made at assembling records of test borings, excavations, etc., in Zurich under the enthusiastic leadership of an interested geologist, Dr. Armin von Moos. The card index thus started was housed in the Research Institute for Earthwork Engineering of the Swiss Federal Institute of Technology (Eidgenossische Technische Hochschule), which is made up of the Hydraulic Research Institute and the Geotechnical Laboratory. All records were related to their position on the excellent basic map of the city, on a scale of 1:5,000. Many were donated by private engineering and construction organizations. The records included photographs and, naturally, copies of all available geological publications dealing with Zurich.

With this modest start, as has been the case with a few other cities, there has now been developed a citywide system of recording all new subsurface information within the limits of the city of Zurich. Maintained by the office Baugrund Daten of the city administration, this excellent assembly of local geological information is greatly aided by the mandatory submission of all boring records obtained in Zurich to the city. The same, or a similar, system is in use in other Swiss localities, such as the Canton of Zurich, the larger administrative unit in which the city is located. There has now been started also a comparable subsurface recording system, still however on a voluntary basis, at the national level. This is known as the Schweizerische Sammelstelle Geologischer Dokumente. It might be thought that, because of the relatively small size of Switzerland, its practice in this matter would not be relevant elsewhere. In this, however, as in so many other activities, there is much to be learned by others from the Swiss approach, experience with which is generally shared.[9.13]

Prague, Czechoslovakia

The city of Prague is located in an area of great geological complexity, and so its development ever since the Middle Ages has been profoundly influenced by its subsurface conditions. The bedrock of the urban area consists of Ordovician folded shales and quartzites. Paleozoic rocks are overlain by Cretaceous sandstones and marls that form the flat-topped hills that surround the central park of the city. The greatest part of the urban area is covered with Quaternary surface deposits, terrace gravels, and strata of loess. Man's activities have contributed to the local subsurface complexity since excavations, demolitions, and the deposition of man-made fills through its thousand years of history have so complicated underground conditions that it is, in some places, difficult to ascertain the original relief of the land.

A complete review of the geological conditions underlying the central part of the city was published in 1948 as *Geologický Podklad a Základové Poměry Vnitřní Prahy* (Geologic Features and Foundation Conditions of the City of Prague). This is an 80-page synthesis (with an excellent English summary) of the personal observations of the author, Dr. Q. Zaruba, through a period of almost 30 years, combined with a critical assessment of previous literature about the city's subsurface, the first paper on the subject appearing in 1905.[9.14] A map to a scale of 1:12,500 accompanies the paper, as do some excellent geological sections illustrating the geological structure beneath the city as deduced from critical study of the borings. One of the sections is reproduced as Fig. 9.8.

Since the end of the Second World War a new map of foundation conditions within the city has been developed under the sponsorship of the Board of Town Planning. It is on a scale of 1:5,000, and it serves as a basis for new regulation plans and for the planning of new districts of the city. The map, which is constantly being improved and expanded, is also available for consultation by interested citizens. Investigation of new building sites is usually carried out by the (Czechoslovak) Institute of Engineering Geology. The results of this investigation work, and of all other subsurface exploration, must be filed with the central Geological Institute of Prague. The index, known as Geofond, is maintained by the Institute, the location of all records being plotted on a 1:5,000 map and coded with their registration numbers. Gradually, therefore, a very detailed picture of the underground conditions beneath this ancient and beautiful city is being obtained. This will be greatly enhanced as a result of the information to be gained from the construction of the new subway system for the city.

Moscow, U.S.S.R.

Almost all subsurface investigations within the area of the great city of Moscow, with its more than 5 million inhabitants, is carried out by the one organization known as Mosgorgeotrest, which is completely equipped for all types of underground exploration and testing. Test drilling is often carried out to a depth of 40 m, but average investigations go usually down to 15 m. The instructions followed by Mosgorgeotrest in its work have been published and are available to anyone interested through government bookstores. This interesting and useful document has been translated by the National Research Council of Canada, and so it can be studied in English by those

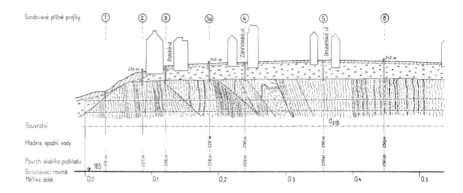

Figure 9.8 Prague, Czechoslovakia. Diagrammatic geological cross section through the city of Prague. *(Courtesy of Q. Zaruba, Prague, based on fig. 2 in reference 3.57.)*

interested in comparing their own procedures with those followed within the Soviet Union.[9.15] The coverage in this 96-page document is remarkably complete. It can well serve as a useful "checklist" for anyone embarking upon this type of investigation for the first time. The details required from subsurface studies within cities, first for overall planning and then in more detail for individual buildings and special structures, as also for studies beneath existing buildings, occupy the last third of the volume. Typical is the Construction Site Registration Document that must be completed for each building operation. Five copies are required—for the builder, the planning organization, the construction organization, Gosarkhstroikontrol' (the State Control for Architecture and Construction Engineering), and for the chief municipal architect. The first two-thirds of the volume gives interesting summary requirements for the prosecution of engineering-geological work in all types of areas, including those underlain by permafrost, this being one special type of terrain that the Soviet Union shares with Canada and Alaska, a large portion of all three geographic areas being perennially frozen beneath the ground surface.

Tokyo, Japan

The frequent references to Japanese cities, and especially to Tokyo, in earlier sections of this volume is an indication of the difficult subsurface conditions with which Japanese architects, engineers, and planners have to contend in the development of their fast-growing cities. It is not surprising, therefore, to find that Japan has made great strides in the development of comprehensive reports on urban geological conditions, providing yet a further example of what other cities can do if their own local circumstances are appropriate. This work started in Tokyo. The heavily developed area around Tokyo Bay includes hills and ridges rising to about 30 m above

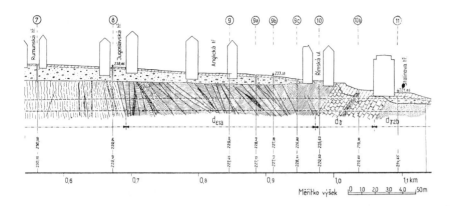

sea level that are partially formed of the Kwanto loam. Between these elevated areas
are wide alluvial plains running down to the sea, the recent alluvial deposits overlying,
usually, the extensive Tokyo beds (Upper and Lower), which consist generally of
alternating sand and gravel strata with some silt layers. These are the beds that have to
be used for many foundations and that create serious problems. In turn, they overlie
Tertiary beds of more competence.

Starting in the early fifties, Dr. Yorihiko Ohsaki, of the Building Research
Institute of Japan, began collecting all the boring records he could find for the
central Tokyo area with the strong support of his director, Dr. Kenzaburo Takeyama.
When over 3,400 records had been assembled, the general results that they presented
after careful study were incorporated into a "Subsoil Map of Tokyo," and this was
published in 1959. This map was published as a supplement to a bound volume,
which contains the logs of all borings, printed in color, a set of double-page maps of
the 32 quadrangles into which the Tokyo area was subdivided on which the locations
of all borings are shown, the map (to a scale of 1:50,000) and vivid geological cross
sections being folded supplements contained in a pocket in the back of the book.
The result is one of the most beautiful engineering-geological volumes that the author
has ever been privileged to see. Even though the text is (naturally) written in Japanese,
the volume is so well produced that its contents can readily be followed and its purpose
fully appreciated even without a working knowledge of the Japanese language.[9.16]

This notable work showed what could be done in thus presenting for public
use a collection of subsurface records for a great urban area, even though initiated
individually and with no guides available as to format. Dr. Takeyama therefore
approached the Japanese Resources Council, who, in turn, made a submission in
October 1957 to the Government of Japan recommending the promotion of a plan
for ground investigation in city areas. The council recommended that (1) a powerful

organization should be established through which the formation and the nature of the ground in every important city should be investigated and ground maps with explanations should be prepared; and (2) the organization should maintain information about the ground beneath cities and take the necessary steps by which this information could be used widely and generally. The submission was favorably considered, with the result that the Ministry of Construction appointed a Special Committee for Ground Investigation in Cities, which had prepared and published by July 1960 a set of "Instructions for Collection and Arrangement of Pre-existing Materials" and also a "Standard Specification for Ground Investigation Works in Cities." These documents have not been translated into English, but they are comprehensive treatments of the two subjects, illustrated as necessary and with typical forms and legends for use in compiling the records of subsurface information. Eight main regions were selected by this national committee for the initial investigations. The speed with which this new major project was attacked is indicated by the fact that by 1963 there were available, in English as well as in Japanese, full accounts of the findings for the first three of the districts selected. Financing was arranged on a 50-50 basis, the National Government paying one half of the costs, the prefectural or municipal government the other half.

In order to illustrate the thoroughness with which this work was done even in its initial stages, the following are the studies made for the northern coastal region of the Bay of Ise: collecting existing boring records, sinking of 11 new borings, electrical prospecting, testing of soil samples from the new borings, geological surveying and associated micropaleontological surveying, observing microtremors in association with national earthquake studies, correlating all this information and the preparation of the resulting ground maps. Appreciation of the importance of subsurface information for urban development is, therefore, well established in all major Japanese cities. Since so much has been published, in English, with great courtesy, it is possible to gain the advantage of sharing the experience of Japanese authorities in developing this nationwide series of invaluable geological records.[9.17]

Johannesburg, South Africa

Brief mention must be made of the start that has been made at assembling subsurface information under civic auspices by another city that has already been mentioned, Johannesburg in South Africa. Local soils include both transported and (underlying) residual soils derived from a variety of bedrock types, as noted in Chap. 3. (See Table 9.1.) The presence of old mine workings within the city limits was noted in Chap. 8, when the ingenious design for the new limited access highway over this part of the city was described. There are, therefore, many geological problems to be faced in this relatively young but rapidly growing city so that it is not surprising that only recently has a start been made at assembling subsurface information obtained as the city has grown. Again, individual effort featured the start of this local interest. Mr. J. de Beer took as the subject of a master's thesis at the University of Witwatersrand

TABLE 9.1
Summary of Geological and Soil Conditions in Johannesburg. (Prepared originally by D. Brigg and revised by A. B. A. Brink; courtesy of the workers cited in text and of the city engineer.)

1. Transported Soils

Generally limited in depth and extent in Johannesburg. Two problems (both peculiar to partly saturated soils) are of sufficient interest to warrant mention:
(a) Lower-lying areas are sometimes underlain by expansive clays.
(b) Sandy hillwash-derived soils often exhibit the phenomenon of collapse of grain structure on wetting and/or loading.

2. Residual Soil Profiles

Deeply weathered residual soil profiles are common. These are tabulated below according to geological origin:

Parent Geological Formation	Approximate Age	Lithology	Extent in Johannesburg	Remarks on Engineering Properties/Problems
Primitive systems	Archean >3,200 m.y.	Assorted metamorphic rocks; chiefly schists and phyllites	Restricted to small area in northeast	Residual soils often expansive but usually shallow (commonly less than 1.53 m)
Basement granite	Proterozoic 3,200 m.y.	Mainly coarse-grained granite-gneiss	Underlies most of the northern suburbs	Collapsible grain structure exhibited on remnants of old erosion surfaces at elevations above 1,525 m above sea level
Witwatersrand system	Proterozoic 2,800 m.y.	Sedimentary succession of quartzites and shales, and bands of auriferous conglomerates. Dips south at ±40–60°. Extensively intruded by diabase dikes and sills	Central city and large areas of southern suburbs	Conglomerates are the source of South Africa's gold. Shales are in many cases deeply weathered (±21.4 m). Diabase intrusions nearly all deeply weathered (±36.6 m) to highly compressible soils
Ventersdorp system	Proterozoic 2,300 m.y.	Amygdaloidal andesite lavas, with minor basal sediments	Fairly extensive band in southern areas, with lava-filled graben running east-west in central area	Deeply weathered (<48.8 m) to compressible soils in graben of central area. Southern area weathering is shallow, but the resulting residual soil is often expansive, causing difficulties with house foundations
Transvaal system	Proterozoic 2,000 m.y.	Thin basal quartzite, overlain by thick beds of dolomitic limestone with subsidiary chert bands	Large area in extreme south	Caverns form in dolomite: these can in some cases give rise to sudden catastrophic sinkholes and very large surface subsidences. This has been very troublesome just west of Johannesburg but limited in Johannesburg as yet

3. Foundation Problems Related to Mining

Johannesburg owes its existence to extensive gold mining, and environment disturbance on such a scale is bound to cause many problems. Those pertinent to soil engineering are, briefly:
(a) Fairly large areas are undermined, some at very shallow depth. Appreciable surface movements occur in these areas.
(b) Earth tremors related to rock falls cause minor disturbance such as plaster cracking.
(c) Mine-waste dumps cover appreciable areas; many are close to the city center. Founding structures on such dumps has proved difficult and expensive. Problems of slope stability have also arisen. On the credit side, such dumps provide sources of easily compacted material for road-building, and are the sole local source of road and concrete stone.

the preparation of a detailed geological and soil map for the Johannesburg city area. He was guided by Prof. T. W. Gevers and Mr. A. B. A. Brink in geological matters and by Professor J. E. Jennings in relation to soil mechanics and foundations. He was able to prepare 200 representative detailed soil profiles and to have access to the subsurface records in the offices of 40 organizations that had worked in the city— government and provincial departments, consultants, contractors, and piling companies. With this information he was able to prepare an engineering-geological map of the central city area to a scale of 1:5,000. The locations of all the soil profiles are shown on this notable map, the value of which is clearly indicated by the fact that the city council arranged for the color printing of the map, copies being sold to engineers, contractors, and others interested.

The map was published in 1965, but before this, from about 1960, the city engineer had been collecting local records of subsurface conditions as a result of voluntary contributions of this information, following an appeal by the city council directed especially to consulting engineers. This collection constituted naturally some of the information used in the preparation of the city map. It has always been publicly available, but shortage of personnel prevented any further development of a central storage and filing system. Early in 1970, however, a special committee was established by the Johannesburg Branch of the South African Institution of Civil Engineers, with the assistant city engineer as chairman, to look into the possibility of establishing and operating a soil parameter and profile bank. A pilot study was initiated late in 1970 to assess the availability and standard of geological information from beneath the city accumulated since 1965. Further studies are in progress, and these may possibly show the feasibility of establishing an effective subsurface-information storage and retrieval system. This has already been done for highway materials in South Africa by the National Institute for Road Research. It will be, if and when established, an example of the idea generally outlined on page 505. Mr. Brink is currently at work on a comprehensive volume describing the engineering geology of the Johannesburg area. The further development of this pioneering work will be watched with interest by all who are concerned with the need for such information about local geological conditions for urban planning as well as for the execution of plans in actual construction projects.[9.18]

Edmonton, Alberta

In addition to what these large urban centers throughout the world are doing with regard to the records of their geological conditions, the situation in Edmonton, Alberta, Canada, may usefully be noted, especially since reference has already been made to the extensive tunnel system that already exists beneath this city and to the problems of planning river-bank development for the University of Alberta. The city is built upon Pleistocene soil deposits of variable thickness underlain by Cretaceous shale, sandstone, and coal. The late Pleistocene deposits consist of well-sorted preglacial sands and gravels, glacial till, and postglacial lake sediments. Depths to bedrock vary up to 36 m and to the till surface up to 9.6 m. The engineering properties of the soils encountered beneath Edmonton exhibit marked variations due to compositional and textural differences. The surficial deposits generally increase in thickness toward the northern part of the city, due to the relief developed on the bedrock surface.

The very rapid development of the city and the erection of an increasing number of multistory buildings in the downtown area in the sixties directed attention to the need for general information on subsurface conditions to supplement the detailed investigations at individual building sites. The Alberta Research Council is concerned with industrial mineral and allied problems within the province. It therefore embarked upon a joint program with the city of Edmonton in 1965. The few available geological reports were carefully studied, the most relevant being a comprehensive report on the surficial deposits of the Edmonton district, excluding the city, published in 1962. A special drilling program was then carried out. Forty-two holes were put down along carefully selected lines, to a total depth of 1,500 m, generally taken to bedrock, soil samples being obtained and groundwater observations made. Logs of existing wells were examined and observations made on existing outcrops and in new excavations. The results were summarized in a 30-page report that gives a general description of the subsurface, logs of all the special holes, and five generalized cross sections along the drilled lines, giving a good general idea of the underlying geology.[9.19] The modest character of this project almost conceals its great value to all who have to build in downtown Edmonton. It can serve as an excellent example of what growing cities can achieve with a minimum of expenditure of money and effort but with the devoted efforts of interested and expert workers.

France

The examples so far given have all been individual cities, some very large and some including large areas around the cities proper. The example of Tokyo showed how activity in correlating subsurface information for the one city led to development of interest on the part of the national government and to its direction of and financial assistance to other Japanese cities following the example of Tokyo. There has been left to the last of this short selection the case of France, for here a national system has been developed serving all the municipalities of that country. To those who do not have the pleasure of knowing France, it may be thought that this arrangement could easily be developed for such a compact and "small" country. It must therefore be pointed out that France is 3½ times the size of England and Wales and only about 20 percent smaller in area than the state of Texas, its total area of 55 million hectares making it the largest of all the continental European countries. Yet despite its size and the diversity of its regions and cities, France has been able to develop a national system for collecting and recording subsurface information beneath all its cities and elsewhere.

This work is carried out within an organization known as the Bureau de Recherches Géologiques et Minières, now established in its own attractive quarters in a small estate at Orléans, 112 km to the south of Paris. BRGM, as it is now widely known, was established in November 1959 through the amalgamation of the existing Bureau de Recherches Géologiques et Geophysiques and three other bureaus concerned with different aspects of mining, the first-named having been in existence since 1942. A letter from the Minister of Industry written at the end of 1965 delineated the exact functions of the bureau, the first of which is "assurer l'infrastructure géologique du territoire national, en collaboration notamment avec les établissements d'enseignement et autres organismes francais de recherche géologique." A decree passed at the end of 1967 further defined the work of the bureau, giving it jurisdiction over the continental shelf off the French coasts. The work of the bureau was centered for the first time at the end of 1969 in a fine group of buildings constructed in an estate of 30 hectares in the department of Loiret close to the city of Orléans.

The Centre Scientifique et Technique d'Orléans-La Source is now the headquarters address of this organization. Here a staff of about 350 work, but their activities are supplemented by the work of 11 regional services employing a further 250 workers, of whom more than one-third (as with the Orléans staff) are professionals. For the regional services, France is divided into 11 geographical regions starting with Region A—Nord Pas-de-Calais. Region C is the Bassin de Paris, the borders of the regions being the borders of groups of departments. One of the principal functions of the 11 regional offices is to "rassembler la documentation sur le sous-sol métropolitain, et a mettre cette documentation en valeur en réalisant des synthèses parmi lesquelles la cartographie géologique tient une place importante." It will be seen that this is exactly the type of service that has been suggested as necessary for every city. It is, therefore, to the regional offices that advice of all proposed boring and excavation programs must be reported, 15 days in advance of the start of work if the anticipated depth is not to exceed 50 m, and 60 days in advance for depths greater than this. Under the Code Minier the staff of BRGM, may have access to the work at all times and may examine samples, etc. Records of the subsurface as determined by the works must be lodged with the bureau. There is naturally a period (up to 10 years) during which subsurface information that must be kept secret is held confidentially, this requirement being naturally of importance in mining exploration. There are reasonable provisions for waiving or reducing the period of secrecy.[9.20]

There is, therefore, for the whole of France an excellent scheme for the collecting, recording, and assessing of all information obtained about geological conditions through test-boring and excavation work in addition to the similar requirements, common to many countries, for such an activity in connection with drilling and exploring for oil and gas. The special service in connection with all foundations in those parts of Paris that are underlain by the old limestone and gypsum quarries (see page 340) is a special supplementary office, but within the same ministry of the French government. In this brief note it has been possible to indicate only the general nature of this service, but it will be clear that it does provide a remarkable example of what can be done in the direction indicated in this chapter when such a service can be considered on a national scale.

In countries throughout the world today, and especially in North America, such a logical extension of a local service to the national scene would be difficult to implement. Accordingly, a more general pattern is for this subsurface information service to be established at the local, municipal, level. The examples cited have shown a number of ways in which the desired results can be achieved, although not one case is identical with the ideal arrangement presented on page 504, i.e., as a public service provided by the municipality through the office of the city engineer. Some difficulties in the way of implementing such a service, clearly of such value as shown by the different ways in which it has already been achieved in major cities, will now be reviewed.

9.7 SOME OBJECTIONS TO BE OVERCOME

With such excellent examples now available from around the world of the collecting, recording, and assessing of subsurface information from beneath cities and its public availability, and with innumerable examples of the vital importance of geology in all aspects of urban planning and city development, why is it that such a system does not exist in an already well-developed state in all cities? Although the answer to this question must always be a local one for each individual city, an answer influenced always by special local circumstances, it is possible to suggest some of the general factors that have militated against the provision of this service. In view of the urgent need for the start of these services in all cities, large and small, it may be helpful if some of the objections that one hears stated are briefly listed—not in any critical sense, for all are understandable to a degree, but in the hope that the mere listing of these misconceptions and misunderstandings will be helpful to those who are inspired to do something about the matter in their own home city. Each of the points to be raised could be discussed at length, but only brief comment should be necessary in view of all the foregoing illustrative material.

Responsibility. It is sometimes suggested, quite seriously, that if a municipality does collect subsurface information and make it available for public use, this implies some sort of responsibility for its accuracy, with possible claims against the city if the information is found to be inaccurate or is improperly used. To many readers such a suggestion will be thought to border on the absurd, but there is at least one city in which this point of view has prevailed. Why exactly the same sort of argument should not be used to halt all land-survey recording, all subsurface utility recording, and many other regular municipal services is an unsolved mystery. Possibly the idea of treating subsurface geological information in the same way as other factual information necessary for urban planning and development is so new that the similarity of this service to many existing services has not yet been appreciated. In answer it can be pointed out that the provision of this civic service is not intended to replace individual professional examination of each building site but rather to increase the efficiency of such private endeavors by providing the general geological framework while giving city officials an invaluable overall view of the geology of their city for control purposes, for planning, and for assisting with their own underground works; that the use by the public of all subsurface records can be so clearly provided on the basis of the city's not guaranteeing the information but rather making it available as a convenience; and that any possible risk of a complaint being registered, a complaint that should have no legal validity, will be far more than repaid by the benefits that the service will confer on the whole city.

Privacy. An equally unusual suggestion is that information obtained by test borings put down for foundation exploration is the private property of those who pay for the borings and so cannot be made available for public use. If there are readers who think that this is ridiculous, the author can testify from his own experience of a large engineering firm that took this view and held to it, impeding (although not seriously) studies of the geology of an important Canadian city. It has already been explained that such records from boreholes put down for gas and oil exploration, and in many areas those put down in the search for water, must legally be lodged with a public authority and made available for public consultation, always with due safeguards for the confidential character of the information for a relatively short initial period. If this can be done for such critical borehole information as that obtained in the highly competitive search for natural petroleum products, there would seem to be no good reason at all for withholding information obtained in foundation studies. If construction is proceeded with on a site that has been drilled, the excavation itself will reveal far more than the preliminary boreholes and this can readily be seen by anyone interested. What makes this particular objection so weak is that those who do not wish to disclose the results of their borings were in all probability aided in the planning of their own boring program by the general information available from adjacent sites that had been made available to them. It is an objection that, almost certainly, will disappear as the general concept of knowing what lies beneath a city comes to be generally accepted.

Unwillingness. Much more substantial is the suggestion that cities are already doing enough to serve the public and that any subsurface information service is just one more task that an already overburdened civic administration is unwilling to shoulder. It is an undoubted fact that the demands upon civic administrations are constantly growing, but this is inevitable with the physical growth of cities, the increasing complexity of modern buildings, and the services that the "affluent society" has led the average citizen to expect. It is, however, impossible to turn back the hands of the clock or, as Charles Lamb put it more poetically over 150 years ago: "Can we unlearn the arts that pretend to civilize and then burn the world? There is a march to science; but who shall beat the drum of its retreat?" Who, indeed? These advances must be accepted and priorities determined among the many new and pressing claims upon city coffers and available manpower. It is here that the facts of the case must be brought to bear on determinations of priority, facts such as it has been the purpose of this volume to provide. If the cities of the future, if the expansion of the cities of today, and if the rebuilding of outmoded parts of older city areas are to be well planned and safely built, then it is essential that the geological conditions of the areas to be built upon shall be known with accuracy and with certainty. It is difficult to imagine any service with a higher claim to priority than this, especially since the cost in money and man-hours is so small.

Not a civic responsibility. If the importance of the service is granted and its essential priority admitted, another argument is sometimes heard—that such a service is not a civic responsibility but should be undertaken by some other body. It is perfectly natural for those charged with the direction of city services to seek to avoid assuming any more responsibilities if anyone else can be found to do the job that is admitted to be desirable or even essential. Examples cited give some support for this view. London has had the great advantage of the continuing interest of the Geological Survey with its headquarters in the city. French cities have had the service provided for them by their own national organization. Edmonton has the advantage of being the headquarters of the Alberta Research Council, which has a lively interest in all the geology of Alberta and, so, that underlying its own city. These can all be regarded as special cases. Japan points the way to a pattern that might well be widely copied, the initial inspiration having come from individual professional interest, taken up, supported, and guided by a national organization in association with individual cities on a cost-sharing basis in the initial phase. When a project has been well started, however, it cannot be gainsaid that the major benefit of the resulting coordinated information will be to the city itself so that convenience will be served, efficiency assured, and costs allocated appropriately if the service is maintained directly by the city, possibly with some financial support from senior government or from specially interested national agencies such as geological surveys. The fact that every city is responsible for the granting of all approvals for all building within its boundaries gives to each city a specific public responsibility for seeing to it that all such building is well and safely done, while at the same time giving to the city a degree of control over relevant information that, as already explained, can make the procurement of the necessary information a relatively easy and convenient matter. That the provision of a subsurface information system is ultimately a civic responsibility cannot really be questioned, but if the operation can be shared to a degree, while remaining under civic authority, possibly with some sharing of costs, a singularly satisfactory arrangement can result.

Cost. The cost of the service being advocated is naturally the final, and in the eyes of those who make it, the final and absolute, objection. The city has got on all right up to now without such a service; why burden the taxpayers with this additional uncalled-for expense? So runs the familiar argument, applied so often to needed municipal or governmental services. It is a good and sound argument, to a degree, and one that should always be posed, since unless a new service can be shown to be truly economically and socially essential, then it can rightly be questioned.

Cities all over the world have indeed developed to their present stages in most cases without anything like such a service as is now being considered—but at what extra cost, with what waste of manpower, and, in some cases, with what subsequent difficulties because the necessary subsurface information was not available in advance of planning or of construction? It is impossible to imagine what this loss has been, what more could have been done, and what improvements in city development might have been achieved if only good subsurface information had been more generally available. It requires only a leafing through the pages of a book such as this to show all too many examples of troubles, or inefficiencies, that could have been avoided had there been some means available of collating information already available about underground conditions within city boundaries. Housing developments built on old fills; sewer installations called for in design but impossible to construct without the blasting of trenches in solid rock after houses had been built; mud runs into city streets because of failures in design—the list is, unfortunately, endless.

It will usually require only one such unfortunate example for any one municipality to justify, economically, the initiation of the service that is herein proposed. And it would be difficult to find any municipality in which some feature could not have been better built, or some difficulties in planning or building avoided, had proper underground information been available. Rather than deal in generalities, the suggestion may therefore be advanced that, in order to counter this particular argument, those desirous of seeing such a service started in their own city should search the records to find one or more examples of what the lack of information has done. If the cost thus incurred be compared with the total operating cost of a geological information service, the answer to the argument will be clear for all to see. In a medium-sized city, the cost might well be that of one professional worker, necessary clerical assistance and office supplies, and any expenses in connection with the operation of the necessary geological advisory committee. It can be seen that expenditure of the order of $50,000 a year is all that is involved in such an average case, plus the cost of printing any necessary publications. Clearly, this figure is not even a guide but merely an indication that, in comparison with the cost of other municipal services, the provision of subsurface geological information on an orderly basis is a very small charge indeed against the taxpayers. They must, however, be convinced that even so small an expenditure is justified and their interest in the project ensured. Herein lies probably the greatest difficulty of all.

Lack of local interest. In the government of modern cities, just as of states and countries, those charged with the responsibility of representing the views of the electorate will naturally do their best to give the citizens they represent good administration and the provision of those municipal and other services that meet with public favor. Roads are essential; expenditure upon them is rarely questioned. In northern areas even the expenditure today of very large sums of money on the clearing of snow from city streets is now accepted without question (but with protest if it is not well done), whereas but a short time ago snow was left as a cover for streets until the spring thaw. Water supply is essential; all citizens know that money must be spent on a good and safe waterworks system for every city. So also with sewers and sewage treatment, even though it must be admitted that there are all too many cities that have as yet failed to measure up to their full responsibilities for this latter service. This situation, too, is changing under the influence of public interest in doing away with unnecessary pollution—and this despite the high costs involved. All these, and many other well-established municipal services, are well understood by the average citizen, who will not usually question the voting of money for their provision, operation, and maintenance. Elected representatives do their best to see that available funds are properly allocated and efficiently used.

It might be thought that so small an item as the money required for a subsurface information service could easily be "buried" in one of the sums for major civic services. It probably could, but all concerned with the expenditure of funds know that this is a procedure that is not only incorrect but also unsound. Someday, some astute critic will spot the new item of expenditure and it will be assailed as a "frill." This is not the way, assuredly, to win public approval of what will be, in so many cities, a new service, even though attached to and operated within the office of the city engineer.

When the project has been approved by civic authorities, it should be listed as a separate item in its own right, small though it is, so that all may see what is involved. For this course to be successful, the public must be aware—at least in a general way— of what is involved and their interest in its potential aroused. Even geology itself is but little known by the mythical man in the street, let alone the service that it can perform for his city. How, then, is public interest, without which no such project can win real acceptance, to be aroused? This opens up many interesting avenues of inquiry that go far beyond the immediate matter of concern, but to the specific task of developing public interest in geology, and its application especially in service to cities, the remainder of this chapter will be devoted. It will be found that this very mundane approach leads to socially desirable results of widespread influence.

9.8 LOCAL PROFESSIONAL INTEREST

Engineers and architects have a natural professional interest in the foundation bed conditions beneath the cities in which they practice. They must know what these conditions are before they can complete the designs of the structures for which they are responsible. It is common practice today to employ a specialist in foundation investigation to conduct the necessary site investigation and the associated soil and rock testing, then reporting upon his findings to the architect or engineer who will incorporate the essence of the information thus received in his contract documents. It is to the benefit of all three of these professional groups to have as much geological information as can possibly be assembled before any expenditure is committed on work at a building site. In this way economy can be introduced into the work that is necessary, and the overall program can be planned with all the more certainty. Geologists will also have a real professional interest in the subsurface of cities, either because of their own professional work as engineering geologists or through their interest in the scientific information that can be obtained only in this way.

In many cities those with such special interests in the ground are associated in local groups organized under a variety of auspices. The work of the Boston Society of Civil Engineers in its city, in association with local geologists, has already been appreciatively mentioned. In Philadelphia a corresponding group of members of the American Society of Civil Engineers has taken a lively interest in local foundation records. In the larger Canadian cities there are now active geotechnical groups that bring together those from various disciplines who share interest in geotechnical problems. It was one of these groups that was responsible for inaugurating work on what developed into the Saskatoon Folio that was mentioned in Chap. 3 (page 98). These Canadian groups, some in their second decade of service, are following in a good tradition, for as early as 1937 a representative committee of engineers was established under the auspices of the Engineering Institute of Canada to make a study of foundation conditions in Winnipeg; architects were also included in its membership, as was a testing engineer. The first recommendation of this committee (in 1937) was "That the public be given more information on foundation problems in the Greater Winnipeg area"—yet another reminder that there is, in so many ways, nothing new under the sun.

There must be many other cities throughout the world in which, through the initial enthusiasm of a few keen men, similar groups have been formed to share experiences with local foundations. Some have gone further and reported upon local subsoil conditions. Others, like the BSCE Committee, have actually engaged in the collection of boring and excavation records and in the publication of this information for public use. This final step requires financing and an office to provide continuing logistic support. The society provides the latter in Boston; on page 515 the financial support was noted. In most cases it may not prove possible to take such an active interest in the assembling of records as has been done for so many years in Boston. In any case, this is a function that can be so much more easily carried out under civic auspices, but the interest and support of such local groups as have been mentioned can be of the greatest assistance to the local city engineer, both directly and in developing a public awareness of the need for providing a subsurface information service. As always in such matters, the progress that can be made depends ultimately on the interest and enthusiasm of individual workers.

Whenever a local group can be started to foster interest in local geological conditions, the auspices under which it meets are therefore not nearly so important as is attracting the right people to the group. It is most desirable that groups be interdisciplinary. If confined merely to engineers, or even to geotechnical experts, group activity can soon devolve into "preaching to the converted." If architects can be persuaded to join, they will learn much and can make their own percipient contributions to discussion. So also can experts in agricultural soil science, for the science of pedology, as explained in Chap. 3, has much to contribute in this important field of work. Geologists, above all, should be persuaded to join in discussions as active group participants. Their training and their discipline will give them a usefully contrasting outlook on the matters discussed. They can show the scientific interest and significance of what might otherwise be regarded merely as "nuisance conditions" in the ground. Above all, they can take from the group an appreciation that the works of architects, engineers, and contractors within their city present real possibilities for geological study, possibilities that should not be lost but (in cooperation with those responsible) exploited to the full for the benefit of the science. They can take away also the practical evidence to which they will be introduced as to how geology can be, and is being, applied in the future planning and actual building of their city. If they can pass on the sense of this cooperative work to their colleagues, to their classes, and in their ordinary social contacts, they can perform a great service to their city while aiding the public recognition of their science, a recognition that is so strangely and so sadly lacking in almost all parts of the world.

9.9 LOCAL PUBLIC INTEREST IN GEOLOGY

In the first of the lectures by the Reverend Charles Kingsley given to "young men of the city of Chester," mentioned at the outset of this chapter, there is an eloquent statement about the science of geology that is relevant here, especially since it was made over 100 years ago: "The facts of Geology . . . may be studied in every bank, every grot, every quarry, every railway cutting, by any one who has eyes and common sense, and who chooses to copy the late illustrious Hugh Miller, who made himself, a great geologist out of a poor stonemason . . . thus Geology is (or ought to be) in popular parlance, the people's science . . . ." The people's science—a splendid concept that yet may be! But Kingsley's hopes have not yet been realized as he so confidently expected. If geology had only been given its place in school curricula as the first, and most readily appreciated, of the natural sciences the situation today would be different.

Past neglect of geology in the schools is probably one of the most important reasons for the lack of public recognition of geology today, but it is only one of many causes. It would not be profitable to explore these; the situation has to be accepted, but it is a situation that, fortunately, is changing and changing rapidly. This public disregard for geology must be responsible, however, at least in part, for its neglect by cities. As the public comes to appreciate the interest of geology, its fascination to all lovers of the outdoors and the contribution it can make to the enjoyment of scenery, then its importance to the development of cities will also become obvious—with some assistance from those with special interest in this application—so that public support for the provision of subsurface information services may be expected to grow with increasing public awareness of the science.

Science training in many school systems is today undergoing drastic revision. The earth sciences (the more general term that includes geology and its associated sciences) are at last being given due recognition as one of the principal areas of scientific study. As a recent report has stated:

> The fast-growing interest in our physical environment, the mounting pressures concerning landscape preservation and anti-pollution, the need for improved urban planning, and the importance of natural resource development . . . highlight the relevance of earth sciences . . . . Students in our secondary schools should be given the opportunity to learn the principles of science through discovery of the physical world in which they live—the atmosphere, the lakes and rivers, the oceans, the mountains, the rocks, the minerals—so that science can be seen to be relevant and useful.[9.21]

There have always been some devoted science teachers who appreciated the significance of the earth sciences and did what they could in their classes to get their students to "look out the window." There have been some who knew what geology meant to the city in which they lived and regularly took their students out to see interesting geological exposures nearby. But they were the exception rather than the rule. Today their interest is being recognized. Training courses in the earth sciences are being given, supported by pioneer work of the American Geological Institute. Curricula are being revised so as to link the earth sciences with the other basic physical sciences in a total approach to science. Teachers will be looking for illustrative material to serve this new and growing interest. Where better can they look than in their own community and especially so if the utility of the basic science can thus be demonstrated.

Lest the foregoing appear to be idealistic stargazing, let the author recount what he was told by a devoted, young high school teacher in a small New England town. When this young man first taught his course on the earth sciences, he had to overcome great objections on the ground that it was a superficial subject of little relevance. His principal supported him. After his first term he began to get calls from parents asking why their children had got so fired with enthusiasm for geology, and what was geology anyway. He set stiff examinations, including small projects that meant field visits by the students to places where geology was involved in the development of their town. The course is now one of the most highly respected in that school. Geological field trips around the town are a regular feature. Parents are beginning to be shown by their children what geology means in their town. So it can be done. And it must be done to an increasing extent not only to make citizens aware of the importance of geology to the development of their city but, of even more importance, so that an appreciation of the essential geological setting of all natural resources may be appreciated against which public efforts in conservation measures can be properly directed.

Education, and that is really the matter under discussion, is not confined to the schools. Museums occupy a singularly important place in the educational system of all but the smallest communities. They, too, are changing and developing in the face of increasing interest and demand, arising in part from the increased amount of leisure now available to so many. And there are few museums that do not feature the earth sciences in some way, sometimes with great imagination. Despite all the attractions offered by television, museums are more than holding their own in public esteem and in public use. Anyone who had anything to do with the displays of samples of the recently acquired "moon rocks" at museums across North America must have been amazed by the public interest shown in these relatively small exhibits. "Moon rocks" have little to do with urban geology, it is true, but they were geological exhibits and as such must have had some effect upon the multitudes of people who waited so long, in so many places, to see them. More relevant, and more effective in achieving that degree of public interest in geology that has been shown to be so desirable, are special museum displays that feature some specific aspect of local geology in relation to building in the area. The display in the Royal Ontario Museum in Toronto illustrating the geological aspects of some phases of the construction of the Toronto subway was first opened in 1960. And it is still attracting much public interest, although naturally updated and changed from time to time. Museum curators can have a continuing source of new ideas for displays once they recognize that the urban geology of their city does have relevance and is of public interest.

There are many who do not go into museums but who prefer to make their study of natural history (to use, once again, the good old title, outmoded though it is now often thought to be) in the great outdoors. Here, too, there are signs of growing interest in the earth sciences. One of the many interesting sociocultural phenomena of North American cities in recent years has been the remarkable growth in the number and activity of "rockhounds," the modern name for those who band together for the study of rocks and minerals. Their studies are not utilitarian but scientific and aesthetic. Inevitably, however, rockhounds cannot follow their calling without at least a general appreciation of the fact that there is more to geology than merely the collecting of specimens of rocks and minerals. A number of rockhound groups have, therefore, extended their interest and exhibited a lively concern for geological features of a more general character in their areas. Correspondingly, naturalists' clubs are being reminded by their members that there is more to the study of nature than the proverbial "birds and the bees," with the result that many of these clubs now have active geological sections. Experience has shown the interest that can be generated by talks to club audiences about the geology of their own city. Even though purely descriptive, such talks will inevitably touch upon the way in which local geological conditions have influenced the development of the city, thus making a few more citizens aware of the need for good subsurface information if their community is to develop along sound lines.

There is a steadily increasing supply of excellent handbooks, issued by geological surveys and similar organizations, to serve as guides to the study of geology out-of-doors. Some of these are collectors' guides, explaining where unusual minerals are to be found along well-used highways. Others are guides to the geology to be seen when driving along scenic highways (when traffic permits), of which there are now good examples in most parts of North America. These are, admittedly, getting far outside cities, but they will be used by city dwellers so that their influence in bringing home the reality of geological study and its influence on the works of man, such as highway construction, can only be beneficial and will be slowly cumulative.[9.22]

It is, however, within cities that the education of citizens in geology can most easily be carried out. In this context, that word "education" has an austere and formal connotation that is the reverse of the informal and pleasant process of information that can add so much to the "atmosphere" of a city while inconspicuously giving to all observant citizens an appreciation of the importance of what lies beneath the streets on which they walk. It is quite possible—only a psychologist could tell with certainty—that this book is being written because the author, when a schoolboy, regularly used to pass one of the largest glacial erratics he has ever seen, carefully mounted on a pedestal at an important traffic intersection. He knew nothing about geology then; he was given no instruction in it in his school, excellent though this was in other respects; but the memory of the "Big Stone" has always remained with him and so may possibly have led to his deep-seated interest in geology in more recent years.

The stone is a block of gypsum weighing 18 tonnes discovered in boulder clay in a brickyard about 24 m below the ground surface. Its unusual character was appreciated and brought to the attention of a local geologist-engineer. He arranged to have it carefully measured and located *in situ* and then, with the aid of local authorities, to have it moved to the location noted, mounted on a masonry pedestal in exactly the orientation in which it was found in the ground, and suitably protected by a fence in view of its composition. T. Mellard Reade was the enthusiast who achieved this result in 1898; he had published 10 years before one of the first known papers on the value to civil engineers of a study of geology.[9.23]

The mounting of glacial erratics is not uncommon; they form striking monuments. Presentation of outcrops of bedrock in public gardens and parks can be effective, the more so if they are well marked as to their geological character. The use of unusual building stones, especially for interior decoration, is always attractive; it can be of interest also if small labels are used to show whence the stone has come. This is the sort of information that can so easily be incorporated in the guidebooks that are now available for almost every city. If geology has played a part in the historical development of the city, this can be a key feature of any popular description. Historical walking tours are frequently an intriguing feature of such guides; they can be all the more interesting if geology is also featured, appropriately. There are some guidebooks that have special walking tours just to illustrate the variety of building stones used in the central parts of larger cities. And if there are any notable fossil beds within a city's boundaries, these can prove to be a feature of unusual interest and value.[9.24]

In selecting a few examples with which to illustrate the foregoing general

Figure 9.9   Great Crosby, Lancashire, England. The "Big Stone" of Crosby, an erratic block of gypsum discovered in a brick pit, preserved, and mounted in public view in the same orientation as it had *in situ*. *(Courtesy of H. O. Roberts, Town Clerk, Borough of Crosby.)*

observations, a remarkable exposure of fossil dinosaur tracks and its preservation for public interest and benefit may well be first described. In Rocky Hill, a small urban community about 12.8 km to the south of the center of Hartford, Connecticut, the State Highway Department had selected a site for the construction of a new testing laboratory. A construction contract was awarded and excavation started. On 24 August 1966 the operator of a bulldozer, Edward McCarthy by name, noticed as he was scraping soil off the bedrock, which he had exposed about 3.6 m below the natural ground level, that it was covered with some strange marks. These were recognized as ancient footprints embedded in the sandstone. He drew them to the attention of the engineer and architect on the site. They, in turn, called the Peabody Museum at Yale University and the newspapers. That same evening a large number of people came to the site to collect specimens; one man is said to have started up the contractor's bulldozer in his enthusiasm to collect more efficiently. The next afternoon, after morning consultations, Dr. J. W. Peoples, Director of the State's Geological and Natural History Survey, met other state officials at the site; collecting was still going on. Scientists had assessed the value of the site, paleontologically and geologically; with this support Dr. Peoples recommended to the State Commissioner of Public Works that an effort should be made to save the area for public benefit.

The various state officials then took very quickly the necessary steps to halt any further excavation, to put up a temporary fence around the site, and to have the State Police guard the site on a 24-hour basis. A conference of interested state officials with interested scientists was held on 29 August. It was then decided to seek another site for the laboratory building. Yale University made available the services

Figure 9.10 Hartford, Connecticut. The dinosaur tracks noticed by a bull-dozer operator and saved for public benefit, now preserved in Dinosaur Park. *(Photograph by J. Howard, courtesy of J. W. Peoples, Director, Connecticut Geological and Natural History Survey.)*

of their chief preparator to supervise the uncovering of more tracks, down the dipping bedrock as more excavation was carefully done. On 13 September, the Governor of Connecticut announced that the 3.1-hectare site that contained the tracks would be set aside as a state park. This was only three weeks from the initial find, a truly remarkable example of what interested and concerned cooperation can achieve. By the time excavation on the site had to stop late in October, an area of 850 m² of the fossil horizon had been exposed, on which were about 1,000 footprints. At least three reptiles have been recognized by their tracks, the most common being a dinosaur about 7.5 m long. It is only rarely that so many tracks of ancient animals are found in such profusion in so small an area.

During the first winter, the site was covered with a special electric blanket in order to preserve the surface. Excavation and preparation continued during the following summer. The state legislature voted the money necessary for the construction of a temporary exhibit building over the site and for site facilities for public convenience. On 17 October 1968 the temporary building (of somewhat unusual design) was officially opened. The site was declared by the National Parks Service to be a Registered

Natural Landmark, a suitable plaque being erected on the same day. Even without these facilities, 50,000 visitors came to the site during each of the first 2 years; with the new facilities and informed guides now available, attendance is expected to exceed 100,000 per year. Dinosaur State Park is therefore a well-established attraction in Connecticut, already well known throughout New England and to visitors from many other parts of North America. Plans have been drawn up for its permanent development so that it will be continually available as a public attraction and as an invaluable outdoor museum for school children from a wide area, a constant reminder to all thoughtful visitors of what can be found in excavating for a building—if your bulldozer is operated by a man who recognizes a dinosaur footprint when he sees one.[9.25]

This whole story is so delightful an example—of percipient observation, quick action, splendid cooperation, and enlightened administration—that it has been told in some detail, even though dinosaur parks will continue to be a rarity. But there are many other excavations to be made as cities expand and develop that will have their own geological significance and interest. The citizens of Birmingham, Alabama, for example, watched through a period of several years the construction close to their city of one of the largest rock cuts ever made for a highway. This is on the Red Mountain Expressway that is part of an interchange system of major highways serving this important southern city. More than 1.5 million m³ of rock were excavated at a cost of about $19 million, forming a cut 555 m long, 63 m deep, 45 m wide at the bottom, and 141 m wide at the top. An unusually interesting geological section is

Figure 9.11 Hartford, Connecticut. The plaque of the National Parks Service at Dinosaur Park, indicative of its public significance. *(Photograph by R. Arnold, courtesy of J. W. Peoples.)*

exposed, a geological period of 440 million years being represented by the rocks now to be seen in the length of the cut. Rocks vary from the Chickamauga limestone of Middle Ordovician age through the Red Mountain (Silurian) formation to shales, cherts, limestones, and sandstone of Mississippian age. A committee of public-spirited citizens was formed to establish a Birmingham Geological Monument Commission. The cut is being developed by constructing a series of steps and platforms, with access to viewing platforms at several levels. A guidebook is being prepared and other arrangements developed to form this engineering feature into an outdoor natural history museum and geological exhibit of outstanding interest and grandeur, tribute indeed to another splendid cooperative local effort.[9.26] W. M. Spencer, a local lawyer, was one of the leaders in this community venture; the local committee was assisted by the Geological Survey of Alabama, of which P. E. LaMoreaux is State Geologist.

It will be said that these great highway projects do not occur in more than a few cities, so what is the ordinary city to do? For any writer to select any city as "ordinary" places him in an invidious position unless he chooses his own city; that solution is the only possible course to follow here, and so the situation in Ottawa, Canada, will be briefly reviewed. Ottawa itself has a population of about 300,000. The city is going through a transitional stage since the province of Ontario is in the course of establishing regional governments throughout the province. Ottawa is now included within the Ottawa-Carleton region, an area of 285,000 hectares, including 16 organized municipalities having a population of almost 500,000. The regional government has assumed responsibility for some municipal services, including regional planning, but this merely serves to increase the need for attention to local geology, and the eminent desirability of developing local public interest in geology.

As the capital city of the Dominion of Canada, Ottawa has been for a very long time the headquarters location for the Geological Survey of Canada. Study of the geology of the Ottawa region has naturally been an active project of the Survey for many years. All recent workers in this area would subscribe to the desirability of mentioning as the pioneer worker Dr. Alice Wilson, the first woman to be a member of the Survey staff. By her talks to many groups through many years, her teaching at a local university after her official "retirement" until almost her eightieth year, by her leadership of field trips throughout the area, and by her geological reports, she had a profound and lasting influence upon general appreciation of the geology of Ottawa. Her geological maps of the region are the starting point for all further studies; one was mentioned in connection with engineering problems on page 222.

It is not, therefore, surprising to find that in addition to an active "rockhounds club" there is an active geological section in the Ottawa Field Naturalists Club, one of the oldest of such societies in Canada. The members of these clubs, as do other citizens, have the advantage of having the National Museums in Ottawa, with geological and mineralogical collections, providing convenient environments for meetings. Field trips can range from the Precambrian of the Shield, several kilometers to the north, over exposures of Paleozoic limestones, shales, and sandstones, with faults

Figure 9.12 Birmingham, Alabama. Rock cut on the Red Mountain Expressway, with some of the city in the background, a natural geological exhibit now preserved for public benefit. *(Courtesy of the Geological Survey of Alabama. P. E. LaMoreaux, State Geologist.)*

in clear view and some good fossil collecting locations, to complex exposures of the local soils, which include the sensitive Leda clay. Dr. Wilson herself prepared an excellent guide to the geology of the area that was published by the Naturalists Club in 1956.[9.27] It was later supplemented by two excellent guides to mineral collecting in the area to the north of the city, all three guides being useful aids to field trips around the city, Dr. Wilson giving complete details of eight trips.[9.28]

Within the city itself, there are many splendid exposures, for all to see, of the local Paleozoic limestone; one adjacent to the building that houses the Geological Survey has been tastefully arranged to show clearly its bedded structure so obviously supporting the large building behind. A fine glacial erratic block is the mounting for a memorial tablet to Sir William Logan, the first and great director of the Survey. And in the newly developed shopping mall, right in the center of the city, there has been arranged a collection of large block specimens of typical rocks from each of the 10 provinces of Canada, well marked by means of a bronze plaque. There is now available a more modern guide, aided by color printing, written by Dr. David Baird, that is without question the best example of a guide to the geology of a city that the author has ever seen.[9.29]

These somewhat personal and detailed comments are given to show what an "ordinary" city is doing in developing public interest in geology. Most of the items mentioned can be done by any city if there are a few citizens—preferably with an inspiring pioneer such as Dr. Alice Wilson—interested enough to get things moving. In the forties, an undergraduate engineer, Gordon McRostie, who had gained summer experience on construction in Ottawa prepared an unusually good thesis on the geological conditions met with in Ottawa foundation work, and he prepared, for this, the first large-scale maps of the subsurface. These were later used by the Geological Survey and one of the committees of the National Research Council as the basis for a more extended survey. In 1958 a preliminary map of bedrock contours throughout the city was issued by the Survey based upon records of more than 500 borings. In 1959 a more complete map of the same type showing the whole city and based on

Figure 9.13 Ottawa, Canada. Headquarters Building of the Geological Survey of Canada, showing in the foreground an exposure of the limestone bedrock on which the building is founded; the plaque that may be seen in the center foreground to the right of the steps explains that this is rock of the Cobourg beds of the Ottawa formation and the Barnveld stage of Ordovician time, and is about 440 million years old. *(Courtesy of the Geological Survey of Canada, Y. Fortier, Director.)*

Figure 9.14 Ottawa, Canada. "Stones of the Provinces" in Ottawa's Sparks Street Mall; a block of a typical stone from each of Canada's provinces and territories, pleasantly arranged in a small garden with an explanatory bronze plaque. *(Courtesy of Helmer and Tutton, architects, Ottawa.)*

a study of over 1,000 borings was published.[9.30] Other records have been lodged with the Geological Survey, which is carrying out a regional study along the lines given in Chap. 3; this will be of great value in relation to the future planning of the rapidly expanding regional area. Local foundation engineers have, therefore, much useful information available in addition to their own experience.

Denver, Colorado, is no ordinary city, but it does call for brief mention, in conclusion, not only because of the special interest of its urban geology but also because of what has been done about it. Lying close to the eastern front of the Rocky Mountains, the city has a most picturesque setting and one of great geological interest. Not only are there interesting soils to be seen, but the bedrock ranges from the geologically young rocks of the Great Plains to the older rocks of the foothills (of Paleocene and Cretaceous and Jurassic age) and then to the ancient Precambrian rocks of the mountains. The Alameda Parkway is one of the roads leading out to the mountains to the west. In its route, it cuts across 10 geological formations before reaching the Precambrian, starting with the relatively young Denver formation. Every important geological exposure on this scenic roadway has been clearly marked, and

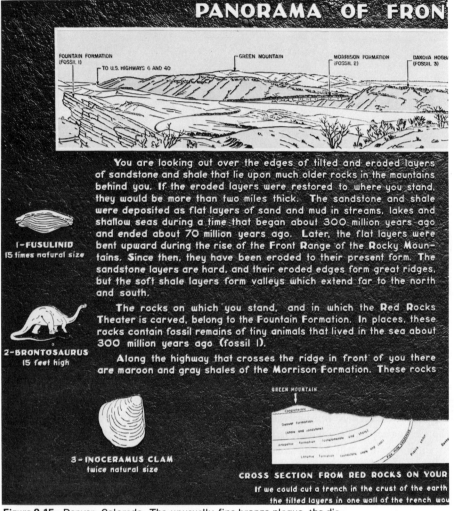

Figure 9.15 Denver, Colorado. The unusually fine bronze plaque, the diagrams in color, mounted on a pedestal in full view of the mountain scene that it describes so vividly for the benefit of all visitors to the Red Rocks park. *(Courtesy of John R. Stacy, the Colorado Scientific Society, and H. E. Simpson, Denver.)*

the U.S. Geological Survey has provided an excellent leaflet to serve as a guide. A drive along the parkway, therefore, is one of the most interesting geological experiences that a visitor can wish to have, especially when he realizes that the rocks over which he is driving represent a geological time duration of over 500 million years. The Alameda road leads to the famous Red Rocks Park, in which is located the superb

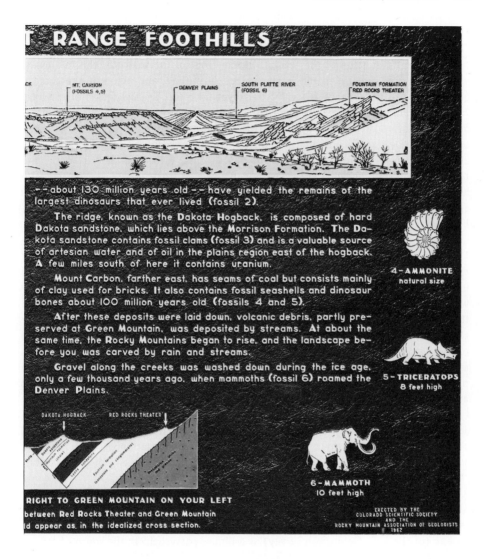

RANGE FOOTHILLS

MT. CARSON
(FOSSILS 4,5)   DENVER PLAINS   SOUTH PLATTE RIVER
(FOSSIL 6)   FOUNTAIN FORMATION
RED ROCKS THEATER

-- about 130 million years old -- have yielded the remains of the largest dinosaurs that ever lived (fossil 2).

The ridge, known as the Dakota Hogback, is composed of hard Dakota sandstone, which lies above the Morrison Formation. The Dakota sandstone contains fossil clams (fossil 3) and is a valuable source of artesian water and of oil in the plains region east of the hogback. A few miles south of here it contains uranium.

Mount Carbon, farther east, has seams of coal but consists mainly of clay used for bricks. It also contains fossil seashells and dinosaur bones about 100 million years old (fossils 4 and 5).

After these deposits were laid down, volcanic debris, partly preserved at Green Mountain, was deposited by streams. At about the same time, the Rocky Mountains began to rise, and the landscape before you was carved by rain and streams.

Gravel along the creeks was washed down during the ice age, only a few thousand years ago, when mammoths (fossil 6) roamed the Denver Plains.

4-AMMONITE
natural size

5-TRICERATOPS
8 feet high

6-MAMMOTH
10 feet high

DAKOTA HOGBACK   RED ROCKS THEATER

RIGHT TO GREEN MOUNTAIN ON YOUR LEFT
between Red Rocks Theater and Green Mountain
ld appear as, in the idealized cross section.

ERECTED BY THE
COLORADO SCIENTIFIC SOCIETY
AND THE
ROCKY MOUNTAIN ASSOCIATION OF GEOLOGISTS
1962

outdoor natural amphitheater in the Fountain formation, naturally a red sandstone, of Paleozoic age. Here, too, are markers, one showing a beautiful contact with the massive Precambrian rocks of the mountains.

Less than 0.8 km away there is a special lookout point at which has been erected one of the most vivid geological plaques that can be seen in North America, a joint effort by the Colorado Scientific Society and the Rocky Mountain Association of Geologists, with the assistance of the Denver Department of Parks and Recreation. A magnificent panorama of the foothills lies in front of the visitor to this interesting spot. On the plaque the scene is reproduced in outline, and below it the geology hidden beneath the surface is vividly portrayed in color. Typical fossils of the local rocks decorate the sides of the plaque, the inscription on which is a clearly written, brief explanation of the geology thus presented so interestingly. The author has been assured by Denver friends that, in their years in elementary school, every child attending Denver schools is brought out by bus to this lookout at least once, and the geology of this magnificent scene is explained to them. There can be few who have had this experience who will ever forget the appreciation that this gives to one's enjoyment of the scenery all around. One wishes that every child could sometime have a similar meaningful experience.

It is small wonder, then, that geology and scenery are widely appreciated in the Denver area, so widely indeed that when the State Highway Department announced that they were going to excavate a deep wide cut through the most famous of all local "hogsback" hills, this one even being known merely as the Hogsback, there was an immediate outcry on the part of local conservationists who soon showed that they were a militant group of citizens. The great road cut has been made, as may be seen from the accompanying photograph. It will be seen, however, that this is no ordinary cut. A closer look at the benches would show that some are finished roadways and walkways with lookouts located at strategic points, useful signs indicating the nature of the geology that is so vividly displayed by the sections of the dipping beds exposed on both sides of the dual highway. Opened only in 1970, "the Hogsback Cut" has already taken its place as one of the leading scenic attractions of the Denver area. The State Highway Department was able to use the intended route for this section of Interstate Highway No. 70. The fears of conservationists were assuaged, and the entire region is the beneficiary of one of the finest natural geological exhibits that the author has ever seen. How was this fine result achieved?

Since the story illustrates so well and so delightfully what a meeting of the minds—of interested and informed citizens—can achieve, the author counts it a privilege to be able to relate what followed from the attendance of Dr. Edwin D. McKee (of the U.S. Geological Survey) at a dinner party held in the south of Denver when the Hogsback Cut was still merely a proposal. In Dr. McKee's own words:

> I sat next to Mrs. Estelle Brown, project coordinator for the Association of Beautiful Colorado Roads (ABCR). During our conversation Mrs. Brown was bemoaning the fact that a major highway into the mountains was about to be constructed through the hogsbacks which are one of the really fine scenic features of this area. I replied that this might not necessarily be bad from the standpoint of human values, and that geologists are constantly searching for roadcuts that expose the internal structure of mountains in order to understand the story behind the scenery. I further explained that if properly handled, this

Figure 9.16 Denver, Colorado. The Hogsback cut on Interstate Highway
70 but without the varied colors that add so much to this natural geological
exhibit. *(Courtesy of the Colorado Division of Highways, C. E. Shumate,
Chief Engineer.)*

might constitute a fine opportunity for developing a significant educational
exhibit that would illustrate under very favourable conditions something of the
history of the earth.

Continuing, Dr. McKee relates

Mrs. Brown evidently thought over this statement carefully, because a day after
the party she phoned me to ask for elaboration of my comments, and soon after
that went into action. She did a tremendous job, enlisting the interest and help
of highway officials, landscape architects, engineers, geologists and educators.
Furthermore, she promoted plans with the help of many experts for the exhibit
installation, parking areas, walk ways, and lookout points, and arranged for the
necessary funding. Through her great energy, enthusiasm and hard work, the
entire project was made a reality . . . . Many people and organizations have
contributed in various ways, but Estelle Brown was mainly responsible for
changing what might have been an unsightly road scar into an attractive and
valuable roadside feature of considerable human interest.[9.31]

And all this from a dinner table conversation.

9.10   GEOLOGY AND CONSERVATION

The march of roads through the hills cannot be stopped. It is but a reflection of the growth of cities, a summary picture of which was presented as the outset of this volume. And it is only one small part of what is involved in urban development. It will be well to glance back at the overall view that was then summarized—how that within less than the next 30 years, or by the end of the century (for the twenty-first century is that close), the cities of the world, and so of North America, are going to double in population at least, if not indeed more than this. Something like 140,000 square miles of land is going to be covered up in the United States alone, even within the boundaries of cities, with streets and buildings, before that year 2000 arrives. The "covering up" must be well done and efficiently prosecuted if the expansion of cities is to keep pace with the demands of expanding population. Geology, as can now be seen, has a vital role to play in assisting in all phases of urban and regional planning, in the building and rebuilding of cities, and in ensuring that the geological features that are thus to be hidden for all time are studied and recorded as a part of the never-ending search for a full understanding of the nature of the crust of the earth. But all this is not enough.

The Roman city of Thamugadi, the site of which in Algeria is now known as Timgad, was a completely planned city, established by the Emperor Trajan about A.D. 100. It was laid out with its streets in regular pattern; it had a magnificent forum, a public library, 17 Roman baths with magnificent mosaic floors, a theater seating 2,500, and even marble flush latrines. It was supported by produce from the fertile land around, grain from the valley fields, olives from the orchards in the hills. The Berbers captured the city in the year 430. After an Arab invasion of the seventh century, the city was lost to human ken, buried in dust and sand—the products of soil erosion; water erosion, from occasional storms, has taken its toll also. It was a magnificent city, as can now be seen from the ruins that have been brought to light through patient archeological excavations during the last four decades, but it remains as one of the supreme demonstrations of the fact that a city cannot exist of itself.

A city is and must always be interdependent with all the country around. Protection and conservation of the renewable natural resources throughout the entire region served by every city must be recognized as a civic concern of paramount importance. It will be said that Thamugadi is an extreme example. Perhaps—but it was not alone. Carthage, the North African city that produced Hannibal and that at one time rivaled Rome itself, has disappeared, a small village now occupying its great site. Kish was one of the most important cities in the entire world 6,000 years ago. Only in recent years has it come to be known again as its ruins have been revealed beneath the desert sands of Mesopotamia. Babylon itself passed from its glory into disuse, finally disappearing beneath the sands of the desert—not because it was razed by an enemy but because the irrigation canals that watered its supporting lands were allowed to fill with silt. The "Hundred Dead Cities of Syria" are well known, if only through their tragic communal name, to all students of archeology. Located on the rolling country between Hama, Aleppo, and Antioch, the underlying limestone on more than 405,000 hectares has been exposed to view through critical soil erosion, these ancient towns (not "cities" as the word is understood today) were not buried but deserted. This area is one of the most seriously eroded areas anywhere in the ancient world, neglect of the measures that had been taken to conserve soil and water following upon invasions by the Persians and later by desert nomads.

The vision of Moses as he stood on Mount Nebo and saw a land flowing with milk and honey—"a land of brooks and water, of fountains and depths that spring out of valleys and hills; a land of wheat, and barley, and vines and fig-trees and pomegranites; a land of oil-olive, and honey; a land wherein thou shalt eat bread without scarceness"—was a true picture of a lovely land that only in these recent years is having some of its former resources slowly and laboriously restored. All who have been privileged to visit the Israel of today must find it hard to believe that this is the land described so eloquently by Moses, as they see the bare hillsides, the muddy water of the Jordan, and note the efforts at reforestation now being carried on. The "cedars of Lebanon" must have been one of the glories of this ancient land, long, long ago.

Figure 9.17 The ruins of Timgad in North Africa, excavated from the sand that once covered this ancient city. *(Photograph by W. C. Lowdermilk, courtesy of the U.S. Soil Conservation Service.)*

It is related that prior to 2900 B.C. 40 ships arrived in Egypt loaded with timber from this famous forest that is believed to have covered 520,000 hectares. Solomon supplied over 100,000 men to work in the forest of Lebanon and in shipping the logs then cut down. Today? There are four small groves, with about 400 trees left. The hills of Lebanon are bare. And in the Far East—for the picture is a worldwide one—thought has only to be given to the Yellow River, "China's Sorrow," carrying eroded silt to the sea in such quantities that it has even given the great river its name, to see what dire effect man's actions can have upon the land.[9.32]

These are not hypothetical examples. All these things happened, and many more, to untold ancient cities. It will be said that all this happened long ago, that things are different now, that modern man knows better than to waste his heritage, that reference to such matters is just alarmist and has no place in a book like this. Would that this were so. It is true that the few cases cited did happen long ago, but records of bad soil erosion in relatively recent years from all too many parts of North America could be given if space permitted. All readers who can remember the thirties will never have to be reminded of what dust storms then did to the Midwest and the Prairies. Fortunately, the lesson was learned at least in part and much rehabilitation work has been done since then, the pioneering efforts of the U.S. Soil Conservation Service being especially noteworthy. Much remains to be done still in the conservation of soil, in the developing of forests on land suited to them, in the protection of sources of water supply, and (perhaps above all) in the cleansing of polluted waters. And cities, and those who plan cities, cannot but be vitally concerned about such efforts.

Soil conservation and forest development are two essential ingredients of all plans for flood control. If floods can be reduced, all downstream cities and towns will benefit. Water-supply areas, such as the catchment areas of rivers used for supply and the intake areas for important groundwater basins, must be conserved and protected if safe water is to be ensured for use in cities. Cities and their industrial plants are often themselves the worst offenders in polluting running waters, all too many major municipalities still dumping their raw sewage into the waterways with which they are blessed, to the detriment of everything downstream. Geology enters into all these measures since without accurate knowledge of the land, rehabilitation efforts and conservation measures may prove to be poorly planned. After the recital of cases throughout this volume, this relevance of geology even to conservation need not be labored. And such uses of geology will still be geology in the service of cities.

Much good progress has been made but so much more remains to be done, perhaps above all a general realization by the public of the complete interdependence of cities and country. For not only is it essential that the two shall be never separated in major planning, for strictly utilitarian reasons such as have already been given, but their linkage should be a part of the human aspects of all planning. What will be the future of people if, with the best possible planned cities, there are no forests nearby in which to roam, no green fields to enjoy, no running streams in which to fish, no quiet and lovely trails along which to wander and renew one's spirit? The poets have said this in many delightful ways and with pointed words. Many plans do provide for just the attention to the need for open spaces that is here suggested by the inclusion of *green belts* around their cities. On how many master plans have excellent green belts been shown? In how many modern cities have they been brought into actual existence? Around Warsaw there is a green belt that effectively, and deliberately, limits the expansion of this old-modern city. Ottawa is gradually developing a fine green belt through the efforts of the National Capital Commission, possibly just because it is a national capital. There are other examples, but still all too few. In the selection of areas that can be set aside for such communal purposes, knowledge of the ground itself is, as always, a first essential.

This general thinking about "the land" must extend far beyond the cities if the good things of the earth are to continue so that they may be enjoyed by those who dwell in cities. "It is desirable that some large and easily accessible region of American soil should remain, as far as possible, in its primitive condition, at once a museum for the instruction of the student, a garden for the recreation of the lover of nature, and an asylum where indigenous tree, and humble plant that loves the shade, and fish and fowl and four-footed beast, may dwell and perpetuate their kind, in the enjoyment of such imperfect protection as the laws of a people jealous of restraint can afford them." These are not words of this author, even though he subscribes wholeheartedly to them. Nor are they from an officer of the Wilderness Society, although doubtless he, too, would agree with them. They come from a book that was published over 100 years ago. Its author was George Perkins Marsh, a most remarkable man from Vermont. Entitled, variously, *The Earth and Man, Man and Nature*, and *The Earth as Modified by Human Action*, published in English and Italian, and reaching its third edition in a relatively few years, this 650-page volume could have been and should have been a guidepost to the planners of cities in the latter part of the nineteenth century. But it was forgotten, its clarion call for conservation measures for the protection of water, soil, and forests—the message that is again being sounded today—being passed by in the scramble of unrestricted industrial development. Only as the centenary of its publication came round did it again receive any attention, apart from an occasional footnote in writings by historically minded conservationists.[9.33]

The temptation to quote further from this visionary book is difficult to resist since here, over a century old, is the message with which this book must close, clearly written and supported by examples from a score of countries—and all this at a time when steps could have been taken to secure the land around cities that should have been preserved, when lands well suited to agriculture could have been delineated and urban growth planned in other directions. The despoiling with industrial plants of the irreplaceable fruit lands of the Niagara garden belt in southwestern Ontario would rightly have called down the resounding wrath of Marsh had he lived to see it, as would comparable misuse of land in a hundred cities. He knew the place of geology (the "emphatically modern science," as he then called it) in all efforts aimed at the conservation of renewable natural resources. He had thought about the matter of cost, for even in those days there must have been some who questioned whether the country could "afford" such measures. "The cost of one year's warfare," commented Marsh, "—or in some countries of that armed peace which has been called 'Platonic war'—if judiciously expended in a combination of [both] methods of improvement, would secure, to almost every country that man has exhausted, an amelioration of climate, a renovated fertility of soil, and a general physical improvement, which might almost be characterized as a new creation." Making every allowance for the cadences of Victorian prose, there is still a message here that has yet to be learned.

Science has given man the ability to predict. His intellect and accumulated experience have enabled him to use the predictions of science in his planning for the future. So it is that in the conscious planning of how existing cities shall develop, how new towns and cities shall be developed, and how the regions around cities shall be conserved for general benefit, man is able to call upon the findings and predictions of many sciences and disciplines. Another glance at Fig. 3.1 (page 48) will be a useful final reminder of the complexity of urban and regional planning and of the many professional groups that should be called upon to assist in the planning process. Engineering-geologists are just one of these groups; their work must be coordinated with that of other disciplines, even though it has naturally been desirable to present this overview of their work in relative isolation. But, as will now be evident, unless geological conditions are suitable for urban growth, and unless urban development is planned in full coordination with the best possible predictions as to the geological conditions beneath and around the area to be built upon for human use, all other aspects of planning may not be as effective as they should.

So also with the regions around cities, and the areas that should serve cities for the recreation of their citizens. If these are to be conserved—and to conserve means "to keep alive and flourishing"—an understanding of the ground, its nature and what lies beneath it, must be the starting point for this stewardship of the land that is so essential for human happiness and well-being in the future. That this was not done in the past can be regretted and much must be undone, to the extent that is now possible. Man has indeed acted as a destructive geological agent in all too many instances in the past. But in the years ahead, he can be well guided by this experience from the past and remember that it is in his hands to see that cities of the future are indeed designed with nature and not in opposition to it, that the good land around cities is indeed husbanded and conserved so that Nature can continue her beneficence. As his guide he can take words from an English poet who is shared with the world, John Milton, who, in *Paradise Lost*, put these words into the mouth of the Angel (with the "contracted brow"):

> *Accuse not nature, she hath done her part;*
> *Do thou but thine, and be not diffident*
> *Of wisdom, she deserts thee not, if thou*
> *Dismiss not her.*

References
Cited in
Text

A General Note on References

Every effort has been made to cite references that will be generally available, such as *Engineering News-Record* and *Civil Engineering,* for the convenience of readers who wish to have more information on cases mentioned in summary form. There will generally be available more detailed accounts in more technical sources; a few indications of this further information have been given (such as reference 8.6) so that readers may see the wealth of information that is available in a wide variety of journals and proceedings.

Chapter One

1.1   Shelley, Percy Bysshe: Lines 61–67 from *Ode to Liberty.*

1.2   Information kindly provided by Professor S. D. Lash, Kingston.

1.3   United Nations: *18th Demographic Yearbook 1966,* New York, p. 95.

1.4   Shebeski, L. H., and N. B. Hutcheon: *The Future for Agriculture and Building,* DBR Technical Paper 266, National Research Council of Canada, Ottawa, 1967.

1.5   United Nations: *21st Demographic Yearbook 1969,* New York, p. 115.

1.6   Fagley, R. M.: *The Population Explosion and Christian Responsibility,* Oxford University Press, New York, 1960, p. 16.

1.7   Jones, Emrys: *Towns and Cities,* Oxford University Press, Oxford, 1966, p. 2.

1.8   U.S. Bureau of the Census: *Estimates of the Population of 100 Large Metropolitan Areas: 1967 and 1968,* series P-25, no. 432, October 1969.

1.9   United Nations (Economic and Social Council): *Housing, Building and Planning in the Second United Nations Development Decade,* Document E/C.6/90, July 1969, p. 36.

1.10 Charlier, R., and C. Schwartz: "Man and his Cities," *Habitat* (CMHC, Ottawa), **12,** 2–10, 1969.

1.11 Information kindly provided by G. H. Brown, Director, U.S. Bureau of the Census, 1971.

1.12 Sherlock, R. L.: *Man's Influence on the Earth,* T. Thornton Butterworth, Ltd., London, 1931.

1.13   Arvill, R.: *Man and Environment*, (Pelican original) Penguin Books, Harmonds-worth, rev. ed., 1969, p. 38.

1.14   News Release (19849-69), U.S. Department of the Interior, *San Francisco Selected for Pilot Urban Study*, 1969.

Chapter Two

2.1   Handcock, P. (ed.): *The Code of Hammurabi*, Macmillan Texts for Students, New York, 1920, p. 35.

2.2   Hughes, J. Q.: *The Building of Malta 1530–1795*, Academy Edit., London, 1967.

2.3   *Ibid.*, p. 194.

2.4   Hyde, H. P. T.: *Geology of the Maltese Islands*, Lux Press, Malta, 1955.

2.5   Berghinz, C.: "Venice is Sinking into the Sea," *Civil Engineering* (New York), **41**, 67–71, March 1971.

2.6   Reuter's Press Reports in Canadian daily newspapers 22 and 23 October 1971.

2.7   Zaruba, Q., and K. Hromada: "Technicko-Geologicky Rozbor Území Města Kutné Hory" (Geologico-Technical Surveying of the Town of Kutna Hora), Svasek 9, Geotechnica, Prague, 1950; and information in private communication from Dr. Quido Zaruba.

2.8   Hoskins, W. G.: *Local History in England*, Longmans, Green & Co. Ltd., London, 1959, pp. 72–74.

2.9   Thomas, W. N.: *Jour. Inst. Mun. and County Engs.* (London), **54**, 2, 1927.

2.10   Dowrick, D. J., and P. Beckmann: "York Minister Structural Restoration," *Proc. Inst. Civil Engs.*, 1971 Supp. Paper 7415S, 93–156, 1971.

2.11   Morton, H. V.: *In Search of England*, 13th ed., Methuen & Co. Ltd., London, 1931, p. 54; and Hoskins, W. G.: *op. cit.*, p. 72.

2.12   Begbie, Joan: "The Quarrylands of Purbeck," *The Countryman* (Idbury, England), **74**, 115–124, Spring 1970.

2.13   Blythe, F. G. H.: *A Geology for Engineers*, Edward Arnold & Co., London, 1943, pp. 125 and 208; and Morton, H. V.: *op. cit.*, p. 61.

2.14   Cunliffe, B.: *Guide to the Roman Remains of Bath*, Molly J. Gerard, Bath, 1970.

2.15   Kellaway, G. A., and J. H. Taylor: "The Influence of Landslipping on the Development of the City of Bath," *Proc. XXIII Int. Geol. Cong.*, Sec. 12, Prague, 1968, pp. 65–76.

2.16   Knill, J. L., D. G. Price, and I. E. Higginbottom: "Aspects of the Engineering Geology of the City of Bristol," *Proc. XXIII Int. Geol. Cong.*, Sec. 12, Prague, 1968, pp. 77–88.

2.17   In a private communication from Frank Slater, Bristol.

2.18   Vitruvius: *The Ten Books on Architecture*, trans. by M. H. Morgan, Dover Publications Inc., New York, 1960.

2.19   Kingsley, Charles: *Town Geology*, Daldy, Isbister & Co., London, 1877, p. 81.

2.20   Smith, W. (ed.): *A Scientific Survey of Merseyside*, University Press, Liverpool, 1953, p. 215ff.

2.21   *Ibid.*, p. 167.

2.22   Kirkpatrick, Sir C. R. S.: *The Development of Dock and Harbour Engineering*, Inst. Civil Engs., London, 1926.

2.23 Hunter, W. H.: *Rivers and Estuaries*, Longmans, Green & Co. Ltd., London, 1913.

2.24 Gest, A. P.: *Engineering* (Our Debt to Greece and Rome Series), Longmans, Green & Co., New York, 1930, p. 187.

2.25 Sheppard, T.: *The Lost Towns of the Yorkshire Coast*, A. Brown & Sons Ltd., London, 1912.

2.26 Steers, J. A.: *The Sea Coast*, Collins, London, 1953, p. 24; see also *The Coastline of England and Wales*, Cambridge University Press, Cambridge, 1946.

2.27 *Idem*, p. 148.

2.28 Royal Commission on Coast Erosion, Third (and final) Report, H. M. Stationery Office, London, 1911.

2.29 Wilson, Allison: "The Lesson of Hallsands," *New Scientist*, **45**, 311, 12 February 1970.

2.30 Marsh, G. P.: *The Earth as Modified by Human Action*, 2d ed., Sampson, Low, Marston, Low, and Searle, London, 1874.

2.31 Prescott, W. H.: *History of the Conquest of Peru*, J. M. Dent & Sons Ltd., London, 1942, pp. 38, 94. (A modern edition; first published in 1847.)

2.32 Schatz, A., and V. Schatz: "Some Biogeochemical Considerations Concerning the Inca Stonework," *Abstract Vol. Geol. Soc. Amer. Annual Meeting*, Miami Beach, 1964, p. 174.

2.33 Millon, R.: "Teotihuacan; Completion of Map of Giant Ancient City in the Valley of Mexico," *Science*, **170**, 1077–1082, 4 December 1970.

2.34 Fisk, H. N.: "Geologic setting of New Orleans," *Abstract Vol. Geol. Soc. Amer. Annual Meeting*, New Orleans, 1955, p. 35A.

2.35 Information in a private communication from Dr. Clifford A. Kaye.

2.36 Kantrowitz, I. H., and W. G. Weist: "Geological Factors Affecting Urbanization in New York State," *Abstract Vol. Geol. Soc. Amer., N.E. Section, Annual Meeting*, Albany, N.Y., 1969.

Chapter Three

3.1 Wordsworth, W.: Sonnet Composed on Westminster Bridge, *Miscellaneous Sonnets*, pt. II, xxxvi.

3.2 From a speech in 1932 by Franklin D. Roosevelt reported in the daily press.

3.3 Mumford, Lewis: *The Culture of Cities*, Harcourt, Brace and Company, New York, 1938, p. 336.

3.4 Pollard, W. S., and D. W. Moore: "The State of the Art of Planning," *Proc. Amer. Soc. Civil Engs., Urban Planning Div.*, **95**, UP 1, Paper 6517, April 1969.

3.5 Kellett, J. R.: *The Impact of Railways on Victorian Cities*, Routledge and Kegan Paul, London, 1969.

3.6 Mumford, Lewis: *The City in History*, Harcourt, Brace & World, Inc., New York, 1961.

3.7 Mumford, Lewis: *The Culture of Cities*, Harcourt, Brace and Company, New York, 1938.

3.8 Claire, W. H. (ed.): *ASCE Urban Planning Guide,* Amer. Soc. Civ. Engs., Manuals and Reports on Engineering Practice, no. 49, 1969.

3.9 Peterson, G. L., R. S. Gemmell, R. D. Worrall, and D. S. Berry: "Civil Engineering and Urban Systems," *Proc. Amer. Soc. Civil Engs., Urban Planning Div.,* **95**, UP 1, Paper 6501, April 1969.

3.10 Chandler, R. J.: "The Degradation of Lias Clay Slopes in an Area of the East Midlands," *Quat. Jour. Eng. Geol.,* **2**, no. 3, 161, 1970.

3.11 Information received privately from Dr. Quido Zaruba.

3.12 McHarg, Ian: *Design with Nature,* Natural History Press for the American Museum of Natural History, New York, 1969.

3.13 See, for example, *Civil Engineering,* **40**, no. 8, 44, August 1970.

3.14 *Natural Features of the Washington Metropolitan Area,* Metropolitan Washington Council of Governments, Washington, D.C., 1968.

3.15 Darton, N. H.: "Configuration of the Bedrock Surface of the District of Columbia and Vicinity," *USGS Prof. Paper 217,* 1950; see also, "Sedimentary Formations of Washington, D.C., and Vicinity," USGS map, 1947.

3.16 Gould, J. P.: "Geology and the Construction of the Metropolitan Washington, D.C., Rapid Transit System," *Abstract Vol. Geol. Soc. Amer., N.E. Section, Annual Meeting,* Albany, N.Y., 1969.

3.17 Schlocker, J., M. G. Bonilla, and D. H. Radbruch: "Geology of the San Francisco North Quadrangle, California," map I-272, USGS, Washington, D.C., 1958; see also, Radbruch, D. H.: "Areal and Engineering Geology of the Oakland West Quadrangle, California," map I-239, USGS, Washington, D.C., 1957.

3.18 U.S. Department of the Interior, "San Francisco Selected for Pilot Urban Study," Press Release, 29 October 1969.

3.19 Trimble, D. E.: "Geology of Portland, Oregon, and Adjacent Areas," *USGS, Bulletin 1119,* 1963.

3.20 Wooltorton, F. L. D.: "Foundations in Mandalay," *The Structural Engineer,* **18**, 659, September 1940.

3.21 *Symposium on Hong Kong Soils,* Hong Kong Joint Group (of the Institutions of Civil, Mechanical, and Electrical Engineers), May 1962.

3.22 Dastidar, A. G., and P. K. Ghosh: "Subsoil Conditions of Calcutta," *Jour. Institution of Engineers* (India), **48**, no. 3, pt. CI 2, 692, November 1967. (One of the papers presented at a symposium on "The Study of Soil Properties in the Calcutta Region" held in September 1964.)

3.23 Little, I. P., and R. R. Storrier: "A Soil Survey of the Municipality of Ku-Ring-Gai, Sydney," 2d ed., *Bulletin No. 1,* Soil Survey Unit, Chemists Branch, Dept. of Agriculture, New South Wales, 1959; see also, "Suggested Footings for Use in the Municipality of Ku-Ring-Gai," *Technical Record* (not for publication) *of the Commonwealth Experimental Building Station,* Sydney, N.S.W., November 1953.

3.24 *Field Manual of Soil Engineering,* 4th ed., Michigan State Highway Commission, Lansing, 1960.

3.25 McComas, M. R., K. C. Hinkley, and J. P. Kempton: "Coordinated Mapping of Geology and Soils for Land-Use Planning," *Environmental Geology Note No. 29,* Illinois State Geological Survey, December 1969.

3.26 Hilpman, P. L. (ed.): "A Pilot Study of Land-Use Planning and Environmental

Geology," *Report No. 15D* ("701" Project No. Kans. P-43), State Geological Survey of Kansas, June 1968.

3.27 Lutzen, E. E.: "Engineering Geology of the Maxville Quadrangle, Jefferson and St. Louis Counties, Missouri," 2 maps and leaflet, *Engineering Geology Series No. 1*, Missouri Division of Geological Survey and Water Resources, May 1968.

3.28 Mozola, A. J.: "Geology for Environment Planning in Monroe County, Michigan," *Report of Investigation 13*, Michigan Geological Survey Division, 1970.

3.29 Mozola, A. J.: "Geology for Land and Ground-Water Development in Wayne County, Michigan," *Report of Investigation 3*, Michigan Geological Survey Division, 1969.

3.30 Gross, D. L.: "Geology for Planning in DeKalb County, Illinois," *Environmental Geology Note No. 33*, Illinois Stage Geological Survey, April 1970.

3.31 White, G. W.: "Glacial Geology of Wayne County, Ohio," *Report of Investigations No. 62*, Ohio Division of Geological Survey, 1967.

3.32 Willman, H. B., and J. C. Frye: "Pleistocene Stratigraphy of Illinois," *Bulletin 94*, Illinois State Geological Survey, 1970.

3.33 "Environmental Geology and Hydrology, Madison County, Alabama, Meridianville Quadrangle," *Atlas Series 1*, Geological Survey of Alabama, 1971.

3.34 "Physical Characteristics of the Region," *Bulletin Technique No. 4*, Service d'Urbanisme, Montreal, February 1966.

3.35 Prest, V. K., and J. Hode Keyser: "Surficial Geology and Soils of the Montreal Area, Quebec," Presented to the 15th Canadian Soil Mechanics Conference, Montreal, November 1961, separate paper.

3.36 Hode Keyser J.: "Geologie de Montreal," *Proc. Sixth Int. Conf. on Soil Mech. and Found. Eng.*, Montreal, **3**, 114, Montreal, 1965.

3.37 Christiansen, E. A. (ed.): "Physical Environment of Saskatoon, Canada," Sask. Research Council and National Research Council of Canada, Ottawa, 1970.

3.38 Hughes, G. T.: "Geology and the Engineering Properties of Soils in the Kingston Area," Royal Military College, Kingston, 1958; see also, Joliffe, A. W., and D. L. Townsend: "Geotechnical Notes of the Kingston Area," Queen's University, Kingston, 1969.

3.39 Karrow, P. F.: "Pleistocene Geology of the Galt Map-Area," *Geological Circular No. 9*, Dept. of Mines, Toronto, Ont., 1961.

3.40 Karrow, P. F.: "Pleistocene Geology of the Scarborough Area," *Geological Report 46*, Dept. of Mines, Toronto, Ont., 1967.

3.41 Bergstrom, R. E. (ed.): "Geology for Planning at Crescent City," *Environmental Geology Note No. 36*, Illinois State Geological Survey, September 1970.

3.42 Varnes, D. J., and G. R. Scott: "General and Engineering Geology of the United States Air Force Academy Site, Colorado," *USGS Prof. Paper 551*, 1967.

3.43 Gerlach, A. C. (ed.): "Environmental Conditions and Resources of Southwestern Mississippi," USGS, Geographic Applications Program, February 1970.

3.44 McLerran, J. H.: "Airphoto Interpretation for Airfield Site Location," *Proc. Amer. Soc. Civil Engs., Air Transport Div.*, **66**, AT 1, Paper 2467, 73, May 1960.

3.45 Merrill, C. L., J. A. Pihlainen, and R. F. Legget: "The New Aklavik—Search for the Site," *Engineering Jour.*, **43**, 52, January 1960.

3.46 Brown, R. J. E.: *Permafrost in Canada*, University of Toronto Press, 1970.

3.47 *Permafrost in Canada* (Map at 1 inch to 120 miles): map no. 1246A of the Geol. Survey of Canada and pub. no. NRC 9769 of the Div. of Building Research, National Research Council of Canada, 1967, reprinted 1969.

3.48 MacFarlane, I. C. (ed.): *Muskeg Engineering Handbook*, University of Toronto Press, 1969.

3.49 Aitchison, G. D., and K. Grant: "The P.U.C.E. Programme of Terrain Description, Evaluation and Interpretation for Engineering Purposes," *Proc. Fourth Regional Conf. for Africa on Soil Mechanics and Foundation Engineering*, Cape Town, December 1967, p. 1.

3.50 Stewart, G. A. (ed.): *Land Evaluation*, Macmillan of Australia, 1968.

3.51 Lung, R., and R. Proctor (eds.): *Engineering Geology in Southern California*, Assoc. of Eng. Geologists, Glendale, Calif., 1966.

3.52 Gardner, M. E.: "Preliminary Engineering Geologic Map of the Boulder Quadrangle, Boulder County, Colorado," USGS, Open File 1968.

3.53 "An Act concerning the Adoption of Subdivision Regulations" (Senate Bill No. 105), State of Colorado, 1967.

3.54 City of Lakewood Comprehensive Plan, General Design Considerations; City of Lakewood Planning Commission, 1970.

3.55 Hruska, J. (ed.): *Bibliography and Index of Engineering Geological Mapping; Part 1: Czechoslovakia, German Democratic Republic, Hungary, Poland*, Geofond, Prague, 1970.

3.56 Sujkowski, Z., and S. Z. Rozycki: Mapa Geologiczna Warszawy, Warszawa, 1936.

3.57 Zaruba, Q.: "Geologický Podklad a Základove Pomery Vnitrní Prahy" (Geologic Features and Foundation Conditions of the City of Prague), Svazek 5, Geotechnica, Prague, 1948.

3.58 Goldodkovskaya, G. A., N. V. Kolomenskii, I. V. Popov, and M. V. Churinov: "Engineering Geological Mapping in the U.S.S.R.," *Proc. XXIII Int. Geol. Cong.*, Sec. 12, Prague, 1968, p. 57.

3.59 Czoray, G.: "A Mernoekgeologiai Terkepezes Helyzete es Kerdesei az Alfdelden" (Present State and Problems of Engineering-Geological Mapping in the Great Hungarian Plain), *Relat. Inst. Geol. Hungary*, 513, Budapest, 1964.

3.60 Personal communication from Professor Quido Zaruba.

3.61 Gazel, J., and A. Peter: "Essais de Cartographie Geotechnique," *Annales des Mines*, 41, Paris, December 1969.

3.62 Matula, M.: *Regional Engineering Geology of Czechoslovak Carpathians*, Slovak Acad. of Sciences, Bratislava, 1969.

Chapter Four

4.1 Aristotle: *Politics*, trans. by B. Jowett, Modern Library, New York, 1943, p. 300 (book VII, chap. 11).

4.2 Morris, W. V.: *Water*, Dept. of Energy, Mines and Resources, Ottawa, 1968.

4.3 Thomson, D. H.: "Water and Water Power," *Trans. Liverpool Eng. Soc.*, **44**, 105, 1923.

4.4   Quoted in Blake, N. M.: *Water for the Cities*, Syracuse University Press, 1956.

4.5   *Ibid.*, p. 35.

4.6   See Swenson, E. G. (ed.): *Performance of Concrete*, University of Toronto Press, 1968.

4.7   Distillers-Corporation Seagrams Ltd., *Annual Report*, Montreal, 1969, p. 27.

4.8   Daiches, D.: *Scotch Whisky*, Andre Deutsch, London, 1969.

4.9   "Hot Well Water Cooled for Use in City Distribution Systems," *Eng. News-Record*, **118**, 130, 1957.

4.10 Personal communication from Dr. Jan Silar, Prague; see also, Silar J., "Czechoslovak Mineral Springs," *Geotimes,* **13**, 10, May–June 1968.

4.11 Koenig, J. B.: "Geothermal Development," *Geotimes,* **16**, 10, March 1971; see also, Garrison, L. E., "Geothermal Steam in the Geysers, Clear Lake Region, California," *Bull. Geol. Soc. Amer.*, **83**, 1449–1468, May 1972.

4.12 Zoega, J., and G. Kristinsson: "The Reykjavik District Heating System," *Proc. U.N. Conference on Resources*, **2**, 3, Rome, August 1961.

4.13 Render, F. W.: "Geohydrology of the Metropolitan Winnipeg Area as Related to Groundwater Supply and Construction," *Can. Geotechnical Jour.*, **7**, no. 3, 243, 1970.

4.14 Savini, J., and J. C. Kammerer: "Urban Growth and the Water Regimen," *USGS Water-Supply Paper 1591-A*, 1961.

4.15 "The New Filter Gallery at Des Moines, Iowa," *Eng. News-Record*, **65**, 468, 1912.

4.16 Gourlay, H. J. F.: "The Water-Supply of Kano, Northern Nigeria," *Min. Proc. Inst. Civil Engs.*, London, **237**, 454, 1935.

4.17 Lloyd, J. G., "River Authorities and Their Work," *Jour. Inst. Water Engineers*, **22**, 1, 1968.

4.18 *Water Management in Ontario*, Ont. Water Resources Commission, Toronto (no date).

4.19 *The Water Supply of London*, London, Metropolitan Water Board, 1961.

4.20 Gough, J. W.: *Sir Hugh Myddleton*, Oxford University Press, Oxford, 1964.

4.21 *Thames Conservancy Water Plan: Pilot Scheme Successfully Completed*, Thames Conservancy, Reading, May 1970.

4.22 See 4.4, p. 100.

4.23 Cohen, P., O. L. Franke, and B. L. Foxworthy: "An Atlas of Long Island's Water Resources," *N.Y. Water Resources Commission Bulletin 62*, 1968.

4.24 *Water for Sydney*, Metropolitan Water, Sewerage and Drainage Board, Sydney, N.S.W., Australia, 1959.

4.25 "Hong Kong Stores Water in Sea," *Eng. News-Record*, **172**, 26, 9 January 1964.

4.26 Personal information from the late G. Chiappe, City Engineer, and others at Gibraltar.

4.27 "Miner's Mistake is Modern Blessing," *Eng. News-Record*, **168**, 37, 8 March 1962.

4.28 *Greater Vancouver Water District*, folder, 1958.

4.29 Aten, R. E., and R. E. Bergstrom, "Ground-Water Hydrology of Kuwait," *ASCE Reprint 152*, Water Resources Conference, Mobile, Alabama, March 1965.

4.30 *The Water Resources of Oahu*, The Honolulu Board of Water Supply, 1960.

4.31 Bruington, A. E., and F. D. Seares: "Operating a Sea Water Barrier Project," *Proc. Amer. Soc. Civil Engs., Irrigation and Drainage Div.*, Paper 4264, 117, March 1965.

4.32 Bruington, A. E.: "Progress on Barrier to Sea Water Intrusion," *Proc. Amer. Soc. Civil Engs., Irrigation and Drainage Div.*, Paper 2159, 89, September 1959; see also, "Wall of Wells Will Hold Back Pacific," *Eng. News-Record*, **167**, 28, 13 July 1961.

4.33 "Israel Turns to Sewage for Water," *Eng. News-Record*, **183**, 42, 6 November 1969.

4.34 Evans, D. M.: "Man-made Earthquakes in Denver," *Geotimes*, **11**, 11, May-June 1966; see also, Evans, D. M.: "Man-made Earthquakes—a Progress Report," *Geotimes*, **13**, 19, July-August 1967.

4.35 "Unusual Flood in Ohio Town," *Eng. News-Record*, **119**, 40, 1937.

4.36 "Dig Deep to Store Storm Water," *Eng. News-Record*, **175**, 18, 22 July 1965; see also, Sorenson, K. E.: "Underground Reservoirs: Pumped Storage of the Future?" *Civil Engineering*, **39**, 66, March 1969.

4.37 Ackenheil, A. C.: "Pennsylvania Erases Its Mining Scars," *Civil Engineering*, **40**, 54, October 1970.

4.38 Boughner, C. C.: "Hurricane Hazel," *Weather*, **10**, 200, June 1955.

4.39 Goddard, J. E.: "Flood-plain Management," *Civil Engineering*, **41**, 81, September 1971.

4.40 Vogt, E. Z., and R. Hyman: *Water Witching U.S.A.*, University of Chicago Press, 1959

Chapter Five

5.1 Vitruvius: *The Ten Books of Architecture*, trans. by M. H. Morgan, Dover Publications Inc., New York, 1960, p. 88.

5.2 Harton, F. P.: *The Pictorial History of Wells Cathedral*, Pitkin Pictorials Ltd. (no date); and in personal communications from The Very Reverend the Dean of Wells and G. A. Kellaway.

5.3 Price, D. G., and J. L. Knill: "The Engineering Geology of Edinburgh Castle Rock," *Geotechnique*, **17**, 411, December 1967.

5.4 Personal communication from Dr. L Bjerrum, Oslo.

5.5 See Terzaghi, K., and R. B. Peck: *Soil Mechanics in Engineering Practice*, John Wiley & Sons, New York, 1948.

5.6 Farquhar, O. C.: "Rhode Island Formation in Rock Excavation, Massachusetts," *Abstract Vol. Geol. Soc. Amer. Annual Meeting*, Kansas City, 1965, p. 65.

5.7 Higginbottom, I. E., and P. G. Fookes: "Engineering Aspects of Periglacial Features in Britain," *Quat. Jour. Eng. Geology*, **3**, 85, December 1970.

5.8 Thomson, S.: "Riverbank Stability Study at the University of Alberta, Edmonton," *Can. Geotechnical Jour.*, **7**, 157, June 1970.

5.9 "Leaning Tower of Pisa," *Eng. News-Record*, **150**, 40, 2 April 1953.

5.10 Gillette, D. H.: "Washington Monument Facts Brought up to Date," *Eng. News-Record*, **109**, 501, 1933.

5.11 Cummings, R. J.: "Design of San Jacinto Monument," *Civil Engineering*, **7**, 484, July 1937; Dawson, R. F.: "Settlement Studies on San Jacinto Monument," *Civil Engineering*, **8**, 589, September 1938; and private information from Professor R. F. Dawson.

5.12 Fox, Sir Francis: *Sixty Three Years of Engineering*, John Murray, London, 1924, p. 125.

5.13 Green, E. E.: "An Account of the Problems Caused by Ground Water, Encountered during the Construction of the New Wessex Hotel at Winchester, for Trust Houses Limited," *Proc. Institution Civil Engs.*, London, **28**, 171, June 1964.

5.14 Zeevaert, L.: "Foundation Design and Behavior of Tower Latino Americana in Mexico City," *Geotechnique*, **7**, 115, September 1957; see also, Thornley, J. H., G. B. Spencer, and P. Albin: "Mexico's Palace of Fine Arts Settles 10 ft.," *Civil Engineering*, **25**, 357, June 1955.

5.15 Crawford, C. B.: "Settlement Studies on the National Museum Building, Ottawa, Canada," *Proc. Third Int. Conf. on Soil Mech. and Found. Eng.*, Zurich, **1**, 338, 1953.

5.16 Crawford, C. B., and J. G. Sutherland: "The Empress Hotel, Victoria, British Columbia; Sixty-Five Years of Foundation Settlements," *Can. Geotechnical Jour.*, **8**, 77, February 1971.

5.17 Heydenrych, R. A., and B. Isaacs: "The Excavation and Stabilizing of the Carlton Centre Basement," unpublished paper 1967; see also, "Record Slip Formed Core Rises from a Tricky Excavation," *Eng. News-Record*, **185**, 22, 3 December 1970.

5.18 Nicoletti, J. P., and J. M. Keith: "External 'Shell' Stops Soil Movement and Saves Tunnel," *Civil Engineering*, **39**, 72, April 1969.

5.19 Legget, R. F.: "The Wellpoint System; Application to an Excavation in Waterlogged Ground in Canada," *Civil Eng. and Public Works Review*, London, **31**, 229, 1936.

5.20 Dixon, H. H., and R. H. S. Robertson: "Some Engineering Experiences in Tropical Soils," *Quat. Jour, Eng. Geol.*, **3**, no. 3, 137–150, December 1970.

5.21 "Haste Pays Off in Hong Kong," *Eng. News-Record*, **173**, 42, 27 August 1964.

5.22 Nowson, W. J. R.: "The History and Construction of the Foundations of the Asia Insurance Building, Singapore," *Proc. Inst. Civil Engs.*, pt. 1, **3**, 407, 1954.

5.23 Feld, J.: "Report on International Conference on Rock Mechanics," *Civil Engineering*, **36**, 59, December 1966.

5.24 "Anchoring Unstable Foundations," *Civil Eng. and Public Works Review*, London, **55**, 893, July 1960.

5.25 Wilson, A. E.: "Geology of the Ottawa-St. Lawrence Lowland, Ontario and Quebec," *Memoir 241*, Geol. Survey of Canada, Ottawa, 1946.

5.26 Reitz, H. M.: "Foundations on Fissured Limestone—How They Were Selected," *Civil Engineering*, **35**, 52, September 1965.

5.27 Peterson, R.: "Rebound in the Bearpaw Shale, Western Canada," *Bull. Geol. Soc. Amer.*, **69**, 1113, 1958.

5.28 Hardy, R. M.: "Engineering Problems Involving Preconsolidated Clay Shales," *Trans. Eng. Inst. Canada*, **1**, 1, 1957.

5.29 Penner, E., J. E. Gillott, and W. J. Eden: "Investigation of Heave in Billings Shale by Mineralogical and Biogeochemical Methods," *Can. Geotechnical Jour.*, 7, 333, September 1970.

5.30 Brune, G.: "Anhydrite and Gypsum Problems in Engineering Geology," *Eng. Geol.* (now *Bull. Assoc. Eng. Geol.*) 2, 26–38, 1965.

5.31 Rutledge, P. C.: "Utilization of Marginal Lands for Urban Development," *Proc. Amer. Soc. Civil Engs., Soil Mech. Div.*, 96, SM 1, Paper 7000, 3, January 1970.

5.32 *From Fisherman's Paradise to Farmer's Pride*, a 1959 publication of the Netherlands Government Information Service, is an excellent introduction to this great work. For more details see 8.18.

5.33 Lobdell, H. L.: "Settlement of Buildings constructed in Hackensack Meadows," *Proc. Amer. Soc. Civil Engs., Soil Mech. Div.*, 96, SM 4, Paper 7398, 1235, July 1970; see also, Widmer, K., and D. G. Parrillo: "Pre-Pleistocene Topography of the Hackensack Meadows, New Jersey," Abstract Vol. *Geol. Soc. Amer. Annual Meeting*, Pittsburgh, 1959, p. 140A.

5.34 Wood, E. D.: "Wellpoints Master Oolite," *Eng. News-Record*, 152, 35, 6 May 1954.

5.35 "Permanent Wellpoints Keep Sewage Tanks from Floating," *Eng. News-Record*, 150, 47, 26 March 1953.

5.36 "Modern Engineering to Save Mediaeval Tower," *Eng. News-Record*, 91, 505, 1923.

5.37 Snow, B. F.: "Tracing Loss of Groundwater," *Eng. News-Record*, 117, 1, 1936; see also, "Drainage in Reverse at Copley Square," *Eng. News-Record*, 154, 47, 28 April 1955.

5.38 "Artificial Groundwater for Wood Piles," *Eng. News-Record*, 107, 70, 1931; and also information given personally by L. Clarey, Building Superintendent.

5.39 Legget, R. F., and C. B. Crawford: "Trees and Buildings," *Canadian Building Digest No. 62*, Ottawa, February 1965.

5.40 Bozozuk, M., and K. N. Burn: "Vertical Ground Movement near Elm Trees," *Geotechnique*, 10, 19, 1960.

5.41 Skempton, A. W.: "A Foundation Failure due to Clay Shrinkage Caused by Poplar Trees," *Proc. Inst. Civil Engs.*, pt 1, 3, 66, 1954; see also, Hammer, M. J., and U. B. Thomson: "Foundation Clay Shrinkage Caused by Large Trees," *Proc. Amer. Soc. Civil Engs., Soil Mech. Div.*, 92, SM 6, Paper 4956, November 1966.

5.42 "Foundation Reinstatement without Interference to Services," *The Engineer*, London, 220, 791, 12 November 1965.

5.43 McMahon, C. A.: "Los Angeles Constructs 2,000-Car Underground Garage," *Civil Engineering*, 21, 689, December 1951.

5.44 Kapp, M. S.: "Slurry-Trench Construction for Basement Wall of World Trade Centre," *Civil Engineering*, 39, 36, April 1969.

5.45 Skempton, A. W.: "The Albion Mill Foundations," *Geotechnique*, 21, 203, September 1971.

5.46 Glick, G. W.: "Rigid Rectangular Frame Foundation for Albany Telephone Building," *Eng. News-Record*, 105, 836, 27 November 1930.

5.47 Golder, H. Q.: "State of the Art of Floating Foundations," *Proc. Amer. Soc.*

Civil Engs., Soil Mech. Div., **91**, SM 2, Paper 4278, 81, March 1965.

5.48 "Five-Story Basement Sinks Below Grade," *Eng. News-Record*, **169**, 43, 6 December 1962.

5.49 "Caissons Dig Out a Seven-Story Basement," *Eng. News-Record*, **166**, 42, 6 July 1961; see also, Brugger, M. A.: "Garage Rive-Centre à Genéve," *L'Enterprise*, Zurich, no. 15–16, 1, 1961.

5.50 Johnson, S. D.: "Precompression for Improving Foundation Soils," *Proc. Amer. Soc. Civil Engs., Soil Mech. Div.*, **96**, SM 1, Paper 7020, January 1970.

5.51 "Surcharging a Big Warehouse Floor Saves $1 Million," *Eng. News-Record*, **176**, 22, 3 March 1966.

5.52 Ellis, D. R., and J. McConnell: "The Use of Freezing Process in the Construction of a Pumping Station and Stormwater Overflow at Fleetwood, Lancashire," *Proc. Inst. Civil Engs.*, **12**, 175, February 1959.

5.53 Prentis, E. A., and L. White: *Underpinning*, 2d. ed., Columbia University Press, New York, 1950.

5.54 "Sweden's Royal Palace Gets Underpinning to Stop Settling," *Eng. News-Record*, **175**, 48, 23 September 1965.

5.55 White, G. W., S. M. Totten, and D. L. Gross: "Pleistocene Stratigraphy of Northwestern Pennsylvania," *General Geology Report G 55*, Pennsylvania Bureau of Topographic and Geologic Survey, 1969.

5.56 Upson, J. E., E. B. Leopold, and M. Rubin: "Postglacial Change of Sealevel in New Haven Harbour, Connecticut," *Amer. Jour. Science*, **262**, 121, January 1964.

5.57 Kaye, C. A.: "Kaolinization of Bedrock of the Boston, Massachusetts, Area," *USGS Prof. Paper 575-C*, p. C165, 1967.

Chapter Six

6.1 Murray, M. A.: *Petra, the Rock City of Eden,* Blackie and Son, London, 1939; see also, Kennedy, Sir A.: *Petra, Its History and Monuments,* Country Life, London, 1925.

6.2 White, E. E.: "Saving the Temples of Abu Simbel," *Civil Engineering*, **32**, 34–38, August 1962.

6.3 Prelini, C.: *Tunnelling*, 6th ed., D. Van Nostrand Company, Inc., Princeton, N.J., 1912.

6.4 Blake, N. M.: *Water for the Cities*, Syracuse University Press, 1956, p. 3; see also, Taylor, E. J.: "The Beginnings of Philadelphia's Water Supply," *Jour. Amer. Water Works Assoc.*, **42**, 633, July 1950. Additional notes from S. J. Schwartz through the kindness of S. G. Baxter of Philadelphia.

6.5 Laurie, P.: *Beneath the City Streets*, Allen Lane The Penguin Press, London, 1970.

6.6 Crawford, C. B., and R. F. Legget: "Ground Temperature Investigations in Canada," *Engineering Jour.*, **40**, 263, 1957.

6.7 *A New Concept in Space*, Missouri Resources and Development Commission, Jefferson City, 1961; see also, *Guidebook to the Geology and Utilization of Underground Space in the Kansas City Area, Missouri*, Assoc. of Missouri Geologists, 1971.

6.8 "Building Underground: Factories and Offices in a Cave," *Eng. News-Record*, **166**, 58, 18 May 1961.

6.9 Reuters: "Russia Puts Old Salt Mine to New Use as a Hospital," *Globe and Mail*, Toronto, 16 November 1970.

6.10 Albert, O.: "Shelters in Sweden," *Civil Engineering*, **31**, 63, November 1961.

6.11 Morfeldt, C.-O.: "Significance of Groundwater at Rock Constructions of Different Types," *Proc. Int. Symp. on Large Permanent Underground Openings*, Oslo, 1969, p. 311.

6.12 Blaschke, T. O.: "Underground Command Centre," *Civil Engineering*, **34**, 36, May 1964; see also, "Builders Blast Out Underground Fortress," *Eng. News-Record*, **167**, 38, 16 November 1961.

6.13 "Huge Underground Vaults Built Oiltight," *Eng. News-Record*, **135**, 873, 1945.

6.14 *Power from Labrador*, Churchill Falls (Labrador) Corp. Ltd., Montreal, 1969.

6.15 Anderson, D.: "The Construction of the Mersey Tunnel," *Jour. Inst. Civil Engs.*, 2, 473, 1936; see also, Boswell, P. G. H.: "The Geology of the New Mersey Tunnel," *Proc. Liverpool. Geol. Soc.*, **17**, 160, 1937.

6.16 Morgan, H. D., and J. V. Bartlett: "The Victoria Line; Part Three, Tunnel Design," *Proc. Inst. Civil Engs.*, Supp. Vol., 1969, Paper 7270 S, 377, 1969.

6.17 Follenfant, H.: "The Victoria Line; The Project," *Proc. Inst. Civil Engs.*, Supp. Vol., 1969, Paper 7270 S, 337, 1969, with four companion papers.

6.18 James, L., J. W. Marlette, and E. Weber: "Investigation of Alternative Aqueduct Systems to Serve Southern California: Appendix C, Procedure for Estimating Cost of Tunnel Construction," Calif. Dep't of Water Resources, September 1959.

6.19 Thomas, H. H.: "Machine Tunneling in Tasmania," *Civil Engineering*, **33**, 60, March 1963.

6.20 "Chicago Report: 6 ft per hour of 16 ft. 10 in. dia. Tunnel," *Eng. News-Record*, **185**, 44, 12 November 1970.

6.21 "Mole Bests Mexico City's Treacherous Subsoil," *Eng. News-Record*, **185**, 20, 2 July 1970.

6.22 "Regional Sewer System Is No Dream in Detroit," *Eng. News-Record*, **185**, 24, 10 December 1970.

6.23 Mair, A.: "U.S. 'Mole' Bores 18 ft. Edmonton Tunnel," *Eng. and Contract Record*, Toronto, **52**, 82, March, 1968.

6.24 Eden, W. J., and M. Bozozuk: "Earth Pressures on Ottawa Outfall Sewer Tunnel," *Can. Geotechnical Jour.*, **6**, 17, February 1969.

6.25 Montgomery, T. J.: "Tunnelers Dig Past Heavy Structures," *Eng. News-Record*, **162**, 43, 21 May 1959.

6.26 Rahm, D. A.: "Geology of the Main Drainage Tunnel, Boston, Massachusetts," *Jour. Boston Soc. Civil Engs.*, **49**, 319, October 1962.

6.27 Billings, M. P., and F. L. Tierney: "Geology of the City Tunnel Extension, Greater Boston, Massachusetts," *Jour. Boston Soc. Civil Engs.*, **51**, 111, April 1964.

6.28 Billings, M. P., and D. A. Rahm: "Geology of the Malden Tunnel, Massachusetts," *Jour. Boston Soc. Civil Engs.*, **53**, 116, April 1966.

6.29 "On-schedule at Niagara," *Eng. News-Record*, **151**, 33, 10 September 1953.

6.30 Cerutti, H. P.: "Twin Conduits for Niagara," *Civil Engineering*, **30**, 50, July 1960.

6.31 Busfield, J. L.: "The Mount Royal Tunnel," *Engineering Jour.*, **2**, 267, 1919.

6.32 Low, G. J.: "Soil Freezing to Reconstruct a Railway Tunnel," *Proc. Amer. Soc. Civil Engs., Constr. Div.*, **86**, CO 3, Paper 2639, November 1960.

6.33 Clark, J. A. M., G. S. Hook, J. J. Lee, P. L. Mason, and D. G. Thomas: "The Victoria Line; Part Four, Some Modern Developments in Tunnelling Construction," *Proc. Inst. Civil Engs.,* Supp. Vol., 1969, Paper 7270 S, 397, 1969.

6.34 "Digging Foundation Around Bridge Approach and Subway Tunnels," *Eng. News-Record*, **162**, 60, 18 June 1959.

6.35 Legget, R. F., and W. R. Schriever: "Site Investigations for Canada's First Underground Railway," *Civil Eng. Public Works Rev.,* London, **55**, 73, 1960.

6.36 Information received privately from G. Connel, Seattle, Consulting Engineer.

6.37 "Twin Highway Tunnels are Driven from One End Only," *Eng. News-Record*, **160**, 34, 16 January 1958.

6.38 Page, B. N.: "Geology of the Broadway Tunnel, Berkeley Hills, California," *Econ. Geology*, **45**, 142, March-April 1950.

6.39 Baker, C. O., and D. A. Howells: "The Gibraltar Hill Tunnel, Monmouth (Great Britain)," *Eng. Geology*, Amsterdam, **3**, 121, 1969.

6.40 Parry, R. R., and G. D. Thornton: "Construction of the Monmouth Tunnels in Soft Rock," *Proc. Inst. Civil Engs.*, **47**, 25, September 1970.

6.41 Schneider, A.: *Railways Through the Mountains of Europe*, Ian Allan Ltd., London, 1967, p. 126.

6.42 "Dynamiters Blast Out a Tunnel . . . but Delicately," *Eng. News-Record*, **161**, 58, 11 December 1958.

6.43 Rolt, L. T. C.: *Isambard Kingdom Brunel*, Arrow Books, London, 1961, p. 33.

6.44 Noble, C. B.: *The Brunels; Father and Son*, Cobden-Sanderson, London, 1938, p. 80.

6.45 Haswell, C. K.: "Thames Cable Tunnel," *Proc. Inst. Civil Engs.*, **44**, 323, December 1969.

6.46 Smaill, W., and R. M. Wynne-Edwards: "Difficult Caisson Sinking for Vancouver Water Tunnel," *Eng. News-Record*, **111**, 9, 6 July 1933.

6.47 Richardson, C. A.: "Constructing a Soft-Ground Tunnel under Boston Harbour," *Civil Engineering*, **31**, 42, January 1961.

6.48 "Driving the Queens Midtown Tunnel," *Eng. News-Record*, **124**, 29, 1940.

6.49 See 6.15; see also, McKenzie, J. C., and G. S. Dodds: "Mersey Kingsway Tunnel Construction" (with two companion papers), *Proc. Inst. Civil Engs.*, **51**, 503–533, March 1972.

6.50 Murphy, G. J., and I. W. Tarshansky: "Foundation Problems on the Second Elizabeth River Tunnel," *Civil Engineering*, **33**, 54, July 1963.

6.51 Plantema, G.: "Rotterdam's Rapid Transit Tunnel Built by Sunken-Tube Method," *Civil Engineering*, **35**, 34, August 1965; supplemented by information from Dr. G. Plantema.

6.52 *Report on the Collapse of Clifton Hall Tunnel*, H. M. Stationery Office, Ministry of Transport and Civil Aviation, London, 1964.

6.53 See 6.26 to 6.28.

6.54 Gorrell, H. A.: "Ordovician Dundas Formation as Exposed in the Excavations for the Toronto Subway," p. 62; Schriever, W. R.: "Soil Mechanics Studies for the Toronto Subway," p. 105; Watt, A. K.: "Correlation of the Pleistocene

Geology as Seen in the Subway with that of the Toronto Region, Canada," p. 122. All in *Abstract Vol. Geol. Soc. Amer. Annual Meeting*, Toronto, 1953.

6.55 Kloos, H.: *Conversation with the Earth*, Routledge and Kegan Paul Ltd., London, 1954, p. 309; © R. Piper & Co. Verlag, München, 1947.

Chapter Seven

7.1 Salzman, L. F.: *Building in England Down to 1540; A Documentary History*, Oxford University Press, 1952, p. 126.

7.2 *Canada 1968* (Official Handbook of Present Conditions and Recent Progress), Dominion Bureau of Statistics, Ottawa, 1969, p. 111.

7.3 See 6.43, p. 149.

7.4 Cotham Caving Group, *Box Freestone Mines*, Free Troglophile Assoc., Bristol, 1966.

7.5 *Stone and the Architect*, 5th ed., The Stone Firms Ltd., London and Corsham, Wilts., 1967.

7.6 Sherlock, R. L.: *Man's Influence on the Earth*, T. Thornton Butterworth, Ltd., London, 1931.

7.7 Brindley, J., probably, as explained with the quotation at the head of Chap. 6 (p. 253).

7.8 Legget, R. F.: *Rideau Waterway*, University of Toronto Press, 1955, p. 49.

7.9 "Precast Window Frames Cover Hotel," *Eng. News-Record*, **163**, 38, 22 October 1959.

7.10 Gross, M. G.: "New York Metropolitan Region—A Major Sediment Source," *Water Resources Research*, **6**, 927–931, 1970.

7.11 In a personal communication from Prof. A. F. Byers, Saskatoon.

7.12 In a personal communication from Dr. Clifford A. Kaye, Boston.

7.13 See, for example, "ASTM Standard C568-67 Dimension Limestone" and "ASTM Standard C170-50 Standard Method of Test for Compressive Strength of Natural Building Stone," both in *ASTM Book of Standards*, Part 12, Philadelphia, 1969.

7.14 Hudson, K.: *The Fashionable Stone*, Adams and Dart, Bath, 1971.

7.15 Schaffer, R. J.: *The Weathering of Natural Building Stones*, 2d ed., Special Report no. 18 of the Building Research Station, H. M. Stationery Office, London, 1933.

7.16 Information kindly supplied by George M. White, Architect to the Capitol, Washington, D.C.

7.17 Information kindly supplied by A. J. Henshaw, Surveyor, Houses of Parliament, London.

7.18 Baird, D.: "Guide to the Geology and Scenery of the National Capital Area," *Misc. Report No. 15*, Geol. Survey of Canada, 1968.

7.19 Information kindly supplied by B. Tawse, Aberdeen.

7.20 Shadmon, A.: "Quarry Site Surveys in Relation to Country Planning," *Proc. XXIII Int. Geol., Cong.*, Sec. 12, Prague, 1968, p. 125.

7.21 Lafay, M.: "L'Inspection Générale des Carrières de la Seine," *Travaux*, p. 3, Paris, 1958.

7.22 Vitruvius: *The Ten Books of Architecture*, trans. by M. H. Morgan, Dover Publications Inc., New York, 1960, p. 42.

7.23 Biggar, H. P. (ed.): *The Works of Samuel de Champlain*, vol. V (1608–1620), The Champlain Society, Toronto, 1932, p. 128.

7.24 Prescott, W. H.: *The Conquest of Peru*, J. M. Dent & Sons, Ltd., London, 1942, p. 39; see also 2.32.

7.25 Patty, T. S.: "Industrial Mineral Utilization by the Texas Highway Department," unpublished paper given to *Fourth Annual Meeting Geol. Soc. Amer., S. Central Section*, College Station, Texas, April 1970.

7.26 Kerr, L. and P. Brown: "Process Building over Faulted Rock," *Eng. News-Record*, **135**, 795, 1945.

7.27 See, for example, R. A. Lohnes, R. O. Fish, and T. Demirel: "Geotechnical Properties of Selected Puerto Rican Soils in Relation to Climate and Parent Rock," *Bull. Geol. Soc. Amer.*, **82**, 2617, September 1971.

7.28 See, for example, D. A. Cawsey, "Volcanic Road-making Materials in the Tropics," *Proc. Geol. Soc. London*, no. 1662, p. 13, 1970.

7.29 Pliny: *Natural History*, XXXVI, sec. 173 in vol. X, Loeb Classical Library, D. E. Eichholz (ed.), William Heinemann Ltd., London, 1962, p. 137.

7.30 Smeaton, J.: *A Narrative of the Building and a Description of the Construction of the Edystone Lighthouse with Stone . . .*, printed by H. Hughs, sold by G. Nicol, London, 1791.

7.31 "Chewing Up a Mountain, Cheaply," *Eng. News-Record*, **180**, 56, 23 May 1968.

7.32 See 4.6.

7.33 Duncan, M. A. G., and E. G. Swenson: "Investigation of Concrete Expansion in Nova Scotia," *Prof. Eng. Nova Scotia*, Halifax, **10**, no. 2, 16, May 1969.

7.34 Legget, R. F.: *Geology and Engineering*, 2d ed., McGraw-Hill Book Company, New York, 1962, p. 270.

7.35 Williams, H., and J. N. Stothard: "Rock Excavation and Specification Trials for the Lancashire-Yorkshire Motorway, Yorkshire (West Riding) Section," *Proc. Inst. Civil Engs.*, **36**, 607, March 1967.

7.36 Withington, C. F.: "Engineering Geology in Urban Affairs," *Abstract Vol. Geol. Soc. Amer. N.E. Section, Annual Meeting*, Albany, N.Y., March 1969.

7.37 Hewitt, D. F., and P. F. Karrow: "Sand and Gravel in Southern Ontario," *Industrial Mineral Report No. 11*, Dept. of Mines, Ont., Toronto, 1963.

7.38 See "Test Methods" in *ASTM Book of Standards*, Part 10, Concrete and Mineral Aggregates (including Manual of Concrete Testing), Philadelphia, 1971.

7.39 Hanes, F. E., and R. A. Wyman: "The Application of Heavy Media Separation to Concrete Aggregate," *Bull. Can. Inst. Mining and Metal.*, **55**, no. 603, 489, July 1962.

7.40 Information kindly supplied by Shipping and World Traffic Publications Ltd., Basle.

7.41 Hewitt, D. F., and S. E. Yundt: "Mineral Resources of the Toronto-Centered Region," *Industrial Mineral Report No. 38,* Dept. of Mines Ontario, Toronto, 1971; see also 7.52.

7.42 Duane, D. B.: "Sand and Gravel Deposits in the Nearshore Continental Shelf, Sandy Hook to Cape May, New Jersey," *Abstract Vol. Geol. Soc. Amer. Annual Meeting*, Atlantic City, 1969, p. 53.

7.43 Lewis, A. F. G. (ed.): *Sea-Dredged Aggregates for Concrete*, Proc. of a Symposium, Sand and Gravel Assoc. of Great Britain, London, 1969.

7.44 Ahearn, V. P.: *Land Use Planning and the Sand and Gravel Producer,* Nat. Sand and Gravel Assoc., Washington, D.C., 1964.

7.45 Bauer, A. A.: "A Guide to Site Development and Rehabilitation of Pits and Quarries," *Industrial Mineral Report No. 33,* Dept. of Mines, Ont., Toronto, 1970.

7.46 Hayes, W. C., and J. D. Vineyard: "Environmental Geology in Town and Country," *Educational Series No. 2,* Missouri Geological Survey and Water Resources, Rolla, Mo., August 1969.

7.47 Peck, R. B.: "Foundation Exploration–Denver Coliseum," *Proc. Amer. Soc. Civil Engs.,* **79,** sep. no. 326, November 1953.

7.48 Fisher, W. L., and L. E. Garner: "Bloating Characteristics of East Texas Clays," *Abstract Vol. Geol. Soc. Amer. Annual Meeting,* Miami Beach, 1969, p. 62.

7.49 Powell, D. J.: "Hertfordshire Lime Kilns," *The Countryman,* **75,** no. 1, 52, Autumn 1970.

7.50 Ciborowski, A., and S. Jankowski: *Warsaw Rebuilt,* Polonia Publishing House, Warsaw, 1962.

7.51 "Japan's Pollution Grows with Population," *Eng. News-Record,* **185,** 26, 17 December 1970.

7.52 Jones, J. H.: *A Bold Concept for the Development of the Toronto Waterfront,* Toronto Harbour Commissioners, January 1968; see also, *Report on Coastal Engineering Studies and Design in the Toronto Area,* Eng. Dept., Toronto Harbour Commissioners, 1968.

7.53 "Solid Wastes Pile Up While Laws Crack Down and Engineers Gear Up," *Eng. News-Record,* **182,** 28, 12 June 1969.

7.54 *Ibid.,* p. 31.

7.55 Information from U.S. Public Health Service, cited in 7.53.

7.56 Emrich, G. H.: "What is a Geologist Doing in a Health Department?" unpublished paper given at Geol. Soc. Amer. Annual Meeting, Milwaukee (from Bureau of Sanitary Engineering, Penna. Dept. of Health), 1970.

7.57 Pitt, M. E.: "Portsmouth Harbour Reclamation Scheme," *Proc. Inst. Civil Engs.,* **47,** 157, October 1970; see also, for discussion, **49,** 539, 1971.

7.58 *Otterspool Riverside Promenade,* City of Liverpool, May 1970.

7.59 O'Sullivan, P. M.: "Recent Development Works In Dublin Port," *Proc. Inst. Civil Engs., Supp. Vol.,* 1970, p. 153, 1970.

7.60 See 7.51.

7.61 Piburn, M. D.: "New Beaches from Old Bottles," *Natural History,* **LXXXI,** no. 4, April 1972.

7.62 Crawford, C. B., and K. N. Burn: "Building Damage from Expansive Steel Slag Backfill," *Proc. Amer. Soc. Civil Engs., Soil Mech. Div.,* **95,** SM 6, p. 1325, November 1969; see also, for discussion, SM 4, p. 1470, July 1970, SM 5, p. 1808, September 1970, and SM 6, p. 2131, November 1970.

7.63 Sutherland, H. B., and P. N. Gaskin: "Factors Affecting the Frost Susceptibility Characteristics of Pulverized Fuel Ash," *Can. Geotechnical Jour.,* **7,** 69, February 1970; see also, "Fly-Ash to Fletton," *Railway Magazine,* London, **125,** 319, June 1970.

7.64 Hansen, T. C., C. W. Richards, and S. Mindess: "Sand-Lime Bricks and Aerated Lightweight Concrete from Gold Mine Waste," *Materials, Research and Standards,* **10,** 21, August 1970.

7.65 "Medieval Church Founded on Coal Must Go," *Eng. News-Record*, **184**, 28, 14 May 1970.

7.66 Legget, R. F.: "Duisburg Harbour Lowered by Coal Mining," *Can. Geotechnical Journal*, **9**, November 1972.

Chapter Eight

8.1 Yokoyama, L.: "Pozzuoli Event in 1970," *Nature*, **229**, 532, 19 February 1971.

8.2 *San Andreas Fault*, 1965. (One of a popular leaflet series of the U.S. Geological Survey; it can be supplemented by reference to many papers in the geological literature, such as in the *Bulletin of the Geological Society of America.)*

8.3 Cluff, L. S., and K. V. Steinbrugge: "Hayward Fault Slippage in the Irvington-Niles Districts of Fremont, California," *Abstract Vol. Geol. Soc. Amer. Cordilleran Section, Annual Meeting*, Reno, 1966, p. 27; see also in same volume, Bonilla, M. G.: "Slippage on Hayward Fault Indicated by Deformation of Railroad Tracks in the Niles District of Fremont, California," 1966, p. 22.

8.4 Hodgson, J. H.: *Earthquakes and Earth Structure*, Prentice Hall, Inc., Englewood Cliffs, N.J., 1964.

8.5 Kunze, W. E., M. Fintel, and J. E. Amrhein: "Skopje Earthquake Damage," *Civil Engineering*, **33**, 56, December 1963.

8.6 Degenkolb, H. J.: "Seismic Tremor Shook Caracas Severely," *Eng. News-Record*, **179**, 16, 24 August 1967. (The American Iron and Steel Institute has published a more detailed report on this earthquake in volume form.)

8.7 Slemmons, D. B.: "Structural and Geomorphic Effects of the Dixie Valley-Fairview Peak Earthquakes of December 16, 1954, Churchill County, Nevada," *Abstract Vol. Geol. Soc. Amer. Annual Meeting*, New Orleans, 1955, p. 94A.

8.8 Barney, K. R.: "Madison Canyon Slide," *Civil Engineering*, **30**, 72, August 1960; see also, Sherard, J. L.: "What the Earthquake Did to Hegben Dam," *Eng. News-Record*, **163**, 26, 10 September 1959.

8.9 Legget, R. F.: "Earthquake Damage at Cornwall," *Engineering Jour.*, **27**, 572, 1944.

8.10 Eckel, E. B.: "The Alaska Earthquake: March 27, 1964, Lessons and Conclusions," *USGS Prof. Paper 546*, 1970; see also, Grantz, A., G. Plafker, and R. Kachadoorian: "Alaska's Good Friday Earthquake; March 27, 1964; a Preliminary Geologic Evaluation," *USGS Circular 491*, 1964.

8.11 Scott, J. D., and F. W. Render: "Effect of an Alaskan Earthquake on Water Levels in Wells at Winnipeg and Ottawa, Canada," *Jour. Hydrology*, Amsterdam, 2, 262, 1964.

8.12 Dobrovolny, E., and H. R. Schmoll: "Geology as Applied to Urban Planning: an Example from the Greater Anchorage Area Borough, Alaska," *Proc. XXIII Int. Geol. Cong.*, Sec. 12, 39, Prague, 1968.

8.13 Miller, R. D., and E. Dobrovolny: "Surficial Geology of Anchorage and Vicinity, Alaska," *USGS Bulletin 1093*, 1959.

8.14 *National Building Code of Canada 1970*, 5th ed., National Research Council of Canada, Ottawa, 1970, p. 150.

8.15 *Report of the Special Committee for the Study of the Fukui Earthquake, 1948*, National Research Council of Japan, 1950; see also, Seed, H. B., and I. M.

Idriss: "Influence of Soil Conditions on Building Damage Potential during Earthquakes," *Proc. Amer. Soc. Civil Engs., Structural Div.,* **97**, ST 2, Paper 7909, 639, February 1971.

8.16 Beard, F. D.: "Microseismic Forecasting of Excavation Failures," *Civil Engineering,* **32**, 50, May 1962.

8.17 Bernstein, J.: "Tsunamis," *Scientific American,* **191**, 60, August 1954.

8.18 Legget, R. F.: *Geology and Engineering,* 2d ed., McGraw-Hill Book Company, New York, 1962, p. 785 (a summary only). For current situation in the Netherlands, see Bazlen, K. A.: "How the Dutch Live Below Sea-Level," *Build. International,* **2**, 137, May/June 1971.

8.19 Kiersch, G. A.: "Vaiont Reservoir Disaster," *Civil Engineering,* **34**, 32, March 1964.

8.20 Information received from various Indian sources through the kindness of the late Lt. General Sir Harold Williams.

8.21 "Russians Blast through Landslide Dam," *Eng. News-Record,* **172**, 24, 7 May 1964.

8.22 *Tangiwai Railway Disaster: Report of the Board of Inquiry,* Govt. Printing Office, Wellington, New Zealand, 1954.

8.23 Stowe, L. "The Ordeal of Huaraz," *Reader's Digest,* **94**, 63, June 1969.

8.24 Mann, J. F., and R. O. Stone: "Von Trigger-Cadiz Mudflow of July 1953," *Abstract Vol. Geol. Soc. Amer. Annual Meeting,* Los Angeles, 1954, p. 77.

8.25 Mason, A. C., and H. L. Foster: "Extruded Mudflow Hills of Nirasaki, Japan," *Abstract Vol. Geol. Soc. Amer. Annual Meeting,* Los Angeles, 1954, p. 78.

8.26 Collin, A.: *Landslides in Clays,* trans. by W. R. Schriever, University of Toronto Press, 1956.

8.27 Crawford, C. B., and W. J. Eden: "Nicolet Landslide of November 1955, Quebec, Canada," *Eng. Geol. Case Histories No. 4,* Geol. Soc. Amer., Boulder, 1963, p. 45.

8.28 Tavenas, F., J.-Y. Chagnon, and P. LaRochelle: "The Saint-Jean-Vianney Landslide: Observations and Eyewitness Accounts," *Can. Geotechnical Jour.,* **8**, 463, August 1971.

8.29 Zaruba, Q., and V. Mencl: *Landslides and Their Control,* Elsevier and Academia, Prague, 1969.

8.30 *Ibid.,* p. 42.

8.31 See, for example, Lung, R., and R. Proctor (eds.): *Engineering Geology in Southern California,* Assoc. Eng. Geologists, Glendale, Calif., 1966.

8.32 *Report of the Commission Appointed to Investigate Turtle Mountain, Frank, Alberta,* Geological Survey of Canada Memoir 27, 1912.

8.33 Mathews, W. H., and K. C. McTaggart: "The Hope Land-Slide, British Columbia," *Proc. Geol. Assoc. Canada,* **20**, 65, February 1969.

8.34 "Chalk Cliffs Are Being Stabilized at Dover," *The Engineer,* **225**, 627, 19 April 1968.

8.35 Lee, C. S.: "Chalk Falls between Folkstone and Dover," *The Railway Magazine,* London, **87**, 531, October 1940.

8.36 Mohr, C., and R. Haefeli: "Umbau der Landquartbrucke der Rhatischen Bahn in Klosters," *Schweitzerische Bauzeitung,* **65**, 5 and 32, 1947; see also, Haefeli, R., C. Schaerer, and G. Amberg: "The Behavior under the Influence of Soil

Creep Pressure of the Concrete Bridge Built at Klosters by the Rhaetian Railway Company, Switzerland," *Proc. Third Int. Conf. on Soil Mech. and Found. Eng.*, **2**, 175, Zurich, 1953.

8.37 Henkel, D. J.: "Slide Movements on an Inclined Clay Layer in the Avon Gorge in Bristol," *Proc. Fifth Int. Conf. on Soil Mech. and Found. Eng.*, Paris, **2**, 619, 1961.

8.38 *Report of the Tribunal Appointed to Inquire into the Disaster at Aberfan on October 21st, 1966*, H. M. Stationery Office, London, 1967; and *A Selection of Technical Reports submitted to the Aberfan Tribunal*, 2 vols., H. M. Stationery Office, London, 1969; see also a masterly review by Glossop, R.: *Geotechnique*, **20**, 218, June 1970.

8.39 Watkins, G. L.: "The Stability of Colliery Spoilbanks," *Colliery Engineering*, **36**, 493, 1959; and reprinted in same journal, **43**, 459, 1966.

8.40 Davies, W. E.: "Geologic Hazards of Coal Refuse Banks," *Abstract Vol. Geol. Soc. Amer. Annual Meeting*, New Orleans, 1967, p. 43.

8.41 Schaerer, P. A.: "Planning Defences against Avalanches," *Can. Geotechnical Jour.*, **7**, 397, November 1970.

8.42 Christiansen, E. A.: "Geology of the Crater Lake Collapse Structure in Southeastern Saskatchewan," *Can. Jour. Earth Sci.*, **8**, 1505, 1971.

8.43 Flint, R. F., C. R. Longwell, and J. E. Sanders: *Physical Geology*, John Wiley & Sons Inc., New York, 1969, p. 250.

8.44 From a press report in *The Globe and Mail*, Toronto, for 12 December 1970, by K. Dzeguze.

8.45 "Sinkhole Causes Roof Failure," *Eng. News-Record*, **183**, 23, 11 December 1969.

8.46 Grant, L. F.: "Solution in Bedrock at the Calhoun, Tenn., Plant of Bowaters' Southern Paper Corp.," *Bull. Geol. Soc. Amer.*, **67**, 1751, 1956.

8.47 Brucker, E. E.: "Geology and Treatment of Sinkholes in Land Development," *Missouri Mineral Industry News*, **10**, 125, July 1970.

8.48 "Underground Channels Utilized for Airport Drainage," *Eng. News-Record*, **130**, 498, 1943.

8.49 Legget, R. F.: *Geology and Engineering*, 2d ed., McGraw-Hill Book Company, New York, 1962, p. 160.

8.50 See 4.35.

8.51 Foose, R. M.: "Ground Water Behavior in the Hershey Valley," *Bull. Geol. Soc. Amer.*, **64**, 623, 1953.

8.52 Jennings, J. E.: "Building on Dolomites in the Transvaal," *The Civil Eng. in S. Africa*, **8**, 41, January 1966; supplemented by information from Prof. Jennings.

8.53 Kennedy, J. M.: "A Microwave Radiometric Study of Buried Karst Topography," *Bull. Geol. Soc. Amer.*, **79**, 735, 1968.

8.54 News report in *The Lancaster Guardian* for 24 September 1892, and personal communication from E. H. Scholes, Lancaster.

8.55 News report in *The New York Times* for 12 February 1970, p. 49.

8.56 Mansur, C. I., and M. C. Skouby: "Mine Grouting to Control Building Settlement," *Proc. Amer. Soc. Civil Engs., Soil Mech. Div.*, **96**, SM 2, Paper 7166, 511, March 1970.

8.57 Gray, R. E., and J. F. Meyers: "Mine Subsidence and Support Methods in Pittsburgh Area," *Proc. Amer. Soc. Civil Engs., Soil Mech. Div.*, **96**, SM 4, Paper 7407, 1267, July 1970.

8.58 Heathcote, F. W. L.: "Movement of Articulated Building on Subsidence Sites," *Proc. Inst. Civil Engs.*, **30**, 347, February 1965; see also discussion in **33**, 492–517, March 1966.

8.59 Price, D. G., A. B. Malkin, and J. L. Knill: "Foundations of Multi-storey Blocks on the Coal Measures with Special Reference to Old Mine Workings," *Quart. Jour. Eng. Geology*, London, **1**, 271, June 1969.

8.60 News report in *The Globe and Mail*, Toronto, and other papers, for 21 February 1954.

8.61 Calvert, A. J.: *Salt in Cheshire*, E. and F. N. Spon, London, 1915.

8.62 "Elevated Roadway Adjusts to Bad Ground," *Eng. News-Record*, **178**, 50, 27 April 1967.

8.63 Gifford, E. W. H., M. V. Wooley, and A. A. W. Butler, "The Design and Construction of the Calder Bridge on the M1 Motorway," *Proc. Inst. Civil Engs.*, **43**, 527, August 1969.

8.64 Poland, J. F., and G. H. Davis: "Land Subsidence due to Withdrawal of Fluids," in *Reviews in Engineering Geology II*, Geol. Soc. Amer., Boulder, 1969, p. 187; see also, Allen, A. S.: "Geologic Settings of Subsidence" in same volume, p. 305.

8.65 *Ibid.*, p. 200ff for an excellent review.

8.66 *Ibid.*, p. 199.

8.67 Collins, J. J.: "New Type Seawall Built for Subsiding Lake Shore in Venezuela," *Eng. News-Record*, **114**, 405, 1935.

8.68 See 8.64, p. 216.

8.69 Weaver, P., and M. M. Sheets: *Guide Book for Field Excursion No. 5, Nov. 1962*, for Annual Meeting, Geol. Soc. Amer., Houston, 1962.

8.70 Davis, G. H., J. B. Small, and H. B. Counts: "Land Subsidence Related to Decline of Artesian Head in the Ocala Limestone at Savannah, Georgia," *Abstract Vol. Geol. Soc. Amer. Annual Meeting*, Pittsburgh, 1959, p. 27A.

8.71 Hardy, R. M.: "Construction Problems in Silty Soils," *Eng. Journal*, Montreal **33**, 775, September 1950; see also, Clevenger, W. A., "Experiences with Loess as Foundation Material," *Proc. Amer. Soc. Civil Engs., Soil Mech. Div.*, **82**, SM 3, Paper 1025, July 1956.

8.72 *Progress Report Land-Subsidence Investigations, San Joaquin Valley, California, through 1957*, Inter-Agency Committee on Land Subsidence in the San Joaquin Valley, c/o U.S. Geological Survey, 1958; see also, Lofgren, B. E.: p. 271 of 8.64.

8.73 Whitman, R. V., D. R. Casagrande, K. Karlsrud, and R. Simon: "Performance of Foundation for Altair Radio," *Proc. Amer. Soc. Civil Engs., Soil Mech. Div.*, **97**, SM 1, Paper 7809, 1, January 1971.

8.74 Kassiff, G., M. Livneh, and G. Wiseman: *Pavements on Expansive Clays*, Jerusalem Academic Press, 1970.

8.75 Mencl, V.: "Mechanics of Landslides with Non-circular Slip Surfaces with Special Reference to the Vaiont Slide," *Geotechnique*, **16**, 329, December 1966.

8.76 Chandler, R. J.: "The Degradation of Lias Clay Slopes in an Area of the East Midlands," *Quart. Jour. Eng. Geol.*, London, 2, 161, February 1970.

8.77 Skempton, A. W.: "Long Term Stability of Clay Slopes," Fourth Rankine Lecture, *Geotechnique*, **14**, no. 2, 75–101, June 1964.

8.78 MacGregor, W. M., and F. H. Lyra: "Furnas Hydro-electric Scheme, Brazil; Closure of Diversion Tunnels," *Proc. Inst. Civil Engs.*, **36**, 21, January 1967.

8.79 Kuznetsov, A. M.: "The Phenomena of Gas Formation in the Foundations of Concrete Dams," *Tech. Trans. No. 1310*, National Research Council of Canada, Ottawa, 1967 (trans. from *Gidrotekh. Stroit.*).

8.80 "Florida Bridge Pile Explosions Traced to River Water Bacteria," *Eng. News-Record*, **186**, 14, 4 February 1971.

8.81 Bechtold, I. C., and R. H. Jahns: "Geologic Environment of HVDC Ground Currents as Related to Buried Pipelines," *Paper No. 42*, Nat. Assoc. of Corrosion Engs., Conference at Cleveland, Houston, 1968.

8.82 Watts, G. M.: "Mechanical Bypassing of Littoral Drift on Inlets," *Proc. Amer. Soc. Civil Engs.*, Waterworks Div., **88**, WW 1, Paper 3058, 83, February 1962.

8.83 Howard, E. A.: "Permeable Groynes of Concrete Check Beach Erosion," *Eng. News-Record*, **114**, 594, 1935; and information kindly supplied by Prof. W. G. Murphy, Milwaukee.

8.84 Kamel, A. M.: "Use of Natural Radioactivity in Tracing the Source and Direction of Littoral Drift," *Abstract Vol. Geol. Soc. Amer. Annual Meeting*, Houston, 1962, p. 84A.

8.85 Shumway, G., G. B. Dowling, G. Salsman, and R. H. Payne: "Submerged Forest of Mid-Wisconsin Age on the Continental Shelf off Panama City, Florida," *Abstract Vol. Geol. Soc. Amer. Annual Meeting*, Cincinnati, 1961, p. 147A.

8.86 Wilkinson, D.: *The Arctic Coast*, Illus. Nat. Hist. of Canada, Toronto, 1970, p. 50.

8.87 Fairbridge, R. W.: "The Changing Level of the Sea," *Scientific American*, **202**, 70, May 1960.

8.88 Jessup, W. E.: "Baldwin Hills Dam Failure," *Civil Engineering,* **34**, 62, February 1964; and press reports of legal decisions. See also, Hamilton, D. H., and R. L. Meehan: "Ground Rupture in the Baldwin Hills," *Science,* **172**, 333, 23 April 1971.

Chapter Nine

9.1 Kingsley, C.: *Town Geology*, Daldy, Isbister & Co., London, 1877.

9.2 Ami, H. M.: "On the Geology of the Major Cities of Canada," *Trans. Royal Soc. Canada,* Second Series VI, Section IV, 125, 1900.

9.3 Grice, R. H.: "Geological Data Handling in Urban Geology," *Can. Geotechnical Jour.*, 8, 134, February 1971.

9.4 Brisbin, W. C., and N. M. Ediger: *A National System for Storage and Retrieval of Geological Data for Canada*, National Advisory Comm. on Research in Geol. Sciences c/o Geol. Survey of Canada, Ottawa, 1967.

9.5 Kassner, J. J.: "Relocating Substreet Utility Lines," *Civil Engineering*, 38, 86, April 1968.

9.6 Missimer, H. C.: "Avoiding Utility Interference Underground," *Civil Engineering*, **35**, 36, September 1965.

9.7 Stover, P. (chairman): *Activities of the City of Ottawa Underground Public Utilities Coordinating Committee*, City Hall, Ottawa, 1969.

9.8 Worcester, J. R.: "Boston Foundations," *Jour. Boston Soc. Civil Engs.*, **1**, 1, 1914.

9.9 "Report of Committee on Boston Subsoils," *Jour. Boston Soc. Civil Engs.*, **18**, 243, 1931.

9.10 "Boring Data from Greater Boston" (prepared by the Committee on Subsoils of Boston in cooperation with the USGS), *Jour. Boston Soc. Civil Engs.*, **56**, 131, July-October 1969.

9.11 *Geological Survey: Information from Trial Holes*, Circular no. 18/62, Ministry of Housing and Local Government, London, 6 April 1962.

9.12 *Colour-Printed Geological Maps of the London District*, Geological Survey of Great Britain, 1935.

9.13 Information kindly provided by Dr. Armin von Moos, Zurich; see also his paper "Engineering Geology in Switzerland," *Geotechnique*, **1**, 40, June 1948.

9.14 See 3.57.

9.15 Kos'kov, B. I., and A. N. Nalivkin (eds.): "Instructions on Engineering Surveys for Municipal and Settlement Construction (SN 211-62)," *Tech. Trans. No. 1206*, National Research Council of Canada, Ottawa, 1965.

9.16 Since this volume is printed entirely in Japanese, it cannot be referenced in the usual way, but it could be identified as *"The Subsurface of Tokyo."*

9.17 Information kindly supplied by Dr. Ohsaki Yorihiko, Tokyo.

9.18 Information kindly supplied by Prof. J. E. Jennings, A. B. A. Brink, and associates, Johannesburg.

9.19 Bayrock, L. A., and T. E. Berg: "Geology of the City of Edmonton: Part 1, Central Edmonton," *Report 66-1*, Research Council of Alberta, Edmonton, 1966.

9.20 Information kindly supplied by Dr. J. D. Scott, Ottawa, and Dr. J. Rigour, BRGM.

9.21 "Earth Sciences Serving the Nation," *Report No. 7* of the Science Council of Canada, Ottawa, April 1970.

9.22 See, for example, *West Texas Geological Society Road Log, Del Rio, El Paso*, W. Texas Geol. Soc., Midland, 1958.

9.23 Reade, T. M.: "The Gypsum Boulder of Great Crosby," *Proc. Liverpool Geol. Soc.*, **8**, 347, 1899.

9.24 See 7.18.

9.25 See *Thirty Fourth Biennial Report of the Commissioners of the State Geological and Natural History Survey*, Bulletin 104 of the Connecticut State Geological and Natural History Survey, p. 3, Hartford, 1971; and also *Dinosaur State Park*, leaflet of the Connecticut State Park and Forest Commission (no date).

9.26 LaMoreaux, P. E., and T. A. Simpson: "Birmingham's Red Mountain Cut," *Geotimes*, **15**, 10, October 1970.

9.27 Wilson, A. E.: "A Guide to the Geology of the Ottawa District," *Can. Field-Naturalist*, **70**, 1, January-March 1956.

9.28 Hogarth, D. D.: "A Guide to the Geology of the Gatineau-Lievre District," *Can. Field-Naturalist*, **76**, 1, January-March 1962; Sabina, A. P.: "Rocks and Minerals for the Collector; Buckingham . . . Ottawa, Ontario," *Paper 68-51*, Geol. Survey of Canada, Ottawa, 1969.

9.29 See 7.18.

9.30 *Drift-Thickness Contours; City of Ottawa, Carleton County, Ontario*, map 39-1959, Geol. Survey of Canada, Ottawa, 1959.

9.31 In a personal communication from Dr. E. McKee, Denver.

9.32 Lowdermilk, W. C.: "Lessons from the Old World to the Americas in Land Use," *Smithsonian Report for 1943* (Publication no. 3756), 413, Smithsonian Institution, Washington, D.C., 1944.

9.33 See 2.30.

SOME SUGGESTIONS FOR FURTHER READING

This brief list gives titles of some books and pamphlets of a general, rather than a technical, character that the author has found useful and of interest. The listing is a very personal one and is therefore suggestive only; it is hoped that it may be helpful.

Chapter One

The Population Challenge; what it means to America (Conservation Yearbook No. 2 of the Department of the Interior, 1966, Government Printing Office, Washington) should be on the shelves of every reader of this book. Statistical information on population growth is readily available in publications of the United Nations, especially the *Demographic Yearbooks*. The significance of this growth is well discussed in *Population: Resources and Environment,* by Paul R. Ehrlich and Anne H. Ehrlich (W. H. Freeman and Company, San Francisco, 1970), and in other writings of Paul Ehrlich, such as his paperback *The Population Bomb* (Sierra Club-Ballantyne, New York, 1971). *The Population Explosion and Christian Responsibility,* by R. M. Fagley (Oxford University Press, New York), is still relevant, even though published in 1960.

The growth of cities was featured in the September 1965 issue of *Scientific American* (**213**, no. 3), a most interesting review. *Towns and Cities,* by Emrys Jones (Oxford University Press, Oxford, 1966), and *World Cities,* by Peter Hall (World University Library, McGraw-Hill Book Company, New York, 1966), are excellent concise reviews, as indicated by their mention in the text. *Urbanization in the Second United Nations Development Decade* (United Nations, New York, 1970) is a convenient printed and edited version of the working paper noted as reference 1.9.

Chapter Two

The City in History, by Lewis Mumford (Harcourt, Brace & World, Inc., New York, 1961), is a fine starting point for studying the development of cities. All major cities will be found to have some publications on their history, often of great interest. *Local History in England* (Longmans, Green & Co., Ltd., London, 1959) and *Fieldwork in Local History* (Faber & Faber, Ltd., London, 1969), both by W. G. Hoskins, are stimulating introductions to the fascination of local historical inquiry.

Chapter Three

The Culture of Cities (Harcourt, Brace and Company, New York, 1938) is another of Lewis Mumford's master works. His introduction increases the interest of *Design with Nature,* by Ian McHarg (Natural History Press, New York, 1969), to which tribute is paid in the text. Introductions to geology will be found at the end of this list, but the volume noted in the text is *The Earth's Crust,* by L. Dudley Stamp (George G. Harrap & Co., Ltd., London, 1951). From the many general treatments of *Man and Environment* now happily available, a pocket book with this title by R. Arvill (Penguin Books, Inc., London, 1969) can be commended as showing the problem through British eyes.

One of the very best introductions to what geology can do in urban develop-ment is *Environmental Geology in Towne and Country*, by W. C. Hayes and J. D. Vineyard, a well-printed pamphlet that is No. 2 of the Educational Series of the Missouri Geological Survey (Rolla, Missouri, 1969).

Chapter Four

Water and Life is the arresting, but accurate, title of the UNESCO "Courier" for July-August 1964. It gives a well-illustrated introduction to this vital topic. *Urban Growth and the Water Regime,* by J. Savini and J. C. Kammerer (Water Supply Paper No. 1591-A of the U.S. Geological Survey, 1961), is a good overall review of its quantitative aspect. Another useful USGS paper, of 1963, is *A Primer on Ground Water,* by Helene L. Baldwin and C. C. McGuiness, a helpful introduction to this least familiar part of the hydrological cycle. The *Atlas* noted as reference 4.23 is a vivid presentation of the groundwater situation below Long Island. Indicative of the excellent information available from industry in this, as in other fields, is a 440-page volume *Groundwater and Wells,* second printing 1972, available from the Johnson Division, Universal Oil Products, St. Paul, Minnesota 55165. The sixth Interior Conservation Yearbook (see above), *River of Life,* is another fine general treatment and the occasional Yearbooks of the U.S. Department of Agriculture devoted to *Water* (such as that for 1955) are valuable encyclopedic references.

Chapter Six

Tunneling does not lend itself readily to description other than technical, but *Beneath the City Streets,* by Peter Lawrie (Allen Lane, The Penguin Press, London, 1970), is an interesting "private enquiry into the nuclear preoccupations of Govern-ment" (that of the U.K.) that includes results of the writer's studies of tunnels and other excavations as used in England for shelter.

Chapter Seven

Building stone is the only material used for cities that appears to have attracted the attention of general writers, but the only recent book on stone that the author has seen is *The Fashionable Stone,* by K. Hudson (Adams and Dart, Bath, 1971), a delightful review of the wide use in England of the oolitic limestone mentioned in the text. As showing how important building stone still is, *Marble in the Philippines,* by A. Shadmon, may be mentioned, a fine report on the UNDP Marble Development Project published in 1969 by the Bureau of Mines in Manila.

Chapter Eight

In contrast, there is now such an extensive literature on geological hazards and their effects (of which reference 8.4 is a good example) that it may be preferable to indicate the public attention that is now being given to these vital matters. Special Study No. 32 of the Utah Geological and Mineralogical Survey (Salt Lake City, 1970) is an illustrated record of the *Governor's Conference on Geological Hazards in Utah, December 14, 1967.* A corresponding record is Special Publication No. 1 of the Colorado Geological Survey (Denver, 1967) on the *Governor's Conference on Environmental Geology.*

Indicative of the importance with which geological hazards are now viewed was the establishment of the *Smithsonian Institution, Center for Short-lived Phenomena.* This somewhat unusual title indicates an information center, with worldwide resources, on such hazards as landslides, landrises, storm surges, and tsunamis. Full particulars may be obtained from the Center at 60 Garden Street, Cambridge, Massachusetts 02138.

Chapter Nine

The Earth and Man, by George Perkins Marsh, must be mentioned again for the inspiration and challenge it presents to all thoughtful readers. Marsh would have welcomed Circular 645 of the USGS (1971) since it is a concise *Procedure for Evaluating Environmental Impact* by L. B. Leopold, F. E. Clarke, B. B. Hanshaw, and J. R. Balsley. Well used, this can be a powerful tool for good in all urban development and other engineering works. Almost at the other end of the scale, for those city dwellers to whom conservation is still just a word, is *Living with your Land, a Guide to Conservation for the City's Fringe* by John Vosburgh, Bulletin No. 53 of the Cranbrook Institute of Science (Bloomfield Hills, Michigan, 1968).

Geology

From the many currently available splendid volumes providing an introduction to the science of geology, three will be noted, not in any invidious distinction but because the author knows them well and has found them especially helpful: *Physical Geology,* by C. R. Longwell, R. F. Flint, and J. E. Saunders (John Wiley & Sons, Inc.,

New York, 1969); *Principles of Physical Geology*, second edition, by Arthur Holmes (Thomas Nelson & Sons, New York, 1965); and *Geology*, Second edition, by W. C. Putnam as revised by Ann B. Bassett (Oxford University Press, New York, 1971). *Geology—Science and Profession*, a compact brochure, is one of the helpful publications of the American Geological Institute (1444 N. Street N.W., Washington, D.C. 20005). *The Earth and its Surface* (American Book Company, New York, 1969) is a good example of material now available for use in high schools. *Rocks and Minerals*, one of the Golden Nature Guides (Golden Press, New York, 1957) is an admirable "pocket guide." *Glacial and Quaternary Geology*, by R. F. Flint (John Wiley & Sons, Inc., New York, 1971), includes Pleistocene geology in its masterly coverage. And for local and specific information, the state surveys should be remembered, as well as the national service of the U.S. Geological Survey, with its information offices in Denver, Salt Lake City, Anchorage, Dallas, Los Angeles, San Francisco, and Spokane, all in addition to its main center in Washington, D.C.

Name Index

Place Index

Subject Index